Macworld
Illustrator 5.0/5.5
Bible

Macworld
Illustrator 5.0/5.5 Bible

by Ted Alspach
Foreword by Pierre Bézier

IDG BOOKS

IDG Books Worldwide, Inc.
An International Data Group Company

San Mateo, California ✦ Indianapolis, Indiana ✦ Boston, Massachusetts

Macworld Illustrator 5.0/5.5 Bible

Published by
IDG Books Worldwide, Inc.
An International Data Group Company
155 Bovet Road, Suite 310
San Mateo, CA 94402

Library of Congress Catalog Card No.: 94-75905

ISBN: 1-56884-097-7

Printed in the United States of America

10 9 8 7 6 5 4 3 2 1

1C/QV/RX/ZU

Distributed in the United States by IDG Books Worldwide, Inc.

Distributed in Canada by Macmillan of Canada, a Division of Canada Publishing Corporation; by Computer and Technical Books in Miami, Florida, for South America and the Caribbean; by Longman Singapore in Singapore, Malaysia, Thailand, and Korea; by Toppan Co. Ltd. in Japan; by Asia Computerworld in Hong Kong; by Woodslane Pty. Ltd. in Australia and New Zealand; and by Transword Publishers Ltd. in the U.K. and Europe.

For general information on IDG Books in the U.S., including information on discounts and premiums, contact IDG Books at 800-762-2974 or 415-312-0650.

For information on where to purchase IDG Books outside the U.S., contact Christina Turner at 415-312-0633.

For information on translations, contact Marc Jeffrey Mikulich, Foreign Rights Manager, at IDG Books Worldwide; FAX NUMBER 415-358-1260.

For sales inquiries and special prices for bulk quantities, write to the address above or call IDG Books Worldwide at 415-312-0650.

 is a registered trademark of IDG Books Worldwide, Inc.

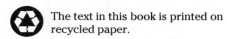 The text in this book is printed on recycled paper.

About the Author

Ted Alspach has been using and abusing Adobe Illustrator since the beginning of time (well, since the late '80s, at least). An expert at logo and font design, Ted has trained thousands of people in all areas of graphics and desktop publishing for the Macintosh. He is the owner of Bézier Graphic Experts, the Southwest's leading graphics training company. Ted is unbearably enthusiastic about Illustrator, Macs, and desktop publishing, to the point where you're better off not asking his opinion about any of these topics. In his spare time, Ted has been known to juggle torches, bowling balls, razor sharp knives and razor sharp small children high above his head as their parents look on in approval. He avoids chainsaws because "someone could get hurt."

And, yes, Ted drinks lots of CHO.

About IDG Books Worldwide

Welcome to the world of IDG Books Worldwide.

IDG Books Worldwide, Inc., is a subsidiary of International Data Group, the world's largest publisher of computer-related information and the leading global provider of information services on information technology. International Data Group publishes over 200 computer publications in 63 countries. Forty million people read one or more International Data Group publications each month.

If you use personal computers, IDG Books is committed to publishing quality books that meet your needs. We rely on our extensive network of publications, including such leading periodicals as *Macworld*, *InfoWorld*, *PC World*, *Computerworld*, *Publish*, *Network World*, and *SunWorld*, to help us make informed and timely decisions in creating useful computer books that meet your needs.

Every IDG book strives to bring extra value and skill-building instructions to the reader. Our books are written by experts, with the backing of IDG periodicals, and with careful thought devoted to issues such as audience, interior design, use of icons, and illustrations. Our editorial staff is a careful mix of high-tech journalists and experienced book people. Our close contact with the makers of computer products helps ensure accuracy and thorough coverage. Our heavy use of personal computers at every step in production means we can deliver books in the most timely manner.

We are delivering books of high quality at competitive prices on topics customers want. At IDG, we believe in quality, and we have been delivering quality for over 25 years. You'll find no better book on a subject than an IDG book.

John Kilcullen
President and CEO
IDG Books Worldwide, Inc.

IDG Books Worldwide, Inc. is a subsidiary of International Data Group. The officers are Patrick J. McGovern, Founder and Board Chairman; Walter Boyd, President. International Data Group's publications include: **ARGENTINA'S** Computerworld Argentina, Infoworld Argentina; **AUSTRALIA'S** Computerworld Australia, Australian PC World, Australian Macworld, Network World, Mobile Business Australia, Reseller, IDG Sources; **AUSTRIA'S** Computerwelt Oesterreich, PC Test; **BRAZIL'S** Computerworld, Gamepro, Game Power, Mundo IBM, Mundo Unix, PC World, Super Game; **BELGIUM'S** Data News (CW) **BULGARIA'S** Computerworld Bulgaria, Ediworld, PC & Mac World Bulgaria, Network World Bulgaria; **CANADA'S** CIO Canada, Computerworld Canada, Graduate Computerworld, InfoCanada, Network World Canada; **CHILE'S** Computerworld Chile, Informatica; **COLOMBIA'S** Computerworld Colombia, PC World; **CZECH REPUBLIC'S** Computerworld, Elektronika, PC World; **DENMARK'S** Communications World, Computerworld Danmark, Macintosh Produktkatalog, Macworld Danmark, PC World Danmark, PC World Produktguide, Tech World, Windows World; **ECUADOR'S** PC World Ecuador; **EGYPT'S** Computerworld (CW) Middle East, PC World Middle East; **FINLAND'S** MikroPC, Tietoviikko, Tietoverkko; **FRANCE'S** Distributique, GOLDEN MAC, InfoPC, Languages & Systems, Le Guide du Monde Informatique, Le Monde Informatique, Telecoms & Reseaux; **GERMANY'S** Computerwoche, Computerwoche Focus, Computerwoche Extra, Computerwoche Karriere, Information Management, Macwelt, Netzwelt, PC Welt, PC Woche, Publish, Unit; **GREECE'S** Infoworld, PC Games; **HUNGARY'S** Computerworld SZT, PC World; **HONG KONG'S** Computerworld Hong Kong, PC World Hong Kong; **INDIA'S** Computers & Communications; **IRELAND'S** ComputerScope; **ISRAEL'S** Computerworld Israel, PC World Israel; **ITALY'S** Computerworld Italia, Lotus Magazine, Macworld Italia, Networking Italia, PC Shopping, PC World Italia; **JAPAN'S** Computerworld Today, Information Systems World, Macworld Japan, Nikkei Personal Computing, SunWorld Japan, Windows World; **KENYA'S** East African Computer News; **KOREA'S** Computerworld Korea, Macworld Korea, PC World Korea; **MEXICO'S** Compu Edicion, Compu Manufactura, Computacion/Punto de Venta, Computerworld Mexico, MacWorld, Mundo Unix, PC World, Windows; **THE NETHER-LANDS'** Computer! Totaal, Computable (CW), LAN Magazine, MacWorld, Totaal "Windows"; **NEW ZEALAND'S** Computer Listings, Computerworld New Zealand, New Zealand PC World, Network World; **NIGERIA'S** PC World Africa; **NORWAY'S** Computerworld Norge, C/World, Lotusworld Norge, Macworld Norge, Networld, PC World Ekspress, PC World Norge, PC World's Produktguide, Publish&Multimedia World, Student Data, Unix World, Windowsworld; IDG Direct Response; **PAKISTAN'S** PC World Pakistan; **PANAMA'S** PC World Panama; **PERU'S** Computerworld Peru, PC World; **PEOPLE'S REPUBLIC OF CHINA'S** China Computerworld, China Infoworld, Electronics Today/Multimedia World, Electronics International, Electronic Product World, China Network World, PC and Communications Magazine, PC World China, Software World Magazine, Telecom Product World; IDG HIGH TECH BEIJING'S New Product World; IDG SHENZHEN'S Computer News Digest; **PHILIPPINES'** Computerworld Philippines, PC Digest (PCW); **POLAND'S** Computerworld Poland, PC World/Komputer; **PORTUGAL'S** Cerebro/PC World, Correio Informatico/Computerworld, Informatica & Comunicacoes Catalogo, MacIn, Nacional de Produtos; **ROMANIA'S** Computerworld, PC World; **RUSSIA'S** Computerworld-Moscow, Mir - PC, Sety; **SINGAPORE'S** Computerworld Southeast Asia, PC World Singapore; **SLOVENIA'S** Monitor Magazine; **SOUTH AFRICA'S** Computer Mail (CIO),Computing S.A.,Network World S.A., Software World; **SPAIN'S** Advanced Systems, Amiga World, Computerworld Espana, Communicaciones World, Macworld Espana, NeXTWORLD, Super Juegos Magazine (GamePro), PC World Espana, Publish; **SWEDEN'S** Attack, ComputerSweden, Corporate Computing, Natverk & Kommunikation, Macworld, Mikrodatorn, PC World, Publishing & Design (CAP), Dataingenjoren, Maxi Data,Windows World; **SWITZERLAND'S** Computerworld Schweiz, Macworld Schweiz, PC Tip; **TAIWAN'S** Computerworld Taiwan, PC World Taiwan; **THAILAND'S** Thai Computerworld; **TURKEY'S** Computerworld Monitor, Macworld Turkiye, PC World Turkiye; **UKRAINE'S** Computerworld; **UNITED KINGDOM'S** Computing /Computerworld, Connexion/Network World, Lotus Magazine, Macworld, Open Computing/Sunworld; **UNITED STATES'** Advanced Systems, AmigaWorld, Cable in the Classroom, CD Review, CIO, Computerworld, Digital Video, DOS Resource Guide, Electronic Entertainment Magazine, Federal Computer Week, Federal Integrator, GamePro, IDG Books, Infoworld, Infoworld Direct, Laser Event, Macworld, Multimedia World, Network World, PC Letter, PC World, PlayRight, Power PC World, Publish, SWATPro, Video Event; **VENEZUELA'S** Computerworld Venezuela, PC World; **VIETNAM'S** PC World Vietnam

Dedication

To Toulouse, Linus, Pyro Louise, and Lucy Ann, for whom it is more than just second nature to use a mouse.

Acknowledgments

Many, many, many people (a whole heckuva lot of 'em) contributed to different areas of the *Macworld Illustrator 5.0/5.5 Bible*. I thank each and every one of them for their contributions, both great and small.

The most significant of these people is Jennifer Garling, whose incredible illustrations grace this entire book. From the colorful loony bird to the technically precise drawings that illustrate the different kinds of anchor points, Jennifer was flexible and imaginative enough to do the wide variety of artwork throughout this book. She took tons of nasty criticism, such as: "That's not the type of illustration I was looking for in this figure at all, Jen. Maybe you should try something else." Jennifer would always respond thoughtfully and politely to these remarks with, "Yes, it *is* what you were looking for, Ted. Maybe *you* should draw this figure." If there is one thing that distinguishes this book from the rest, it is the amazing illustrations, each one created in Adobe Illustrator, and most of them created by Jennifer.

For help in making this book *the* final word on Illustrator: Marta Partington of IDG Books Worldwide. Marta's contributions to this book range from the organization and content of the text, to the thematic style and overall quality of the artwork. Beyond that, she has pushed and pushed (well into the wee hours of the night) to make this book better than I could have possibly imagined.

For their countless hours of editing and patience without whom this book would never have been finished: Patricia A. Seiler, Barbara Potter, and Shawn MacLaren.

For the basics of Illustrator and desktop publishing taught to me eons ago, without which I would currently be writing about dBASE programming, the nesting habits of Indonesian carpenter bees, how to tie shoelaces with one hand, or something else that I *don't* love doing: Rob Teeple of Teeple Graphics.

For getting answers to some pretty ridiculous questions and taking the time to sink them into my skull and for incorporating some of my suggestions into the latest versions of Illustrator and Dimensions: Sean McKenna (the only person I know with as much Illustrator enthusiasm as my own, and whom I owe my thanks for molding Illustrator into way-cool software), Ellen Ablow (who has made Dimensions 2 into the heavyweight-class 3-D software it is today), Erik Gibson (who knows more about the inner workings of Illustrator than most of the engineers who wrote the software), and all the technical support people I whined to at Adobe Systems, Inc. (who are good-natured enough not to mind a running joke and are probably reading these acknowledgments while ignoring their ringing phones).

For providing me with the Filter Charts that are included on the CD-ROM, as well as some great insights into Illustrator: Sandee Cohen.

For selling enough copies of *The Omni* so that I could learn more about Illustrator: Wayde S. Delafield.

For providing me with two great case studies: Tim Freed of Freed Design and Royce Copenheaver of Academy ArtWorks.

For not knowing how to tint process colors and then leaving town unexpectedly under cover of darkness, owing everyone money: Michael Miller.

For inspiring me to write this book on Illustrator: all the clients I have had the fortune of training in the past, too many to mention, particularly those (especially Lisa T.) who kept bugging me to get an Illustrator book written.

For providing printing expertise regarding color separations, trapping and printing presses, as well as going on a skiing vacation one fateful January: Terry "Encyclopedia of Printing Trivia" Zerphey of Y/Z Printing.

For steering me in the right direction in regard to content and for being a great "editor-of-the-month": Janna Custer of IDG Books Worldwide.

For his initial — albeit unknown at the time — contribution to Illustrator and his willingness to be a part of this book: Pierre E. Bézier. His foreword eloquently states how the creation of Bézier curves came about from a need for surface design in the automobile industry of the '50s and '60s that was computer based. He then goes on to explain that although Bézier curves are the basis for PostScript and Illustrator, the users of Illustrator don't need to have the mathematical knowledge of how Bézier curves are created in order to use them. I, for one, thank him for doing all that nasty work so that computer illustrators can be illustrators and not mathematicians.

(The publisher would like to give special thanks to Patrick J. McGovern, without whom this book would not have been possible.)

Credits

Publisher
David Solomon

Managing Editor
Mary Bednarek

Acquisitions Editor
Janna Custer

Production Director
Beth Jenkins

Senior Editors
Tracy L. Barr
Sandra Blackthorn
Diane Graves Steele

Production Coordinator
Cindy L. Phipps

Associate Acquisitions Editor
Megg Bonar

Editorial Assistant
Darlene Cunningham

Project Editor
Marta Justak Partington

Editors
Patricia A. Seiler
Barbara L. Potter
Shawn MacLaren
A. Timothy Gallan

Technical Review
Michael J. Partington

Production Staff
Tony Augsburger
Valery Bourke
Mary Breidenbach
Chris Collins
Sherry Gomoll
Drew Moore
Steve Peake
Kathie Schnorr
Gina Scott

Proofreader
Carlos A. Huerta

Indexer
Sharon Hilgenberg

Cover Illustrator
Steve Lyons

Cover Design
Kavish + Kavish

Contents at a Glance

Foreword from Pierre Bézier xxxiii

Introduction 1

Part I: Basic Illustrator Stuff Everyone Should Know **11**

Chapter 1: The Macintosh Computer 13

Chapter 2: The Basics of Adobe Illustrator 47

Chapter 3: Tools 85

Chapter 4: Menus 125

Part II: Getting Started **197**

Chapter 5: Drawing Basic Shapes and Painting 199

Chapter 6: Drawing and Manipulating Paths 239

Chapter 7: Templates, Tracing, Measuring, and Manipulating 277

Chapter 8: Type 293

Chapter 9: Working with Illustrator Files 343

Part III: Advanced Areas **383**

Chapter 10: Path Editing and Transforming 385

Chapter 11: Compound Paths and Masking 405

Chapter 12: Blends and Gradations 425

Chapter 13: Patterns and Graphs 471

Chapter 14: Preferences and Layers 499

Part IV: Filters **525**

Chapter 15: Filter Basics 527

Chapter 16: The Color and Create Filters 539

Chapter 17: The Distort and Stylize Filters 567

Chapter 18: The Object and Pathfinder Filters 589

Chapter 19: The Select and Text Filters 607

Part V: Areas Related to Illustrator 627

Chapter 20: Strokes and Backgrounds 629

Chapter 21: Printing Separations and Traps 655

Chapter 22: Adobe Streamline™ 699

Chapter 23: Case Studies and Discovering Cool Stuff on Your Own 707

Part VI: Appendices 733

Appendix A: Your System and Illustrator 735

Appendix B: Resources 745

Appendix C: How Illustrator Versions 5.0 and 5.5 Differ 749

Appendix D: Taking Files from a Mac to a PC and Back 757

Appendix E: About the Enclosed CD-ROM 759

Appendix F: Keyboard Commands and Shortcuts 763

Index 773
Reader Response Card .... Back of Book

Table of Contents

Introduction 1

I Have a Dream 2
What Is Adobe Illustrator? 2
What's with the 5.0/5.5 Thing on the Cover? 2
A Little More about This Book 3
How to Read This Book 4
How Come There's a Silver Frisbee in the Back? 4
What's Where in the Book 4
Part I: Basic Illustrator Stuff Everyone Should Know 5
Part II: Getting Started 5
Part III: Advanced Areas 6
Part IV: Filters 6
Part V: Areas Related to Illustrator 7
Part VI: Appendices 7
Icons 8
Yo, Ted! 9
Before You Dive into the Book 9

Part I: Basic Illustrator Stuff Everyone Should Know 11

Chapter 1: The Macintosh Computer 13

An End to Traditional Work 13
Why Macintosh? 14
Basic Macintosh Concepts 15
 Consistency 15
 Mousing around 16
 The cursor 17
 Windows 17
 Dialog boxes 19
 Tools 20
 Selecting before doing 21
 Pulling down menus 21
 Keyboard commands 21

Macintosh Terminology 22
Macintosh Hardware 23
    The computer 24
    Keyboards 24
    Of mice and trackballs 25
    Monitors 26
    Floppy disk drives 27
    Hard disk drives 27
    Syquest drives 27
    Optical drives 28
    CD-ROM drives 28
    Tape drives 29
    Scanners 29
    Laser printers, imagesetters, and PostScript 30
    Other strange attachments 31
System Software 32
    System 7, System 7.1, and System 7.5 32
    System 6 32
    What system software should I use? 33
The Finder 33
    The Mac is a Mac because of the Finder 33
    Stuff that happens in the Finder 34
Fonts 35
    Bitmap fonts 35
    PostScript fonts 36
    TrueType fonts 38
    Fonts and Adobe Illustrator 39
        ATM 39
        Multiple Master Fonts 40
        Super ATM 41
Applications 41
    How applications work 41
    Quitting applications 42
Heavens to Megabytes! 42
    Memory terminology 43
    Floppy disk and hard drive memory 43
    RAM (random access memory) 44
    Programs and memory 44

Chapter 2: The Basics of Adobe Ilustrator 47

The Learning Curve 47
That was then; this is not then 48
Techniques for learning more 48
PostScript and Printing 51
What PostScript does 52
Why PostScript is so cool 54
Paths 56
Anchor Points 63
Bézier Curves 67
Direction Points and Direction Lines 68
Clear, Cut, Copy, and Paste 73
Clear 73
Cut, Copy, and Paste 73
The magic Clipboard 74
Undo and Redo 76
Artwork and Preview Modes 77
Artwork mode 77
Preview mode 77
Palettes versus Windows 79
The Document Window 81
Pasteboard 81
Artboard 82
Miscellaneous window stuff 83

Chapter 3: Tools 85

The Toolbox 85
The Selection Tools 89
The Selection tool 93
The Direct Selection tool 94
The Group Selection tool 94
The Viewing Tools 96
The Hand tool 96
The Zoom tool 97
The Path Creation and Editing Tools 100
The mighty Pen tool 100
The path editing tools 101
The Brush tool 103
The Freehand tool 104

The Auto Trace tool 106
The shape creation tools 108
The Measure Tool 108
The Type Tools 109
The Type tool 110
The Path Type tool 111
The Area Type tool 111
The Transformation Tools 111
The Rotate tool 113
The Scale tool 115
The Reflect tool 116
The Shear tool 117
The Paint Bucket and Eyedropper Tools 119
The Eyedropper tool 120
The Paint Bucket tool 120
The Gradient Vector and Blend Tools 120
The Gradient Vector tool 121
The Blend tool 122
The Graph Tools 122
The Page Tool 124

Chapter 4: Menus **125**

Menus That Make Sense 125
Menu rules 127
Using menus effectively 127
The File Menu 129
Preferences 134
The Edit Menu 135
Publishing 138
The Arrange Menu 139
The View Menu 141
The Object Menu 148
Guides 152
Masks 154
Compound paths 155
Crop marks 155
Graphs 157
The Type Menu 159
Alignment 162

The Filter Menu 169
   Missing filters in Illustrator 5.0 170
   Colors 171
   Create 174
   Distort filters 177
   Objects 181
   Pathfinder filters 184
   Select filters 188
   Stylize filters 189
   Text filters 193
The Window Menu 194
The Apple Menu 196

Part II: Getting Started 197

Chapter 5: Drawing Basic Shapes and Painting 199
Making Basic Shapes 199
   Drawing rectangles 201
   Drawing rectangles from their centers 205
   Drawing a perfect square 206
   Drawing rounded rectangles and squares 206
   Rounding corners the other way 210
   Drawing ovals and circles 211
   Creating an entire illustration 215
Creating Cool Shapes 217
   Creating polygons 218
   Creating stars 220
   Angling basic shapes 222
Filling and Stroking Shapes 223
   Fills 223
   Strokes 224
   Combining strokes and fills 226
Using the Paint Style Palette 226
   The many faces of the Paint Style palette 227
   The Stroke and Fill squares 229
   The Apply button and the Auto check box 230
   The Main panel 230
   Slider magic 235
   The Color Swatch panel 236
   Stroke attributes 237

Chapter 6: Drawing and Manipulating Paths 239

Drawing Paths in Illustrator 239
Drawing with the Brush Tool 241
    Calligraphy drawn to order 245
    Bends and ends 246
    Variable widths and pressure-sensitive tablets 247
Drawing with the Freehand Tool 247
    Using the Freehand tool 248
    Drawing open paths and closed paths 250
    Drawing semistraight segments 251
    Erasing in real time 252
    Drawing jagged paths and smooth paths 252
    Adding to an existing open path 254
Drawing Precisely with the Pen Tool 255
    Drawing straight lines 258
    Closing paths 259
    Drawing curves 259
    Knowing the Pen Commandments 262
    Closing curved paths with the Pen tool 265
    Creating curved-corner points 265
    Creating combination-corner points 267
    Using the Pen tool 267
Selecting, Moving, and Deleting Entire Paths 268
Selecting and Moving Portions of Paths 269
The Foreground and the Background 271
Grouping and Ungrouping 274
    Ungrouping 275
    Using the Group Selection tool 276

Chapter 7: Templates, Tracing, Measuring, and Manipulating 277

Using Templates 277
    Tracing templates 281
    When is a template not a template? 282
Measuring 285
    Using the Measure tool 285
    Using the rulers 285
    Using objects 286
    Using the Offset Path filter (for equidistant measuring) 287

Guides 288
    Creating guides 288
    Moving guides 289
    Releasing guides 289
Locking, Hiding, and Moving Objects 290
    Locking 290
    Hiding 291
    Moving 291

Chapter 8: Type **293**
Type Areas 293
Point Type 294
Rectangle Type 295
Area Type 296
    Choosing the good shapes for Area type 297
    Outlining areas of Area type 297
    Doing bizarre things to Area type 299
    Coloring type that is anchored to a path 301
    Designing with Area type 301
Path Type 303
    Type on the top and bottom of a circle 304
    Avoiding Path type trouble 307
    Reversing Path type 307
Selecting Type 309
Editing Type 311
Changing Character Attributes 312
    Using the Character palette 312
    Character palette features 313
    Tracking and kerning 316
Changing Paragraph Attributes 320
    Using the Paragraph palette 320
    Alignment 321
    Indentation, paragraph spacing, and hanging punctuation 322
    Hyphenation 323
    Spacing 324
Controlling the Flow of Type 324
    Type wrapping 325
    Text linking 325
    The trouble with tabs in Illustrator 5.0 326
    The Tab Ruler palette 327

Creating Editable Type Outlines 329
    Making letters that normally appear in your worst nightmares 330
    Creating logos from type outlines 331
    Arcing words and phrases 332
    Masking and other effects 333
    Avoiding font conflicts by creating outlines 334
    Amazing type (and path) effects 335
Special Characters 335
    Symbol typefaces 336
Customizing Fonts 339
Text Filters 340
Other Type Considerations 340

Chapter 9: Working with Illustrator Files 343
Setting up a New Document 343
Changing the Document Setup 346
    Artboard options 346
    View options 347
    Path splitting options 348
    Ruler units 351
    Using the printer's default screen 352
Navigating through the Document 353
    Who's zoomin' who? 353
    The Zoom tools 353
    Other zooming techniques 355
    Using the scroll bars 357
    Scrolling with the Hand tool 357
Artwork Mode versus Preview Mode 358
    Artwork (only) mode 359
    Preview mode 359
    Preview Selection mode 360
    Combining Artwork and Preview modes 362
Now You See It 362
Using Custom Views 364
Managing Files 364
Saving Files 365
    The Save As command 367
    File types 367
    Preview options 368
    Compatibility options 370

Opening and Closing Illustrator Files 372
Opening PICT Templates 373
Placing EPS Files 374
Importing Styles 375
Printing from Illustrator 375
    The Chooser 376
    The Document Setup dialog box 377
    The Page Setup dialog box for Apple LaserWriters 378
    The Page Setup dialog box for PS Printers 380
    The Page Setup dialog box for ImageWriters 380
    Printing with the Apple LaserWriter driver 380
    Printing with the PS Printer driver 381

Part III: Advanced Areas 383

Chapter 10: Path Editing and Transforming 385

Adding and Removing Anchor Points 385
    Adding anchor points 386
    Removing anchor points 387
Splitting Paths 388
Averaging Points and Joining 389
    Averaging points 389
    Joining 390
Converting Direction Points 393
    Converting smooth points 393
    Converting straight corner points 394
    Converting combination corner points 395
    Converting curved corner points 395
Transforming Objects 395
    Creating shadows 396
    Transforming gradients 398
    Rotating into a path 398
    Making tiles using the Reflect tool 399
    Using transformation tools on portions of paths 401
    Rotating into kaleidoscopes 403
    Transforming patterns 404

Chapter 11: Compound Paths and Masking 405

Compound Paths 405
    Creating compound paths 405
    Releasing compound paths 407
    Understanding holes 408
    Overlapping holes 409
    Creating compound paths from separate sets of paths 409
    Type and compound paths 410
Path Directions 411
    The Even-Odd rule, or what happened to my fills? 412
    Reversing path directions 413
Faking a Compound Path 414
Masks 414
    Creating masks 414
    Masking EPS images 416
    Masking blends and other masks 416
    Stroking and filling masking objects 417
    Releasing masks 419
    Masks and printing 419
    Masking with compound paths 420
    Using compound paths and masks in an illustration 421

Chapter 12: Blends and Gradations 425

Understanding Blends and Gradations 425
Blends 428
Creating Linear Blends 431
    Multiple colors with linear blends 432
    Nonlinear blends 433
    Masking blends 435
    New and improved pseudolinear blends 436
    Guidelines for creating color linear blends 437
    End paths for linear blends 439
    Calculating the number of steps 440
    Creating radial blends 442
Creating Shape Blends 443
    Shape blend #1: computer vents 443
    Shape blend #2: circle to star 445
    Complex shape blending 446
    Shape blend #3: cheating 447
    Creating realism with shape blends 450

Airbrushing and the Magic of Stroke Blends 453
   Tubular blends 454
   Spring tube blends 456
   Airbrushed shadows 457
   Creating glows 458
   Softening edges 459
   Neon effects 460
   Backlighting 461
Gradations 462
   The Gradient Vector tool 462
   Using preset gradients 463
   Using the Gradient palette 463
   Shadows, highlights, ghosting, and embossing 465

Chapter 13: Patterns and Graphs 471

Patterns 471
   Using the default patterns 472
   Creating custom patterns 474
   Making seamless patterns 477
   Symmetrical patterns 480
   Line patterns and grids 483
   Diagonal line and grid patterns 484
   Transparency and patterns 484
   Modifying existing patterns 485
   Putting patterns and gradients into patterns 485
   Transforming patterns 486
Graphs 487
   The six types of graphs 490
      Grouped column graphs 490
      Stacked column graphs 490
      Line graphs 492
      Pie graphs 493
      Area graphs 494
      Scatter graphs 494
   Customizing graphs 494
   Using the Graph Data dialog box 495
   Using marker and column designs 496

Chapter 14: Preferences and Layers 499

Preferences 499
Modifying the Start-up File 500
Changing Application Preferences 502
   The General Preferences dialog box 502
      The Constrain angle option 503
      The Corner radius option 505
      The Freehand tolerance option 506
      The Auto Trace gap option 507
      The Snap to point option 507
      The Transform pattern tiles option 508
      The Scale line weight option 508
      The Area select option 509
      The Use precise cursors option 509
      The Ruler units option 511
      The Indent/shift units option 512
      The Cursor key option 512
      The Size/leading option 512
      The Baseline shift option 513
      The Tracking option 513
      The Undo levels option 513
      The Paste remembers layers option 514
      The Greek text limit option 514
   Other application preferences 515
      The Color Matching dialog box 515
      The Hyphenation Options dialog box 517
      The Plug-Ins Folder preference 517
      Placement and Toolbox value preferences 517
   Things you can't customize 517
Layers 518
Getting started with layers 518
The Layers palette 520
   The main section of the Layers palette 521
   The pop-up menu of the Layers palette 522
   Layer advice and strategies 523

Part IV: Filters 525

Chapter 15: Filter Basics 527

Filters in Illustrator 527
66 Filters and No One Uses Them 528

Comparing and Contrasting Illustrator and Photoshop Filters 529
The Plug-Ins Folder 531
The Great FPU Scare 532
Third-Party Filters 533
Filter Combinations and Relations 533
Why You Can Choose the Last Filter but Never "Last Filter" 534
Those Other Filters and Plug-Ins 535
    Acrobat PDF File Format (5.5 only) 535
    Artwork View Speedup 535
    Document Info (5.5 only) 535
    Overprint Black (5.5 only) 536
    PICT File Format (5.5 only) 537
    Pressure Support 537
    Make/Delete Riders 537

Chapter 16: The Color and Create Filters 539

Manipulating Colors with the Color Filters 539
    Techniques for creating shadows and highlights 541
    Creating extruded multiple path objects 541
    Creating negatives 543
Instant Creations with the Create Filters 544
    Adding strokes and fills to masks 544
    Creating mosaics 545
    Adding trim marks 553
Creating Polygons, Stars, and Spirals 554
    Using the Create filters to produce special effects 555
    Creating patterns with polygons 559

Chapter 17: The Distort and Stylize Filters 567

See, I Told You So: There Are Real Filters in Illustrator 567
The Distort Filters 568
    The Free Distort filter 568
    The Twirl filter 571
    The Random Mangle filters 574
        The Roughen filter 576
        The Scribble and Tweak filters 578
The Stylize Filters 580
    The Add Arrowheads filter 581
    The Drop Shadows filter 583
    The Punk and Bloat filters 584

The Round Corners filter 586
The Calligraphy filter 587

Chapter 18: The Object and Pathfinder Filters 589

The Object and Pathfinder Filters 589
Using the Object Filters 590
    The Add Anchor Points filter 591
    The alignment and distribution filters 591
    The transform each filters 593
    The "pathfinder" object filters 594
        The Offset Path filter 595
        The Outline Stroked Path filter 596
The Pathfinder Filters 596
    Changes from Version 5.0 to Version 5.5 597
    The Pathfinder Options dialog box 597
    The combine filters 599
    The overlay filters 600
        The Divide filter 601
        The Outline filter 602
        The Reduce and Merge filters 603
The Mix Filters 604
The Trap Filter 605

Chapter 19: The Select and Text Filters 607

The Select Filters 607
The Paint Style Selection Filters 608
    The Same Fill Color filter 608
    The Same Paint Style filter 609
    The Same Stroke Color filter 609
    The Same Stroke Weight filter 610
    Combining the Paint Style selection filters 610
The Select Inverse Filter 611
    The Select Masks filter 611
    The Select Stray Points filter 612
The Text Filters 613
    The Text Export filter 613
    The Text Find filter 613
    The Change Case filter 615
    The Check Spelling filter 616
    The Find Font filter 618

The Revert Text Paths filter 619
The Rows & Columns filter 620
The Smart Punctuation filter 624

Part V: Areas Related to Illustrator 627

Chapter 20: Strokes and Backgrounds 629

Using Strokes 629
The secret magic of strokes 630
Using the stroke charts 632
Stroking type 638
Creating rough edges 640
Using fills to create half-stroked paths 641
Workin' on the railroad 642
The wild river 644
The highway 644
Putting type into strokes 650
Creating Backgrounds for Illustrations 651
Using gradients for backgrounds 652
Using blends and blend effects for backgrounds 653

Chapter 21: Printing Separations and Traps 655

Printing 655
Printing composites 655
Printing color separations 657
Spot color separation 658
Process color separation 659
Combining both spot and process color separations 662
Adobe Separator 663
Using Separator 664
The main Separator window 666
Margin marks 666
The bounding box, bleed, and page direction 669
Changing printer information 670
Changing page size 671
Changing the orientation 672
Understanding emulsion 674
Setting the halftone screen 674

Changing from positive to negative to positive 679
Modifying the Transfer function 680
Working with Different Color Separations 682
Getting information about an illustration 684
Printing separations 685
Saving separations 686
Separator secrets 686
Printing Separations from Other Applications 687
Traps 687
Understanding what traps do 687
Trapping Illustrator 5.0 files 691
Complex trapping techniques in Illustrator 5.0 694
Trapping in Illustrator 5.5 698

Chapter 22: Adobe Streamline 699

The Streamline Software 699
The Streamline Toolbox and Menu Items 700
Streamline tools 700
Streamline menus 703
Using Streamline 706

Chapter 23: Case Studies and Discovering Cool Stuff on Your Own 707

Case Study #1: "A Natural Form of Expression" 707
The concept 708
The animals 708
The fish 709
The bug 709
The salamander and its rock 710
The snake 712
The parrot 713
The background 714
The type 715
The production 715
Case Study #2: "VW Corrado" 716
Preparing to illustrate 717
Creating the body 719
Creating the panel gradients 720
Molding and pieces 720

Interior design 720
Glass and taillights 721
Creating the trunk lock 722
Adding all the little things 723
The wheels 723
Getting the lighting just right 724
Creating the background 724
Case Study #3: The Bézier Logo, Business Cards,
 Letterhead, and Envelopes 724
The concept and the logo 725
Designing the cards, letterhead, and envelopes 725
Printing the job 727
Discovering Cool Stuff on Your Own 728
How I figured out cool stuff 728
Knowing versus memorizing 729
What you can do to learn more 730
Getting answers and information from Adobe 731

Part VI: Appendices 733

Appendix A: Your System and Illustrator 735

System Requirements 735
The computer 735
RAM 736
Other attachments 736
System Recommendations 736
CPU and FPU 737
Too much RAM is never enough 738
Adobe Illustrator on Floppy Disks 738
Installing Illustrator from disks 738
Disk 1 739
Disk 2 739
Disk 3 739
Disk 4 740
Disk 5 740
Disk 6 740
Disk 7 740
Custom installation 740
Illustrator on CD-ROM 742

Appendix B: Resources 745

People and Service Company Resources 745
Software Company Resources 746

Appendix C: How Illustrator Versions 5.0 and 5.5 Differ 749

Illustrator 5.0 749
    New stuff 750
    Tools 750
    Menus 751
    Shortcuts 752
Illustrator 5.5 752
    New features in 5.5 753
        Text changes 753
        Pathfinder filter changes 754
        Other filter changes 754
        Other changes 754
    Illustrator 5.5 tools 755
    Illustrator 5.5 menus 755
    Illustrator 5.5 shortcuts 755
Upcoming Versions 755

Appendix D: Taking Files from a Mac to a PC and Back 757

A Brief History of Computing's "Tower of Babel" 757
Transferring Illustrator Files across Platforms 758

Appendix E: About the Enclosed CD-ROM 759

Running the Tutorials 759
Examining the Artwork 760
The Filter Charts 760
The Fonts 761
    Lefty Casual 2.1 761
    Ransom Note 2.1 761
The Clip Art 762
The Demo Software 762

Appendix F: Keyboard Commands and Shortcuts 763

Menu Commands 763
Tool Time 764
    Accessing tools 765
    Using tools 765
Viewing Shortcuts 767
Generic Dialog Box Commands 767
Type Command Shortcuts 768
Palette Commands and Shortcuts 769
Miscellaneous 771

Index 773

Reader Response Card .... Back of Book

Foreword by Pierre Bézier

Around 1960, engineers and technicians in the European car industry were divided into two groups: those who worked on mechanical parts and those who worked on car body parts.

For the mechanical group, the surfaces that could be manufactured were clearly defined with dimensions and limits — there was no place for haggling or bargaining at inspection time, and the verdict was simple: GOOD or SCRAP.

For the body-design group, things were far from being simple. From the stylist's small scale mock-up to the full scale drawing of the "skin," to the clay model, to the final drawing, to the master model, to the stamping tools — each rendering was supposed to be in accordance with the preceding one. Designers used french curves, sweeps, and lathes (plastic splines), but small discrepancies could not be avoided at each step. These minor errors added up, to the detriment of the final product.

Although these problems had gone on for decades, people were not satisfied and still looked for a solution. They believed, as Plato said, that "Number is the expression of everything," and, as Lord William Kelvin said, that "No one can claim to have mastered a phenomenon as long as he has not been able to express it with figures."

By 1960, a small number of people believed that the computer could provide an acceptable solution to the problem of discrepancies in measurements. The aircraft industry was probably the first industry in the U.S. to use computers, but the automotive industry rapidly followed suit.

At this time, two solutions were considered. The first solution was to keep the general process of manufacturing and, with the help of computers (CRT or numerically controlled machine tools), improve one or two steps. The second solution was to forget the existing scheme and start from scratch to take full advantage of the computer's capabilities. This step entailed greater risks but also had greater advantages.

For those who chose the latter solution, the first task was to build a list of requirements that included the following:

- Creating or adopting a mathematical system that could be easily understood and operated by draftsmen, designers, and methods people. The system needed to describe space curves — not only conics and surfaces — and to provide an accurate, complete, and distortion-free definition of the curves. It needed to be easily transmitted between offices, shops, and subcontractors.

- Providing the body- and tool-drawing offices with full-scale drawing machines, controlled completely by computers that work in interactive mode, such as those capable of tracing curves at a speed of one foot per second.

- Equipping the drawing offices, not the tool shops, with rapid milling machines that could carve large portions of a car — the top, the hood, and so on — in a soft material, such as Styrofoam, urethane foam, or plaster.

- Devising the relevant software.

- Equipping the tool shops with heavy NC milling machines for manufacturing stamping units.

In 1960, the mathematical theory was based on the use of conics — nonrational polynomials with vector coefficients. Mathematical theory now includes B-splines and NURBS, but mathematicians still search for other solutions.

By the end of the '60s, some simple systems were operative, but a complete system was not fully operative until the end of the '70s. Since that time, many basic improvements in car design have been developed, including color, reflection lines, perspective viewing, animation, finite elements, crash simulation, aerodynamics, stress and strain, vibration and noise, and so on.

No doubt, the advent of CAD/CAM has been one of the most important changes that took place in the industry during the present century. Of course, it is not necessary for the lay user to master the complete theory — one can play basketball without referring to Galileo, Newton, Keppler, or Einstein — but students and engineers who take part in the development or improvement of a system will find plenty of food for thought in this book.

Pierre E. Bézier

Introduction

If I were stranded on a desert island with a Power Mac 8100 and I had to choose one software package to have with me, I would choose Adobe Illustrator. Of course, contemplating such a thing says something (and not a good something) about my increasingly fragile state of mind, but it also lets you know how much I enjoy using this software. When you understand that Adobe Illustrator won out over F/A-18 Hornet, a fighter simulation game, and Spaceward Ho!, a conquer-the-galaxy game, it should become even more apparent to you that Illustrator is "good stuff."

I wasn't always this enamored with Illustrator. After the first several months of using the software in 1988, I grumbled every time I had to jump out of PageMaker to use Illustrator for what I thought was its primary function: rotating type. Since that time, I've learned that Illustrator isn't just about rotating type (although it does this procedure exceedingly well), but it is also about creating almost anything that you can imagine with a few basic tools.

So what took me so long? Well, in contrast to most Macintosh users, I read and followed the tutorial provided with the software. But I never really got the hang of masks, the Pen tool, or those silly little round points and lines sticking out from the silly little square points. It took several years before Illustrator techniques began to sink into my overly thick skull.

Part of the problem was that there wasn't anyone to show me exactly what to do and why — no one else seemed to know any more than I did. The other problem was that I couldn't find any good books on Illustrator. The first problem was never really solved, although I have managed to keep myself busy in my spare time training others in most desktop publishing applications, including Illustrator.

This book is meant to solve the second problem. If there is something I have learned about the way Illustrator works, I have crammed it in this book somewhere. The facts-per-page ratio rivals that of Webster's new edition, but I think you'll find the *Macworld Illustrator 5.0/5.5 Bible* a little more readable.

I Have a Dream . . .

My goal in writing this book is not only to tell you how to do the basics, the advanced stuff, and the really cool techniques of Illustrator, but also to spread my enthusiasm for the program to everyone who reads this book. If you're up until 2 a.m. one morning trying to improve upon that reflective chrome effect you've blended, then my goal has been achieved.

If I can help you figure out how to make that stubborn line of type appear on both the top and the bottom of that #$%#@! circle, I'll sleep better. After you draw your first cloverleaf with the Pen tool, you'll begin to understand the potential of what you can do with Illustrator.

What Is Adobe Illustrator?

Technically, Adobe Illustrator is a vector-based drawing software. Huh? Because technical definitions are boring, a real definition is in order: Adobe Illustrator is a program that allows you easily and precisely to create full color or black-and-white artwork. Type can be added and manipulated in any way imaginable. Photographic images can be imported and transformed in a number of ways. Finished artwork can be printed at any size with no loss in quality.

You can use Adobe Illustrator to create giant billboards, brochures, and business cards in full color. Adobe Illustrator is used by most advertising agencies to design logos, packages, and advertisements.

When combined with other software, such as Adobe Dimensions, Adobe Streamline, and Adobe Separator (also discussed in this book), Illustrator becomes the most powerful design tool at an artist's disposal. If you can imagine something, Illustrator allows you to put it on paper.

What's with the 5.0/5.5 Thing on the Cover?

In the course of my writing this book, Adobe developed an upgrade for Illustrator, which it christened 5.5. I discuss all the cool stuff found in 5.5 in this book, with indicators to show what the differences are.

Appendix D contains a summary of all the great new features that Adobe includes in Version 5.5. One thing that is really important: If you're thinking about purchasing a Power Mac, do it and get the 5.5 upgrade to Illustrator. Version 5.5 was written *for* the PowerPC computers and hums along quite nicely on a lowly Power Mac 6100, currently the bottom of the barrel in Power Macs, but a step above the fastest Quadra.

Because the version upgrade was compartmentalized, very few changes affect the way you use the program. If you have Version 5.5, you have more to read in this book.

A Little More about This Book

This book is written in contemporary language so that most Homo sapiens can comprehend the information within. As you read along, think of me talking directly to you about Illustrator and visualize yourself listening, with the occasional nod to show that you haven't fallen asleep.

One of my former Illustrator trainees told me to write the way I talk. Fortunately for you, it's hard to mumble when I type (although my editors may disagree). I've tried to make this book as interesting as possible and have even included the occasional pun ("Now rotate that as far as you're *inclined* to") to keep topics, such as the dreaded compound paths, as upbeat as possible.

You don't need to be an artist to use Illustrator, and you don't need to be one to read this book. If you aren't an artist, maybe you can pick up some design tips from the illustrations, most of which were done by an exceptional graphic artist. If you are an artist, you may enjoy verbally ripping the enclosed artwork to shreds — something most of my artist friends seem to enjoy — and creating your own.

You don't need to be a computer techie, either. If you are, great; you can skip over the explanations of FPUs, RAM caches and MHz that pop up occasionally. If not, you can still skip over those explanations.

This book was written to appeal to every Illustrator user out there, from the novice who is having trouble with that blasted shrink wrap to the guy providing Illustrator tech support at Adobe who wants something to do when he doesn't feel like answering his ringing telephone. If you use Illustrator all the time or just once a month, this book has something in it for you.

How to Read This Book

If you're a novice user of Illustrator, start at the beginning and read through the whole book. If you've been using Illustrator for a while but you hate the Pen tool, skim through the first section and then dive into Chapter 6, which should replace your hatred with desire — if not all-out lust for the Pen tool. If you're familiar with most aspects of Illustrator, jump ahead to Parts III and IV, which have all sorts of tasty new techniques and helpful hints (heck, even I learned something when I read it). If you're an experienced Illustrator user, go right to the sections that interest you the most . . . there aren't any special code words given out in the earlier chapters that allow you to read the later ones.

How Come There's a Silver Frisbee in the Back?

I've included a CD-ROM with this book because I know that there are a few things that even a book of this magnitude can't cover. I've packed all sorts of cool stuff into the CD, the most important being QuickTime demonstrations of many examples in this book and other demonstrations of things we couldn't squeeze into the book.

If this isn't enough, all the artwork used in the color insert of the book is available in Illustrator format for your perusal. Several clip art companies that use Adobe Illustrator to create their clip art have made samples of their artwork on the CD. Software for connecting to America Online and a demo version of Adobe Streamline are included. Finally, two high-quality shareware fonts, RansomNote and LeftyCasual, are also included.

What's Where in the Book

This book has been designed so that if you were the one stranded on the desert island with a Power Mac 8100 and Illustrator, this is the book you would read while waiting for your RAM (or whatever the local ComputerMart was out of before you took that fateful trip on the Minnow) from Airborne Express. We are assuming, probably unfairly, that the Professor couldn't fashion some 70ns RAM from papaya seeds and explain to you himself the inner workings of PostScript Level 2.

The book, all six million pages of it, has been divided into five parts, and those parts each contain about five chapters. At the end of the book is a supplementary part of appendices, ranging in topics from installing the software to a comprehensive listing of key commands.

Part I: Basic Illustrator Stuff Everyone Should Know

If you want to learn Illustrator from the ground up, start here. I've even thrown in a chapter (no charge) on the Macintosh computer. These chapters contain the fundamentals that deliver all that great background information and also serve as a quick reference to the tools and menus in the software.

Chapter 1: The Macintosh Computer is a summary of the important things about Macintosh computers. The good, the bad, and the mouse, as it were.

Chapter 2: The Basics of Adobe Illustrator discusses the program's fundamental features. Some concepts critical to understanding Illustrator are included here. All sorts of topics are covered, from PostScript to combination corner points.

Chapter 3: Tools is devoted to all the powerful and unusual tools Illustrator has to offer. If you aren't sure how to use a tool, look here for a quick summary. In addition to each tool's function and use, basic techniques for using the tools are discussed, as well.

Chapter 4: Menus is the end-all summary of the menus in Adobe Illustrator.

Part II: Getting Started

Now it's time to put muscle to the mouse and create an illustration. Drawing, working with type, and most of the basic techniques that you need to know for doing the cool stuff in later parts are explained here.

Chapter 5: Drawing Basic Shapes and Painting gets your mouse wet by creating ovals, rectangles, polygons, and stars and coloring them.

Chapter 6: Drawing and Manipulating Paths is where you get to use the Brush tool, the Freehand tool, and (gasp!) the Pen tool to create some really cool illustrations.

Chapter 7: Templates, Tracing, Measuring, and Manipulating serves as a catchall for the different things you can do now that you can create basic shapes and draw.

Chapter 8: Type is all about using type in Illustrator. Designing with type is one of the most fun and rewarding activities in Illustrator.

Chapter 9: Working with Illustrator Files shows you what to do after the award-winning design has been completed and you want to stop drawing and fly your World-War-II-era Hellcat over the Pacific.

Part III: Advanced Areas

Sure, this is a scary title, but you shouldn't be intimidated. This part contains the *fun* stuff.

Chapter 10: Path Editing and Transforming contains all the techniques that you need to fix mistakes in your artwork as well as move, stretch, rotate, flip, and skew your illustration all over the place.

Chapter 11: Compound Paths and Masking tackles these feared areas with an arrogance that frightens paths into the right directions. Learn how to put holes in your paths and how to hide everything outside a certain path.

Chapter 12: Blends and Gradations is *the* fun chapter. Illustrator is at its most enjoyable here as you blend paths from shape to shape and color to color.

Chapter 13: Patterns and Graphs seems to link an unlikely pair, but these two items have more than a few things in common. Learn to use patterns to fill objects with seamless, repeating designs and how to take advantage of Illustrator's customizable graphing capabilities.

Chapter 14: Preferences and Layers shows you how to make Illustrator sit up and bark like it's supposed to when you create a new document and how to organize artwork on separate layers.

Part IV: Filters

The huge menu full of Filters was the most powerful and significant feature to be implemented by Illustrator 5.0 back in 1993. I've given filters their own part because they are an incredibly powerful addition to the software.

Chapter 15: Filter Basics tells you all you need to know about filters and includes information on the filters that don't fall into any of the other filter chapters.

Chapter 16: The Color and Create Filters chapter explains how to use the color adjustment filters and the create filters.

Chapter 17: The Distort and Stylize Filters chapter is about *real* filters. The filters in these categories are similar to their Photoshop cousins.

Chapter 18: The Object and Pathfinder Filters chapter discusses Illustrator's power filters. These filters are Illustrator-specific and do things that would normally take hours to accomplish manually.

Chapter 19: The Select and Text Filters chapter explains the selection and text filters. The selection filters make selecting difficulties a thing of the past, and the text filters (especially the 5.5 filters) make working with text almost as easy as using a word processor.

Part V: Areas Related to Illustrator

This part includes all sorts of topics that needed to be discussed but didn't fit in any other category. Adobe Dimensions and Adobe Streamline, both companion products to Illustrator, are explained.

Chapter 20: Strokes and Backgrounds is another fun chapter in this book. Read this chapter if you want to amaze your family and friends with your Illustrator expertise.

Chapter 21: Printing Separations and Traps is an in-depth look at how to create color illustrations that will eventually be color separated and printed. Adobe Separator, color separation software included with Illustrator, is explained in detail.

Chapter 22: Adobe Streamline is a rundown on the Streamline software, which takes scanned images and automatically converts them into editable outline format that Illustrator can read.

Chapter 23: Case Studies and Discovering Cool Stuff on Your Own dissects two different illustrations by prominent illustrators and looks at how a problematic trapping situation was dealt with.

Part VI: Appendices

This part has several different appendices that contain all sorts of useful reference information.

Appendix A: Your System and Illustrator contains information on what type of system Illustrator works best on, how to get the best performance from Illustrator, and how to install the software.

Appendix B: Resources contains information on how to contact contributing artists, software vendors, and other companies that may provide useful information.

Appendix C: How Illustrator Versions 5.0 and 5.5 differ lists the changes in versions from Version 5.0 to Version 5.5.

Appendix D: Taking Files from a Mac to a PC and Back shows you step by step how to do this procedure.

Appendix E: About the Enclosed CD-ROM provides information on the contents of the CD-ROM that is included with this book.

Appendix F: Keyboard Commands and Shortcuts isn't just a listing of keyboard commands; it also explains why a particular command is used for a certain function.

Icons

Most computer books use funny little pictures, called *icons,* to lure the unsuspecting reader into reading some small tidbit of information. Not wanting to be politically incorrect, the *Macworld Illustrator 5.0/5.5 Bible* uses several of these icons.

The Power Tip icon highlights concepts and techniques that I was just pleased as punch to come up with because I think they are particularly helpful for using the program. By reading the information in this icon, you are spoon-feeding my ego. If you're the type that eats the icing before the cake, skim through the book looking for these icons first.

Bad things can sometimes happen when you use Illustrator, and reading the Caution icons can help you avoid running into a lot of trouble. If you're a manic depressive, you'll feel right at home skimming through the book looking *just* for these icons.

The Note icon gives you additional information on the topic I'm writing about at the time. Read these icons if you're a trivia buff.

The Cross Reference icon points you to someplace else where there is related information. If you are a naturally fidgety person, skim through the book and follow the Cross Reference icons through the book to where they take you.

The 5.5 icon points out significant differences between Versions 5.0 and 5.5 of Illustrator. If you have just upgraded or will do so soon, skim through the book looking for these icons.

Yo, Ted!

If you would like to get in touch with me, whether to complain that I didn't use your favorite font or because you think I should have included a chapter just on Gaussian blurs (which, of course, are a part of Photoshop and not Illustrator), there are several ways to contact me.

The best and fastest way is by e-mail on America Online at Toulouse or via the Internet at toulouse@aol.com. If you must use snail mail, do so at P.O. Box 4428, Scottsdale, AZ 85261. E-mail always gets a response. Snail mail might but usually doesn't.

Before You Dive into the Book . . .

Be at peace with your inner self and take a moment of silence to reflect (or to shear) on the great undertaking you are about to venture in to. There is no turning back, great warrior.

Seriously, though, take your time ingesting the material in this book — there's an awful lot of it. Watch a few demos. Try to do some of the steps that lead you throughout the book. Look at the pretty pictures and try to figure out how they were drawn. Draw your own pretty pictures.

Last, but far from least, *have fun*. Though you may not know it yet, that's what Illustrator is really all about.

Basic Illustrator Stuff Everyone Should Know

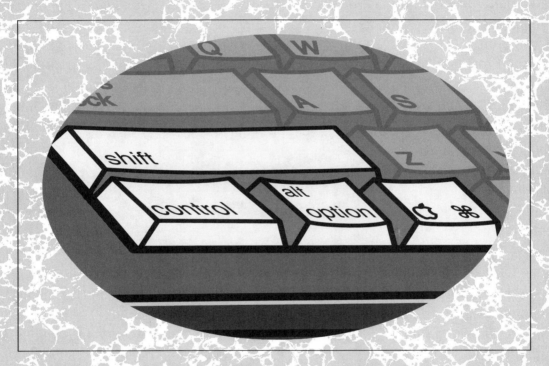

The first time you open up Adobe Illustrator on-screen, you may be overwhelmed by the number of tools and menu items that you have to choose from. As if that weren't bad enough, you also have a blank white page staring you in the face, daring you to create something — anything.

In this section, I discuss the fundamental principles of the Macintosh and Illustrator. If you feel comfortable in your knowledge of the basics, skim through this part; however, you may find something that interests you or provides you with a different perspective.

There are many fundamental concepts and techniques in Illustrator, and you'll find the basis for these concepts and techniques in the first few chapters of this section. In Illustrator, more than most other major applications, a fundamental understanding of the program is needed to be able to get the most out of it. After the basics are understood, there are no limits with Adobe Illustrator.

The Macintosh Computer

CHAPTER 1

In This Chapter

- Why graphic artists prefer Macintosh computers
- Some Macintosh computer basics
- The pieces of a Macintosh computer system
- How system software and the Finder work
- All about fonts
- What programs are and how they work
- Memory: disks and chips

An End to Traditional Work

Today, most graphic designers work on Macintosh computer systems. Not too long ago, however, artists and illustrators worked by hand, not on computers. It may seem hard to believe, but artists spent hours and hours with T squares, rulers, french curves, and type galleys from their local typesetters (see Figure 1-1).

Now, of course, artists and artist wanna-bes spend hours and hours with their Macintosh, a mouse, a monitor, and type on-screen that they've set themselves. Some traditional artists are still out there . . . although they seem to be a dying breed. In our world of overnight deliveries and impossible-to-meet deadlines, high-speed Macintosh computers have become a necessity.

Figure 1-1:
The shift to
computerized
drawing.

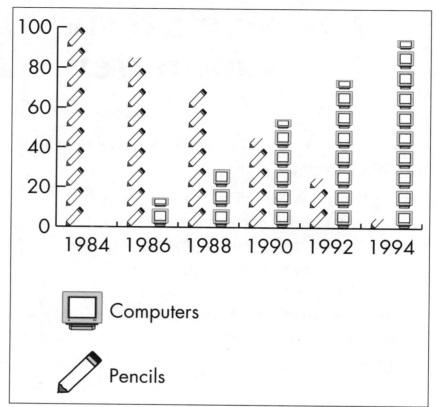

Why Macintosh?

Why not use a Pentium PC with Windows? Why not a Sun Sparc 10 workstation? Remember the old Life cereal commercials with the kid Mikey? The point of those commercials was that if you didn't like Life cereal, you probably had never tried Life cereal. The same can be said for the Macintosh. I have used Windows systems and Sun systems, as well as Commodore Amiga and Atari ST systems. I like the Mac better. It just feels right.

From a business standpoint, the Macintosh is definitely the system to have if you are involved in graphic design, photo retouching, image manipulation, and, of course, desktop publishing. Macs are the standard by which all other systems with similar purposes are measured, and they are more popular than any other system for graphic design work. Macintosh systems are now being used as high-end prepress color systems, and most publishers use them as their core system. In addition, Apple Computer's vision of the future is one in which Macintosh computers outsell Windows-based computers; currently, Windows systems outnumber Macintosh systems about eight to one.

If your primary concern is having a computer that is user friendly, well, that's what the Macintosh is all about. "The Computer for the Rest of Us" is still the easiest system to unpack, assemble, and configure of any computers that are available today. Because of the strict guidelines that Macintosh developers must follow when they create software for the Mac, a common, consistent interface enables users to pick up new software quickly.

 On the subject of PCs, back in the early 1980s, it was PC (*politically correct*, in this case) to own and use a PC. In the mid-'80s, it was PC to own and use a Mac. In the late '80s/early '90s, it became PC to use a PC. And now, in the mid 90s, it is once again PC to use a Mac. Jeesh.

Basic Macintosh Concepts

Before you work with Macintosh programs, you need to get a few basic concepts under your belt. Even if you are an experienced Mac user, now is a good time to review; you may be surprised at what you learn!

Consistency

The consistency between various types of software is most apparent in the menus that you can pull down in all Mac programs. Every Mac program has at least two menus: the File menu and the Edit menu. The File menu (see Figure 1-2) usually contains options for New, Open, Close, Save, Print, and Quit. The Edit menu (see Figure 1-3) contains Undo, Cut, Copy, Paste, and Clear choices. These commands work about the same way in every piece of Macintosh software, so you can perform these basic operations in every program as soon as you load it onto your system.

Figure 1-2:
The File menu from the Finder.

File	
New Folder	⌘N
Open	⌘O
Print	⌘P
Close Window	⌘W
Get Info	⌘I
Sharing...	
Duplicate	⌘D
Make Alias	⌘M
Put Away	⌘Y
Find...	⌘F
Find Again	⌘G
Page Setup...	
Print Window...	

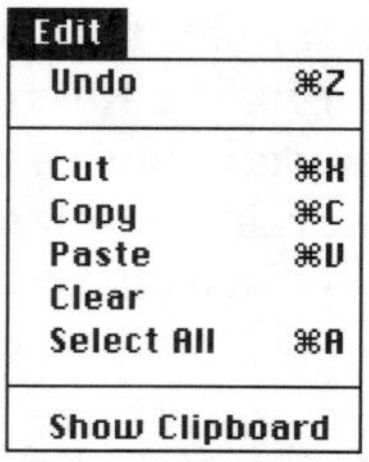

Figure 1-3:
The Edit menu from the Finder.

Edit	
Undo	⌘Z
Cut	⌘H
Copy	⌘C
Paste	⌘U
Clear	
Select All	⌘A
Show Clipboard	

Other types of consistency are not quite so obvious:

- Double-clicking a program's icon to run a program

- The Save As and Open dialog boxes

- Window functions

- Basic command keys for the basic menu commands (for commands on the File and Edit menus, for example)

- The Automatic adaptation of programs to their environment (multiple monitors and so on)

- Several ways to do an action (for example, clicking the mouse, typing a command, and pulling down a menu)

Mousing around

Most applications on a Macintosh require a mouse for selecting items, pulling down menus, moving objects, and clicking buttons.

Learning to use the mouse efficiently can require a great deal of patience, practice, and persistence. In most programs, you can master the mouse quickly, but using the mouse with Illustrator's Pen tool takes patience, practice, and persistence to a new extreme. A fun way to get used to working with a mouse is by playing a Macintosh mouse-driven game, such as Eric's Ultimate Solitaire from Delta Tao. After several hours of play (providing you don't get fired by your employer or kicked out of the house by your irritated spouse), you will become a mouse master.

You use the mouse to perform three basic functions:

- **Clicking,** which is pressing and releasing the mouse button in one step.

- **Dragging,** which is pressing the mouse button and keeping it pressed while you move the mouse.

- **Double-clicking,** which is quickly pressing and releasing the mouse button twice in the same location.

The cursor

Although one of the most oft-used phrases when people are using a Macintosh is "@#&*%!!," that isn't what I mean when I refer to a cursor. The cursor is the little animated picture that moves in the same direction as the mouse. (If the cursor seems to be moving in the opposite direction from the mouse, check to make sure that the mouse isn't upside down, or, heaven forbid, that you aren't upside down.) Usually, the cursor is in the shape of an arrow, and when the computer is busy — doing whatever it is a computer does when it is busy (computing?) — an ugly little watch takes its place. Many times, the cursor takes the form of a tool that you are using. Figure 1-4 shows some of the cursors that appear in Adobe Illustrator.

Figure 1-4:
An assortment of cursors from Adobe Illustrator.

Windows

All windows in the Macintosh follow similar rules. The most important rule is that the active window (the one in which you are currently working) is always in front of any other windows. If the window that you want to work in is not in front of the other windows on the screen, just click it once with the mouse to bring it to the front. You use the window's title bar to move the window around, and moving a window usually makes it active. Figure 1-5 shows an active window.

Windows is an operating system for IBM-compatible PCs that is similar in form and function to the Macintosh Operating System. Most graphic artists shy away from the "clunky" feel of Windows compared to the "precise" feel of a Mac.

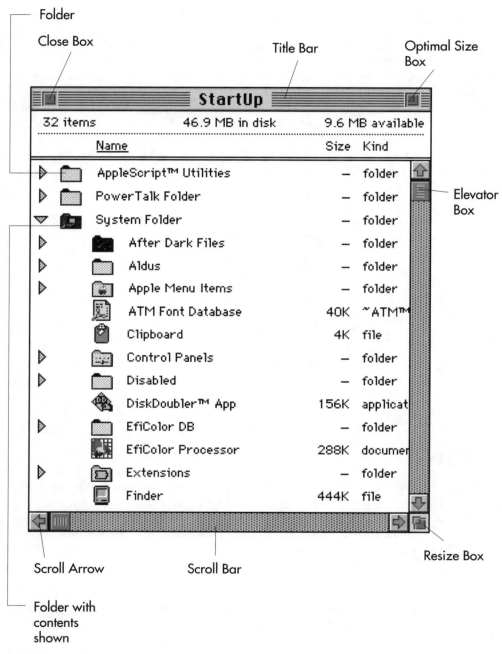

Figure 1-5: An active window in the Finder.

The corner boxes on the windows behave the same way in all programs. Clicking in the upper lefthand corner box closes the window; if you have made changes since the last time you saved your work, a dialog box appears, asking whether you want to save changes. Clicking and dragging in the lower righthand corner of a window resizes the window. Clicking in the upper righthand corner of a window toggles between the current size and a preset "good" size, which may be the size of the document or the size of the entire screen.

You use the scroll bars and their arrows to move through the information in a window when the document contains more information than you can view in that size window. Clicking the arrows shows the hidden information slowly; clicking on the gray bars moves the information about the distance of the open window; and dragging the little scroll box (also known as an elevator box) moves to the part of the document that is proportional to the distance you drag.

Dialog boxes

Dialog boxes are sometimes referred to incorrectly as windows, but they share very little in common with a standard window. A dialog box usually appears when the computer is giving you information or asking you to verify or change information. The dialog box creates a "dialog" between you and the system.

Dialog boxes normally don't have a title bar at the top; many dialog boxes have no title at all (see Figure 1-6). The most common dialog box is the type that appears when you do something that the computer perceives as wrong; it asks you to click an OK button to tell the computer that you have read the dialog box information and understand it. A rather annoying characteristic of dialog boxes makes ignoring the contents of the box difficult: Normally, you have to click OK before you can do anything else, even if you disagree with the information in the box.

Figure 1-6:
An alert dialog box.

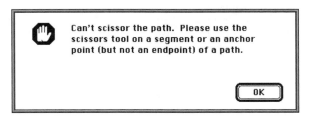

Some dialog boxes have areas where you can choose options by checking check boxes and selecting radio buttons (see Figure 1-7). Check boxes come in sets where any combination of choices is possible. You can choose all of the options, none of them, or any number in between, in any order. Radio buttons also come in sets, but only one radio button can be selected at any given time.

Figure 1-7:
A standard dialog
box.

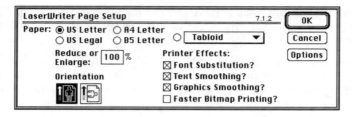

Adobe Illustrator's dialog boxes often have editable text fields, which are areas where you can enter values in the form of numbers or, sometimes, text. When you enter text information in a dialog box, it becomes second nature to press Tab to move to the next box, Shift-Tab to move to the preceeding box, and Return when you finish making changes. If you enter a number or character that is out of range (too high, too low, or the wrong type of character — for example, letters in a box that requires numbers), Illustrator shows you another dialog box that explains what the original box requires. When text in a dialog box is highlighted, you do not need to delete that text before typing; highlighted text is automatically deleted when you press any key on the keyboard.

Tools

Most programs for the Macintosh have a Toolbox (see Figure 1-8) that contains various types of tools that you use to create and manipulate objects on the screen. Although the tools vary widely from one application to another, the way that you use the Toolbox in each program is the same. You simply click the tool once, and you can then use that tool for the next operation you perform in that program. Normally, the tool remains selected until you choose another tool, but in certain software (for example, QuarkXPress), the tool may "jump back" to another tool. In many programs, certain key combinations enable you to select a tool temporarily (Illustrator has many of these key combinations).

Figure 1-8:
The Adobe Illustrator Toolbox.

Selecting before doing

Possibly the most common concept in the Macintosh world is *selecting before doing*. In order to change any existing icon, picture, object, or text, you first have to select it. You can select items in many ways, but the most common method is to click an object. Visual clues, such as handles, are usually present to indicate that an object is selected. You select text by dragging the cursor across characters; the text will either reverse or be surrounded by a selection color (see Figure 1-9). Double-clicking a word usually selects that word; this technique also works for a stand-alone number.

Figure 1-9:
Highlighted
text.

Part of this line of type is selected.

Pulling down menus

All Macintosh applications have menus, and most applications have a File menu and an Edit menu. To see what is in a menu, point to the menu item (for example, the word *File*) and press and hold down the mouse button. A list of choices appears. Keeping the button pressed, pull down to select a menu item (for example, the word *Save*) and then release the mouse button.

An ellipsis (three periods [. . .]) after a menu item means that a dialog box will appear to give you choices or ask you to verify information.

Special symbols and characters that are to the far right side of a menu item are the keyboard command for that menu item.

If you see a little sideways triangle at the right side of a menu item, a pop-up menu will appear when you pull down to that menu item. You then pull over to the pop-up menu and then up or down to select an item on the pop-up menu before you let go of the mouse.

Keyboard commands

Keyboard commands are shortcuts for common activities that you perform on the Macintosh. Ninety percent of the shortcuts use the Command key (the one with the cloverleaf symbol ⌘ and the apple) in combination with other keys.

Many menu items have keyboard shortcuts listed next to their names. Pressing the key combination does the same thing as choosing that menu item from the menu. Some menu items do not have keyboard commands; usually, you have to choose those items from the menu.

Common keys that are used with the Command key are the Option key (located handily next to the Command key) and the Shift key. The Control key has also been used much more recently than it was in the past (long ago — circa 1986 — Macintosh keyboards did not have a Control key). You hold down these keys while you press another key or click the mouse. Figure 1-10 shows these four modifier keys.

Figure 1-10:
The four modifier
keys on an
extended
keyboard.

Keyboard commands are as important to the Macintosh operator as the mouse is, and with a little practice you can get into a habit of memorizing them as soon as you start using a new application. Besides, many keyboard commands are the same from program to program, which makes you an instant expert in software that you haven't even used yet!

Macintosh Terminology

The language of Macintosh users sounds kinda funny to normal people and Windows users. (Did you detect a note of sarcasm there?) In this book, Macintoshes are called *Macs* where appropriate.

Sometimes Mac users, in their enthusiasm, start spouting off all manner of ungodly terms, such as *RAM, megabytes, DPI,* and *Option-clicking.* Then there are the Power Users, who are into *megahertz, gigabytes, line screens,* and *Command-Option-Shift-clicking.* In this book, such terms are discussed as they come up.

Macintosh Hardware

In the old days (once again, the mid-'80s) owning a Macintosh was easy: You bought the latest model (either the 512K "Fat Mac" or the Mac Plus with . . . *one megabyte of RAM!!!*), took it home, turned it on, and you were in business. The computer came complete with monitor, keyboard, mouse, and floppy disk drive. It was truly an "all in one" computer.

In the mid-'90s, your purchases consist of the following (see Figure 1-11):

- A CPU (the actual computer)
- A keyboard
- A third-party mouse, trackball, or other pointing device
- A monitor
- An external hard drive and/or Syquest drives, CD-ROM players, and tape backup units
- A scanner
- A laser printer
- Various strange attachments

Figure 1-11:
The computer of yesteryear and today's average system.

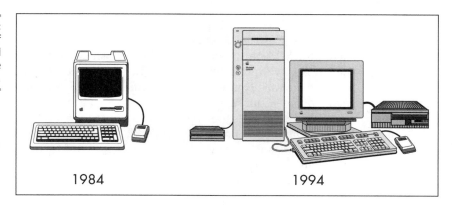

1984   1994

The computer

These days, the CPU, monitor, keyboard, mouse, hard drives, and other miscellaneous pieces are referred to by most people as the *computer*. Technically, the computer is just the part that contains the main logic board, and on that main logic board is the CPU — the *c*entral *p*rocessing *u*nit. The CPU is a silicon chip that is the brains of the computer. The faster the CPU, the faster the computer.

CPU speeds are measured in two ways: by the processor's type and by the processor's speed. Prior to 1994, all Macintoshes were based on a processor called the 68000 that was made by Motorola. The 68000 evolved over its ten-year life span to the 68020, the 68030, and then the 68040. Other computer systems, most notably the Atari ST and Commodore Amiga lines, also were based on this processor. The Power Macintosh computers are now based on the PowerPC 601 and 603 line of processors, again from Motorola. The speed of these processors is measured in megahertz (MHz), millions of cycles per second. The higher the MHz, the fast the processor can operate.

All of this talk about processor type and MHz is confusing enough, but then a real wrench is thrown into the mess: A computer with a processor that has a certain fixed MHz is a different speed than a computer with a different processor and the same MHz. For example, a 25MHz 68040 is more than twice as fast as a 25MHz 68030.

The speed of a computer also depends on the design of its logic board, how fast the RAM is, and the speed of the hard drives that are attached to it. In addition, certain programs work faster on certain computers, and others run at about the same speed on several different systems.

It is generally acceptable nowadays to refer to the case that has the word *Macintosh* imprinted on it as the computer.

Keyboards

Some Macintosh systems (Performas and LCs) may come with a keyboard. The PowerBook has a built-in keyboard, but all other Macintosh computers arrive in their brand spankin' new boxes without a keyboard. Apple sells different types of keyboards for different types of users (see Figure 1-12). For home users and people who use their computers for minor business tasks, the standard keyboard is sufficient. Extended keyboards contain 15 function keys that you can program to perform certain commands or macros (combinations of repetitive tasks) as well as a "middle" section that contains arrow keys and six special keys. An extended keyboard is the best type to use for Illustrator, especially if you have a macro-creating utility like QuicKeys.

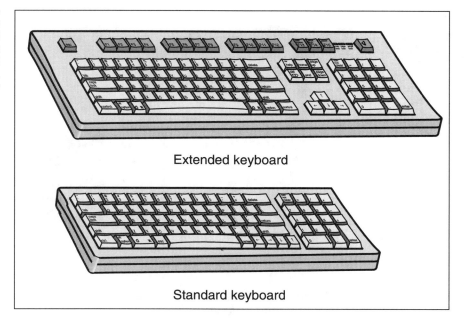

Figure 1-12:
An extended
keyboard and a
standard
keyboard.

Extended keyboard

Standard keyboard

Keyboards from third-party manufacturers cost a bit less than the Apple keyboards. The most important thing about selecting a keyboard is how it feels to you. Certain keyboards feel mushy to some people; others offer too much resistance. If you have used a typewriter, the Mac keyboard will seem soft. Some keyboards also have a more audible click when you press a key; the click reinforces that you did indeed press that key.

Of mice and trackballs

Macintosh computers currently ship with the Desktop Mouse II, a rounder, "fit the shape of your hand" version of the Desktop Mouse I. The majority of mice work by having a ball under the mouse. It rolls along easily (more easily on a soft mouse pad) and sends signals to the computer to move the cursor in the direction that the mouse is moving. Most Macintosh users find this mouse an adequate pointing device for their Mac work, but some find it hard to use.

If you don't like using a mouse, several trackballs are available from third-party manufacturers. A trackball is an upside-down mouse — you move the ball in the direction that you want to go, not the base underneath it. Trackballs usually have an extra button that serves as a "lock" button. Pressing and releasing this button is the same as holding down the normal button. This feature enables you to be more accurate when you are dragging. Figure 1-13 shows a mouse and a trackball.

Figure 1-13:
A mouse and a
trackball.

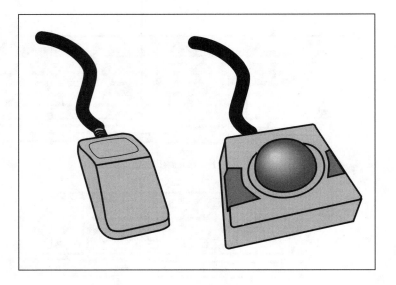

Joysticks also move the cursor around the screen, but they are much more suited to games than to business and graphic applications.

Monitors

The monitor is one of the most important parts of the computer setup because it tells you what is happening on the computer.

Color monitors are a must for graphics and desktop publishing applications. The three standard sizes for color monitors are 13/14 inches, 16/17 inches, and 20/21 inches. Monitors are measured like you measure a TV, from corner to corner. Although you can use a 14-inch monitor for most software, the proliferation of palettes in high-end software has made these monitors seem confining.

You commonly attach monitors to Macintosh computers through on-board video ports. Macs with built-in monitors and older Macs (Mac II, IIx, IIcx, and IIfx) do not have built-in video; the only way to hook up a monitor to these Macs is through a video card. On most machines, the on-board video limits the size of the monitor and the number of colors. Check before you buy to make sure that the monitor and computer are compatible so that you don't have to invest in a video card for a computer that is already set up for on-board video.

Most Macintosh computers enable you to use a video card to hook up more than one monitor at a time to a system. When more than one monitor is attached, your workspace is actually increased by the size of the additional monitor. Some computers, such as the Quadra 950, enable you to run six monitors at once. Many people find that having more than one monitor increases their productivity.

Floppy disk drives

All Macintosh computers have a built-in floppy disk drive (except the PowerBook Duo series and the PowerBook 100), and computers manufactured after 1989 came with Superdrives that read double-density, high-density, and IBM-formatted 3½-inch floppy disks. The disks don't appear to be floppy because of their hard plastic shell, but inside that shell is a thin plastic disk that is floppy.

Usually, you do not need an additional floppy disk drive. On systems that don't have a Superdrive, replacing the current drive with a Superdrive is usually better and cheaper.

Hard disk drives

A hard disk gets its name from being . . . well, hard. Instead of being made of plastic, a hard disk is made from metal, which is usually permanently affixed within a mechanism called a hard drive. There can be several hard disk "platters" inside a hard drive; the more platters, the more storage space is available. There is usually at least one hard drive inside most Macs, and it can be any size in terms of storage space.

Hard drives come in three standard physical sizes: 2½ inches, 3½ inches, and 5¼ inches. You can get 3½-inch and 5¼-inch drives in both full-height and half-height sizes. Certain computers may have three drives connected within the main housing of the computer. The Macintosh is normally limited to having seven additional devices attached to it, which includes hard drives and scanners, so the largest number of hard drives that can be connected is seven.

Though hard disks are made from metal, the drive mechanism that spins the disk and reads and writes information to it can be easily damaged by jostling, bumping, or dropping the drive. The information on a hard disk is stored even when no power is going to the drive.

Syquest drives

To be quite honest, this section should be labeled "Removable Cartridge Drives," of which Syquest drives are just one brand name. But like Kleenex is to tissues and Xerox is to copiers, Syquest is the name people think of when they see a cartridge drive (see Figure 1-14).

Figure 1-14:
A Syquest cartridge
and cartridge
drive.

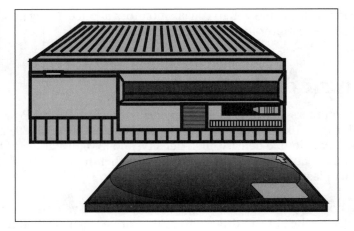

A removable cartridge drive is a hard disk drive with removable disks. The metal disks are protected in a smoky plastic shell that opens when inserted in the drive. The use of multiple cartridges provides for unlimited storage.

Syquest cartridge drives are by far the most popular drives that are currently available. They come in three sizes: 44MB, 88MB, and 128MB. The 44MB and 88MB cartridges measure 5¼ inches, and the 128MB cartridge measures 3½ inches. (No, that isn't a misprint; the smaller cartridges hold more than the larger cartridges.)

The 5¼-inch mechanisms (produced since 1993) can read and write to both 44MB and 88MB cartridges.

Drives and cartridges from other cartridge drive manufacturers are not interchangeable with Syquest's drives and cartridges or with each other.

Optical drives

Instead of using magnetic media, as do floppy and hard disk drives, optical drives use lasers to imprint code on a hard silvery disk. Most optical drives use removable optical cartridges, though sizes and capacities vary throughout the industry.

CD-ROM drives

CD-ROM disks (see Figure 1-15) hold up to 650MB of information, which make them extremely useful for multimedia presentations. A CD-ROM is included with this book.

Figure 1-15:
A CD-ROM disk and a
CD-ROM drive.

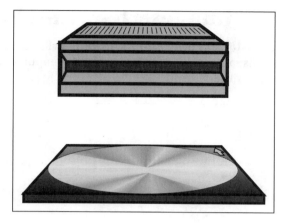

In the past few years, Apple Computer and innovative software companies, including game manufacturers, clip art providers, and even Adobe, have spurred the growth in the use of CD-ROM drives.

A major difference between most other media and CD-ROMs is that you usually cannot write information to a CD. Prices on CD-ROM drives that have write capabilities are continuing to fall, and soon they should be priced reasonably for most businesses.

Tape drives

Tape drives are usually designed to back up a computer system. Most tape drives are now in DAT (*d*igital *a*udio *t*ape) format, which enables each tape to hold up to 2.5 gigabytes of information.

Scanners

Scanners bring printed images into a computer. The two types of scanners are flatbed scanners and drum scanners. Flatbed scanners are relatively inexpensive (you can purchase good ones for less than $2,000), but their clarity and resolution are limited. Drum scanners range from $25,000 to $300,000, depending on the size and quality. The difference between images scanned on a drum scanner and images scanned on a flatbed scanner is huge.

You hook scanners up to Macintoshes through the SCSI port the same way that you connect hard drives. Make sure that the scanner is always the last device in the SCSI chain.

Laser printers, imagesetters, and PostScript

Laser printers (see Figure 1-16) and imagesetters are not part of a certain computer system; instead, they are usually part of a network. Many computers on the same network can use one laser printer to print documents.

Figure 1-16:
A LaserWriter II printer.

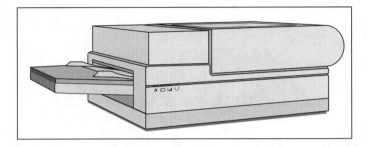

Laser printers and imagesetters are based on PostScript, the page description language that is also the core of Adobe Illustrator.

Although laser printers and imagesetters print individual dots, the number of dots on a given page is incredible. Consider a standard, low-end, 300 dpi (*dot per inch*) laser printer. Three hundred dpi means that every square inch has 300 x 300 dots, or 90,000 dots, in it. An 8½ x 11-inch page has 93.5 square inches on it. At 90,000 dots per square inch, that is 8.5 million dots. An imagesetter that prints at 2,540 dpi (currently the standard for four-color work, but the dpi for some imagesetters is higher) needs to lay down more than 600 million dots on a page. How long does a computer take to put down all of those dots? A heckuva long time. If the computer were capable of plotting 10,000 points a second (a relatively high figure), it would need about 16 hours to plot that 8½ x 11-inch page.

Adobe developed the PostScript language to resolve this problem. PostScript is a system that works with shapes instead of with dots.

The main difference between laser printers and imagesetters is that laser printers apply toner to a plain piece of paper with a laser and imagesetters use a laser to etch an image onto RC (*resin coated*) paper, film, or plates that must then be run through a chemical processor before the image appears. For a comparison of images produced by a laser printer and by an imagesetter, see Figure 1-17.

Three things to consider when you are purchasing a laser printer are page size, processing power, and dpi. The norm for laser printers is becoming 600 dpi.

When you are considering the purchase of an imagesetter, you need to think about a wealth of factors, the first of them being whether owning an imagesetter is worth the cost when you can have pages run out by a local service bureau.

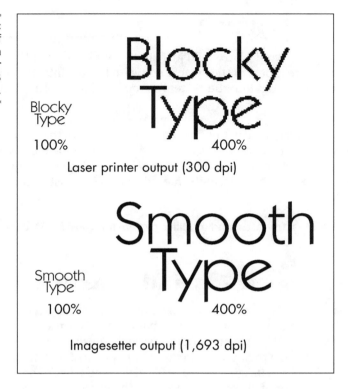

Figure 1-17:
A close-up view of output from a 300 dpi laser printer and a 1,693 dpi imagesetter.

Other strange attachments

As Macintosh computers increase in popularity and number, more and more devices are being produced that hook up to various ports on the computer:

- Pressure-sensitive tablets, which enable you to simulate drawing with a pen, are among the most popular attachments. Some programs, most notably Fractal Design Painter, integrate pressure-sensitive tablets with drawing to such an extent that they simulate natural media on the computer screen exactly.

- You can attach external speakers and microphones to most Macs.

- Video in and out (for importing and exporting video on the desktop) is available, and is even built in on the AV (*a*udio *v*isual) Macs.

- You can use modems to communicate via the computer over phone lines.

- The Geo-port on the AV Macs enables you to attach a telephone so that the computer can act like an answering machine or voice mail system.

System Software

Without system software, your Mac would just sit on your desk, unable to do the simplest of actions. A great deal of the system software for Macintosh computers is disk-based; you have to load it into the system's memory before you can use the computer.

System software consists of instructions that apply to the ways the computer acts when an activity takes place. For example, when you click a word in the menu bar, and the menu pulls down, the system software controls this action. System software controls how the computer works with icons, fonts, files, disks, and almost everything else that users take for granted.

Apple Computer creates, updates, and modifies system software for Macintosh computers.

System 7, System 7.1, and System 7.5

The current version of system software (as of summer, 1994) is System 7.5. System software on the Mac has gone through several major revisions, the most recent being the change from System 6.0.X to System 7.0. (Any time you see the letter X in a version number, the text is referring to any version number in place of that X. For example, 6.0.X refers to Systems 6.0, 6.0.1, 6.0.2, 6.0.3, 6.0.4, 6.0.5, 6.0.7, and 6.0.8.) The most recent revision includes a number of changes, but most of the changes that users notice are the cosmetic changes to the Finder, which is discussed later in this chapter.

System 7 (when "System 7" is written, it usually refers to systems 7.0, 7.0.1, 7.1, 7.1.1, and 7.5) has many features that have never been available to Mac users before, including file-sharing, built-in 32-bit addressing, and an organized, flexible System Folder. Most of the other new capabilities are beyond even the seasoned Mac user, as well as the scope of this book. Overall, System 7's capabilities are a drastic improvement over System 6's capabilities.

System 6

Apple stopped shipping computer systems with System 6 on them in the summer of 1991. System 6 has some limitations for professional graphic artists, the most important being a built-in limit of 8MB of RAM.

System 6 does not work on the computers that have been released since that fateful summer, but System 7 works on all Macintoshes back to the lowly Mac Plus.

What system software should I use?

As of 1993, Mac users no longer had to think about this question. Much of the software that is being produced will work only with System 7, which makes new software purchases difficult for System 6 owners.

The main reason that users hesitated to upgrade to System 7 in the past was that a great deal of Macintosh software was not compatible with System 7. As stated previously, the reverse is true now. Another concern was that System 7 requires more memory (about 2MB as opposed to System 6's 1MB) to run, and memory costs a great deal of money. Memory prices are fairly reasonable now; and to use the current crop of software, you need at least 16MB of RAM, which would have been considered an excessive amount two years ago.

Unless your computer can't handle more than 4MB of RAM, you should be using System 7. If your computer can't use more than 4MB (the Mac Plus and SE), you won't be able to run current programs, such as Adobe Illustrator, that require a faster processor than the ones included with those older machines.

The Finder

As soon as you turn on a Macintosh, you are using the Finder. A misnomer of grand proportions, the Finder doesn't *find* anything. Instead, the Finder enables you to organize all the information on your hard drives, floppy disks, Syquest drives, and so on so that you can find the information easily at a later time. The Finder is always available in System 7, even when you are running several other programs at once. The Finder is considered a program, or application, like Illustrator, QuarkXPress, and Microsoft Word.

The Mac is a Mac because of the Finder

If there is one piece of software that identifies your computer as being a Macintosh, it is the Finder. The Finder houses icons, windows, menus — everything that is Mac-like (see Figure 1-18).

The main function of the Finder is to make file organization of your disks easier than is possible with other operating systems. The Finder was the first major GUI (*graphical user interface*) environment, and the most popular until Microsoft starting forcing Windows on PC owners. The Finder is what most people think of when they think about the Macintosh, with the hard drive icons in the upper righthand corner and that cute little trash can in the lower righthand corner.

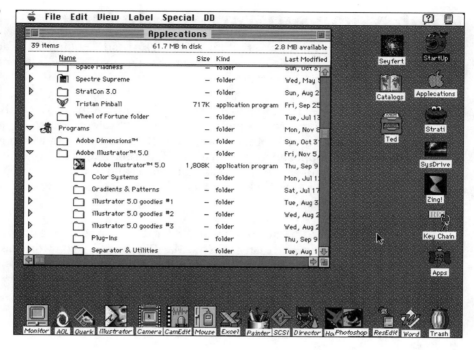

Figure 1-18:
The Finder
Desktop with
an open
window (the
start-up file
on the hard
drive).

Stuff that happens in the Finder

What do you use the Finder for? Moving files (including folders, applications, programs, and documents) from one location to another, copying files from one disk to another, deleting unwanted files from disks, and opening and modifying documents.

The Finder's menus deal primarily with file manipulation. You use them to create new folders to organize your work, print the contents of a window, open a file or folder, restart or shut down the system, empty the trash can, and label files and folders. You also can set up file-sharing capabilities for disks, make aliases of files (icons that serve as a link to original files), view folders and files in different ways, and get more information about certain icons.

The *Find* in the Finder is the menu option called, appropriately, Find. This option provides a way for you to find files by name, kind, date, or various other delimiters. A Find Again feature will find multiple files that meet the criteria you specify.

Fonts

Fonts are a big deal to Macintosh users. Not only is a huge selection of typefaces available, but until System 7.1, users had to contend with huge problems with font ID numbers, font formats, and the location of the parts of a font. System 7.1 squished the font ID number and location problems into nothingness, but font format problems still exist.

For the seasoned graphic artist, the thousands of typefaces that are available for the Mac provide a typesetting heaven on earth. For a newcomer to Macs, art, and type-setting, fonts are overwhelming. Macs ship with about 20 fonts; others are available for purchase at costs that range from about $2 per face to hundreds of dollars for a family.

Fonts for the Macintosh come in various formats, each format having advantages and disadvantages over other formats. Fonts fall into the following categories:

- Bitmap fonts, also known as screen fonts
- PostScript fonts, also called Type 1 or Type 3
- TrueType fonts

Fonts are very important to the way Adobe Illustrator works because a large part of the software deals with typefaces and manipulating type.

Bitmap fonts

A bitmap font is a font that is made up of a series of dots inside a grid pattern. Bitmap fonts were the original fonts for the Macintosh, and they worked well on both the screen and the dot-matrix printers that were prevalent at the time they were introduced.

Each character in a bitmap font has a certain number of square black dots that define its shape. Some bitmap fonts include different point sizes, with the smaller point sizes having fewer dots than the larger point sizes. The larger the point size, the more detail is available, and the better the letter looks.

A problem arises when a point size is specified for which no corresponding bitmap font is available. Then dots from the point size that is closest to the specified size are scaled to the new size. The result is usually large, blocky-looking letters. The larger the size specified, the larger the "blocks" (see Figure 1-19).

Figure 1-19:
Different point sizes of bitmap fonts. At 48 points, the font is hideous looking.

Because bitmap fonts were originally designed for a Macintosh screen, the dots in a bitmap font are set at 72 dpi, as are most Macintosh screens. When you print a bitmap font on a laser printer, which has a resolution of at least 300 dpi, the letters look blocky, even when their sizes are supported by the typeface. People usually refer to them as "Bitmapped. Yuck."

PostScript fonts

PostScript fonts are the most popular font format (see Figure 1-20), but they also are the most confusing and frustrating fonts to use because they have two parts, the screen font (which is really a bitmap font) and the printer font.

Figure 1-20:
Three PostScript typefaces.

The screen font needs to be installed in order for the computer to recognize the font in the different programs you use. If the printer font is installed but the screen font is not installed, you can't use the font at all. Screen fonts for PostScript fonts are usually in little suitcases. Double-clicking on the suitcases reveals the bitmap fonts inside the suitcase, and each point size has its own file. Double-clicking on a bitmap font (in System 7) displays a screen with that font in that point size and a sentence that contains all the letters in the alphabet (see Figure 1-21). This makes for sentences that are pretty, well, bizarre. Nothing like reading "How razorback-jumping frogs can level six piqued gymnasts!"

Figure 1-21:
Inside a
PostScript font
suitcase.

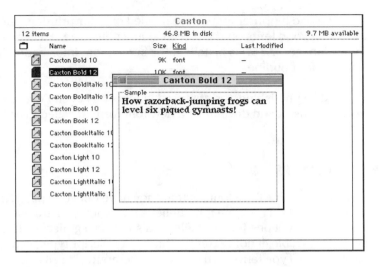

Printer fonts are needed, as their name implies, for printing. Printer fonts consist of outlined shapes that get filled with as many dots as the printer can stuff in that particular shape. Because these printer fonts are outlines, and not a certain number of dots, they make characters look good at any point size. In fact, PostScript printer fonts are *device independent,* meaning that the quality of the type depends on the dpi of the printer (also known as device dependent). The higher the dpi, the smoother the curves and diagonal lines look. If printer fonts are missing, the printer either uses the corresponding bitmap font or substitutes another font whose printer font is available. Figure 1-22 shows the same words as they appear on-screen and when printed.

Figure 1-22:
Screen fonts
and their
PostScript
printer font
counterparts.

PostScript fonts were developed by Adobe, who, just by coincidence, created the PostScript page description language, which is also, just by coincidence, based on outlines instead of dots. Adobe also created typefaces in PostScript format, called Type 1 format. They released a set of specifications for third-party manufacturers to use in creating other fonts, called Type 3 fonts. Type 3 fonts have an advantage over Type 1 fonts in that the outlines of these fonts can be stroked, not just filled, and they can be filled with various shades of gray instead of just black. Then Adobe released the specifications for Type 1 fonts, and third-party manufacturers having been creating fonts in the Type 1 format ever since.

Things wouldn't be so bad if printer fonts were needed only for printing, but they also are needed for drawing good fonts on the screen at any point size. If a control panel called Adobe Type Manager (ATM) is installed, the screen font information is supplemented by the printer font outline.

Since the rise of desktop publishing, the standard in fonts has been PostScript. In 1990, Apple teamed with Microsoft and developed a new font format, called TrueType.

TrueType fonts

The greatest advantage of TrueType fonts is that they have only one part. No screen font and printer font, just the TrueType font. Believe me, when you are used to finding two of everything, this idea of one font, one file, and so on, is a godsend. The quality of TrueType fonts is comparable, if not better, to that of PostScript typefaces (see Figure 1-23). Apple includes TrueType fonts with every new computer it sells. So TrueType, and not PostScript, should be the standard format, right?

Figure 1-23:
Three TrueType typefaces.

Remember back in the early '80s when VCRs were starting to become popular? There was Beta, and there was VHS. Beta was better, hands down. But VHS became the standard videotape format. Why? One reason is that more people had VHS than Beta. Video stores had every movie in VHS and just a select few in Beta. People who were going to buy VCRs saw that more movies were available for VHS recorders, and so they bought VHS recorders. Now VHS is the standard.

A similar thing happened with fonts for the Macintosh. PostScript fonts were the only ones available (besides bitmaps), and companies, including service bureaus, invested large amounts of money in them. After Apple introduced TrueType, it never really caught on, even though its technology is better. TrueType requires that the printer have more memory; its spacing is different from PostScript faces; and most people already owned PostScript. Why throw out thousands of dollars of perfectly good fonts? Most companies shrugged their shoulders and continued to buy PostScript fonts.

Battles between the two formats are still raging, but PostScript appears to be winning the war. In this case, competition is not better for the consumer, just confusing.

Fonts and Adobe Illustrator

Adobe makes PostScript. Adobe makes Illustrator. What type of fonts should you use? Although PostScript is the correct answer, Illustrator does support the use of TrueType fonts. One thing that Illustrator does not support is having two fonts with the same name, one in PostScript and one in TrueType. If this scenario happens, strange things occur on the screen (invisible type, for example). Make sure that you have only one type of font format per typeface.

ATM

Adobe Type Manager (see Figure 1-24) is to computer screens what PostScript is to printers. Before ATM, PostScript typefaces would look just dandy when displayed on-screen in one of the standard screen font sizes (usually 10, 12, 14, 18, and 24 points). But pick a size larger, smaller, or in between, and the result was terrible. Until ATM was released in 1989, this situation was acceptable. Most Mac users had never known anything different (although Type 3 faces were smooth on the screens of QuarkXPress 2 users), and "bitmapped" fonts on the screen were just something that couldn't be changed.

Figure 1-24:
If this ATM icon appears as you are starting up a Mac, ATM is installed.

ATM is a sort of link between the screen fonts and the printer fonts. If the point size that you choose is unavailable for a certain typeface, the screen font references the printer font for its outline and fills the outline with dots. The result is a smooth character, whatever the point size on-screen (see Figure 1-25).

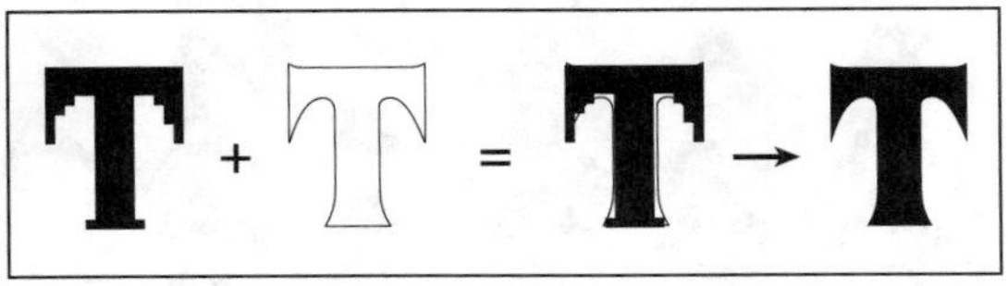

Figure 1-25:
ATM works by comparing screen fonts to printer fonts and filling in the outlines.

$$\mathbf{T} + \mathbb{T} = \mathbf{T} \rightarrow \mathbf{T}$$

Because of screen resolution limitations (72 dpi), type below 8 points can be hard to read, even with ATM. When type gets below this size, many software applications use *greeking*, which changes small type into gray bars, saving the application a great deal of processing time. (They figure that if you can't read it anyway, no reason exists to put all those dots in the right places.)

A side benefit to using ATM is that non-PostScript printers can print beautiful, smooth type. Instead of having the printer do the work, the ATM software has already done it.

TrueType automatically renders type at various point sizes without the use of ATM. Adobe bundles ATM free with most software packages and will send it to most users for a $7.50 handling/shipping fee. Because of the abundance of rendering techniques, Mac users expect on-screen type to have smooth edges at any point size.

If you start up a Macintosh with extensions off (by pressing Shift until the "Welcome To Macintosh" screen appears), ATM will be disabled, and you can see bitmap fonts in all their glory.

Multiple Master Fonts

Multiple Master Fonts, again from Adobe, provide an impressive, if not somewhat complex, way to vary typestyles. Normally, a typeface may come in several weights, such as bold, regular, light, and black. But what if you want a weight that is in between bold and black? Usually, you are out of luck.

The theory behind Multiple Master Fonts is that a font has two extremes — for example, black and light. Multiple Master technology creates any number of in-betweens that range from one extreme to the other. Multiple Masters don't stop with weights, though. They also work to step between regular and oblique, wide and condensed, and serif or sans serif. Figure 1-26 is an example of a two-dimensional Multiple Master Font (a font that has two scalable qualities, in this case width and obliqueness).

Figure 1-26: Multiple Master Font typeface variations of width and obliqueness.

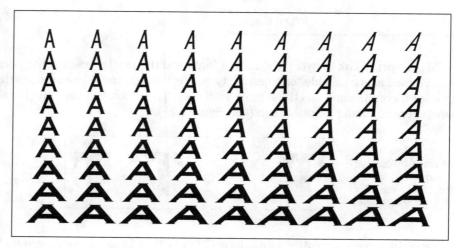

Multiple Master Font capabilities are built into many high-end graphics applications, such as Illustrator and QuarkXPress.

Super ATM

Although ATM is a very good product, Super ATM is even better. ATM creates smooth fonts for the screen from corresponding printer fonts on the system. But when the corresponding printer font is not available, you get bitmapped fonts.

Super ATM creates smooth fonts for both the screen and the printer, even when you don't have printer fonts for a typeface (see Figure 1-27). How? By using Multiple Master technology to simulate the typeface that you specify. Unfortunately, having Super ATM doesn't mean that you can get away with not buying any more fonts; the outlines that Super ATM makes usually aren't that good. Why use it then? Because, unlike printing bitmaps or substitute fonts, Super ATM provides a close approximation to the original, and what's more important, Super ATM retains the spacing of the originally selected font.

Figure 1-27:
The ATM Font Database icon, automatically installed as part of Acrobat Reader (which came with Version 5.0 of Illustrator).

Super ATM is useful for people who get a number of documents to print and don't have the printer fonts for those documents. Super ATM is not good for service bureaus because the quality of its output is not high enough to satisfy customers.

Applications

Without applications, which also are called *programs* — the two words are used interchangeably — your computer wouldn't do much but sit there. Sure, you might be able to move the cursor on the screen, but you wouldn't have anything to point it at. The Finder, discussed previously, is an application. Adobe Illustrator is an application. Other examples of popular applications are QuarkXPress (a page layout program), Adobe Photoshop (an image editing application), Microsoft Word (a word processing program), F/A-18 Hornet (a flight simulation program), and Macromedia Director (a multimedia production application).

How applications work

In order to use a program, you need to *launch,* or *run,* it. The Finder program is automatically launched when you start up the system. From the Finder, you can launch other applications by double-clicking either the program or a document created in the program.

When you double-click a program, that program is copied into the system's RAM. After it has been copied (or parts of it have been copied) into RAM, you can use it. To run additional programs, simply go back to the Finder and double-click the next program. Usually, you return to the Finder through the Application menu in the upper righthand corner of the screen. Figure 1-28 shows this menu.

Figure 1-28:
This Application menu lists a few programs that are running.

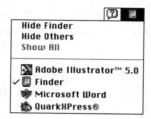

The amount of RAM that you have limits the number of applications that you can run at one time. If you don't have enough RAM, a dialog box will appear, telling you that you need to quit another program in order for the new one to have enough space to run.

Quitting applications

After you load an application into RAM and it is running, it continues to run until you choose Quit from its File menu or press ⌘-Q. You can never quit the Finder (Quit does not appear on its File menu). Many people believe that closing open documents in a program quits that program, but that is not the case. If you click the desktop of the Finder, you zip out of the program that you are using and into the Finder, making it appear as if you have quit the program that you were using. If you are unsure whether any programs are running in the background, go to the Application menu and make sure that the Finder is the only program that is listed.

Heavens to Megabytes!

When dealing with memory issues, people often fail to specify what type of memory they are referring to. The Macintosh makes use of two types of memory:

- Storage memory, which takes the form of both floppy and hard disks
- Random access memory (RAM), which also is known as application memory and system memory

Memory terminology

Many terms are used in referring to memory. The following list explains a few of them. If you aren't interested, don't care, or if you consistently run out of toes when you are counting, skip down to kilobyte.

- **Bit:** A bit is the smallest unit of computer storage. A combination of bits makes up everything that computers do. Computers think in terms of 1 or 0, on or off. Because computers work with just two numbers, they are considered to be working in Base 2 (sometimes called *binary*). You work in a Base 10 system, because you use 10 different numbers. Using Base 2 makes most computer numbers some exponent of the number 2, usually in the form of 2 to the third power (2^3, or 2 x 2 x 2, or 8), 2 to the tenth power (2^{10}, or 2 x 2 x 2 x 2 x 2 x 2 x 2 x 2 x 2 x 2, or 1024), and so on.

- **Byte:** A byte is a set of 8 bits in a row. To a computer, a byte looks like this: 01010110. A computer counts this way: 00000000 = 0, 00000001 = 1, 00000010 = 2, 00000011 = 3, and 00000100 = 4. The highest number a byte can represent in bits is 11111111, which is 256.

- **Kilobyte, or K:** The kilobyte is one of the most common terms that is in use today for measuring memory. It is a tiny component of memory — 1K = 1,024 bytes (K for a thousand). Most people just say that 1K = 1,000 bytes and leave it at that. This method makes math much easier.

- **Megabyte, or MB:** 1,024K = 1MB, or more simply, 1,000K = approximately 1MB. The relationship between K and MB is one of the most fundamental; fortunately, it is the most basic. (Megabyte means 1 million bytes.) Just remember that 1MB = 1,000K.

- **Gigabyte, or GB:** 1,024MB = 1GB, or once again, 1,000MB = approximately 1GB. (Gigabyte means 1 billion bytes.) Don't fool yourself. Gigabytes are big. If you can afford a gigabyte of anything, consider yourself fortunate.

- **Terrabyte:** 1,024GB = 1 terrabyte. Terrabytes are so big that there really isn't an official abbreviation for them (TB is a disease). Gigabytes are really big, but terrabytes are just plain silly. But, hey, that's what they said about gigabytes a few years back. . . .

Floppy disk and hard drive memory

Information that is stored on floppy disks and hard disks takes up part of the available memory of those disks. Floppy disks have a much smaller capacity than hard disks have. Information on disks is considered permanent; it will not leave the disk unless you remove it.

Double-density floppy disks for the Macintosh hold about 780K of information. A double-spaced page of type takes up about 1K, which means that a double-density floppy disk can hold all the text in this book.

High-density floppy disks (they have an *HD* imprinted on the top that looks like *CH* if you are holding the disk upside down) contain up to 1.3MB (1,300K) of data.

Hard drives can be any size from about 40MB to 5.5GB. Some old hard drives of the 10MB and 20MB range are still floating around, but they are too small for any real work. Macintosh computers used to come with 40MB or 80MB hard drives until the '90s. Now they come with a minimum 230MB drive and a current maximum of 1.2GB.

CD-ROMs hold 650MB of information; DAT tape drives hold 1 – 5GB of data; and of course, 44MB, 88MB, and 128MB Syquests hold 44MB, 88MB, and 128MB of data, respectively.

RAM (*random access memory*)

One of the most often used but least understood terms in the world of computers is *RAM*. RAM is temporary memory. When power is shut off to the device that holds RAM, the information in RAM is gone. Magically.

Instead of using a mechanical device to read and write information to disks magnetically, RAM uses SIMMs (*single in-line memory modules*), which are little green boards that have microchips arranged on them in rows. Information is passed to and from SIMMs electronically; no physical movement is needed.

RAM is much faster than floppy disks and hard disks, which is why it is used, instead of hard disks, as system memory. Hard drives are measured in milliseconds (thousandths of a second), and RAM is measured in nanoseconds (billionths of a second). RAM is literally a million times faster than a hard disk.

SIMMs come in various sizes and speeds. There are many different types of SIMMs and many different ways that RAM works and doesn't work, and then there are things such as low-profile SIMMs and composite SIMMs. It's all rather overwhelming. Suffice to say that the more RAM you have, the better. No one ever complains about having too much RAM or too many SIMMs.

Programs and memory

The applications that you use are stored permanently on the hard drive. When you launch a program, it is temporarily loaded into RAM. The amount of RAM that it needs is not the same as the amount of disk space that it needs. Confused?

When programs are installed on the hard drive, the program and associated files may take up to 10MB of space. Of course, this amount includes tutorials, samples, Read Me files, and all sorts of other little things that you don't need to use the software. When you launch a program, certain parts of it and parts of other files (in the case of Illustrator, Plug-In files) get loaded into RAM. If this information were to equal 2MB, then you would need 2MB of RAM, right? Well, kinda. You see, you need additional RAM for loading the documents that you are working on, as well as RAM for doing complex procedures (for example, the Mosaic filter in Illustrator).

Figuring out how much RAM you need for a program is up to you. The Get Info box (select the program and choose File⇨Get Info in the Finder) contains guidelines that say what the Suggested, Minimum, and Preferred sizes are. Never type a number in the Minimum or Preferred box that is less than what is in the Suggested box. The Suggested box value is a good starting point for the Minimum box value, and you should add a couple thousand K for the Preferred box. This formula, of course, varies from application to application.

In 1986, most software needed about 200K of RAM to run. Most of the computers at that time had 1MB of RAM, which was an acceptable amount. When the Mac II premiered in 1987, things began to change. At that time, you could upgrade the Mac II to 8MB of RAM. What in the world would anyone need all that memory for? No program at the time needed 1MB, let alone 8MB. Then big bulky programs, such as PageMaker and Photoshop, appeared. QuarkXPress, Illustrator, and others followed, all wanting more than their fair share of memory. In 1994, major applications such as QuarkXPress and PageMaker need 3MB apiece, and Illustrator and Photoshop need a minimum of 5MB. Couple these requirements with everyone's desire to run three or four programs at the same time, and you have a system that needs at least 20MB in order to work at the level your programs demand. To find out how much RAM your computer has, quit all applications and then access the About This Macintosh dialog box from the Apple menu (see Figure 1-29). The amount of memory in your computer is listed as the "Total Memory" in kilobytes (K). Divide that number by 1,024 to find out how many megabytes of memory are in your system.

Figure 1-29:
About This Macintosh
dialog box, from the
Apple menu in the
Finder.

About This Macintosh		
	System Software 7.1.1	
Macintosh Quadra 800	© Apple Computer, Inc. 1983–1993	
Total Memory : 36,864K	**Largest Unused Block :** 1,177K	
Adobe Illustrator...	14,000K	
Microsoft Word	5,000K	
QuarkXPress®	10,974K	
System Software	4,626K	

The Basics of Adobe Ilustrator

In This Chapter

- The length of time it takes to learn a PostScript drawing program
- How to learn faster
- Outline theory
- Pierre Bézier and his curves
- Basic Edit functions: Cut, Copy, Paste, and Clear
- Undoing and redoing
- Working in Preview mode
- Using palettes and windows

The Learning Curve _____

In 1988, I was setting type with PageMaker at the service bureau where I was a college intern. I noticed that the specs called for type to be set at a 15° angle. PageMaker Version 3 had more options and menus than almost any other software at the time, and I spent considerable time searching for "rotate" or something similar. No such luck. I got so desperate that I spied the manual out of the corner of my eye, and I began to reach for it.

"What's the problem?" asked my boss.

Out of instinct, I punched ⌘-S on my keyboard. (The boss, a former soldier, had this thing about saving often; his method of enforcement was a lightning fast flick of my Mac's power switch.) "I can't find where you rotate type in PageMaker," I replied sheepishly.

He nodded. And then he spoke two simple, powerful words: "Adobe Illustrator."

In those days, type at any angle on the computer was a big deal because none of the desktop publishing programs at the time had that capability. That moment was my introduction to Illustrator, and it marked the beginning of my productivity slide.

Figuring out type wasn't too difficult, but then I started playing with some of the other tools and features of the software. Confusion ensued. Hours of staring at an Illustrator document and wondering "Why?" took up most of my time those days. I didn't understand fills and strokes, I didn't understand how to make things certain colors, and I didn't understand why what I drew was so different from what I printed (see Figure 2-1).

Even my boss couldn't help me much with Illustrator; questions to him resulted in a knowing nod and the now-customary tilt and swivel of his head toward the Illustrator manual. I went through the tutorial three times, but when I tried to mask anything but those darn fish, it wouldn't work. I was convinced that the Pen tool was Satan's pitchfork in disguise. Patterns made about as much sense as differential equations. Then there were things like flatness, miter limits, and splitting paths, all subjects that might as well have been written in 3rd-Century Chinese dialect for all I knew.

I had never used or seen software as *different* as Illustrator.

That was then; this is not then

The version of Illustrator I was introduced to was Illustrator 88, an incredible improvement over Illustrator 1.1, but still not a user-friendly piece of software. Version 3, introduced in 1990, was a little better, but most of its improvements were in functionality, not user interface.

Then, in the summer of 1993, Illustrator 5.0 was introduced, with a full load of not just new features but better ways for people to access those features. But there was a problem — although the program was easier for beginners to understand, most of the intermediate and advanced areas of Illustrator were still beyond the scope of the majority of users.

Techniques for learning more

There are a number of ways you can "pick up" Illustrator faster than the average Joe Designer.

"Playing" the right way: I used to hate the term "playing," which has been typically used to describe trying out new features and areas of the software you aren't familiar with. Normally, "playing" is said in a negative way, although if done correctly, it can be the most important and valuable time spent while learning software. When playing with Illustrator, follow these rules for the most effective "playtime":

Figure 2-1:
Artwork as it appears
in Artwork mode (top)
and the printed result.

- Create something that you want to keep, like a business card, a logo for your business (a better logo if your company has a hokey one), a letterhead, or a picture of something you might actually want to keep.

- Even if you don't like what you are doing, *don't* select all and delete. It may look awful, but it could be a starting point for another illustration in the future. Save it.

- Print everything. After an hour of playing, you will (1) feel better about the time your coworkers and boss think you spent playing with new software and (2) eventually have a file of stuff you did that you can review in the future. I love going back to artwork I did three months before and remembering a feature I used for that art that I've just plain forgotten about since then. Imagine if you had years worth of this stuff.

- Don't do real-life projects during playtime. Real-life projects consist of two possible things: artwork you are doing for someone else, which has to be perfect, and artwork you are doing for yourself, which — surprise! — also has to be perfect. Either way, you will invariably select all and delete quite often, and hardly ever print anything but the final product. Try to separate real life from playtime.

- Don't do too much in one sitting. The more you do at one time, the more you will forget. More than a couple hours of play at one time starts becoming detrimental.

Dissect existing illustrations: "How'd they do that?" You can figure out all but the most complex artwork by opening it up in Illustrator and selecting different pieces. You can discover techniques that you probably would never have come across on your own.

Talk to other Illustrator users: By talking to other users, you can discover ways they approach similar illustrations or learn of their pitfalls before they become yours.

Attempt the impossible: If you can successfully create a replica of the ceiling of the Sistine Chapel with a mouse in Illustrator with the proper shading and discoloration associated with aging, you will undoubtedly master the software. Realistically, if you try something that you believe is beyond either your skills or the capabilities of the software, you may be surprised at what you know and what Illustrator can do. And, in the process, you'll probably also come up with new techniques and procedures for creating similar, simpler artwork.

Read the entire *Illustrator Bible*: Just because you never understood masking before, and never thought you would need it in the future, doesn't mean that nothing else in the chapter on masking is going to be of interest to you. The way this book is structured, I've tried to show new and exciting ways of doing everything, from the basics of drawing a line and creating a simple closed shape to reversing gradients and accessing the Convert Direction Point tool while using a pressure-sensitive brush.

Watch the CD-ROM tutorials: Just because you think a tutorial on basic pattern creating is beneath you doesn't mean that there won't be a new way of creating a cloverleaf in a few simple steps. Most of the tutorials on the CD I've included with this book show more tricks on side topics than they do on their main subject.

The CD-ROM tutorials are arranged in the same order as this book, with sections that correspond to the chapters listed here.

PostScript and Printing

Up until the mid-'80s, computer graphics were, well, crusty. Blocky. Jagged. Rough. If a mid-'90s person (you or I) saw graphics that were done on computers in 1981 and printed to a black-and-white printer, gales of laughter would ensue. Of course, in 1981, the world was gaga over the capabilities of computers and computer graphics. Those same pictures were admired, and the average person was generally amazed (the average designer, on the other hand, shuddered and prayed that this whole computer thing wouldn't catch on).

Desktop publishing was pushed to a level of professionalism by a cute little software package called PageMaker in 1985. With PageMaker, you could do typesetting *and* layout on the computer screen, seeing everything on a screen just as it would eventually be printed. Well, almost.

The worst acronym this planet has ever seen was coined at this time: *WYSIWYG,* pronounced about the way it reads (wizzy-wig), and standing for "*w*hat *y*ou *s*ee *i*s *w*hat *y*ou *g*et." Oddly, a more accurate term would have been *Wysisstwygiygial,* (pronounced wizzys-twiggy-guyal), meaning "*w*hat *y*ou *s*ee *i*s *s*omewhat *s*imilar *t*o *w*hat *y*ou *g*et *i*f *y*ou *g*et *i*t *a*t al*l.*" The screen representation was poor, and the likelihood that anything remotely complex would actually print was even poorer. Figure 2-2 shows a common response to these silly acronyms.

Problems aside, PageMaker would not have been a success if the laser printer hadn't handily arrived on the scene. Even so, there were problems inherent with laser printers too: at 300 DPI (*d*ots *p*er *i*nch), there were 90,000 dots in every square inch. An 8.5 x 11-inch paper had 8.5 *million* dots to put down. Computers were finally powerful enough to handle this huge amount of dots, but the time it took to print made computers pretty much useless for any real work.

Figure 2-2:
What you see here is just another unnecessary acronym!

Several systems to handle these large amounts of dots were developed, and the one standout was PostScript from Adobe Systems. Apple licensed PostScript from Adobe for use on its LaserWriter, and a star was born. Installed on every laser printer were two things from Adobe: the PostScript page description language and the Adobe Base fonts, including Times, Helvetica, Courier, and Symbol.

PostScript became fundamental to Apple Macintosh computers and Laser printers, and it was an unchallenged standard. In order to use PostScript, Apple had to pay licensing fees to Adobe for every laser printer it sold. Fonts were PostScript, and if there ever was a standard in graphics, the closest thing to it was PostScript (commonly called EPS, for *E*ncapsulated *P*ostScript).

Today, the majority of fonts for both Macintosh and Windows systems are PostScript, and almost all graphics and desktop publishing software can read PostScript in some form.

What PostScript does

A typical graphic object in "painting" software is based on a certain number of pixels that are a certain color. If you make that graphic larger, the pixels get larger, giving a rough, jagged effect to the art (see Figure 2-3). To prevent the *jaggies,* two things can be done: Make sure that there are enough dots per inch in the image so that when enlarged the dots are too small to appear jagged, or define graphics by mathematical equations instead of dots.

Figure 2-3:
A bitmap image at normal size (left) and enlarged by 300%.

PostScript is a mathematical solution to high-resolution imaging; areas, or *shapes,* are defined, and then these shapes are either filled or stroked with a percentage of color. The shapes are made up of paths, and the paths are defined by a number of points along the path (*anchor points*) and additional points off the path (*direction points,* sometimes called *control handles* or *curve handles*) that control the shape of the curve. Figure 2-4 shows a PostScript outline around a bitmapped image and the enlarged outline filled with black.

Figure 2-4:
A PostScript outline surrounds the original bitmapped image.

Because the anchor points and direction points have real locations on a page, mathematical processes can be used to create the shapes created with these points. The mathematical equation for Bézier curves is quite detailed (at least for someone who fears math, like me) and is shown in Figure 2-5.

PostScript is not just math, though. It is actually a programming language, and more specifically, a *page description language.* Like BASIC, Pascal, or C, PostScript is made of lines of code that are used to describe artwork.

Fortunately, the average user never has to use PostScript code but instead uses a simplified *interface,* like Illustrator. Software that has the capability to save files in PostScript or to print to a PostScript printer writes this PostScript code for you. Printers that are equipped with PostScript then take that PostScript code and convert it to dots on a printed page.

Bézier curves are defined as the curve $\mathbf{P}(u)$ in terms of the locations of $n + 1$ control points $\mathbf{p}_i$

$$\mathbf{P}(u) = \sum_{i=0}^{n} \mathbf{p}_i B_{i,n}(u)$$

where $B_{i,n}(u)$ is a *blending function*

$$B_{i,n}(u) = C(n,i)u^i(1 - u)^{n-i}$$

and $C(n,i)$ is the binomial coefficient, $C(n,i) = n!/(i!(n - i)!)$.

Why PostScript is so cool

Obviously, the fact that most applications can handle EPS files and that most printers can print PostScript is a great benefit to users, but the strength of PostScript is not really in its widespread use.

If you create a 1" circle in Photoshop or any other pixel-based drawing software and then enlarge that same circle in any application, the circle will begin to lose resolution. A 300-DPI circle at twice its original size becomes 150-DPI. This makes those jagged edges more apparent than ever.

If you create a 1" circle in Illustrator, you can enlarge it to *any size possible* without losing one iota of resolution. Figure 2-6 shows 1" circles created both in Illustrator and bitmap graphics software, and both of them are enlarged to twice their original size. The Illustrator circle stays perfectly smooth, even enlarged to 200%. In fact, the resolution of that circle depends on the laser printer or imagesetter that prints it. That means that a perfect 1" circle has the potential to be a perfect 2' circle (providing you can find a printer/imagesetter that can print a 2' x 2' circle).

But scaling objects is only the beginning. You can distort, stretch, rotate, skew, and flip objects created in Illustrator to your heart's content, and still the object will print to the resolution of the output device (see Figure 2-7).

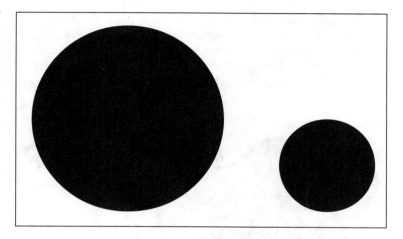

Figure 2-6:
A 1" circle in Illustrator (right) is enlarged to a 2" circle without any loss of quality.

Figure 2-7:
The original mouse (call him "Theme") is in the upper left corner. The other mice are, appropriately, *"Variations on a Theme."*

Here's an example: A company wants its tiny logo, such as the one in Figure 2-8, on a 3' wide poster. Using conventional methods, the edges will become fuzzy and gross looking, pretty much unacceptable to your client. Your other conventional option is to redraw the logo at a larger size or to trace the blown-up version — either way a time-consuming proposition.

Figure 2-8:
The original, fairly crusty logo given to me to scan and fix up and then put on a poster.

The Illustrator solution? Scan the logo, trace it either in Adobe Streamline or with the Auto Trace tool, touch it up, and build your design around it. Afterwards, output the illustration on a printer that can output that size of a poster. As you can see in Figure 2-9, there is no loss of quality. Instead, the curve and the letters look much better. In fact, often the enlarged version from Illustrator will look better than the original that was scanned in.

Figure 2-9:
A poster created in Illustrator by tracing the original, scanned-in image from Figure 2-8.

Paths

The most basic element in Illustrator is a path. A path in Illustrator must have at least one anchor point. Most paths will have a minimum of two anchor points, in which case there will be a line segment between those two anchor points (see Figure 2-10). Depending on the type of anchor points that are on either end of that segment, the line segment may be straight or curved.

Figure 2-10:
Paths with only
two anchor points,
with all anchor
points selected.

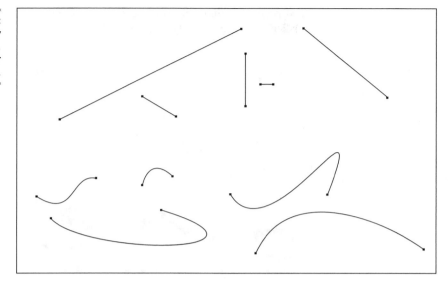

Figure 2-10:
Paths with only
two anchor points,
with all anchor
points selected.

Conceptually, there is no limit to how many anchor points can be in any one path or how many segments can be in one path (see Figure 2-11). There are three major types of paths:

Figure 2-11:
Various open
paths as they
appear in
Artwork mode.

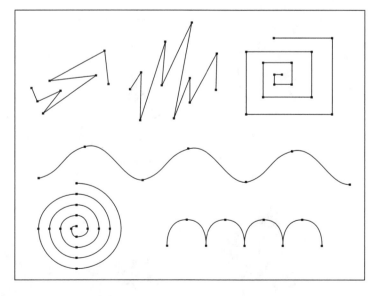

Open paths are paths that have two distinct end points, with any number of anchor points in between. Figure 2-12 shows a variety of open paths as they appear in Artwork mode and when printed.

Figure 2-12:
Several open paths in Artwork mode, with all anchor points selected (top). The paths then were given a black stroke and a gray fill and printed (bottom).

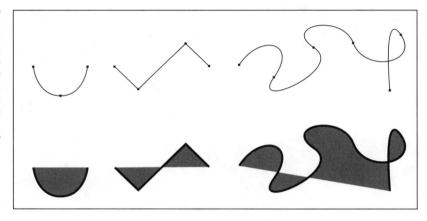

Closed paths are paths that are circular. There are no end points and no start or end to the path — it just continues around and around. Figure 2-13 shows three different closed paths in both Artwork and Preview modes.

Figure 2-13:
Several closed paths in Artwork mode, with all anchor points selected (top). The closed paths were given a black stroke and a gray fill and printed (bottom).

Compound paths are paths that are made up of two or more open or closed paths. Figure 2-14 shows three different compound paths in both Artwork mode and Preview modes.

Figure 2-14:
Several compound paths in front of text in Artwork mode, with all anchor points selected (top). After the compound paths were given a black stroke and a gray fill and the text was given a black fill, the images were printed (bottom).

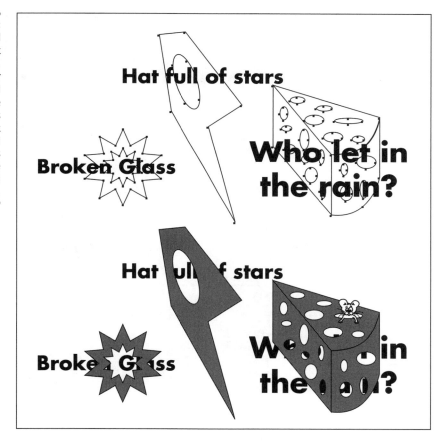

When you are working in Illustrator in Artwork mode (View⇨Artwork), only paths are visible. In Preview mode (View⇨Preview), fills and strokes applied to paths are visible. Unless a path is selected in Preview mode, it isn't visible.

It may be difficult to determine whether a path is a compound path or not; for a detailed look at compound paths, see Chapter 11.

Paths in Illustrator can be filled with a tint of color, a pattern, or a gradient. Closed paths always use the color to fill the inside of the shape they form (see Figure 2-15). Open paths also can be filled; the fill goes straight across the two end points of the path to enclose the object. Figure 2-16 displays how different types of open paths are filled. Filling an open path is usually not desirable, although in some circumstances it may be necessary.

Figure 2-15:
Four closed paths with different fills.

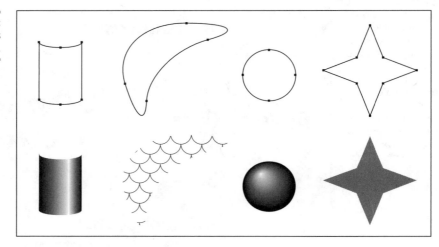

Figure 2-16:
Three open paths with different fills.

Besides filling paths, you can also stroke paths with any tint of any color or a pattern. These strokes can be any weight (thickness), and the width of the stroke is equally distributed over each side of the path. Closed paths with various fills are displayed in Figure 2-17. Open paths have ends on the strokes; these ends can be either cropped, rounded, or extended past the end of the stroke by half the width of the stroke (see Figure 2-18).

Figure 2-17:
Four closed
paths with
various strokes.

Figure 2-18:
Four open
paths with
different
strokes
(don't
expect to
see Gary
Coleman
here).

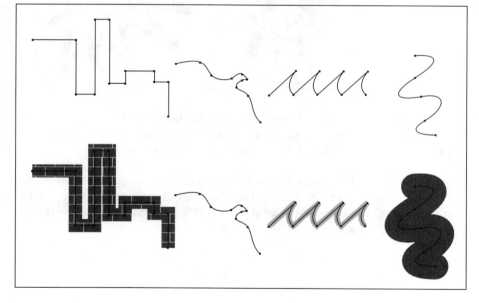

A single point is also considered a path, but in Illustrator single points can have no printable qualities. This isn't readily noticeable because you can assign a fill or stroke color to a single point, although it can't be seen in Preview mode or when printed. When the document is color separated, it will cause a separation of that color to print even if nothing else on that page is using that same color, and that separation will be blank.

Figure 2-19:
The same object with a fill of none (left) and a stroke of none (right) in both Artwork mode (top) and Preview mode.

 If you think you may have individual anchor points floating around your illustration, you can select all of them (if any) at once by selecting Filter⇨Select⇨Select Stray Points and then deleting them.

Fills and strokes in Illustrator can be tints of colors or an opaque white, which knocks out any color underneath it. Fills and strokes may also be *transparent,* in which case the stroke or fill will not be opaque, as in Figure 2-19. Transparency in Illustrator is commonly referred to as a fill or stroke of none.

Anchor Points

Paths are made up of a series of points and the line segments between two points. These points are commonly called anchor points because they anchor the path; paths *always* pass through anchor points. There are two classes of anchor points:

Smooth points are anchor points that have a curved path flowing smoothly through them; most of the time you don't know where a smooth point is unless the path is selected. Smooth points keep the path from changing direction abruptly. There are two *linked direction points* on every smooth point. Direction points never print. Figure 2-20 shows selected smooth points and their corresponding direction points and lines.

Figure 2-20:
Paths made
of smooth
points.

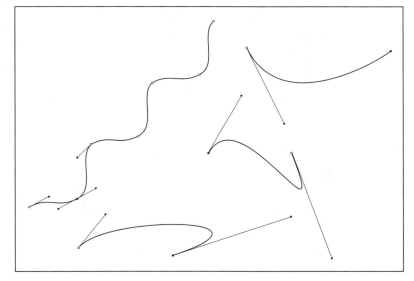

Corner points are a class of anchor points in which the path changes direction noticeably at that specific point. There are three different corner points:

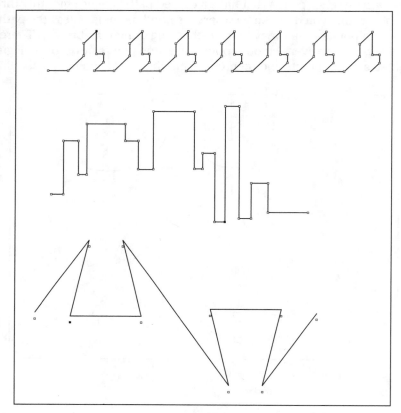

Straight corner points are anchor points where two straight line segments meet at a distinct angle (see Figure 2-21). There are no direction points on this type of anchor point.

Figure 2-21:
Paths made of straight corner points.

> *Curved corner points* are points where two curved line segments meet and abruptly change direction (see Figure 2-22). There are two *independent direction points* on each curved corner point.

Figure 2-22:
Paths made of curved corner points.

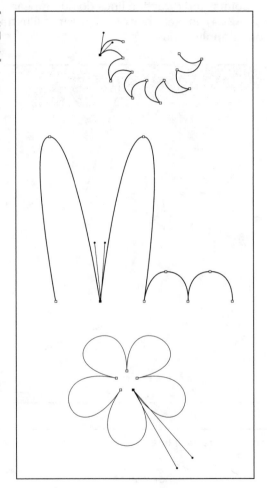

▓ *Combination corner points* are the meeting place for straight and curved line segments (see Figure 23). There is one independent direction point on a combination corner point.

Anchor points, direction points, and direction lines do not appear on the printed output of your artwork (see Figure 2-24). In fact, they only appear in Illustrator, never on artwork imported into other applications.

Figure 2-23:
Paths made of
combination corner
points.

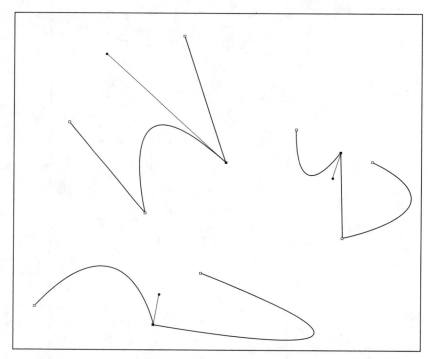

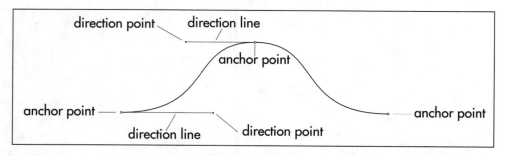

Figure 2-24: Anchor points, direction points, and direction lines on a standard path.

Bézier Curves

Not knowing all that much about geometry (or maybe not remembering that much . . . it was eighth grade, after all), the very concept of creating curves using math frightens me. Most of the curve creation in Illustrator takes place behind the scenes in the PostScript language code we almost never see.

PostScript curves are based on Bézier curves (pronounced Bez-ee-ay), which were created by Pierre Bézier (see Figure 2-25) in the early '70s as a way of controlling mechanical cutting devices, commonly known as Numerical Control. Bézier (see Foreword) worked for Renault (the car manufacturer) in France, and his mission was to streamline the process by which machines were controlled.

Figure 2-25:
Pierre Bézier, who laid the groundwork for PostScript and, thus, Illustrator.

A mathematician and engineer, Bézier developed a method for creating curves using four points for every curved segment. Two of these points lay at either end of the segment (we call them anchor points in Illustrator), and two points just floated around the curve segment, controlling the shape of the curve (direction points). Using these four points, a person could conceivably create any curve; using multiple sets of these curves, one could create any possible shape. The two PostScriptateers (John Warnock and Chuck Geshke) decided that Bézier curves were the best method for creating curves for a page description language, and suddenly those curves were a fundamental part of high-end graphic design.

Bézier curves are anything but intuitive. I believe that Bézier curves represent the most significant stumbling block in learning to use Illustrator well. After you have mastered the concept and use of these curves, everything about Illustrator suddenly becomes easier and friendlier. Don't try to ignore them because they won't go away. You will find it easier in the long run to try to understand how they work.

I've already written about half of what a Bézier curve is: two anchor points. Here comes the hard part (brace yourself).

Direction Points and Direction Lines

If an anchor point has a direction point coming out of it, the next segment will be curved. No direction point, no curve. Couldn't be simpler.

Direction points are connected to anchor points with direction lines. Figure 2-26 shows what happens when an anchor point with no direction point and an anchor point with a direction point are connected to another anchor point. The lines themselves really have no function other than to show you which anchor points the direction points are attached to. You cannot select a direction line. The only way to move a direction line or change the length of a direction line is by moving its corresponding direction point. Figure 2-27 displays how direction points and lines work with curves and anchor points.

Figure 2-26:
An anchor point without a direction point (top left) and an anchor point with a direction point (bottom left) are connected to new anchor points, resulting in a straight line (top right) and a curve (bottom right).

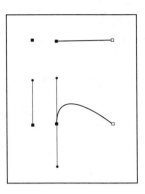

Figure 2-27:
Anchor points, direction points, and direction lines labeled for reference.

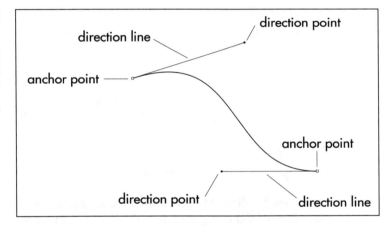

The basic concept concerning direction points is that direction points act as magnets, pulling the curve towards them (see Figure 2-28). This presents an interesting problem because there are usually two direction points per curved line segment. Just as you might suspect, the direction point exerts the greatest amount of force on the half of the curved segment nearest to it. If there is only one direction point, then the segment is curved more on the side of the segment with the direction point than the side with no direction point.

Figure 2-28:
Direction points
act as magnets,
pulling the
curve towards
them.

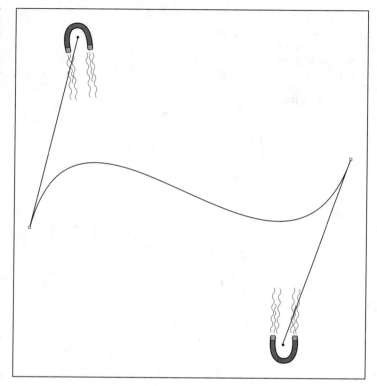

The greater the distance between a direction point and its corresponding anchor point, the farther the curve (on that end of the curve segment) will pull away from an imaginary straight segment between the two points (see Figure 2-29). If the direction points on either end of the segment are on different sides of the curved segment, the curved segment will be somewhat "S" shaped, as the paths in Figure 2-30 show. If the direction points on the ends of the curved segment are on the same side, the curve will be somewhat "U" shaped, the way the segments appear in Figure 2-31.

Direction lines coming out of an anchor point are always *tangent* to the curved segment where it touches the anchor point. By tangent, I'm referring to the angle of both the direction line and the angle of the curved segment as it crosses the anchor point (see Figure 2-32). This is always the case, whether the anchor point is a smooth point, a curved corner anchor point, or a combination corner anchor point.

In Chapter 6, you'll learn how to use the Pen tool for drawing with anchor points, direction points, and direction lines. Rules are also given to help you determine the placement, length, and angle of the various points and direction lines that are encountered using that tool.

Figure 2-29:
Direction points pull
the line segment away
from the straight
segment.

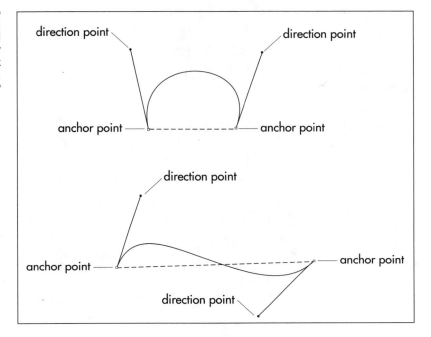

Figure 2-29:
Direction points pull
the line segment away
from the straight
segment.

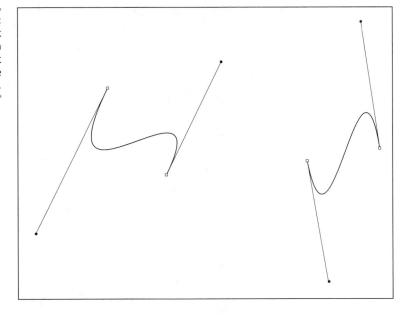

Figure 2-30:
S-shaped curves result
when direction points on
either side of the segment
are pulled in near-opposite
directions.

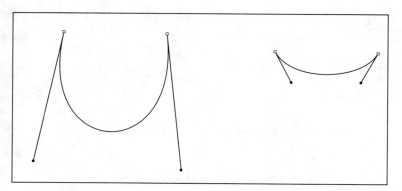

Figure 2-31:
U-shaped
curves result
when
direction
points on
either side of
the segment
are pulled in
almost the
same
direction.

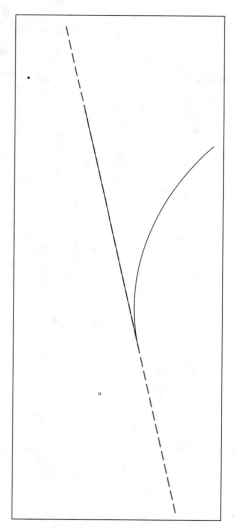

Figure 2-32:
Direction lines run tangent
to the path at the anchor
point.

Clear, Cut, Copy, and Paste

In most Macintosh software, including Illustrator, many of the most basic functions of the Edit menu work the same way. If you have used the Edit menu in QuarkXPress or Microsoft Word, for example, you should have no trouble using the same functions in Illustrator because the menu options are located in the same place in each program.

Clear

The most simplistic of these commands is Clear, which in Illustrator works almost exactly like the Delete key on the keyboard. When something is selected, choosing Clear will delete, or get rid of, what is selected.

You're probably asking yourself: "If the Delete key does the same thing, why do we need Clear?" or "Why didn't they just call the Clear command *Delete*?" Ah, the makers of Illustrator are a step ahead of you in this respect. Note that I said "almost" the same way; there actually is a subtle yet important difference in what the Clear command does and what the Delete key does, due to Illustrator's abundant usage of palettes in Version 5.0.

If you are working on a palette and (1) have just typed in a value in an editable text field or (2) tabbed down or up to an editable text field, highlighting text or (3) dragged across text in an editable text field, highlighting text, the Delete key will (1) delete the last character typed or (2 and 3) delete the highlighted characters. In all these situations, the Clear command will delete anything that is selected in the document.

Cut, Copy, and Paste

Cutting a selected object (or objects) in Illustrator initially does the same thing as Clear: it removes it from the page. But Cut also takes that same object and secretly places it on the *Clipboard*. The Clipboard is a temporary holding place for objects that have been cut or copied. Objects put into the Clipboard by using Cut or Copy stay there until something else gets cut or copied.

After an object is in the Clipboard, it may be pasted into (1) the center of the same document, (2) in the same location as the cut/copied object and (3) pasted into another document in Illustrator, Photoshop, Dimensions, or Streamline thanks to Adobe's PostScript on the Clipboard.

Now, the really cool part: Just because you've pasted the object somewhere doesn't mean it isn't in the Clipboard anymore; it is! You can paste again and again, and keep on pasting until you just get plain bored, or until your page is an indecipherable mess, whichever comes first.

Copy works like Cut, but it doesn't delete the selected object(s). Instead, it just copies them to the Clipboard, at which time you can choose Paste and slap another copy onto your document.

Cut, Copy, and Paste also work with text that you type in a document. Using the Type tools, you can select type, cut or copy it, and then paste it. When you're pasting type, it will go wherever your blinking text cursor is located. If you have type selected (highlighted) and you choose Paste, the type that was selected is replaced by whatever you had on the Clipboard.

You can copy as much or as little of an illustration as you choose; you are only limited to hard disk space for objects that you cut and copy. A good rule of thumb is that if you ever get a message saying you can't cut or copy because you are out of hard disk space, it is time to start throwing out stuff on your hard drive that you don't need or simply get a bigger hard drive.

The most important rule to remember about Cut, Copy, and Paste is that whatever is currently on the Clipboard will be replaced by anything that gets cut or copied subsequently to the Clipboard. Cutting or copying twice will put the second copied object(s) on the Clipboard, and the first will be gone.

The magic Clipboard

You can view the contents of the Clipboard by going under the Edit menu to Show Clipboard. Unfortunately, the only thing you'll usually see in Illustrator is (1) the PostScript logo with the number of objects you have selected and the layers those objects are on (see Figure 2-33) or (2) copied text (see Figure 2-34). In order to see text in the Clipboard, it must be copied using the Type tools. Type that is cut or copied using the selection tools will not appear as type, but instead as an "object." When you view type, it will usually not look like the type you selected; the words are there, but the font and style information won't be present. Instead, the type is displayed in Geneva, at either 12 point or 9 point, depending on what you have copied prior to copying your text.

Figure 2-33:
The Clipboard when several objects on different layers have been copied or cut.

You can't do anything to the Clipboard by displaying this window. You may only resize the window and move it around on your screen for the sole purpose of displaying what you have copied last.

Figure 2-34:
The Clipboard when text selected with a type tool has been copied or cut.

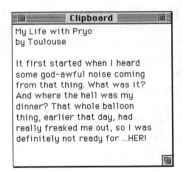

The Clipboard is actually a file in the main (root) level of your system folder called Clipboard.

Undo and Redo

In most Macintosh applications, you can undo the last thing done by choosing Undo from the Edit menu. That works in Illustrator, but Adobe has taken the concept of undo just a little further: you can keep undoing, more than once.

In fact, you can undo in Illustrator up to 200 times, providing your system has enough memory and you have enough patience. After you have undone, you can redo by choosing Redo, right below Undo in the Edit menu. And, guess what, you can redo up to 200 times as well.

The default number of undos in Illustrator is 10. To change the number of undos, go to the General Preferences dialog box (File⇨Preferences⇨General), as shown in Figure 2-35. You *can* set the undo levels to 0, but I wouldn't recommend it; this will disallow any undo/redo operations. If you *do* set the number of undos too low and later realize you want to undo more actions, the cold, hard truth of the Undo levels box will raise its ugly head: You can't increase the number of undos after you have run out of them.

If you undo a couple of times and then *do* something, you won't be able to redo. You have to undo the last thing you did and then actually do everything again. In other words, all the steps that you undid are gone.

It is fine to use the Undo feature to go back and check out what you did, but after you have used multiple undos, don't do anything if you want to redo back to where you started undoing from.

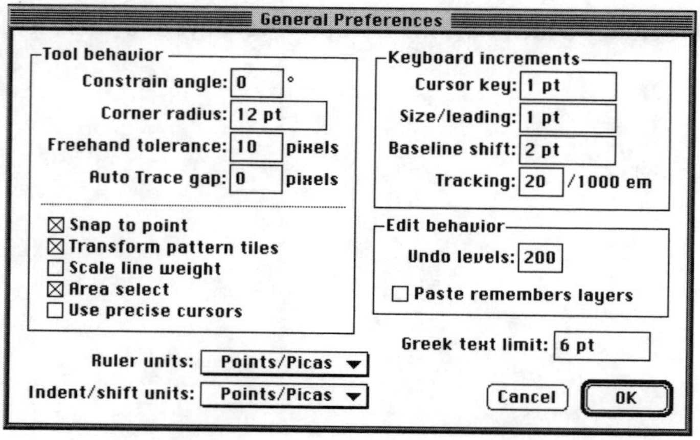

Figure 2-35:
Change the number of allowable undos in Illustrator by entering a number (up to 200) in the Undo levels box.

General Preferences

Tool behavior
Constrain angle: 0 °
Corner radius: 12 pt
Freehand tolerance: 10 pixels
Auto Trace gap: 0 pixels

☒ Snap to point
☒ Transform pattern tiles
☐ Scale line weight
☒ Area select
☐ Use precise cursors

Ruler units: Points/Picas ▾
Indent/shift units: Points/Picas ▾

Keyboard increments
Cursor key: 1 pt
Size/leading: 1 pt
Baseline shift: 2 pt
Tracking: 20 /1000 em

Edit behavior
Undo levels: 200
☐ Paste remembers layers

Greek text limit: 6 pt

Cancel   OK

Saving, unlike most other software, has no impact on Undo/Redo. Saving is not considered to be an option that can be undone, or done again, so its very existence is ignored by Undo/Redo. After you save, you may easily undo the last thing you did before you saved.

Artwork and Preview Modes

Ah, sigh. Gone are the days of working blind, having to wait to see what you were illustrating until you chose Preview and then not being able to work again until you chose Artwork. I'm being sarcastic, of course. Aldus FreeHand has allowed artists to work in Preview for just over a million years (since 1989, to be exact), and Adobe finally included that capability for Macintosh owners in 1993 with the release of Illustrator Version 5.

Artwork mode

Many artists who have used Illustrator in the older versions (1.1, 88, 3.2) actually *like* working in Artwork mode. Why? It's faster, you can see every path in the document (and select those same paths), and the anchor points and direction points stand out more. Artwork mode (see Figure 2-36) is much closer to what the printer sees: paths that define the edges of the objects you are working with.

Artwork seems to be a misnomer. Wireframe mode would be more descriptive — or maybe Paths mode. The only thing visible in Artwork mode is the paths that make up the objects, and all paths are always visible.

Preview mode

In Preview mode, you see on-screen what your illustration really looks like when it prints, with the exception of any selected paths that you see on-screen (see Figure 2-37).

Instead of selecting a path by clicking it, you can also select entire paths by clicking the inside of those paths in a filled area. It becomes a little more difficult to select certain points on paths because the strokes on those paths are also visible. Sometimes, there is so much stuff on your screen in Preview that you don't know what to click.

Figure 2-36: Four illustrations as they appear in Artwork mode.

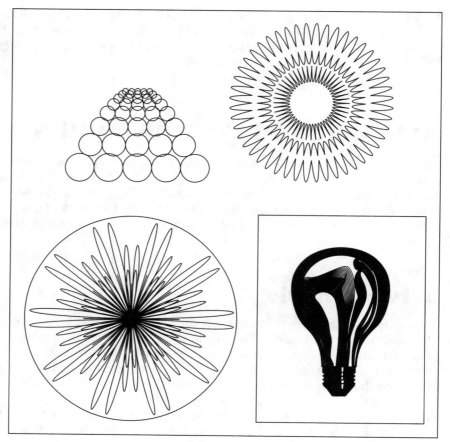

The major drawback to Preview mode is not the inability to select paths or parts of paths, but the amount of time it takes for certain types of fills and blends to redraw accurately on your screen. The first time a slow redraw takes place in your document, you hardly notice it; you are too busy looking at how that object looks now that it has, say, a pattern fill. After that, though, you may not be working with that object but others, and you still have to wait for that pattern-filled object to completely redraw every time you change views, move that object, or move something in front of that object.

Fortunately, Illustrator has a saving grace that makes this slowness almost acceptable. Whenever the screen is in this redraw mode, you can do other things. If your patterned, filled object is redrawing, for example, Illustrator lets you go to the Type menu to change typefaces you've selected; when you are done selecting the type, the image finishes redrawing. This process is called *interruptable redraw,* and it is a godsend for Illustrator users.

Figure 2-37:
The illustrations
from Figure 2-36
as they appear,
unselected, in
Preview mode.

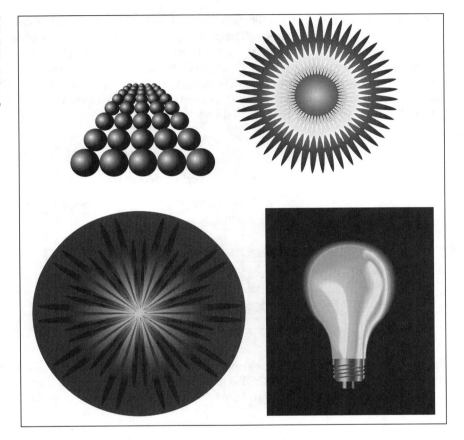

Palettes versus Windows

If there is a trend in graphics programs, it's the trend toward using palettes for everything possible. It started becoming noticeable with Fractal Design Painter, which has 12 palettes that can be on the screen at the same time. QuarkXPress soon followed with a half-dozen palettes, and Photoshop 2.5 has five. Illustrator 5 has seven palettes, all of which can remain open while you work on your document (providing you can still see your document through all those palettes!).

In many respects, palettes are like windows. They have a title bar that can be clicked and dragged to move the palette. There is usually a close box in the upper left corner of the palette, and in the upper right corner there is often an auto-resize box, which makes the palette smaller or larger than its original size. Occasionally, a manual resize box will be located in the lower right corner for dragging the palette to a new size. Options for hiding and showing palettes are even located under the Window menu. Figure 2-38 shows the Character palette with all its parts labeled.

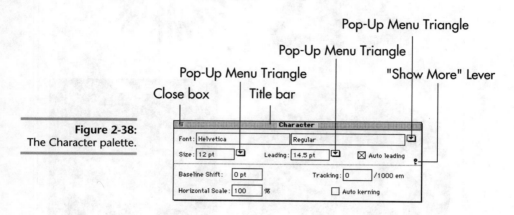

Figure 2-38:
The Character palette.

Palettes are unlike windows in several ways. Palettes seldom have scroll bars, although the Layers palette (see Figure 2-39) is an exception. When you hop from one program to another, palettes automatically hide, while windows remain visible.

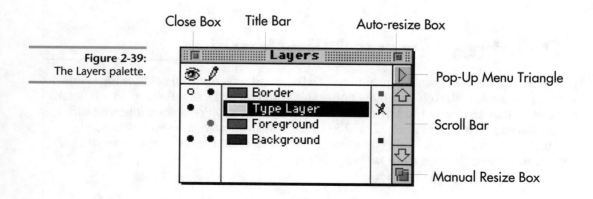

Figure 2-39:
The Layers palette.

The Toolbox in Illustrator is also a palette; it can be hidden by clicking the close box in the upper left corner.

Unlike windows, palettes are never really "active." Instead, the one you are working in will be in the front, and if it has editable text fields, one will be highlighted or a blinking text cursor will appear. To bring a palette to the forefront, simply click on it anywhere.

The Document Window

 Getting around your documents in Illustrator can be a little confusing at first, especially if you have a monitor that is not the common 13"/14" color monitor from Apple. If you have a larger monitor, initially the Illustrator window will only take up about half of the available screen space. Clicking in the upper right corner of the document window is a quick fix; for a permanent one, see Chapter 14, which deals with Preferences.

Pasteboard

Probably the worst thing that can possibly happen when you are using Illustrator is for you to lose everything you've worked on. This seems to happen very easily in Illustrator just by clicking a few times on the gray part of the scroll bars at the bottom of the document window. What happens when you click here is that you are moving about half the width of your window with every click, and three clicks later your page and everything on it is no longer in front of you. Instead, you see the Pasteboard, a vast expanse of white nothingness.

The Pasteboard measures 120 x 120 inches, which works out to 100 square feet of drawing space. At actual size, you only see a very small section of the Pasteboard. A little letter-sized document looks extremely tiny on a pasteboard that is this big. If you get lost on the Pasteboard, a quick way back is by selecting View➪Actual Size. This puts your page in the center of the window at 100% view at which time you should be able to see at least part of your drawing. To see the whole page quickly, select View➪Fit In Window; this resizes your page down to where you can see the entire page. To see the entire Pasteboard, press Option while double-clicking the Zoom tool.

Artboard

In the center of the Pasteboard is a black-bordered box called the Artboard. The Artboard represents the largest area that will actually print out of Illustrator. If you are taking your Illustrator artwork into another application, such as Photoshop or QuarkXPress, the size of the Artboard is irrelevant; your entire illustration will appear in most other software applications even if that artwork is larger than the Artboard. The Artboard, Pasteboard, and page areas of a document are labeled in Figure 2-40.

Figure 2-40:
The main parts of the inside of a document window.

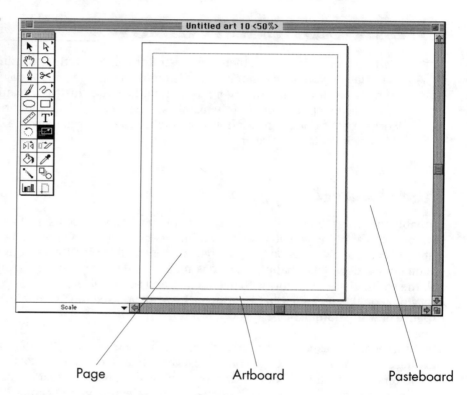

Page   Artboard   Pasteboard

The dotted lines on the Artboard represent which area will print and the size of your printer's paper, referencing the printer options you have chosen in Page Setup for this information. There are two sets of dotted lines on the Artboard, although normally you can only see the inside line. The inside line represents what will actually print; the outside line is the size of the paper you have chosen in Page Setup.

The dimensions of the Artboard can be changed by selecting File⇨Document Setup and typing in different values in the width and height box.

Miscellaneous window stuff

Illustrator windows act like windows in most other programs. The close box is in the upper left corner, and the manual resize box is in the lower right corner. The box in the upper right corner will toggle between your current window size and full-screen size. The title bar at the top of the window is used to move the window around your screen. On the title bar is the name of the document; if you have not yet saved your document, the name of the document is "Untitled Art 1," with the number changing for each new document you create. Next to the title of the document is the current viewing zoom percentage relative to actual size.

The scroll bars on the right side of the window allow you to see what is above and below the current viewing area. The scroll bars at the bottom of the window control panning from side to side. The arrows on each scroll bar let you see just a bit more with every click; holding down the mouse on an arrow slowly scrolls to other parts of the document. Dragging the elevator box takes you to another part of the document, relative to the direction you are dragging. Clicking either side of the elevator box in the gray bars changes your view by chunks of about half the width or height of your window.

In the lower left corner is the status bar. The status bar tells you all sorts of neat information that you just can't get anywhere else. The default is usually set to display the name of the tool you are working with.

Tools

3

In This Chapter

❖ Understanding the Toolbox

❖ Using the selection tools properly

❖ Navigating in your document with the viewing tools

❖ The differences between the path creation and editing tools

❖ Using the Measure tool

❖ What the different tools are used for

❖ Transforming selected objects with the four transformation tools

❖ Sampling paint style attributes with the Eyedropper tool and painting them with the Paint Bucket tool

❖ The differences between the Gradient Vector tool and the Blend tool

❖ Using the Graph tool

❖ Changing the printable page area with the Page tool

The Toolbox

The Illustrator 5.0 Toolbox (see Figure 3-1) is quite different from its predecessors in previous versions. Many new tools have been added, certain tools have been removed, and the way the selection tools work has been totally revamped. It may seem that the Toolbox has been randomly thrown together and that nothing makes any sense in the Toolbox structure, but that is not the case at all.

The Toolbox has two columns of tools, with the tools on each row related to each other. The viewing tools — the Hand tool and the Zoom tool, for example — are next to each other. The Blend tool and the Gradient Vector tool are also side by side. In fact, only two sets of tools are *not* related on the Toolbar: the Measure tool and the Type tool, and the Graph tool and the Page tool.

Figure 3-1:
The Illustrator 5.0
Toolbox.

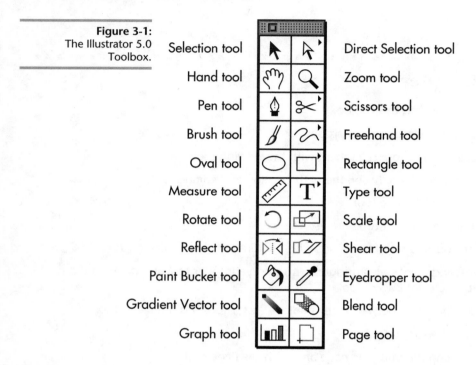

Selection tool	Direct Selection tool
Hand tool	Zoom tool
Pen tool	Scissors tool
Brush tool	Freehand tool
Oval tool	Rectangle tool
Measure tool	Type tool
Rotate tool	Scale tool
Reflect tool	Shear tool
Paint Bucket tool	Eyedropper tool
Gradient Vector tool	Blend tool
Graph tool	Page tool

To choose a tool, click the one you want to use in the Toolbox and release the mouse button. You can use this tool until you click another.

Unlike most applications, Illustrator lets you click and drag from the tool of your choice across other tools and keep selected the tool you clicked initially. But there is no need to drag, and a better habit to develop is to just click the desired tool, release the mouse button, and use the tool in the document window.

Many tools have additional *pop-up tools*, tools that appear only when you click and hold down the mouse on the default tool. The default tools that have pop-ups are located in the right column and are indicated with a little triangle in the upper righthand corner of the tool. To select a pop-up tool, click and hold on a tool with a triangle until the pop-up tools appear; then drag the pop-up tool you want over to the Toolbar. The new pop-up tool replaces the default tool in its slot. This procedure is demonstrated in Figure 3-2.

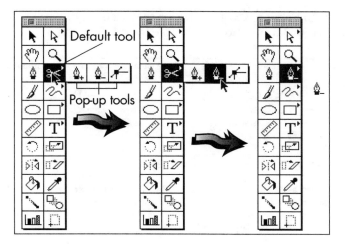

Figure 3-2:
Selecting a pop-up tool.

To change a pop-up tool back to its default, press Shift while you double-click the tool you want to reset. To change all the tools back to their defaults, press ⌘-Shift while double-clicking any tool, even ones without pop-up tools. You can see a complete list of all pop-up tools in Figure 3-3.

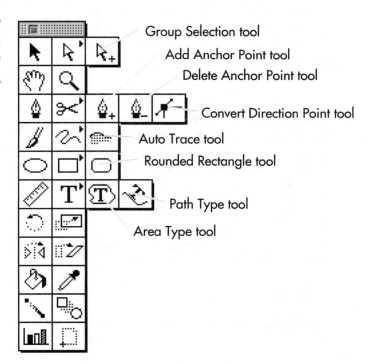

Figure 3-3:
The pop-up tools in the Toolbox.

Group Selection tool
Add Anchor Point tool
Delete Anchor Point tool
Convert Direction Point tool
Auto Trace tool
Rounded Rectangle tool
Path Type tool
Area Type tool

Most of the tools from Version 3.2 of Illustrator are available in Version 5. Figure 3-4 shows all the tools from 3.2 and the comparable tools in Version 5.

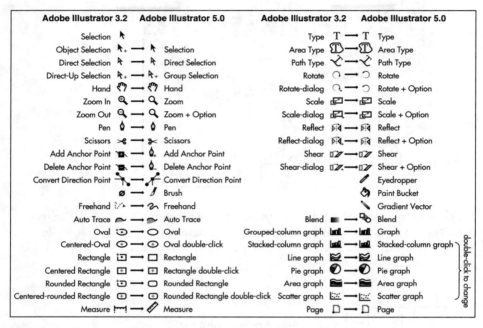

Figure 3-4: The tools from Version 3.2 as compared to Version 5.

The Toolbox appears on top of your document window, covering up part of your illustration in the upper lefthand corner. Now that the Toolbox is two columns wide, it takes up much more space than it did in previous versions of Illustrator. Clicking the close box in the upper lefthand corner of the Toolbox hides it from view; selecting Window⇨Show Toolbox causes it to appear in the same location it was before it was hidden. When the Toolbox is on-screen, the option under Window reads Hide Toolbox. Just as with most other palettes in Illustrator, you can use a key command, ⌘-Control-T, to show and hide the Toolbox.

If you hide the Toolbox, you still can use whichever tool you last selected. By using different key commands, you can access even more tools.

Most key commands let you use a certain tool while you hold down certain keys. For example, pressing ⌘-spacebar activates the Zoom In tool, and pressing the spacebar activates the Hand tool. After those keys are released, the tool originally selected again becomes the active tool.

Although there are many key commands for temporarily selecting tools in the Toolbox, only one command can *permanently* change a tool. ⌘-Tab toggles between the Selection and Direct Selection tools.

 Selecting different tools and Showing/Hiding the Toolbox is not something that can be undone. Instead, Undo will undo the last action prior to your Toolbox changes.

The Selection Tools

If there is one group of tools in Illustrator you absolutely *must* have, it is the set of three selection tools. As in most Macintosh applications, to change or alter something (move, transform, and so on), you must first select it. When you draw a new path or when you paste in Illustrator, the program automatically selects the object you're working on; however, as soon as you draw another path, the preceding object is deselected and Illustrator automatically selects the object with the new path. The selection tools allow you to select paths and perform additional manipulations on them. Illustrator 5.0 has three selection tools: the Selection tool, the Direct Selection tool, and the Group Selection tool.

There are several different ways to select a path in Illustrator, depending on what you wish to change:

First-level selecting: *First-level selecting* means at least one point or segment of a path is selected, usually with the Direct Selection tool. First-level selecting is used to adjust individual points, segments, and series of points.

Even though just a portion of the path is selected, many changes will affect the entire path — not just the selected points. For example, most of the attributes available in the Object menu (including Paint Style, Masking, and Compound Paths) will affect the entire path when only a point or segment is selected.

First-level selecting also allows you to use most of the functions in the Arrange menu, such as hiding, locking, or grouping.

Selected anchor points on first-level selected paths are solid squares; unselected points are hollow squares. Selected segments are indicated by visible direction points and direction lines on either side of the segment if the selected segment is curved. If the selected segment is not curved, no indication that the segment is selected appears on-screen. If you delete a segment or point, the entire remaining path becomes selected at the second level.

Figure 3-5 shows first-level selection by using the Direct Selection tool to select a line segment, to select an anchor point, and to drag a marquee around portions of paths.

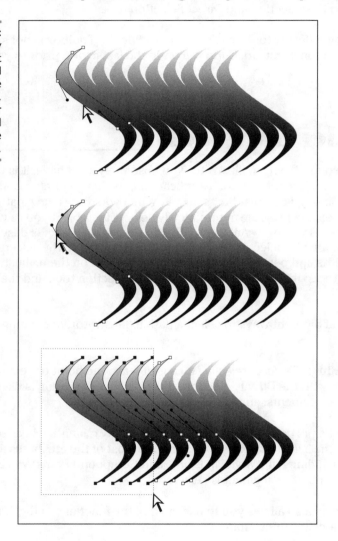

Figure 3-5:
First-level selection by using the Direct Selection tool and clicking a line segment (top), clicking an anchor point (middle), and drawing a marquee (bottom).

Second-level selecting: *Second-level selecting* means that all points and segments on a path are selected. When a path is clicked by using the Group Selection tool or the Selection tool, the entire path will automatically be selected. (Drawing a marquee entirely around a path with the Direct Selection tool will also select the entire path.)

All the capabilities from first-level selecting are available, such as the entire Object menu and the Arrange menu and most of the functions in the Filter menu.

After you select a path on the second level, the entire path is affected by moving, transforming, cutting, copying and pasting, and deleting. An example of second-level selecting is shown in Figure 3-6.

Figure 3-6:
Second-level selection by using the Selection tool and clicking a line segment (top) and dragging a marquee around the objects.

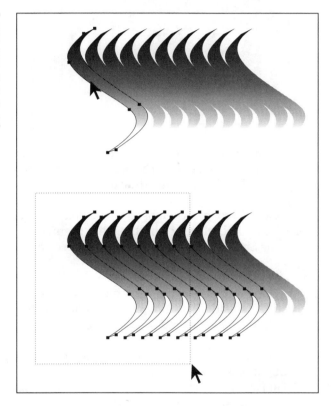

Third-level selecting: You can select and affect any series of grouped paths as one path in *third-level selecting*. All paths in the group are affected in the same way as paths that you select in the second level. The Selection tool will select entire groups of paths at once. If you use the Group Selection tool instead, you will need a series of clicks to select a group of paths. Refer to Figure 3-7 to see what you can accomplish with third-level selecting.

To select everything in your document that hasn't been hidden or locked, choose Edit⇨Select All (⌘-A), which selects all the points and segments on every path in the document. You also can select everything in the document by drawing a marquee around all the paths with any selection tool.

Figure 3-7:
Third-level selection by
using the Selection tool and
clicking a line segment.

Normally, after you select something new, everything that you have previously selected becomes *deselected*. To continue to select additional points, paths, or segments, you must hold down the Shift key while clicking and dragging.

The Shift key normally works as a toggle when used with a selection tool, selecting anything that is not selected and deselecting anything that is currently selected. Each selection tool works with the Shift key a little differently, as described in the following sections.

To deselect everything that is selected, click a part of the document that is empty (where you can see the Pasteboard or Artboard) without using the Shift key. You also can deselect everything by choosing Edit⇨Deselect All (⌘-Shift-A).

You can use the selection tools for manually moving selected points, segments, and paths. Personally, the thought of manual labor terrifies me, but when I do something *manually* in Illustrator, I am usually referring to the process of dragging or clicking with the mouse. You use *automatic* or *computer-assisted manipulations* when you enter in specific values in the Move dialog box (Arrange⇨Move), for example. The Move Dialog box can also be accessed by Option-clicking the Selection tool.

There were four selection tools in Illustrator 3.2, but all the functions of those four tools have been incorporated into the three selection tools in Illustrator 5.0. The missing tool is the Object Selection tool, which appeared as a solid arrow with a little plus symbol in the lower righthand corner. This tool's functionality has been put into Illustrator 5.0's Selection tool, and the Selection tool from 3.2 has been eliminated. The next few sections cover the breakdown of the selection tools and their functions.

The Selection tool

The Selection tool in Version 5.0 performs the functions of the Object Selection tool in Version 3.2 (with no plus symbol). The Selection tool selects entire paths or complete groups at one time, as illustrated in Figure 3-8. You can't select just one point or a few points on a path with the Selection tool. Instead, the entire path on which that point lies is selected (all the anchor points turn black). Drawing a marquee (clicking and dragging as a box forms behind the cursor) around parts of paths or entire paths also selects those entire paths.

Figure 3-8:
Using the Selection tool to select an entire path.

If you press the Shift key, the Selection tool works as a toggle between selecting and deselecting paths. While you hold down the Shift key and click on paths that are not selected, they become selected. When paths that are selected are Shift-clicked, they become deselected. The Shift key can be used in this way to add to or subtract from a series of selected paths.

You can access either the Selection tool or the Direct Selection tool from the keyboard by holding down the Command key (⌘). Technically, the Command key causes the selection tool that you last used — either the Selection tool or the Direct Selection tool — to appear. You can toggle back and forth between the two tools from the keyboard by pressing ⌘-Tab.

 The Group Selection tool can be accessed from the keyboard when the Direct Selection tool is selected by pressing the Option key along with the Command key.

The Direct Selection tool

To select individual points, line segments, or a series of specific points within a path, you need to use the Direct Selection tool. It is the *only* tool that allows you to select something less than an entire path, as you can see in Figure 3-9. You can also draw a marquee over a portion of a path to select only those points and segments within the area of the marquee. If the marquee surrounds an entire path, the entire path is selected. Individual points or a series of points on different paths also can be selected by drawing a marquee around just those points.

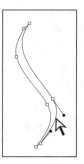

Figure 3-9:
Using the Direct Selection tool to select individual points on a path.

The Shift key is used with the Direct Selection tool to select additional points or segments or to deselect previously selected points. If only one segment or point on a path is selected and you Shift-click on that segment or point with the Direct Selection tool, the entire path is deselected.

Selecting items with the Direct Selection tool can be a little intimidating because anchor points show up as *solid* when selected and *hollow* when deselected. Furthermore, a selected segment does not have any anchor points selected; instead, any direction points and direction lines associated with that segment become selected. If there are no direction points associated with a segment, such as a segment that is in between two straight corner points, then it is difficult to tell which segment is selected.

After you select a point or series of points, those selected points can be manipulated in a number of ways, including being moved and transformed (via the transformation tools) and having certain filters applied to them. Individual segments and series of segments can be selected and modified in the same way points are transformed.

 # The Group Selection tool

Before Version 5.0, I had never met anyone who used the Group Selection tool very much, in any version of Illustrator, because it was not available as a pop-up selection tool. The only way to access it was by acquiring the Direct Selection tool and holding down the Option key to use it, which is another way of accessing the Group Selection tool in Version 5. But the main reason no one used it is because it had not been explained very well in the Illustrator manuals or in other third-party books. In addition, Adobe named the tool with the mystical title Direct-up Selection tool, which probably prevented people from using the tool right off the bat.

The Group Selection tool is driven by a very cool concept: it first selects a path, then the group that the path is in, then the group that the other group with the path is in, and so on. On second thought, the name Direct-up Selection wasn't inappropriate for what the tool does because it clicks "up" through groups.

For the Group Selection tool to work properly, the first path or paths can be chosen by either clicking them or drawing a marquee around them. To select the group that a particular path is in, however, requires you to click one of the initially selected paths. To select the next group also requires a click; if you drag at any point, only the paths you drag over are selected.

This process may seem a little fuzzy at first, but it will get easier the more you use the Group Selection tool. Remember: the first time you select something with the Group Selection tool, you select only the paths you click or drag over. The next time you click an already selected path, all the paths in its group will be selected.

Let's look at a prime example in Figure 3-10. In the first graph, nothing is selected. The second graph shows what happens after one click with the Group Selection tool to select the little bar. The third graph shows the results of the second click with the Group Selection tool on the sample bar; notice how all bars of the same color are now selected. Another click in the fourth graph shows how the Electronic art box is now selected, as well.

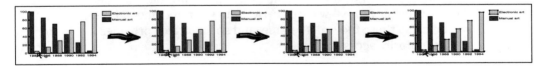

Figure 3-10: A sample Group Selection sequence.

 Still confused about how the Shift key selects and deselects paths? I can make it worse. The Shift key is an odd duck when used with the Group Selection tool. What happens when you click an unselected path with this tool while holding down the Shift key? The path is selected. But what happens when you click a selected path? The process deselects *just one path*. What makes more sense to me is if you would click again with the Shift key, and it then would deselect the entire group. Nope. Ain't gonna happen. The Shift key works as a toggle between the one path you are clicking on: select it, deselect it, and so on.

Dragging a marquee around paths with the Group Selection tool works only for the first series of clicks; dragging another marquee, even over the already selected paths, just reselects those paths.

If you have selected several paths at once, clicking a selected path will select only the group that the selected path is in. If other selected paths are in different groups, those groups will not be selected until you click those paths with the Group Selection tool. However, clicking multiple times on any of the paths in the selected group continues to select "up" in the group that the selected path is part of.

The Group Selection tool is the most useful when dealing with graphs and blends, but it can be used in a number of other situations to greatly enhance your control of what is and is not selected. People who always are ungrouping and regrouping paths (I believe they're called groupies) can greatly benefit from using the Group Selection tool. In fact, proper use of this tool prevents you from ever having to ungroup and regroup objects for cosmetic (that is, paint style) reasons.

You can access the Group Selection tool when the Direct Selection tool is selected by holding down the Option key. If the Direct Selection tool is not chosen, then select it by holding down the Command key (you may have to press ⌘-Tab to toggle from the Selection tool to the Direct Selection tool) and pressing the Option key at the same time.

The Viewing Tools

In order for you to work with your document easily, Illustrator has included a number of tools used for changing your view of the artwork in your document. Like the selection tools, you will be using these tools all the time, and so Illustrator provides keyboard commands to temporarily access them all.

In Illustrator 5.0, there are only two viewing tools visible, the Zoom tool and the Hand tool; in Illustrator 3.2 there were three viewing tools visible. (For some reason — known only to the gods of PostScript — Adobe incorporated both the Zoom In and the Zoom Out tools of Illustrator 3 into the one Zoom tool of Illustrator 5.0.)

 ## The Hand tool

Scroll bars are evil. Really. What happens when you want to move diagonally within your document? You have to use both scroll bars. Half the time you go too far and have to click the arrow in the opposite direction, and the other half you drag that &#*@! elevator box too far and become totally disoriented.

The Hand tool (called the Scroll tool in many other programs) allows you to move around inside your document without having to use those nasty bars at all. And it couldn't be simpler to use. Just select the Hand tool, click somewhere in your document, and drag (notice how the Hand tool looks like it is grabbing the page when you click the mouse button). The document moves inside the window in the direction you drag. As you drag, the elevator boxes in the scroll bars move along proportionately.

The Hand tool does not affect anything in your document, but it does show you different areas of your artwork.

 A good strategy for using the Hand tool to move around in your document is to click the opposite side of your document window from where you want to move. If you want to push your page down, for example, go to the top of the window, click, and drag down. You can move the document much farther this way.

In addition, if you drag outside the window (maybe your window isn't as big as your screen or you have two or more screens), the document continues to scroll in the same direction that you are moving.

 The Hand tool is extremely useful when you have zoomed in to a high magnification because using the scroll bars at this time can get you instantly disoriented.

 The Hand tool can be accessed from the keyboard by pressing the spacebar. If the Type tool is chosen, however, and you are in the middle of a text box, pressing the spacebar results in a series of spaces instead of the Hand tool, as expected. To get around this, press ⌘-spacebar and, while keeping the spacebar depressed, release the Command key.

The Zoom tool

OK, the Zoom tool is really just a funky name for a magnifying glass. (Inconsistency runs abundant in the viewing tools: the Hand tool is named for what it looks like, not what it does; and the Zoom tool is named for what it does, not what it looks like . . . hmmm.) Choosing the Zoom tool results in a cursor that looks like a magnifying glass with a plus sign in it. This is really the Zoom In tool, although the status bar still just says it's the plain old Zoom tool.

 Using the Zoom tool does not change anything in your document. You are just seeing a close-up perspective of your artwork when you zoom in and a far away perspective when you zoom out.

Clicking with the Zoom tool magnifies the document one increment per click. The increments of viewing percentages are as follows: 6.25%, 8.33%, 12.5%, 16.67%, 25%, 33.33%, 50%, 66%, 100%, 150%, 200%, 300%, 400%, 600%, 800%, 1200%, and 1600%. You can continue to click with the Zoom tool until the title bar reads <1600%>, at which time you are at the highest possible magnification.

To zoom out, hold down the Option key and click the document with the Zoom tool, which decreases the magnification one increment with each click — just the opposite of how the zoom in function works. Notice how the cursor is marked with a minus sign rather than a plus sign. Continue zooming out until the title bar reads the smallest percentage, <6.25%>.

All that clicking is nice, but the real strength of the Zoom tool is when you use it to draw a marquee around something in your document. The area you surround with the Zoom marquee fills your window at the largest percentage possible, as in Figure 3-11. Drawing a marquee works only with the Zoom tool set to zoom in. If you press the Option key when drawing a box with the Zoom tool, you won't see the marquee lines, and you will just zoom out one magnification step.

 The Zoom Marquee can be repositioned at any time while the mouse button is pressed by pressing the spacebar and moving the cursor. The entire marquee will move until the spacebar is released.

To quickly zoom to "fit in window" magnification — where your entire Artboard fits inside the window — double-click the Hand tool. You can also select View⇨Fit in Window (⌘-M). The viewing percentage here depends on the size of your window (and the size of your screen).

To go back to the actual size (100%) of the figure, double-click the Zoom tool. To go to the actual size and center the page at the same time, select View⇨Actual Size (⌘-H).

By holding down the Option key while double-clicking the Zoom tool, the document resizes itself so that you can see the entire Pasteboard in your window. (On 14" and smaller monitors, you can never see the entire Pasteboard, even at 6.25% magnification; the screen is just too small.)

 Remember that what the computer says is actual size and what is actual size in real life are similar, but rarely exact. It is next to useless to hold up a pica sample stick to your computer monitor to measure your computer's type size. (Don't laugh; I've seen people do this — what really scares me are the ones who use that same pica stick to draw straight lines on their monitors. If you do this, turn to Chapter 7, which discusses guides.) If your monitor is exactly 72 ppi (pixels per inch), then the Actual Size (100%) setting is fairly accurate. If there are more than 72 pixels per inch, images on your monitor will be smaller than the output; if the pixels per inch is less than 72, the image on-screen will be larger than real life. To find out the ppi of your monitor, consult its operating manual. Most Apple color monitors (13", 14", 16", and 21") are 72 dpi, although the 12" color monitor is less.

Figure 3-11:
Using the Zoom tool by
drawing a marquee.

The Path Creation and Editing Tools

The next six tools and their corresponding pop-up tools on the toolbar contain path creation and adjustment tools. Aside from filters, these tools represent the only way you can make new paths in Illustrator. Most of these tools, except the Brush tool, have been part of Adobe Illustrator since Illustrator 88. The path creation and editing tools are as follows: Pen, Scissors, Add Anchor Point, Delete Anchor Point, Convert Direction Point, Brush, Freehand, Auto Trace, Oval, Rectangle, and Rounded Rectangle.

For detailed lessons on path creation with these tools, refer to Chapters 5 and 6; for more information on the path editing tools, see Chapter 10.

 ## The mighty Pen tool

The Pen tool is the most powerful tool in Illustrator's arsenal and also the hardest to master. With the Pen tool, you are dealing more directly with Bézier curves than with any other tool. It is one thing to adjust paths, anchor points, and direction points with the Direct Selection tool, but using the Pen tool to create paths out of nothing is dumbfounding.

For the first several months of my experience using Illustrator, I avoided the Pen tool like the plague. Then I slowly worked up to where I could draw straight lines with it comfortably, and finally curved segments. Even after I had been drawing curved segments for a while, I really didn't understand how the tool worked, and I was missing out on a lot of its capabilities because of that lack of knowledge. The manuals for Illustrator really weren't very clear on how to use the Pen tool, and no one I knew could do any better. To learn how to use it, I forced myself to use the Pen tool to draw objects that I could draw with the Auto Trace tool.

While practicing with the Pen tool, I necessarily learned about the four types of anchor points — smooth points, straight corner points, curved corner points, and combination corner points — because the key to using the Pen tool is understanding how anchor points work (see Figure 3-12). Refer to Chapter 6 for an in-depth explanation of anchor points.

Figure 3-12:
The four
kinds of
anchor
points.

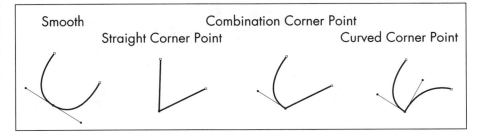

The Pen tool draws points one at a time. The first click of the Pen tool produces one anchor point. The second click (usually in a different location) creates a second anchor point that is joined to the first anchor point by a line segment. Clicking without dragging produces a straight corner anchor point.

For detailed information on drawing with the Pen tool and creating the different anchor points, see Chapter 9.

The path editing tools

The path editing tools are the Scissors tool and its three pop-up tools: the Add Anchor Point, Delete Anchor Point, and Convert Direction Point tools. Clicking and holding down the Scissors tool (also known as the Split Paths tool) displays all four tools. Dragging out to a certain path editing tool replaces the default Scissors tool with the newly selected pop-up tool. If the Caps Lock key is pressed when a path editing tool is chosen, the tools resemble crosshairs, as you can see in Figure 3-13. The crosshair cursors enable precision positioning of cursors.

The Scissors tool is used for splitting paths. Clicking with the Scissors tool on a closed path makes that path an open path with the end points directly overlapping each other where the click occurred. Using the Scissors tool on an open path splits that open path into two separate open paths, each with an end point that overlaps the other open path's end point.

The Add Anchor Point tool is used for adding anchor points to an existing path. If an anchor point is added to a straight segment (one that has no direction points on either end), then the anchor point will be a straight corner anchor point. If the segment is curved — meaning that you have at least one direction point for that segment — then the new anchor point will be a smooth anchor point.

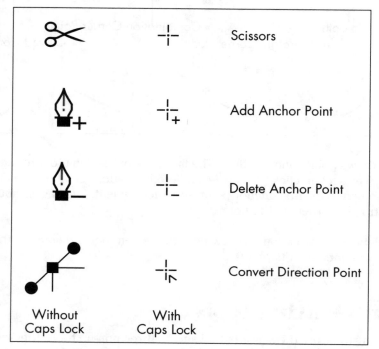

Figure 3-13:
The path
editing tools.

The Delete Anchor Point tool gets rid of the anchor point that you click. A new segment is created between the anchor points that were on either side of the anchor point you clicked. If the anchor point you clicked on is an end point, no new segment is drawn; instead, the next anchor point on the path becomes the new end point.

If there are only two points on an *open* path, the anchor point you clicked is deleted and so is the segment connecting it to the sole remaining anchor point. If there are only two points on a *closed* path, both line segments from the anchor point you clicked are deleted along with that point, leaving only one anchor point remaining.

The Convert Direction Point tool has two functions. The first is to simply change an anchor point from its current type of anchor point to a straight corner anchor point by clicking and releasing it. You can also change the current type to smooth by clicking and dragging on the anchor point. The second function is to move direction points individually by changing smooth anchor points to curved corner anchor points and by changing combination anchor points and curved corner anchor points to smooth anchor points. (Straight corner anchor points don't have any direction points, so they can't be changed by using this method.)

Figure 3-14 shows what each tool can do to a certain path (see Chapter 12 for more information on how to use these tools).

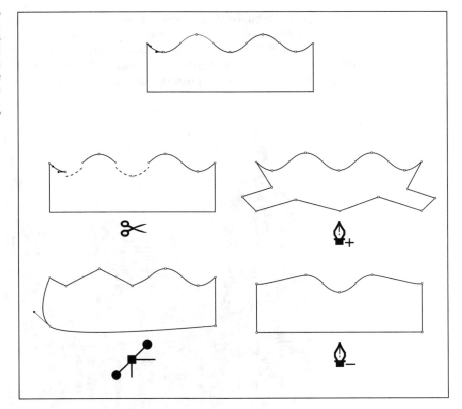

Figure 3-14:
A path as it is
originally and
after being
changed by the
four path editing
tools.

  Using the path editing tools is discussed in detail in Chapter 11.

The Brush tool

The Brush tool is the latest addition to Illustrator's drawing tools. The Brush tool is more similar to the Rectangle and Oval tools than it is the Pen or Freehand tools because it draws closed paths, and closed paths only.

The Brush tool is similar to brush-type tools in painting programs; the brush has a certain width, and you can paint with this brush at this width anywhere in your document. The big difference between paint programs' brushes and Illustrator's brush is that when you finish drawing with Illustrator's Brush tool, a filled, outlined area has been created.

The following options are available by double-clicking on the Brush tool: the weight of the brush, the calligraphic option (painting with a flat brush), the type of joins and miters on ends and angles, and (if you have a pressure-sensitive tablet) the width of the brush in proportion to the amount of pressure from your tablet. Figure 3-15 was drawn entirely with the Brush tool and a Wacom pressure-sensitive tablet.

Figure 3-15:
This building was drawn with the Brush tool.

The Freehand tool

When you need to draw rough edges or realistic illustrations that don't look "computery," the Freehand tool is the tool to use. It draws a path wherever you drag the tool with the mouse, creating smooth points and corner anchor points relative to how you draw. Although the Pen tool is the tool to use to get precise, super-straight lines, it is difficult to use. The Freehand tool is much easier to use, but it draws lines that are far from perfect. The tree in Figure 3-16 was drawn with the Freehand tool.

Figure 3-16:
This tree was
drawn with the
Freehand tool.

Figure 3-16:
This tree was
drawn with the
Freehand tool.

The number of anchor points produced by using the Freehand tool is relative to the speed of the cursor and the Freehand Tolerance setting. The Freehand Tolerance setting can be changed by selecting File⇨Preferences⇨General and typing in a number between 0 and 10 in the Constrain Angle text box. A value close to 0 results in a jagged path with many anchor points; a value near 10 creates a path with few anchor points and very smooth curves. The drawings in Figure 3-17 show the difference between a Freehand Tolerance set at 10 in the top drawing and a Freehand Tolerance set at 0 in the bottom drawing.

While drawing with the Freehand tool, you can erase what you have drawn as long as the mouse button has not been released and you are holding down the Command key as you retrace your path. Releasing the Command is the signal for the Freehand tool to continue to add to the path, from the node point where the Command key last erased.

Figure 3-17:
A freehand drawing with a tolerance of 10 (top), another with a tolerance of 0.

 # The Auto Trace tool

Illustrator provides a very basic and simplistic way of tracing images or artwork created in paint programs: the Auto Trace tool. Unfortunately, you can only trace PICT and MacPaint images. Both types of images are limited in their resolution (72 dpi), making tracing images rough at best.

To trace artwork, it must first be opened as a template in Illustrator. To trace an image, choose the Auto Trace tool and click the edge of the artwork. The tool automatically traces in between black and white edges, filling with whatever color was chosen last.

Chapter 7 covers templates and manual tracing with the Auto Trace tool and Illustrator's other drawing tools. Adobe Streamline™ does this tracing much better and is discussed in Chapter 22. Figure 3-18 shows the difference when a template is traced with the Auto Trace tool and Streamline.

Figure 3-18:
A logo as it appears as a template (top), traced with Auto Trace (middle), and run through Streamline (bottom).

The shape creation tools

Three different shapes can be created in Illustrator through the use of three shape creation tools: the Oval tool, the Rectangle tool, and the Rounded Rectangle tool. Drawing with these tools is discussed in Chapter 5.

To draw with any of these tools, select it and click and drag; the shape gets larger the farther you pull away from the location that you originally clicked. To constrain the shape to equal dimensions (such as a circle or square), hold down the Shift key as you drag.

To draw from the center of the shapes, hold down the Option key and drag. In addition, double-clicking any of these tools toggles to Draw from Center mode, in which you draw a shape from the center out. In Draw from Center mode, pressing the Option key toggles back to Draw from Corner mode. Although these tools seem quite limiting, all sorts of neat and weird illustrations can be created with them.

Clicking anywhere in an Illustrator document (without dragging) with one of the shape creation tools brings up a box where exact measurements can be entered. Creating shapes with these tools gives the resulting shapes a displayed center point. Unlike previous versions of Illustrator, this center point is not an actual point grouped to the shape, but a center point marker, which moves as the shape is resized. The center point display can be turned on and off by choosing Object⇨Attributes (⌘-Control-A) and unchecking the Show center point box.

The Measure Tool

The Measure tool has one function, and it does this function quite well: to measure the distance between two points on the page. Using the Measure tool automatically displays the Info palette (or, if already displayed, brings the Info palette to the front). To hide the Info palette, just click the close box in its upper lefthand corner or select Window⇨Hide Info (⌘-Control-I).

There are two ways to use the Measure tool:

▨ Click first in the location you are measuring *from* and then click the point you want to measure *to.* You don't have to click a point, path, or any object in your document for the Measure tool to work.

※ Click in the location you are measuring *from* and then drag to the location you want to measure *to*. As you drag, the numbers in the Info palette change to display your current distance.

The Measuring line will jump directly to (that is, *snap to*) points and paths when near them if the Snap to Point option is checked (to check, select File⇨Preferences⇨General or ⌘-K).

If you hold down the Shift key, you can constrain the movement of the measuring line to the following:

※ In Preview mode, the measuring line defines a 45° or 90° angle if no paths or filled parts of paths are under the cursor.

※ In Artwork mode, your cursor will snap to the paths.

※ In Preview mode, the cursor will snap to any filled part of any path.

 The Measuring tool is linked to the Move dialog box. As long as you don't move any objects in between measuring and choosing Move (Arrange⇨Move or ⌘-Shift-M), the same distance and angle appear in the Move dialog box. Just click OK and your selected objects move as far as you have measured. Figure 3-19 shows the corresponding values in both the Info palette and the Move dialog box.

Figure 3-19:
The Move dialog box mirrors the values in the Info palette when you use the Measure tool.

The Type Tools

The three different type tools in Illustrator can do almost anything to the way type appears in an Illustrator document. Initially, the type tools are used to create type, and then later they can be used to edit that very same type. The default tool is the standard Type tool, which creates both Point type and Rectangle type. The two pop-up tools are the Area Type tool and the Path Type tool.

Each of the type tools displays a different cursor, as shown in Figure 3-20, when it is used for creating Point or Rectangle type, Area type, or Path type.

Figure 3-20:
The Type cursors. The top cursor is present when creating Point or Rectangle type.

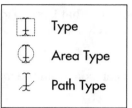

Type can be selected in Illustrator with the Selection tool, in which case all the type in the *story* (a contiguous set of type in either Point type, Rectangle type, Area type, or Path type — to be explained later in this chapter) is modified.

Selecting type with a type tool is done either by dragging across characters or lines; every character from the initial click until the release of the mouse button is selected. Double-clicking with a type tool selects the entire word you clicked, including the space after it. Triple-clicking (clicking three times in the same place) selects an entire paragraph.

New type can be entered into an existing story by clicking with a type tool where you want the new type to begin and then typing. If type is highlighted when you begin typing, the highlighted type is replaced with the new type that you type in from the keyboard.

⊤ The Type tool

With the Type tool, you can do everything you need to do with type. Clicking in any empty part of your document creates Point type, an anchor point that type aligns to. Type created as Point type does not wrap automatically; instead, you must manually press the Return key and start typing the next line.

Clicking and dragging with the Type tool creates Rectangle type — type that is bordered by a box, which you create when you click and drag the Type tool.

As the Type tool is passed over a closed path, it changes automatically into the Area Type tool. Clicking a closed path results in type that fills the shape of the area you clicked. Holding down the Option key as you pass over a closed path changes the tool into the Path Type tool. This "intelligent" switching of type tools by Illustrator prevents you from having to choose different type tools when you want a different type of type.

If the Type tool crosses over an open path, it becomes the Path Type tool. Clicking an open path places type *on the path,* with the baseline of the type aligning along the curves and angles of the path. Holding down the Option key when the Type tool is over an open path changes it into the Area Type tool.

The Path Type tool

The Path Type tool is used for running type along any path in Illustrator. This is a great tool for putting type on the edges of a circle.

 You can toggle between the Path Type tool and the Area Type tool by pressing the Option key. Pressing the Control key changes the Path Type tool to the standard Type tool.

The Area Type tool

The Area Type tool is used for filling closed or open paths with type. Even compound paths can be filled in Illustrator.

 You can toggle between the Area Type tool and the Path Type tool by pressing the Option key. Pressing the Control key changes the Area Type tool to the standard Type tool.

Figure 3-21 shows the same sentence as Point type, Rectangle type, Area type, and Path type.

The Transformation Tools

The following four tools in the Illustrator Toolbox have been a staple of PostScript drawing applications for years because they address four fundamental functions: the Rotate tool, the Scale tool, the Reflect tool, and the Shear tool.

Before any of these tools can be used, one or more objects (including paths, points, and segments) must be selected. The selected paths are the paths that are transformed.

Figure 3-21:
Type created as
Point type,
Rectangle type,
Area type and
Path type.

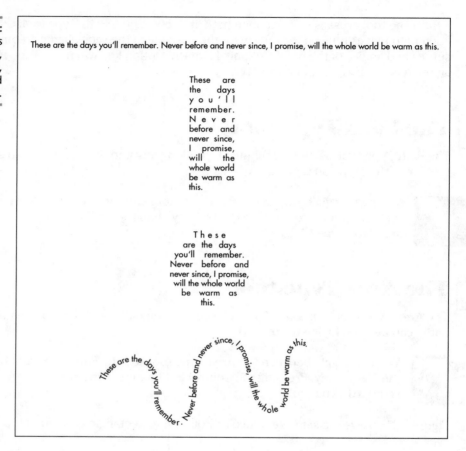

Figure 3-21: Type created as Point type, Rectangle type, Area type and Path type.

There are three ways to transform selected objects:

- Click with the transformation tool to set an origin point and then drag (called manual transformations).

- Option-click to set the origin and then enter exact information in the tool's transformation dialog box (this method is more precise than manually transforming).

- Double-click a transformation tool to set the origin in the center of the selected object(s); then you can enter information in the tool's transformation dialog box.

All the transformation tools work on a relative basis. For instance, if an object is scaled to 150% and then is scaled again to 150%, the object is now 225% of its original size (150% x 150% = 225%). If the object is initially scaled to 150% of its original size and you want to take it back to that original size, you must do the math and figure out what percentage is needed to resize it — in this case, 66.7% (100% ÷ 150% = 66.7%). Entering 100% in the Scale dialog box leaves the selected objects unchanged.

When manually transforming objects, you can make a copy of the selected object (and thus leave the original untransformed) by holding down the Option key before and after releasing the mouse button. In a transformation dialog box, you can make a copy by clicking the Copy button, pressing Option-Return, or Option-clicking OK.

If the Pattern Tiles check box is available (you must have a pattern for the option not to be grayed out) inside any of the transformation dialog boxes, you can check its option box to transform your pattern along with the object. You can also transform the pattern only, leaving the object untransformed, by unchecking the Objects box.

Manually transforming objects is fairly simple if you keep in mind that the first place you click (the point of origin) and the second place should be a fair distance apart. The further your second click is from the point of origin, the more control you have when dragging to transform. The Shear tool is an exception — although it does matter where you click — because you can lose control of your shape anywhere.

All the transformation tools perform certain operations that rely on the Constrain Angle setting as a point of reference. Normally, this setting is set to 0°, which makes your Illustrator world act normally. The setting can be changed by selecting File⇨Preferences⇨General (⌘-K).

 # The Rotate tool

The Rotate tool rotates selected objects within a document. Double-clicking on the Rotate tool displays the Rotate tool dialog box, where the precise angle of the selected item's rotation can be entered in the Angle box. The object rotates around its mathematical center. A positive number between 0 and 180 rotates the object counterclockwise that many degrees. A negative number between 0 and –180 rotates the selected object clockwise. The rotation tool works on a standard 360° circle of rotation, although it is usually easier to type in numbers between 0 and 180 and 0 and –180 than numbers like 270, which is the same as –90°.

Holding down the Option key and clicking somewhere in the document also brings up the Rotate tool dialog box; however, the object now rotates around the point where the Rotate tool was clicked. This point can be on or off the selected object. Be careful because it is quite easy to rotate an object right out of your viewing area! Illustrator has many precautions, however, that prevent you from transforming or moving an object off the Pasteboard.

Click once to set the origin point from where the object's center of rotation should be and then click fairly far from the origin and drag in a circle. The selected object spins along with the cursor. To constrain the angle to 45° or 90° as you are dragging, hold down the Shift key. This angle is dependent on the Constrain Angle box (File⇨Preferences⇨General or ⌘-K), and is 45° or 90° plus the angle in this box. Figure 3-22 shows an illustration before and after being rotated.

Figure 3-22:
An illustration
rotated with the
Rotate tool.

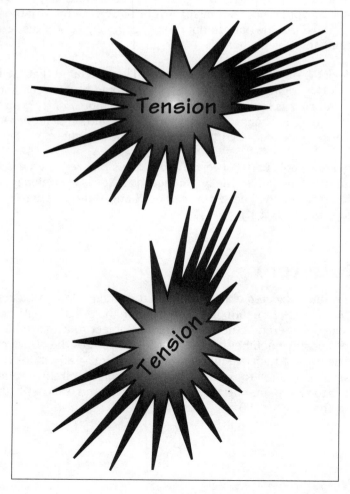

The Scale tool

The Scale tool resizes objects both proportionally and nonproportionally. You can also use the Scale tool to "flip" objects, but without the precision of the Reflect tool (it is impossible to keep the size and proportions of an object constant while scaling).

Double-clicking on the Scale tool brings up the Scale dialog box, shown in Figure 3-23. All selected objects are scaled from the mathematical center of the objects. If the Uniform radio button is checked, numbers typed into the text field result in proportionately scaled objects (where the width and height of the object remain proportional to each other). Numbers less than 100% shrink the object; numbers greater than 100% enlarge it. When the Uniform radio button is chosen, you may check the box called Scale line weight; this option is grayed out if nonproportional scaling is used.

Figure 3-23:
The Scale dialog box.

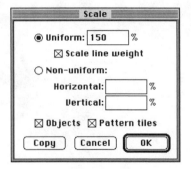

Nonproportional scaling resizes the horizontal and vertical dimensions of the selected objects separately, distorting the image. The way nonproportional scaling works is related to the Constrain Angle Box (File⇨Preferences⇨General or ⌘-K), where the angle is the horizontal scaling, and the vertical scaling is 90° from that angle.

 Pressing the Option key and clicking in the document window also brings up the Scale Dialog box, but now the objects are scaled from the location in the document that was Option-clicked.

Manual resizing is achieved by clicking your point of origin and then clicking away and dragging to scale. If you cross the horizontal or vertical axis of the point of origin, the selected object flips over in that direction. Holding down the Shift key constrains the objects to equal proportions (if the cursor is dragged at approximately 45° from the point of origin) or constrains the scaling to either horizontal or vertical scaling only (providing the cursor is being dragged along at about a 90° angle from the point of origin relative to the constrain angle). Figure 3-24 shows an illustration before and after being scaled.

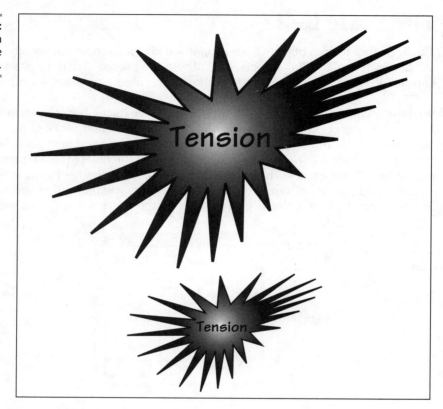

Figure 3-24:
An illustration
scaled with the
Scale tool.

 # The Reflect tool

The Reflect tool makes a mirror image of the selected objects, reflected across an axis of reflection. Double-clicking on the Reflect tool reflects selected objects across an axis of reflection that runs through the center of the selected objects. In the Reflect dialog box, you can enter the axis of rotation. If you want to rotate the object along either the horizontal or vertical axis, click the appropriate radio button.

 Option-clicking in the document window also brings up the Reflect dialog box, but the axis of reflection is not now in the center of the selected object, but in the location in the document where you Option-clicked.

Manual reflecting is done by clicking once to set the origin point (center of the axis of reflection) and again somewhere along the axis of reflection. If you click and drag after setting your origin point, you can rotate the axis of reflection and see what your objects look like reflected across various axes. The Shift key constrains the axis of reflection to 90° angles, relative to the constrain angle (File⇨Preferences⇨General or ⌘-K). Holding down the Option key during the release of the click leaves a copy of the original object. Figure 3-25 shows an illustration before and after being reflected.

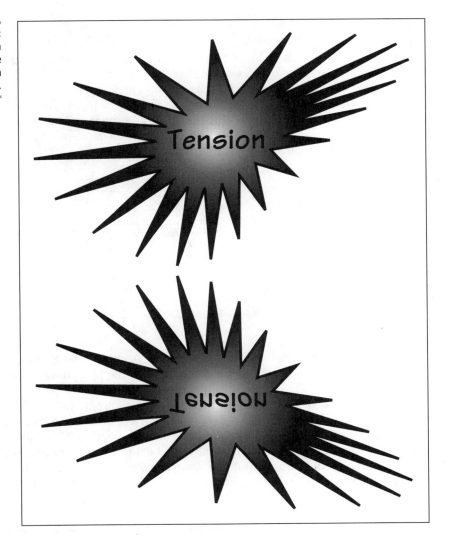

The Shear tool

The "Swear" tool causes more cursing (no, not cursoring; that's different) than all tools but the mighty Pen tool. Another good name for the Shear tool (one that I have heard many people use) is the "Stupid" tool because that's usually how you feel when trying to get good results from its use. It's a terrifying feeling to see the artwork you spent an hour touching up until it's just right go zinging off the screen, seemingly all by itself.

The Shear tool is rightfully distrusted because using it manually is usually a quick lesson in futility. Double-clicking on the Shear tool brings up the Shear dialog box, shown in Figure 3-26, which is much more controllable. Double-clicking causes the origin to be in the center of the selected object. The Angle box is simple enough; in its text box, you enter the angle amount the object should shear. Any amount over 75° or less than –75° renders the object into an indecipherable mess. The Shear tool reverses the positive-numbers-are-counterclockwise rule: To shear an object clockwise, enter a positive number; to shear counterclockwise, enter a negative number. The Axis Angle box is for shearing an object along an axis of shearing.

Figure 3-26:
The Shear dialog box.

Option-clicking in the document window brings up the Shear dialog box, with the origin of the shear being the location of the preceding Option-click.

Manual shearing is something else again because you are doing two things at once: changing both the angle of shearing (the distance from the beginning of the second click until it is released) and the angle of the axis of shearing (the angle the mouse is dragged during the second click). Usually, it's best to start your second click fairly far away from the point of origin. Holding down the Shift key constrains the axis of shearing to a 45° angle, relative to the constraining angle. Figure 3-27 shows an illustration before and after being sheared.

More details and samples for using the transformation tools appear in Chapter 10.

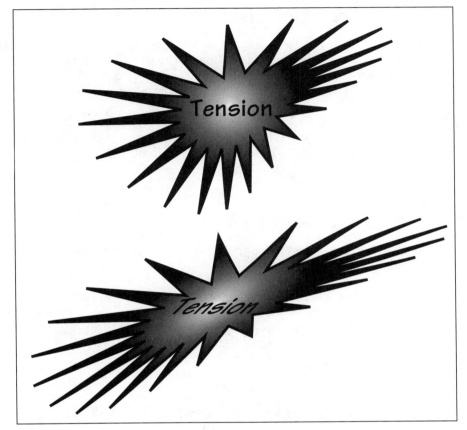

Figure 3-27:
An illustration
sheared with
the Shear tool.

The Paint Bucket and Eyedropper Tools

The Paint Bucket and Eyedropper tools are lifesavers for those of us who are constantly using up notes to jot down what the percentages of CMYK (cyan, magenta, yellow, and black) are in one path so that we can apply those same amounts to another path. Double-clicking on either tool brings up the Paint Bucket/Eyedropper dialog box, where multiple options regarding paint style information are selected or deselected.

The Eyedropper tool

The Eyedropper tool samples paint style information from a path and stores it in the Paint Style palette, without selecting that path. The information stays in the Paint Style palette until the information in the palette itself is changed, another path with different paint style information is selected, or if you click any other path with a different paint style.

If the Option key is held down, the Eyedropper tool toggles to the Paint Bucket tool. If the Eyedropper tool is double-clicked on any path, all selected objects in the document are changed to the paint style of the path that you double-clicked with the Eyedropper tool.

 # The Paint Bucket tool

The Paint Bucket tool is used for applying the paint style that is currently in the Paint Style palette.

Holding down the Shift key when clicking a path fills the Paint Bucket tool with the current paint style and also selects that path. If the path was already selected, a Shift-click deselects it. Pressing the Option key toggles from the Paint Bucket tool to the Eyedropper tool.

The Gradient Vector and Blend Tools

Technically, the Gradient Vector and Blend tools do two very different things, but they have been grouped together because the results from the two tools are similar.

Of course, before Version 5 of Illustrator, there was no way of making gradients except with the Blend tool, and for simple color-to-color blends, using the Blend tool was an incredible hassle. Now the Gradient Vector tool takes some of the burden off the Blend tool and does most of the basic functions of the Blend tool (at least, what most people used the Blend tool for). The Gradient Vector tool, with the whole concept of gradients, is much easier to comprehend and use effectively than the Blend tool, but the Blend tool can give you results not possible with the Gradient Vector tool. An example of the same image created with both the Gradient Vector and the Blend tools is shown in Figure 3-28. The images on the left of the figure are Artwork mode displays; the images on the right are the printed output.

Figure 3-28:
The difference between
using the Gradient Vector
tool and the Blend tool.

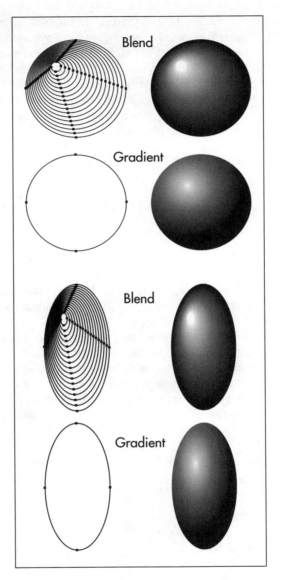

Blend

Gradient

Blend

Gradient

 # The Gradient Vector tool

The Gradient Vector tool is used to change the angle and the starting and ending points
for a linear gradient as well as the location of the center and edges of a radial gradient.
The tool is also used to offset the "highlight" on a radial gradient.

Paths must be filled with a gradient and selected to be affected by the Gradient Vector tool. To use the tool to change the location or angle of any gradient, click anywhere in the document (not necessarily in a selected path) and drag for the length of the gradient in the direction you wish the gradient to go. In the case of a linear gradient, the gradient begins where you clicked and ends where you released the mouse button. When you're using the Gradient Vector tool with radial gradients, the center color of the gradient circle of the radial gradient is where you click initially, and the outside color of the gradient circle is where you release the button.

To change the highlight color on a radial gradient, just click where you want the highlight to be.

Double-clicking the Gradient Vector tool displays the Gradient palette.

 # The Blend tool

The Blend tool creates in-between steps in the area between two paths, where the paint style and shape of one path transform into the paint style and shape of the second path.

You can blend only between two paths at a time, as long as both paths are either open or closed. To blend between two closed paths, select both objects, click one point on one path, and then click another point on another path. A dialog box appears, displaying the recommended number of steps to properly blend the paint styles. Blend paths created with the Blend tool are automatically grouped together, but the two source paths remain independent paths. To blend between two open paths, follow the preceding steps and make sure to click the end points of the two objects only.

 The process of blending and using gradients is covered in much more detail in Chapter 12.

 # The Graph Tools

 Illustrator seems to have done away with most of the graph tools from Version 3, but fear not — the tools are there; you just can't get to them in the same way. The six graph tools are as follows: Graph, Stacked-column Graph, Line Graph, Pie Graph, Area Graph, and Scatter Graph.

    All the graph tools work in a similar manner as the shape creation tools: click and drag to set the size of the graph, or click to display the Graph Size dialog box and then enter the size information. If you press the Shift key while you drag, the graph is constrained to a perfect square (or circle, if it's a pie graph). If you press the Option key while you drag, you will drag from the center of the graph out. If you Option-click, the graph you create is centered at the point you Option-clicked. That's it. That's all you have to do to use the graph tools. Neat, huh?

 Entering data for graphs is discussed in Chapter 13.

Double-clicking on the Graph tool brings up the Graph Style dialog box, shown in Figure 3-29. Choosing a different graph style at this point and clicking OK changes the tool to represent the type of graph you selected. You can choose from six graph styles; the grouped-column graph is the default. Figure 3-30 shows a sample grouped-column graph.

Figure 3-29:
The Graph Style dialog box.

Figure 3-30:
A sample grouped-column graph.

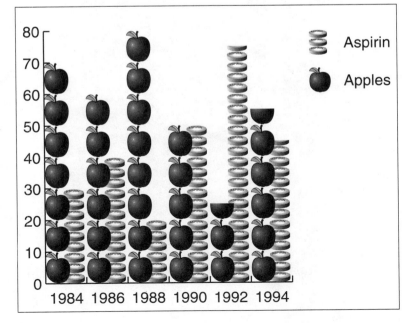

The Page Tool

The Page tool works differently in Illustrator 5.0 than it did in other versions, thanks to the way Illustrator handles documents and paging via the Document Setup and Page Setup dialog boxes.

The Page tool changes the printable area of your document by moving the printable area of the document, without moving any of the printable objects in the document. Clicking and dragging the lower lefthand corner of the page relocates the page to the place where you release the mouse button.

 This tool is useful when your document is larger than the biggest image area your printer can print to. The tool allows you to *tile* several pages to create one large page out of several sheets of paper.

Menus

In This Chapter

- ✽ How menus are organized
- ✽ How to learn the menus faster
- ✽ The File menu
- ✽ The Edit menu
- ✽ The Arrange menu
- ✽ The View menu
- ✽ The Object menu
- ✽ The Type menu
- ✽ The Filter menu
- ✽ The Window menu
- ✽ The Apple menu

Menus That Make Sense

In the years prior to the release of Illustrator 5.0, Adobe's method of organizing their menus had been questioned as being illogical in many respects. First, the Bring To Front and Send To Back commands were placed illogically in the Edit menu, not the Arrange menu. The Move option also was in the Edit menu instead of Move. There was a tiny menu called Paint, which in Version 3 contained Make Compound and Release Compound, which technically have nothing at all to do with Paint. A few other oddities existed, but Adobe has squashed most of these by adding a new menu, Object, and getting rid of the old Paint and Graph menus. There is also a separate menu item just for fonts, appropriately called the Font menu, which contains nothing but lists of your typefaces. Figure 4-1 shows the File menu with all its parts labeled.

Furthermore, Adobe's main products, Illustrator, Photoshop, Premiere, Dimensions, and Streamline, all have a fairly consistent interface, including menus, palettes, and dialog boxes. It appears that Adobe has listened carefully to their end users and made certain that Illustrator is not so *different* anymore in almost all respects.

 Illustrator 5.5 contains a new Save As dialog box, which closely resembles the Save As dialog box in Photoshop. The new dialog box has only one pop-up menu, which shows all the different formats. If you select a format not native to Illustrator, another dialog box appears, asking for specifics.

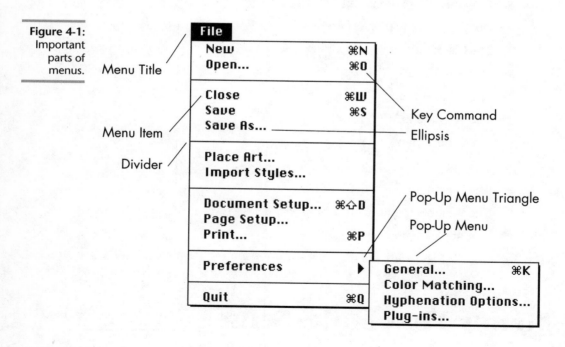

Figure 4-1:
Important
parts of
menus.

Menu rules

Some general rules apply to Illustrator menus:

- To select a menu item, pull down to that item and release the mouse button. If the cursor is not on that item, but it is still highlighted, the command will not take effect.

- Whenever an *ellipsis* appears (three little dots that look like …), choosing that menu item will bring up a dialog box where you must verify the current information or enter more information, by clicking on an "OK" button when you are done. If there is no ellipsis, the action you select will take place right away.

- Anytime there is a *key command* listed on the right side — usually the Command (⌘) symbol and a character, sometimes the Command symbol and other modifier keys and a character — instead of using the mouse to pull down this menu, you can type this key command. Using key commands for menu items works just like clicking the menu bar and pulling down to that item.

- If you see a little *triangle* next to a menu item, it means there is a *pop-up menu* associated with it. Items in the pop-up menu can be chosen by pulling over to the menu and then pulling up or down to select the menu item needed. Pop-up menus usually appear on the right side of the menu, but due to space limitations on your monitor, they may appear on the left side for certain menus.

Using menus effectively

If you can never remember what is on which menu, and you are constantly holding down the mouse button and slowly running along the menu bar, reading every menu item, looking for a certain command, you have a disease. Every year millions of people become afflicted with Menu Bar Scanning Syndrome (MBSS): the need to continually search and hunt for special menu items that they just can't remember. MBSS is a disease that can be treated fairly easily, but it wastes valuable production time costing companies billions of dollars a year. Don't be surprised if the next time you flip on *60 Minutes,* Steve Kroft is doing an inside investigation into the mysteries of MBSS.

MBSS is deadly not only because it wastes time, but because the user is forced to read every single menu and pop-up menu. Sure, in the File menu you *know* that Page Setup is where to go to change the size of the page, but as you work your way over things begin to get a little fuzzy. By the time you get to the Filter menu, your mind is mush. You see the Distort category and figure that all the pop-up menu items in there are legal functions. If you can manage to get to the Windows menu, thewordswouldjustruntogetherlikethis, making no sense whatsoever. If Figure 4-2 looks familiar, then you are probably one of the afflicted.

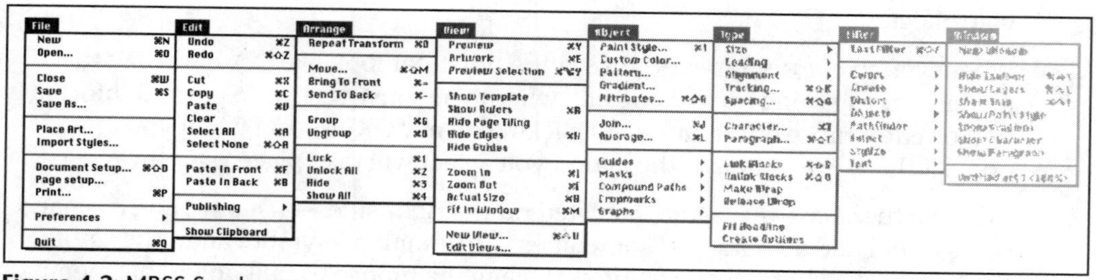

Figure 4-2: MBSS Syndrome.

You can help prevent MBSS by doing a bunch of different activities:

Memorize what is in each menu. This is the hardest thing to do, but a few hours spent memorizing each menu item and where it goes will eventually save countless MBSS-related searches. Make sentences out of the first letter of each menu item if it helps. The File menu is either "New, Old, Close, Save, Save As, Place Art, Import Styles, Document Setup, Page Setup, Print, Preferences, Quit" or "Nine Old Cats See Silly People Icing Danish Pieces of Prune Pit Quiche." (I know, I know. You're not supposed to put icing on prune pit quiche. That's why the people are *silly*.)

Think of what you want in noun/verb terms. If you break down what you want to do in its most basic form of noun and verb, often the noun or verb will relate directly to the correct menu. For example, if you want to save a file onto your hard disk, the noun/verb would be "Save File." There is no "save" menu, but there is a File menu, and under that there is, of course, "Save." It/Easy. You/Understand?

Use the menus as little as possible. Instead, memorize key commands. Most of the menu items have them (if you don't include the Filter menu, more than half do), so now you only need to go up to the menu bar when a menu item doesn't have a key command.

The File Menu _____

```
┌─────────────────────────────────┐
│ File                            │
├─────────────────────────────────┤
│ New                        ⌘N   │
│ Open...                    ⌘O   │
├─────────────────────────────────┤
│ Close                      ⌘W   │
│ Save                       ⌘S   │
│ Save As...                      │
├─────────────────────────────────┤
│ Place Art...                    │
│ Import Styles...                │
├─────────────────────────────────┤
│ Document Setup...          ⌘⇧D  │
│ Page Setup...                   │
│ Print...                   ⌘P   │
├─────────────────────────────────┤
│ Preferences           ▶  General...              ⌘K  │
├──────────────────────────┤ Color Matching...         │
│ Quit                 ⌘Q   │ Hyphenation Options...   │
└──────────────────────────┤ Plug-ins...               │
                           └──────────────────────────────┘
```

Most of the menu items in the File menu are related directly to the file on which you are working. You can save the file, print the file, close the file, and so on. Two exceptions to this are the Preferences submenu and the Quit command: Quit exits the entire program (this is a pseudo-flaw in all Macintosh applications), and the Preferences submenu affects the way the entire Illustrator program works, regardless of which document you have displayed. In reality, Document Setup contains the preferences for that particular document.

New (⌘-N) creates a brand new document and makes that document the *active* document. In previous versions of Illustrator, users were hit with an evil dialog box, where they had to indicate which template they wanted to use. Because most users do not normally use templates, this command was altered to instantly create a new document with no questions asked. Many other graphics and desktop publishing programs, including FreeHand, Photoshop, and QuarkXPress, all ask you to set up your document size before the document is created. In Illustrator, the document defaults to the size document in your Document Setup file, located in the Plug-Ins folder.

Open (⌘-O) enables you to open a document already created in Illustrator or a template that can be traced. Using this command, you can only open Illustrator files saved in 1.1, 88, 3.2, 4, or 5 formats.

Close (⌘-W) closes the *active* document. The active document is the one that is in front of all other documents and has a title bar with lines on it and text in black. Nonactive documents don't display any lines in their title bar, and the text in the title bar is gray. Closing an Illustrator document does *not* "close" Illustrator; it continues running until you "Quit." If you haven't saved changes to your active document when you choose Close, a dialog box appears (see Figure 4-3), asking whether you would like to save changes. If you want to save, click Yes and Illustrator updates the file (or brings up the Save As dialog box if you have yet to save the document); clicking No closes the file without saving any work that you have done since you last saved (if you saved at all). Clicking Cancel does not close the document; instead you are returned to where you were before you chose Close.

Figure 4-3:
The Save Changes dialog box.

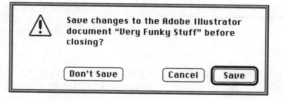

Save (⌘-S) updates the saved file of the active document. If the document has not been saved yet, the Save As box appears.

Save As brings up the Save As dialog box (see Figure 4-4). If you have not saved your file, Save As lets you name the file and choose where the file is to be saved. If the file has already been saved, Save As allows you to do the following:

- Save a new copy of the file with a different name in the same or a different location.

- Save a new copy of the file with the same name in a different location.

- Replace the existing file by saving it with the same name in the same location.

Save As also lets you change the preview and compatibility of the file, but if you save with the same name, you will actually be replacing the saved file with the new version. A dialog box will always appear to warn you if you are going to replace an existing file.

 The Save As box in Version 5.5 looks different. Although the changes are mainly cosmetic, 5.5 users can save files as Adobe Acrobat PDF files.

 Detailed information on saving and file types is provided in Chapter 9.

Figure 4-4:
The Version
5.5 Save As
dialog box.

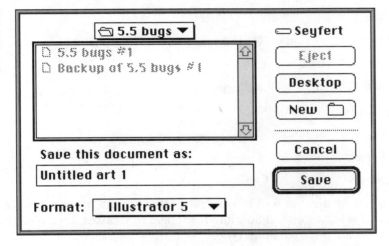

Revert To Saved is an option that automatically closes the document and opens the last saved Version of it. This option will be grayed out if the file has not been saved yet. When it is selected, a dialog box appears, asking you to confirm that you *do* want to revert to the last saved Version of the document. This feature was not available with the initial release of 5.0; it was implemented in Version 5.0.1.

 A Revert To Saved cannot be undone.

Place Art brings an EPS (Encapsulated PostScript) file into your document. In order for EPS artwork to be seen in Illustrator, the EPS file must have been saved with a preview. EPS files that have been "placed" can be manipulated using the four transform tools, but their contents cannot be changed. Placed art is often masked within Illustrator.

Change Placed Art appears in place of Place Art if placed artwork within the Illustrator document is currently selected. Selecting Change Art replaces the selected EPS artwork with a different EPS file.

 The really cool part about Change Placed Art is that if you have placed artwork that has been transformed, the artwork you exchange with it via Change Placed Art will have the exact same transformation attributes! For example, if you scale down placed artwork to 50% and rotate it 45°, artwork that is exchanged with that artwork is also scaled down 50% and rotated 45°.

Import Text takes the place of Place Art when a type tool is being used within a story. Type can be imported if it is in the following formats:

- ASCII (American Standard Code for Information Interchange)
- MacWrite 4, 5, and II
- Microsoft Word 3, 4, 5 (including 5.1)
- RTF (Rich Text Format)
- WordPerfect 2 for Macintosh
- WordPerfect 5.1 for PCs
- WriteNow 3

Formatted text (bold, italic, and so on) will retain that formatting unless saved in ASCII format. Text that is imported will flow into Rectangle type boxes, Area type shapes, onto Type paths, and out from Point type.

 If Point type is selected, paragraph type will flow onto one line. At the end of each paragraph (in the original text document), the text will start a second line. This is usually undesirable for long amounts of text, and more likely than not will cause your type to go flying out the edges of your document window.

 Make sure that you have a folder called Claris XTend in your System Folder, or you won't be able to import *any* text. Illustrator automatically installs this when you install Illustrator.

Import Styles imports certain attributes from other Illustrator documents, including custom colors, gradients, and patterns into your document. To use this, select File⇨Import Styles and find the document that has the styles you want to import. Only different styles will be imported.

Different styles with the same name as styles in your current document get replaced with styles from the imported file. This can be a big problem if documents have paths with these styles that are being changed because this can adversely affect an entire document. Import Styles cannot be Undone, so Save before you Import Styles. That way if there is a problem, you can close the file without saving and open it again, restoring the original styles. Another method is to change the names of all your styles to different names before importing other styles.

Document Setup (⌘-Shift-D) brings up the Document Setup dialog box (see Figure 4-5). Here you can change the size of the Artboard and make changes to preferences that affect this document only.

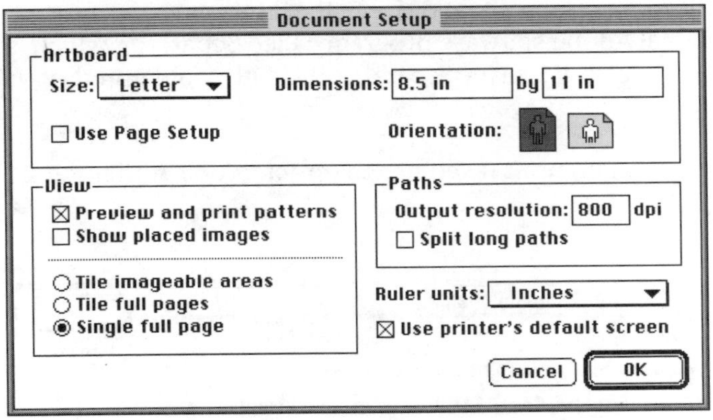

Figure 4-5:
The Document Setup dialog box.

> **Document Setup**
>
> ┌─ **Artboard** ──────────────────────────
> │ Size: [Letter ▼]   Dimensions: [8.5 in] by [11 in]
> │
> │ ☐ **Use Page Setup**   Orientation: [👤] [👤]
> └──────────────────────────────────────
>
> ┌─ **View** ────────────── ┌─ **Paths** ──────────────
> │ ☒ **Preview and print patterns** │ Output resolution: [800] dpi
> │ ☐ **Show placed images**   │ ☐ **Split long paths**
> │   └──────────────────
> │ ○ **Tile imageable areas**
> │ ○ **Tile full pages**   Ruler units: [Inches ▼]
> │ ● **Single full page**
> └────────────────── ☒ **Use printer's default screen**
>
>   [Cancel] [**OK**]

Page Setup displays the current printer's Page Setup dialog box (see Figure 4-6). If you have PS Printer 8.01 or Laserwriter 8.0.1 installed, the Page Setup dialog box will look very different than if you are using the standard Apple LaserWriter extension (see Figure 4-7). If you are printing to a non-PostScript printer, this box will also look different.

If you have Laserwriter 8.0.0 or PSPrinter 8.0, you should upgrade to 8.0.1 immediately. There are numerous technical problems with Version 8.0.0.

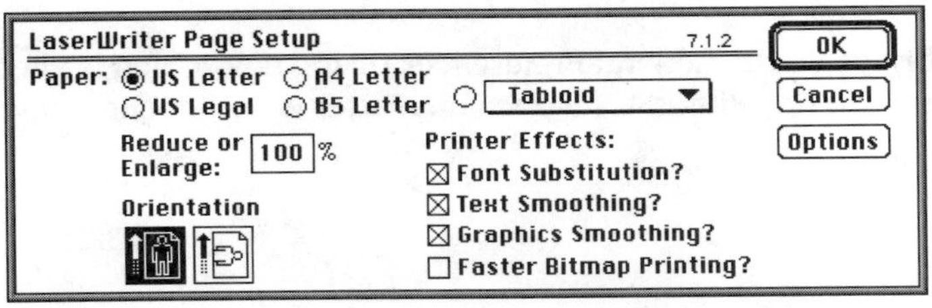

Figure 4-6:
The LaserWriter Page Setup dialog box.

> **LaserWriter Page Setup**   7.1.2   [**OK**]
> Paper: ● US Letter ○ A4 Letter   ┌─────────┐ [Cancel]
>   ○ US Legal   ○ B5 Letter   ○ [Tabloid ▼]
>   [Options]
> Reduce or [100] %   **Printer Effects:**
> Enlarge: ☒ **Font Substitution?**
> **Orientation**   ☒ **Text Smoothing?**
> [👤] [👤]   ☒ **Graphics Smoothing?**
>   ☐ **Faster Bitmap Printing?**

Figure 4-7:
The PS Printer
dialog box.

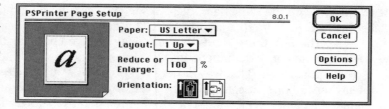

Figure 4-7:
The PS Printer
dialog box.

Print (⌘-P) prints the active document to the printer that was selected from the Chooser. A dialog box with printing options appears, similar to the one in Figure 4-8. This box lets you specify which pages (if your pages are set to tile) will print, how many copies of those same pages will print, and various other printing-related specifications.

You *cannot* print color separations with the Print command. Instead, you must use an additional Adobe software program called Separator, which is included with Illustrator (usually it is in the Separator & Utilities folder in the System Folder).

For information on printing color separations, look at Chapter 21.

Figure 4-8:
The Print dialog
box.

Preferences

Preferences pulls out to a submenu of four different preference options.

Preferences are discussed in detail in Chapter 14.

General (⌘-K) brings up the General Preferences dialog box, which is filled with options that affect the way Illustrator works, no matter which document you have open.

Color Matching displays the Color Matching dialog box, which is designed to let you represent colors more accurately on your screen than they would naturally appear.

Hyphenation Options brings up the Hyphenation Options dialog box. In this dialog box, you can choose which language you are using (there are 11 to pick from besides English!). You also can enter any words here that you don't want to be hyphenated, called *hyphenation exceptions.*

Plug-Ins is a dialog box that tells Illustrator where the Plug-Ins Folder is, or, if you have changed the name of the Plug-Ins Folder, what the name of that folder is by means of a simple Open/Save As dialog box.

Quit (⌘-Q) quits Illustrator and returns you to the Finder or to the program you were last in that is still running. If documents that have not been saved recently are open, a dialog box appears, asking whether you would like to save those documents.

 If you accidentally hit ⌘-Q after saving, your document closes and Illustrator quits without warning. Be careful with the dialog box that appears when you haven't saved yet. Clicking No will quit Illustrator without saving your document.

The Edit Menu

Edit	
Undo	⌘Z
Redo	⌘⇧Z
Cut	⌘X
Copy	⌘C
Paste	⌘U
Clear	
Select All	⌘A
Select None	⌘⇧A
Paste In Front	⌘F
Paste In Back	⌘B
Publishing ▶	Create Publisher...
	Subscribe To...
Show Clipboard	Publisher Options...
	Show Borders

The Edit menu pretty much conforms to the standard Macintosh software Edit menus, though there are some unusual commands that are specific to the way that Illustrator works.

Undo (⌘-Z) undoes the last activity that was performed on the document. Successive undos undo more and more activities, until (1) the document is at the point where it was opened or created or (2) you have reached the undo limit, set in the General Preferences dialog box (File⇨Preferences⇨General or ⌘-K).

Redo (⌘-Shift-Z) redoes the last undo. You can continue to redo undos until (1) you are back to the point where you started undoing or (2) you perform another activity, at which time you can no longer redo any previous undos.

Cut (⌘-X) deletes the selected objects and copies them to the Clipboard, where they are stored until another object is cut or copied or the Macintosh is shut down or restarted. Quitting Illustrator *does not* remove objects from the Clipboard. Cut is not available when no object is selected.

Copy (⌘-C) copies selected objects to the Clipboard, leaving the selected objects untouched. Objects copied to the Clipboard stay there until another object is cut or copied or the Macintosh is shut down or restarted. Quitting Illustrator *does not* remove objects from the Clipboard. Copy is not available when no object is selected.

 Illustrator can copy paths (and paths only!) to other Adobe software, including Dimensions, Streamline, and Photoshop.

Paste (⌘-V) places any objects on the Clipboard into the center of the document window. If type is selected with the Type tool or highlighted in another application on the pasteboard, either a Rectangle type, Area type, Path type, or Point type area must be selected with the Type tool. Paste is not available if nothing is in the Clipboard or if the contents of the Clipboard were copied there from another application.

 Just as Illustrator can copy paths to other Adobe software, paths from Dimensions, Streamline, and Photoshop can be pasted into Illustrator.

Clear (Clear on the numerical keypad) clears selected objects on the Artboard.

Normally, the Delete key can be used instead of the Clear command or Clear key. However, when a text field in a palette is active (highlighted or containing a blinking indent cursor), Delete will delete highlighted text or work as a Backspace key. In those cases the Clear command or the Clear key *must* be chosen to clear an object from the Artboard.

Select All (⌘-A or ⌘-period when the screen is not redrawing) selects all paths in the active document (as in Figure 4-9). If a type tool is selected and there is an insertion point in the text, all the type in that story will be selected (see Figure 4-10).

Figure 4-9:
Select All with paths in Preview mode selected.

Figure 4-10:
Select All with type selected.

The Painted desert can wait till summer. We've played this game of just imagine long enough. Wait till summer?

Select None (⌘-Shift-A) deselects all selected objects. Select None does *not* work with type selected with a type tool.

Paste In Front (⌘-F) pastes any objects on the Clipboard on top of any selected objects, or on the top of the current layer if no objects are selected. In addition, Paste In Front pastes objects *in the same* location as the copied object, even from document to document. If the documents are different sizes, Illustrator pastes them in the same location relative to the center of each document. If the Clipboard is empty, or if type selected with a type tool is on the Clipboard, this option is not available.

Paste In Back (⌘-B) pastes any objects on the Clipboard behind any selected objects, or on the bottom of the current layer if no objects are selected. In addition, Paste In Back pastes objects *in the same* location as the copied object, even from document to document. If the documents are different sizes, Illustrator pastes them in the same location relative to the center of each document. If the Clipboard is empty, or if type selected with a type tool is on the Clipboard, Paste In Back is not available.

Publishing

Publishing displays a category with four submenu items, all related to System 7's Publish and Subscribe feature. Publish and Subscribe allows certain users to publish documents that are subscribed to by others. As the Publisher changes its *edition*, the Subscriber receives updated information about that edition. You may neither publish nor subscribe text only, but you may publish and subscribe to entire type objects (such as a Area type or Path type).

Create Publisher creates an edition file that other users can subscribe to (by choosing Subscribe in their application). The edition includes any selected objects at the time Create Publisher is chosen. After the edition is created, a light gray border appears around the edition's objects when one or more of those objects is selected. After you have created an edition using the Create Publisher command, it will be updated every time you save the file that the edition is contained within. An edition border is a fixed size and cannot be changed.

Subscribe To lets your document subscribe to an edition. A dark gray border will appear around editions you have subscribed to if that edition is selected. Your document is updated instantly whenever the edition is updated, even if your document is open.

Publisher Options gives you the ability to manually update the edition, even without saving your file. You can also choose to Unpublish your edition at this point.

Show Borders always shows the borders of both edition files you have published (light gray) and edition files you have subscribed to (darker gray).

Hide Borders reverses the Show Borders option.

Show Clipboard opens a window that shows the current contents of the Clipboard. This window can remain open and be put anywhere on the screen, but it will always be behind all palettes and the active document after the document or any of the palettes are clicked. When the Clipboard is visible behind the palettes or document window, either clicking on a visible part of it or selecting the Show Clipboard option will bring it back to the front. The Clipboard can be resized with the box in the lower righthand corner, toggled between the current size and the full screen with the box in the upper righthand corner, and closed with the box in the upper righthand corner. The contents of the Clipboard cannot be changed in the Clipboard window; the only way the information there can be altered is when something is cut or copied. Figure 4-11 shows two examples of how the Clipboard can look when different things are copied.

Hide Clipboard hides the Clipboard. This option is available only if the Clipboard is *active* — that is, in front of all open documents.

Figure 4-11:
The Clipboard on the left contains type copied with a type tool; the other contains paths or other objects from Illustrator.

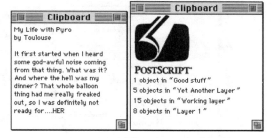

The Arrange Menu

The Arrange menu contains menu items that alter the way objects on a page are distributed. Selected objects can be moved to any location on the document, and can be moved to the top and bottom of the working layer with Arrange commands. Objects can also be grouped together or ungrouped, as well as hidden and locked.

Repeat Transform (⌘-D) redoes the last transformation that was done to a selected object. Transformations include Move (mouse-dragging or Move command), Rotate, Scale, Reflect, and Shear. Repeat Transform also will make a transformed copy if a copy was made (1) manually or (2) by pressing the Copy button in a transformation dialog box.

Repeat Transform remembers the last transformation, no matter what else you do, and it can apply those same transformations to other objects.

Move (⌘-Shift-M, Option-click Selection tool) brings up the Move dialog box, shown in Figure 4-12. Selected objects are moved by the distance and angle specified in their respective text fields. By default, the Move dialog box will contain the distance and angle that you have last moved an object, whether manually or in the Move dialog box. The Move command can only be chosen if something is selected.

Figure 4-12:
The Move dialog box.

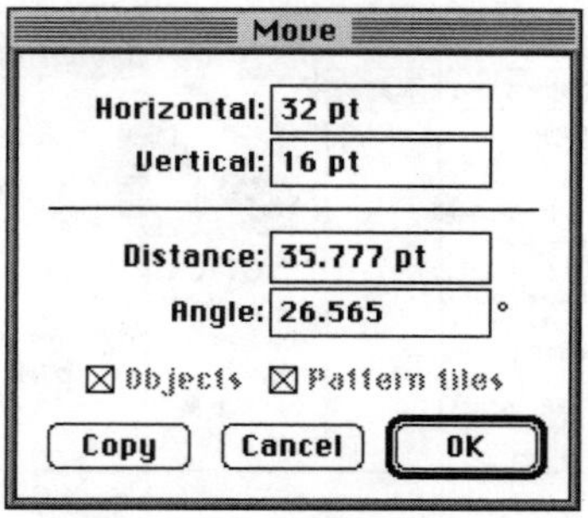

Move
Horizontal: 32 pt
Vertical: 16 pt
Distance: 35.777 pt
Angle: 26.565 °
☒ Objects ☒ Pattern tiles
[Copy] [Cancel] [OK]

Bring To Front (⌘-=) brings any paths or objects that have at least one point or segment selected to the front of the current layer. Bring To Front is not available when no objects are selected. Multiple-selected paths and grouped paths still retain their front/back position relative to each other.

Send To Back (⌘-hyphen) sends any paths or objects that have at least one point or segment selected to the back of the current layer. Send To Back is not available when there are no objects selected. Multiple selected paths and grouped paths still retain their front/back position relative to each other.

Group (⌘-G) groups selected paths together. The Selection tool will select an entire group at one time when you click any point or segment or drag the marquee. Groups can be grouped with other groups or paths to form new groups. When paths or groups are grouped, all the paths in the new group are brought forward until they are right behind the frontmost object in the group.

If you choose Group again after the selected objects have already been grouped, nothing will happen.

Ungroup (⌘-U) ungroups groups. Huh? If a group is selected, that group will be ungrouped. Ungrouping again will ungroup the next level of groups. Ungrouping paths that are not grouped (by typing ⌘-U, because the menu option will be gray) has no effect.

Lock (⌘-1) makes the selected objects *unselectable,* making it impossible to modify or delete these objects. Locked objects cannot be moved or changed, but they are always visible and will always print (locked objects cannot be hidden).

Holding down Option and choosing Arrange⇨Lock or typing ⌘-Option-1 will lock all the objects that are not selected.

Locked items remain locked when the document is closed and then reopened at a later time.

Unlock (⌘-2) unlocks all locked objects, selecting them all at once. There is no way to unlock just a few objects locked with the Lock command.

Hide (⌘-3) hides any selected objects, making them invisible in both Artwork and Preview modes. Hidden objects will not print out of Illustrator. If you close a file with hidden objects, the hidden objects can be seen (visible) the next time you open the document.

Holding down Option and choosing Arrange⇨Hide or typing ⌘-Option-3 will hide all the objects that are *not* selected.

Show All (⌘-4) shows any hidden objects. Think of it as "unhide." There is no way to show just a few of the hidden objects.

The View Menu

View	
Preview	⌘Y
Artwork	⌘E
Preview Selection	⌘⌥Y
Show Template	
Show Rulers	⌘R
Hide Page Tiling	
Hide Edges	⌘⇧H
Hide Guides	
Zoom In	⌘]
Zoom Out	⌘[
Actual Size	⌘H
Fit In Window	⌘M
New View...	⌘⌃V
Edit Views...	

In the View menu are all the different commands for viewing artwork within the active document at different sizes, showing certain attributes and objects.

New to Illustrator 5.0 is the ability to create custom views: views that are certain magnifications at certain locations with various other viewing criteria. This can be used for showing a client various layouts of an illustration in different sizes, with different backgrounds all in the same illustration, saving time and disk space. By typing a key command, the user can flip instantly to any custom view.

Preview (⌘-Y) Selecting Preview mode shows your artwork the way it will print out of Illustrator.

 Preview can't show some things, such as patterns on strokes or patterns in type that haven't been turned into outlines; these attributes can be printed from Illustrator. Preview shows guides and templates, but these will not print.

Preview also does not show any *overprinting*, which can't be printed just out of Illustrator. Overprinting can only be printed from an application that prints color separations, such as Adobe Separator (included with Illustrator) or QuarkXPress. To see overprinting on the screen, open an Illustrator 5.0 EPS file in Photoshop (remember that gradients and patterns will not appear in Photoshop).

Unlike previous versions of Illustrator, you *can* edit your artwork in Preview mode. To select a path or object in Illustrator's Preview mode, click either the fill of the artwork or the path itself.

 While Illustrator is drawing the preview, you may click ⌘-period to cancel the redrawing; this changes the mode to Artwork mode instantly.

 Be careful not to click ⌘-period to cancel previewing when the illustration has already been redrawn; this action will cause all objects to become selected.

Figure 4-13 shows artwork in Preview mode with a small area selected using the Direct Selection tool.

Artwork (⌘-E) is more of a *wireframe* mode because you see all the shapes of all the objects and paths created in black, and all anchor points, direction points, and direction lines in blue (a light blue is the default color, which can be changed to the color of your choice via the Layers palette).

 If you have a Plug-In called Artwork Speedup (originally located in the Separator & Utilities folder) installed, your anchor points, direction points, and direction lines will be black.

Placed artwork will be displayed in black and white only, and templates will be grayer than before. The main advantage to working in Artwork mode is the speed increase over Preview mode. The speed that you gain is even greater when the artwork contains gradients, patterns, placed artwork, and blends. In addition, you can select paths that were hidden by the fills of other objects.

To select paths in Artwork mode, you must click the paths or draw a marquee across them. Figure 4-14 shows artwork in Artwork mode with a small area selected using the Direct Selection tool.

Preview Selection (⌘-Option-Y) previews only the selected objects in your document; the unselected objects remain in Artwork mode. This is useful when you are working in Artwork mode and want to check how a gradient or pattern is filling a path. ⌘-period cancels any redrawing that is taking too long, returning you to Artwork mode. In Illustrator 5.0, you can create new paths and adjust existing ones while in Preview Selection mode. ⌘-period performs a Select All when the screen is not redrawing. Figure 4-15 shows artwork in Preview Selection mode with a small area selected using the Direct Selection tool.

Figure 4-14:
The drawing from
Figure 4-13 in
Artwork mode.

Figure 4-15:
The drawing from
Figure 4-13 in
Preview Selection
mode. Only the
selected paths are
previewed.

Show Template shows the template in the document (if there is a template) when this option is selected. After you select Show Template, the menu item changes to Hide Template.

Hide Template hides the template in the document (if there is a template) and changes the name of this menu item back to Show Template.

Show Rulers (⌘-R) shows the rulers if they are not displayed. Ruler increments are in whichever unit of measurement was set in General Preferences (⌘-K) in Ruler Units. Guides can be dragged out from the rulers with any tool. When Show Rulers is chosen, the menu item changes to Hide Rulers.

 To change the increments that the rulers display quickly, use ⌘-Shift-P to change to picas, ⌘-Shift-I to change to inches, and ⌘-Shift-N to change to centimeters.

Hide Rulers (⌘-R) hides rulers if they are displayed. When Hide Rulers is chosen, the menu item changes to Show Rulers.

 You can change Ruler Units even if rulers are not displayed by typing ⌘-Shift-P for picas, ⌘-Shift-I for inches, and ⌘-Shift-N for centimeters.

Hide Page Tiling hides the edges of the printable area if they are currently showing. Use of the Page tool automatically turns off Hide Page Tiling. When Hide Page Tiling is chosen, the menu item switches back to Show Page Tiling.

Show Page Tiling shows the edges of the printable area if they are currently not visible. Use of the Page tool automatically enables Show Page Tiling. When Show Page Tiling is chosen, the menu item switches to Hide Page Tiling.

Hide Edges (⌘-Shift-H) should probably be called Hide Selected Paths, which would be technically correct. This command works differently in Artwork and Preview modes.

In Artwork mode, Hide Edges hides the anchor points, direction points, and direction lines in selected paths. In Preview mode, Hide Edges hides the anchor points, direction points, and direction lines in selected paths as well as the paths themselves.

When Hide Edges is on, you are actually working normally, creating new objects and editing existing ones by selecting them. The problem is that you can't tell which objects are selected and which objects aren't selected unless you are in Preview Selection mode.

 Be careful to note when you have this feature enabled, as it can appear to the unwary that they are unable to select anything just because Hide Edges has been activated.

Hide Edges only affects the active document when it is turned on.

As with the Hide command (Arrange➪Hide), whether Hide Edges is selected or not is *not* saved with the document. Hide Edges becomes Show Edges after Hide Edges is chosen.

Show Edges (⌘-Shift-H) shows all paths, anchor points, direction points, and direction lines in the document where it is chosen. After Show Edges is chosen, the menu item flips to Hide Edges.

Hide Guides makes all *guides* (dotted lines useful for aligning objects within your document) invisible. The weird thing is that you can still create guides either by selecting Object➪Guides➪Make or by pulling them out from the ruler, but you won't be able to see them.

Remember when this function is on so that you don't unwittingly pull guide after guide onto your document, wondering why they don't show up. Or you may choose Make Guides and wonder if you accidentally chose Hide instead because paths changed into guides when Hide Guides is on simply disappear.

Show Guides takes the place of Hide Guides after Hide Guides is selected.

Show Guides shows Guides that are hidden via Hide Guides. After you choose Show Guides, the menu item switches back to Hide Guides. Even though guides are showing, they *will not print.* Unless, that is, they are converted back into normal paths and given a stroke.

Zoom In (⌘-]) increases the zoom level to the next highest zoom level. There are 17 zoom levels in Illustrator, ranging from 6.25% on up to 1600%. The Zoom In feature zooms from the center out. Choosing Zoom In does not affect the document in any way; it just changes the way you are viewing it. The Zoom In command is available (not grayed out) at 1600%, but choosing it will do nothing. Clicking once with the Zoom In tool in the exact center of the document window will do the same thing as Zoom In.

Zoom Out (⌘ [) decreases the zoom level to the next lowest zoom level. The Zoom Out feature zooms from the center In. Choosing Zoom Out at 6.25% does nothing. Clicking once with the Zoom Out (Option-Zoom) tool in the exact center of the document window will do the same thing as Zoom Out.

Actual Size (⌘ H) takes the document back to 100% size. At this view, you can hold an 8.5" x 11" piece of paper, and it should fit squarely over an 8.5" x 11" document on your Illustrator screen. The accuracy of the fit depends on the pixels per inch of your monitor.

Choosing Actual Size also centers the document in your window (this is unlike double-clicking the Zoom tool, which resizes the page to 100% but brings the current center at the smaller or larger size to the center when resizing).

Fit In Window (⌘-M) changes the size of the document so that the entire Artboard fits in the current window, as in Figure 4-16. An 8.5" x 11" Artboard (the default size) on a 13" monitor with the window as big as possible is scaled to 50% of actual size. The viewing scale percentage varies depending on both screen size and window size. There is no difference between using Fit In Window and double-clicking on the Hand tool.

New View (⌘-Control-V) brings up the New View dialog box. In this box, you can enter the name of your custom view. The settings of view menu (either Artwork or Preview, as well as the viewing magnification and location of the artwork) are all recorded into this custom view.

 You cannot create a custom view with the Preview Selection mode in operation. Your new custom view name will be displayed at the bottom of the View menu.

Figure 4-16:
A tabloid-sized document (11" x 17") is reduced significantly to fit within the document window in Fit In Window mode.

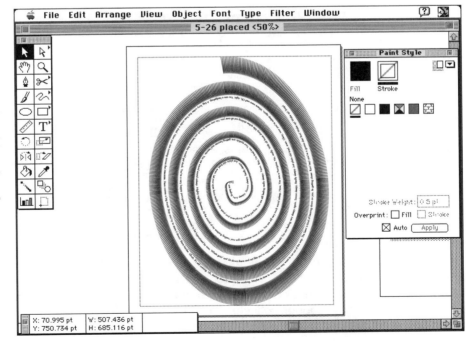

Edit Views displays the Edit Views dialog box, which lets you delete or rename your custom views. To delete more than one view at a time, drag over the names appearing in the Edit Views dialog box and click Delete. You cannot use the Delete key in the Edit Views dialog box.

 Strangely enough, you can choose Edit Views even when there are no custom views to edit!

New View 1 (⌘-Control-1) is the first custom view you create. You may name the custom view anything you like when creating it by typing in a different name than New View # (number) or editing it later using the Edit Views command.

You can create up to 25 custom views. The first 10 will have keyboard command equivalents, such as ⌘-Control-2, ⌘-Control-3, ⌘-Control 4, and so on.

The Object Menu

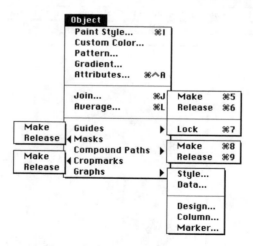

The Object menu is chock-full of options that directly affect different objects that are selected in the documents. The first section deals with objects and their paint attributes, the middle section is concerned with moving objects and points, and the third section is a kind of hodgepodge collection of object-related activities.

Paint Style (⌘-I) shows the Paint Style palette (see Figure 4-17) if it is not already currently displayed. If the Paint Style palette is behind other palettes, choosing Paint Style brings it to the forefront. If the Paint Style palette has just been chosen, it will disappear if Paint Style is chosen.

In the Paint Style palette, you may change the Paint Style attributes of selected objects, including the fill (white, black, process color, custom color, pattern, and gradient) and stroke (white, black, process color, custom color, and pattern). In the Paint Style palette, you specify whether fills and strokes overprint and what, if any, dash patterns are within strokes.

 Selected objects have their attributes changed in real time, as soon as you make a change, as long as the Auto box is checked. If the Auto check box is unchecked, then the Apply button must be pressed when all the changes have been entered.

There are four different ways to display the Paint Style palette, chosen by two different methods in the upper righthand corner of the palette. The Paint Style palette replaces the Paint Style dialog box from Versions 3.2 and before, and many of the little extras have been removed, including Masks, Reverse (direction of paths), and Flatness settings.

Figure 4-17:
The Paint Style palette.

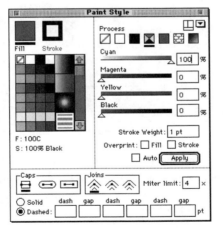

Custom Color brings up the Custom Color dialog box (see Figure 4-18), which displays the current custom colors in the document and allows you to add or delete from the current Custom Color palette. The Custom Color dialog box can also be accessed by double-clicking on a custom color in the Paint Style palette.

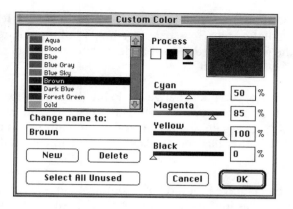

Figure 4-18:
The Custom Color
dialog box.

Pattern brings up the Pattern dialog box (see Figure 4-19). New patterns that have been defined in your document appear here. You should go here to initially define the pattern. Patterns in the document also can be deleted here.

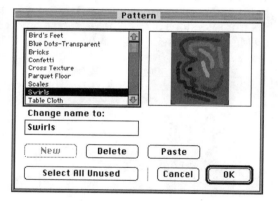

Figure 4-19:
The Pattern dialog box.

Gradient displays the Gradient palette (see Figure 4-20). If the Gradient palette is behind other palettes, selecting Gradient from the Object menu brings it to the front of the other palettes. If the Gradient palette has just been selected, then it will disappear if Gradient is selected from the Object menu.

Contrary to what you may think, you don't choose gradients for selected objects with the Gradients palette. Instead, you modify existing gradients, create new gradients, or delete existing gradients. To apply a gradient to a selected object, you must use the Paint Style palette.

Figure 4-20:
The Gradient palette.

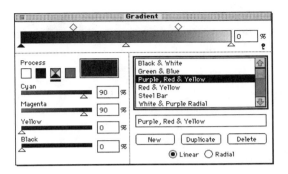

Attributes (⌘-Control-A) brings up the Attributes dialog box. In this box, notes can be added to any selected object, the path can be reversed (if the object is part of a compound path), the center point of the object can be made to display or hide, and the split path characteristics (output dpi) can be changed. At least one object must be selected in order to select Attributes.

Join (⌘-J) joins two separate end points in a number of ways:

 If two points are selected and directly on top of each other, and are end points in the same or two different open paths, the points will become one point. Doing so brings up a dialog box that asks whether the point should be a corner point or a smooth point.

The best way to select two points that are directly above one another is to draw a marquee around them with the Direct Selection tool. The difference between two points joined as corner or smooth points is shown in Figure 4-21.

 If one open path has been chosen with the regular Selection tool or Group Selection tool or if all points in a path have been selected with the Direct Selection tool, the path will become a closed path. If the two end points were overlapping, they will become one point, and the dialog box will appear asking what type of point the joined point should become, smooth or corner. If the two points were not overlapping, a straight segment is drawn between the two end points.

 If two selected end points on the same or different open paths are not overlapping, a straight segment will be drawn between them.

If the Option key is held down while selecting Join (or ⌘-Option-J is pressed), then the selected points will average on top of each other (vertically and horizontally) and join at the same time.

Average (⌘-L) takes the selected points and averages their location. You can average any number of points at one time. When the Average command is selected, a dialog box will appear, asking how you want the points averaged: Horizontal only, Vertical only, or Both. Choosing Both places the points on top of each other.

It is usually not a good idea to select a path with the regular Selection tool or the Group Selection tool or to select all the points in a path with the Direct Selection tool, as this will bring all the points that are selected to the center of the location.

 Average works on a "mean" basis, averaging the location of all the points selected to determine where the average will be. For instance, if there are four points on the right side of a path and one point on the left side of the path and the path is averaged vertically only, the path will lean more heavily towards the left side than the right side.

Figure 4-21:
Points joined as corner points (top) and smooth points.

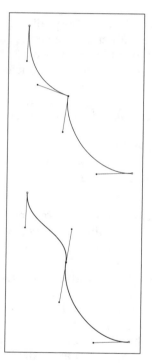

Guides

Guides are teeny tiny little people that show you around Illustrator, as shown in Figure 4-22. The more of them you make, the easier it is to use the program. Uh huh. I know, let you know when the shuttle lands. Sigh.

The guides commands make new guides and release and lock any existing guides that you have created in your document, either by dragging them from the rulers or choosing a path and selecting Make Guides. Guides will not print, and they will be saved with documents. Guides usually display as dotted lines, although paths that are made into guides will display their anchor points, direction points, and direction lines when selected.

Figure 4-22:
Guides are just plain
helpful.

Guides⇨Make (⌘-5) creates guides out of all selected paths. Guides cannot be made out of text. Only paths themselves appear as guides; no fills or strokes affect guides.

Guides⇨Release (⌘-6) releases all selected guides that have been made, as well as all selected guides that have been pulled from the rulers. Releasing a guide changes it back to its original Paint Style. Guides that were dragged from rulers have a fill and stroke of none when released. When guides are released, they are selected.

To release all guides in a document, select Edit⇨Select All and then Object⇨Release. To release one guide, Control-Shift-double-click it.

Guides⇨Lock (⌘-7) toggles between locking and unlocking all guides in *all open documents*. Guides are either in a state of being locked or unlocked: when locked, they cannot be selected or released using Release guides at all; when unlocked, they can easily be selected and moved. Guides that are locked can be moved independently if Control-Shift-dragged on. Locked guides can be released by Control-Shift double-clicking them.

Masks

Masks are objects that *mask* out everything but the path(s) made up by the mask (see Figure 4-23). Masks can be open, closed, or compound paths. The masking object is the object whose paths make up the mask, and this object must be in front of all the objects that are being masked.

Figure 4-23:
An objects, its mask, and the resulting masked object.

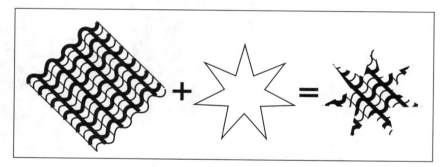

Masks⇨Make creates masks from the selected objects in the document. The topmost object (the *masking object)* will mask out only the selected objects beneath it. Masked objects are *not* grouped together; all objects within a mask are independent from one another. Masking objects lose their Paint Style attributes when they become part of a mask.

Masks⇨Release releases masked objects that are selected from their masked objects. If more than one masking object is selected, only the topmost masking object will be released. With each successive release, another selected masked object is released moving from top to bottom. A mask that has been released will contain a fill and a stroke of None.

Compound paths

Compound paths are paths made up of two or more open or closed paths. Where the paths cross or every other fill area exists is a "hole," which is transparent. You can specify which paths create the holes by changing the direction of the paths via the Reverse option in Object⇨Attributes. The general rule is that holes are formed by paths traveling in the opposite direction of any adjoining paths. Compound paths can be fun or frustrating, depending on the day.

 You can find a complete discussion of compound paths in Chapter 11.

Compound Paths⇨Make (⌘-8) creates a compound path out of two or more selected open or closed paths. If paths were previously part of a compound path, that entire compound path is now a part of the newly created compound path. The Paint Style from the rearmost path is applied to the newly created compound path.

 Paths belonging to different groups cannot be made into a compound path, unless all paths in all the groups are selected.

Compound Paths⇨Release (⌘-9) releases existing selected compound paths and transforms them back into normal paths. If this option is gray, it means that the paths selected are not compound paths. When a compound path is released, all paths inside of it have the same Paint Style as the compound path did. To release multiple compound paths, keep choosing Release until the option is grayed out.

Crop marks

Crop marks are little lines that are designed to help you cut (or crop) along the edges of your illustration after the document has been printed (see Figure 4-24).

 Unfortunately, you can only create one set of crop marks per document. Making multiple crop marks by drawing them yourself or using the Trim Marks filter (Filter⇨Create⇨Trim Marks) isn't enough for color separations; black crop marks that you create by drawing may be 100% of process colors but will not contain any other spot colors you may have in your illustration. (This problem is the result of a serious limitation in Illustrator; the program does not allow you to choose "registration" as a color, which would print on every different color plate.) Trim Marks created with the Trim Marks filter are only 100% black.

Figure 4-24:
Cropmarks
on an
illustration.

Here's a workaround: Choose the crop marks/trim marks you create and stroke them with 100% of all four process colors when you are printing out four-color separations. If you are printing out spot-color separations, you must copy the crop marks, select Edit⇨Paste In Front or Edit⇨Paste In Back and then color the stroke of the crops with the spot color you are using, choosing the Overprint Strokes option in the Paint Style palette. Additional crop marks need to be Pasted in Front or Pasted in Back for every additional color separation in your document.

Crop marks⇨Make transforms a selected rectangle drawn with the rectangle tool.

That rectangle can only be modified prior to becoming crop marks by moving it or resizing it via the Scale tool. If any transformation is done to the rectangle, a message will appear saying that you can only make crop marks out of a single rectangle. If a rectangle is drawn with a constrain angle set to an angle other than 0°, 90°, 180°, or 270° (–90°), you will not be able to make crop marks out of that rectangle.

If nothing is selected, crop marks will appear around the edge of the single full page. If Tile Imageable Areas is chosen in Document Setup, the crop marks will appear only around the first page. If crops are set to the size of the page and the page is moved with the Page tool or if the document has been resized with the Document Setup dialog box, the crop marks *will not move*.

Crop marks⇨Release releases the crop marks that were set. If the crop marks were created from a rectangle, then that rectangle is an editable path, which can be resized and changed back into crop marks, deleted, or modified. Any rectangle that has been changed back from being a set of crop marks will have a fill and stroke of None.

 You cannot choose Crop marks⇨Release when no crop marks are in your document. In addition, Crop marks⇨Release will not release trim marks made with the Filter⇨Create⇨Trim Marks command.

Graphs

Illustrator is great for making graphs quickly. While not as full-featured as other graphing software, notably Delta Graph, there are some amazing capabilities hidden away in Illustrator's graphing functions.

Graphs⇨Style (double-click the Graph tool) shows the Graph Style dialog box (see Figure 4-25). In the Graph Style dialog box, you specify the type of graph you are going to create (graph types include Grouped Column, Stacked Column, Line, Pie, Area, and Scatter). You also tell Illustrator how you want to alter the current graph.

The Graph Style dialog box has options relative to each graph style except Area. For example, you can specify where you want the axis — left, right, or both sides. Cosmetic options (such as Drop Shadow and Legends across top) are modified by clicking the appropriate options in the lower right corner.

 Changing the graph type in the Graph Style dialog box will change the Graph tool's appearance to that type of graph. All graphs drawn with the new tool will be that tool's graph type.

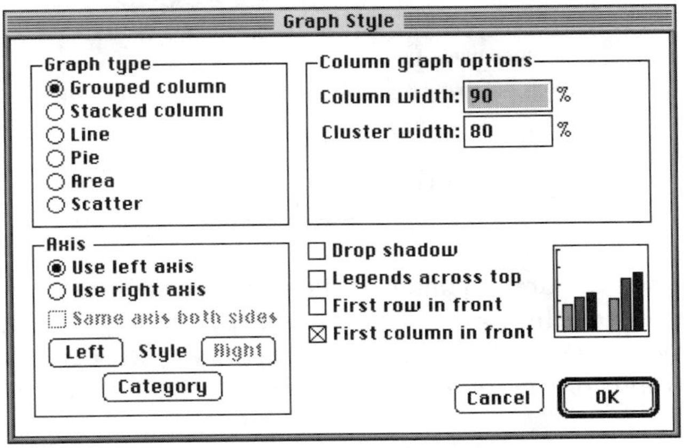

Figure 4-25:
The Graph Style dialog box.

Graph⇨Data (dragging with the Graph tool in the document) displays the Graph data dialog box (see Figure 4-26), where you enter all the statistical information relevant to the graph that you are creating.

Graph⇨Design brings up the Design dialog box (see Figure 4-27) where you can specify the type of graph that you will be using as either a column or marker design. The design must be bordered by a rectangle, and that rectangle must be behind all the selected design elements to use the selected objects as Graph Designs.

Figure 4-26:
The Graph data dialog box.

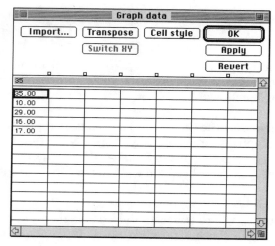

Figure 4-27:
The Design dialog box.

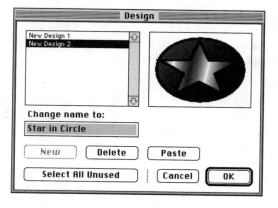

Graph⇨Column shows the Graph Column Design dialog box (see Figure 4-28). In this dialog box, you may specify how your Graph design appears in your graph (either column type). Many options are available, including the way the design is cropped or scaled within the graph columns and how the design is repeated (if at all).

Graph⇨Marker displays the Graph Marker Design dialog box, where you select which design to use for graph markers of data points in both line graphs and scatter graphs.

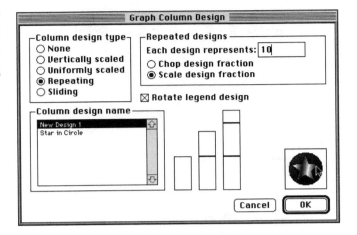

Figure 4-28:
The Graph
Column Design
dialog box.

The Type Menu

If you have a 12" or smaller monitor, you only have one menu with type information on it, called the Type menu. If you have a larger monitor, though, you will have two type menus: the Font menu and the Type menu. The Font menu lists all the fonts that you currently have installed on your computer, while the Type menu contains all sorts of cool menu items that affect type on your system. But don't be too concerned if you have a smaller monitor; fonts are available by pulling down the Font submenu from the Type menu.

Type is discussed in detail in Chapter 8.

Most of the Type options can be changed in the Character palette (Type⇨Character), shown in Figure 4-29. The Character palette can be accessed by various menu functions.

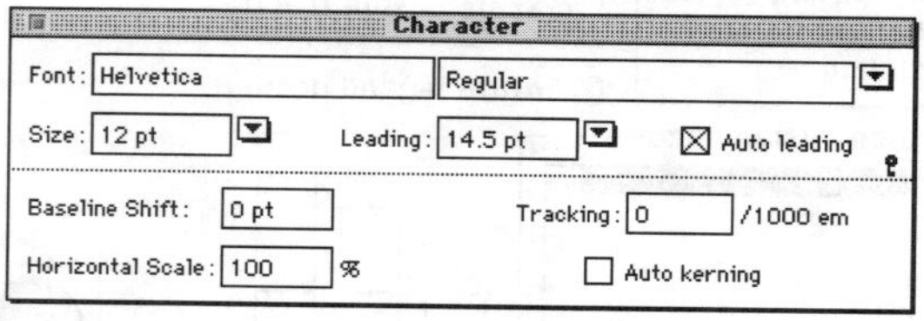

Figure 4-29:
The Character palette.

Character		
Font: Helvetica	Regular	
Size: 12 pt	Leading: 14.5 pt	☒ Auto leading
Baseline Shift: 0 pt	Tracking: 0	/1000 em
Horizontal Scale: 100 %	☐ Auto kerning	

Type is set in Illustrator in sets of *stories*. A story is a set of continuous, linked text.

When the term *paragraph* is mentioned, it is usually referring to the characters that are between returns. If there are no returns in a story, then that story is said to have one paragraph. Returns end paragraphs and begin new ones. There is always exactly one more paragraph in a story than there are returns.

Font (⌘-Shift-F, ⌘-Option-Shift-M) displays a submenu with all the fonts that are currently installed on the Macintosh you are using. Pressing ⌘-Shift-F or ⌘-Option-Shift-M automatically highlights the Font field on the Character palette. A check mark will appear next to the font that is currently selected. If no check mark appears next to any of the fonts, more than one font is currently selected.

If you are wondering why the folks at Claris Corp. chose such an odd combination of keys and commands, you probably don't use QuarkXPress too much. Quark's key command for highlighting the font field in its measurement palette is ⌘-Option-Shift-M.

Size (⌘-Shift-S) displays a submenu with "Other" listed and various point sizes. When Other is chosen, the Character palette appears and the Size field is highlighted, in which you can type any point size from .1 to 1296.

Type created in Illustrator may be scaled to any size, but it must first be converted into outline paths by using the Create Outlines command.

A check mark will appear next to the point size that is currently selected. If the point size currently selected does not correspond to a point size in the Size submenu, a check mark will appear next to the Other menu item. Point size for type is measured from the top of the ascenders (like the top of a capital letter *T*) to the bottom of the descenders (like the bottom of a lowercase *g*). If no check mark appears next to any of the sizes, more than one size is currently selected (even if the different sizes are all Other sizes).

You can also increase and decrease the point size of type by using the keyboard shortcut ⌘-Shift->, which increases the point size by the amount specified in General Preferences, and ⌘-Shift-<, which decreases the point size by the amount specified in General Preferences.

Yet another way to change point size is to use the Scale tool. Using the Scale tool to change point size lets you change to any size; that size is displayed in the Character palette as soon as you are done scaling. Once again, keep in mind that the limit in scaling type is 1296 points, and you cannot exceed that even with the Scale tool (unless, of course, the type is already outlined paths).

Leading displays a pop-up menu with leading sizes that correspond to the point sizes for type, along with an Auto item and an option called Other. *Leading* is the distance between the baseline of one line of type and the baseline of the preceding line of type (see Figure 4-30).

When you are changing the leading option, you are affecting an entire paragraph at once, not just a word or a sentence, but the entire paragraph (in fact, with the type tools being used to select type, you must actually triple-click or drag over all the characters in the entire paragraph, including the return at the end, for the leading to be decreased).

The leading for the entire paragraph is always the greatest leading within that paragraph. When Auto is chosen, the leading is always 20% greater than the point size of the type. If Other is chosen, the Character palette will be displayed, and the leading field will be highlighted.

 Technically, you cannot enter in a number in the leading field that is less than .1 point or greater than 1296 points. But if you check the Auto leading box or choose Auto in the Leading submenu, the Leading will go as high as 1555 points!

Unfortunately, when you take off Auto leading, the leading automatically changes back to 1296. Once again, if you convert your type to outlined paths, you can choose any leading you desire merely by dragging the lines apart. If no check mark appears next to any of the leading sizes, more than one leading size is currently selected (even if the different leading sizes are all Other sizes).

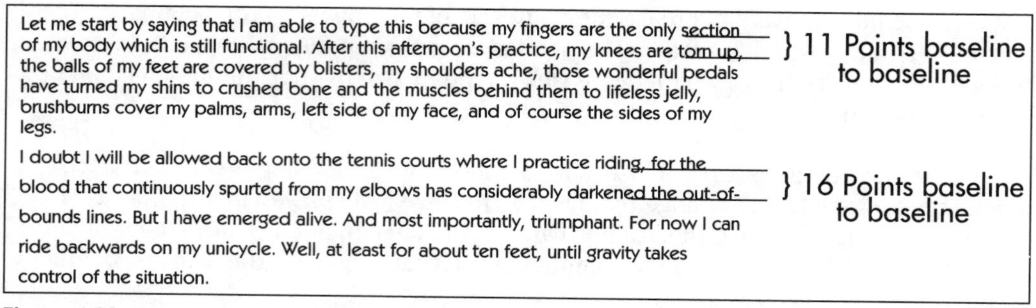

Let me start by saying that I am able to type this because my fingers are the only section of my body which is still functional. After this afternoon's practice, my knees are torn up, the balls of my feet are covered by blisters, my shoulders ache, those wonderful pedals have turned my shins to crushed bone and the muscles behind them to lifeless jelly, brushburns cover my palms, arms, left side of my face, and of course the sides of my legs. } 11 Points baseline to baseline

I doubt I will be allowed back onto the tennis courts where I practice riding, for the blood that continuously spurted from my elbows has considerably darkened the out-of-bounds lines. But I have emerged alive. And most importantly, triumphant. For now I can ride backwards on my unicycle. Well, at least for about ten feet, until gravity takes control of the situation. } 16 Points baseline to baseline

Figure 4-30: Two paragraphs with different leading.

Alignment

Alignment displays a pop-up menu with five different choices. *Alignment* refers to the horizontal positioning of type in relation to either the Point in Point type, the Path Bar in Path type, or the left and right edges in Rectangle type and Area type.

Alignment always affects an entire paragraph at a time if the following conditions are met:

- At least one character is selected with a type tool.
- An insertion point is blinking in that paragraph or the type is chosen with a selection tool.

 Alignment directions are always relevant to the direction the type is rotated. For example, Rectangle type rotated 90° (it would read from bottom to top) and aligned flush left would be flush at the current bottom of the rectangle.

A check mark appears next to the alignment that is currently chosen. If no check mark appears next to any of the alignments, more than one alignment is currently selected. The five different types of alignment are shown in Figure 4-31.

Alignment⇨Left (⌘-Shift-L) makes selected type *flush left.* Point type will align to the right of the point, and successive lines will be placed evenly on the left side of the type. Path type will align to the right of the Path Bar. Rectangle type and Area type will align as far as possible to the leftmost edge of the shape the type is within.

Alignment⇨Center (⌘-Shift-C) makes selected type *centered.* Point type will align at the center of the point, and successive lines will be centered in relation to the first line. Path type will be centered on the Path Bar. Rectangle type and Area type will be centered in their respective shapes. Flush-left type is sometimes referred to as ragged right because the left side is smooth and straight, while the right side is uneven.

Alignment⇨Right (⌘-Shift-R) makes all selected type *flush right*. Point type will align to the left of the point, and successive lines will be even on the right side of the type. Path type will align to the left of the Path Bar. Rectangle type and Area type will align as far as possible to the rightmost edge of the shape the type is within. Flush-right type is often referred to as ragged left because the right side is smooth and straight, while the left side is uneven.

Alignment⇨Justified (⌘-Shift-J) makes all selected type *justified*. In justified type, words are evenly spaced out in all lines in a paragraph — except the last line, which is flush left. The type can be considered to be both left and right justified. Justified type only works with Rectangle type and Area type.

Figure 4-31:
Type set up in
the five
different
Alignment
options.

Left	Center	Right
She gave me life	She gave me life	She gave me life
I gave her death	I gave her death	I gave her death
My beautiful Marquise.	My beautiful Marquise.	My beautiful Marquise.
And on the Devil's Road	And on the Devil's Road	And on the Devil's Road
we walked. Two orphans	we walked. Two orphans	we walked. Two orphans
together.	together.	together.
And does she hear my hymns	And does she hear my hymns	And does she hear my hymns
tonight of Kings and Queens	tonight of Kings and Queens	tonight of Kings and Queens
and Ancient truths?	and Ancient truths?	and Ancient truths?
Of broken vows and sorrow	Of broken vows and sorrow	Of broken vows and sorrow
Or does she climb some	Or does she climb some	Or does she climb some
distant	distant	distant
path where rhyme and song	path where rhyme and song	path where rhyme and song
can't find her?	can't find her?	can't find her?

Justify	Justify Last Line
She gave me life	She gave me life
I gave her death	I gave her death
My beautiful Marquise.	My beautiful Marquise.
And on the Devil's Road	And on the Devil's Road
we walked. Two orphans	we walked. Two orphans
together.	t o g e t h e r .
And does she hear my	And does she hear my
hymns	h y m n s
tonight of Kings and	tonight of Kings and
Queens	Q u e e n s
and Ancient truths?	and Ancient truths?
Of broken vows and	Of broken vows and
sorrow	s o r r o w
Or does she climb some	Or does she climb some
distant	d i s t a n t
path where rhyme and	path where rhyme and
song	s o n g
can't find her?	

Choosing Alignment⇨Justified for Point type or Path type will result in no activity taking place.

If a justified paragraph has only one line of type, that line is the last line in the paragraph and so will appear flush left.

Alignment⇨Justify Last Line (⌘-Shift-B) makes all selected type *justified,* even the last line of a paragraph. Justify Last Line only works with Rectangle type and Area type.

Choosing Alignment⇨Justify Last Line for Point type or Path type will result in no activity taking place.

Justify Last Line will usually put extra space between words, not letters, when justifying. To put space evenly between letters as well as words, use the Fit Headline command.

Character (⌘-T) brings up the Character palette and highlights the Font field. In the Character palette, you can change fonts, styles, point size, leading, baseline shift, horizontal scale, and tracking/kerning values, all at one time! If the Character palette has just been brought to the front, used, or clicked before Character is selected, the Character command will close (hide) the Character palette.

Paragraph (⌘-Shift-T in Version 5.0, ⌘-Shift-P in Version 5.5) displays the Paragraph palette (see Figure 4-32) and highlights the left indentation field. Changes can be made in the Paragraph palette to the alignment by clicking different alignment boxes, and the left, right, and first line indents can be changed. In addition, the Leading before paragraph (a fancy name for "space before paragraph"), Hang punctuation, and Auto hyphenate options are available. In the bottom part of the palette (click the little lever in the lower right corner of the palette to see the bottom part), hyphenation and spacing limitations and guidelines can be set. If the Paragraph palette has just been brought to the front, used, or clicked before Paragraph is selected, the Paragraph command will close (hide) the Paragraph palette.

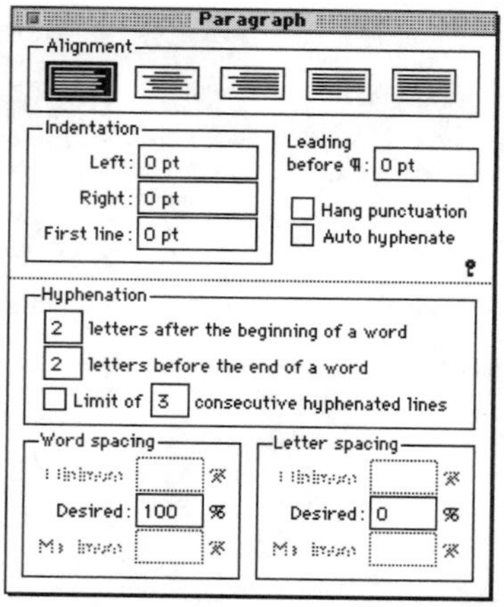

Figure 4-32:
The Paragraph palette.

Link Blocks (⌘-Shift-G) links text from one area or rectangle to another, continuing a story from one area or rectangle to another (see Figure 4-33). Linked blocks act like groups, and using the regular Selection tool and clicking on just one area will select all areas. Individual blocks *can* be selected with the Direct Selection tool. Whenever more text is available than can fit into a text area, a tiny little plus sign in a box appears, alerting you that there is more text in the box than you see.

Figure 4-33:
Text blocks linked together in the order of the arrows.

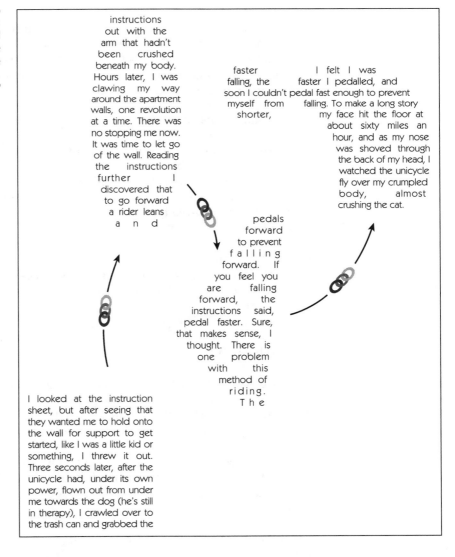

To use Link Blocks, select a text area or rectangle and any other shapes, even text rectangles and areas, and choose Link Blocks. Text will flow from the backmost shape to the frontmost in any group of linked blocks, so be careful to order your boxes correctly when setting up linked text. In fact, if you send a box to the back, that will be where the text starts from, going to the next box forward, and then the next, and so on. You cannot select Link Blocks if at least one text area and one other path or text area is not selected.

Unlink Blocks (⌘-Shift-U) destroys the links made with the Link Blocks command. Blocks can only be unlinked when all boxes linked together are chosen. This is done quite easily with the regular Selection tool. When blocks are unlinked, the text inside them is split into several stories, one for each block. If the boxes are later relinked with the Link blocks command, they will be separated by paragraph returns.

Make Wrap wraps text around any paths, as shown in Figure 4-34. To use Make Wrap, select both the type and the paths you want the type to wrap around. The paths that the type wraps around must be in front of the type in order for them to wrap around the paths. The objects then act like a grouped object; the regular Selection tool will select all objects in a Make Wrap area. Make Wrap only works with Area type and Rectangle type. The selection will be dimmed if Path type or Point type is chosen. You can choose Make Wrap if no object is chosen but the Area type or the Rectangle type, but selecting Make Wrap at this point will display an error message.

Remember that Make Wrap only wraps around paths; regardless of how thick the stroke on your path is, the wrap will not change. This can cause the Wrapping object to run into the text if the object has a heavy stroke.

Make Wrap works in levels; you can Make Wrap with one type area or rectangle to a path and then Make Path again with the same type area or rectangle to another path, and the type will wrap around both paths.

Release Wrap releases any text wraps that are selected, all at one time. Release Wrap does *not* release wraps in the order that they were created. Because paths wrapped to type areas and rectangles do not lose or change attributes when they become wrapped paths, those paths retain their original Paint Style attributes when released.

Fit Headline is designed to automatically increase the weight and width of type using Multiple Master fonts in order to fit type perfectly from the left side of a type area or rectangle to the right side of that same type area or rectangle. Of course, for this to work, you must have Multiple Master typefaces.

Personally, I think this feature would have been great if it just increased the point size of any type, Multiple Master or not, so that the type fit from left to right.

If you don't have Multiple Master typefaces, you can still use Fit Headline. Although the command only increases the tracking of the type until it is justified, it actually does a lot better job than the Type⇨Alignment⇨Justify Last Line command, which only puts space in between words.

Figure 4-34: Text wrapped around different objects.

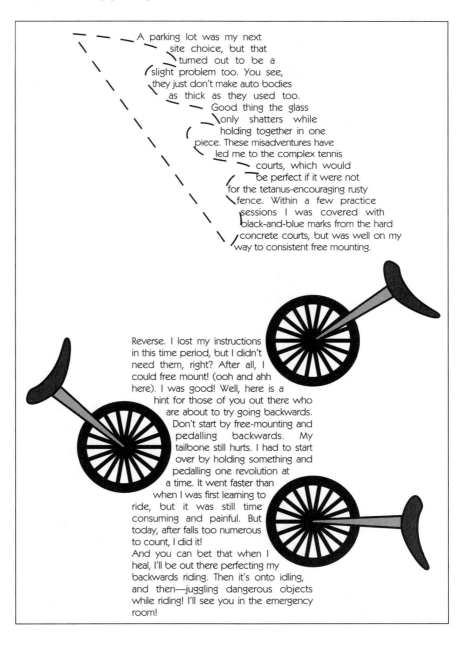

A parking lot was my next site choice, but that turned out to be a slight problem too. You see, they just don't make auto bodies as thick as they used too. Good thing the glass only shatters while holding together in one piece. These misadventures have led me to the complex tennis courts, which would be perfect if it were not for the tetanus-encouraging rusty fence. Within a few practice sessions I was covered with black-and-blue marks from the hard concrete courts, but was well on my way to consistent free mounting.

Reverse. I lost my instructions in this time period, but I didn't need them, right? After all, I could free mount! (ooh and ahh here). I was good! Well, here is a hint for those of you out there who are about to try going backwards. Don't start by free-mounting and pedalling backwards. My tailbone still hurts. I had to start over by holding something and pedalling one revolution at a time. It went faster than when I was first learning to ride, but it was still time consuming and painful. But today, after falls too numerous to count, I did it! And you can bet that when I heal, I'll be out there perfecting my backwards riding. Then it's onto idling, and then—juggling dangerous objects while riding! I'll see you in the emergency room!

Create Outlines needs a key command because it is one of the handiest capabilities of Illustrator. After your type is set (and spelled correctly), choose Create Outlines and the type selected is converted into *editable paths* (see Figure 4-35). To convert type to outlines, the type needs to be selected with a selection tool, not a type tool. Each letter is its own compound path, and each path can be edited with the Direct Selection tool.

Create Outlines only works with Type 1 PostScript and TrueType fonts, not bitmaps or Type 3 PostScript fonts. For Create Outlines to work with PostScript Type 1 fonts, you must have Adobe Type Manager installed and active (extensions on), and you must have both the screen and printer fonts for those fonts. (TrueType combines the screen and printer fonts into one piece — if you can choose a TrueType font, you can create outlines with it, regardless whether of ATM is installed or not.)

When type has been converted to outlines, you can apply gradients to its fill, as well as apply patterns to its fill that you can preview on-screen. (Patterns can be applied to type that is not outlines, but you cannot see those patterns in the type. Instead the type becomes a dingy gray color.)

Figure 4-35:
Type converted into outlines with the Create Outlines command.

While you can Undo Create Outlines, be forewarned that there is no way to convert back to type in case you made a spelling error or wish to change the font or any other type attributes.

All forms of type including Point type, Path type, Area type and Rectangle type may be converted to outlines.

 Creating outlines out of type is also very useful when you want to send the file to be output and the person doing the output does not have the font you are using. Simply Create Outlines before you send the file, and it will print just fine.

The Filter Menu

The most exciting additions to Illustrator 5.0 and 5.5 are the items contained in the Filter menu. *Filters* in Illustrator are additional functions. Many filters in Illustrator automate repetitive tasks and adjust paths automatically in ways that would take hours manually (in other words, when using the path editing tools). Other filters create objects automatically, adjust colors, and select specific objects.

 Filters in Illustrator are based on entirely different concepts than the filters in Adobe Photoshop. In Photoshop, filters enable you to change an image in ways that are impossible to duplicate when working with any other software.

 Filter techniques are discussed in detail in Chapters 15–19.

So why are all these functions in the Filter menu? Because none is really integrated into Illustrator; instead, each filter is an individual file called a *Plug-In*, which resides in the Plug-Ins folder. For a filter to be available, the Plug-In must be in the Plug-Ins folder.

By the way, there really aren't 60 *different* filters. Some of the filters just don't have to be there. You can Distribute Horizontally and Distribute Vertically, for instance, by choosing Align Objects and selecting "distribute" in either the horizontal or the vertical side. In addition, Bloat and Punk are inverses of each other, so if you enter a negative value in Bloat or Punk, you get Punked or Bloated (yuck!). And Scribble and Tweak (two more really great names) each do the same thing, except Scribble uses a percentage and Tweak uses a unit of measurement. Desaturate/Desaturate More and Saturate/Saturate More are variations on the original; the More Version is 2.5 times more than the original, but because you can't apply Desaturate or Saturate 2.5 times, it's OK, right?

Last Filter (⌘-Shift-E) reapplies the last filter chosen. If no filters have been chosen yet, this option will be grayed out. Last Filter stays in place even while you are undoing, so you can undo several steps and still apply the last filter you have chosen; the Last Filter will change only when you pick a new filter. If you have picked a filter, this option will not read Last Filter, but instead it will read the name of the last filter you picked. One difference is that if you chose a filter that had an ellipsis, which meant that there was additional information entered into a dialog box before the filter was performed, there will be no ellipsis in the Last Filter spot. Instead, if the last filter you chose was Rotate Each..., then the top spot in the Filter menu will read Rotate Each without the three dots. In this case, the information you entered last into the Rotate Each dialog box will be used again for this application of the filter.

Last Filter... (Press the Option key while choosing the Last Filter command) brings up the filter dialog box for that particular filter. The Option key must be pressed *before* you click on the menu bar. If that filter had no dialog box, the filter will be reapplied. Like Last Filter, Last Filter... will display the name of the last filter that was applied, and if applicable it will have three dots after it. For instance, if the last filter you used was Free Distort..., holding down the Option key before clicking on the Filter menu will display Free Distort.... If the Option key was not held down, the top line of the Filter menu will then read Free Distort with no ellipsis.

You cannot press ⌘-Option-Shift-E to access the Last Filter... command.

Holding down the Option key and clicking on the Filter menu when no filters have been used in one session will display only Last Filter grayed out.

Missing filters in Illustrator 5.0

When Illustrator 5.0 is installed, the installer program checks the computer to see if an FPU (Floating Point Unit, Math Coprocessor) is available. If not, the following filters will not be installed:

- In the Objects submenu: The Offset Path and Outline Stroked Path filters

- The entire Pathfinder submenu and all 13 filters that are part of that submenu

These filters will work only if an FPU is present, so Illustrator's installer figures that if you can't use them anyway, why install them? Well, if you have Software FPU, a shareware product available on most on-line services, you can use most of these filters. To install these filters, go to the installer, choose Custom, and then install the FPU-based Plug-Ins. If the FPU-based Plug-In filters are present on your computer and your computer does not have either an FPU or Software FPU, the filters will not load and will not be available. (A quick way to see whether your computer has either an FPU or Software FPU: check whether there is a Pathfinder submenu in the Filter menu. If not, then no FPU or Software FPU exists.)

 Certain computers do not have FPUs; others have them as an option; and still others have their FPUs integrated within the main processor (most notably, 68040s).

 All filters in Version 5.5 are present whether your computer has an FPU or not.

Colors

The Colors submenu (Filter⇨Colors) contains nine filters that allow you to modify the color to existing paths that contain either black, process, or custom colors. On the filters that work with custom colors, the new colors created with the Colors filters will result in process color combinations.

Adjust Colors brings up the Adjust Colors dialog box (see Figure 4-36). Adjust Colors increases and decreases process color fills in each individual four-color part. The percentages entered in Adjust Color are absolute changes, meaning that a 10% decrease of cyan when cyan is 100% will result in 90%, and a 10% decrease of cyan when cyan is 50% will result in 40%, not 45%. If the increase makes the tint of a color greater than 100%, it will stay at 100%, but other colors may still increase, if they are not yet at 100%. If the decrease makes the tint of a color less than 0%, that color will remain at 0%, but other colors may still decrease, as long as they are not yet at 0%. For example, a 25% increase to both yellow and magenta to a path with 80% yellow and 50% magenta will result in the colors being 100% yellow and 75% magenta. Reapplying this filter will result in 100% yellow and 100% magenta. Reapplying this filter at this point will result in no change at all.

Entering negative numbers when the Increase button is active will not decrease the value. If you wish to increase the cyan by 10% and decrease the black by 5%, you must use the Adjust Colors filter twice: once to increase the cyan and once to decrease the black.

Figure 4-36: The Adjust Colors dialog box.

Adjust Colors

Cyan: 10 %
Magenta: 25 %
Yellow: 0 %
Black: 0 %

◉ Increase by %
○ Decrease by %

Apply   Reset

Cancel   OK

Blend Front To Back blends the colors of at least three objects whose backmost and frontmost objects are both process tints or both black tints. Blend Front To Back does not work with custom colors, patterns, or gradients. Blend Front To Back is very similar to using the Blend tool, but instead of making different shape *and* color blends, the Blend Front To Back creates new colors inside the objects automatically. If the frontmost and backmost colors are different color *types,* Blend Front To Back will produce undesirable results.

Blend Horizontally blends the colors of at least three objects whose leftmost and rightmost objects are both process tints or both black tints. Blend Horizontally does not work with custom colors, patterns, or gradients. Blend Horizontally is very similar to using the Blend tool, but instead of making different shape *and* color blends, the Blend Horizontally command creates new colors inside the objects automatically. If the leftmost and rightmost colors are different color *types,* Blend Horizontally will produce undesirable results.

Blend Vertically blends the colors of at least three objects whose topmost and bottom-most objects are both process tints or both black tints. Blend Vertically does not work with custom colors, patterns, or gradients. Blend Vertically is very similar to using the Blend tool, but instead of making different shape *and* color blends, the Blend Vertically command creates new colors inside the objects automatically. If the topmost and bottom-most colors are different color *types,* Blend Vertically will produce undesirable results.

Custom To Process: Illustrator 5.5 has an optional color filter called Custom To Process, which converts custom colors into their process color equivalents. Because this filter is not usually in the Plug-Ins folder, you must copy it from the Optional Plug-Ins folder to the Plug-Ins folder in order to use it. The next time you restart Illustrator, the Custom To Process filter will appear in the Color submenu.

Desaturate removes equal amounts of color from the selected objects. This filter does not correspond in any way to saturation changes made by Photoshop. The color removed is proportional to each color in a path, so using Desaturate works very similarly to holding the Shift key down and dragging a triangle in the Paint Style palette. Desaturate does not work with patterns or gradients. Desaturate takes away 10% of the color with the highest percentage, and every other color has 10% removed proportionately to the first one (Color1 = Color1 – 10%, Color2 = Color2 – 10% of original Color2). Using this formula, you can only use Desaturate 10 times before everything selected is white.

Desaturate More desaturates 2.5 times as much as the Desaturate filter. The color with the largest percentage gets an absolute value of 25% taken away, and the next color gets 25% taken away relative to that. Using this formula, Desaturate can only be used four times before the selected paths are white.

Invert Colors works in strange and mysterious ways on selected paths. Whatever the color of the path, Invert Colors takes the first three colors in the Paint palette (cyan, magenta, yellow) and subtracts them from 100. If the original color was a shade of red (for example, where cyan = 0%, magenta = 100%, and yellow = 100%, then Invert Colors makes the new color cyan = 100%, magenta = 0%, and yellow = 0%.

The percentage of black is not affected by Invert colors. Therefore, this is *not* the same as getting a negative image.

Saturate adds equal amounts of color to the selected objects. This filter does not correspond in any way to saturation changes made by Photoshop. The color added is proportional to each color in a path, so using Saturate works very similarly to holding the Shift key down and dragging a triangle to the right in the Paint Style palette. Saturate does not work with patterns or gradients.

Saturate adds an absolute amount of 10% to the color with the highest percentage, and every other color gets 10% added proportionately to that. (Color1 = Color1 + 10%, Color2 = Color2 + 10% of original Color2). After any color reaches 100%, Saturate no longer has any effect. Using this formula, you can only use Saturate 10 times before everything selected is fully saturated (that is, one of the colors in each path is at 100%).

There must be some color in an object for Saturate to work.

Saturate More adds equal amounts of color to the selected objects, working at 2.5 times more than the Saturate filter. The color with the highest percentage gets 25% added; each other color gets 25% of that current color's percentage added. Saturate More can be used no more than four times, at which point at least one color in an object must be 100%.

There must be some color in an object for Saturate More to work.

Create

Most of the filters in the Create submenu (Filter⇨Create) make it easier to create special shapes than with Illustrator's drawing tools. The Fill & Stroke for Mask filter makes two copies of any selected mask and gives one a fill and the other a stroke. The Mosaic filter converts a PICT image into Illustrator squares filled with an average paint color.

Fill and Stroke for Mask takes any selected masks and copies them. The mask is then seemingly given the Paint Style attributes currently in the Paint Style palette. But because masks cannot be filled or stroked, this filter at first glance seems to be working some really great magic.

Of course, Fill and Stroke for Mask really doesn't do anything all that spectacular. After it copies the mask, it does a Paste Behind for the fill (this object is made into the bottommost part of the mask). If a stroke is specified, the filter also does a Paste In Front for the stroke — but this path is not masked and is not part of the masking object.

Before choosing Fill and Stroke for Mask, make sure that you have only the mask you want to fill and stroke selected, and that you have chosen the proper Paint Style attributes that you wish the mask to be colored.

It is a good idea to get into the habit of grouping the new stroke and fill paths to the mask. To do so, you will have to group everything that is part of the mask. Of course, the Group Selection tool will allow you to move anything necessary, even if everything is grouped together.

Mosaic creates a series of tiles out of a PICT image, as shown in Figure 4-37. Any size or color PICT image may be used. When an image is converted through the Mosaic filter, it becomes a series of rectangles and each rectangle is filled with a different color.

In the Mosaic dialog box (see Figure 4-38), you can specify the number of tiles that the image is made up of and the space between the tiles. You also can specify a different size for the entire mosaic.

Be careful with Mosaic, for this filter, unlike almost any other, will run out of memory if the source image or number of tiles is too large. This is the one filter in Illustrator that does almost exactly what its counterpart in Photoshop does.

Figure 4-37:
An original
PICT image
(left) and
the image
after Mosaic
has been
applied.

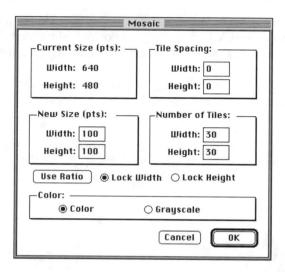

Figure 4-38:
The Mosaic dialog box.

Chapter 16 shows many useful techniques that involve the Mosaic filter.

Polygon automatically creates a polygon. In the Create Polygon dialog box, you specify the number of sides and the polygon's radius. People who have tried to create an equilateral triangle in previous versions of Illustrator with any combination of tools will just love this filter.

Spiral creates a spiral. In the Create Spiral dialog box, you specify the spiral's radius, the number of times the spiral spirals, and whether the spiral spirals clockwise or counterclockwise. The spiral direction measures from the center out, so a spiral set to spiral clockwise will start spiraling clockwise at the center. Be sure to give a stroke, not just a fill, to spirals, or they will look like a circle with a lump.

Star automatically creates a star shape. In the Create Star dialog box, you specify the number of points, the difference between the star's inside points and its outside points.

If the smaller of the two radiuses is set in the 1st Radius field, stars with odd numbers of points will have their center point on the top. If the larger of the two radiuses is set in the 1st Radius field, stars with odd numbers of points will have their center point on the bottom (that is, stars appear upside down).

Trim Marks creates automatic Trim Marks around any selected objects, including text areas selected with one of the selection tools.

Trim Marks are *huge* compared to crop marks, measuring an astounding ½" long. Normal crop marks are about ¼" long.

When Trim Marks are created, they have a 100% black stroke of .3 point. For Trim Marks to appear on every color separation in four-color process printing, the trim marks need to be stroked with process colors of 100% cyan, magenta, yellow, and black. If the illustration contains spot colors that are to print on separate plates, trim marks need to be copied, pasted in back, stroked with the spot color, and set to overprint stroke, for every spot color in the document.

Distort filters

The Distort filters are filters that alter the appearance of a selected path. Free Distort gives you the most control when changing the shape of a path. Roughen, Scribble, and Tweak work in similar ways, changing the appearance of paths automatically and randomly. Twirl spins the selected paths around the mathematical center of those paths.

Free Distort displays the Free Distort dialog box (see Figure 4-39), where you control how much you want to distort the selected paths.

If the Show Me box is checked, you will see what the image looks like as it is distorted. To distort the selected paths, click and drag the four corner points of the box surrounding the artwork (see Figure 4-40). Those handles can be pulled anywhere, including right out of the dialog box onto the document — and even off the document!

 If you pull the handles too far, you will have to click the Reset button to get to your handles again. Doing so resets the image to its original shape.

 Text can be distorted using Free Distort, but it must first be converted into outlines.

Roughen brings up the Roughen dialog box (see Figure 4-41), where you can enter information to literally "roughen up" the illustration.

Figure 4-39:
The Free Distort dialog
box, before distorting.

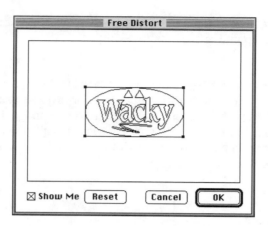

Figure 4-40:
Distorting an image.

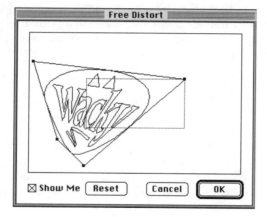

Three options are available here:

- Size: How far points may move when roughed relative to the width or height (whichever is greater) of the selected path.

- Detail: How many points are moved. For example, if you have a 1" by 1" square, the number of points added would be 36. (4" — top, bottom, left, right — at 10 points per inch equals 40 points. There are already 4 points on a rectangle, so you only need 36 more points.)

- How points are joined: rounded or jagged. If rounded, all the anchor points added will be smooth points. If jagged, all the points added will be straight corner points.

Roughen will never take away points when roughening a path.

Figure 4-41:
The Roughen dialog box.

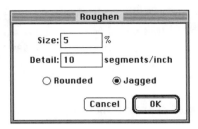

The Roughen filter can be used as a very hip Version of the Add Anchor Points filter. If the Size box is set to 0%, all points added will be added along the existing path all at once. Instead of going to Add Anchor Points again and again, just try entering a value of 25 into the segments/inch field of the Roughen filter. You have instant multiple Add Anchor Points. This is a great technique for Twirl, Scribble, Tweak, or anything else where you need a bunch of anchor points fast.

Scribble displays the Scribble dialog box (see Figure 4-42), where you define the amount of scribble, including how much horizontal and vertical scribble and which points are moved (Anchor Points, In Control Points, or Out Control Points).

No anchor points are added with the Scribble dialog box.

The percentages of Horizontal and Vertical correspond to the movement of the selected points. If 0% is entered in either field, no movement will occur in that direction. The percentage is based on the width or height of the shape, whichever is longest. If Anchor Points is checked, then all anchor points on the selected path will be moved in a random distance corresponding to the amounts set in the Horizontal and Vertical text field boxes. If In or Out Control Points is checked, then those points will be moved the specified distance as well. The *In Control Points* are the points on one side of the anchor point, while *Out Control Points* refers to the points on the other side of the anchor point.

Figure 4-42:
The Scribble dialog box.

Tweak brings up the Tweak dialog box, which looks like the Scribble dialog box. In fact, Tweak works muck like Scribble. Instead of specifying a distance based on percentage, however, Tweak lets you enter in the distance in real measurements, in whatever unit your measurement system is currently using. All the options in the Tweak dialog box have the same effects as the same options in the Scribble dialog box.

Figure 4-43 shows an object and the resulting Roughened, Scribbled, and Tweaked images.

Twirl displays the Twirl dialog box, where you specify how much the selected objects will spin. You can set the twirl angle from −4000° up to 4000°. The very center of the selected objects will rotate the degree specified, while the objects on the edges will rotate around the center very little. Positive values rotate the selected paths clockwise; negative values rotate the selected paths counterclockwise.

 You achieve a "going down the drain" effect when you set the Twirl very high.

Figure 4-43:
The original
image is
Roughened,
Scribbled, and
Tweaked.

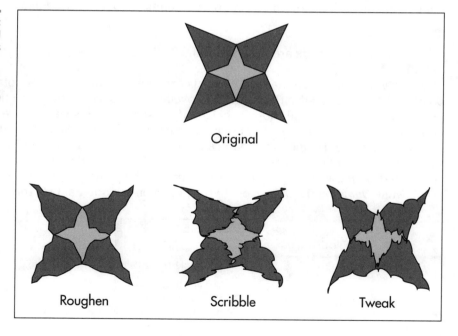

The more anchor points on your path, the better your result. I usually either Add Anchor Points several times or add anchor points via the Roughen filter before applying the Twirl filter.

Figure 4-44 shows an object before and after being Twirled.

Figure 4-44:
The original object (top) is Twirled.

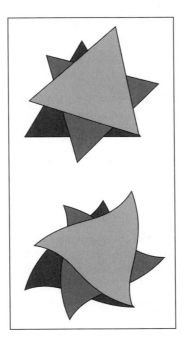

Objects

Most of the Objects filters control how objects are aligned and how they are positioned, scaled, and rotated in the document. Other Objects filters add anchor points to paths and outline strokes or create a new path that is offset from the original.

Add Anchor Points adds new anchor points between every pair of existing anchor points it can find. For example, if you have one line segment with an anchor point on each end, Add Anchor Points will add one anchor point to the segment, exactly in the middle of the two anchor points. If a rectangle is drawn and Add Anchor Points is applied, it will have four new anchor points: one at the top, one at the bottom, one on the left side, and one on the right side.

Add Anchor Points is related to the Add Anchor Point tool. The filter adds anchor points the same way as the tool does, only more efficiently. Points that are added to a smooth segment are automatically smooth points; points added to a straight segment are automatically corner points.

Want to know how many points are being added to your path when Add Anchor Points is applied? Each time the filter is reapplied, the number of anchor points doubles on a closed path and is one less than doubled on an open path.

Align Objects brings up the Align Objects dialog box (see Figure 4-45), which contains radio buttons that enable you to determine horizontal and vertical alignment. The dialog box also has a preview box, where you can see what will happen when you choose certain options.

You must select at least two objects for Align Objects to work. You can align selected objects horizontally (flush left, centered, or flush right) and vertically (flush to the top, center, or bottom). The objects also can be distributed evenly from left to right if Distribute is checked.

Unfortunately, choosing Distribute distributes the *centers* of the paths, not the edges. There is no option for automatically distributing the objects so that there are even amounts of space between them.

Figure 4-45:
The Align Objects dialog box.

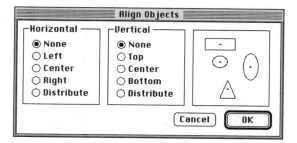

Distribute Horizontally and **Distribute Vertically** enable you to quickly distribute the centers of the objects without accessing the Align Objects dialog box. These filters work essentially the same as the Distribute options in the Align Objects dialog box.

Move Each moves an entire path at one time. Move Each also has the capability of moving paths *randomly*. If you check the Random check box, each path selected will move any amount up to the number of points selected in the horizontal and vertical text fields.

You *cannot* move individual points with the Move Each filter. To move individual points, use the Move command (⌘-Shift-M) or the Direct Selection tool.

 Continuously reapplying the Move Each filter when the Random box is checked will result in a truly random placement of all selected paths.

Offset Path is a tough filter to understand fully, but what it does is fairly straightforward. Here is a brief, basic explanation of what it is supposed to do.

Choosing the Offset Path command displays the Offset Path dialog box (see Figure 4-46), where you enter how far and which way you want the new path to be offset from the original. In a sense, you are creating a stroke, outlining it, and uniting it with the original all in one swoop. You can specify the distance the path is to be offset by entering a value (in points, mils, or millimeters) in the Offset box.

 The Line join and Miter limit are the same types of options available for strokes in the Paint Style palette.

 Offset Path is an FPU-only filter for Illustrator 5.0 users. It will not work unless your computer has an FPU or the software equivalent.

Figure 4-46:
The Offset Path dialog box.

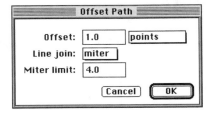

Outline Path (called Outline Stroked Path in Version 5.0) automatically creates an outline around any stroke on a selected path. The width of the stroke is surrounded by a path, which is then filled with the original color of the stroke, with no color (None) given to the new stroke.

 This filter does not work for dashed lines. For a tough workaround (which sort of works), see Chapter 20.

 Outline Stroked Path in Illustrator 5.0 is another FPU-only filter that will not work unless your computer has an FPU or the software equivalent.

Rotate Each is a handy little filter that rotates each selected object individually. In other words, all selected paths rotate *independently of each other.* In the Rotate Each dialog box, you indicate how much you want to rotate.

For example, if you have 100 squares set just where you want them on the page and then decide you want the squares to be diamonds, select all 100 and then choose Rotate Each, entering 45° in the Angle text field. Each square will spin in place until it is a diamond, but the objects will not change location (see Figure 4-47).

If you check the Random box, the boxes will rotate up to 45° in *both directions.*

 Rotate Each works differently than the Rotate tool. The Rotate tool rotates the entire grid of squares as one object.

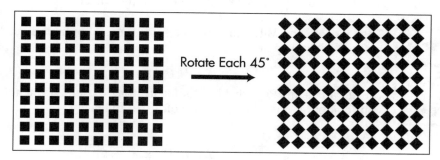

Figure 4-47:
A series of squares set to Rotate Each by 45°.

Rotate Each 45°

Scale Each brings up the Scale Each dialog box, where you can specify how each selected path scales independently. Each path scales from its center. You can scale horizontally and vertically, entering in any percentage from 0% to 4000%. If you check the Random box, the selected paths will scale anywhere up or down to the percentage you specify.

For example, you can change the grid of diamonds in Figure 4-47 into a grid of better-looking diamonds by squeezing the horizontal measurement just a little (see Figure 4-48). If you enter 70% in the horizontal field and 100% in the vertical field, the diamonds keep the same height but are condensed. As a result, the diamonds look more like real diamonds. Or at least more like playing card diamonds.

Pathfinder filters

The Pathfinder filters are the biggest time-savers in Illustrator. But you need an FPU or Software FPU to run them with Illustrator 5.0. And it's pretty darn hard to figure out which filter to use for which job.

Figure 4-48:
The diamonds from Figure 4-47
Scaled Each by 70%.

Figure 4-48:
The diamonds from Figure 4-47
Scaled Each by 70%.

Take a second to look at the Pathfinder submenu, shown in Figure 4-49. Not too confusing (really, I'm serious). The filters are arranged into four distinct sections: Combine, Overlay, Mix, and Trap.

Figure 4-49:
The gigantic Pathfinder submenu.

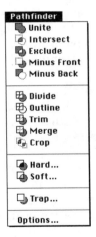

The Pathfinder filters take the place of doing mundane path editing that could take hours. Everything that the Pathfinder filters do can be done manually with Illustrator tools, but the Pathfinder filters do them much more quickly. Common activities like joining two paths together correctly and breaking a path into two pieces are done in a snap.

In Version 3.2, trapping was confusing, difficult, annoying, and extremely time consuming. Thanks to the Divide Stroke filter, trapping in Illustrator 5.0 was only confusing, difficult, annoying, and *mildly* time consuming. In fact, I could trap in a quarter of the time it took in Version 3.2.

Illustrator 5.5 includes a Trap filter, which should eliminate the fear of trapping for most users.

Trapping is discussed fully in Chapter 21.

When should you avoid the Pathfinder filters? When you don't have a path — for example, when you have type selected that has not been converted into outlines.

Unite unites the selected objects if they are overlapping. A new path outlines all the previously selected objects. There are no paths where the original paths intersected. The new object takes the Paint Style attributes of the topmost object. If any objects are within other objects, those objects will be assimilated. If there are "holes" in the object, the holes will become reversed out of a compound path.

Intersect creates only the intersection of the selected paths. Any part of a selected path that does not intersect is deleted. If two paths are intersecting and selected, only the area that intersects between the two paths will remain. If three or more paths are selected, all must intersect at a common area for the filter to produce results. If the paths selected do not intersect at all, nothing will happen. If one selected path is contained within all the other selected paths, the result will be that contained path. The resulting path will have the Paint Style attributes of the topmost path.

Exclude is pretty much the opposite of Intersect. Choosing Exclude deletes the intersecting areas, grouping together the outside pieces. If you are having trouble making a compound path, try using Exclude; any path within another path will be reversed, creating a compound path automatically.

Back Minus (Back Minus Front in Version 5.0) subtracts all the selected paths in front of the backmost selected path from the backmost selected path. With two objects, it is quite simple; the object in front is deleted, and the area where the object in front was located is also deleted. It gets a little more confusing when you have more objects, but it does the same thing, all at once to all the selected paths. If the area to be subtracted is totally within the path it will subtract *from,* then a compound path results.

Front Minus (Front Minus Back in Version 5.0) is the opposite of Back Minus Front: it subtracts all the selected paths behind the frontmost selected path from the frontmost selected path. With two objects, it is also quite simple; the object in the back is deleted, and the area where the object in back was placed is also deleted. It gets a little more confusing when you have more objects, but it does the same thing, all at once to all the selected paths. If the area to be subtracted is totally within the path it will subtract *from,* then a compound path results.

Divide (Divide Fill in Version 5.0) checks to see where the selected paths overlap and then creates new paths at all intersections where the paths crossed, creating new paths if necessary. Fills are kept, but any strokes are changed to None. In the process, Divide Fill also groups the pieces of the fill together. Divide Fill also keeps sections their original colors; the illustration appears to look the same unless it previously had strokes. To keep the strokes, copy before performing the filter, Divide Fill, and then Paste In Back.

Outline (Divide Stroke in Version 5.0) creates small sections of paths wherever paths cross and colors the strokes, using the fill of the path they were part of, giving the strokes a weight of 1 point. Divide Stroke is very useful for trapping in Version 5.0, as it will automatically create the sections needed that have to be chosen for overprinting, although many times the colors will be incorrect. (Actually, Merge Stroke is better, but Divide Stroke will give you more pieces to work with, which can be more useful.)

 If you are going to use Divide Stroke for trapping, be sure to make a copy first. Then, after making paint attribute changes to the strokes and deleting the ones you don't need, Paste In Back.

 Trim (available in Version 5.5 only) removes sections of paths that are overlapped by other paths. Frontmost paths are the only ones that will remain. This filter is very useful for cleaning up complex overlapping illustrations.

Merge (Merge Fill in Version 5.0) merges paths that overlap that have the exact same fill applied to them. Even if the fill is different by as little as one percent, Merge Fill will create two separate paths. This method is much more efficient than Unite for making areas of the same color into one object.

Merge Stroke (only available in Version 5.0) merges paths that have the same fill into paths with a continuous stroke. That stroke is broken up wherever Merge Stroke encounters another path with a different fill. Merge Stroke is even better for trapping than Divide Fill in Illustrator 5.0, usually because there are fewer segments to delete.

Crop (Crop Fill in Version 5.0) works very similar to the way masks work, except that anything outside the cropped area is deleted, not just hidden. To use Crop Fill, bring the object that you wish to use as a cropper (ugh! you can call it a mask if it makes you feel better) to the front, select all the paths you wish to crop with it and the cropper itself, and choose Crop Fill. Everything outside the cropper will be deleted. The objects that were cropped are grouped together in the shape of the crop.

Unlike masks, there is no outside shape after a crop is made. The cropper used to crop the image is deleted when Crop Fill is chosen.

Crop Stroke (available in Version 5.0 only) works just like Crop Fill, but instead of the paths remaining being filled with a color, they are stroked with a color.

Hard (Mix Hard in Version 5.0) adds the values of overlapping path fills. The more objects that are overlapping, the darker the fill. Each section that overlaps is a new path, just like what happens when you choose Divide Fill. Any strokes are changed to none and ignored.

Soft (Mix Soft in Version 5.0) adds colors together based on a percentage you enter into the Mix Soft dialog box.

Trap (available in Version 5.5 only) automatically creates a trap between abutting shapes of different colors. You set the amount of trap in a dialog box that appears after choosing the Trap item.

Options (available in Version 5.5 only) displays a dialog box, where you may specify how exact the Pathfinder filters are (in increments of one point).

Select filters

The Select filters are used for selecting paths with common attributes. The first four select filters select paths based on Paint Style. The Select Inverse filter selects everything that is currently *not* selected. The Select Masks and Select Stray Points filter select masks and stray points, respectively.

Same Fill Color selects all objects that have the same fill color as the currently selected object. You cannot select objects with different fills for Same Fill Color to work, but you may select two objects that have the same fill.

Same Paint Style selects all objects that have the same Paint Style attributes as the currently selected object. You cannot select objects with different Paint Style attributes for Same Paint Style to work, but you may select two objects that have the same Paint Style attributes. *All* the attributes must be the same, including line weight and stroke options.

Same Stroke Color selects all objects that have the same stroke color as the currently selected object. You cannot select objects with different strokes for Same Stroke Color to work, but you may select two objects that have the same stroke color.

Same Stroke Weight selects all objects that have the same stroke weight as the currently selected object. You cannot select objects with different stroke weights for Same Stroke Weight to work, but you may select two or more objects that have the same stroke weight.

Select Inverse selects everything that is not selected. If nothing is selected, this filter works like Select All. If everything is selected, this works as Select None. The same effect can be achieved by Shift-dragging a marquee across everything in the document.

Select Masks selects all objects currently being used as masking objects. Select Masks will *not* select paths that are made from masks, such as paths created with the Fill and Stroke Mask filter.

Select Stray Points selects all anchor points that are *stray* — that is, all anchor points that are not connected to any other anchor points in the document.

Stylize filters

The Stylize filters are used for a variety of functions, kind of a catchall for filters that really couldn't go anywhere else. Add Arrowheads puts arrowheads (all sorts!) onto the ends of open paths. Calligraphy changes the selection into something that could have been drawn with a calligraphy pen. Drop Shadow adds a darkened shadow to the selected path. Bloat, Punk, and Round corners all seem like they may be better suited to the Distort submenu, but Adobe has chosen to put them here.

Add Arrowheads adds an arrowhead (or two) to any selected open paths. If more than one path is selected, Arrowheads will be added to each open path. To use Add Arrowheads, select an open path and choose Add Arrowheads. The Add Arrowheads dialog box appears, as shown in Figure 4-50. In this box, you can pick which of the 27 different arrowheads you want to stick on the end of your path. Scale refers to the size of the arrowhead relative to the stroke weight of the path; you may enter any number between 1% and 1000% in this box. Choosing Start places the arrowhead on the beginning of the path (where you first clicked to draw it), choosing End places the arrowhead on the ending of the path (where you last clicked to draw it), and choosing Start and End places the same arrowhead on both the beginning and ending of the path. Reapplying this filter to the same paths will continue to put arrowheads on top of arrowheads.

 Add Arrowheads *does not* work on closed paths.

Arrowheads are grouped to the paths that were selected when they were created; it is sometimes necessary to rotate the arrowhead by either ungrouping it or choosing it with the Group Selection tool or the Direct Selection tool.

Figure 4-50:
The Add Arrowheads dialog
box.

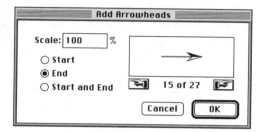

Bloat brings up the Bloat dialog box, where you may specify a percentage that you want the selected paths to be bloated. Bloating causes the segments between anchor points to expand outwards. The higher the percentage, the more bloated the selection. Several paths have been bloated in Figure 4-51. You can bloat from –200% up to 200%.

If you choose a negative percentage to bloat by, you are actually punking (see below), not bloating. Go figure.

Figure 4-51:
Bloated paths.

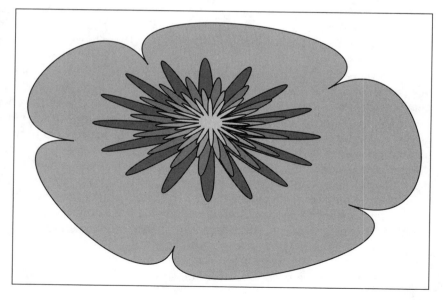

Calligraphy brings up the Calligraphy dialog box, where you specify the width and angle of the pen you want to use. Calligraphy works with paths, not fills or strokes, and is entirely dependent on the shape of the path for its results.

 Drawing with the Brush tool over the same area with the same settings will have a similar effect as using the Calligraphy filter, but the results will be slightly better with the Brush tool.

The maximum thickness of the calligraphic line is called Pen Width, and Pen Angle is the angle at which the pen is at its thickest.

Drop Shadow affects both stroke and fill, unlike most other filters. In the Drop Shadow dialog box (see Figure 4-52), you may specify the offset of the drop shadow by entering values for how far across the drop shadow should move (X Offset) and how far up or down it should move (Y Offset). Positive numbers will move the shadow to the right and down; negative numbers will move the shadow to the left and up.

Figure 4-52:
The Drop Shadow dialog box.

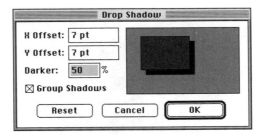

The general rule in drop shadowing is that the more offset the drop shadow is, the higher the original object looks. To make an object look like it is floating far above the page, enter high offset values.

The percentage entered in Darker is how much black is added to the fill and stroke colors. Darker does not affect any of the other custom or process colors. If Group Shadows is checked, the drop shadow is grouped to the original object, which is a good idea, since you shouldn't just leave your shadow lying around.

Punk is the opposite of Bloat. While Bloat makes rounded, bubble-like extrusions appear on the surface of your object, Punk makes tall spikes appear on its path. When you choose Punk, you can enter how much you want to Punk the drawing. Punk amounts can range from –200% to 200%. The number of spikes is based on the number of anchor points in your drawing. Figure 4-53 shows several Punked objects.

When a negative value is entered for Punk, you are really Bloating, not Punking. Hmmm.

Round Corners changes all types of corner points to smooth points. This filter works on any path that has corner points, but the best results seem to be on polygons and stars. In the Round Corners dialog box, you specify what the radius of the Round Corners should be. The larger the number, the bigger the curve.

 Don't apply the Round Corners filter to a Rounded Rectangle to make the corners "more rounded." Instead of making the corners rounder, the flat sides of the Rounded Rectangle will curve slightly.

Figure 4-53:
Several Punked objects.

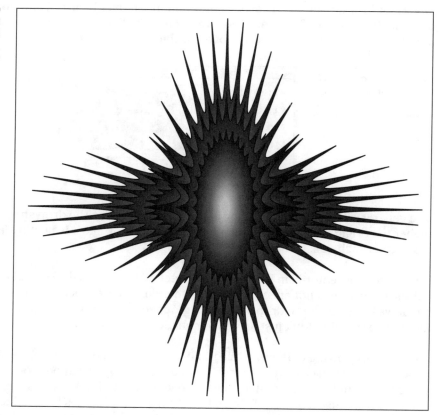

Text filters

The two text filters are odd ducks because they are not filters but Plug-Ins. In fact, they probably should be in the Type menu because they work with type only.

Export brings up the Export dialog box, where you may choose the format to save text in your document, give the new text document a name, and save it.

 Export is not available if you do not have the Claris XTend filters installed.

Find brings up the Text Find dialog box (see Figure 4-54). In this box, type what you are looking for and then click Find Next. The next occurrence in the text box that you are in will be highlighted. To search backwards, click the Search Backward check box, and the search will go from where you are in the text to the beginning. If Whole Word is checked, then the characters you type must be a whole word and not part of any other word. If Case Sensitive is checked, the word you are searching for must match the case of your characters exactly. If Wrap Around is checked, the search will continue through the end of the type and begin at the start of the story.

Choosing Replace and then Find replaces the selected word with whatever is in the Replace with text field and then highlights the next word. Replace just replaces the word but does not find the next word. Replace All finds all the occurrences of that word and replaces them.

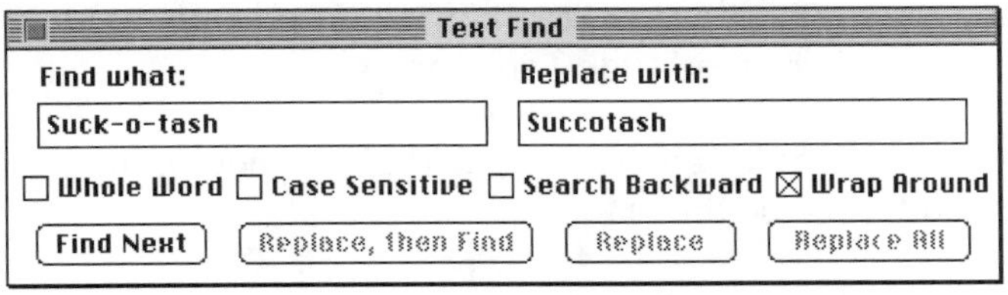

Figure 4-54:
The Text Find dialog
box.

Text Find
Find what: **Replace with:**
Suck-o-tash   Succotash
☐ Whole Word ☐ Case Sensitive ☐ Search Backward ☒ Wrap Around
[Find Next] [Replace, then Find] [Replace] [Replace All]

The Window Menu

```
Window
New Window

Hide Toolbox    ⌘⌃T
Show Layers     ⌘⌃L
Show Info       ⌘⌃I
Show Paint Style
Show Gradient
Show Character
Show Paragraph

✓Untitled art 1 <100%>
```

The Window menu contains the various options for displaying the different palettes available in Illustrator, as well as any documents that are currently open. Another command in the Window menu is New Window, used to create a duplicate window of the current file.

New Window creates a new window that displays the current document, usually at a different viewing percentage or at a different mode. This new window will initially be the same size and viewing options as the existing, frontmost window, but the viewing options can be changed without affecting the other window.

Hide Toolbox (⌘-Control-T) hides the toolbox from view. If the toolbox is hidden, this command will read Show Toolbox.

Show Toolbox (⌘-Control-T) shows the toolbox if it is currently hidden. If the toolbox is showing, this command will read Hide Toolbox.

Hide Layers (⌘-Control-L) hides the Layers palette from view. If the Layers palette is hidden, this command will read Show Layers.

Show Layers (⌘-Control-L) shows the Layers palette if it is currently hidden. If the Layers palette is showing currently, this command will read Hide Layers.

Hide Info (⌘-Control-I) hides the Info palette from view. If the Info palette is hidden, this command will read Show Info.

Show Info (⌘-Control-I) shows the Info palette if it is currently hidden. If the Info palette is showing currently, this command will read Hide Info. The Info palette appears automatically when the Measure tool is used.

Hide Paint Style (⌘-I) hides the Paint Style palette from view. If the Paint Style palette is hidden, this command will read Show Paint Style.

Show Paint Style (⌘-I) shows the Paint Style palette if it is currently hidden. If the Paint Style palette is currently showing, this command will read Hide Paint Style.

Hide Gradient hides the Gradient palette from view. If the Gradient palette is hidden, this command will read Show Gradient.

Show Gradient shows the Gradient palette if it is currently hidden. If the Gradient palette is currently showing, this command will read Hide Gradient.

 The Gradient palette also appears automatically when the Gradient tool is clicked or if a gradient in the Paint Style box is double-clicked.

Hide Character (⌘-T) hides the Character palette from view. If the Character palette is hidden, this command will read Show Character.

Show Character (⌘-T) shows the Character palette if it is currently hidden. If the Character palette is showing, this command will read Hide Character. If any of the options for type are chosen that have to be entered through the keyboard (that is, leading, size, font, and so on), then the Character palette appears.

Hide Paragraph (⌘-Shift-P in Version 5.5, ⌘-Shift-T in Version 5.0) hides the Paragraph palette from view. If the Paragraph palette is hidden, this command will read Show Paragraph.

Show Paragraph (⌘-Shift-P in Version 5.5, ⌘-Shift-T in Version 5.0) shows the Paragraph palette if it is currently hidden. If the Paragraph palette is showing, this command will read Hide Paragraph.

 Show Tab Ruler (⌘-Shift-T) shows the Tab Ruler palette if it is hidden.

Untitled Art 1 and all other titles below this dotted line are referencing the open Illustrator documents and duplicate document windows. A check mark appears in front of the title that is the title of the active document or window.

The Apple Menu

Everyone's Apple menu looks different, depending on which files are in your Apple Menu Items folder in your System Folder. Nonetheless, there should be two items under your Apple menu that are specific to Illustrator: About Adobe Illustrator and About Plug-Ins. When Illustrator is running, going to the Finder and choosing About This Macintosh is also useful.

About Adobe Illustrator displays a dialog box with the user information and scrolling credits for everyone, absolutely everyone, who had any teeny tiny little thing to do with Illustrator.

About Plug-Ins displays a submenu that lists all the installed Plug-Ins. Choosing one of the items in the Plug-Ins submenu displays who made the Plug-In.

About this Macintosh (in the Finder, while Illustrator is running) displays how much memory is allocated to Illustrator, and how much Illustrator is actually using of that allocated amount.

Now that the basics are ingrained in your skull, it's time to start experimenting with the features in Illustrator. This section takes you step by step through creating basic shapes, paths, and text. You'll learn how to manipulate and organize your creations.

Drawing Basic Shapes and Painting

In This Chapter

- How to draw basic ovals and rectangles
- How to use filters to create instant polygons and stars
- How to use fills and strokes
- How to use the Paint Style palette
- How to color the fill of objects with Paint Style
- How to color the stroke of objects with Paint Style

Making Basic Shapes

Technically, the name of this section should really be "Placing and Sizing Preformatted Closed Paths," but then no one would read it. And this is an important chapter because it introduces many concepts that are built upon in future chapters.

Drawing the most basic shapes — rectangles, ovals, polygons, and stars — is precisely what a computer is for. Try drawing a perfect oval by hand. Troublesome, isn't it? How about a square that doesn't have ink bubbles or splotches at the corners? How about a nine-point star? Yuck. Drawing these objects and then coloring them in Illustrator is so easy and so basic that after a few weeks of using Illustrator, you'll never be able to draw a shape by hand again without wincing. Figure 5-1 compares shapes drawn by hand with those drawn by a computer.

Figure 5-1:
Hand-drawn
shapes, their
computer-
drawn
counterparts,
and the same
shapes
transformed.

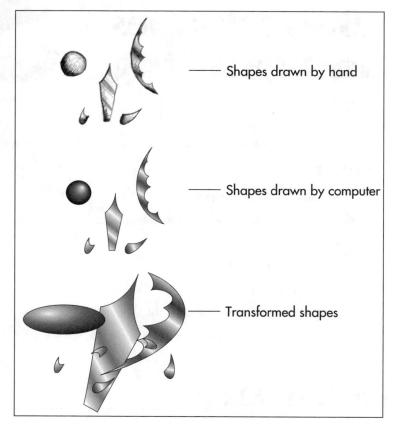

Figure 5-1: Hand-drawn shapes, their computer-drawn counterparts, and the same shapes transformed.

Shapes drawn by hand

Shapes drawn by computer

Transformed shapes

Getting rid of the shape you've drawn is even easier than creating it in the first place. And after the shape is created, it can be moved, rotated, scaled, and manipulated in any way you like.

The true power of object-oriented drawing programs is exemplified in Illustrator. No matter what you draw, you can adjust and move each piece of the drawing independently until it's just right. Don't like the sun so high in your background? Pull it down and tuck it in just a bit behind those mountains. Is the tree too small for the house in your illustration? Scale it up a bit. This feature is great not only for artists, but also for your pesky client (or boss) who demands that everything be moved but that darned tree. Figure 5-2 shows an illustration drawn one way and then modified in a matter of seconds by moving and transforming existing elements.

Figure 5-2:
An original
illustration and
its trans-
formation.

A bitmap paint application does not have this capability to move pieces of a drawing (with the exception of Fractal Design Painter's X2). After an image is moved in a bitmap program, a *hole* appears in the place where the section used to be. And if there is anything under the section where the image was moved to, that information is gone when the section is replaced with the new image.

Drawing rectangles

The most basic shape you can draw is a rectangle. To draw a quick rectangle, select the Rectangle tool (highlighted in the toolbox shown in Figure 5-3) by clicking it in the toolbox and dragging diagonally on the document. (If the toolbox is not visible, press ⌘-Control-T.) Figure 5-3 shows the steps to take to draw a rectangle: 1. Click to set the origin while holding down the mouse button; 2. Drag diagonally to the size you desire; 3. Release the mouse button. The farther the distance from the initial click until the point where you release the mouse button, the larger the rectangle.

After you release the mouse button, a black rectangle appears with four blue points in the corners and one blue point in the center (if you are in Preview mode). The edge of the rectangle has thin blue lines surrounding it. The blue points in the corners are *straight corner anchor points.* The blue point in the center is the *center point.* The blue lines are *straight line segments* that connect the anchor points of the rectangle. The blue points and blue lines together are considered a *path.* In Artwork mode, the rectangle has no fill or stroke, and the points and path appear black.

Figure 5-3:
Drawing a
rectangle.

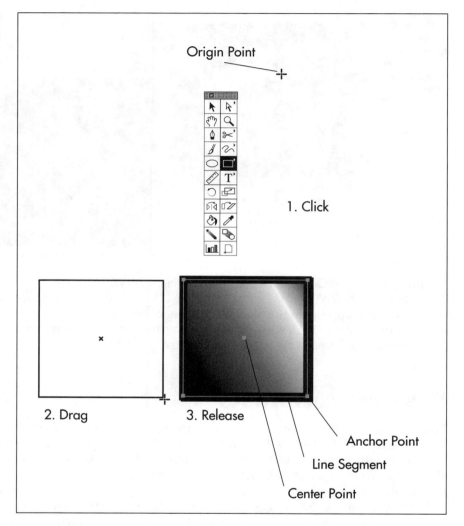

The initial click you made with the Rectangle tool is called the *origin point*. While you drag a figure, the origin point never moves; however, the rest of the rectangle is fluid, changing shape as you drag in different directions and to different distances with your mouse. Dragging horizontally with almost no vertical movement results in a long, flat rectangle. Dragging vertically with very little horizontal movement creates a rectangle that is tall and thin. Dragging at a 45° angle (diagonally) results in a squared rectangle.

Rectangles can be drawn from any corner by clicking and dragging in the opposite direction of where you want that corner to be. For instance, to draw a rectangle from the lower righthand corner, click and drag up and to the left. As long as you have the Rectangle tool, dragging with it in the document window produces a new rectangle.

If you need to draw a rectangle that is an exact size, instead of dragging with the Rectangle tool, just click it where you want the upper lefthand corner to be. The Rectangle dialog box appears, as shown in Figure 5-4. Type in the width and height, click OK, and the rectangle draws itself, becoming precisely the size that you typed in.

Figure 5-4:
The Rectangle dialog
box.

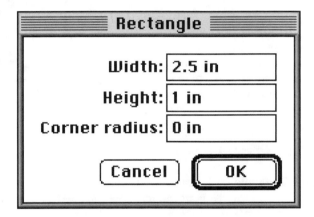

The third text field in the Rectangle dialog box is for the size of the corner radius. This option makes the corners of the rectangle curved, although leaving the setting at a value of 0 keeps the corners straight. Rectangles whose sizes are specified in the Rectangle size dialog box are always drawn from the upper lefthand corner unless you press the Option key when drawing the rectangle (see "Drawing rectangles from their centers" in the next section). The largest rectangle you can draw is 10 feet by 10 feet. It's a wonder you can get anything done at all with these limitations.

When the Rectangle dialog box appears, values are usually already inside the text fields. Those numbers correspond to the size of the rectangle you have drawn last. To create another rectangle the exact same size, just click OK (or press Return or Enter). To make the rectangle a different size, replace the values with your own measurements. If a text field is highlighted, typing replaces the text in the text field and deletes what had been highlighted. To highlight the next field in a dialog box, press the Tab key. You can also highlight the preceding field in a dialog box by pressing Shift-Tab. To accept the options in the dialog box, click OK or press Return or Enter.

When you first run Illustrator, all measurements are set to points and picas. This means that the values inside the Rectangle dialog box appear in so many points (12 points in a pica). You can work in inches in two ways. The first way, before you bring up the Rectangle dialog box, is to select File⇨Preferences⇨General and choose inches as the measurement system you would like to work with. All dialog boxes will then express their measurements in inches, not points. The second way is to type either the inch symbol (") or **in** after the number, even though the text fields show points. Illustrator does points/inches/centimeters conversions on the fly, so after you enter an inch value, the program converts the inches into points as soon as you press the Tab key. This little feature can be an excellent way for you to become more comfortable with points and picas.

To get out of the Rectangle dialog box without drawing a rectangle, click the Cancel button. Whenever you see a Cancel button in a dialog box, pressing ⌘-period acts just like clicking that Cancel button. Anything you have typed in that dialog box is then forgotten; the next time the dialog box is opened, it still has the size of the previously drawn rectangle inside it.

STEPS:	Creating a Drop Shadow Box

Step 1. Using the Rectangle tool, draw a rectangle that is about 1 inch wide by ¾ inch tall. If the rectangle is not black, select Object⇨Paint Style, and in the Paint Style palette, click the Fill square and then click on the smaller black box below it. Then click the Stroke square and click the box with a slash below it.

Step 2. Choose the Selection tool and drag up and to the right just a little while holding down the Option key. The farther you drag, the greater the depth of the drop shadow.

Step 3. After you release the mouse button, you should have two overlapping rectangles. Change the color of the top one by clicking the Fill square and changing the color in the first gray box to **25%** black. Put a border around the top box by clicking the Stroke square and clicking the black box below it. Your drop shadow box should look like the one in Figure 5-5.

Figure 5-5:
A drop shadow box.

Drawing rectangles from their centers

Instead of drawing a rectangle from a corner, you can also draw one from its center. Rectangles are often placed on top of or under certain other objects, and there needs to be an even amount of space between the rectangle and the object it is surrounding. Drawing from the corner forces you to "eyeball" the space around the object, while drawing from the center of the other object ensures that space surrounding the object is the same.

To draw a rectangle from its center, hold down the Option key, click, and drag. The origin point is now the center of the rectangle. The farther you drag in one direction, the farther the edges of the rectangle go out in the opposite direction. Drawing from the center of a rectangle lets you draw a rectangle twice as big as the one you can draw if you were dragging from a corner. As long as the Option key is pressed, the rectangle continues to be drawn from its center. If you release the Option key before you release the mouse button, the origin of the rectangle changes back to a corner. You can press and release the Option key at any time while drawing, toggling back and forth between drawing a corner rectangle and a centered rectangle. The important criteria is *when* to release the Option key. If the Option key is pressed when the mouse button is released, the rectangle is a centered rectangle. If the Option key is *not* pressed until after the mouse button is released, the rectangle is a corner rectangle.

 If you click without dragging when the Option key is pressed, the Rectangle dialog box appears. The center of the rectangle is now where you clicked (normally, the corner of the rectangle is where you click). Unlike manually drawing (dragging) centered rectangles, the values you enter for width and height are the actual width and height of the rectangle. The value is *not* doubled, like it is when you are dragging a centered rectangle, which is created twice as fast as one drawn from a corner.

You can also draw a rectangle from its center by double-clicking the Rectangle tool. The tool changes from the Corner Rectangle tool to the Centered Rectangle tool. Drawing with the Centered Rectangle tool automatically draws a rectangle from its center. Now the Option key toggles from drawing from the middle to drawing from the corner. So if the Option key is pressed when the mouse button is released, the rectangle is drawn from the corner, not the center.

Drawing a perfect square

Few things in life really are perfect, but squares in Illustrator are pretty darn close. The difference between a square and a rectangle is that a square is a rectangle with four sides of exactly the same length. If you are really careful, you can drag out from a corner or from the center of a rectangle to create a square, but chances are it will be off just a little.

If you are entering the width and height into the Rectangle dialog box to draw a perfect square, just make sure that the values are equal. Only then will you have a perfect square.

When drawing, you can force Illustrator to create perfect squares by holding down the Shift key as you draw. When the Shift key is pressed while a rectangle is being drawn, it conforms to a square, with all four sides being equal. The Shift key must be pressed when the mouse button is released for a square to result.

To draw a square from its center, hold down the Option and Shift keys while drawing. Make sure that *both* keys are still pressed when the mouse button is released. If you are using the Centered Rectangle tool and you press Option-Shift, the square is drawn from a corner.

Drawing rounded rectangles and squares

Sometimes, straight corners just aren't good enough. That's when it's time to create a rectangle with *rounded corners*. Why? Maybe you want your rectangles to look less "computery." A tiny bit of rounding of the corners (2 or 3 points) can do this quite easily.

To draw a rectangle with rounded corners, choose the Rounded Rectangle tool, a pop-up tool from the Rectangle tool. Click and drag with this tool as if you were drawing a standard rectangle; the only difference is that this rectangle has rounded corners. The point at which you clicked is where the corner is — if there were a corner. Of course, with rounded corners, there is no real "corner," so the computer uses an imaginary point, called the *origin point*, on-screen as the real corner. Figure 5-6 shows the origin point and its relationship to the curve of a rounded rectangle.

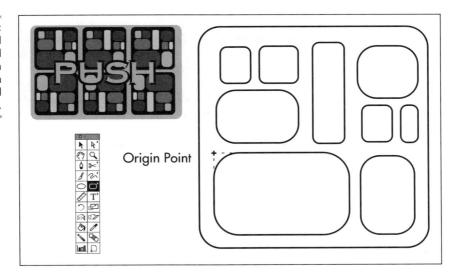

Figure 5-6:
The Rounded
Rectangle tool
and the origin
point on a
rounded
rectangle.

The *corner radius* in Illustrator is the length from that imaginary corner, the origin point, to where the curve begins, as shown in Figure 5-7. The larger the value you enter in the Corner radius field of the Rectangle dialog box, the farther the rectangle starts from the imaginary corner, and the bigger the curve is.

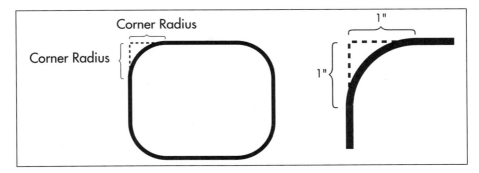

Figure 5-7:
The corner
radius.

For example, if you set the corner radius at 1 inch, the edge of the rectangle would start curving 1 inch from where a "real" corner would normally appear.

To draw a rounded rectangle from the center, press the Option key. Make sure that the Option key is pressed when the mouse button is released, or the rounded rectangle snaps back to being drawn from a corner.

To change the tool so that it *always* draws rounded rectangles from the center, double-click the Rounded Rectangle tool. When you see a plus mark in the center of the Rounded Rectangle tool, it has changed into the Centered Rounded Rectangle tool.

To draw a rounded square, hold the Shift key while dragging and do not release it until the mouse button has been released. Drawing a rounded square from its center requires that you press both the Option and Shift keys until the mouse button is released.

The *roundness* of the corners is determined by two things: the radius of the corners drawn in the last rounded rectangle, or the radius set in the General Preferences dialog box (File⇨Preferences⇨General or ⌘-Shift-D). The corner radius in the General Preferences dialog box changes each time the radius is changed by the Rounded Rectangle tool. To change the radius of the next rounded rectangle to be drawn, go to the General Preferences dialog box and enter the new corner radius value. All rounded rectangles are now drawn with this new corner radius until this value is changed.

The corner radius can also be changed by clicking with the Rounded Rectangle tool in the document, which brings up the Rectangle dialog box. Changing the value in the Corner radius field box not only changes the current rounded rectangle's corner radius, but also changes the radius in the General Preferences box and makes all subsequently drawn rounded rectangles have this corner radius until the radius is changed again by either method.

One cautionary note to all this rounding of corners: if the corner radius is more than one half the length of either the length or width of the rectangle, the rectangle will appear to have perfectly round ends on at least two sides. If the corner radius is more than one half the length of both the length or width of the rectangle, then the rectangle will be a circle!

You are limited to a maximum of a 4320-point corner radius, which works out to 5 feet. The largest rectangle you can create has a 10-foot length (the size of the Illustrator Pasteboard). So a 10-foot square with a 5-foot radius is another circle. Who ever said that Adobe wasn't clever?

If you have a rectangle with straight corners and you want it to have rounded corners, neither of the preceding methods will work. Instead, you must choose Filter⇨Stylize⇨Round Corners, which brings up the Round Corners dialog box. In this dialog box, shown in Figure 5-8, enter the value of the corner radius you would like for the existing rectangle. Using this filter allows you to change straight corner rectangles to rounded corner rectangles, not rounded corner rectangles to straight corner rectangles. Using this filter does not affect rectangles that already have rounded corners.

Furthermore, this filter cannot change corners that have been rounded with either the Rounded Rectangle tool or by previous use of the Round Corners dialog box. Using this dialog box affects corners that are *not* round. Figure 5-8 shows the Round Corners filter applied to various rectangles and the results.

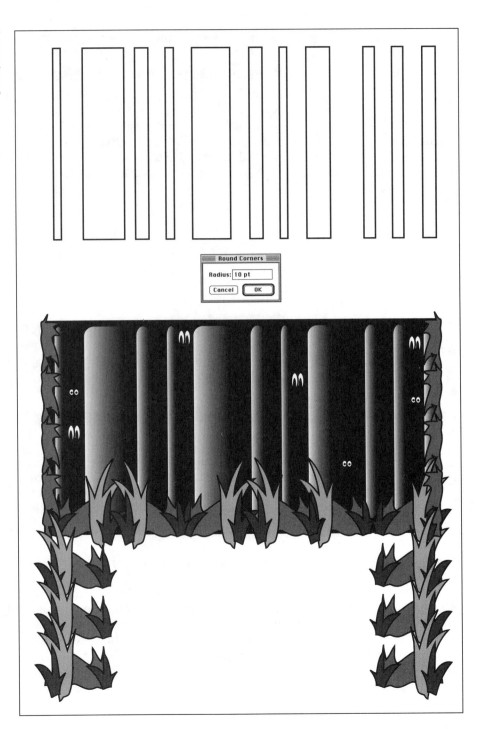

Figure 5-8:
The Round Corners filter and its results.

How a corner radius *really* works

Now for all you geometry buffs, this is the real way that this whole corner radius business works: The width of any circle is called the *diameter* of that circle. Half the diameter is the *radius* of the circle, as shown in the accompanying figure. If you create a circle with a radius of 1 inch, the circle actually has a width (diameter) of 2 inches. Put this 2-inch circle into the corner of the rectangle, as in the next figure, and the curve of the circle matches the curve of the rounded rectangle that has a corner radius of 1 inch. Huh?

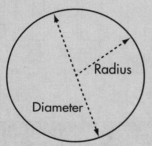 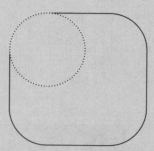

To realistically determine the way a round corner will look, use the method that measures the distance from the imaginary corner to the place where the curve starts.

 The program has a neat intuitive feature here: If you are in the Rectangle dialog box and enter a value of 0 in the Corner Radius text field, the Rounded Rectangle tool is replaced by the standard Rectangle tool in the toolbox. If a value greater than 0 is entered, the Rounded Rectangle tool takes over that slot in the toolbox.

Rounding corners the other way

What if you want your corners to round "in" instead of out? Well, it would seem that you are initially out of luck, for Illustrator doesn't provide any way to automatically enter a "negative" value for corner radius values. Instead, you need to manipulate the corners manually with the Rotate tool. The following steps explain how to create a reverse rounded rectangle, as you can see in Figure 5-9.

Figure 5-9:
The process of creating a reverse rounded rectangle.

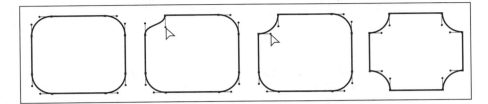

STEPS: Creating a Reverse Rounded Rectangle

Step 1. Choose File⇨Preferences⇨General and set the corner radius to **.25"**. Draw a rounded rectangle that is about 3 inches wide by 1 inch tall.

Step 2. Select the rightmost point on the left side of the rounded rectangle with the Direct Selection tool (hollow arrow). One direction point appears, sticking out to the left.

Step 3. Using the Rotate tool, click the anchor point once to set the origin. Click the direction point again and drag it down below the anchor point. Press the Shift key to ensure that the direction line is perfectly vertical and then release the mouse button.

Step 4. Select the topmost point on the left side with the Direct Selection tool. A direction point appears, sticking out of this anchor point straight up.

Step 5. Using the Rotate tool, click the anchor point once to set the origin. Click the direction point again and drag it to the right of the anchor point. Press the Shift key to ensure that the direction line is perfectly horizontal and then release the mouse button.

Step 6. Repeat this process for each of the corners. After you get the hang of it, the points start flying into position almost by themselves. Your reverse rounded rectangle should look something like the one in Figure 5-9.

Drawing ovals and circles

Drawing ovals and circles is *almost* as easy as drawing rectangles and squares. You can create a wide variety of ovals and squares in Illustrator. To draw an oval, choose the Oval tool, click, and drag diagonally. The outline of an oval forms, and when the mouse button is released, an oval appears on-screen.

Ovals, like rectangles, have four anchor points, but the anchor points on an oval are at the top, bottom, left, and right of the oval. The anchor points on a rectangle are on the corners.

Drawing an oval is harder than drawing a rectangle because the point or origin on an oval is outside the oval. With a rectangle, the point of origin corresponds to either a corner of the rectangle, which also happens to be an anchor point, or the center of the rectangle. On an oval, there are no corners. This means that clicking and dragging does not align the top or bottom, or left or right, but one of the 45° curves to the origin point (an *arc*). Figure 5-10 shows that the top of the curve extends above the origin point; the bottom of the curve extends below the origin point; the right edge extends to the right of the origin point; and the left edge extends to the left of the origin point. More detailed (and fairly unnecessary) math is available at the end of this section.

Figure 5-10:
The curves of an oval
extend beyond the
boundaries of the
dragged area.

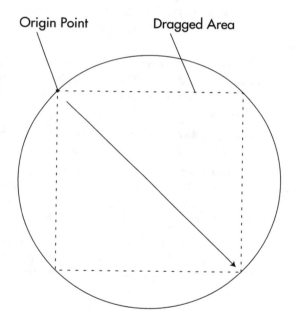

Origin Point   Dragged Area

Drawing an oval from its "corner" is a difficult task when the top, bottom, left, and right edges of the oval need to be at a specific location. On the other hand, tracing oval objects is easier because clicking and dragging on the edge of an existing oval object results in a close-to-perfect match (see Figure 5-11).

For easier tracing of circles, change the constrain angle (File➪General Preferences) to 45°. Now you can place the cursor on the top, bottom, or sides of the circle, and drag horizontally or vertically for a perfect fit. This technique doesn't work for ovals because the oval will be angled at 45° if drawn this way.

Figure 5-11:
Tracing a dimmed EPS image with the Rectangle and Oval tools.

STEPS: **Tracing an EPS Image with Basic Shapes**

Step 1. Place the Horses/snowman file from the Artwork folder on the *Macworld Illustrator Bible 5.0/5.5* CD-ROM. Choose Window⇨Show Layers. In the Layers palette, double-click Layer 1 and check the Dim EPS images option.

Step 2. Use the Rectangle tool to trace the frame of the picture, the walls, and the pieces of the snowman's arms. Place the cursor in a corner of the object to be traced and drag towards the opposite corner. Use the Rotate tool to rotate the arms. For the hat, choose File⇨General Preferences (⌘-K) and change the constrain angle to **14°**. Trace the hat and brim at this angle and then change the constrain angle back to **0°**.

Step 3. Use the Oval tool in the same way as the Rectangle tool to trace the snowman circles, the eyes, nose, mouth, snowballs, and snow drifts. If you can't see an entire circle, such as with most of the snow drifts and the bottom section of the snowman, just estimate.

To draw from the center of an oval, press the Option key and drag. As long as you are holding down the Option key when the mouse button is released, the oval uses the initial click as the origin point, and the oval is drawn from its center.

To change the Oval tool so that it *always* draws ovals from the center, double-click the Oval tool, and it changes to the Centered Oval Tool (an oval with a plus sign in its center). Double-clicking the tool again transforms it back to the standard Oval tool.

Clicking without dragging with the Oval tool brings up the Oval dialog box, shown in Figure 5-12, where you can enter any value for the width and height of your oval. The oval is drawn from the upper left arc. Entering identical values results in a circle. Option-clicking brings up the same dialog box, but the oval is now drawn from the center instead of the left arc.

To draw a perfect circle, hold down the Shift key as you drag; the oval has equal width and height, making it a circle. Make sure that the Shift key is pressed when the mouse button is released; otherwise, the oval loses its equal proportions. To draw a circle from the center with the Oval tool, hold down both the Option and Shift keys and drag diagonally.

Ovals are drawn from the upper lefthand corner and extend about 20 percent of the total height above the origin point and about 20 percent of the total width to the left of the origin point. It's not just a coincidence that the right edge and bottom also extend 20 percent past the release point. The way this works out in mathematics (numerophobics should skip ahead to the next section now) is that the height and width of the oval will be the square root of 2 (about 1.414) times the height and width of the "box" that is dragged from corner to corner.

Figure 5-12:
The Oval dialog box.

Creating an entire illustration

To create the illustration in Figure 5-13, I used only rectangles and ovals. Through a creative use of fills, the illustration comes alive.

Figure 5-13:
An illustration drawn with rectangles and ovals only.

STEPS: Drawing the Juggler with Rectangles and Ovals

Step 1. Change the Paint Style to a fill of None and a stroke of 1 point black in the Paint Style palette.

Step 2. Using the Oval tool, drag to create the juggler's body and then his head (see Figure 5-14).

Step 3. To tilt back the juggler's head, select the "head" oval and double-click the Rotate tool. Then enter a value of **30°**, which angles the head back.

Step 4. Next, create one of the rings by pressing the Shift key and dragging to create a perfect circle.

Step 5. Duplicate the circles by pressing the Option key and dragging one of the circles to a new location. As long as the Option key is pressed when you release the mouse button, the circle is duplicated rather than moved.

Step 6. Draw a much smaller circle for one of the balls the juggler is balancing on his head. Option-copy the balls in the same way you copied the rings.

Step 7. Option-copy two more ball-sized circles to create hands, the white area of the eye, and the mouth.

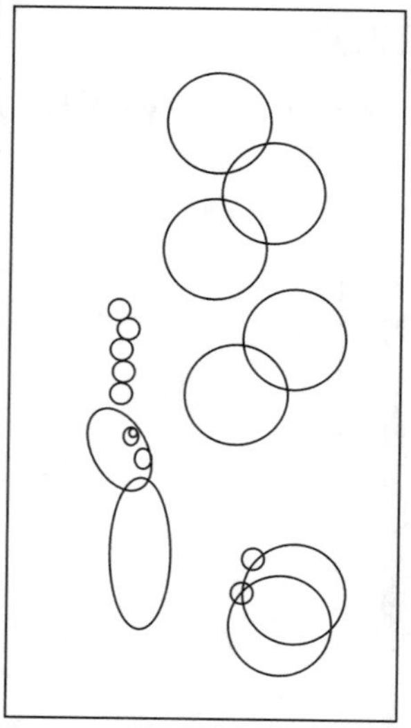

Figure 5-14: Using the Oval tool.

Step 8. Choose File⇨General Preferences (⌘-K) and change the constrain angle to **45°**.

Step 9. Using the Rectangle tool, create first the top part of the hat and then the rim of the hat (see Figure 5-15). The pieces will automatically be angled at 45°.

Step 10. Change the constrain angle back to **0°** and draw both arms. They may need to be rotated individually, depending on the location of the rings.

Step 11. Draw the rectangular background and select Arrange⇨Send To Back (⌘-minus sign).

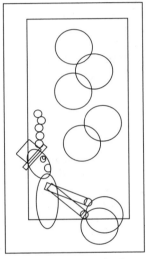

Figure 5-15: Using the Rectangle tool.

Step 12. Select individual paths and fill them with different colors and gradients.

Creating Cool Shapes

Although it is just loads of fun to create more and more ovals, rectangles, and rounded rectangles, sooner or later you're gonna get bored. There are other, dare I say, more interesting shapes that you can create automatically by using filters.

Filters are discussed in Chapters 15–19.

Like most of the filters in Illustrator, the two filters discussed here, Star and Polygon, don't do anything you couldn't have done without them, but they help you create the shapes in an easier and more accurate way. The Polygon and Star filters are located under the Create submenu (Filter⇨Create). Unfortunately, creating a perfect five-point star is anything but simple with Illustrator's standard tools (in the case of the five-point star, the Pen tool would be the best choice). With the Star filter, however, it's as easy as specifying the number of points in the star and specifying the size of the star. You get a perfect star every time.

The main difference between creating a shape with a filter and creating a rectangle, rounded rectangle, or an oval is that shapes created with Filter⇨Create are *equilateral*. For those of you without a dictionary handy, that means that all the shapes have sides of equal length. Any shape created with these filters, whether a star or a polygon, has segments that are the same length. For example, a four-sided polygon is *always* a square. A three-sided triangle is an equilateral triangle, with all three sides an equal length.

Creating polygons

Polygons are created by choosing Filter⇨Create⇨Polygon. The Create Polygon dialog box appears, displayed in Figure 5-16, where you can enter the number of sides and the radius of the polygon. The radius is the distance from the center of the polygon to the corners of the polygon. For even-sided shapes (4, 6, 8, 10 sides, and so on), the radius is half the width of the object, from one corner to the opposite corner. For odd-sided shapes, the radius is *not* half the width of the object, but instead can *only* be measured by going from one corner point to the center.

The maximum number of sides on the polygon that you can create with the Polygon filter is 4000. Of course, at that point the polygon is pretty much a circle. The fewest sides a polygon can have is 3, which happens to be a triangle.

Polygons created with the Polygon filter always appear in the center of the document window. To experiment with a polygon, try adding the barn to the snow scene in Figure 5-11. Just follow these steps.

STEPS:	**Adding a Polygon to the Snow Scene**
Step 1.	To add a barn to the background of the snow scene, select Filter⇨Create⇨Polygon. Type in **6** for the number of sides and **1.5"** for the radius. These measurements create a hexagon, but the top half is pretty much the shape of the barn. You'll hide the bottom half a little later.

Step 2. Choose the Pen tool and click the top of the hexagon. Press the Shift key and click about 1 inch above there to create a post for a weathervane.

Step 3. Click the Pen tool again to tell Illustrator you are done with the first line segment and then click about ½ inch to the right of the line segment and a little below the top. Press the Shift key and click about 1 inch to the left. You have now completed the weathervane.

Figure 5-16: Various polygons created with the settings in the Create Polygon dialog box.

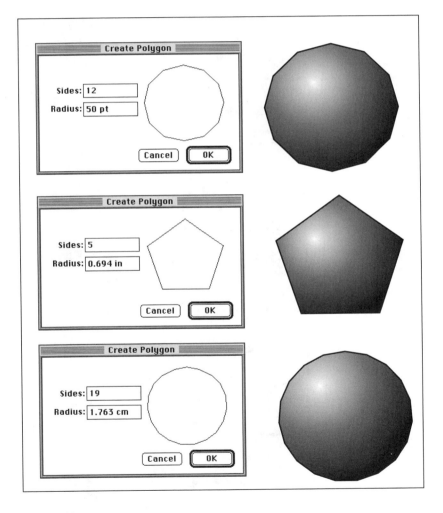

Creating stars

Stars, like the ones in Figure 5-17, are created by selecting Filter⇨Create⇨Stars. The Create Star dialog box appears, where you can now determine how many points you want on the star and what the radius of the tips and the inside corners of the stars will be.

Figure 5-17:
Various stars created with the settings in the Create Star dialog box.

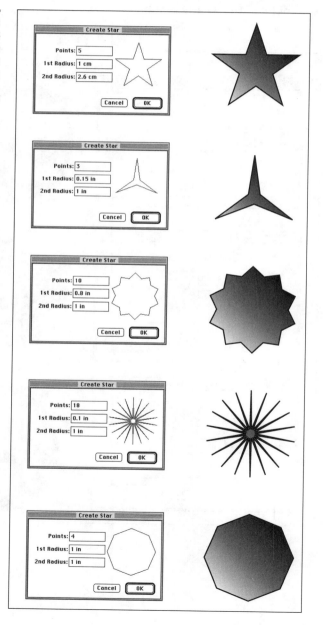

The number of points you enter is relevant to how many *tips* there are on the star, not the number of anchor points. Actually, the number of anchor points is twice the number of tips that you specify in the Points text field. For a five-point star, you enter a **5** in the Points text field, but you actually will have 10 anchor points on the star. Stars can have up to 4000 points but must have at least 3 points.

The two radius fields represent the "innie" anchor points and the "outie" anchor points of the star. The 1st Radius option is usually for the inner anchor points, or corners; the 2nd Radius option is typically for the outer anchor points, or tips. Whichever of the two numbers is greatest will be the tips.

If the two radiuses (radii?) have equal values, the resultant star is a polygon with twice the number of sides than the number of points entered in the Point field.

Like the Polygon filter, the Star filter's radiuses represent how far the anchor points are from the center of the star. In stars with even numbers of points, the first radius is half the distance between the innie points, and the second radius is half the distance between the outie points. With stars with odd numbers of points, the distance between the innie point and the corresponding outie point is one half of both radius values added together.

In stars with odd numbers of points, entering a larger number in the 2nd Radius box results in an "upside down" star, where the center point is at the bottom center of the star, instead of the top center.

The following steps tell you how to create different stars in the snowman's sky (see Figure 5-18).

Figure 5-18:
Adding stars to the winter scene.

STEPS:	Drawing the Sky

Step 1.   To create different stars across the sky, choose Filter⇨Create⇨Star. In the Create Star dialog box, enter **4** for the number of points, **.02"** for the first radius, and **.2"** for the 2nd radius. Choose Filter⇨Star (⌘-Shift-E) a few more times to create more four-pointed stars.

Step 2.   Press the Option key and select Filter⇨Star. When the Option key is pressed, the Last Filter dialog box appears. In the dialog box, enter **5** for the number of points and keep the radiuses the same. Create a few other different stars by pressing the Option key, selecting Filter⇨Star, and changing the measurements.

Step 3.   Using the Selection tool, move the stars around evenly throughout the top (sky) of the illustration.

Step 4.   Select all the stars by clicking each of them while holding down the Shift key. Choose Filter⇨Object⇨Rotate. Type in **90** in the angle field and check the Random check box. Click OK, and all the stars rotate a random amount. The illustration should look something like the one in Figure 5-18.

Angling basic shapes

Normally, when you draw a rectangle or another basic shape, it appears to be oriented with the document and the document window. For instance, the bottom of a square is parallel to the bottom of the document window.

But what if you want to draw shapes that are all angled at 45° on the page? Well, one possibility is to rotate them after they are drawn. Better than this alternative, however, is the ability to set up your document so that every new shape is automatically angled.

The angle of the shapes is dependent on the *constrain angle*. Normally, the constrain angle is 0°, where all shapes appear to align evenly with the borders of the document. To change the constrain angle, choose File⇨Preferences⇨General and enter a new value in the Constrain Angle text field inside the General Preferences dialog box. Figure 5-19 shows an illustration with the constrain angle changed several times.

When you are done drawing these angled shapes, make sure that you change the constrain angle back to 0°, or all new shapes will be created at the altered constrain angle.

Figure 5-19:
Shapes drawn
with different
constrain
angles.

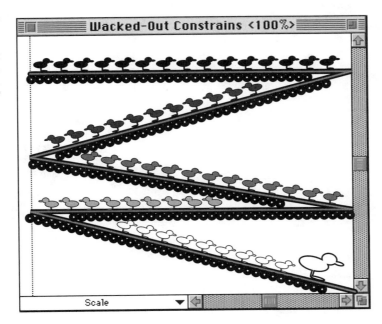

Filling and Stroking Shapes

One of the most powerful capabilities of Illustrator is its capability to color objects. In Adobe Illustrator, you can color both the fill and the stroke of the paths you have created.

Fills

The *fill* of an object is the color inside the shape. If a path is closed, the fill exists only on the inside of the path. If the path is open (meaning that it has two end points), the fill exists between an imaginary line drawn from end point to end point and the path itself. Fills in open paths can provide some very interesting results when the path crosses itself, or the imaginary line crosses the path. Figure 5-20 shows an example of fills in open and closed paths and how the paths appear in Artwork mode. For text, the fill is the color of the text. Fills do not appear in Artwork mode, only in Preview mode. Depending on the complexity of the path and the type of fill, Illustrator may refuse to preview the fill and will automatically switch to Artwork mode.

Fills can be a number of different types, including white, black, a tint of black, process colors, custom colors, patterns, or gradients. The fill of an object can also be none, where the fill is transparent. This is useful when the stroke of an object is to be the visible part, and the inside is transparent.

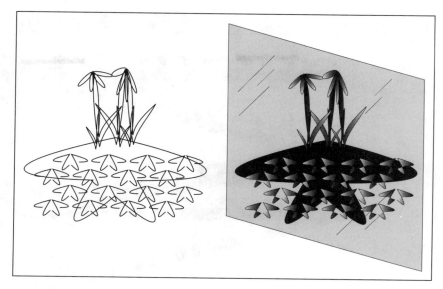

Figure 5-20: Fills in open and closed paths (right) and how the paths appear in Artwork mode.

Strokes

The *stroke* of an object is made up of three parts: its color, weight, and style. Strokes appear where there are paths, or around the edges of type. Like fills, any one path or object may have only one type of stroke on it; the color, weight, and style of the stroke are consistent throughout the length of the path or the entire text object.

The color of a stroke is similar to the colors available to fills. Colors for strokes may be white, black, a tint of black, process colors, custom colors, or patterns. The stroke of an object can also be none, where the stroke is transparent. When the stroke is set to none, then the object is said to have no stroke. Strokes cannot display patterns in Preview mode. Strokes cannot be filled with gradients, either.

The weight of a stroke is how thick the stroke is. On a path, the stroke is centered on that path, with half the thickness of the stroke on one side of the path and half the thickness on the other side of the path. Strokes can be anywhere from 0 to 1000 points thick.

The style of a stroke consists of several parts, including the cap style, join style, miter limit, and dash pattern (see the "Stroke attributes" section later in this chapter). The *cap style* is the way that the ends of a stroke look and can be either butt cap, rounded cap, or projected cap. The *join style* is the way that corner points on paths appear when stroked and can be either mitered join, rounded join, or beveled join. Figure 5-21 shows examples of the cap styles and join styles.

The *miter limit* is the length at which miter joins are cropped. Normally, the dash pattern for a stroke is solid, but various dash patterns can be created for different effects. Figure 5-22 shows different miter limits on different corners.

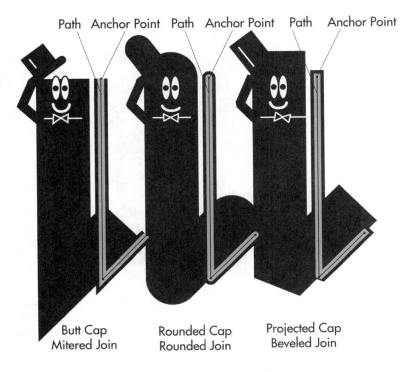

Path Anchor Point Path Anchor Point Path Anchor Point

Figure 5-21:
The three different cap
and join styles for strokes.

Butt Cap
Mitered Join

Rounded Cap
Rounded Join

Projected Cap
Beveled Join

Figure 5-22:
A sampling of all the
different cap styles, join
styles, miter limits, and dash
patterns for strokes.

Combining strokes and fills

Many times, the paths in Illustrator require both fills and strokes. When you give both a fill and a stroke to a single path, the stroke knocks out the fill at the edges of the path by one half the weight of the stroke. Figure 5-23 demonstrates this.

Figure 5-23:
Strokes knock out fill by one half the weight of the stroke.

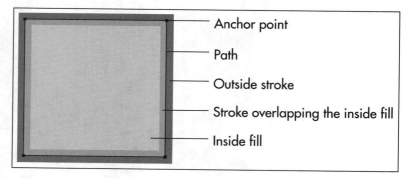

- Anchor point
- Path
- Outside stroke
- Stroke overlapping the inside fill
- Inside fill

 A method for fixing this problem is to copy the path and paste it in front, removing the frontmost path's stroke. The filled path, on top of the stroked path, knocks out the "inner" half of the stroke. This technique is discussed in detail in Chapter 20.

Using the Paint Style Palette _____

To give objects in Illustrator fills and strokes, you usually use the Paint Style palette, shown in Figure 5-24. The Paint Style palette works in two ways: It can be used to change the current Paint Style attributes of selected objects to something else, and it lists the current Paint Style attributes of an object.

To view the Paint Style palette, choose Object⇨Paint Style (⌘-I) or choose Window⇨Show Paint Style. To hide the Paint Style palette, click the close box in the upper lefthand corner of the palette or select Window⇨Hide Paint Style. When the Paint Style palette is visible and no text fields in it are selected, ⌘-I also hides the Paint Style palette. The Paint Style palette can be moved around your screen by clicking the title bar and dragging. The Paint Style palette cannot be dragged off the screen.

To change the Paint Style attributes of an object, first select it and then make the changes in the Paint Style palette. If the Auto check box is checked, those changes occur automatically; if not, the Apply button must be clicked.

Color Swatch Panel Main Panel Show/Hide Display

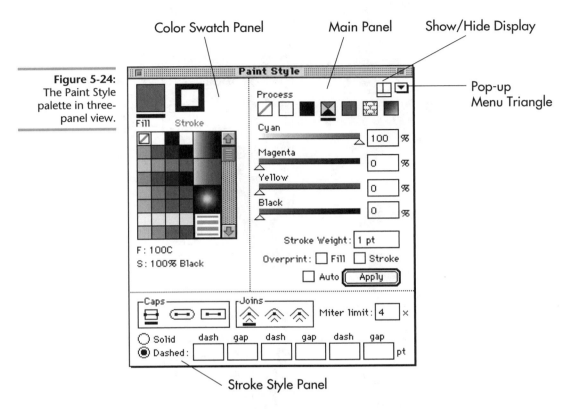

Figure 5-24:
The Paint Style
palette in three-
panel view.

Pop-up
Menu Triangle

Stroke Style Panel

To view the current attributes of an object, select the object. The Paint Style palette's information changes to accurately reflect how the object is "painted." Figure 5-25 shows three different paths with different Paint Style attributes. The fourth illustration at the bottom of the figure has different paths with different fills and strokes, so question marks appear in the Fill and Stroke squares. If either the Fill or Stroke squares are changed at this point, all objects selected will have the new fill or stroke. Changing the fill for several objects does not affect the stroke on any of them; changing the stroke for several objects does not affect the fill on any of them.

The many faces of the Paint Style palette

The Paint Style palette is the most flexible palette I've used in *any* program. You can view the panel in four different ways, depending on which of the three panels you want to see.

The left panel is the Color Swatch panel, where different preset color swatches are available. The right panel is the Main panel, where most choices for color and fill and stroke type are available. The bottom panel is the Stroke Style panel, where the different options for stroke styles are available.

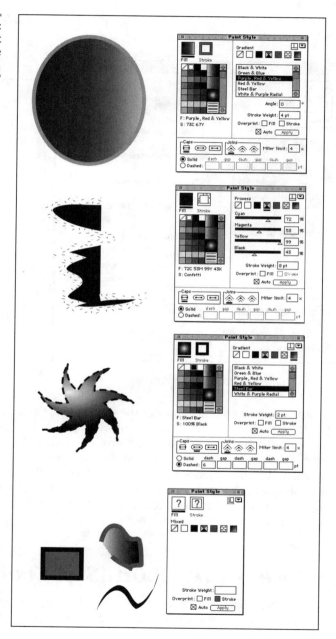

Figure 5-25: Paths with different Paint Style attributes.

The default view of the Paint Style palette is the three-panel view, where all three panels of the Paint Style palette are visible. This view takes up the most space on-screen, and it is the only view where you can see the Stroke Style panel. The two-panel view displays the Color Swatch panel and the Main panel. The third view is the Color Swatch panel view, which shows only the Color Swatch panel. The last view is the Main panel view, which displays only the Main panel.

To change the views of the panels, click and hold on the little triangle in the upper righthand corner of the palette and then drag over and out to the right, where a pop-up menu appears. On this pop-up menu, you can choose any one of the four available views.

You can also choose different views by clicking different sections of the Show/Hide display to the left of the pop-up menu triangle. The current view is made of white boxes with black outlines. Any areas that are currently not being displayed are shown as gray boxes with darker gray borders.

When the Paint Style palette is displayed, it always appears the way it was viewed last. For instance, if you were viewing the Paint Style palette in the two-panel view and closed it (hid it), then the next time it was opened, even if the computer was shut down between sessions, the Paint Style palette would be displayed in two-panel view.

The Stroke and Fill squares

When using the Paint Style palette, you can make changes to either the stroke or fill, but not to both at the same time.

In the top section of the Color Swatch panel, there are two squares, the Fill square and the Stroke square. The Stroke square has a heavy stroke around it. There is an underline under the square that is currently being used. To change from Fill to Stroke, click the Stroke square. To change from Stroke to Fill, click the Fill square.

No matter which view you use, the two Fill and Stroke squares are always visible. If the Main Panel is the only panel visible, the Fill and Stroke squares are at the top of it. Every view also has the Stroke Weight text field. Although it normally appears in the Main panel, if only the Color Swatch panel is showing, the Stroke Weight text field also appears at the bottom of that field.

The panel selectors, the pop-up menu, and the diagram of the displayed panels appear in all views of the Paint Style palette, as well.

The Apply button and the Auto check box

In the lower righthand corner of the Paint Style palette is the Auto check box. When this check box is checked, any changes in the Paint Style palette take place instantly to any selected objects. When the Auto check box is selected (has an X inside it), the Apply button remains dimmed.

When Auto is not checked, the Apply button becomes available. Changes in the Paint Style palette do not affect selected objects until the Apply button is clicked. You can also achieve the results of the Apply button by pressing Return or Enter on the keyboard. The Apply button can be clicked only when changes have been made to options in the Paint Style palette.

The Main panel

The Main panel of the Paint Style palette contains all the major options for fill and stroke colors. Along the top of the Main panel are seven boxes, shown in Figure 5-26, each with a different type of color for fills and strokes. When the Stroke option is chosen, there are only six boxes because strokes can't have gradients. The box that is currently selected has an underline under it, similar to the underlines under the Stroke and Fill squares. Only one of the seven boxes can be chosen at one time.

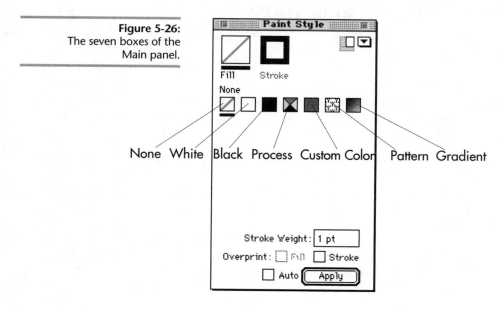

Figure 5-26:
The seven boxes of the
Main panel.

The first box has a slash in it, which corresponds to "none." Fills painted with the None option are transparent, while strokes painted with None are considered to have "no stroke." Objects and paths can have both no stroke and no fill and still exist in your illustration. (Of course, they won't print. . . .) Paths with no fill or stroke are used for several different things, including masks, pattern and graph design borders, and pathfinder shapes.

The second box is the White option. When this box is chosen for either a fill or a stroke, the result is 0% color in that area. White is different from None in that anything colored with white is opaque. When an object with a white fill is placed on top of any other object, the white object obscures anything underneath it. Also, an object with a fill has the fill reduced by half the width of a white stroke on that object. When the White box is chosen, a *slider bar* appears, allowing you to make, well, a darker white. A triangle (*slider*) is at the far left of the bar, and the number to the right in the text field is 0%. Any number greater than 0 results in a shade of black, even though you initially chose the white square. If you deselect the object after changing the slider to a higher position, the next time the object is selected, the Black box will be underlined, not the White box. When entering a value in the text field, you must press Return or Enter for the value to be accepted. Moving the sliders, though, is instantaneous.

The following steps show you how to add color to the snowman in the winter scene.

STEPS:	Coloring the Snow and the Snowman
Step 1.	To color the snow and the snowman, select the snowman and the round drifts of snow with the Selection tool.
Step 2.	Choose the Fill square and click the White box in the Main panel.
Step 3.	Select the Stroke square and click the None box in the Main panel.

The third box is the Black option, and choosing this box allows you to specify exactly what tint of black (gray) you would like, from 0% (which happens to be white) to 100%. When the box is first selected, the slider on this slider bar is at the far right, and the text field reads 100%. Entering a value less than 100 results in that particular tint. If the value entered is 0, then the next time the object is selected, the White box is highlighted. When more than one object is selected and all have a tint of black, the triangle slider does not show up, and the text field will be empty. In this case, the Stroke or Fill square, whichever is underlined, has a question mark inside it. This happens only because some of the objects selected have *different* tints of black. Entering a value in the text field changes all selected objects to that tint. Clicking once on the left end of the slider bar places the triangle at the left end of the slider bar and changes the number in the text field to 0%, transforming all selected objects to white strokes or fills, whichever is chosen. Another click repositions the slider to a different location.

Now you can add more color to the winter scene by following these steps.

STEPS: **Coloring the Hat and the Barn**

Step 1. Select the two pieces of the hat with the Selection tool and move them on to the head of the snowman.

Step 2. Press the Shift key and select the barn, the eyes, and the mouth.

Step 3. Change the fill to black, and the stroke to none.

The fourth box is made of four different triangles, each a different color. This is the Process box, with four different slider bars. Each of the slider bars represents a different process color: cyan, magenta, yellow, and black. These four process colors correspond to the four process colors used in printing. Different combinations of these four colors result in a large variety of colors, covering about half the colors that the human eye can see. Various combinations of these colors can closely represent Pantone colors, a spot color system that is widely used in the printing industry. For instance, to get a bright red color, set the cyan and black settings to 0%, and the magenta and yellow settings to 100%. For a dark forest green, change the cyan setting to 100%, the magenta setting to 0%, and the yellow and black settings to 50%. 0% of all four process colors results in process white, which is different than regular white mainly through how it relates to other colors, especially in the areas of blends, gradients, and color adjustments through the color filters.

The fifth box is the Custom Color box. A custom color is a color that is set up to print as either a spot color, a color on a separate plate, or a color to be split into process colors when printed. If process color printing is to be used, the advantage to using custom colors instead of process colors is that colors can remain much more consistent throughout the illustration if only custom colors are used. When the Custom Color box is selected (underlined), a scroll box appears, listing all the custom colors in the document. To choose a custom color, click the color of your choice with the cursor or type the first few letters of the custom color to select it. When a custom color is chosen, a triangle appears on the slider bar beneath the scroll box. The position of the triangle represents the *tint* of the custom color. At 0%, the color resembles white, in that it will look white and will be opaque, but according to Illustrator, the color is still just that custom color with a tint of 0%. Double-clicking a custom color brings up the Custom Color dialog box.

Follow the steps to add color to the stars in the winter scene.

STEPS: Coloring the Stars

Step 1. Select all the stars with the Selection tool.

Step 2. Change the Fill square to the gold custom color and the Stroke square to none.

The sixth box is the Pattern box, used for giving a pattern to a stroke or a fill. Patterns given to strokes appear in Preview mode as solid gray, although the width of the stroke is represented accurately. After the Pattern box is selected, a scroll box appears, listing all the patterns in the document. To choose a pattern, click the pattern name of your choice with the cursor or type the first few letters of the pattern's name to select it. There are no tint options for patterns; the tint of the pattern is determined when it is created. I discuss creating and modifying patterns in Chapter 13.

Even the barn can be a different color if you follow these steps.

STEPS: Coloring the Walls

Step 1. Select the two walls of the barn with the Selection tool.

Step 2. Change the Fill square to the brick pattern and the Stroke square to none.

Step 3. Deselect the top wall by Shift-clicking it with the Selection tool.

Step 4. Double-click the Scale tool. In the Scale dialog box, type **300** in the Uniform text field. Uncheck the Object check box and click OK. This step changes the size of the bricks in the lower wall so that they are three times the size of the ones in the back, producing the illusion that the lower wall is closer.

The seventh box is the Gradient box. Only fills — not strokes — of objects can have gradients as attributes. (After the Stroke option is chosen, only six boxes appear, all except the Gradient box.) After the Gradient box is selected for a fill, a list of gradients appears in a scroll box. Select a gradient by clicking its name or typing the first few letters of the gradient. You cannot change the tint of a gradient; instead you must change the gradient itself in the Gradient palette. To quickly access the Gradient palette, double-click the gradient you want to modify and the Gradient palette appears, with that gradient selected. Gradients are explained in detail in Chapter 12.

STEPS: Coloring the Background and the Sign

Step 1.   Select the background rectangle with the Selection tool.

Step 2.   Change the Fill square to the black-and-white gradient, change the angle to 90°, and change the Stroke square to none.

Step 3.   Select the sign and change the Fill square to the steel bar gradient with an angle of 160°.

STEPS: Finishing Touches

Step 1.   Select the snow drift ovals and choose Arrange⇨Bring To Front.

Step 2.   Select the three snowman circles and select Arrange-Bring To Front (⌘-plus sign).

Step 3.   Select the brick wall, the hat, and the sign and Bring To Front.

Step 4.   Select the horizontal path and select Filter⇨Stylize⇨Add Arrowheads. Click OK.

Step 5.   Press the Option key and choose Filter⇨Add Arrowheads. In the Add Arrowheads dialog box, check the Start button and select arrowhead number 19.

Step 6.   To give the illustration more interest, add some custom gradients to the background and white radial gradients to the snow. Figure 5-27 show the final illustration. The color insert shows the final illustration, as well.

Overprinting options are available only in the Main panel. If these boxes are available, you may choose to overprint a stroke, fill, or both. Overprint is available only when the Black, Process, Custom Color, or Gradient boxes are selected. When Overprint is checked, the object does not knock out anything directly under or above it but, instead, mixes with anything it overlaps. Overprinting is mostly useful for trapping; see Chapter 21 for more information on trapping.

Figure 5-27:
The completed
illustration.

Slider magic

Moving the sliders around can be done in so many different ways that I've devoted a small section to it. If you thought all you could do with the little triangles on the slider bars was drag them to different places, you'll be astounded by the next few paragraphs.

The most basic way to move the sliders around is by dragging them. Clicking a triangle and dragging it is beneficial because you actually see the Stroke or Fill square (whichever you have chosen) on the Paint Style palette change as you drag.

After you stop dragging the slider, you can drag the others (if you have chosen the Process box) to see what changes occur if you adjust the other sliders. Just watch the Fill or Stroke square. This process allows for much less guesswork than in previous versions of Illustrator.

When a value is entered in the text field to the right of each slider bar, the slider moves to that position. In the Process area, with its four slider bars, you can press Tab to move to the next slider bar text field and Shift-Tab to move to the preceding one.

You can move a slider much faster by clicking the slider bar where you want the slider to be. The slider instantly relocates to the position you clicked and shows the appropriate value in the text field.

To move a slider in *tiny* increments, hold down the Option key and click either side of the triangle. The triangle moves along the slider bar in 1% increments for every click. To move a slider in *small* increments, press Shift-Option and click either side of the triangle. The triangle moves along the slider bar in 5% increments for every click made with the Option and Shift keys pressed.

Now, the really amazing slider trick: When working with process colors, press the Shift key and drag the slider with the highest percentage of color. The colors on the slider bars change to show only a tint of that color, and all the sliders with a percentage of color greater than 0 move proportionally to the one being dragged.

The Color Swatch panel

The Color Swatch panel, shown in detail in Figure 5-28, is made up mainly of little squares that have *color swatches* in them. In each color swatch is a color that was created in the Main panel. Color swatches can be made from any of the seven boxes in the Main panel and from any options in those boxes. Overprinting is not part of a color swatch, nor are any stroke attributes.

Figure 5-28:
The Color Swatch panel.

There are two different types of color swatch boxes: little ones and big ones. The only difference between the different color swatch boxes is their size. Large boxes are good for patterns and gradients because they show more detail than the smaller boxes. You can put patterns and gradients in the little boxes, and most two-color gradients look fine. You can also put solid colors in the larger boxes.

To use the color swatches, first click either the Stroke or Fill squares. Then, as you pass the cursor over the color swatches, the cursor changes into an Eyedropper. Clicking a color swatch changes the selected square (Fill or Stroke) to that color.

To add a new color swatch to the existing color swatches, set up the color by using the Main panel and then drag the new color from the appropriate square, either Fill or Stroke, to an empty (white) color swatch box at the bottom of the color swatches. To see empty color swatch boxes, you may have to scroll down in the swatch listing. Technically, the swatch boxes are really never "empty"; instead, they have, at the very least, the process white color in them.

To replace an existing color swatch with a new color, drag the new color from the Fill or Stroke square to an existing color. The new color replaces the existing color.

To remove a color, hold down the Command key as you pass over the color swatches. The cursor turns into a scissors. Clicking a color swatch displays a warning box that says you cannot undo this operation! Click OK (or press Return or Enter) to delete the swatch permanently. You can delete a swatch without seeing a dialog box by pressing ⌘-Option and then clicking. To delete several colors at once, click and drag with the Command key pressed. To delete several colors without a warning dialog box, press ⌘-Option and drag across the color swatches you wish to delete. To reset the Paint Style color swatches, press ⌘-Shift and click any color swatch.

Underneath the color swatch boxes are the coolest things you'll see in Illustrator: the color information lines. One line (F:) tells you exactly what your fill is, and another line (S:) tells you what your stroke is. Process colors are specified by percentages and the first letter of the color. For instance, 100% cyan, 50% magenta, 50% yellow and 0% black would be: 100C 50M 50Y. If a process color has a value of 0%, it does not appear in the color information line. Custom colors, gradients, and patterns appear by displaying the name of the color, gradient, or pattern.

Stroke attributes

At the bottom of the three-panel view of the Paint Style palette (and visible only in this view, no others) is the Stroke Style panel, which contains information about the stroke attributes for the selected paths and objects.

The weight of the stroke is always changed at either the bottom of the Main panel or, if that is not visible, in the Color Swatch panel. Everything else relevant to strokes is changed in the Stroke Style panel.

In the Caps box, there are three different types of end caps. Caps apply only to the end points on open paths. The first cap is a butt cap (wouldn't a pair of modest boxers have been just as suitable?), which is a flat end of the stroke, cut off perpendicularly to the direction the path is traveling at its end point. The second type of cap is a rounded cap, which is a smooth, round cap whose farthest distance from the end point is half the weight of the stroke. The last type of cap is the projected cap, named so because the end of the cap projects from the end point half the width of the stroke and is squared off. Each path can have only one type of end cap on both ends.

There are three different types of joins in the Join box. Joins apply to corner anchor points *only*. The first type of join is a mitered join, where the edges of the stroke meet at a point. The next type of join is a rounded join, where instead of meeting in a point, stroked edges meet in a smooth curve. The last type of join is the beveled join, where the edges appear to have been mitered but then chopped off. Each path can have only one type of miter for all its joins.

The Miter limit text field shows how far a miter can go past its corner point, relative to the width of the corner point. If the end of the miter exceeds the set miter limit, the miter is cropped off near the corner point. The Miter limit setting can never be more than 500, and it can never be more than the stroke width times the Miter limit exceeding 1800 points. The miter limit affects all the corner points on an entire path.

The bottom of the Stroke Style panel contains information about whether the stroke is solid or dashed. If dashed, the length of the dashes and the strokes can be specified.

 Strokes are covered completely in Chapter 20.

Drawing and Manipulating Paths

In This Chapter

- Drawing shapes with the Brush tool
- Drawing with the Freehand tool
- Using the Pen tool
- Learning the laws of the Pen tool
- Selecting, moving, and deleting entire paths
- Selecting, moving, and deleting portions of paths
- Understanding foreground and background
- Grouping and ungrouping paths
- Using the Group Selection tool

Drawing Paths in Illustrator

The most challenging way to create paths is to draw them with one of the drawing tools. The Brush tool, the Freehand tool, and the Pen tool are Illustrator's primary drawing tools, shown in Figure 6-1. Using the Brush tool is the easiest, but also the most limiting, unless you use it with a pressure-sensitive tablet. The Freehand tool is simple to use to create paths, but the results can be questionable. The Pen tool is the most difficult to use, but the results from it can be better than from either the Brush or the Freehand tools.

Each drawing tool has something it does better than the others, as well as having its own limitations, too. However tempting it may be, do not ignore any of these tools because you think that another tool can perform the same function. The one tool that most people avoid is the Pen tool. Mastering Illustrator becomes impossible when you avoid this tool.

Figure 6-1:
Illustrator's drawing
tools.

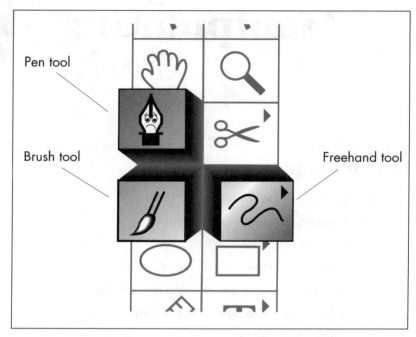

Pen tool

Brush tool

Freehand tool

Hey, I won't kid you. Mastering the Pen tool is like mastering calculus: it makes no sense at first and even less sense when people explain it to you. But, like calculus, the more you use the Pen tool, the more you like it, and the more technically amazing things you can do with it. Personally, I think the Pen tool is easier to learn than calculus.

 Understanding how the Pen tool works helps you understand not only how Illustrator works but also how PostScript and many other tools in other programs work. Adobe Photoshop has a Path tool, which is virtually identical to Illustrator's Pen tool; by understanding and using the Pen tool in Illustrator, you've already learned one of the most difficult tools to use in Photoshop.

Figure 6-2 was drawn with a combination of all three drawing tools. Throughout this chapter, you will examine how the parts of this illustration were drawn and how they were manipulated to produce the final drawing.

Figure 6-2:
This illustration
was drawn
using a
combination of
the Brush,
Freehand, and
Pen tools.

Drawing with the Brush Tool _____

In this section, you will create the grass and the horse outlines from Figure 6-2. Both can be drawn with or without a pressure-sensitive tablet — which I discuss in the "Variable widths and pressure-sensitive tablets" section later in this chapter — but you can achieve better effects with a pressure-sensitive tablet.

STEPS: Drawing the Horse and Tall Grass Outlines

Step 1.   Double-click the Brush tool and set the width to 3 points. If the variable option can be checked (if you have a pressure-sensitive tablet), make the minimum 1 point and the maximum 10 points. Change your Paint Style to a Fill of black and a Stroke of none in the Paint Style palette.

Step 2.   Using the Brush tool, draw each piece of the basic shape of the horses, as shown in Figure 6-3. The more individual pieces you draw, the easier it is to use the Brush. Long strokes are difficult to produce and aren't as appealing as shorter strokes. Don't worry about filling in the horses with color at this point. You are using the Brush tool only to create the smoothly flowing outlines of the horse. If you make a mistake, select Edit⇨Undo (⌘-Z).

Step 3. To draw the tall blades of grass, just draw a few select blade outlines to create a "clump" of grass. Drag the anchor points from the base of the clump up and outward with the Scale tool and the Option key pressed for the best effects.

Figure 6-3: Horse outlines and outlines of blades of grass created with the Brush tool.

The Brush tool is a most welcome addition to Illustrator 5.0's new tools. Coupled with the ability to preview what you are drawing, you can use the Brush tool as soon as you start the program. Just choose the tool and start drawing. A freeform path appears wherever you drag. That's all there is to it. Kinda. Figure 6-4 shows a drawing I created with the Brush tool set to a variable width with a pressure-sensitive stylus.

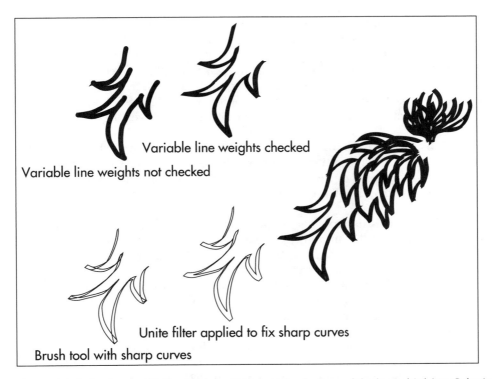

Variable line weights checked

Variable line weights not checked

Unite filter applied to fix sharp curves

Brush tool with sharp curves

Figure 6-4: Paths drawn with the Brush tool to create the feathers of the loony bird (see Color Insert).

Drawing with the Brush tool is a bit more complicated than I just explained. The most important consideration is the width of the brush stroke. The brush stroke can be as narrow as 0 points and as wide as 1,296 points.

 Although 0 is the smallest width, a brush stroke drawn with a width of 0 points actually has a width bigger than 0 points. To change the brush stroke width, double-click the Brush tool and enter a number in the Width text field.

The term *stroke* in Illustrator and *brush strokes* drawn with the Brush tool are entirely different critters. In fact, brush strokes are usually filled, not stroked. Brush strokes are made of paths that surround the edges of the stroke, and the width of the brush stroke is the distance between the path on either side of the brush stroke. Brush strokes created with the Brush tool are always closed paths. After the mouse button is released, several anchor points appear. These anchor points and their corresponding direction points shape the path.

A strange thing happens when the Brush tool is used: Paths at sharp turns and corners overlap each other, sometimes extensively. If the brush stroke is just filled, this usually isn't much of a problem. But if you wish to give the brush stroke a regular stroke, the stroke goes into the middle of the brush stroke and looks, well, bad. Of course, you don't want your art to look bad, so there is a way around this problem. Use the Unite filter on individual brush strokes that have overlapping pieces. Figure 6-4 shows how paths overlap around sharp corners and how the Unite filter removes these overlaps.

To use the Unite filter on brush strokes, draw your brush stroke with the Brush tool and then immediately select Filter⇨Pathfinder⇨Unite. All the overlapping paths magically disappear. Make sure that only one path is selected when the Unite filter is applied, or any intersecting brush strokes will be joined.

Results achieved with the Brush tool vary depending on two very important character-istics: your artistic ability and your ability to control the mouse. If you can't draw with a pencil or other forms of traditional media, there is very little possibility that using a mouse will turn you into a Michelangelo (the artist, not the turtle). If Michelangelo had to use a mouse to draw, he probably would have become a philosopher or sunk so low as to be an editor for a Macintosh magazine, constantly complaining about the ineffi-cient means by which cursors are controlled.

A mouse is *not* an intuitive drawing tool, and not being able to draw in the first place makes it even more difficult to draw with the Brush tool. So if artists have trouble with the mouse, what's the point of having the Brush tool at all? Well, instead of a mouse, you can use several types of alternative drawing devices. The best of these is a pres-sure-sensitive tablet, pictured in Figure 6-5. Trackballs with locking buttons are also good for drawing with the Brush tool (this allows more control over the direction and speed of the brush).

When you're drawing with any of the tools in Illustrator, dragging off the edge of the window causes the window to scroll, which creates a frightening effect for the uninitiated. If you don't want the window to scroll, don't let go of the mouse; instead, just drag in the opposite direction. To scroll the other way while still using a tool, drag off the other side of the window.

To help you draw more precisely, you have the option of changing the cursor from the cute little brush into a crosshair. Press the Caps Lock key (to engage it), and the cursor changes into the crosshair with a dot in the center. Press the Caps Lock key again (to release it), and the cursor returns to the brush shape. The dot at the center of the crosshair is the center of any brush stroke drawn with the Brush tool. Normally, when the cursor is in the shape of a brush, the tip is the center of the brush stroke. Some people find it easier to draw when the brush is replaced with the precise crosshair.

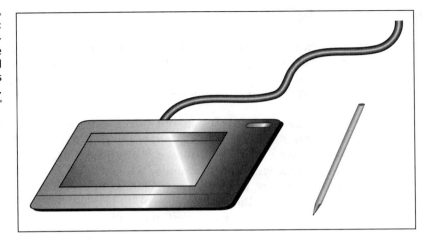

Figure 6-5:
A pressure-sensitive tablet and cordless stylus.

The best and, at the same time, the most limiting capability of the Brush tool is its consistency of width. If you make the width 18 points, the brush creates a brush stroke that is 18 points wide for the length you draw it. No other tool in Illustrator can be this precise, even the Pen tool with all its precision capabilities.

Of course, there are options that allow you to change this width. . . .

Calligraphy drawn to order

Double-clicking the Brush tool brings up the Brush dialog box, in which the little Calligraphic check box appears. If this box is checked, the Brush tool no longer creates brush strokes with even widths; instead, it creates brush strokes that vary according to the angle that they are drawn. The feathers in Figure 6-4 were created with the Calligraphic box selected.

When the Calligraphic box is checked, another box appears, asking what angle the calligraphic brush should be set to. The angle chosen depends on what is going to be drawn. To mimic hand-drawn lettering in a calligraphic style, the angle should be set to 45° (if you're left-handed, it should be set to –45°).

You can also use the Calligraphy filter in the Stylize menu of the Filters menu; however, the result achieved with the Brush tool and the Calligraphic option is much better than any possible result obtained from using the filter.

Bends and ends

Something that brush strokes and regular strokes have in common is that you can specify how the corners and ends appear. Instead of three options for each, as with strokes, there are only two options. You can't change end and corner options when calligraphic styles are chosen in the Brush dialog box.

Caps are the way the ends of each brush stroke should appear — either rounded (the default) or straight. If straight is chosen, the ends appear perpendicular to the direction of the brush stroke at its ends. When straight is chosen, the brush stroke can be a little disconcerting to draw because the ends appear rounded while you are drawing the brush stroke, but the ends are promptly cut off after the mouse button is released. The feathers in Figure 6-4 were drawn with the straight caps option chosen, while the pinwheels in Figure 6-6 were drawn with the rounded caps option chosen.

Joins can be made round (default) or straight. When the joins are set to straight, the width of the brush is usually much less at the point where the corner is straightened out. The difference between the two settings is shown in the pinwheels in Figure 6-6.

Figure 6-6:
The left pinwheel was drawn with the straight caps option chosen, while the right pinwheel was drawn with the rounded caps option chosen.

Straight Joins

Rounded Joins

Straight Joins

Rounded Joins

Variable widths and pressure-sensitive tablets

If you have a pressure-sensitive tablet — a Wacom (walk 'em) tablet, some call them, because a large majority seem to be made by Wacom — you can select the Variable check box in the Brush dialog box. If you don't have a pressure-sensitive tablet, this option is grayed out.

 Pressure-sensitive tablets are flat, rectangular devices which a special stylus is passed over. The more pressure exerted by the stylus on the tablet, the wider a brush stroke will be, providing the Variable option in the Brush dialog box is checked.

After you check the Variable option, two new text fields appear, giving you an option to specify the minimum and maximum width of the brush stroke as it is drawn. The minimum width is as narrow as the stroke can appear when you are pressing the pen as lightly as possible; the maximum width is as wide as the stroke can appear when you are pressing the pen as hard as possible. Different widths are shown in Figure 6-4, which compares fixed line weight feathers with variable line weight feathers.

 When using the Variable option, try to set the minimum and maximum widths fairly close to get the most realistic brush look for your drawings.

Drawing with the Freehand Tool ___

The Freehand tool initially seems to be a poor version of the Brush tool. Like the Brush tool, the Freehand tool draws a freeform path wherever the cursor is dragged, but instead of creating a closed path that is a certain width, the result is a single path following approximately the path you've taken with the cursor. Approximately? Well, you can get the resulting path to follow your cursor-drawn line exactly by using free-hand tolerance — but trust me, you really don't want to use this.

The Freehand tool has the unique capability to make the lines you draw with the cursor look, well, good. A swooping, uneven, jagged line that looks terrible as it is being drawn can be instantly transformed into a beautifully curved piece of artwork reminiscent of lines drawn traditionally with a French curve.

Still, the Freehand tool has some limitations: The main limitation is that, unlike the Pen tool, it is an *imprecise* path-drawing tool. It is difficult to draw a straight line with the Freehand tool. It is even more difficult to draw a shape with precise curves. The location of a path drawn with the Freehand tool is directly relevant to the direction and speed that the cursor is moving.

Using the Freehand tool

Before you use the Freehand tool for the first time, it is a good idea to change the Paint Style attributes in the Paint Style palette to a Fill of none and a Stroke of black, 1 point. Having a Fill other than none while drawing with the Freehand tool can make the results look bizarre (causing you to forget where you last left your cloth sack of miniature round balls).

To use the Freehand tool, select it from the Toolbox, click in the document window, and begin dragging the mouse. As you drag, you see a series of dots following the cursor. These dots show the approximate location of the path you have drawn. After the mouse button is released, the path of dots is transformed into a path with anchor points, all with direction lines and direction points shooting off from them. The faster you draw with the Freehand tool, the fewer points are created. The slower you draw, the more points are used to define the path.

In Figure 6-2, the tree and the short grass were both drawn with the Freehand tool.

STEPS: Drawing Grass and a Tree with the Freehand Tool

Step 1.   Select File⇨Preferences⇨General (⌘-K) and set the Freehand tolerance setting to 2, which allows for detail in the paths without making all the segments straight lines. Set the Paint Style to a Fill of green and Stroke of black, 1 point in the Paint Style palette.

Step 2.   The short grass was created by drawing three different clumps of grass (see the top of Figure 6-7) and then duplicating the clumps to create the appearance of random blades. Select the Freehand tool and drag up and down to create the blades; then drag across under the blades to connect the bottom to form a closed path. Repeat this procedure to create three or four clumps of different sizes. Be sure to change the Fill color to a slightly different green each time.

Step 3.   Using the Selection tool, click the clumps of grass and Option-drag them side by side, overlapping them slightly. Pressing the Option key duplicates the dragged clumps. Repeat this process until there are enough clumps to resemble a grassy area.

Step 4.   To create the tree, first change the Freehand tolerance setting to 7 in the General Preferences dialog box (⌘-K). Drag with the Freehand tool to create the outline of the tree branch, trunk, and roots. Connect the ends of the path to close it and change the Fill to a dark brown, keeping the Stroke black.

Step 5.   To create the textured areas of the bark on the tree, change the Fill to none and the Stroke to a dark shade of gray. Drag along the contours of the tree, which creates circles and wavy patterns.

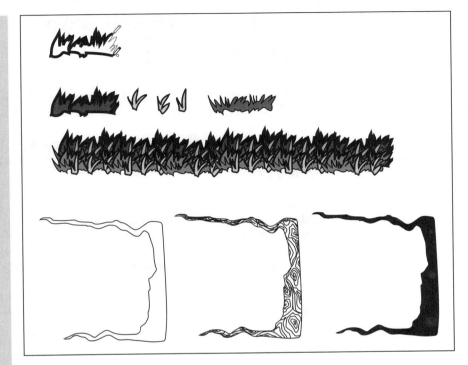

Figure 6-7: Clumps of grass and tree bark created with the Freehand tool.

Every anchor point created with the Freehand tool has two direction points shooting out of it; this means that straight-corner anchor points *cannot* be drawn with the Freehand tool. This lack of straight-corner anchor points makes constructing precise objects not only difficult, but impossible. Also, though they may appear to exist at first glance, smooth anchor points are also not created with the Freehand tool, which can be especially deceiving when the Freehand tolerance option is set to a high number, and all the anchor points look like they *have* to be smooth. Not the case. In fact, all anchor points created with the Freehand tool — except for its end points — are curved-corner points, which are anchor points with two *independent* direction points shooting out.

Normally, the Freehand tool resembles a little pencil when you are drawing with it in the document. (I guess it would look pretty silly to draw with a squiggle, the shape of the tool in the Toolbox.) The line of dots that are drawn comes directly from the point (tip) of the pencil. Pressing the Caps Lock key (engaging it) changes the cursor from the pencil shape to a crosshair, which looks suspiciously like the crosshair from the Brush tool. The line of points comes from the dot in the center of the crosshair when you press the Caps Lock key.

Drawing open paths and closed paths

You can draw both open and closed paths with the Freehand tool. An open path has two separate, distinct end points. A closed path has no end points.

To change an open path into a closed path, the end points must be joined together. Joining is discussed in Chapter 7.

Paths in Illustrator may cross themselves (no, not to protect against vampires). When the paths cross, the fills on these paths may look a little unusual. Strokes look normal, just blending together where paths cross.

To create an open path, draw a path with the Freehand tool, but make sure that the beginning and end of the path are two separate points at different locations. Open paths with fills may look a little bizarre because Illustrator automatically fills in between the end points on the path, even if the imaginary line between the end points crosses the path itself. Figure 6-8 shows both open and closed paths drawn with the Freehand tool.

Figure 6-8:
Open and closed paths drawn with the Freehand tool.

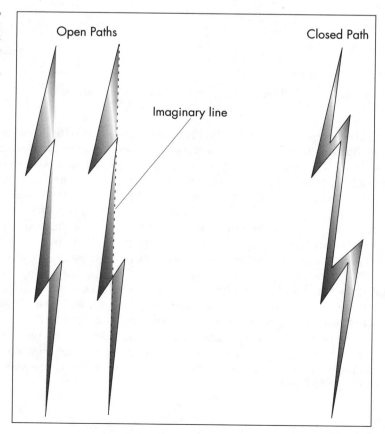

To create a closed path, end your path at the same place that you started the path. When the pencil cursor is directly over the location where the line begins, the eraser end of the pencil (opposite end from the tip) turns black, and a little circle appears to the lower right of the pencil. This change means that the path is a closed path if you release the mouse button when that particular cursor is showing.

Drawing semistraight segments

You can draw semistraight segments — that is, segments that look straight but, upon closer inspection, are really just a teeny bit curved — with the Freehand tool. To draw these segments, start drawing with the Freehand tool and press the Command key at the point where you want the semistraight segment to begin. The cursor changes to an eraser (see the next section for details on erasing). Keep dragging to where you want the semistraight segment to end and release the Command key to continue drawing with the Freehand tool.

Notice that the dots that normally appear along the path that the Freehand tool takes do not appear between the area where you first pressed the Command key and where you released the Command key; this is normal. After you are done drawing, release the mouse button and a semistraight line segment appears between the locations where you pressed and then released the Command key. Upon further inspection with the Direct Selection tool, notice that direction points extend out from the anchor points on either side of the semistraight segment.

One of the important things to remember in this process is that the mouse button should never be released while the Command key is pressed. You can create as many semistraight segments in a path drawn with the Freehand tool as you like by pressing and holding the Command key for each of them. Keep in mind, however, that when drawing multiple semistraight segments, there must be some movement of the mouse between drawing the semistraight segments. After you press the Command key, move the mouse, and then release the Command key, the mouse *must* be moved before you press the Command key again to create a new segment. If the mouse is not moved between Command-key presses, only one segment is drawn, from the location where the Command key was initially pressed to the location where it is ultimately released.

A problem with drawing semistraight segments is that it is difficult to see exactly where to place the endpoint of the segment because the cursor looks like a huge eraser, the type you were given in first grade that you needed two hands to hold onto and use properly (those erasers always seemed to take the varnish right off the desk under the paper after they tore through that wonderful Grade Triple Z paper that still had tree bark in it). If you press the Caps Lock key before the Command key, the big fat eraser cursor becomes the suave dotted crosshair cursor.

Of course, it is my belief that the Command key was never intended to be used with the Freehand tool to draw these semistraight lines. In fact, the only real reason the Command key does anything like this at all is because it is used for erasing.

Erasing in real time

The Freehand tool has a capability not found in any of Illustrator's other tools: the capability to erase itself right away while being drawn. Some people think they are erasing when they draw a rectangle or oval and then decide they don't want the figure, so they make it so tiny that it seems to disappear. Of course, the shape isn't erased; instead, a tiny rectangle or oval is created, which is visible only in Artwork mode and on final output. The Brush tool doesn't erase, nor does the Pen tool.

To erase a path as it is being drawn with the Freehand tool, press the Command key (that's right, the Command key again) and while the mouse button is still pressed, retrace over the line of dots that you just drew. The dots that the cursor, now an eraser shape, passes over are deleted. After the Command key is released (the mouse button is still pressed), the dots again begin to form wherever the cursor is being dragged. While the Command key is pressed, the cursor appears as an eraser — a big ugly eraser, but an eraser nonetheless. If the Caps Lock key was engaged first, the cursor appears not as an eraser but as a dotted crosshair. Like when I'm drawing semistraight segments, I find the dotted crosshair much easier to use for erasing than the big fat eraser cursor.

 Erasing works *only* if you haven't let go of the mouse button yet. Releasing the mouse button results in a path with points that can't be erased with the Command key and the Freehand tool, only by deleting selected anchor points.

Drawing jagged paths and smooth paths

Because drawing nice-looking paths with the Freehand tool and a mouse is just a tad difficult and frustrating ("Really?" you ask sarcastically . . .), Illustrator provides ways to roughen or smooth out paths while they are being drawn.

Normally, paths that appear from the dotted lines created with the Freehand tool are fairly similar to those dotted lines in direction and curves and such. When lines are being drawn, though, human error can cause all sorts of little bumps and "skiddles" (a *skiddle* is a little round misdrawn section resembling a small fruit-flavored candy) to appear, making the path appear lumpy. In some cases, lumpy is good. More often than not, though, lumpy is an undesirable state for your illustrations.

The smoothness of the resulting paths drawn with the Freehand tool relies on the Freehand tolerance option in the General Preferences dialog box (⌘-K), which determines how jagged or smooth each section will appear from the dotted line to the path.

The smoothness of the resulting paths drawn with the Freehand tool rely on *Freehand Tolerance* to determine how jagged or smooth each section will be converted from dotted line to path.

Freehand tolerance is a value, between 0 and 10, that determines the smoothness of the paths drawn, with 0 being rough, and 10 being really smooth. To change the Freehand tolerance setting, select File⇨Preferences⇨General (⌘-K) and enter a number between 0 and 10 in the Freehand tolerance text field. Figure 6-9 shows the same clump of grass created with different Freehand tolerance settings. After the number is changed, the new setting affects all paths drawn *after* the new value has been entered. Previously drawn Freehand paths are not affected by a change in the Freehand tolerance setting. The default value is 2, which is a good all-around value, supplying partially smooth curves and some detail.

Figure 6-9: Freehand tolerance settings and the resulting paths.

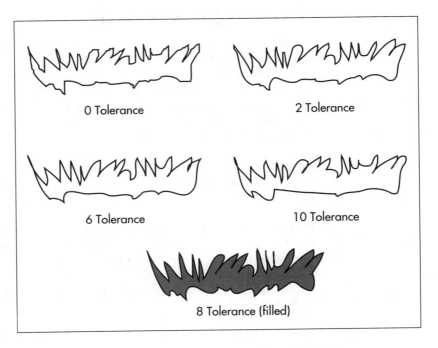

At a Freehand tolerance setting of 0, paths appear jagged and rough. Also, many more anchor points are present, although there are still no straight-corner anchor points. A setting of 0 is great for creating some photo-realistic illustrations of complex, detailed objects, such as tree leaves and textures. When the setting is this low, the resulting path follows the dotted line as closely as possible.

When the Freehand tolerance option is set to 10, paths created with the Freehand tool appear extremely smooth. The smallest number of anchor points are used, and the curve of the line appears to be very graceful. Because so few anchor points are used, much detail is lost, and the path wavers from the original dotted line of the Freehand tool by a significant amount. Even though it appears that all the anchor points are smooth anchor points, they are actually curved-corner anchor points, with two independent direction points.

Because the Freehand tolerance setting is changed in the General Preferences dialog box, it retains its current value until it is changed, even if you quit Illustrator or restart the entire system.

 Freehand tolerance affects the way the Auto Trace tool works in the same way as it affects the Freehand tool (higher numbers for smooth paths with few anchor points and lower numbers for jagged paths with many anchor points).

Adding to an existing open path

To continue drawing on an existing path (which could have been drawn with the Pen tool or the Freehand tool), the existing path must first be an open path with two distinct end points. After you pass your drawing tool over one end of the path with the Free-hand tool, the pencil cursor changes into a pencil with a black eraser. This action means that if you click and drag, you can now extend the path with the Freehand tool, as shown in the grass clump at the top of Figure 6-7. If the Caps Lock key is engaged, the cursor looks like a crosshair with a hollow box in the center.

Although you are continuing with the same path, you may not erase that part of the path that was in place before you added to it. You may, however, press the Command key and erase any part of the dotted line that appears from the new add-on segment.

So far, all the points in paths drawn with the Freehand tool have been curved-corner anchor points. This changes when you add to an existing path with the Freehand tool. The point that connects the existing path to the newly drawn path is a smooth point. No matter which way you drag, the point always is a smooth point. However, you can force a curved-corner anchor point in place of the smooth point by pressing the Option key while clicking the end of the existing path.

If you drag to the other open end of the existing path, you have the opportunity to make the path(s) into a closed path. This point will also be a smooth point — unless the Option key is pressed — at which time it changes into a curved-corner point.

You can add on only to end points on an existing path. Anchor points that are within paths cannot be connected to new (or existing, for that matter) segments. If you attempt to draw from an anchor point that is not an end point, you create an end point for the path you are drawing that is overlapping but not connected to the anchor point you clicked.

 Illustrator's pencil cursor changes the eraser to black whenever the pencil tip passes over any anchor point, not just end points on open paths. This change can be a little confusing at first, so try to remember that you *absolutely cannot* add a new path to an existing path on an anchor point that is not an end point.

Drawing Precisely with the Pen Tool

After you get the hang of it, the Pen tool isn't so bad. Go ahead, ask anyone who has been using Illustrator for, say, two years or longer. They like the Pen tool. I use the Pen tool more than the Brush, Auto Trace, and Freehand tools combined.

I have approached this tool delicately because, although it is a little frustrating and confusing to use well, it is the most important tool to learn, and this is the one section of this book that you should really read well. (On the enclosed CD-ROM, there are several examples that should help to clarify its use.)

In our sample illustration from Figure 6-2, the weeds in the upper righthand corner were created with the Pen tool. The weeds are composed entirely out of straight lines and were duplicated in clumps, just as the long and short grasses were. Figure 6-10 shows the process used for creating the mass of weeds in the illustration.

Figure 6-10:
A clump of weeds as drawn with the Pen tool.

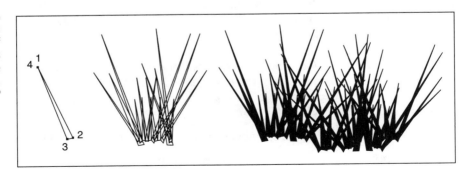

Steps:	Drawing Weeds with the Pen Tool
Step 1.	Change the Paint Style to a Fill of black and a Stroke of none. Using the Pen tool, click (don't drag!) at the top of the first weed (1). Then click lower at the bottom right of the first weed (2). Click to the right (3) and click back at the start point (4) to complete the weed. When the last weed in the clump has been finished, click the first anchor point to close the path.
Step 2.	Create additional weeds in this same way, making clumps of them like the one in Figure 6-10.
Step 3.	With the Selection tool, Option-drag the clumps a few times to create a mass of weeds.

When drawing straight lines with the Pen tool, *never* drag the mouse when the button is pressed. Doing so results in at least one curved segment.

The Pen tool draws precise lines, both curved and straight. With a little practice and with using the tips given in these pages, you can master the tool. In the process, you will understand Illustrator much better than is possible otherwise.

It would be really simple if the Pen tool did *all* the work, but you do have to do some of the labor involved in creating curves and straight lines yourself. Actually, using the Pen tool is easier than I have been letting on. All you have to do is place anchor points where you want the path to go.

OK, now I oversimplified it a bit. Drawing with the Pen tool isn't *just* placing anchor points. The first obstacle is to figure out where the heck those anchor points are going to go. Two drawings with the same number of anchor points can look totally different depending on where they're placed. You have to think ahead to determine what the path will look like before you draw it.

Points should always be located where there is a change in the path. That change can be a different curve or a corner. The three changes to look for are

- A corner of any type

- The point where a curve changes from clockwise to counterclockwise or vice versa

- The point where a curve changes *intensity:* from tight to loose or loose to tight (by far, the hardest change to judge)

The second obstacle is to decide what type of anchor point you want to use. Remember, there are four different anchor points to choose from when drawing with the Pen tool. If the path is smoothly curving, you use a smooth point. If there is a corner, use one of the corner points. Figure 6-11 shows each of the anchor point types.

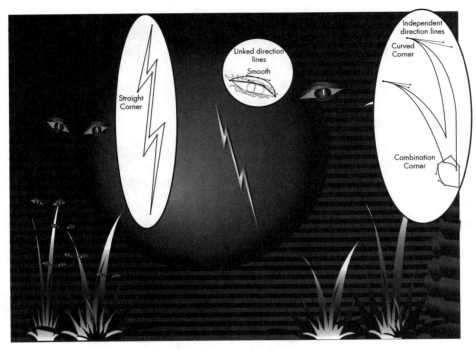

Figure 6-11: The four types of anchor points used in this illustration.

Smooth anchor points are anchor points with two connected direction points sticking out, resulting in a path that moves smoothly through the anchor point. Changing the angle of one direction point changes the angle of the other direction point. Changing the length of the direction line does not affect the other direction point. A smooth anchor point guides the path along its journey but doesn't severely or suddenly alter that path's direction.

Straight-corner anchor points are anchor points where two line segments meet in a corner. The line segments are not curved where they reach the anchor point, and there are no direction points. Straight-corner anchor points usually, but not always, distinctly change the direction of the path at the location where it passes through the anchor point.

Curved-corner anchor points are anchor points where two different curved segments meet in a corner. There are two direction points coming out of a curved-corner anchor point, but the direction points are independent of each other. Moving one direction point does not affect the other.

Combination-corner anchor points are anchor points where two segments meet, one curved and one straight. There is one direction point on a combination-corner anchor point. That direction point affects only the curved segment, not the straight segment.

The third obstacle arises when you decide that the anchor point should be anything but a straight-corner anchor point. All the other anchor points have direction points, you see. The third obstacle is how to drag the direction points, how far to drag them, and which direction to drag them.

Drawing straight lines

The easiest place to start learning to use the Pen tool is with drawing straight lines. The lightning bolt in Figure 6-12 was created entirely with straight lines. The great thing about straight lines drawn with the Pen tool is that there are no direction points to worry about or fuss over.

To draw the lightning bolt in Figure 6-12, click at each number with the Pen tool in order. Before you click at number 11, the Pen tool changes to a pen cursor with a little circle in the lower righthand corner. This change signifies that the path is going to close when you click this point.

Figure 6-12:
A lightning bolt drawn
entirely with straight lines.

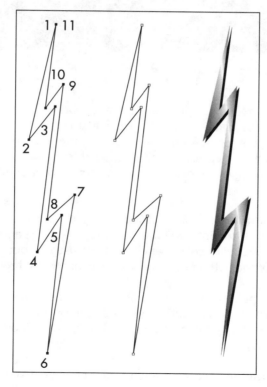

The simplest straight line is a line drawn with only two anchor points. To draw a line like this, select the Pen tool and click and release where you want the first end point (the beginning of the line) to appear. Then click and release where you want the second end point (the end of the line) to appear. A line appears between the two points. Too easy, isn't it?

To draw another separate line, first click the Pen tool in the Toolbox or hold down the Command key and click. Either action tells Illustrator that you are done drawing the first line. Clicking and releasing again in one spot and then another draws a second line with two end points. Be careful not to drag when clicking the Pen tool to form straight lines.

Paths drawn with the Pen tool, like the Freehand tool, may cross themselves. The only strange result you may see involves the fills for objects whose paths cross. In open paths created with the Pen tool, fills may look unusual because of the imaginary line between the two end points and any paths that the imaginary line crosses, as shown in Figure 6-8.

To draw a straight segment that is angled at 0°, 45°, 90°, and so on, press Shift before you click. The segment drawn will be at the closest 45° angle.

Closing paths

If you want to create a closed path (one with no end points), return to the first anchor point in that segment and click. As the Pen tool crosses over the beginning anchor point, the cursor changes to a pen with a circle in the lower righthand corner. After you have created a closed path, there is no need to click the Pen tool again. Instead, the next click of the Pen tool in the document automatically begins a new path.

You must have at least two anchor points to create a closed path with straight lines, but the irony is that a path with two straight-corner anchor points is a line. You can change the identity of one of these points to a different type of anchor point by curving one of the segments and giving the closed path some substance.

Drawing curves

Initially, the worst thing about drawing curves with the Pen tool is that the whole process is rather disorienting. You actually have to think differently to grasp what the Pen tool is doing. The difference that you notice right away between drawing straight lines and drawing curves is that to draw a curve, you need to drag with the Pen tool; whereas, when drawing straight lines, you click and release.

The most basic of curves is the bump (a curved segment between just two points). A bump was used to create a path to fill the horses' rears in Figure 6-2. Follow the next steps to create the bump that is illustrated in Figure 6-13.

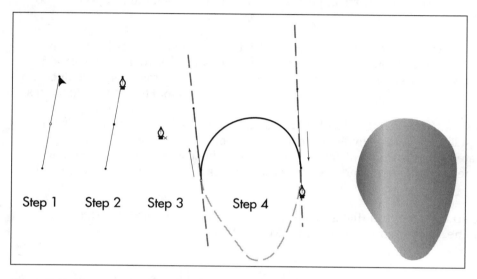

Figure 6-13: The four steps for creating a basic bump curve.

STEPS: Creating a Basic Curve

Step 1.   Click with the Pen tool and drag up about ½ inch. You see an anchor point and a line extending from it as you drag.

Step 2.   When you release the mouse button, you see the anchor point and a line extending to where you dragged, with a direction point at its end.

Step 3.   Position the cursor about 1 inch to the right of the place you first clicked.

Step 4.   Click with the mouse and drag down about ½ inch. As you drag, you see a curve forming that resembles a bump. When the mouse is released, the curve is filled with the current fill color. You see the direction point you just dragged.

Before you try to draw another curve, remember that the Pen tool is still in a mode that continues the current path, not starts a new one. To start a new path, click the Pen tool once or hold down Command and click an empty spot. The next time you use the Pen tool, you will now draw a separate path.

To create an S shape, one more step is needed. The steps for creating the S shape are illustrated in Figure 6-14.

STEPS: Creating a Basic S Curve

Step 1. Click and drag with the Pen tool about ½ inch to the left.

Step 2. Release the mouse button. You should see the anchor point and the direction point that you just drew, with a direction line between them.

Step 3. Position the cursor about 1 inch below where you first clicked.

Step 4. Click and drag to the right about ½ inch.

Step 5. Release the mouse button.

Step 6. Position the cursor about ½ inch below the last point you clicked.

Step 7. Click and drag to the left, about ½ inch. Now you have an S shape. To make the S look more like a real S, change the Fill to none and the Stroke to black in the Paint Style palette, 1 pt.

Figure 6-14:
The seven steps for creating a basic S curve.

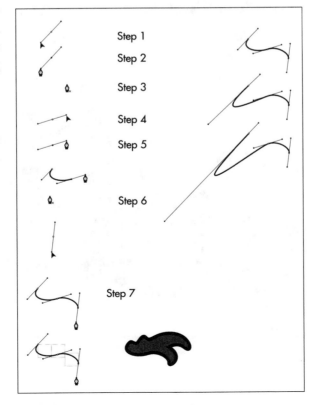

All the anchor points we have created in these two examples are smooth points. The direction points that were dragged were dragged in the direction of the next curve that was to be drawn, and the length of the direction lines on either side of the anchor point was the same.

The length of the direction lines on either side of the smooth point does not have to be the same. Instead, a smooth point may have both long and short direction lines coming out of it. The length of the direction line affects the curve, as shown on the S curve from Figure 6-14.

To create a smooth point with two direction lines of different lengths, first create a smooth point along a path. Go back to this point after it has been created and click and drag it again. You can adjust the angle for both direction lines and the length for the new direction line that you are dragging. Note that as you are dragging out this direction line, the other direction line wobbles to the angle that you are dragging. This happens because on any smooth point, the direction lines *must* be at the same angle, and as you drag out the new direction line, you are changing the angle for both direction lines simultaneously.

Knowing the Pen Commandments

The Pen Commandments are laws to live by — or, at least, to draw by — as shown dramatically in Figure 6-15.

Figure 6-15: The Pen Commandments.

Thou shalt drag approximately one third of the length of the next curved segment.
Huh? What this means, as shown at the bottom of Figure 6-14 (in the gridded area), is
that the direction point you drag from the anchor point should be about one third of
the distance between this anchor point and the next one you click. (This technique
takes some planning ahead.) In fact, you have to be aware of where the next anchor
point is going to be located before you can determine the length of the direction line
you are dragging. Dragging by one third is always an approximation — a little more or a
little less doesn't hurt and, in fact, is sometimes quite necessary. You might run into
trouble when the direction line is more than ½ or less than ¼ of the next segment.

 If your direction line is the length of the line segment, chances are the line will
curve erratically. Remember not to drag where the next point will be placed,
just one third of that distance.

**Thou shalt remember that direction lines are always tangent to the curved segment
they are guiding.** Tangent? Well, a simpler way of putting this commandment may be
that direction lines go in the same direction as the curve and that they are always
outside of the curve, as shown in Step 4 of Figure 6-13. Don't get the outside of the curve
and the outside of the shape you are drawing confused — they may well be two different things. If your direction point lies inside the curve you are drawing, it will be too
short and overpowered by the next anchor point. Direction points *pull* the curve toward
themselves; this makes them naturally curve out toward the direction lines. If you fight
this natural pull, your illustrations can look loopy and silly.

**Thou shalt always drag the direction point in the direction that you want the curve to
travel at that anchor point.** Once again, the direction point pulls the curve toward itself
by its very nature; doing otherwise will certainly cause some trouble. If you drag
backwards toward the preceding segment, you will create a little curved spike that
sticks out from the anchor point. This commandment applies *only* to smooth points, as
shown in Step 4 of Figure 6-13. If the anchor point is to be a curved-corner point, then
the initial drag should be in the direction the curve was traveling, and the next drag (an
Option-drag) should go in the direction that the curve is going to travel. If the anchor
point is a combination-curve point and the next segment is straight, then the dragging
motion should be in the direction that the curve was traveling; then the anchor point
should be clicked and released. If the combination-curve point's next segment is
curved, the first click should be clicked and released, and the second click should be
dragged in the direction of the next curve.

Thou shalt make segments as long as possible. If your illustration calls for smooth, flowing curves, use very few anchor points. If, on the other hand, your illustration should be
rough and gritty, use more anchor points. The fewer anchor points you have, the smoother
the final result, as demonstrated in Figure 6-16. When there are only a few anchor points
on a path, changing its shape is easier and faster. More anchor points means a bigger
file and longer printing times, as well. If you're not sure if you need more anchor points,
don't add them. You can always add them later with the Add Anchor Point tool.

Figure 6-16:
The path on the left was created with twelve anchor points; the one on the right, with sixty. The results speak for themselves.

Thou shalt place anchor points at the beginning of each "different" curve. Anchor points should be used as *transitional* points, where the curve either changes direction or increases or decreases in size dramatically. If it looks as though the curve will change from one type of curve to another, then the location to place an anchor point is in the middle of that transitional section. The top drawing in Figure 6-17 shows good locations to place anchor points on a curved path.

Thou shalt not overcompensate for a previously misdrawn curve. If you really screw up on the last anchor point you've drawn, don't panic and try to undo the mistake by dragging in the wrong direction or by dragging the direction point out to some ridiculous length. Doing either of these two things may temporarily fix the preceding curve but usually wrecks the next curve, causing you to have to overcompensate yet again. The results of just minor overcompensation are shown in the bottom drawing in Figure 6-17.

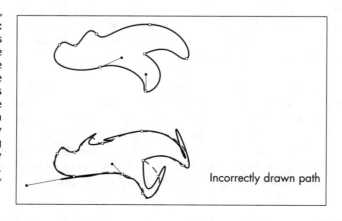

Figure 6-17:
The anchor points on the top path are placed where the curve changes. The path at the top was drawn correctly; the one on the bottom was drawn by overcompensating for previously misdrawn curves.

Incorrectly drawn path

Closing curved paths with the Pen tool

The majority of the paths you draw with the Pen tool will be closed paths, not the open ones we've drawn so far. Like open curved paths, any closed curved path must have at least two anchor points, just as paths with straight corner points need three distinct points to create a closed path.

When the Pen tool is placed over the starting point of the path while you draw, a little circle appears to the right of the pen shape. This is an indicator that the path will become a closed path if you click this anchor point.

Of course, to ensure that the initial anchor point remains a smooth anchor point, you need to click and drag on the initial anchor point. Simply clicking produces a combination corner point, which only has one direction point associated with it.

Creating curved-corner points

Curved-corner points are points where two different, usually distinct, curved segments meet at an anchor point. Because the two curves meet this way, a smooth point does not provide the means for their joining correctly. Instead, a smooth point would make the two different curves blend into each other smoothly.

The main difference between a curved-corner point and a smooth point is that a smooth point has two linked direction lines with direction points on their ends; a curved-corner point has two *independent* direction points, as shown in Figure 6-11. Like the word indicates, the direction points and their associated direction lines move independently of each other, creating the capability for two different, distinct types of curves to come from the same anchor point.

To create a curved-corner anchor point, create a smooth point in a path and then Option-drag on that same anchor point. As you Option-drag from the anchor point, you are creating a new, independent direction point. The next segment will curve as controlled by this direction point, not by the original one.

Option-dragging on a direction point attached to a curved-corner point changes the anchor point back to a smooth point, where the direction lines and direction points are linked once again.

The clumps of grass from Figure 6-2 were created by using curved-corner points. The process is explained in the following steps.

STEPS: Creating Paths with Curved-Corner Points

Step 1. As shown in Figure 6-18, click the first point (1) and drag up and to the left. Try to duplicate the locations of all the points for the best results.

Step 2. Click at (2) and drag left and down just a little bit, which creates the curved segment between (1) and (2). You won't see the direction point you are dragging on the figure on the right because Step 3 replaces it.

Step 3. To create the first curved-corner point, Option-click on (2) and drag up and to the right.

Step 4. Click at (3) and drag to the lower right.

Step 5. Continue to Option-click when starting to draw a new segment, effectively creating independent direction points until you have created a clump of grass.

Step 6. Option-copy and transform the clumps to create several clumps of grass.

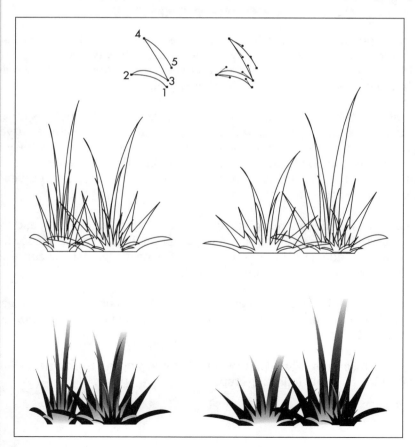

Figure 6-18: How to create paths with curved-corner points.

When creating curved-corner points, you can press the Option key (to create independent points) all the time, not just when starting a new segment.

Creating combination-corner points

A combination-corner point is a point where a curved segment and a straight segment meet each other. At this corner point, there is one direction point coming from the anchor point from the side where the curved segment is located and, on the other side, there is no direction point, indicating a straight segment.

To create a combination-corner point with the Pen tool, draw a few curved segments and then go back to the last anchor point. There should be two linked direction points displayed at this point. Simply click once on the anchor point, and one of the two direction points will disappear. The next segment then starts out straight.

 You can change existing smooth and curved-corner points into combination-corner points simply by dragging one of the direction points into the anchor points.

Using the Pen tool

In the sample illustration in Figure 6-2, the Pen tool was used not only to draw the spiky weeds but also to draw the horses on the hill and the fill shapes for the hill. The horse outlines and the blade outlines were created with the Brush tool.

To fill the hillside, click where the left edge of the hill should begin and drag down and to the right about ½ inch. Next, click at the top of the hill and drag just a tiny bit (less than ¼ inch) to the right. Click again at about halfway down the hill and drag at about the same angle as the hill. Click again at the base of the hill and drag to the right 1 inch. Click without dragging on the far side of the illustration. To finish off the hillside fill, click the lower righthand and lower lefthand corners and then click the starting point. Fill the path with a gradient that complements a hillside and change the Stroke to none.

To create the horse fill shape, create a path with the Pen tool by using mostly smooth points that go right through the center of the horse outlines. Make separate shapes for the head area, manes, body area, and the tails. Fill the paths with gradients or solid colors and choose a Stroke of none.

To create the long grass blade fills, use the Pen tool to draw paths that go right through the center of the blades of grass. Create separate paths for each blade, and fill the blades with a green linear gradient.

Selecting, Moving, and Deleting Entire Paths

Usually, the best way to select a path that is not currently selected is by clicking it with the regular Selection tool, which highlights the points on the path and allows you to move, transform, or delete that entire path.

To select more than one path, you can use a number of different methods. The most basic method is to hold down the Shift key and click the successive paths with the Selection tool, selecting one more path with each Shift-click. Shift-clicking a selected path with the Selection tool deselects that particular path. Drawing a marquee around paths with the Selection tool selects all paths that at least partially fall into the area drawn by the marquee. When drawing a marquee, be sure to place the cursor in an area where there is nothing. Finding an empty spot may be difficult to do in Preview mode because fills from various paths may cover any white space available. Drawing a marquee with the Selection tool when the Shift key is depressed selects nonselected paths and deselects currently selected paths.

If paths are part of either a compound path or a group, all other paths in that compound path or group are also selected, as shown in Figure 6-19.

To move a path, click the path and drag in one motion with the Selection tool. To move several paths, select the paths and then click a selected path with the regular Selection tool or the Direct Selection tool and drag.

Figure 6-19:
On the left is a compound path when selected; on the right is the same path when deselected.

If you have been selecting multiple paths by using the Shift key, be sure to release it before clicking and dragging on the selected paths. If the Shift key is still pressed, the clicked path becomes deselected, and no paths move. If this does happen, just Shift-click the paths that were deselected and drag.

To delete an entire path, select it with the Selection tool and press the Delete key. To delete multiple paths, select them and press the Delete key.

In our sample illustrations, many of the objects needed to be moved and duplicated. To duplicate paths when moving them, press the Option key while the mouse button is released.

Duplicate the spiky weeds by clicking them and dragging to the left or right. When the weeds are at a visually good distance, press Option and release the mouse button. Select Arrange➪Repeat Transform to create another set of weeds at the same distance, if necessary.

The short grass, long grass, and silhouetted horses can be duplicated the same way, by selecting one and dragging it to the left or right and pressing Option while the mouse button is released.

Selecting and Moving Portions of Paths

To select just a portion of a path, you *must* use the Direct Selection tool. To select an anchor point or a line segment, simply click it. To select several individual points or paths, click the points or paths to be selected while holding down the Shift key. Series of points and paths can be selected by dragging a marquee across the paths that are to be selected.

Individual points that are selected become solid squares. If these points are smooth, curved-corner, or combination-corner anchor points, direction lines or handles appear from the selected anchor point.

Line segments that have at least one anchor point that is either a smooth, curved-corner, or combination-corner anchor point may display a direction line and direction point coming out from that anchor point. Samples of each of these selected types of anchor points are shown in Figure 6-20.

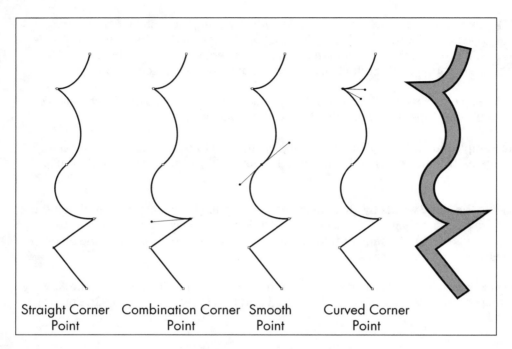

Straight Corner Point   Combination Corner Point   Smooth Point   Curved Corner Point

Figure 6-20: The four different types of anchor points when selected.

To move these selected points or paths, release the Shift key and click a selected path or point and drag.

 Illustrator doesn't tell you when a straight line segment is selected or which one is selected. The first time you click a straight line segment, all the anchor points on the path appear as hollow squares, which is just telling you that *something* on that path is selected. Selected points turn black, and curved line segments have one or more direction points and lines sticking out from the ending anchor points, but straight line segments don't do anything when selected. The inventive side of you may think that you can get around this problem by dragging the selected segments to a new location or by copying and pasting them and then undoing — but this solution doesn't work because of Illustrator's habit of selecting all points on paths when undoing operations on those paths.

 When you run into this problem of not knowing if a straight segment is selected, do the following: Instead of moving, copying, or pasting, simply whack the good ol' Delete key, and whatever disappears is what you had selected. Now when you undo, just the segments that were selected before the deletion are still selected, not the entire path.

To delete points and segments, select them as described above and then press Delete. Remember that line segments exist only when there is one point on either side of the segment. Even if the line segment is not selected, if one of its anchor points is deleted, the line segment is deleted, as well. A path is made up of points, and those points are connected via segments. If the points are gone, the paths disappear along with them. But if you delete all the segments, all the points remain.

 If points need to be changed from one type of anchor point to another (such as smooth to curved-corner), refer to Chapter 10.

Portions of paths can be duplicated when pressing the Option key while the mouse button is being released. Duplicating segments also duplicates the anchor points on either side of that segment.

The Foreground and the Background

One of the crucial concepts that you need to understand in the world of Adobe Illustrator is that of foreground and background. This concept is not the same as the layer concept that is discussed in Chapter 14, but it is rather the forward/backward relationship between objects within each layer.

After you create the first object in Illustrator, the next object is created *above* the first object, or on top of it. The third object is created above both the first and second objects. This cycle continues indefinitely.

A great deal of planning goes into creating an illustration so that the object you draw first is on the bottom of the pile, and the last thing you draw ends up on the top. To make your life much more pleasant, Illustrator has the capability to move objects up and down (forward or backward) through the mass of objects. In fact, Illustrator's method of moving objects up and down is so simplistic and basic that it is also quite limiting.

You can move objects in Illustrator relative to foreground and background either all the way to the bottom or all the way to the top. You may not move an object up a bit or down just a little; you can move the objects only to the extremes. Figure 6-21 shows the same illustration with the loony bird moved forward and backward.

To move an object to the front, select Arrange⇨Bring to Front (⌘-=). The selected object is brought forward so that it is in front of every other object (but only in that layer — Chapter 14 explains how layers work). If more than one object is selected, the topmost object of the selected group will be at the very top and the bottommost object of the selected group will be beneath all the other selected objects — but all the selected objects will be on top of all the nonselected objects.

To move an object to the back, select Arrange⇨Send to Back (⌘-hyphen). The selected object is sent backwards so that it is behind every other object.

Individual characters in a string of text work in a similar manner to their object cousins when it comes to front/back placement. The first character typed is placed at the bottom of the text block, and the last character typed is placed at the top, as shown in Figure 6-22. To move individual characters forward or backward, you must first select Type⇨Create Outline and select the outline of the character you wish to arrange.

Figure 6-22: The letters in a word are bottom to top, from left to right.

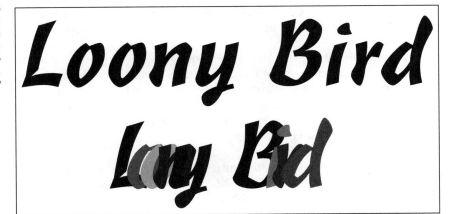

Try as you might, you cannot change the forward/backward relationship of strokes and fills. Strokes are always in front of fills for the same path. To get the fill to cover or overlap the stroke, you must copy the path, use the Paste In Front command (select Edit⇨Paste In Front, ⌘-F), and then remove the stroke from the path you just copied.

 To understand more about how the foreground and background works with layers, see Chapter 14.

Grouping and Ungrouping

Grouping is the process of putting together a series of objects that need to remain spatially constant in relationship to each other. Groups can be made up of as little as one path, and they may contain an unlimited number of objects.

To group objects together, they should first be selected with any of the selection tools. After you select the objects, select Arrange⇨Group (⌘-G) to make the separate objects stay together when selected.

Selecting any object in a group with the regular Selection tool selects all the objects in that group and makes all the points in a path solid (selected). To see how the Group Selection tool works with selecting groups, see "Using the Group Selection tool," at the end of this chapter.

Not only can several objects be grouped together, but groups can be grouped together to form a "group of groups," in which there is a hierarchical series of grouped groups. In addition, groups can be grouped to individual objects or to several other objects.

After a set of objects or groups is grouped together, grouping it again produces no effect. The computer does not beep at you, display a dialog box, or otherwise indicate that the objects/groups you are attempting to group together are already grouped. Of course, it never hurts to select Arrange⇨Group (⌘-G) again, if you are not sure if they are grouped. If they weren't grouped before, they now are, and if they were grouped before, nothing unusual or unexpected happens.

In our example illustration from Figure 6-2, the objects will be much easier to manipulate if they are grouped. Group the short grass together as one group, the long grass as one group, the horse outlines and fills as one group, and the hillside outline and fills as one group. The tree outline and bark detail should be one group as well.

If you are having trouble selecting all the objects for each type in a group, select Fill⇨Select⇨Same Paint Style after one object is selected. This process usually (but not always) selects all the objects of one type.

Grouping similar areas is helpful for moving entire areas forward or backward as well as doing any type of horizontal or vertical movement or transformation upon a set of objects.

Grouping is helpful for controlling blends. Figure 6-23 shows a blend that is grouped to its end paths.

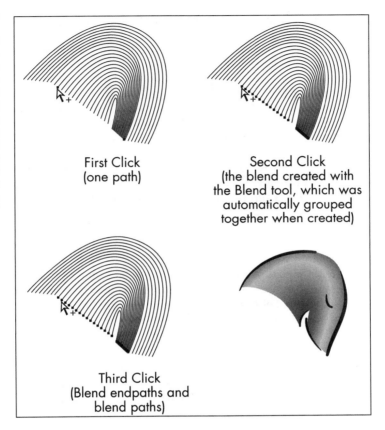

Figure 6-23:
Blends
grouped with
end paths. The
Group
Selection tool
is being used
to select one
path, the
blend, and
then the entire
blend and end
paths
together.

First Click
(one path)

Second Click
(the blend created with
the Blend tool, which was
automatically grouped
together when created)

Third Click
(Blend endpaths and
blend paths)

Ungrouping

To ungroup groups, select Arrange⇨Ungroup (⌘-U), and any selected groups become ungrouped. Ungrouping, like grouping, works on one set of groups at a time. For example, if you have two groups that are grouped together, ungrouping that group results in the two original groups. If Ungroup is selected again, those two groups will also become ungrouped.

When you absolutely do not want anything in a group grouped with anything else — and you suspect that there may be several minigroups within the group you have selected — simply press ⌘-U several times. You do not need to select the subgroups individually to ungroup them. To get rid of all the groups in your illustration, select Edit⇨Select All (⌘-A) and then proceed to ungroup (⌘-U) several times.

When you're ungrouping, groups must be selected with either the Group Selection tool or the regular Selection tool.

Using the Group Selection tool

The Group Selection tool is used primarily to select groups within other groups or individual paths within groups. To access the Group Selection tool, click the Direct Selection tool in the Toolbox and drag to the right to the Group Selection tool. Clicking once with the Group Selection tool on any path selects that particular path. Clicking again with the Group Selection tool on the same path selects the group that path is in. Clicking yet again selects the group that the previously selected group is in.

To move a path that is part of a group, do not ungroup the path; instead, select the path with the Group Selection tool and move it.

If you select a path in a group with the Group Selection tool and then click the same path again to move it, the group that path is in will be selected, instead. To avoid this problem, either select and move at one time or use the Direct Selection tool for moving.

If several different paths are selected with the Group Selection tool either by dragging a marquee or Shift-clicking, clicking again on a selected path or object selects the group that object is in. If that object's group is already selected, then the group that the selected group is in will be selected. Figure 6-23 shows the results after one click, two clicks, and then three clicks on the same object in a graph, which is made up of several groups.

The Group Selection tool also selects compound paths. One click selects an individual path within the compound path, and the second click selects the entire compound path.

Using the Shift key with the Group Selection tool on selected paths or objects deselects just one path at a time. Shift-clicking a path that has just been deselected reselects that path, not deselects the group that path is in.

For quick access to the Group Selection tool, press the Option key when the Direct Selection Tool is the active tool. But release the Option key before the mouse button is released, or you'll have a duplicated path or object. The Direct Selection tool can be selected by pressing the Command key (⌘-Tab toggles between the Direct Selection and regular Selection tools). Pressing the Command and Option keys together can be used to access the Group Selection tool, no matter which tool is selected in the toolbox!

Templates, Tracing, Measuring, and Manipulating

■ ■

In This Chapter

※ What templates are and how they are used

※ Creating high-quality templates

※ Manual tracing versus autotracing

※ Measuring by using the Measure tool

※ Measuring by using circles and using the Offset Path filter

※ Creating and using guides

※ Locking, hiding, and moving objects

■ ■

Using Templates

An Illustrator *template* is a gray image that sits underneath the drawing plane — that is, a template is a background object — and serves as a model for your illustration. (In other words, Illustrator turns your computer into a glorified version of tracing paper.) Using a template eliminates the guesswork and measuring usually needed when you want to re-create an image. With a template, you can easily match or even improve upon the original art.

The downside: Template quality is rather poor. Templates are always gray with a resolution of 72 dpi at 100%; as a result, zooming in on a template does not display any more detail than you see at 100%. Templates with fine details appear as so much mush.

Nonetheless, a template enables you to quickly reconstruct an image that was created by other means. For example, a template can help you convert a scanned illustration (see Figure 7-1) or logo into Illustrator paths.

Figure 7-1:
A template in
Illustrator.

Images used as templates do not print; nor are they saved inside the new Illustrator file. (Instead, Illustrator creates a link between the file and the template.)

Any illustration created in another application usually can be imported into Illustrator as a template. An Illustrator template can have one of two file formats: Paint or PICT. (The only difference between these formats is how other applications save them.) Paint images are often cropped, and PICT images are sometimes stretched, reducing their resolution, or even distorted, making them unusable as templates.

Much better clarity can be achieved in Illustrator by using an enlarged template, effectively increasing the detail available in the template. When creating a template, open an image in Photoshop and save it in either Paint or PICT format in bitmap mode at 75 dpi. For most images scanned at 300 dpi, this rule of thumb quadruples their relative size in Illustrator. After tracing the template, simply select the new image and scale it down to 25% to see it at the original size.

Setting up Illustrator templates in Photoshop

A template's usefulness is directly related to the quality of its scan. You can scan any image and stick it in Illustrator as a template for you to trace, but the quality of your final image will be based on the way the scan looks in Illustrator.

To achieve the best results, try the following:

1. Scan the black-and-white artwork as grayscale.

   Yes, doing so takes up more memory (on average, black-and-white bitmap images take up ⅛ the space as their grayscale counterparts) — but only temporarily (until Step 5).

2. Open the scanned grayscale image in an image editing program, such as Photoshop. In Photoshop, open the Levels dialog box (see figure below) by selecting Image⇨Adjust⇨Levels (⌘-L).

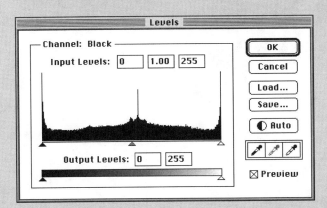

3. In this dialog box, you can adjust the appearance of the scanned grayscale image by moving the three triangle sliders. Move the three sliders so that they overlap, changing the grayscale image into a black-and-white image.

4. After clicking OK in the Levels dialog box, choose Mode⇨Bitmap and make sure that the DPI is 75 and the Method is set to 50% Threshold. These settings eliminate any unsightly little stray pixels.

5. Save the image as either a PICT or Paint file.

   I like saving as MacPaint because Photoshop first must convert the image to bitmap. It's easy to forget about changing the mode from Grayscale to Bitmap (see Step 4) because the image already looks like a bitmap. Both file formats when saved as bitmap images take up the exact same amount of disk space.

continued

(continued)

6. Open the bitmap file in Illustrator; it appears as a template.

The difference in quality between an original scan and one touched up in Photoshop is illustrated in the figure below. The top scanned image was opened directly in Illustrator as a template. The sharper scanned image (notice the space between leaves) was touched up in Photoshop and then brought into Illustrator as a template.

Tracing templates

You can trace templates in two ways: manually and automatically. Manually tracing consists of using the Freehand and Pen tools to tediously trace the edges of a template — often a very time-consuming task. Using the Auto Trace tool, though, speeds up the process.

The Auto Trace tool seems simple to use at first: clicking on the edge of the template causes Illustrator to outline the template with a path. The Auto Trace tool appears to outline both white and gray areas within the template, but it actually creates a path between the two contrasting areas. After all the paths have been drawn, the paths can be selected and transformed into a compound path. This process often automatically colors the alternating black and white areas correctly (where black is the "fill" and white appears as the "holes").

For more information on compound paths, see Chapter 11.

The Freehand Tolerance setting in the General Preferences dialog box (⌘-K) directly affects the Auto Trace tool much like it affects the Freehand tool — the higher the number, the less precise the tracing.

A Freehand Tolerance setting of 2 or 3 works pretty well for autotracing templates accurately, but neither setting enables the Auto Trace tool to follow the ridges created from the template's diagonal and curved edges.

Most designers prefer manually tracing. Using the Pen and Freehand tools provides illustrators with a level of precision not found with the Auto Trace tool. Furthermore, illustrators may add detail, remove oddities, and change curves, angles, and the like to their satisfaction. After Illustrator autotraces a template, however, the image already has a final appearance to it, lessening its "editability."

I've found that a combination of manual tracing and autotracing works quite nicely for drawing fairly basic illustrations, especially those with type and straight lines. Autotrace the basic shapes first and then use the path editing tools to add or remove anchor points and move paths so that the image has a consistent look. After fixing the autotraced section, use the Pen and Freehand tools to draw in the intricate shapes.

Figure 7-2 shows an original scanned image, the paths comprising the image in Illustrator, and the final illustration.

Of course, the best way by far to trace images is to use Streamline, an Adobe product designed specifically for outlining images. In Chapter 22, I discuss Streamline and how to get the most out of it with Illustrator.

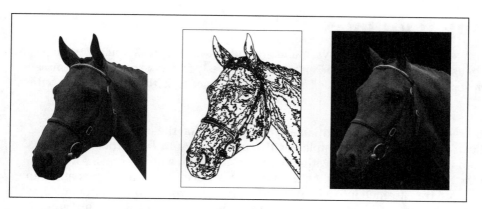

Figure 7-2: (l-r) Original scan, image with traced paths, and resulting image with filled paths.

When is a template not a template?

The best Illustrator templates aren't templates: they're imported EPS files set to "dim" in the Layers palette. Dimming EPS images is discussed in more detail in Chapter 14. (Refer to Figure 7-3 to see the difference between a regular EPS image and a dimmed EPS image.)

STEPS: Dimming an EPS Image for Tracing

Step 1. Place an EPS image into the document by choosing File⇨Place Art and selecting the EPS image.

Step 2. Move the EPS image into the proper position and transform it if necessary.

Step 3. Open the Layers palette by selecting Window⇨Show Layers (⌘-Control-L). In the Layers palette, double-click on Layer 1. In the Layer Options dialog box, select both the Dim Placed Images check box and the Lock check box and then click OK. If you lock the layer, the EPS image cannot be moved or selected.

Step 4. Click on the Layers palette's pop-up menu and select New Layer. Click OK in the New Layer dialog box. Any drawing done with any tool will now take place on the new layer, which sits on top of the layer with the dimmed EPS image.

Figure 7-3:
Tracing a regular EPS image (top) and a dimmed EPS image.

Placed EPS images work well as templates because their resolution is independent of the Illustrator document. Although placed EPS files still are imported at 72 dpi, you can scale them up or down, *changing their on-screen resolution* as you change their size. For instance, if you scale a 72 dpi image down to one-fourth of its imported size (making the dpi of the placed image 4 X 72 dpi, or 288 dpi), you may zoom in on the image in Illustrator at 400%. At 400% the placed EPS image still has a 72 dpi resolution because one-fourth of 288 dpi is 72 dpi. The more the placed image's dpi is increased by scaling it down, the more you may zoom in to see the details of the image.

This works exceedingly well if you think ahead enough to scan at 200% or 400%. When the image is then reduced in Illustrator by 50% or 25% respectively, it will be the actual size of the original artwork, and you will be able to zoom in to 200% or 400% to see the detail of that artwork, without making the artwork smaller than the original size.

Another plus: An EPS template is a full-color template (well, it's a 256 color or 256 gray template, which should be fine for most applications) while PICT and Paint templates are black/white only (and the black appears kind of gray). Keeping all the shading and colors allows you to see all the fine details easily.

The one drawback: You can't autotrace placed EPS files because Illustrator doesn't consider them templates. Unless you constantly use the Auto Trace tool, though, this problem is just an oddity.

 For the best results, scan an image at four or eight times screen resolution (288 or 576, respectively). Then open the image in Photoshop and select Image⇨Image Size. Make sure that both Proportions and File size are checked, and then change the dpi to 72 (doing so keeps the file the same physical disk size but changes its measured size). Save the image as EPS and then import it into Illustrator. You may now zoom up to 400 or 800 percent with no loss of quality.

The illustrations in Figure 7-4 were created by tracing an EPS image.

When you are done tracing, select Layer 1, click the pop-up menu, and choose Delete Layer to eliminate the EPS image (and anything else on the same layer).

Figure 7-4: An EPS style image as it normally appears when placed (top left) and how it appears after tracing with the Brush, Pen, and Freehand tools.

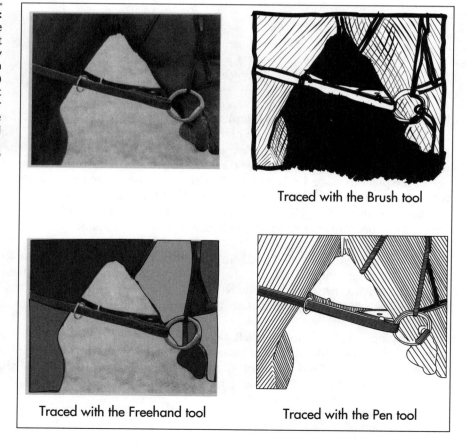

Traced with the Brush tool

Traced with the Freehand tool

Traced with the Pen tool

Measuring

You can measure distances in Illustrator in three ways:

- Use the Measure tool
- Use the rulers along the side of the document window
- Place objects whose dimensions are known against the edges
- Eyeball it (popular since the first artist painted his recollections of the preceding day's battle with the saber-toothed animals of his time)

 Believe it or not, computer users who don't know that there are measuring tools in graphics software use rulers taped to their monitor screens. This practice almost works at actual size, but it looks *really* silly.

Using the Measure tool

The fastest way to obtain a precise, exact measurement in Illustrator is to use the Measure tool. As soon as you click an object with the Measure tool, the Info palette appears, showing the distance between the location first clicked and the next location clicked or the distance between where the tool was first clicked and where the mouse was released.

If the Snap to point option in the General Preferences dialog box is checked, the Measure tool automatically snaps to nearby paths and points. If the Shift key is pressed, the measuring line created when you drag the Measure tool snaps to a 45° or 90° angle on any paths or any visible fills of any path.

As soon as the Measure tool measures a distance, it routes that information to the Move dialog box. The next time you open the Move dialog box (select Arrange⇨Move, Option-click on the Selection tool, or press ⌘-Shift-M), it will hold the values sent by the Measure tool.

Using the rulers

You can toggle rulers on and off by selecting View⇨Show/Hide Rulers (⌘-R). Normally, the rulers measure up and across from the document's lower left corner; you can alter this orientation by dragging the ruler origin (where the zeros are) from its position in the lower right corner, between the rulers.

Because rulers take up valuable on-screen real estate, it's usually a good idea to leave them turned off unless you are constantly measuring things or you want to display your illustration at a higher magnification. Rulers are easy to show and hide: just press ⌘-R when you want to see them; press ⌘-R again to lose them.

One of the rulers' nicest features is the display of dotted lines corresponding to the cursor's position. And yet, at times, measuring with rulers works no better than eyeballing: although the process requires precision, you are limited by the rulers' hash marks in pinpointing the cursor's exact position. The rulers are best suited for measuring when the document is at a very high zoom level.

 If you change the ruler origin to the middle of the document page, try to move it back to a corner when you are finished. When you zoom in, rulers may be your only indicator of your location within the document.

 To change the rulers' measurement system without selecting File⇨Preferences⇨General, you can use key commands to toggle between the three measurement systems. To change to inches, press ⌘-Shift-I; to change to millimeters, press ⌘-Shift-N; to change to picas, press ⌘-Shift-P. These key commands work whether the rulers are showing or not. These commands only work in Illustrator 5.0, not 5.5.

Using objects

Using objects to compare distances can be more effective than using either the Measure tool or the rulers, especially when you need to place objects precisely — for example, when you want several objects to be the same distance from one another.

If you place a circle adjacent to an object (so that the objects' edges touch), you know that a second object is placed correctly when it's aligned to the circle's other side. (A circle is the object most commonly used because the diameter is constant.)

You can use other objects for measuring, including the following:

▧ Squares — when you need to measure horizontal and vertical distances

▧ Rectangles — when the horizontal and vertical distances are different

▧ Lines — when the distance applies to only one direction

 To enable better precision, turn the measuring object into a guide. To transform an existing path into a guide, select the path and choose Object⇨Guides⇨Make (see the "Guides" section later in this chapter). To move the "guided" object, press Control-Shift and drag.

In Figure 7-5, circles are used to ensure that the stems have the same width.

Using the Offset Path filter (for equidistant measuring)

Sometimes, you may want to place several objects the same distance from a central object. But using any of the previously mentioned measuring techniques can be time-consuming and even inaccurate, especially when you deal with complex images. Illustrator's Offset Path filter, however, enables you to automatically align objects equidistantly from a central object.

Figure 7-5: Circles made into guides are effective measuring tools.

First, select the central object. Then choose Filter⇨Object⇨Offset Path and enter the desired distance in the Offset text field. Enter the distance in points, millimeters, or mils. After the new path is created, check the corner areas to see whether there are any overlapping areas that appear as loops. If so, select Filter⇨Pathfinder⇨Unite; the Unite filter eliminates these unsightly aberrations. Change the new path into a guide and align your objects to this guide.

Guides

Guides are dotted lines that serve to help you align artwork. In Illustrator and most desktop publishing software, guides are straight lines extending from one edge of a document to the other. But in Illustrator, you also can turn any path into a guide (see the following section). Figure 7-6 shows how a guide (the dotted circle) can help you line up objects (the triangles) in a perfect curve.

Creating guides

You can create guides in two ways: by pulling them out from the rulers and by transforming paths into guides.

Figure 7-6: You can use guides to align objects and to make sure that the edge of one object (in this case, the triangle) perfectly fits a curve or other path.

To pull a guide from a ruler, first make the vertical and horizontal rulers visible by selecting Objects⇨Show Rulers (⌘-R). To create guides that span the entire pasteboard, click on the vertical or horizontal ruler and drag out.

To transform an existing path into a guide, select the path and choose Object⇨Guides⇨Make (⌘-5).

 The Magic Rotating Guide (possibly the coolest tip you'll ever learn): When you drag a guide out from the vertical ruler, hold down Option and the vertical guide becomes a horizontal guide. And vice versa.

Moving guides

Moving an unlocked guide is simple — click on it and drag. If the guide is locked, press Control-Shift and then click and drag.

If you aren't sure whether the guides in your document are locked or unlocked, select Object⇨Guides. If you see a check mark next to Lock, the guides are locked (***Note:*** All new guides also will be locked). Unchecking the Lock option (choose Object⇨Guides⇨ Lock or press ⌘-7) unlocks all the document's guides. To lock guides again, choose Object⇨Guides⇨Lock or press ⌘-7.

All guides in a document have a special status of "lockedness," where all guides are either locked or unlocked. Weirdly enough, however, guides can be locked and unlocked individually as well (see the "Locking" section later in this chapter).

Releasing guides

To *release* a guide, or change it into a path, press Control-Shift and double-click the guide or select the guide and choose Object⇨Guides⇨Release (⌘-6).

To release multiple guides: First, make sure that the guides are unlocked; in other words, make sure that there's no check mark next to Lock in the Object⇨Guides submenu. Then select the guides (you do so in the same way you select multiple paths: either drag a marquee around the guides or Shift-click each guide) and choose Object⇨Guides⇨Release (⌘-6).

Selecting *all* guides — even those that are currently paths — by dragging a marquee or Shift-clicking can be a chore. Here's another way: Make sure that the guides are not locked and choose Edit⇨Select All (⌘-A). Then select Object⇨Guides⇨Release (⌘-6), releasing all guides and, more important, selecting all paths that were formerly guides; all other paths and objects are deselected. Then select Object⇨Guides⇨Make (⌘-5) and all guides become guides again and are selected.

For the most part, guides behave exactly like their counterparts, paths. As long as guides are unlocked, you may select them, hide them, group them, and even paint them (although paint attributes will not be visible on-screen or on a printout until the guides are converted back into paths).

Locking, Hiding, and Moving Objects

All objects in Illustrator (except templates, which always seem to be locked) can be locked, hidden, and moved — including guides (see preceding section). Locking and hiding work about the same, and the results are only marginally different, but you can move objects in Illustrator in several ways.

Locking

To lock an object, select it and choose Arrange⇨Lock (⌘-1). The selected object is not only locked but also deselected. In fact, an object is unselectable when locked.

A locked object remains locked when the document is saved and closed. As a result, locked objects are still locked the next time the document is opened. Locked objects do print, with no indication whether they are locked or not.

Because a locked object can't be selected, it can't be changed: in Illustrator, as in most Macintosh applications, objects can be modified only when selected. To change a locked object, choose Arrange⇨Unlock (⌘-2), unlocking (and selecting) all objects.

Hiding

Sometimes, you don't want to see certain objects on your document page — perhaps because they obstruct your view of other objects or they take a long time to redraw. In these cases, it's a good idea to hide the objects in question. To do so, select them and then select Arrange⇨Hide (⌘-3).

Hidden objects are invisible and unselectable; they still exist in the document, but they do not print. When a document is reopened, hidden objects reappear.

To show (and select) all hidden objects, select Arrange⇨Show (⌘-4).

 To lock or hide all *nonselected* objects, press Option while locking or hiding.

Moving

The most common way to move an object is to use a selection tool and drag the selected points, segments, and paths from one location to another.

The most precise way to move an object is to use the Move dialog box. Select the object you want to move and then choose Arrange⇨Move (⌘-Shift-M). The Move dialog box appears, and you can enter the appropriate values in either the horizontal or vertical text fields. If you want to move an object diagonally, enter a number in the Distance text field and then enter the angle of movement direction in the Angle text field.

Any object (except for text selected with a type tool) can be moved via the Move dialog box, including anchor points and line segments.

 The numbers that appear in the Move dialog box as defaults are a recording of the last move made with a selection tool in that document.

 If you have used the Measure tool prior to using the Move dialog box, the numbers in the Move dialog box correspond to the numbers that appeared in the Info palette when you used the Measure tool.

In the Move dialog box, positive numbers in the horizontal text field move an object from left to right, while negative numbers move an object from right to left. Positive numbers in the vertical text field move an object from bottom to top, while negative numbers move an object from top to bottom. Negative numbers in the Distance text field move an object in the direction opposite of that entered in the Angle text field. The Angle text field works a bit differently. Negative numbers in the Angle text field move the angle in the opposite direction from 0° (so entering –45° is the same as entering 315° and entering –180° is the same as entering 180°).

The measurement system in the Move dialog box matches the system set in the General Preferences dialog box. To enter a measurement different from the current measurement system, use the following indicators:

For inches	1″ or 1in (one inch)
For picas	1p or 1pica (one pica)
For points	1pt or 0p1 (one point)
For picas/points	1p1 (one pica, one point)
For millimeters	1mm (one millimeter)
For centimeters	1cm (one centimeter)

The horizontal and vertical text fields are linked to the Distance and Angle text fields; when one of the fields is changed, the others are altered accordingly.

Pressing the Copy button duplicates selected objects in the direction and distance indicated, just as holding down Option when dragging duplicates the selected objects.

 The Move dialog box is a great place to enter everything via the keyboard. Press Tab to move from text field to text field, press Return to push the OK button, and press ⌘-Period or ESC to push the Cancel button. Pressing Option-Return or pressing Option while clicking OK pushes the Copy button.

Type **8**

In This Chapter

* Methods of entering type in a document
* Creating Point type
* Creating Rectangle type
* Placing type within areas
* How to create type on a path
* Selecting type and changing type attributes
* Importing type
* Converting type into editable outlines
* Designing with the Type tool
* Special characters
* Avoiding type compatibility problems
* Creating custom fonts

Type Areas

In order for type to exist in Illustrator, there must first be a *type area* defined. Type can never be outside these areas because type is treated very differently than any other objects in Illustrator.

There are four different kinds of type areas: Point type, Rectangle type, Area type, and Path type. Point type exists around a single point clicked with the standard Type tool. Rectangle type is type constricted to a rectangular area — also drawn with the standard Type tool. Area type is type that flows within a specific open or closed path. Path type is type whose baseline is attached to a specific open or closed path.

Point Type

To create type with a single point defining its location, use the Type tool and click on one single location within the document window where there are no paths. A blinking *insertion point* appears, signifying that type will appear where that point is located (see Figure 8-1). By typing on the keyboard, text will now appear in the document at that insertion point. Type cannot be entered when a selection tool is being used. Type selected with a selection tool appears at the bottom of Figure 8-1.

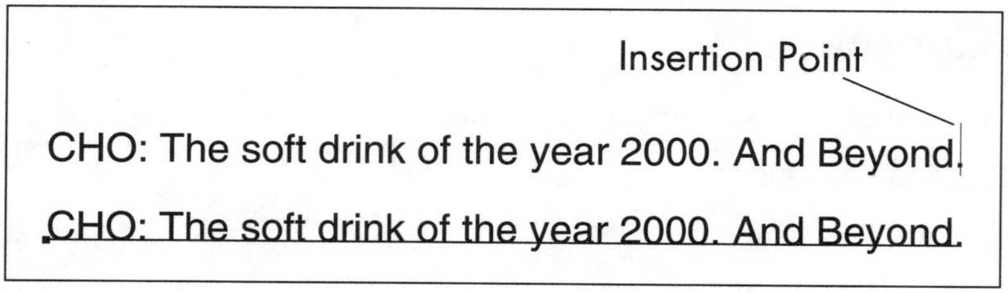

Figure 8-1:
Point type
with an
insertion
point at
the end of
the line,
and the
same line
of type
selected
with a
selection
tool.

Insertion Point

CHO: The soft drink of the year 2000. And Beyond.

CHO: The soft drink of the year 2000. And Beyond.

When the Illustrator program is first booted, text defaults into the following values: 12 Helvetica, Flush left, Auto Leading on, Spacing 0, Baseline Shift 0, Tracking/Kerning 0, Horizontal Scale 100%, Auto Kerning off, no indentation or paragraph spacing. There is no method within Illustrator to automatically change this default upon start-up.

Point type that is flush left will have its left side flush against the vertical location of the point initially clicked. Centered type will be centered left to right on the vertical location of the point. Flush right type will have its right edge flush with the vertical location of the point. Point type cannot be justified with either of the two methods available.

When creating Point type, keep in mind that only hard returns will force a new line of text to be created. If no returns are used, eventually text will run right off the document. When importing text, be sure that the text contains these hard returns, or the text will run into oblivion. Hard returns can be added after importing, but it may be difficult to do so.

Rectangle Type

There are two ways to create Rectangle type (see Figure 8-2). The easiest way is by clicking and dragging the Type tool diagonally, which creates a rectangle as you drag. The blinking insertion point appears in the top row of text, with its horizontal location dependent on the text alignment choice. Choosing flush right forces the insertion point to appear in the upper righthand corner; centered puts the insertion point in the center of the row; and flush left or one of the justification methods makes the insertion point appear in the upper lefthand corner.

If the Shift key is pressed, the rectangle is constrained to a perfect square. There is no need to drag from upper left to lower right — you can drag from any corner to its opposite — whichever way is most convenient.

Figure 8-2:
Rectangle type
(the dotted line is
the border of the
rectangle).

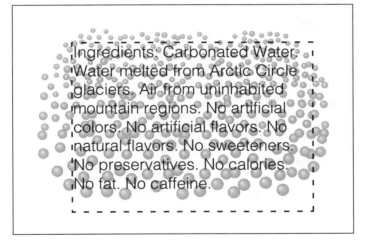

STEPS: Creating Rectangle Type in an Area of Specific Proportions

Step 1. Using the Rectangle tool, click without dragging to get the Rectangle dialog box. Enter the exact dimensions of the type area.

Step 2. Choose the Type tool and click the Type cursor on the edge of the rectangle. Any type entered into this box will be constrained to that particular rectangle.

Once a rectangle has been used as a type rectangle, it can never be a non-type rectangle again.

To create type in a rectangle of specific proportions, draw a rectangle with the Rectangle tool by clicking once in the document window. This will display the Rectangle Size dialog box, where you can enter the information needed. Then choose the Area Type tool and click on the edge of the rectangle. The type will fill the rectangle perfectly.

If you need to create a Rectangle type area that is a precise size but don't want to draw a rectangle first, open the Info palette by selecting Window⇨Show Info (⌘-Control-I) and as you drag the type cursor, watch the information in the Info palette, which will display the dimensions of the type area.

Area Type

The cabability of placing type within any area is one of the "cooler" features of Illustrator, right up there with the fact that the program comes in a purple box.

To create type within an area, first create the path that will be the area that confines the type. The path can be closed or open and any size. Keep in mind that the area of the path should be close to the size needed for the amount of text (at the point size that it needs to fit). After the path has been created, choose the Area Type tool and position the type cursor over the edge of the path and click.

The type in Figure 8-3 has been flowed into the outline of the CHO logo. Using text wraps, the type exists only inside the letters yet reads across all of them.

Figure 8-3:
Area type created so that the text flows inside the outlines of the word CHO.

Choosing the good shapes for Area type

What exactly constitutes a "good" shape to be used for Area type? As a rule of thumb, gently curved shapes are better than harsh, jagged ones. Type tends to flow better into the larger lumps created by smoothly curving paths.

Try to avoid creating paths with wild or tight curves. Other designs that can cause problems are "hourglass" shapes or any closed path that has an area where the sides are almost touching. Figure 8-4 shows how type flows into a smoothly curved area and how it has trouble flowing into a sharp, spiky shape.

Figure 8-4:
Type flows much better into a smoothly curved area (left) than a sharp, spiky one.

Try to make the top and bottom boundaries of the path have less "bumpiness" than the sides; use of this technique will reduce the number of times that type jumps from one area across another.

For the best results with Area type, make the type small and justify it (⌘-Shift-J). This will ensure that the type flows up against the edges of the path.

Outlining areas of Area type

Placing a stroke on the path surrounding Area type can be a great visual effect, but doing so and getting good results can be a bit tricky.

If the stroke is thicker than a point or two, and you don't want the type to run into the edges of the stroke, there are a few things you can do.

The fastest way to do this (although it requires a bit of math) is to copy the stroked path that the type is inside of and paste it in front. Fill the shape with the background color and a stroke equal to twice the amount of white space you would like between the stroke and the text. Then hide the path and the type, and select the original path. Delete the text from this path and make the stroke the width according to this formula:

(Desired Width + White Space size) X 2 = Bottom layer stroke weight

So if you want a stroke that is 6 points wide on a shape and has 3 points of white space between the stroke and the text, the bottom shape will have a stroke of (6 + 3) X 2 = 18. The top layer will have a "white" stroke of 6, with a fill the same color as the stroke.

The second way to do this is by using the Offset Path filter. This is better for two reasons: first, it requires much less math, and second, you don't have to worry about background color (especially if the background is a bunch of other objects or a placed EPS image). Of course, there is a catch: The path cannot be turned into a text area boundary before the Offset Path filter is applied to it.

STEPS:	**Creating Inset Type Areas with the Offset Path Filter**
Step 1.	Create a path for your Area type with any drawing tool. Close the path for the best results when using the Offset Path filter.
Step 2.	Do *not* make the path into a type area by clicking on the path with a type tool at this point. Select the path you wish to use for Area type with the Selection tool and then select Filter⇨Object⇨Offset Path.
Step 3.	Determine the distance that you wish your text to be from the edge of the real path. If there is a stroke on the edge of the real path, add half the width of the stroke to your distance. In the Offset field, enter this distance in negative form. For example, if you want the distance from the edge of the path to be 6 points and the width of the stroke is 10 points, the number you enter in the Offset field will be –11 points (6+10/2).
Step 4.	After you click OK, a new path will be created inside the original. Click on this path with the Area Type tool, and the text will be "inside" the edge, with a buffer (see Figure 8-5).

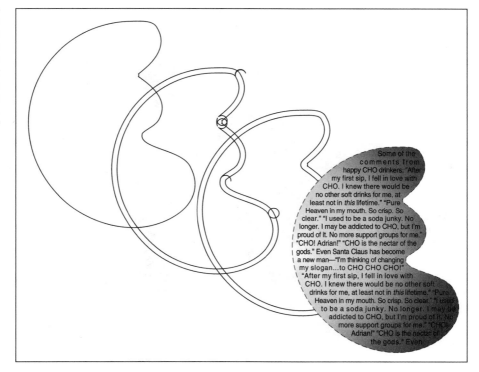

Doing bizarre things to Area type

Probably the most overlooked rule when it comes to manipulating Area type and the paths that create the type boundaries is the simple fact that the path and the type are treated equally, unless the path is chosen with the Direct Selection (or Group Selection) tool.

When using the transformation tools, be sure that if you don't want to change any of the characteristics of the type, that you select just the path. Use the Group Selection tool to just click once on the deselected path, and only the path will be selected, not the type.

If the type is selected as well as the path, then the transformations will affect both the type and the path. Figure 8-6 shows transformations taking place to both type and its surrounding path and transformations taking place to just the surrounding path.

Figure 8-6:
Both the
path and
the type of
the figure
on the top
have been
trans-
formed,
although
just the
path has
been
trans-
formed on
the figure
on the
bottom.
The figure
on the left
has not
been
trans-
formed at
all.

Area type is selected when there is an underline under all the characters in the area.

Type color *and* the color of type

There is a difference between the *color of type* and *type's color*. Type can be painted in Illustrator to be any one of millions of different shades, which determines the color we normally think of.

The color of type, on the other hand, is the way the type appears in the document and is more indicative of the light or dark attributes of the text. The actual red-green-blue colors of the type do work into this appearance, but many times the weight of the type and the tracking/kerning have a much more profound effect on color.

To easily see the color of type, unfocus your eyes as you look at your document. This works better on a printed area than on-screen, but you can still get the gist of the way it will appear when viewing it on your monitor. Dark and light areas become much more apparent when you can't read the actual words on the path. This method of unfocusing your eyes to look at a page also works well when trying to see the "look" of a page and how it was designed. Many times, unfocusing will emphasize the fact that you don't have enough white space or that all the copy seems to blend together.

Heavy type weights, such as bold, heavy, and black, make type feel darker on a page. Type kerned and tracked very tightly also seems to give the type a darker feel.

The x-height of type (the height to which the lowercase letters, such as an "x," rise) is another factor that determines the color of type. Certain italic versions of typefaces can make the text seem lighter, although a few make text look darker because of the additional area that the thin strokes of the italic type covers.

Combined with red-green-blue colors, type can be made to stand out by appearing darker, or blend into the page when lighter. When you add smartly placed images near the type, your page can come alive with *color*.

Coloring type that is anchored to a path

When type is anchored to a path, either as Area type or Path type, there are some important considerations to think of before filling and stroking the type.

First, if just the type or just the path is selected with the regular Selection tool, the other (path or type) will be selected as well. Do you want to put a stroke along that path that surrounds your type? If you select the path with the regular Selection tool, then the type will be selected as well, and each character in the type area will have the same stroke you meant to apply to the path.

For changing just the path's Paint attributes, be sure to use the Direct Selection tool to select the path. If no underlines appear under the text, then the text is *not* selected. To change all the text, you must choose a type tool, click within the text area, and then Select All (⌘-A). Only then will just the text be affected.

Designing with Area type

All sorts of nifty things can be done with type that has been flowed into areas — from unusual column designs to fascinating shapes.

A publication can be livened up quite easily by using nonrectangular columns. *Mondo 2000* magazine uses curved columns that are easy to read and lend a futuristic, hip look to the publication. Angled and curved columns are simple to create in Illustrator by creating the shape of the column and flowing Area type from one shape to the next.

Traditionally, forcing type into an irregular (nonrectangular) area was quite a task. The typesetter had to set several individual lines of type, each specced by the art director or client to be a certain specific length so that when all the text was put together, the text formed the shape (see Figure 8-7). This is probably the main reason the world has not seen too much of this, except in overly zealous art students' portfolios.

Figure 8-7: The subject matter fit into a related shape.

As cold waters to a thirsty soul, so is good news from a far country. —Proverbs 25:25

Water is Excellent. —Pindar

A little water clears us of this deed. —William Shakespeare

But somewhere, beyond space and time, Is wetter water, slimier slime! —Rupert Brooke

Water, water every where, And all the boards did shrink; Water, water, every where, Nor any drop to drink. —Samuel Taylor Coleridge

"What's the water in French, sir?" "L'eau," replied Nicholas. "Ah!" said Mr. Lillywick, shaking his head mournfully. "I thought as much. Lo, eh? I don't think anything of that language—nothing at all."—Charles Dickens

For example, you can give a report on toxic waste in New Jersey more impact by shaping the text into the form of a hypodermic needle. Or you can make a seasonal ad in the shape of a Christmas tree. Look at some of the Absolut Vodka ads to see what they've done to flow text into that all-too-familiar bottle. Figure 8-7 shows quotes about water fit into water droplets.

Path Type

The unique thing about type on a path is that when the path is not visible, the type *becomes* the path, as in Figure 8-8. This can produce some really fascinating results, especially when combined with various fonts of different weights, styles, colors, and special characters.

To create Path type, first create a path in your document. Then click on the path with the Path Type tool to create an insertion point along the path. This will work whether the path is a closed path or an open path.

Figure 8-8:
Type, when set on a path, can actually *become* the path.

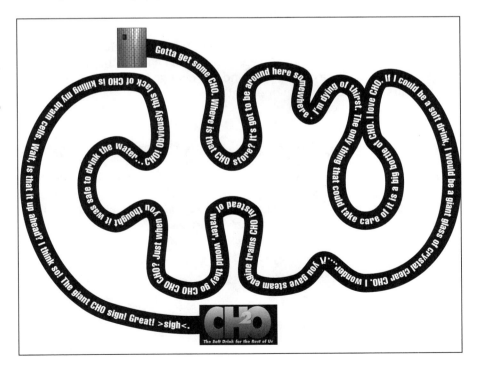

Type will align to the insertion point; if the type is set to flush left, the left edge of the type will align to the location where the Path Type tool was first clicked. Unlike Point type, where a hard return sent the type to the next line, hard returns send the rest of the type into never-never land, only to be retrieved by deleting the hard return or selecting all and cutting and pasting in a standard text block.

Path type can be flowed along the path it is aligned to by clicking on the Insertion bar with any selection tool and dragging along the path. If the Insertion bar is dragged to the other side of the path, then the type will flip over in the direction of the bar. For this reason, it is a good idea to click on the topmost part of the Insertion bar before dragging.

 As with other objects in Illustrator that can be moved by dragging, pressing the Option key before releasing the mouse will cause the object being dragged to duplicate instead of just move. This works with the Type Insertion bar, as well.

If you would like the type you are dragging to appear below the path but not get flipped upside down and change direction, use baseline shift (found in the Character palette) to raise and lower the type to your liking. The key commands for baseline shift (Option-↑ and Option-↓ to move up and down by increments set in the General Preferences dialog box) are particularly useful when adjusting Path type.

 Even though there are three different type tools, you only need to choose one. If you have the standard Type tool, it will change into the Area Type tool when you pass over a closed path and will change into a Path Type tool when the cursor passes over an open path.

Type on the top and bottom of a circle

Everyone's doing it. Peer pressure is going to make you succumb as well. If you can put type on the top and the bottom of a circle so that it runs along the same path, you are quite the designer, or so thinks the average guy on the street. The simple type-on-a-circle shown in Figure 8-9 can be created quite easily.

Figure 8-9:
Type on the
top and
bottom of a
circle.

Follow these steps, and with a little practice, you can create type on a circle (Selection tool selected) in under 15 seconds. Pretty impressive to even those who understand how it's done.

STEPS:	Creating Type on the Top and Bottom of a Circle
Step 1.	Draw a circle with the Oval tool (hold down the Shift key to make sure it is a perfect circle). Then choose the Path Type tool and click on the top center of the circle. The blinking insertion point will appear at that point on the circle.

Step 2. Type the text that is to appear at the top of the circle and press ⌘-Shift-C (or select Type⇨Alignment⇨Centered), which will center the type at the top of the circle.

Step 3. Choose the Selection tool and click on the top of the I-bar marker, dragging it down to the bottom center of the circle. Before letting go of the mouse button, center the type, making sure that it is readable from left to right, and press the Option key. When you do release the mouse button, there will be type along the top *and* the bottom of the circle, but the type on the bottom will be *inside* the circle.

The key here is that the Option key is pressed. The Option key *duplicates* the text and circle, moving it to a new location in the process. If the Option key were not pressed, the type would have just moved to the bottom of the circle.

Step 4. Select the bottom text with the Type tool and slowly "scoot" the type down below the baseline by pressing Option-Shift-↓. This will push the type down the baseline in increments that were set in the General Preferences dialog box (the default is 2). Keep pressing the key combination until the type is vertically positioned to mimic the type on the top of the circle.

Step 5. Select the text along the bottom of the circle with the Type tool. Type in the text that is to appear at the bottom of the circle. It will replace the selected text. Figure 8-10 shows these steps.

You're finished. Amazing, isn't it? Just remember that you now have *two* circles with type on them, not one circle with two type paths (that can't happen).

Figure 8-10:
The steps for creating type on the top and bottom of a circle.

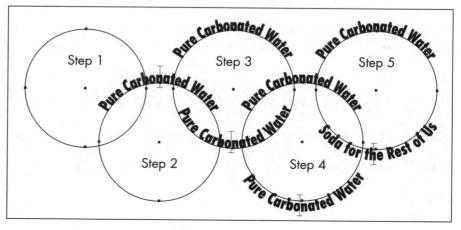

Avoiding Path type trouble

The most common trouble with Path type usually occurs when the path has either corner anchor points or very sharp curves. Letters will often crash (run into one another) when this occurs.

Besides the most obvious way to avoid this problem, which is to not use paths with corner anchor points and sharp curves, the areas where the letters crash can sometimes be kerned apart until they aren't touching anymore.

 When kerning Path type, be sure to kern from the "flush" side first. For instance, if the type is Flush Left, start your kerning from the left side and work to the right. If you start on the wrong end, the letters you kern apart will move along the path until they aren't in an area that needs kerning, but instead other letters will appear there.

Another method of fixing crashed letters is to "tweak" the path with the Direct Selection tool. Careful adjusting of both anchor points and direction points can easily fix crashes and letters that have huge amounts of space between them.

 If the path that is the base of the letters doesn't need to be directly under the letters, use the baseline shift keyboard commands (Option-Shift-↑, Option-Shift-↓) to move the type until the path runs through the center of the text. This can automatically fix the spacing problems encountered by text that crashes over sharp turns and corners.

Reversing Path type

One of the most desirable effects with Path type (and, in my opinion, much cooler than type on a circle) is Path type that is reversed, as shown in Figure 8-11.

Figure 8-11:
Steps for
creating type
reversed on a
path.

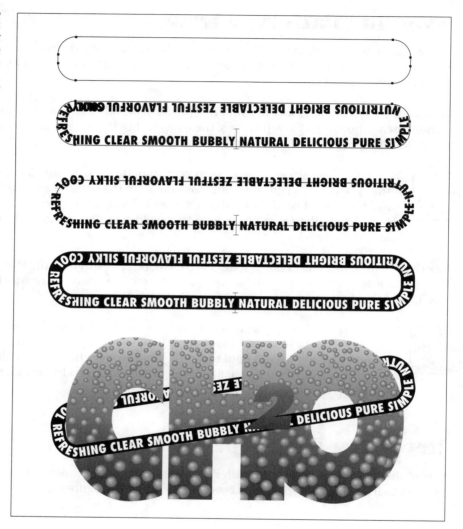

STEPS: Creating Reversed Path Type

Step 1.   Create the path to use for the Path type. In my example, I used a rounded
rectangle. Your path can be open or closed.

Step 2. Click on the path with the Path Type tool and type in the type for the path. Type with no descenders works better than type with descenders.

Step 3. Vertically center the type on the path by adjusting baseline shift (Option-Shift-↑ or ↓ Arrow). If there are descenders, make sure the type is centered from ascender to descender.

Step 4. Select the type with a type tool and change the fill to white. Select the path with the Direct Selection tool and change the fill to none and the stroke of the path to black. Make the weight of the stroke just greater than the point size of the type.

Selecting Type

In order to make changes to text, it must first be selected. There are two ways of selecting type: Type areas can be selected with a selection tool, which selects every character in the type area, and characters can be selected individually or in groups with any of the type tools.

To select the entire type area or multiple type areas, click on the baseline of a line of type within the type area you want to select. Any changes made in the Type menu, Font menu, Character palette, or Paragraph palette will affect every character in the type areas selected.

If there are blank fields in any of the palettes or no check marks next to some of the menu items (for instance, no font is checked) when type areas are selected, that means that there are different options for each of those fields or menu items within the type area (for instance, Helvetica for some characters, Times for others). Changing a blank field or unchecked menu item to a specific choice will change *all* characters in the type area to that particular choice.

To select characters within a type area, you must be using a Type tool. As you near text that has been typed in the document, the dotted lines surrounding the cursor will disappear. The "hot" point of the Type cursor is the place where the short horizontal bar crosses the vertical bar (see Figure 8-12). It is this hot point that you should use when clicking with the Type cursor.

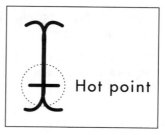

Figure 8-12:
The "hot" point of the Type cursor.

Hot point

To select an individual character, drag across the character to be selected, and it will be reversed (or highlighted, depending on the highlight color in the Colors Control Panel). Any reverse character is a selected character. To select more than one character, drag left or right across multiple characters; all characters from the location you originally clicked to the current location of the cursor will be highlighted. If you drag up with the cursor with straight text, you will select all the characters to the left of the one you selected on that line and all the characters to the right of the cursor's current location. Dragging down does the reverse. The more lines you drag up or down, the more lines will be selected.

To select one word at a time (and the space that follows it), double-click on the word to be selected. The word will reverse and the space after the word will reverse as well. The reason that the space following the word is selected is mainly due to the times you copy, cut, and paste words from within sentences. For example, to remove the word *Lazy* in the phrase "The Lazy Boy," you double-click on the word *Lazy* and press Delete. The phrase will then be "The Boy," which only has one space where the word *Lazy* used to be. To select several words, double-click and drag the Type cursor across additional words. Each word you touch with the cursor will be selected, from the location initially double-clicked to the current location. Dragging to the previous or next line will select additional lines, with at least a word on the first line double-clicked and one word on the line dragged to.

For the nimble-fingered clickers, you may also click three times to select a paragraph. Triple-click anywhere inside the paragraph and the entire paragraph will be selected, including the hard return at the end of the paragraph (if there is one). Triple-clicking and dragging will select successive paragraphs if the cursor is moved up or down while the mouse button is still pressed following the third click.

To select all the text within a type area with a type tool, click once in the type area and choose Edit⇨Select All (⌘-A). All the text in the type area will be reversed.

As in most other Macintosh programs, text can only be selected in contiguous blocks. There is no way to select two words in two different locations of the same type area without selecting all the text between them.

Type can also be selected through use of the Shift key. Click in one spot (we'll call it the beginning) and then Shift-click in another spot. The characters between the beginning and the Shift-click are selected. Successive Shift-clicks will select characters from the beginning to the current location of the most recent Shift-click.

Editing Type

Text editing features in Illustrator are available on a limited scale. By clicking once within a type area, a blinking insertion point appears. If you begin typing, characters will appear where the blinking insertion point is. If you press Delete, you will delete the previous character (if there is one).

The arrow keys on your keyboard move the blinking insertion point around in the direction of the arrow. The right arrow will move the insertion point one character to the right, and the left arrow moves the insertion point one character to the left. The up arrow moves the insertion point to the previous line, while the down arrow moves the insertion point to the next line.

Pressing the ⌘ key while moving the insertion point moves the insertion point much more rapidly than without it. ⌘ –← or → will move the insertion point to the preceding or next word, while ⌘– ↑ or ↓ will move the insertion point to the preceding or next paragraph.

 Pressing the Shift key while moving the insertion point around with the arrows will select all the characters that the insertion point passes over. This works for the ⌘-arrow movements as well.

When characters are selected with a type tool, typing anything will delete the selected characters and replace them with what is currently being typed. When the Delete key is pressed and characters are selected, all the selected characters will be deleted. If type is pasted (⌘-V) when characters are selected, the selected characters will be replaced with the pasted characters.

Changing Character Attributes

The easiest way to change the attributes of characters is by using the Character palette, shown in Figure 8-13. Most of the changes in the Character palette are available as options in the Type menu and the Font menu, but on a limited scale. As a rule, if you have more than one change to make, it is better to do it in the Character palette than the menu, if just for the simple fact that everything you need will be in one place.

Figure 8-13:
The Character palette.

Character attribute changes affect only the letters that are selected, with the exception of leading (see below), which should really be in the Paragraph palette.

 Several character attributes can be changed in increments by using keyboard commands. The increments are set in the General Preferences dialog box (select File⇨Preferences⇨General, or ⌘-K). Increments can be changed for point size, leading, baseline shift, and tracking/kerning values. Where appropriate, the key commands for each attribute change are listed in the paragraphs below.

Using the Character palette

The Character palette can be displayed in a number of different ways. Selecting any of the following menu items will display it or, when displayed, bring it in front of any other palettes: Type⇨Size⇨Other, Type⇨Leading⇨Other, Type⇨Kern, Type⇨Character, and Window⇨Show Character. The following key commands also display the Character palette: ⌘-T, ⌘-Shift-F, ⌘-Shift-S, ⌘-Shift-K, and ⌘-Option-Shift-M.

The Character palette can be displayed in two different modes: full palette or partial palette. Clicking the lever (it looks like a key) in the lower right of the partial palette (top half) displays and hides the rest of the palette. The Character palette remembers which mode the palette was in the last time it was displayed and shows that view the next time you display it. If it is in partial palette mode, selecting Type⇨Kern (⌘-Shift-K) will display the full palette.

The Tab key can be used to tab across the different text fields. When in partial display palette mode, the Tab key works only in the partial palette; when the last field (Leading) is selected, the Tab key then goes back to the Font field. If a field in the lower part of the palette is highlighted when the palette is closed, the Font field will be highlighted. When the palette is in full view, tabbing past the last field (Tracking/Kerning) will highlight the Font field as well. In addition to the Tab key tabbing forward through the text fields, pressing Shift-Tab will tab backward through the text fields.

Selecting Edit⇨Undo (⌘-Z) will *not* undo items typed in the character palette while you are still in the text field. To undo something, you must first move along (tab) to the next field and then undo, and then Shift-Tab back. Canceling (⌘-Period, Escape) will not cancel what you have typed but instead will highlight the field.

Character palette features

The first field on the Character palette, in the upper lefthand corner is the Font family field. When you type the first couple of letters of the font you want to use, Illustrator fills in the rest of the name for you. What happens if you type in a font that you don't have? Illustrator just ignores you, for the most part. In a nice touch, you don't get silly dialog boxes appearing telling you that there is no such typeface (à la QuarkXPress), but instead the blinking insertion point remains in the same location until a letter that works is typed. The Font field can be automatically highlighted (and the Character palette will be displayed if it is not) by pressing either ⌘-T, ⌘-Shift-F, or ⌘-Option-Shift-M.

To close the Character or Paragraph palettes, press ⌘-Return after you enter your last entry in a text field on the palette.

The field in the upper right, next to the font field, is the Style field of the font family. The same rules as entering text for the Font field apply here. Type in the first couple letters of the style, and Illustrator fills in the rest for you. Only if you have the font style installed on your system will you be able to type it in. Illustrator is very strict when it comes to bold and italic versions of typefaces. If there is not a specific type style for what you want, you will *not* be able to type it in, unlike most software, which have "bold" and "italic" check boxes.

For every text field, the information entered may be applied by either tabbing to the next or preceding text field, or by pressing either Enter or Return.

In the upper right corner is a little pop-up menu triangle, which when pressed displays a list of all the typefaces installed on your system. The families are displayed in the main list, and arrows show which families have different styles. To select a font, drag the cursor over it until it is highlighted. To select a specific style of a font family, drag the cursor to the font family name, and then drag to the right to select the style name. The fields to the pop-up menu's left are updated instantly.

The field directly below the Font field is the Size field. Enter in the desired point size (from .1 pt. to 1296 pt., in increments of 1/1000 pt.) and any selected characters will increase or decrease to that particular point size. Next to the Size field is a pop-up menu triangle, which lists the standard point sizes available. Point size for type is always measured from the top of the ascenders to the bottom of the descenders. Type point size can be increased and decreased from the keyboard by typing ⌘-Shift-→ to increase and ⌘-Shift-← to decrease the point size by the increment specified in the General Preferences dialog box.

The keyboard commands for increasing and decreasing typographic attributes, such as point size, leading, baseline shift, and tracking are more than just another way to change those attributes. Instead, they are invaluable to making changes when the selected type has more than one different value of that attribute within it. For example, if some of the characters have a point size of 10 points and some of them have a point size of 20 points, using the keyboard command (with an increment set to 2 points) will change the type to 12 and 22 points. This would be tedious to do separately, especially if there were multiple sizes or just a few sizes scattered widely about.

Measuring type

So, you've finally mastered this whole silly point/pica concept, know that there are 72 points in an inch, and you think you're ready to conquer the world. And you are, as long as no one asks you to spec type.

Type is one of those oddities that is measured from the top of the ascenders (like the top of a capital "T") to the bottom of the descenders, like the bottom of a lowercase "j" (see the sidebar figure). So when people tell you they want a capital "I" that is 1 inch high, you can't just say, "Oh, there are 72 points in an inch, so I will create a 72-point 'I' for them."

A 72-point I is about 50 points tall. In inches that would be just under 3/4". To get better results for specially sized capital letters, a good rule of thumb is that every 100 points is about a 1-inch capital letter. This works for most typefaces, and only for the first several inches, but it is a good start to getting capital letters that are sized pretty accurately.

Curves in capital letters are yet another wrench thrown into the equation. In many typefaces, the bottom and top of the letter "O" will go beneath the baseline and above the ascender height of most squared letters (see the sidebar figure). Serifs on certain typefaces may also cross these lines.

Next to the Size field is the Leading text field. Enter the desired leading value (between .1 pt. and 1296 pt., in increments of 1/1000 pt.). To the right of the leading field is a pop-up menu triangle, from which common leading values can be chosen. In Illustrator, leading is measured from the baseline of the current line up to the baseline of the preceding line, as shown in Figure 8-14. The distance between these two baselines is the amount of leading.

Figure 8-14: Leading is measured from baseline to baseline. The 23 pt. leading was set by selecting the second line and changing the leading. The 14.5 pt. leading was set by selecting the third and fourth lines and changing the leading.

Unlike every other character attribute in the Character palette, leading actually works on entire paragraphs, not just on individual characters. So if one letter in a 12-line paragraph is selected, and the leading for that character is changed, the distance between the lines of every line in that entire paragraph is changed to reflect the new leading value.

If the leading is changed from the number that displays there by default, the box to the leading field's right will become unchecked. This box is the Auto Leading box, which when checked makes the leading exactly 120% of the point size. This is just great when the type is 10 points because the leading is 12 points, a common point size-to-leading relationship. But as point size goes up, leading should become proportionately less, until, at around 72 point, it is less than the point size. Instead, when Auto Leading is checked, 72 point type will have 86.5 point leading. That's a lot of unsightly white space.

Leading increments can be set in the General Preferences dialog box (⌘-K). Pressing the Option-↑ to increase the leading (which pushes lines farther apart) and Option-↓ to decrease the leading.

The bottom portion of the Character palette contains the baseline shift field, which, unlike leading, moves individual characters up and down relative to their baseline (from leading). Positive numbers move the selected characters up, and negative numbers move the characters down by the amount specified. The maximum amount of baseline shift is 1296 points in either direction. Baseline shift is especially useful for Path type. Baseline shift can be changed via the keyboard by pressing Option-Shift-↑ to increase and Option-Shift-↓ to decrease the baseline shift in the increment specified in the General Preferences dialog box.

Directly under baseline shift is the Horizontal Scale field. Horizontal Scale controls the width of the type, causing it to become expanded or condensed horizontally. Values from 1 to 10000% can be entered in this field. Like most other fields in the Character Attributes palette, the values entered are absolute values, so whatever the horizontal scale is, changing it back to 100% will return the type to its original proportions.

Tracking and kerning

To the right of the baseline shift field is the Tracking/Kerning field. The field will read either Tracking or Kerning depending on what is selected in the type area. If the type area is selected with a selection tool, or if one or more characters in the type are selected, then the field will read *Tracking*. If there is a blinking insertion point placed between two characters, the field will read *Kerning*. Figure 8-15 shows tracking/kerning examples.

Figure 8-15:
Examples of
tracking/
kerning.

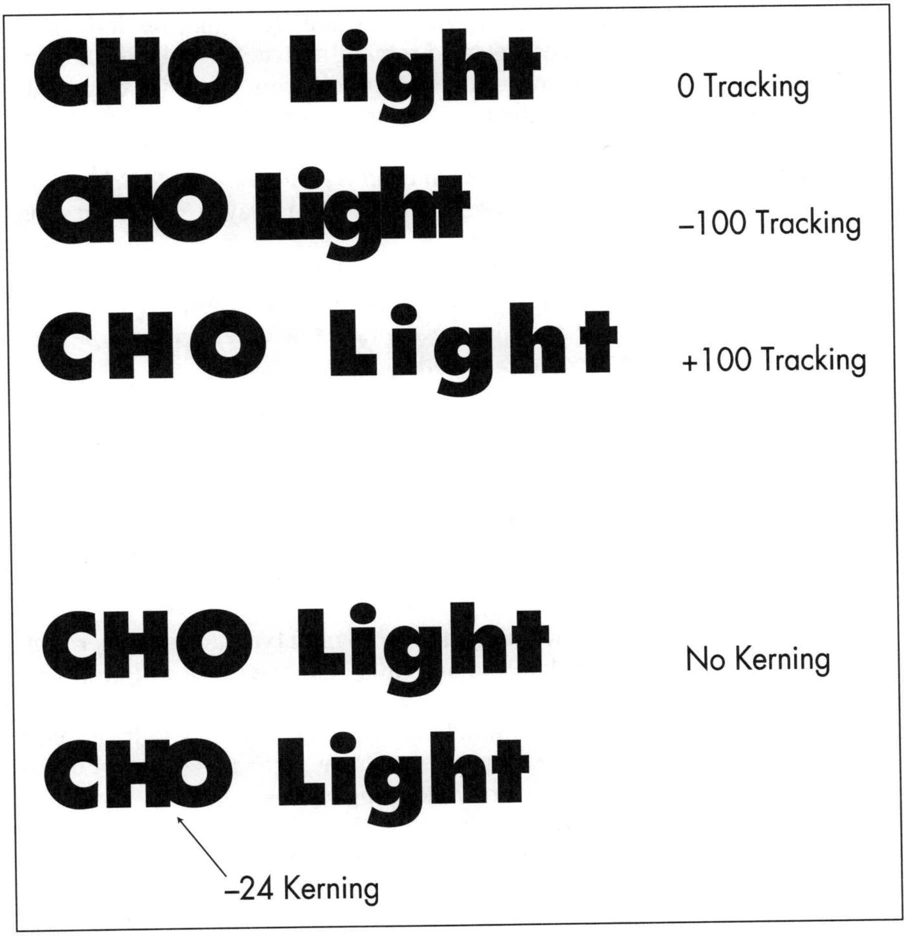

CHO Light   0 Tracking

CHO Light   –100 Tracking

CHO   Light   +100 Tracking

CHO Light   No Kerning

CHO Light

–24 Kerning

To highlight the Tracking/Kerning field and show the Character dialog box, select
Type⇨Track (Kern) (⌘-Shift-K). To increase or decrease the tracking/kerning by the
increments specified in the General Preferences dialog box, press Option-← or Option-→.
To increase or decrease the tracking/kerning by a factor of five times the amount in the
General Preferences dialog box, press ⌘-Option-→ or ⌘-Option-← .

For those QuarkXPress users who have already memorized a slate of key commands, Illustrator makes it easy to remember tracking and kerning increase/decrease commands by adding secondary commands for this option. To increase and decrease the tracking/kerning by the amount set in the General Preferences dialog box, press ⌘-Shift-] and ⌘-Shift-[. In addition, another QuarkXPress-based keyboard command is ⌘-Option-Shift-M to highlight the font field. These same key commands work the same way in QuarkXPress as Illustrator.

Tracking is the amount of space between all the letters currently selected. If the type area is selected with a selection tool, then it refers to all the space between all the characters in the entire type area. If characters are selected with a type tool, tracking only affects the space between the specific letters selected.

Kerning is the amount of space between any specific pair of letters. Kerning can only be changed when there is a blinking insertion point between two characters.

Although they are related, and appear to do basically the same thing, tracking and kerning actually work quite independently of each other. They only *look* like they are affecting each other; they never actually change the amount of one if the other is altered.

The space between letters is normally defined by the typeface designer; different typefaces look like they have different amounts of space between letters. If the Auto Kern check box is checked, then preset kerning values will go into effect for certain letter pairs. There are usually a couple hundred preset kerning pairs for common Adobe typefaces, although their "expert" sets have quite a few more. When the Auto Kern check box is checked, those preset kerning values can be seen by clicking between kerned letter pairs (capital T with most vowels is a good one to check) and reading the value in the Kerning field. Different typefaces have different kerning pairs, and kerning pairs don't only change from typeface to typeface, but even from weight to weight and style to style.

Kerning and tracking values are based on 1/1000 of an *em space*. An *em space* is the width of two numbers (think of two zeros — they tend to be the widest-looking numbers) at that particular point size.

Different software works with kerning and tracking differently. In those programs that *do* offer numerical tracking, it is usually represented in some form of a fraction of an em space, but the denominator varies from software to software. In QuarkXPress, for example, tracking and kerning is measured in 1/200 of an em space. Check the documentation that came with your software to determine the denominator in other software. This can get a little confusing when going from program to program, although the transformation from QuarkXPress to Illustrator is quite simple: to get the same tracking and kerning values in Quark that you used in Illustrator, divide the number you used in Illustrator by 5 (1000/200=5).

The values entered for tracking and kerning must be between –1000 and 10,000. A value of –1000 will result in stacked letters. A value of 10,000 will make enough space between letters for 10 em spaces, or 20 numbers. That's a *lot* of space.

The Language pop-up menu allows you to choose which language your system is native to. This is in support of Apple System 7.1's "World Ready" architecture, which makes it easily adaptable to different languages.

Outlining type the right way

Although at first it seems quite simple to outline characters of type using the stroke option in the Paint Style palette, just slapping on a stroke of a weight that seems to look good on the screen and changing the fill to none or white is technically incorrect.

The right way to outline type is only a little bit more involved. First, select the type that you want outlined and give the type a stroke that is twice the weight you want on the printed piece. Then Copy, Paste in Front, and give the new type a stroke of none and a fill of white. The white fill will knock out the inside half of the stroke, leaving the stroke one-half the width you specified, which is what you really want.

The figure shows both the right way and the wrong way to outline type. The top line is the original type. The middle line is outlined the wrong way with a 1 point stroke and a fill of white. The figure on the bottom has been outlined correctly, with one "100% Natural" outlined with a 2pt. stroke, and another directly on top of it with a white fill and no stroke.

100% Natural
100% Natural
100% Natural

Serif Preservation, as it's known to a select few, requires a teeny bit of math, but it's worth the effort. The white area inside the stroke is exactly the size of the character when done this way, as opposed to being smaller by half the width of the stroke when done normally.

Changing Paragraph Attributes

There are some changes that can be made to text that affect entire paragraphs at the same time. We've already talked about leading, which does this, but there are a number of other areas that are paragraph-specific. Unlike the Character palette, most of the options in the Paragraph palette are available only through the Paragraph palette, and not through a menu choice. The obvious exception to this is alignment, which can be accessed by selecting Type⇨Alignment and then choosing the alignment desired.

Paragraph attributes include alignments, indentation, leading before paragraph (other programs usually refer to this as space between paragraphs), hanging punctuation, hyphenation, and spacing.

Paragraph attributes can be changed if type areas are selected using a selection tool, in which case the changes will affect every paragraph within the entire type area. If the Type tool has selected one or more characters, changes made to paragraph attributes will affect the entire paragraphs of each of the selected characters.

Using the Paragraph palette

The Paragraph palette (see Figure 8-16) can be displayed using the menus by selecting Type⇨Paragraph, Type⇨Spacing, or Window⇨Show Paragraph. To display the Paragraph palette with key commands, type ⌘-Shift-P (⌘-Shift-T for users of Illustrator 5.0) or ⌘-Shift-O.

Figure 8-16:
The Paragraph palette.

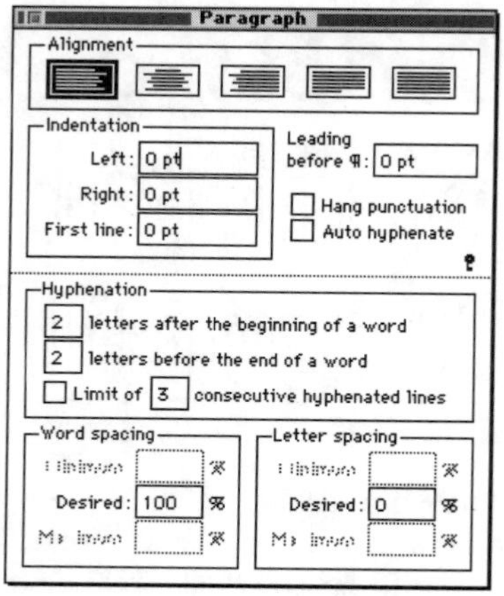

Pressing Tab will tab forward through the text fields, while Shift-Tab will tab backwards through the same text fields. Press Enter or Return to apply the changes that were made.

 To close the Paragraph palette, press ⌘-Return or ⌘-Enter after you enter your last entry in a text field on the palette.

The bottom part of the Paragraph palette contains information that doesn't get changed too often, so for the most part it doesn't need to be displayed. If you wish to display it, click on the small lever on the lower right once to show the bottom portion, and again to hide it.

Alignment

There are five different types of paragraph alignments (see Figure 8-17). Each of them is represented by a graphical representation of what multiple lines of type look like when that particular alignment is applied. The first is the most common: Flush Left, which experienced typesetters often refer to as "ragged right" due to the uneven right side of the text. Flush Left can also be selected by choosing Type⇨Alignment⇨Flush Left (⌘-Shift-L).

Figure 8-17: The five different types of alignments: Flush Left, Flush Right, Centered, Justified, and Justify Last Line.

The next type of alignment is Centered, where all lines of type in the paragraph are centered relative to each other, or to the point clicked, or location of the I-bar in Path type. Centered alignment can also be selected by choosing Type⇨Alignment⇨Centered (⌘-Shift-C).

The middle alignment choice is Flush Right, in which type has a smooth, even right side and an uneven left side (no, "ragged left" isn't really a correct term). Flush Right can also be selected by choosing Type⇨Alignment⇨Flush Right (⌘-Shift-R).

The fourth type of alignment is Justified, where both the left and right sides appear smooth and even. Extra space is added between letters and words, as defined below in "Spacing." The last line in a justified paragraph appears to be flush left. Justified alignment can also be selected by choosing Type⇨Alignment⇨Justify (⌘-Shift-J).

The last alignment is called Justify Last Line, which is the same as Justify except that the last line of every paragraph is justified along with the other lines of the paragraph. This can create some really *awful* looking paragraphs, and is done mainly for artistic emphasis, not as a proper way to justify type. Justify Last Line is particularly useful for stretching a single line of type across a certain width. Justify Last Line can also be selected by choosing Type⇨Alignment⇨Justify Last Line (⌘-Shift-B).

Justification only works on Area type and Rectangle type. Illustrator will not allow you to select Justify or Justify Last Line for Path type or Point type.

Indentation, paragraph spacing, and hanging punctuation

Paragraphs can be indented within the Paragraph palette by choosing different amounts of indentation for the left edge, right edge, and first line of each paragraph. The maximum indentation for all three fields is 1296 points, and the minimum is –1296 points.

Using indents is a great way to offset type, such as quotes, that have smaller margins than the rest of the type surrounding the quote. Changing the indentation values is also useful for creating hanging indents, such as numbered or bulleted text.

To create hanging indents easily, make the left indent as large as the width of a bullet or a number and a space, and then make the first line value the negative value of that. If the left indent were 2 picas, the first line would be –2 picas. This will create great hanging indents every time.

Illustrator allows you to place additional space between paragraphs by entering a number in the Leading before ¶ text field. This measurement is added to the leading to determine the distance from baseline to baseline before the selected paragraphs. You can also enter a negative number to decrease space between paragraphs, if necessary. Values for Leading before ¶ can be between –1296 and 1296 points.

If hanging punctuation is checked, punctuation at the left edge of a Flush Left or Justified/Justified Last Line paragraph will appear outside the type area, like the quotes in Figure 8-18. Punctuation on the right edge of a Flush Right or Justified/Justified Last Line paragraph will also appear outside the type area. Strangely enough, Illustrator is one of the few Macintosh programs that supports this very hip feature.

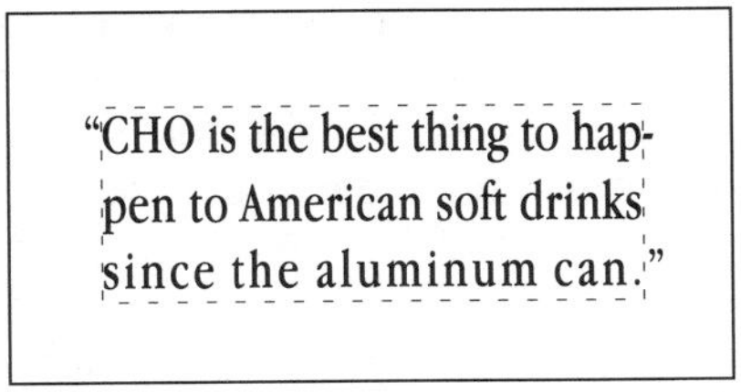

Figure 8-18:
When the Hanging Punctuation box is checked, quotes and hyphens will fall outside the boundary of the type area.

"CHO is the best thing to happen to American soft drinks since the aluminum can."

Hyphenation

Hyphenation? In a drawing program? I couldn't believe it either, but there it was staring me in the face. A nice addition to Illustrator's text-handling capabilities, hyphenation works in the background, silently hyphenating when necessary.

To use Illustrator's hyphenation, you mush check the Auto hyphenate box in the lower righthand corner of the top half of the Paragraph palette. After this is checked for selected text, that text will hyphenate fairly well.

Hyphenation in Illustrator works from a set of hyphenation rules, which you define in the bottom of the Paragraph palette. You can specify how many letters must fall before the hyphen can appear and how many letters must fall after the hyphen. You can also limit the number of hyphens in a row to avoid the "ladder look" of multiple hyphens.

When you need to hyphenate a word at a place where Illustrator doesn't seem to want to hyphenate it, you can create a *discretionary* hyphen. A discretionary hyphen is created by placing the blinking insertion point where the word should break and typing ⌘-Shift-Hyphen. This will cause the word to hyphenate at a certain part of the word only if that word has to be hyphenated. If the word doesn't have to be hyphenated, no hyphen will appear. This is much better than just typing a normal hyphen, which will work temporarily, but if the manually hyphenated word is moved from the edge of the line, the hyphen will remain within it.

Spacing

Illustrator allows you to control the spacing of letters and words in text by editing the Spacing fields at the bottom of the Paragraph palette.

Spacing affects the space between letters and words regardless of the alignment, although Justified text has even more spacing control than Flush Left, Flush Right, and Centered text.

When Flush Left, Flush Right, and Centered alignment are chosen, the only text fields that can be changed are the Desired fields for Letter Spacing and Word Spacing.

The values for Word Spacing may be entered in a number between 0 and 1000%. The Minimum must be less than the amount in the Desired box, and the Maximum must be more than the amount in the Desired box. At 100%, the word space is normal, at less than 100, the word space is reduced, and at a number greater than 100%, the word space is increased.

The values for Letter Spacing must be between –50% and 500%. The Minimum must be less than the amount in the Desired box, and the Maximum must be more than the amount in the Desired box. At 0%, the letter space is normal, at less than 0%, the letter space is reduced, and at a number greater than 0%, the letter space is increased.

The Minimum and Maximum boxes in the Word Spacing and Letter Spacing areas are mainly used to control where the extra space goes and is removed from when stretching out the lines of text and compressing those same lines.

Controlling the Flow of Type

Type can be steered around Illustrator in a number of different ways. In a previous section, "Area Type," I discussed how to make type adhere to specific shapes. In this section, I'll take a look at some other ways to control where type goes.

There are four basic ways to control the flow of type: creating specific areas out of paths in which the type flows, forcing type to wrap around other Illustrator objects, making type jump from one type area to another (text block links), and internal adjustments (indentations, space before paragraphs, and tabs).

Type wrapping

Using text wraps in Illustrator is in some ways the opposite of using type areas. Instead of defining paths for the type to flow through, we define areas that the type cannot flow through. Figure 8-19 shows type wrapped around small bubbles.

Figure 8-19: Type linked through the arrows and wrapped around the small bubbles.

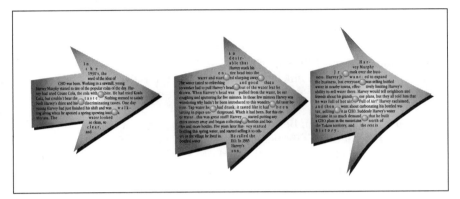

To create wrapped type, first create a block of type anywhere in your document. Then draw the path that you wish for your type to wrap around. The object that the text will wrap around must be closed. The wrapping object must be in front of the text. Select both the wrapping object and the text area with any selection tool, and select Type⇨Make Wrap. The text will flow around the wrapping object.

Additional objects can be used to wrap, just by placing them in front of the type area, selecting both the type area and the new wrapping object, and selecting Type⇨Make Wrap.

Text wrapping objects need no fill or stroke but do need to be closed, so if you would like to use an existing path, but that path is not closed, simply copy the path, select Edit⇨Paste In Front (⌘-F), and change the fill and stroke to none.

Text linking

Text can be linked in Illustrator quite easily, although the program does not give you much feedback about which type areas are linked and what the path of linked blocks is. Text linking is telling Illustrator that, while there isn't enough room in one particular text block for the amount of type you have placed there, the type can continue (be "linked") to another text area within the same document, as shown in Figure 8-19.

Text linking is done most often to link columns of text together. Because Illustrator does not have any other method of creating columns, text linking is often used for this purpose.

Text linking only works for Area type and Rectangle type. If more type is inside a type area than can be displayed, a small square with a plus sign in it appears. This is an indicator to you that there is more text to be seen in this text area.

To create a link between an overstuffed type area and a nice, new, empty one, select both the type area and the closed path or text area you wish to link to and then select Type⇨Link Blocks (⌘-Shift-G). The text will flow from the first type area into the second. To continue the link, select another closed path or type area along with the current type area and select Link Blocks again.

Type in linked blocks can be selected with any type tool by dragging from one type area into another. Selecting Edit⇨Select All (⌘-A) while working with a type tool in a linked type area will select all the type throughout all type areas linked to the one the insertion point is currently in. All other editing and attribute changes will affect type throughout the entire story.

To change the flow of type from one box to another, select individual type areas with the Direct Selection tool and choose Send to Back or Bring to Front. Type will begin in the rearmost type area and end in the frontward type area.

The trouble with Tabs in Illustrator 5.0

There are no tab stops or documented provisions for using the Tab key in Illustrator 5.0. This is a minor problem when typing, especially if you are accustomed to using tabs within your text documents. This is even a bigger problem when importing text that has tab stops, like tabbed text from a chart. Tabs normally work like a line break (a character that forces additional type following the line break to the next line without creating a new paragraph).

The problem with tabs has been accounted for and solved in Version 5.5. The section called "The Tab Ruler palette" is an explanation of how to use the tabs in Version 5.5.

The careful reader would have noticed that I said "documented" in the first paragraph. Well, if you know where to look in the *Beyond the Basics* book for Illustrator 5.0, it's kind of mentioned, but not really. So here, for the first time, is the real lowdown on Tabs in Illustrator 5.0. It seems a little weird at first, but once you get the hang of it, you'll wish all your word processing and layout programs worked with tabs like this.

Start by creating a Rectangle type area and type in five words separated by tabs. Yes, each word will go to the next line. We'll fix that shortly. Next, press Return after the last word entered, Select All (⌘-A), and Copy (⌘-C). Click the last line of type (it should be blank) and then Paste (⌘-V). Paste a few more times (⌘-V, ⌘-V, ⌘-V).

Using the Freehand tool, draw a series of four straight or curved vertical lines that extend above the top and below the bottom of the type area. Select the lines and the type area and select Type⇨Make Wrap. The type should be tabbed to the lines that you drew.

Tabs will tab to the other side of text wrap objects. Play with this a little, and you'll discover that this method is much more flexible than standard word processing tab stops.

 Try as you might, you cannot get tabs to be anything other than flush left in Illustrator 5.0. There is no way to create tab leaders either. Sigh.

The Tab Ruler palette

 In Version 5.5 of Illustrator, there is a wondrous little creature called the Tab Ruler palette, which is used to set tabs the same way you would in your word processing or page layout software.

To access the Tab Ruler palette, select Window⇨Show Tab Ruler or press ⌘-Shift-T.

 If you press ⌘-Shift-T in Version 5.0 of Illustrator, you will display the Paragraph palette.

The Tab Ruler palette is shown in Figure 8-20.

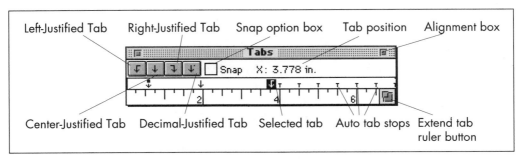

Figure 8-20: The Tab Ruler palette.

To set tabs for type, select the type you wish to set tabs for and select Window⇨Show Tab Ruler or press ⌘-Shift-T. The Tab Ruler palette will appear above the type you have selected and will be the width of the type area automatically.

To change the width of the Tab Ruler palette, click and drag on the Extend Tab Ruler button in the lower right corner of the palette. The Tab Ruler palette can be made wider or thinner, but not taller. To reset the Tab Ruler palette back to the exact size of the type area, click on the Alignment box in the upper righthand corner of the palette.

 The Alignment box will move the Tab Ruler palette to make it flush left with the type and move it up or down so that it is right above the selected text area.

Before you set any tabs, tabs are automatically set at every half inch. These tabs are called *Auto tab* stops. Once you set a tab, all the Auto tab stops to the left of the tab you have set will disappear. The Auto tab stops work like left-justified tabs.

To set a tab, select a tab from the four Tab Style buttons on the upper left of the Tab Ruler palette and click on the ruler below to set exactly where you would like to set the new tab. Once the tab has been set, it can be moved by dragging it along the ruler or removed by dragging it off the top or left edge of the ruler.

 Tabs *cannot* be dragged off the Tab Ruler palette by dragging them off the bottom of the palette, like in most word processing programs and page layout software.

Left-justified tabs make type align to the right side of the tab, with the leftmost character aligning with the tab stop.

Center-justified tabs make type align to the center of the tab, with the center character aligning with the tab stop.

Right-justified tabs make type align to the left side of the tab, with the rightmost character aligning with the tab stop.

Decimal-justified tabs make type align to the left side of the tab, with a decimal or the rightmost character aligning with the tab stop.

If the Snap option box is checked, tab stops will correspond to ruler tick marks.

 The measurement system shown on the ruler is the same system that is used by the rest of the document and can be changed in the General Preferences dialog box or by cycling through the different measurement systems by pressing ⌘-Control-U until the proper measurement system is displayed.

To change a tab from one style to another, select a tab stop and click on the Tab style button that you wish it to change to. To deselect all tabs, click in the area to the right of the Tab position box.

It is a good idea to get in the habit of deselecting tabs after they are set so that defining a new tab style for the next tab stop does not change the tab stop that was just set.

There is no way to create dot leader tabs automatically by using the Tab Ruler palette. We may have to wait for Version 6.0 of Illustrator for this feature to be incorporated. As always, if you think this feature or any other feature that Illustrator lacks would be useful, send them a note (a "feature request") and it *will* be considered. After all, why do you think the Tab Ruler palette was incorporated into Version 5.5?

Creating Editable Type Outlines ____

The process of creating editable type outlines has many uses, the main one that I have seen being the ability to distort mild-mannered characters into grotesque letters. More practical uses for editable type outlines include the following: making type-based logos unique, arcing type (where one side is flat and the other is curved), special effects and masking, and avoiding font compatibility problems.

To change type from being editable text into an Illustrator path (for that is what an editable type outline really is), select the type with a selection tool, not a type tool. Select Type⇨Create Outlines, and the type will change into paths which can be edited. Figure 8-21 shows the CHO logo before and after it has been converted into outlines.

After type has been changed into Illustrator paths using Create Outlines, the only way back is to Undo (⌘-Z). There is no "Convert from Paths to Type" function. Type *cannot* be edited in Outline mode. That means if you misspell somthing, it will remain misspelled.

Initially, when type is converted into outlines, individual characters are turned into compound paths. This ensures that holes in letters such as lowercase *a*s, *b*s, and *d*s are see-through, and not just white-filled paths placed on top of the original objects.

Figure 8-21:
Type that has been converted to outlines and united via the Unite filter.

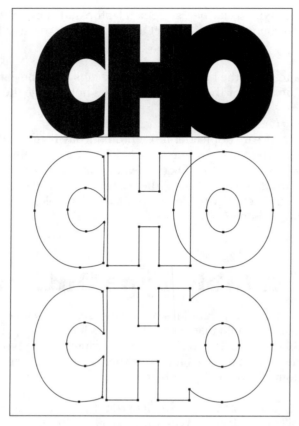

 See Chapter 11 for an in-depth discussion of compound paths.

Making letters that normally appear in your worst nightmares

After letters have been turned into outlines, there is nothing stopping you from distorting them into shapes which only resemble letters in the most simplistic sense of the word, and even then it takes some imagination.

The results of letter distortion usually aren't all that eye-pleasing, but they can be *fun*. Few things in life are as pleasing as taking a boring letter Q and twisting it into *The Letter that Time Forgot*. Or fiddling around with your boss's name until the letters look as evil as he does. Or adding pointed ears and whiskers to a random array of letters and numbers and printing out several sheets or them with the words "Mutant kittens for sale." Some of these samples are shown in Figure 8-22.

Figure 8-22:
Fun with Type
outlines.

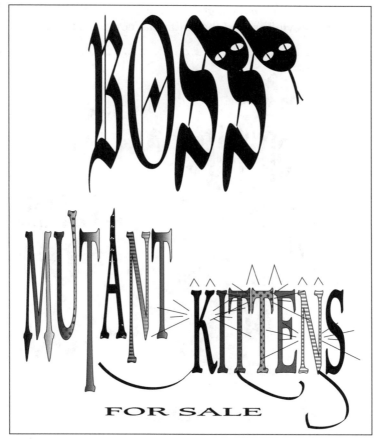

When modifying existing letters, use the Direct Selection tool. Select the points or segments you wish to move and drag them around to your heart's content. This can be great practice for adjusting paths, and you might accidentally stumble onto some really cool designs.

Creating logos from type outlines

Type outlines provide you with the flexibility to manipulate letters to turn an ordinary, boring, letters-only logo into a distinct symbol embodying the company's image.

Outlines are flexible enough that there really are no limits to what can be done with something as simple as a word of type.

The examples in Figure 8-23 show the logos that have been "touched up" by changing them into outlines and moving around the paths that comprise them.

Figure 8-23:
Type converted
to outlines,
edited, and
ready to be
used as a logo.

Arcing words and phrases

The difference between arced words and type on a circle is that while the letters in type on a circle are rotated individually, making each letter line up with one part of the circle; the letters in arced type are not rotated, but instead either the top or bottom of them is stretched to fit to a circular curve, as in the examples at the right of Figure 8-23.

Arcing type is easier and creates better results when the type is created as all capital letters, especially when the tops of the letters are being curved to fit a circle.

To arc type, first convert it into outlines, and then create an oval or circle above or below the outlines. I'll create a circle below the outlines in this example. Make sure that the tip of the top of the circle touches the center letter(s) in the word so that these letters don't need to be changed. Always adjust the horizontal scaling prior to aligning the circle to the outlined type, as this will prevent unnecessary adjustments.

Then, using the scale tool, scale the first letter vertically only (hold down the Shift key) and drag until either the left or right side is even with the path of the circle. Do the same for the remaining letters.

 Scaling and proper use of the Scale tool is discussed in detail in Chapter 10.

After the letters are the correct approximate height, use the Direct Selection tool to adjust the bottoms of the letters to fit the curve well. This can take some time and a bit of practice to get the technique correct, but the results can be outstanding.

Arcing curved letters is much more difficult than arcing straight ones, and arcing letters with serifs is slightly more difficult than arcing letters that are sans serif.

Arcing letters just on one side of a curve can be started easily by selecting just those letters on that half and using the Free Distort filter (select Filter⇨Distort⇨Free Distort). This does the scaling even more accurately than with the Scale tool because the letters aren't just scaled proportionately but angled automatically as well.

Masking and other effects

After type has been converted into outlines, it can then be used as a mask or filled with gradients or patterns. Standard type cannot be used as a mask, filled with gradients, or filled with patterns, like the words in Figure 8-24.

Figure 8-24:
Type that has been converted to outlines and is now filled with a pattern and used as a masking path.

For more detailed information on masks and compound paths, see Chapter 11.

In order for words to work as a single mask, they must first be changed into a compound path. Usually, individual letters of converted type are changed into individual compound paths, whether the letter has a "hole" in it or not. In order for masks to work properly, the entire word or words you will be using as a mask should be selected, and then Object⇨Compound Path⇨Make (⌘-8) should be selected. This will make all the selected letters into one compound path.

In some third-party (non-Adobe) and shareware typefaces, making a compound path out of a series of letters can produce results where the "holes" are not transparent at all. This issue is usually one of path direction, which can be corrected by selecting the inner shape (the "hole") and selecting Object⇨Attributes (⌘-Control-A), and then checking or unchecking the Reverse Path check box.

After the word(s) are a compound path, place them in front of the objects to be masked and select both the word(s) and the masked objects, and then select Object⇨Mask⇨Make.

Avoiding font conflicts by creating outlines

If you ever give your files to a service bureau or to clients, you've probably already run into some font compatibility problems. Font compatibility usually means that the place you gave your file doesn't have a typeface that you've used within your Illustrator document.

This is a problem that there is no great solution to, and if nothing else, the trouble seems to be worsening, as more font manufacturers spring up — TrueType fonts being the Windows standard, and PostScript Type 1 fonts being the Mac standard. And then there are shareware typefaces, some of which resemble Adobe originals to an uncanny degree of accuracy. All this leads to a great deal of confusion and frustration for the average Illustrator user.

 But there is a way around this problem, at least most of the time. By converting your typefaces into outlines before you send them to other people with other systems, they don't need your typefaces for the letters to print correctly. Instead, converted letters aren't really considered type anymore, just outlines.

Save your file before converting the text to outlines and then save as a different filename after converting the text to outlines. This will allow you to do text editing later on the original file, if necessary.

 Converting Type 1 typefaces to outlines removes the hinting system that Adobe has implemented. This hinting system makes small letters on low-resolution (<600 dpi) devices print more accurately, controlling the placement and visibility of serifs and other small, thin strokes in characters. Type at small point sizes will look quite different on laser printers, although it will retain its shape and consistency when it is output to an imagesetter or an output scanner system.

Amazing type (and path) effects

Typefaces edited in Illustrator and certain paths can be given three-dimensional attributes by using Pixar Typestry software after the type and paths have been modified in Illustrator.

Typestry imports Illustrator outlines and extrudes them, adding all sorts of three-dimensional effects to them. The words "Macworld Illustrator Bible" on the main screen of the CD-ROM (and shown on the gatefold of the back cover) were created using Typestry.

 A demo version of Typestry is included on the CD-ROM with this book.

The resulting three-dimensional images can be given different surface effects, special lighting, and can even be animated.

Special Characters

On a Macintosh, there are many special characters available besides the standard letters, numbers, and symbols that appear on your keyboard. To see these special characters, Apple includes a desk accessory called KeyCaps, which displays the keyboard you are using and shows what each character will look like in the typeface you choose.

There are some other popular desk accessories (Apple Menu Items) that allow you to view the character set of each typeface. PopChar is a very popular shareware one, and KeyFinder from Symantec (Part of Norton Utilities) is a good one as well. Both of these have a bit more flexibility than KeyCaps, but all do basically the same thing: They tell you which characters are available in each font and which key combination will result in that character.

There are essentially four sets of characters in each font. The first set is reached by normal typing of the keyboard keys, which include numbers, lowercase letters, and a few symbols. The second set is reached by pressing the Shift key prior to pressing the keyboard key and includes capital letters and symbols that appear on the top half of the keyboard keys. The third set is reached by pressing the Option key before pressing a keyboard key. This set is primarily the common special symbols, such as bullets (•), the cents symbol (¢), an ellipsis (…), and the pi symbol (π). The fourth set of characters can only be reached when both the Option and Shift keys are pressed before a keyboard key is pressed and includes less common symbols, like f-ligatures (fi, fl), the double dagger (‡), and the Apple Computer Apple ().

While almost all typefaces have the first and second sets, many typefaces do not contain very many characters in the third and fourth sets. The list in Figure 8-25 shows the common symbols and their keyboard equivalents, but not all typefaces have all the symbols, and some of the symbols in some of the typefaces may have different keyboard commands.

Symbol typefaces

There are several symbol typefaces available that contain symbols in place of letters and numbers. The most popular of these is the Symbol typeface, which has Greek letters and mathematical operands and symbols. The next most popular symbol font would have to be Zapf Dingbats, which contains a wide variety of different symbols, whose complete character set is shown in Figure 8-26.

Figure 8-25:
The standard keyboard set for most fonts.

1st set	2nd set + Shift	3rd set + Option	4th set +Option–Shift
`	~	`	/
1	!	¡	⁄
2	@	™	°
3	#	£	‹
4	$	¢	›
5	%	∞	fi
6	^	§	fl
7	&	¶	‡
8	*	•	°
9	(	ª	·
0	)	º	‚
-	_	–	—
=	+	≠	±
q	Q	œ	Œ
w	W	∑	„
e	E	´	‰
r	R	®	´
t	T	†	ˇ
y	Y	¥	Á
u	U	¨	¨
i	I	ˆ	ˆ
o	O	ø	Ø
p	P	π	„
[	{	"	"
]	}	'	'
\	|	«	»
a	A	å	Å
s	S	ß	Í
d	D	∂	Î
f	F	ƒ	Ï
g	G	©	˝
h	H	˙	Ó
j	J	∆	Ô
k	K	˚	
l	L	¬	Ò
;	:	…	Ú
'	"	æ	Æ
z	Z	Ω	¸
x	X	≈	˛
c	C	ç	Ç
v	V	√	◊
b	B	∫	ı
n	N	~	˜
m	M	µ	Â
,	<	≤	¯
.	>	≥	˘
/	?	÷	¿

Figure 8-26:
The character set of
Zapf Dingbats.

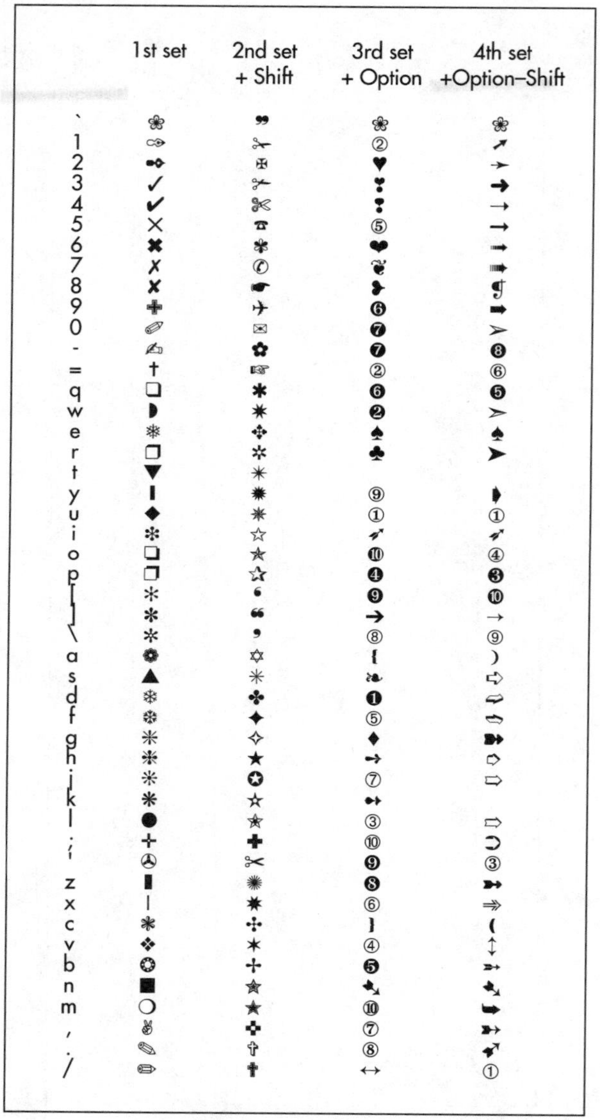

Some other typefaces that contain primarily symbols are Carta, the map symbol
typeface; Bill's Dingbats, a shareware set of symbols that nicely complements Zapf
Dingbats; and Mathematical Pi, a math font containing math symbols.

One of the great things about Symbol typefaces is that individual characters can be
turned into outline characters and edited to create different illustrations.

Customizing Fonts

Typefaces can be created and modified right on your Macintosh, with tools very similar to the ones in Adobe Illustrator. Creating fonts is, in a way, the reverse process of outlining existing fonts because you are taking outlines and turning them into characters in typefaces. Figure 8-27 shows two popular shareware fonts created through a combination of Illustrator and Fontographer: Lefty Casual and Ransom Note were used to create this illustration.

Figure 8-27:
Lefty Casual
and Ransom
Note.

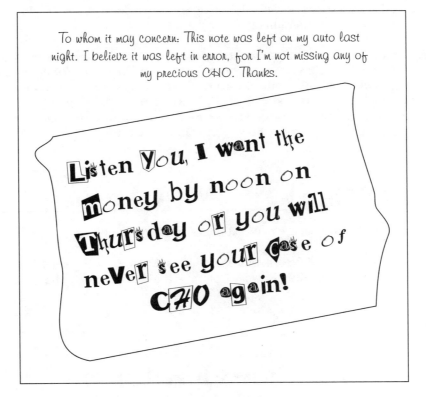

By taking existing typefaces, you can customize the characters, creating a unique typeface. In a typeface you create, all the special characters can be ones you've designed especially for that face. Check with the original typeface manufacturer before doing this to ensure that you will not be violating any copyright laws for that particular font vendor.

There are three major software programs that allow users to create their own fonts: Fontographer, FontStudio, and FontMonger. Each program has certain strengths and weaknesses. Also described is TypeStyler, which is used to manipulate type for special effects.

Fontographer: The most popular of the font-creation software, Fontographer boasts Multiple Master capabilities and very precise Bézier control tools. Now in Version 4.0, the software has proven to be very reliable and is the workhorse of the group.

FontStudio: FontStudio has lingered in the last few years, as its parent company, Letraset, has invested less and less time into its development. Once a favorite, many current type designers haven't even seen the software.

FontMonger: FontMonger has special capabilities that set it apart from Fontographer and FontStudio, including the capability to merge typefaces. It is much easier to use than the other two but rather limited in its feature set.

TypeStyler: TypeStyler is not font-creation software but rather font-manipulation software. The most recent version is about three years old, but minor updates have kept it compatible with the latest software. Although it uses an extremely clunky, dated, and awkward interface, it is easier to use than even Illustrator for creating special shape effects, such as arced type or type in the shape of a fish or wavy pennant. Only shapes of type created in TypeStyler can be imported into Illustrator.

Text Filters

Included with Illustrator 5.0 are two text filters, Find and Export.

Illustrator 5.5 contains six more text filters: Change Case, Check Spelling, Find Font, Revert Text Path, Rows & Columns, and Smart Punctuation.

All text filters are discussed in detail in Chapter 19.

Other Type Considerations

When you're using type in Illustrator, there are a number of things to keep in mind to get good results.

First, make sure that the person you are sending the Illustrator file to has the same fonts you have. It isn't enough just to have the same name of a font; you'll need the exact font that was created by the same manufacturer.

Second, try not to mix TrueType fonts with PostScript fonts. This usually ends up confusing everyone involved.

Third, if the person you are sending Illustrator files to does *not* have your typeface, select the type in that font and select Type⇨Create Outlines.

 It is illegal to give commercial fonts to people who do not own the typeface, even if only for purposes of outputting the job to a high-resolution device. There are no exceptions. After you give a typeface to someone, you have committed software piracy.

Fourth, when you're printing an Illustrator file that has been placed in other software, missing typestyles may go unnoticed until after the job has printed. Be doubly sure that the person outputting the file has all the fonts in the embedded Illustrator file.

Working with Illustrator Files

In This Chapter

- Setting up and viewing documents
- Managing files
- Opening and saving Illustrator files
- Importing and exporting files
- Setting up pages for printing
- Printing illustrations
- Understanding the differences between the LaserWriter and PSPrinter drivers

---

Setting up a New Document

Illustrator currently reigns as the easiest graphics program to start working with. As soon as you run the program, an empty document window appears, ready for you to begin drawing. No hassles. Just an instant drawing area. Creating new documents is equally easy. Just select File⇨New (⌘-N), and a new document window that is ready to use (see Figure 9-1) appears.

Figure 9-1:
The new document
window appears after you
select File⇨New (⌘-N).

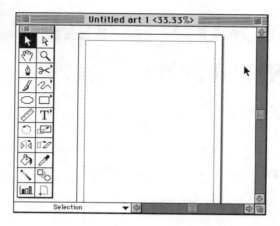

The Dark Ages

Creating a new document hasn't always been easy. Back in the days of Illustrator 88, and even Illustrator 3 to some extent, creating new illustrations was rather annoying. Choosing New Document brought up a dialog box that politely yet sternly asked you to choose a template to trace in Illustrator. Most of the time, though, you didn't want a template, so you had to click the little None button in the dialog box. If you pressed Return, Illustrator would attempt to open a template.

Illustrator 3 was a little more flexible. It enabled you to create a new document without having to deal with the dialog box that asked you to choose a template. All you had to do was hold down Option when you asked for a new document. You either pressed ⌘-Option-N or held down Option when you chose File⇨New. If you forgot about the Option key, you had another chance. Pressing ⌘-N when you were in the dialog box would send the box away and create a new document with no template — as long as you didn't have Directory Assistance, Super Boomerang, or any other utilities that created a new folder when you pressed ⌘-N.

Adobe slowly seemed to realize that you didn't want or need a template to do everything.

Everybody else

In most graphics and desktop publishing software, the program opens to a splash screen, but no document appears. Choosing File⇨New results in a nasty dialog box with options for this, choices for that, conditions for certain occurrences, and confusing terms that seem to have been made up solely to intimidate the user.

In these dialog boxes, you specify page size, units of measurement, margins, columns, output resolution, number of pages, and whether you would like the document to vote Republican, Democratic, or Independent in the next major election. You must check the correct boxes, enter the right figures, and in some cases pray that you aren't wrong about something, because making a change can be a nightmare.

The nice thing about entering all of this information ahead of time is that you can set up the document just as you want it. The bad thing is that you get pummeled with having to enter lots of other information about the document that slows you down right off the bat.

When you create a new Illustrator document, it defaults to the size of the Startup document that is located in the Plug-Ins folder. As a default, this document is 8.5" x 11", and it is in the portrait orientation.

 To change information about the Startup document, see Chapter 18.

The document window initially shows up at "actual size," which is supposedly the same size at which it will be printed. In the title bar at the top of the window, you see Untitled Art 1 <100%>. As soon as you save the document, the title bar will contain the name of the document.

You cannot change the way that some things appear when you first start Illustrator. For example, the Selection tool is always selected in the Toolbox. Another unchangeable item is the initial Paint Style that you begin drawing with: a fill of 100% black, no stroke. The character attributes are always the same: 12-point Helvetica, Auto leading, flush left. In addition, the layer color is always light blue (a color that is just dark enough so that it doesn't conflict a bit with cyan).

Changing the Document Setup

To change almost anything about the document structure and how you work with that document, you need to go to the Document Setup dialog box by selecting File⇨Document Setup or pressing ⌘-Shift-D (see Figure 9-2). In the Document Setup dialog box, you can change the size of the Artboard, define how and when paths are split, change the ruler units, and change the way that printable page edges, patterns, and placed Encapsulated PostScript (EPS) images are viewed.

Any changes that you make in the Document Setup dialog box are saved with the document. The following sections describe the various options that are available in the Document Setup dialog box.

Figure 9-2:
The Document
Setup dialog box.

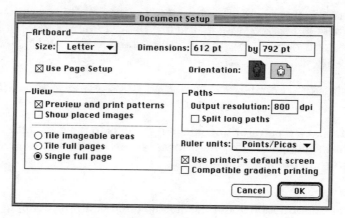

Artboard options

The Artboard in Adobe Illustrator is the drawing area that is defined as the printable area when you print the document through Illustrator.

 Adobe Separator (software included with Illustrator for printing out color separations of Illustrator documents) ignores the Artboard and places crop marks around the entire imagable area. The imagable area, according to Separator, is only the area where artwork exists. It may be within the Artboard, but it also may extend onto the Pasteboard. When you export an illustration to another program, such as QuarkXPress, the Artboard is ignored entirely.

In Illustrator, the Artboard defines the maximum area that can be printed. The Artboard is useful as a guide for where the objects on a page belong. In previous versions of Illustrator, the maximum printable size was 11" x 17"; in Version 5.0, it is 120" x 120" (10 square feet), provided that you can find a printer that prints that big. . . .

To choose the size of the Artboard, you select a preset size from the Size pop-up menu.

- **Letter** is 8.5" x 11".

- **Legal** is 8.5" x 14".

- **Tabloid** is 11" x 17".

- **A4** is 8.268" x 11.693" (21 x 29.7 cm).

- **A3** is 11.693" x 16.535" (29.7 x 42 cm).

- **B5** is 7.165" x 10" (18.2 x 25.4 cm).

- **B4** is 10.118" x 14.331" (55.7 x 36.4 cm).

- **Custom** is whatever size you type in the Dimensions text fields.

A4, A3, B5, and B4 are European paper sizes. If you live and work in the U.S., you will probably never need to choose those sizes.

To define the orientation, you choose one of the two Orientation pages. On the left is the Portrait orientation, where the lesser of the two dimensions goes across the page from left to right, and the greater of the two dimensions goes from top to bottom. On the right is the Landscape orientation, where the greater of the two dimensions goes across the page from left to right, and the lesser of the two dimensions goes from top to bottom. You can put the lesser or the greater value in either of the two Dimensions text fields, but the next time you open the Document Setup box, the lesser of the two will always be on the left.

If you check the Use Page Setup box, then the Artboard will default to the page size and orientation that is selected in the Page Setup dialog box.

View options

You can control how certain things in Illustrator are viewed by checking the appropriate boxes:

- **The Preview and print patterns option** displays patterns that are used as fills in objects when Illustrator is in Preview mode or selected objects that are filled with patterns when Illustrator is in Preview Selection mode. Illustrator also will print patterns when this option is checked. If this option is not checked, it affects only the way that Illustrator sees and prints the pattern objects; it does not affect how other applications see and print them. Choosing this option can dramatically increase screen redraw (Preview mode) times and printing times. If this check box is not checked, patterns will not print or preview in Illustrator, but they will print in other software.

- **The Show placed images option** displays placed images in Artwork mode. It does not affect how placed EPS artwork is viewed in Preview or Preview Selection (when the artwork is selected) modes. When the check box is not checked, placed EPS artwork is represented as a box with an *X* inside it.

- **The Tile imagable areas option** creates a grid on the document, with the size of each *block* equal to the page size that is chosen in the Page Setup dialog box. Little page numbers appear in the lower lefthand corner of each block, representing the pages you would get if you printed page *x* to page *x* in the Print dialog box.

- **The Tile full pages option** creates as many page outlines (from Page Setup) as will completely print. For example, if the Artboard is landscape, 11" x 17", and the selected page size in Page Setup is portrait, 8.5" x 11", then two page outlines will appear side by side in the document.

- **The Single full page option** creates one Page Setup size outline on the page.

Figure 9-3 shows how the Tile imagable areas, Tile full pages, and Single full page options look for the same document.

To move the page outlines, select the Page tool and click and drag in the Artboard. The click point of the page is always the lower lefthand corner.

Path splitting options

Robbie the Robot would be screaming his metal head off if Will Robinson ever thought about clicking the Split long paths check box. The check box looks friendly enough, but the results of checking it can be deadly. If you are quick enough, you can always undo the split paths function, but the actual splitting of paths doesn't always happen when and where you expect it to happen.

Instead, it happens only when you save or print a document. This feature presents some very interesting problems. First, if you save the document and close it right after you save it, the paths are split permanently, and you cannot undo the damage the next time you open the document. Second, after you print a document, saving and closing it is a very natural thing to do. But once again, you cannot get it back to normal. Another problem arises when you are working in Preview mode: if you forget whether you checked the option, sometimes you can't easily determine whether paths have been split.

Figure 9-3:
One document
with the Tile
imagable areas,
Tile full pages,
and Single full
page options
chosen.

Tile imagable areas

Tile full pages

Single full page

The Split long paths function tries to fix paths that are too long or too complex for your laser printer to handle. By entering the final output resolution for the Illustrator document, you can ensure that it will have a better chance of printing than if paths were not split. Every curve in Illustrator is made of tiny straight segments. The higher the resolution of the output device, the more straight segments. The processing power of the laser printer limits how many little straight segments can be in one path. If you exceed that limit, Illustrator chops away at the paths, splitting them into several smaller sections. Because this problem occurs more with high-resolution devices, the greater the number you enter in the Output resolution box, the more paths will be split. Figure 9-4 shows an original document and several examples of path splitting.

Figure 9-4:
A document before path splitting and after path splitting.

Original

300 dpi split paths

1200 dpi split paths

9600 dpi split paths

The only reason to use the Split long paths function is if a document fails to print because of a PostScript error, which is usually a Limitcheck error. But instead of just checking the Split long paths check box, first make a copy of the entire document and then split paths in the new document. Then the original file will not contain split paths. Split paths are extremely difficult to reassemble, and the results from split paths can be horrifying. Please use caution when you split paths.

Points and picas

In my college art classes, I was introduced to a different, frightening method of measurement called *points and picas*. Even cooler than the way it made real numbers of ⅙ inch, was the fact that only artists and professionals in the printing industry knew what I was talking about when I started spouting off measurements in picas.

The point and pica system is a fairly basic concept: a pica is equal to 12 points, and traditionally, an inch is equal to *approximately* 6 picas. Thanks to PostScript and Adobe, I predict that ten years from now an inch will be equal to *exactly* 6 picas.

Adobe points and picas are a bit larger than traditional points and picas, resulting in inaccurate measurements and confusion for the general populace. The only thing consistent about points and picas in the two forms of measurement is the "12 points to a pica" law.

Having two systems of measuring points and picas has created a problem for users who are trying to determine measurements for graphics programs. Pica sticks (also known as pica poles and pica rulers) that are available in art supply stores use traditional points and picas. When you enter measurements in Illustrator that you obtain by using a pica stick, the printed results won't match your original measurements unless you use a special pica stick or make your own measuring device.

Adobe/PostScript point and pica rulers are hard to find. To check whether a ruler is traditional or Adobe/PostScript, use an inch ruler to see whether 72 picas is equal to 12 inches. If it is, the ruler is an Adobe/PostScript ruler.

Some software (for example, QuarkXPress) enables you to change how many points are in one inch. But in Adobe/PostScript points, one inch is equal to exactly 72 points. In traditional measurements, an inch is equal to exactly 72.27 points.

All point and pica measurement references in this book are in Adobe points and picas.

Ruler units

You can view a document in inches, points and picas, or centimeters. The measurement units affect the numbers on the rulers and the locations of the hatch marks on those same rulers. The measurement system also changes the way measurements are displayed in the Info palette and in all dialog boxes where you enter a measurement (other than percentage). Figure 9-5 shows a comparison of the various measurement systems.

Figure 9-5:
The three different
measurement systems
that are available in
Illustrator.

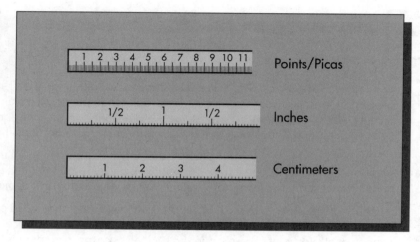

Figure 9-5:
The three different
measurement systems
that are available in
Illustrator.

Points/Picas

Inches

Centimeters

The measurement system is changed in either the General Preferences dialog box (select File⇨Preferences⇨General, or ⌘-K) for all documents, or in the Document Setup dialog box (select File⇨Document Setup, or ⌘-Shift-D) for the currently active document.

To change the unit of measurement in Illustrator 5.0 only, press ⌘-Shift-I to change the measurement system to inches, ⌘-Shift-N to change it to centimeters, or ⌘-Shift-P to change it to points and picas.

Using the printer's default screen

The printer's *default screen* is its built-in line screen setting (also known as the *halftone screen* or *lines per inch*). On a 300 dots-per-inch (dpi) laser printer, the screen setting is usually 53. The line screen affects the size of the dots that make up various tints that can be printed. Usually, the default screen is the highest (smallest dots) value that it can go and still display a large number of grays. The higher the line screen, the fewer grays are available.

Unlike most of the other options in the Document Setup box, the Use printer's default screen option forces the illustration to use the printer's default screen when you print the illustration through page layout software. Even if the page layout software has specified a different line screen for "everything," checking this box makes the illustration print at the printer's default line screen.

For more control over line screens, see the discussion on Adobe Separator, which is in Chapter 23.

Navigating through the Document _

Being able to move through a document easily is a key skill in Illustrator. You rarely can fit the entire illustration in the document window at most magnifications.. Usually, you are zooming in, zooming out, or moving off to the side or above or below.

Who's zoomin' who?

The most basic of navigational concepts in Illustrator is the ability to zoom to different magnification levels. Illustrator's magnification levels actually work very similar to the way that a magnifying glass works. In the real world, you use a magnifying glass to see details that aren't readily visible without it. In the Illustrator world, you use the different magnification levels to see details that aren't readily visible at 100% view. The magnification levels of Illustrator do not affect the illustration. If you zoom in to 200% and print, the illustration will be printed at the same size it would print at if the view were 100%. It will not print twice as large.

The Zoom tools

You use the two Zoom tools, Zoom In and Zoom Out, to magnify a certain area of artwork and then return to the standard view.

To use the Zoom In tool, select it in the Toolbox or press ⌘-spacebar. Either way, the Zoom In tool should appear. It looks like a magnifying glass with a plus sign in it. Clicking any spot in the illustration will enlarge that part of the illustration to the next magnification level. The Zoom Out tool is selected by selecting the Zoom In tool (either way) and pressing Option. Figure 9-6 shows the Zoom In and Zoom Out tools and examples of the 17 different magnification levels that are available in Illustrator. The highest magnification level is 1600%, which shows the illustration at 16 times the size of its original measurements. Of course, the Zoom In feature is not without its pitfall: The more you zoom in on an illustration, the less of that illustration you see at one time.

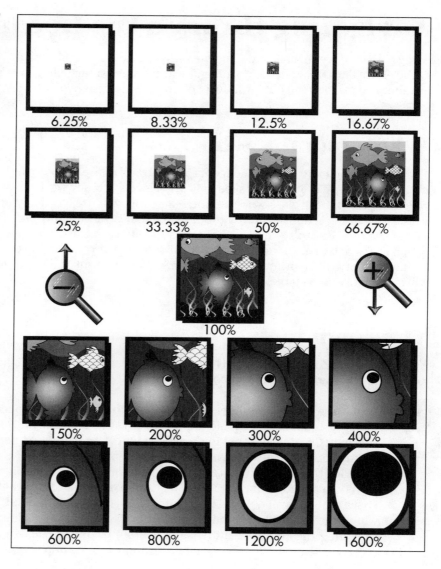

Where you click with the Zoom In tool is very important. Clicking the center of the window will enlarge the illustration to the next magnification level, but the edges (top, bottom, left, and right) will be cropped off as the magnification increases. Clicking the upper righthand corner will crop off mostly the lower left edges, and so forth. If you are interested in seeing a particular part of the illustration close up, click that part at each magnification level to ensure that it remains in the window.

If you zoom in to too high of a magnification level, you can use the Zoom Out tool to zoom out again. To access the Zoom Out tool, press Option while you click the Zoom In tool in the Toolbox or press ⌘-Option-spacebar. Clicking with the Zoom Out tool reduces the magnification level to the next lowest level. You can zoom out to 6.25%, or ¹⁄₁₆ actual size.

When you use the Zoom tools, you change the size of everything in the document, not just the illustration. You change the size of all paths, objects, the Artboard, the Pasteboard, and the Page Setup boundaries relative to the current Magnification level.

If you need to zoom in quite a bit, you can zoom in more easily by using the Zoom In tool to draw a marquee (by clicking and dragging diagonally) around the objects that you want to magnify. The area that is surrounded will magnify as much as possible so that everything inside the box just fits in the window that you have open, as shown in Figure 9-7. Dragging a box with the Zoom Out tool does nothing special; it works the same as if you had just clicked with the Zoom Out tool.

Other zooming techniques

You also can zoom in and zoom out by using commands in the View menu. Select View⇨Zoom In (⌘-]) to zoom in one level at a time until the magnification level is 1600%. Select View⇨Zoom Out (⌘-[) to zoom out one level at a time until the magnification level is 6.25%.

You can use two different methods to automatically zoom to 100%. The first method is to double-click the Zoom tool in the Toolbox. This action changes the view to 100% instantly. A better way to zoom in to 100% is to select View ⇨ Actual Size (⌘-H), which not only changes the magnification level to 100% but also centers the page.

You also can choose from two different methods to change the document view to the Fit In Window size. Fit In Window instantly changes the magnification level of the document so that the entire Artboard fits in the window and is centered in it.

One way to automatically change to the Fit In Window view is to select View⇨Fit In Window (⌘-M). Another way is to double-click on the Hand tool.

You also can instantly zoom out to 6.25% by holding down Option while you double-click the Zoom tool. To instantly zoom in to 1600%, draw a tiny marquee with the Zoom In tool. At actual size, the marquee must be less than ½" x ½" for the magnification level to go instantly to 1600%. It may be necessary to draw more than one marquee if the current magnification level is less than 100%.

Figure 9-7:
The effects of zooming
with the Zoom
marquee.

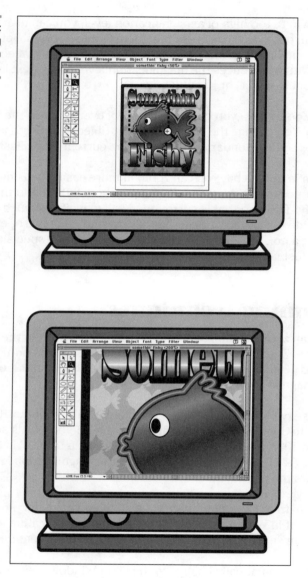

Figure 9-7:
The effects of zooming with the Zoom marquee.

You can never undo any type of magnification level change. Choosing Edit⇨Undo after zooming will undo the last change you made to the document before you changed the magnification level.

Using the scroll bars

Sometimes after you zoom in to a high magnification, part of the drawing that you want to see is outside the window area. Instead of zooming in and out, you can use one of two different scrolling techniques to move around inside the document.

The scroll bar on the right side of the document window controls where you are vertically in the document. Clicking the up arrow displays what is above the window's boundaries by pushing everything in the window *down* in little increments. Clicking the down arrow displays what is below the window's boundaries by pushing the document *up* in little increments. Dragging the little elevator box up displays what is above the window's boundaries by whatever distance proportionately that you drag. Dragging the little elevator box down displays what is below the window's boundaries by whatever distance proportionately that you drag. Clicking on the gray bar above the little elevator box between the arrows displays what is above the window's boundaries in big chunks. Clicking on the gray bar below the little elevator box between the arrows displays what is below the window's boundaries in big chunks.

The gray area of the right scroll bar is proportionate to the size of the Pasteboard. If the little elevator box is at the top of the scroll bar, then you are viewing the top edge of the 120" x 120" Pasteboard. If it is centered, you are viewing the vertical center of the Pasteboard.

The scroll bar on the bottom of the document window controls where you are in the document horizontally. Clicking the left arrow displays what is to the left of the window's boundaries by pushing everything in the window *right* in little increments. Clicking on the right arrow displays what is to the right of the window's boundaries by pushing the document *left* in little increments. Dragging the little elevator box left displays what is left of the window's boundaries by whatever distance proportionately that you drag. Dragging the little *elevator box* right displays what is to the right of the window boundaries by whatever distance proportionately that you drag. Clicking on the gray bar between the arrows that is left of the little elevator box displays what is to the left of the window's boundaries in big chunks. Clicking on the gray bar between the arrows that is right of the little elevator box displays what is to the right of the window's boundaries in big chunks.

Scrolling with the Hand tool

The Hand tool improves upon the scroll bars. Instead of being limited to only horizontal and vertical movement, you can use the Hand tool to scroll diagonally. It is especially useful for finding your way around a document when you are at a high magnification level. The higher the magnification level, the more you will end up using the Hand tool.

To use the Hand tool, either select it in the Toolbox or press the spacebar. (If you are currently using the Type tool, press ⌘-spacebar and then release ⌘, keeping the spacebar pressed.) Clicking and dragging the page will move the document around inside the document window.

 When you click the document, be sure to click on the side that you want to see more of. Clicking at the top of the document and dragging down enables you to scroll down through almost an entire document at a height of one window. Clicking in the center and dragging enables you to scroll through only half a window size at a time. If the window of the document does not take up the entire screen space, you can continue to drag right off the window into the empty screen space. Just be sure that you first click within the document that you want to scroll.

The best thing about the Hand tool is that it works *live*. As you drag, the document moves under your *Hand*. If you don't like where it is going, you can drag it back, still live. The second best thing is that to access it requires only one keystroke, a press of the spacebar.

 You cannot use Undo (⌘-Z) to reverse scrolling that you have done with the scroll bars and the Hand tool.

Artwork Mode versus Preview Mode

In the old days, everyone worked in Artwork mode. You could occasionally check work in progress to see what the illustration would look like by switching to Preview mode. Usually the preview was not quite what you had in mind while you were in Artwork mode, so it was back to Artwork mode to fix everything, and then to Preview again to check. . . .

Illustrator 5 enables you to work in both Artwork and Preview modes. The mode that you are in when documents are printing does not matter. Illustrator will fill and stroke all paths and objects with the colors that are defined in the document, even if the document is in Artwork mode and those colors aren't visible. Saving the document while you are in Artwork mode will not affect anything in the document, but the next time you open it, it will be in Artwork mode. The same thing applies to Preview and Preview Selection modes: Whatever mode you are in will be saved with the artwork.

You cannot undo a Preview or Artwork mode change (going from Preview Selection to Artwork, for example). If you make a Preview or Artwork mode change and then close your document, Illustrator will ask you if you want to save changes, which in this case only refers to the view change.

Artwork (only) mode

To change the current document to Artwork mode, select View⇨Artwork (⌘-E). In Artwork mode, the illustration will disappear and be replaced on-screen by outlines of all the filled and stroked paths. Text that has yet to be converted into outlines will look fine, although it will always be black. Depending on your choice in the Document Setup dialog box (select File⇨Document Setup or press ⌘-Shift-D), a placed EPS image will be displayed as a box with an *X* in it (if Show placed images is not checked) or as a black-and-white-only image, surrounded by a box with an *X* in it (if Show placed images is checked).

Working with a drawing in Artwork mode can be significantly faster than working with it in Preview mode. In more complex drawings, the difference between Artwork mode and Preview mode is significant; on slower computers, working in Preview mode is next to impossible.

Artwork mode enables you to see every path that isn't directly overlapping another path; in Preview mode, many paths can be hidden. In addition, invisible masks are normally visible as paths in Artwork mode.

Artwork mode can take some getting used to. Unless you have been using Illustrator for years and years, you may have a hard time working in Artwork mode.

Artwork mode is better than Preview mainly because it's faster but also because your brain can learn to know what the drawing looks like, and you will be able to envision it from seeing just the outlines, which show all paths, including masks (maskings paths cannot be viewed in Preview).

Preview mode

Selecting View⇨Preview (⌘-Y) changes the view to Preview mode. In Preview mode, the document looks just the way it will look when you print it . . . sort of. Patterns in strokes and patterns in type show as gray areas, and you can't view overprinting.

In Preview mode, the color that you see on the screen represents only marginally what the actual output will be because of the differences between the way computer monitors work (red, green, and blue colors—the more of each color, the brighter each pixel will appear) and the way printing works (cyan, magenta, yellow, and black colors—the more of each color, the darker each area will appear). Monitor manufacturers make a number of calibration tools that decrease the difference between what you see on the monitor and the actual output. You also can use software solutions. One software solution, CIE calibration, is right in Adobe Illustrator (select File⇨Preferences⇨Color Matching).

In Preview mode, you can see which objects overlap, which objects are in front and in back, where gradations begin and end, and how patterns are set up.

Sometimes previewing complex drawings on the screen can take a long time. Usually this problem occurs when you are displaying paths with patterns or a great number of blends. Figure 9-7 takes about three minutes to preview on a Quadra (which is just short of eternity in the computer world). To stop the illustration from being redrawn in Preview mode, press ⌘-period to change the document to Artwork mode.

If the redrawing has been completed before you press ⌘-period, everything will be selected. Objects that were unselected will be selected. This can be especially frustrating when you have spent a good deal of time selecting certain objects, but you didn't group these objects together. The selection or deselection of objects *cannot* be undone.

Preview Selection mode

To change to Preview Selection mode, select View⇨Preview Selection (⌘-Option-Y) to display all selected objects in Preview mode and all unselected objects in Artwork mode. Figure 9-8 shows an illustration in Preview Selection mode.

Figure 9-8: An illustration in Preview Selection mode.

The Preview Selection mode can be useful in a complex illustration when you need to adjust a few object colors and want to see the results without waiting a long time.

Combining Artwork and Preview modes

Using the Layers palette, you can easily combine Artwork and Preview or Artwork and Preview Selection modes. You can force individual layers to display in Preview mode while other layers remain in Artwork mode. This feature can be useful when you have a layer with either a placed EPS image, gradients, or patterns (or all three!) that would normally slow down the work flow. You can place those images on their own layer and set that layer to Artwork mode.

 Chapter 14 discusses layers in detail.

You also can view the same artwork in both Preview mode and Artwork mode at the same time by creating a new window for the current document. Select Window⇨New Window to create a window that is the same size as the original window. You can manipulate these two windows so that they are next to each other, and each window can have different viewing characteristics. One window can be in Preview mode, and the other one can be in Artwork mode. One window can be at Fit in Window size, and you can zoom the other to any percentage.

 Using multiple windows to show Artwork and Preview modes of the same drawing simultaneously was used mainly when Illustrator did not enable artists to edit and create in Preview mode. This function is no longer as helpful as it was before, but you can still use it to preview an illustration when you want to select artwork that is hidden by fills and strokes of other artwork in Preview mode.

Now You See It

Illustrator also provides options that enable you to show and hide various parts of an illustration. Selecting View⇨Show *Item* makes that menu item visible, and selecting View⇨Hide *Item* makes that menu item disappear.

- **Show Template** (select View⇨Show Template) shows the document's template if it has one. When the template is showing, this menu item changes to Hide Template. If a template was hidden the last time you saved the document, it will be hidden the next time you open the document. If a template was showing when you saved the document, the next time you open the document, it will be visible.

Show Rulers (select View⇨Show Rulers or press ⌘-R) displays rulers, in the current measurement system, on the right side of the document and on the bottom of the document window. By default, all rulers measure up and to the right from the lower lefthand corner of the Artboard.

If you're confused about why the rulers in Illustrator are on the right side of the document window — but they measure up from the lower lefthand corner — you're not alone. Undoubtedly the Adobe engineers themselves are confused on this topic, so they set up the rulers this way to confuse the general public.

To change the measurement system that is displayed on the rulers, select File⇨Document Setup (⌘-Shift-D) and choose the new measurement system. In Adobe Illustrator 5.0 (but not 5.5), a quick way to instantly change ruler unit measurement systems is by pressing ⌘-Shift-I for inches, ⌘-Shift-N for centimeters, and ⌘-Shift-P for picas.

To change the origin of the rulers (0 across, 0 up), drag from the box where the rulers meet to the new intersection point.

Pressing ⌘-R toggles between showing and hiding rulers. If rulers are showing, the menu item is Hide Rulers. If rulers are displayed when you save the document, they will be displayed the next time you open it. If rulers are not showing when you save the document, then the next time you open the document, rulers will not be showing.

Show Page Tiling (select View⇨Show Page Tiling) shows the outlines of the page guides from the Page Setup and Document Setup dialog boxes. When Page Tiling is visible, the menu item changes to Hide Page tiling. The condition of Page Tiling is saved with the file.

Hide Edges (select View⇨Hide Edges or press ⌘-Shift-H) does not show paths, anchor points, direction lines, and direction points when it is selected in Preview mode and does not show anchor points, direction points, and direction lines in Artwork mode. When edges are hidden, the menu item reads Show Edges. Pressing ⌘-Shift-H toggles between showing and hiding edges. Edges are always visible when you open a file, regardless of whether they were visible or hidden when you saved it.

Show Guides (select View⇨Show Guides) shows all guides in your artwork, whether you created them by using rulers or by transforming paths into guides. Show guides does not show guides that were hidden with the Hide (⌘-3) command. The alternate, Hide Guides, hides all guides in the document. Whether you save a document with guides visible or hidden, they are always visible when you open a document.

Using Custom Views

Illustrator has a special feature, called *custom views,* that enables you to save special views of an illustration. Custom views contain view information, including magnification, location, and whether the illustration is in Artwork or Preview mode. If you have various layers in Preview mode and others in Artwork mode, custom views also can save that information. However, custom views do not record whether Templates, Rulers, Page Tiling, Edges, or Guides are showing or hidden.

To create a new view, set up the document in the way that you would like to save the view. Then select View⇨New View (⌘-Control-V) and name the view in the New View dialog box. Each of the first 10 views that you create is given a key command of ⌘-Control-1, ⌘-Control-2, and so on. You can create up to 25 custom views, but the last 15 will not have a key command. Custom views are saved with a document as long as you save it in Adobe Illustrator 5 format.

 If you find yourself continuously going to a certain part of a document, zooming in or out, and changing the Preview/Artwork mode, that document is a prime candidate for creating custom views. Custom views are helpful when you show clients artwork that you created in Illustrator. Instead of fumbling around in the client's presence, you can, for example, instantly show the detail in a logo if you have preset the zoom factor and position and saved them in a custom view.

Managing Files

Controlling how files are saved in Illustrator can be a little daunting at first. Although you have many different options for saving file types, you need to follow one basic rule: Save with a color preview if you are going to take the file into other applications. This type of file is not the smallest file type, but it is usually compatible with most software.

Opening files in Illustrator is fairly simple. Illustrator can open and manipulate only files that were created in Illustrator, Streamline, or Dimensions and files that were saved in an Illustrator format. It can open PICT files, but they will always be black-and-white bitmapped templates.

Files placed in Illustrator must be in the EPS file format. PostScript files that are printed to disk usually can't be placed in Illustrator.

Saving Files

Saving Illustrator documents is the most important Illustrator activity you do. Saving often prevents damage to your computer — by keeping you from picking it up and sending it flying across the room. Saving often makes your life less stressful, and backing up your saved files helps you sleep better.

The amount of space that a saved Illustrator file takes up on the hard drive depends on two things: the complexity of the drawing and the Preview option that you selected. Tiny illustrator files take up the smallest amount, about 10K or so. The biggest illustrations are limited only by your storage space, but they can regularly exceed 2MB. As a practice, when you are working on a drawing, save it to the hard drive, not to a floppy disk or a removable cartridge. Hard drives are faster and much more reliable. If you need to place a file on a floppy disk or Syquest cartridge, copy it there in the Finder by dragging the icon of the file from the hard drive to the disk or cartridge.

You should only save the file to another disk if you run out of room on the hard drive. To ensure that you never run out of room, always keep at least 10 percent of the hard drive space free. A hard drive that is too full can cause many problems that are more serious than being unable to save a file.

To save a file, select File⇨Save (⌘-S). If you have previously saved the file, then updating the existing file with the changes that you have made will take just a fraction of a second. If you have not yet saved the file, the Save As dialog box will appear, as shown in Figure 9-9.

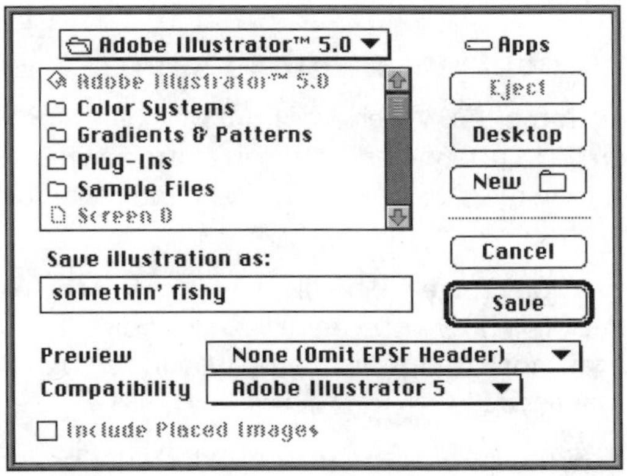

Figure 9-9:
The Save As dialog
box.

STEPS: Saving Illustrator Documents

Step 1. Decide how you are going to save the file. Choose the correct Preview and Compatibility options for the file. (See descriptions in the "Preview options" and "Compatibility options" sections, later in this chapter.)

Step 2. Decide where you are going to save the file and make sure that the name of the folder that you want to save it in is at the top of the file list window. Saving your working files in a location other than the Illustrator folder is a good habit. Otherwise, you can have trouble figuring out which files are yours, which files are tutorial files, and so on.

Step 3. Name the file something distinctive so that if you look for it six months from now you will recognize it. Avoid using *Untitled Art 1, Untitled Art 2,* and so on. The names are nondescriptive, and besides, you can too easily accidentally replace the file at a later date with a file of the same name. For the same reasons, do not use *Document 1, Document 2,* and so on (QuarkXPress's default names). Also avoid using *Test1* (if I had a nickel for every *Test1* or *Test2* I've seen on people's hard drives, I'd have . . . well, I'd have a lot of nickels); *stuff, #$*&!!* (insert your favorite four-letter word here), *picture, drawing,* or your first name. A filename can have up to 32 characters, and you can use all the letters, numbers, and special characters (except a colon [:]), so make the most of them and *describe* the file.

When should I save?

You really can't save too often. Whenever I put off saving for "just a few minutes," that's when the system locks up, or crashes, or gives me a Type 1 error. Depending on your work habits, you may need to save more frequently than other people do. Here are some golden rules about when to save:

⚡ Save as soon as you create a new file. Get it out of the way. The toughest part of saving is deciding how and where you are going to save the file and naming it. If you get those things out of the way in the beginning, pressing ⌘-S later is fairly painless.

⚡ Save before you print. For some reason, PrintMonitor and PostScript errors can crash a system faster than almost anything else.

(continued)

(continued)

▓ Save before you switch to another application. Jostling stuff around in a computer's RAM is an open invitation for the whole system to poop out.

▓ Save right after you do something that you never want to have to do again — such as getting the kerning "just right" on a logo or matching all of the colors in your gradients so that they meet seamlessly.

▓ Save after you use a filter that takes more than a few seconds to complete.

▓ Save before you create a new document or go to another document.

▓ Save before you go to any Apple Menu Item, including the Chooser and Control Panels folder (which are really parts of the Finder, another application).

▓ Save at least every 15 minutes.

The Save As command

The Save As command (File⇨Save As) enables you to save multiple versions of the document at different stages of progress. If you choose Save As and do not rename the file or change the save location, you will be prompted to replace the existing file. If you choose Replace, the file that you saved before will be erased and replaced with the new file that you are saving. Most disk and trash recovery utilities cannot recover a file that you delete this way.

The Save As command is also useful for changing the Preview and Compatibility options (which are described in the "Preview options" and "Compatibility options" sections, later in this chapter). If you have saved in Omit Header Preview and want to change to Color Preview, choose File⇨Save As, don't change the filename or file location, and choose Color from the Preview pop-up menu.

File types

You can save Illustrator 5 files in several ways. Actually, you can save them in 25 different formats . . . though some formats just don't make any sense. You can choose from five different "levels" of Preview in Illustrator 5 and from five different version formats.

Saving your Illustrator files with the wrong options can dramatically affect whether that file can be opened or placed in other software, as well as what features are included with the file when it is reopened in Illustrator. For example, saving the file as Illustrator 1.1 with no header makes it virtually useless to every piece of software but Illustrator, and 60 percent of the features in Illustrator 5 will be lost in an Illustrator 1.1 format file.

Preview options

The following options in Illustrator 5 affect the way that other software programs see Illustrator files. Figure 9-10 shows examples of how files look in QuarkXPress page layout software when you save them in the four Macintosh formats. It also shows the different file sizes for each format.

 Illustrator 5.5 has the same options for saving files as does Illustrator 5.0, but the different options are reached in a different way in 5.5. 5.5 has one pop-up menu in the Save As dialog box, with the different versions of Illustrator listed as well as "EPS" and "Acrobat PDF." Selecting an Illustrator version from the pop-up menu saves the file as the first option below (None-Omit EPSF Header). Selecting EPS brings up a dialog box with different preview and version options, similar to the pop-up menus in Illustrator 5.0 (see Figure 9-11).

 The following listings reflect 5.0's name for the preview and (after the slash) 5.5's names. The names were changed in 5.5 to make Illustrator's EPS file saving more compatible with Photoshop.

- **None-Omit EPSF Header/Any Version** prevents programs other than Illustrator from opening the files. Don't even think about trying to open this type of file for editing in another program, except for other Adobe software, such as Photoshop and Dimensions. Most other software sees a file that you save with Omit EPSF Header as a text-only file that should still print. If you don't need to take the file into other software, save it as Omit EPSF Header.

 EPSF stands for "Encapsulated PostScript File."

- **None-Include EPSF Header/None** lets most software programs recognize the Illustrator document as an EPS file, but instead of viewing it in their software, you see a box the size of the illustration with an X in it. Usually, this box is the same size as the illustration, including any stray anchor points or direction points. The file will print fine out of other software.

None (Omit EPSF Header) 127k   None (Include EPSF Header) 177k

Black & White Macintosh 207k   Color Macintosh 363k

Figure 9-10: How an illustration that was saved with different Preview options appears in QuarkXPress.

▓ **Black & White Macintosh/1-bit Macintosh** saves the EPS file with a PICT file preview as part of the EPS file. A PICT image is embedded within the EPS file (technically, a PICT resource); you do not have two separate files. Page layout software and other software displays this illustration in a black-and-white preview with no shades of gray in it. This file may take up substantially more space than the Include EPSF Header file requires because of the PICT file. The larger the illustration measures, the more storage space the PICT file uses.

Figure 9-11:
The EPS Format
dialog box.

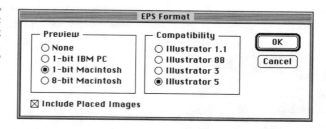

- **Color Macintosh/8-bit Macintosh** saves the file with a color preview that is an embedded PICT image. Page layout and other software displays this file in 8-bit color (256 colors) when you place it in a document. An Illustrator file that you save with a preview that is color takes up more file space than a file saved with any other option.

- **IBM PC/1-bit IBM** saves the file with a preview for IBM systems. Page Layout software or other software for PCs that can import EPS files can preview illustrations that you save with this option.

Compatibility options

Illustrator is one of the few software programs that is almost fully backwards compatible. If you open a file in Illustrator 88 that you created in Illustrator 5.5, it looks almost exactly the same. Most software packages are forward compatible for one major version, but Illustrator is a novelty in that you can open an Illustrator 1.1 file in Version 5 of the software, even though more than seven years passed between those product versions.

There are a number of reasons to save illustrations in older versions of Illustrator. The following list provides information about saving files in each version, and Figure 9-12 shows what happens to artwork that was created in Illustrator 5 when you save it in older versions of the software.

The features added to Version 5.5 do not affect file content. Thus, files created in Version 5.5 have the same structure as files created in Version 5.0.

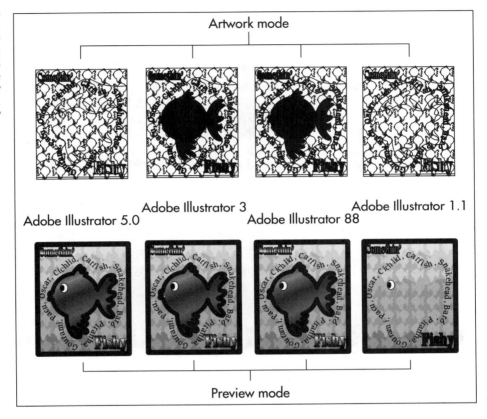

Figure 9-12:
The same
illustration
saved as
each of the
Compatibility
types.

- **Illustrator 5.0** saves the file in the Illustrator 5.0 format, which most applications can read and recognize as an EPS file. Normally, you should save files in the Illustrator 5.0 format unless you have a reason to save them as a different version. Abilities and features that are available only in the Illustrator 5.0 format include gradients, custom views, layers, and custom Artboard sizes.

- **Illustrator 4** saves the file in the Illustrator 4 format, which is a version that is available only for Windows users. Saving a file in the Illustrator 4 format ensures that Illustrator 4 for Windows will open Illustrator files. Gradients, views, layers, and custom Artboard sizes are not supported by the Illustrator 4 format.

- **Illustrator 3** saves the file in the Illustrator 3 format, which is useful not only for taking files into the Illustrator 3 program, but also for taking Illustrator files into FreeHand. The Illustrator 3 format transforms gradients into masks with blends, which is useful when you want to open Illustrator files in Photoshop (Photoshop normally doesn't accept gradients) or other software that doesn't like Illustrator's use of blends. In fact, you can use the Illustrator 3 format for a lot of "cheating" —

doing things that Illustrator normally doesn't enable you to do. For example, technically, you can't put gradients or masks into patterns. But if you save a gradient as an Illustrator 3 file and reopen it in Illustrator 5.0, the gradient becomes a blend, which you *can* use in a pattern.

▓ **Illustrator 88** saves the file in the Illustrator 88 format, which, for about four years (1988 to 1992), was *the* Illustrator standard. Much clip art has been created and saved in the Illustrator 88 format. The main problem with saving in the Illustrator 88 format is that type changes occurred between Illustrator 8 and Illustrator 3. Illustrator 88 cannot handle type on a curve (path type) and doesn't deal correctly with compound paths (type converted to outlines are made up of several compound paths, one for each character).

▓ **Illustrator 1.1** saves the file in the oldest of Adobe Illustrator formats, Version 1.1. Saving in the Illustrator 1.1 format is useful when you want to take files into older versions of Freehand and many other older draw programs.

 See Appendix D for a complete description of the capabilities of each major version of Illustrator, including the differences between Versions 5.0 and 5.5.

Opening and Closing Illustrator Files

You can open any Illustrator file from any version of Illustrator in Illustrator 5.0. Regardless of which Preview options are selected, Illustrator 5.0 can still open the file. When you select File⇨Open or press ⌘-O, the Open dialog box appears and asks you to find an Illustrator file. Find the file and double-click it to have it open into a document window on the screen.

To close an Illustrator file, select File⇨Close (⌘-W). If you saved the file prior to closing it, it will just disappear. If you have modified the file since the last time you saved it, a box appears, asking whether you want to save changes before closing. If you press Return or Enter to save the file, it will be updated. If you have not saved the file at all, the Save As dialog box appears so that you can name the file, choose a location for it, and choose Preview and Compatibility options for the file. If you click the Don't Save button (⌘-D while the dialog box is showing), then any changes that you made to the document since you last saved it (or if you have never saved it, all the changes you made since you created it) are lost. Clicking Cancel (⌘-period) takes you back to the drawing, where you can continue to work on it.

Remember that when you close a document, you do not quit the Illustrator program. To quit Illustrator, you need to select File⇨Quit (⌘-Q). If documents are open, they will close. If you have not yet saved changes to open documents, then a dialog box appears asking if you want to save changes.

Opening PICT Templates

You can bring any PICT image into Illustrator by simply opening it. Unfortunately, all PICT images become templates, which cannot be printed. Instead, you can trace around them, either manually with the drawing tools or automatically with the Auto Trace tool. Only one template can be opened at a time. Templates are visible when you have selected the Show Template option in the View menu and hidden when you have selected the Hide Template option. Files that you save with Hide Template or Show Template will hide or show the template the next time the file is opened. Figure 9-13 shows a template as it appears in Illustrator.

To open a template in a new document, select File ⇨ Open (⌘-O) or press Option and select File ⇨ New (⌘-Option-N). Select a Paint or PICT image, and that image will be brought into Illustrator automatically as a template.

Figure 9-13:
A template (top) and an EPS file (bottom) as they appear in Illustrator.

Placing EPS Files

The only type of file that you can *place* into Illustrator is an EPS (Encapsulated PostScript) format file. To place files, you select File⇨Place Art. A standard Open dialog box appears. Only EPS type files show up in the file window.

After you bring an EPS file into Illustrator, you can transform it (move, scale, rotate, reflect, and shear it) in any way, but you cannot change anything within the EPS file.

The quality of a placed EPS file is as good as the original; if the file was bitmapped (created or saved in a paint program such as Photoshop), then the quality will lessen as the file is scaled up, and the quality will increase as the file is scaled down. If the file was in PostScript outline format (created in Illustrator or FreeHand), then the quality will stay consistent as the file changes in size.

You can use EPS images for tracing, similar to the way that you can use PICT images for tracing, except that the Auto Trace tool does not recognize EPS and will not automatically surround it. In addition, EPS files have a 72 dot-per-inch preview, which can actually become a 144 dot-per-inch preview if the file is reduced to 50 percent of its imported size.

Illustrator shows EPS images differently in Artwork mode and in Preview mode. In Artwork mode, an EPS image is in black and white, and it looks like an outline.

When you save a document with an EPS image in it with a preview, you can link the EPS file to Illustrator or include it in the Illustrator file. Normally, including the EPS file within the Illustrator file is the better choice. This method prevents the two files from being separated; if you have one and not the other, you are out of luck. But you may want to link the file instead of including it because of two reasons. First, EPS images are huge and may make your Illustrator file too large. Second, if you need to make changes to a placed EPS file that you have included in an Illustrator file that you have saved with a preview, you have to replace the placed art in the preview file with the new version. If you have linked the placed art, instead of including it, it is automatically updated when you make changes.

You may want to replace placed images with new versions or completely different artwork. Illustrator has made this process painless. If placed artwork is selected, the menu item that used to read Place Art reads Change Placed Art. You can swap out the currently selected placed art with a new file.

 The menu item in 5.5 always reads "Place Art" but when placed art is selected and this item is selected, a dialog box will appear asking if you would like to replace current artwork or place new artwork, not changing the selected artwork.

When you replace placed art, any transformations that you made to the original placed art are applied to the newly placed art as well.

You can dim placed art by checking the Dim Placed Art check box from the Layer Options on the Layers palette. If you dim placed art, then a ghost of the image appears instead of the solid image. This feature makes tracing placed art easy. Dimming a placed image does not affect its printed output.

Importing Styles

The ability to import styles from other documents can save you enormous amounts of time. Styles that you can import include gradients, patterns, custom colors, and graph designs. This feature is useful for maintaining consistency between illustrations that are related.

If you import styles that have the same name as styles that are in the currently open document, the imported styles will replace the styles that have the same name.

To import styles from another document, select File⇨Import Styles to see the Import Styles dialog box. In the dialog box, select the file that you want to import styles from. The styles that are different from the ones in your document will be imported.

You can use Import Styles to bring in Pantone Colors, Trumatch colors, and so on, by selecting files that include custom colors.

Printing from Illustrator

Printing directly out of Illustrator enables you to see a printed composite (the entire image printed on one sheet, with all colors represented) of an illustration.

You cannot print color separations from inside Adobe Illustrator. To print separations of an illustration, you need to open and print the file through Adobe Separator. You also can print color separations by placing the Illustrator file into a page-layout software or another type of software that prints separations.

Printing out of Illustrator to see the printed illustration is always a good idea. If you have a color printer, the illustration will appear in full color. On a black-and-white printer, colors will appear as various shades of gray.

You use four different dialog boxes to directly affect the way that printed pages appear when you print them from Illustrator:

> ▦ **The Chooser:** You use this part of the Apple System software to select which printer you want to print to.

> ▦ **The Document Setup dialog box:** You use the settings in this box to affect the document's size and what portions of it will print. You can also control whether patterns will print.

> ▦ **The Page Setup dialog box:** Here you change the options for what actually gets printed on the printer's page. There are three main types of Page Setup dialog box: Apple LaserWriter, PS Printer, and ImageWriter. The dialog box that you see depends on the type of printer that you are using.

> ▦ **The Print dialog box:** In the Print dialog box, you specify how many pages and how many copies get printed, as well as other printer-specific information.

The Chooser

To use the Chooser to select different printers, select Apple➪Chooser. The Chooser window appears. If the Chooser option is not available, you may have to reinstall the system software, making sure that you include software for the type of printer that you are using.

On the left side of the Chooser, select the type of printer that you want to print to (that is, laser printers, ImageWriters, and so on). If the printer is a laser printer and you have installed the PS Printer file, you may see both LaserWriter and PS Printer icons in the window on the left. See the sections later in this chapter for information on each of those options.

After you select the type of printer on the left, you see a list on the right that tells you what printers of that type are available. Click any of these printers to select it as the printer to send files to until you choose another printer.

 Choose the Background Printing option if you want to print files in the back-ground. If Background Printing is selected, the file that you are printing is temporarily spooled to a folder in the System Folder. Then the PrintMonitor program, which runs automatically whenever you print something with Back-ground Printing chosen, sends the file to the printer. PrintMonitor is an application that is normally located in the System Folder's Extension folder. To facilitate printing and to ensure that no PrintMonitor-related errors occur, change the amount of application memory PrintMonitor has to at least 300K. (Highlight the PrintMonitor icon when PrintMonitor is *not* running, select File⇨Get Info in the Finder [⌘-I], and type **300** in the Preferred size text box.)

If you have PS Printer installed (or Laserwriter 8) and you want to use that extension to print to laser printers that are equipped with PostScript, a Setup button appears that enables you to specify exactly which type of printer you are printing to.

After you change the printer in the Chooser, the printer will stay the same until you change it in the Chooser.

The Document Setup dialog box

Selecting File⇨Document Setup (⌘-Shift-D) enables you to set the initial page size of an illustration via the Artboard. When you bring up the Document Setup dialog box, you see a wealth of options that assist you in printing. If the Use Page Setup box is checked, then the Artboard size is relative to the size of the page that is selected in the Page Setup dialog box. If the Artboard is smaller than the printable page, then anything entirely outside the edges of the Artboard will be cropped off when you print the illustration through Illustrator. Any objects that are partially on the Artboard will print. Anything outside the Artboard will print when you print the illustration through another application.

Another option in the Document Setup dialog box enables you to choose whether patterns will preview and print. Unchecking this box prevents patterns from printing when you print the illustration from Illustrator.

The Page Tiling options also affect the way that pages appear when a document is printed from Illustrator:

- If you choose Tile imagable areas, a grid appears on the Artboard. Any block of the grid that has a piece of the illustration will print. When this option is chosen, you can specify in the Print dialog box that only certain pages should be printed.

- If you choose Tile full pages, only full pages (as defined in the Page Setup dialog box) that appear on the Artboard will print. If no full pages can fit in the Artboard, everything in the Artboard will print.

- If you choose Single full page, only one page will print.

The Page Setup dialog box for Apple LaserWriters

If the Apple LaserWriter Printer driver is installed and you have chosen a printer that uses it (by clicking on LaserWriter in the Chooser and selecting a printer), then the LaserWriter Page Setup dialog box appears when you select File⇨Page Setup.

You can choose any paper size, even one that your printer does not have the capacity to use. The Tabloid option is the first option in a set of choices in a pop-up menu that also lists envelope sizes and positions. The size that you choose shows up on the document as a dotted line boundary when the Tile full pages or Single full pages options are selected in the Document Setup dialog box. Another dotted line boundary, inside the page size boundary, is the printable area. The printable area also shows up when the Tile imagable areas option is selected in the Document Setup dialog box.

The Reduce or Enlarge option affects how much the illustration is scaled when it's printed. Reducing or enlarging affects the way that the dotted line page boundaries and imagable areas dotted lines appear in the document. This feature is helpful when you want to print everything that's on a large Artboard. If you select a reduced size in the Page Setup dialog box, the dotted lines in the document reflect the reduced size.

Orientation controls how the image is printed on the printed page — whether it is printed in portrait orientation (longest side vertical) or landscape orientation (longest side horizontal).

You don't usually need to check the following printer effects options in the LaserWriter Page Setup dialog box:

- **Font Substitution:** This option replaces any bitmapped fonts with corresponding fonts that are installed on the printer, which usually means that if you have Geneva, New York, and Monaco installed in bitmapped format only, Helvetica, Times, and Courier will take their places. Any other bitmapped font will usually be replaced with Courier. In general, if you don't have the PostScript printer font or the font in TrueType format, you shouldn't use that font with Adobe Illustrator, and you shouldn't check this box.

- **Text Smoothing:** When Font Substitution is not checked and an illustration has a bitmapped font in it, Text Smoothing will make the bitmapped font look slightly better. It will still look bad, but it will look better than just the plain bitmapped font.

- **Graphics Smoothing:** Graphics Smoothing does about the same thing that Text Smoothing does, but it does it to graphics. Because this feature works only with PICT and Paint images, which you cannot print in Illustrator, you should not check this option.

▓ **Faster Bitmap Printing:** This option prints out bitmapped graphics at 36 dpi instead of 72 dpi. You cannot print out these graphics from Illustrator, so do not bother checking this box.

The Options box brings up another slew of options (well, six anyway — in my book that's a slew) that control how the laser printer interprets a document. Next to the options is a page with a dogcow on it. The dogcow changes as you check the options that are next to the page. The dogcow says, "Moof."

▓ **Flip Horizontal:** This option causes the document to print as a mirror image of itself, flipped horizontally. You can use it in combination with the Invert Image option to print negatives from Illustrator.

▓ **Flip Vertical:** This option causes the document to print as a mirror image of itself, flipped vertically. You also can use this option in combination with the Invert Image option to print negatives from Illustrator. Using the Flip Horizontal and Flip Vertical options together causes the document to rotate 180°.

▓ **Invert Image:** This option prints a negative image of the illustration, where all white areas are black and all black areas are white.

▓ **Precision Bitmap Alignment (4% reduction):** This option reduces bitmapped graphics to print better on ImageWriters, which have a resolution of 144 dots per inch. If you reduce graphics that are 300 dpi to 96% of actual size, they are 288 dpi, which is twice the size of the 144 dpi of the ImageWriter. You never need to check this option in Illustrator if you are printing to a laser printer.

▓ **Larger Print Area (Fewer Downloadable Fonts):** This option increases the print area of the document so that it prints closer to the edge of the page. On a standard 8.5" x 11" Apple LaserWriter, not having this box checked results in margins that are approximately ½" on each edge. Checking this box changes the margins to ¼" on the 11" edges and about ⅛" on the 8.5" edges. Of course, this extra printing area takes up a significant amount of printer RAM, so you may have trouble printing complex documents when this option is checked.

▓ **Unlimited Downloadable Fonts in a Document:** This option does more than enable you to use lots of fonts. Checking Unlimited Downloadable Fonts makes the RAM in the laser printer adjustable. As part of the document comes in and is processed, the information that was used to process that part of the document and the fonts that were needed to print it are flushed out of memory. The next section and its needed fonts are then loaded. This method takes longer than loading all of the fonts in the entire document at one time and then processing the document, but it prevents `Out of memory` printing errors.

The Page Setup dialog box for PS Printers

If you are using the PS Printer driver (or the LaserWriter 8 extension), then the Page Setup window will look slightly different from the standard LaserWriter Page Setup dialog box.

PS Printers have the same Reduce/Enlarge and Orientation options as LaserWriters have, but the Paper option is a pop-up menu instead of a series of radio buttons. An additional option called *Layout* changes how the printer puts images on a page.

The Paper option displays only page sizes that your printer can print. For example, my Personal LaserWriter NTR cannot print tabloid size pages, so I can't choose that option.

The Layout pop-up menu displays options of how many pages from the document can fit on the printed page. If you choose any option other than 1-Up, the printed pages are scaled and reoriented so that the pages are printed at the largest possible size.

Clicking the Help button displays another dialog box with all the options explained. Clicking the Options button brings up another dialog box with more options.

All the options in this dialog box are the same as the ones in the LaserWriter Page Setup dialog box; they just appear in different categories. And instead of a dogcow, you see a lowercase *a* that shows what will happen when certain options are checked.

The Page Setup dialog box for ImageWriters

If you are printing to an ImageWriter, you will get poor results from Illustrator unless you have a third-party piece of software, such as Freedom of the Press, that interprets PostScript for non-PostScript printers.

ImageWriter options enable you to pick the paper size and a few special effects that really aren't at all that special. You can change the orientation of the page as well.

Printing with the Apple LaserWriter driver

When all the settings in the Chooser, Document Setup, and Page Setup dialog boxes are correct, the final printing step is to select File⇨Print (⌘-P). This action brings up the Print dialog box, in which you may choose which pages to print, how many of each to print, and a few other options:

▓ **Copies:** The number that you enter here determines how many copies of each page will print. All copies of a single page are printed at one time, so if you enter **4** when you are printing a four-page document, you get four copies of page one, then four copies of page two, and so on.

▓ **Pages:** If you check the All radio button, all the pages that have art on them will print. If you enter numbers in the From and To boxes, only the pages that those numbers refer to will print.

▓ **Cover Page:** If you choose First Page or Last Page, a separate sheet, which contains information about the name of the computer, the name of the file, the number of pages, and the dates, will print. This feature is useful for making each print job easily identifiable when several people share a laser printer.

▓ **Paper Source:** If Paper cassette (the default) is selected, all pages will print on paper from the printer's cassette. If Manual Feed is selected, then the pages will print on paper from the Manual Feed Tray.

▓ **Print:** This option determines the way that the document will print to color or grayscale printers. If Black and White is chosen, no gray or color pixels will print, just patterns of black-and-white pixels.

▓ **Destination:** Choosing Printer prints the document to the laser printer as usual. Choosing PostScript® File prints the document to a PostScript file on the hard disk that you can download to a laser printer at a future time by using a utility such as Font Downloader or LaserWriter Font Utility.

If you click the Cancel button (⌘-period), the dialog box disappears, and no pages are printed. To Print, click the Print button or press Return or Enter.

Printing with the PS Printer driver

The options for printing with PS Printer are almost the same as the options in the LaserWriter Print dialog box, but some helpful additions are included.

The options for copies and the pages to print are exactly the same.

A new box, called *Paper Source,* enables you to print from different paper trays (including the manual feed tray) in the same document. After you choose a tray and click the First from button, the Remaining From pop-up menu appears.

The Destination option is the same as for the LaserWriter, but the setup is a little different; File is a PostScript file.

Clicking the Print button or pressing Return or Enter prints the document. Clicking the Cancel button (⌘-period) closes the Print dialog box and returns you to the illustration. Clicking the Help button brings up an additional dialog box where you can see exactly what each option is about. Clicking the Options button displays another dialog box with additional options.

In the Options dialog box, you can choose whether to print a cover page and whether to print black-and-white documents or documents that are color or grayscale.

The last option is a very innovative feature that enables you to specify how you want PostScript errors to be reported. Summarize On Screen lists the errors on-screen when they occur, and Print Detailed Report prints a report of the errors that occurred while that particular document was being printed.

Always select Print Detailed Report. When an illustration will not print, a paper will come out of the printer with the error message on it.

Always do a Save before you print. Severe problems, when they happen, usually occur when you are printing. Don't let your unsaved document be a victim to one of those severe problems.

For information on printing color separations and dealing with printing problems, see Chapter 25.

Advanced Areas

The most fun you can possibly have using Adobe Illustrator is achieving really incredible special effects. Different, exciting effects can bring an illustration to life, giving it a personality of its very own.

The concepts presented in this section are advanced techniques; in fact, even Illustrator experts may find information in here that they didn't know before. These areas are not particularly difficult to use; it's just that prior to this book they were not all that well explained anywhere else.

Path Editing and Transforming

In This Chapter

- Adding and removing anchor points from paths
- Cutting paths into separate paths
- Averaging points together
- Joining paths
- Changing anchor points into other types of anchor points
- Techniques for using the transformation tools

Adding and Removing Anchor Points

You can add and remove anchor points in two different ways. I've already mentioned one of these methods in Chapters 5 and 6, where I demonstrated how to add anchor points with the drawing tools and remove them simply by selecting them and pressing the Delete key.

The techniques that I cover in this chapter are entirely unlike the method discussed previously. Instead of adding new points that create an extension to an existing path, you will learn how to add points in the middle of existing paths. Instead of deleting points and the line segments connected to them, you will discover how to remove points in between two other anchor points and watch as those two anchor points are connected by a new line segment.

In Figure 10-1, the top row shows a drawing with a point added, resulting in a new curved section. The second row shows a point being removed and then re-added. Adding points, even to the same areas where they were removed, will not change the path back to the shape that it was before the points were removed. That path will have to be altered to resemble the original path. I will discuss these and other issues throughout this chapter.

(Note that Figure 10-1 shows a very simple example. The Delete Anchor Point tool is most often used to remove unnecessary points from overly complicated drawings.)

Figure 10-1:
The Add
Anchor Point
tool adds a
smooth
curve to an
object with
straight
sides.

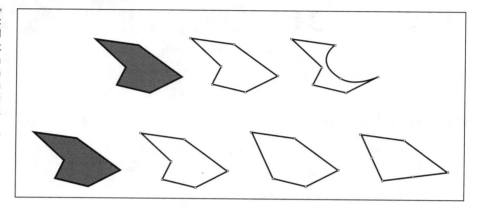

Adding anchor points

To add an anchor point to an existing path, select the Add Anchor Point tool and click a line segment of a path. You may not place an anchor point directly on top of another anchor point, but you can get pretty darn close. Figure 10-2 shows a path before and after several anchor points are added to it.

I like to select the paths to which I am adding anchor points *before* I start adding anchor points. This technique ensures that I don't get the annoying "Can't Add Anchor Point. Please use the Add Anchor Point tool on a segment of a path." message accidentally. It seems that if there is just one point in the middle of a path, that's where I end up clicking to add the point. After I add one point, the path becomes selected automatically.

Anchor points added to paths via the Add Anchor Point tool are either smooth points or straight corner points, depending on the segment where the new anchor point is added. If the segment has two straight corner points on either side of it, then the new anchor point will be a straight corner point. If one of the anchor points is any other type of anchor point than a straight corner anchor point, the new anchor point will be a smooth point.

See Chapters 17 and 18, which discuss the Roughen and Add Anchor Points filters, respectively, for other ways to add anchor points to a path without adding length to it.

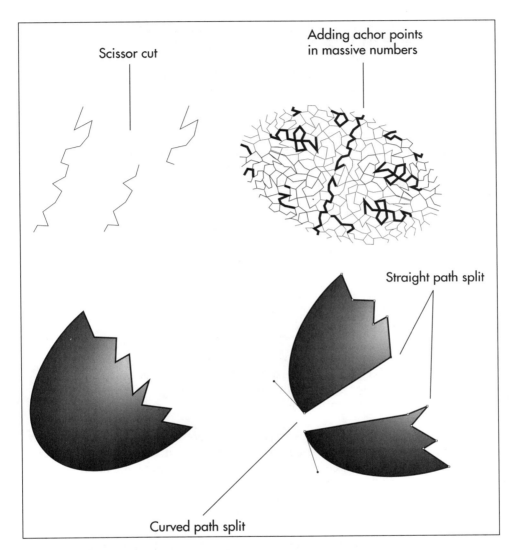

Figure 10-2: Adding anchor points to paths.

Removing anchor points

Removing anchor points is a little trickier than adding them. Depending on where you remove the anchor point, you may adversely change the flow of the line between the two anchor points on either side of it, as shown in the second row of Figure 10-1, where an anchor point has been removed. If the point removed had any direction points, the removal will usually result in more of a drastic change than if the anchor point was a straight anchor point. This situation occurs if direction points on the anchor point being removed controlled at least half the aspect of the curve. A straight corner point would affect only the location of the line, not the shape of its curve.

To remove an anchor point, click an existing anchor point with the Delete Anchor Point tool. Like the Add Anchor Point tool, you can remove points without first selecting the path, but, of course, if the path is not selected, you can't see it or the points that you want to remove. If you miss and don't click an anchor point, you will get a message informing you that to remove an anchor point, you must click one.

After you remove anchor points, you cannot usually just add them back with the Add Anchor Point tool. Considering that the flow of the path will change when you remove a point, adding a point — even the correct type of point — will not give the same result as just undoing the point deletion.

Splitting Paths

To change a single path into two separate paths that together make up a path that is equal in length to the original, you must use the Scissors tool. You can also split paths by selecting and deleting anchor points or line segments, although this method shortens the overall length of the two paths.

To split a path with the Scissors tool, click anywhere on a path. Initially, it doesn't seem like much happens. If you clicked in the middle of a line segment, a new anchor point will appear. (Actually, two will appear, but they are directly on top of one another, so you see only one.) If you clicked directly on top of an existing anchor point, nothing at all seems to have happened, but Illustrator has created another anchor point on top of the one that you have selected.

After clicking with the Scissors tool, you have separated the path into two separate sections, but it will appear that there is still only one path because the two sections are both selected. To see the individual paths, deselect them (⌘-Shift-A) and select just one side with the Selection tool. After a path has been split, one half may be moved independently of the other half (see Figure 10-2).

The anchor point(s) created with the Scissors tool will be either smooth points or straight corner points, depending on the type of anchor point that is next along the path. If the line segment to the next anchor point has a direction point coming out of that anchor point that affects the line segment, then the new end point will be a smooth point. If there is no direction point for the line segment, the end point will be a straight corner point. Figure 10-2 shows the results of splitting paths on both curved and straight segments.

You cannot use the Scissors tool on an end point of a line — only on segments and anchor points that are not end points.

Averaging Points and Joining _____

Averaging points is the process in which Illustrator determines the location of the points and figures out where the center of all the points will be on a mean basis. *Joining* is the process in which either a line segment is drawn between two end points, or two end points are merged into a single anchor point.

Averaging and joining are done together when two end points need to change location to be on top of one another and then merged into one point. You can perform these steps one at a time, or you can have Illustrator do both of them automatically. (Just press ⌘-Option-J or ⌘-Option-L.)

Averaging points

To line up a series of points either horizontally or vertically, use the Average command. The Average command also works to place selected points directly on top of one another. Figure 10-3 shows the different types of averaging.

Figure 10-3:
Different types
of averaging.

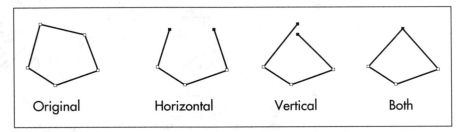

Original   Horizontal   Vertical   Both

To average points horizontally, select the points to be averaged with the Direct Selection tool and select Object ⇨ Average (⌘-L). The Average dialog box will appear, asking which type of averaging that you would like to do. In this case, choose Horizontal, which will move selected points only up and down.

Be sure to select the points to be averaged with the Direct Selection tool. If you select a path with either the Group Selection tool or the regular Selection tool, every point in the path will be averaged! This mistake can do quite a bit of damage when averaging both horizontally and vertically.

To average points vertically, choose the Vertical option in the Average dialog box. To average points both vertically and horizontally, choose Both. The Both option will place all selected points on top of each other.

 When averaging points, Illustrator uses the *mean* method to determine the center. No, Illustrator isn't nasty to the points that it averages; rather, Illustrator adds together the locations of the points and then divides by the number of points, which provides the mean location of the center of the points.

Joining

Joining is a tricky area to define. Illustrator's Join feature does two things: It joins two end points at different locations with a line segment, and it also combines two anchor points into one when they are placed directly on top of each other.

To join two end points with a line segment, select just two end points in different locations (not on top of each other) with the Direct Selection tool and choose Object ➪ Join (⌘-J). A line segment will be formed between the two points, as shown in Figure 10-4.

Figure 10-4:
Joining between
selected points.

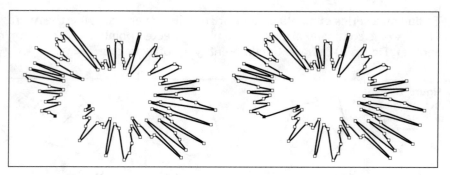

To combine two end points into a single anchor point, select the two points that are *directly* over one another and select Object ➪ Join (⌘-J). The Join dialog box will appear, asking what type of point should be created when the two end points become one anchor point. If you choose smooth point, then the point will become a smooth point with two linked direction points. If you choose corner point, the point will retain any direction line/point that is part of it. And if no direction point is on the line, there will be no direction point on that side of the anchor point.

Not only can you join two separate paths, but you can also join together the end points on the same open path to create a closed path in the same way that two end points from different paths are joined (see Figure 10-5).

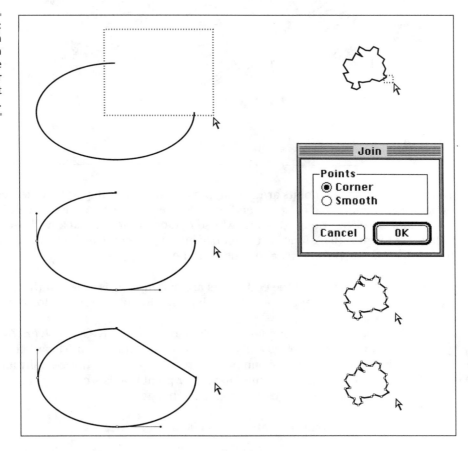

 When creating an anchor point out of two overlapping end points, make sure that the two points are precisely overlapping. If they are even the smallest distance apart, as in Figure 10-4, a line segment will be drawn between the two points instead of transforming the two end points into a single anchor point. You can tell immediately that the points are overlapping correctly when you select Join. If a dialog box appears, the points are overlapping. If no dialog box appears when Join is selected, the points were not overlapping, and it is best to undo the join.

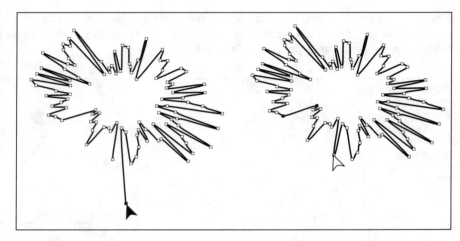

Figure 10-6:
When you drag
over another
point, the
arrowhead
becomes
hollow.

To make sure that end points are overlapping, turn on the Snap to Point feature in General Preferences and drag one end point to the other with a selection tool. When the two points are close enough, the arrowhead cursor (normally black) will become hollow (see Figure 10-6). Release the mouse button when the arrowhead is hollow, and the two points will be directly above one another.

Another way to ensure that the end points are overlapping is to select them and choose Object ⇨ Average (⌘-L) and select the Both option in the Average dialog box.

To make the points overlap and join at once, press ⌘-Option-L or ⌘-Option-J, which will both average and join the selected end points. This method works only on end points. The end points are averaged both horizontally and vertically and are also joined into an anchor point that is a corner point, with direction lines and direction points unchanged.

You can have the following limitations when joining:

- Joins may not take place when one path is part of a different group than the other path.

- If the two paths are in the same base group (that is, not in any other groups before being grouped to the other path, even grouped by themselves), the end points can be joined.

- If one path is grouped to another object and the other object has not been previously grouped to the path, the end points will not join.

- The end points on text paths cannot be joined.

- The end points of guides cannot be joined.

If all the points in an open path are selected (as if the path has been selected with the regular Selection tool), then selecting Object ⇨ Join (⌘-J) will automatically join the end points. If the two end points are located directly over one another, the Join dialog box will appear, asking whether the new anchor point should be either a smooth point or a corner point.

 Joining is also useful for determining the location of end points when the end points are overlapping. Select the entire path, select Object ⇨ Join (⌘-J), and choose smooth point. These steps will usually alter one of the two segments on either side of the new anchor point. Undo the join and you will know the location of the overlapping end points.

Converting Direction Points _____

Technically, the title of this section should be "Converting Anchor Points" because this section deals with changing anchor points from one type of anchor point to another. But to do this task, you will usually use the Convert Direction Point tool.

 See Chapter 2 for detailed definitions of the four different types of anchor points in Illustrator.

You can use the Convert Direction Point tool on either extended direction points or on anchor points. When there are two direction points on an anchor point, clicking either direction point with the Convert Direction Point tool will toggle the direction points from being linked (so that when the angle of one is changed, the other is changed as well) to being independent (the direction point's length from the anchor point and angle can be altered individually). It is generally a good idea to use the Direct Selection tool to move direction points unless you want to toggle between linked and independent points.

Converting smooth points

Smooth points can be changed into the other three types of anchor points by using both the Direct Selection tool and the Convert Direction Point tool. The different types of anchor points are shown in Figure 10-7.

    ▓ To convert smooth points into straight corner points, use the Direct Selection tool to drag the direction points on both sides of the anchor point into the anchor point; then release the mouse button.

Figure 10-7:
The four
types of
anchor
points.

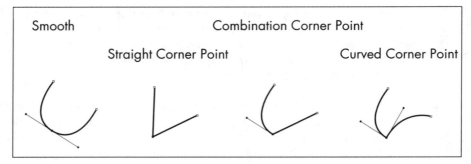

Smooth   Combination Corner Point

Straight Corner Point   Curved Corner Point

> ▩ To convert smooth points into combination corner points, use the Direct Selection tool to drag one direction point into the anchor point.

> ▩ To convert smooth points into curved corner points, use the Convert Direction Point tool to drag one of the direction points. After being dragged with the Convert Direction Point tool, the two direction points become independent of each other. The movement of one *will not* affect the other.

Converting straight corner points

You can change straight corner points into the other three types of anchor points by using both the Convert Direction Point tool and the Direct Selection tool.

> ▩ To convert straight corner points into smooth points, use the Convert Direction Point tool to click and drag on the anchor point. As you drag, linked direction points will appear on both sides of the anchor point.

> ▩ To convert straight corner points into combination corner points, use the Convert Direction Point tool to click and drag on the anchor point. As you drag, linked direction points will appear on both sides of the anchor point. Select one of the direction points with the Direct Selection tool and drag it towards the anchor point until it disappears.

> ▩ To convert straight corner points into curved corner points, use the Convert Direction Point tool to click and drag on the anchor point. As you drag, linked direction points will appear on both sides of the anchor point. Then use the Convert Direction Point tool to drag one of the direction points. After being dragged with the Convert Direction Point tool, the two direction points become independent of each other.

Converting combination corner points

You can change combination corner points into the other three types of anchor points by using both the Convert Direction Point tool and the Direct Selection tool.

- To convert combination corner points into smooth points, use the Convert Direction Point tool to click and drag on the anchor point. As you drag, linked direction points will appear on both sides of the anchor point.

- To convert combination corner points into straight corner points, use the Convert Direction Point tool to click once on the anchor point. The direction point will disappear.

- To convert combination corner points into curved corner points, use the Convert Direction Point tool to click and drag on the anchor point. As you drag, linked direction points will appear on both sides of the anchor point. Then use the Convert Direction Point tool to drag one of the direction points. After being dragged with the Convert Direction Point tool, the two direction points become independent of each other.

Converting curved corner points

You can change curved corner points into the other three types of anchor points by using both the Convert Direction Point tool and the Direct Selection tool.

- To convert curved corner points into smooth points, use the Convert Direction Point tool to click or drag one of the direction points. You can then use the Direct Selection tool to adjust the angle of both direction points at once.

- To convert curved corner points into straight corner points, use the Convert Direction Point tool to click once on the anchor point. The direction points will disappear.

- To convert curved corner points into combination corner points, use the Direct Selection tool to drag one direction point into the anchor point.

Transforming Objects

PostScript has the capability to transform any PostScript object by scaling it, rotating it, reflecting it, and shearing it. Illustrator takes this power and makes it quite usable by providing you the flexibility of using four tools, each of which does one of those transformations.

This section doesn't discuss *how* to use the tools but instead includes steps that detail some neat stuff that you can do with the tools.

 See Chapter 3 for a detailed discussion on how to use the transformation tools.

You can repeat the use of the transformation tools (and the Move function) by selecting Arrange ⇨ Repeat Transform (⌘-D).

Creating shadows

You can create all sorts of shadows by using the Scale, Reflect, and Shear tools, as shown in the illustrations in Figure 10-8.

STEPS:	Creating a Shadow with Transformation Tools
Step 1.	Select the path that will have the shadow and click the bottom of the path once with the Reflect tool. This action will set the origin of reflection at the base of the image. Drag down while pressing the Shift key. The image will flip over, creating a mirror image under the original. Press the Option key (keeping the Shift key pressed) before and during the release of the mouse button.
Step 2.	Using the Shear tool, click the base of the reflected copy to set the origin. Click and drag left or right at the other side of the reflection to set the angle of the reflection.
Step 3.	Using the Scale tool, click once again on the base of the reflected copy to set the origin. Click and drag up or down at the other side of the reflection.
Step 4.	Color the shadow darker than the background that it is on.

When working with type, first vertically scale a copy. Hold down the Option key when releasing the mouse button to create a copy; hold down the Shift key to constrain the scaling to vertical as you drag the mouse up or down. Setting the origin of the scale to the baseline of the type helps, as does using all caps or type with no descenders.

Send the copy to the back (⌘-Hyphen) and shear the shadow off to one side or the other, once again setting the origin at the baseline of the type. Holding down Shift as you shear will prevent the baseline of the copy from angling up or down.

Figure 10-8:
Shadows
created with
the transfor-
mation tools.

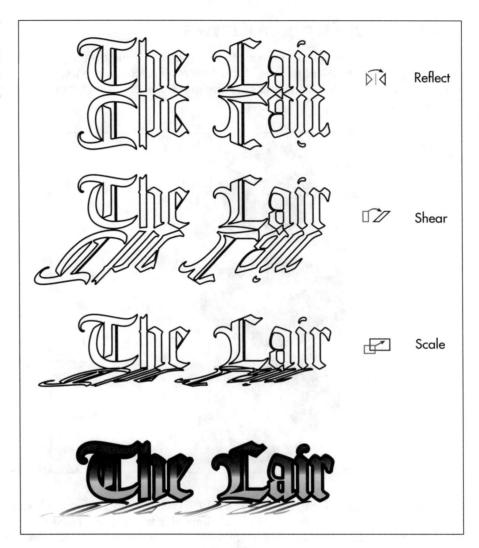

Reflect

Shear

Scale

If you want the shadow in front of the type, to make it appear that the light source is coming from behind the type, use the Reflect tool to flip the copy of the type across the baseline of the type.

Transforming gradients

You can transform gradients in the same way that you transform objects that are colored by gradients. All of the transformation tools affect gradients, but the best effects are achieved by scaling and shearing gradients, especially radial gradients (see Figure 10-9).

Figure 10-9:
Radial blends can be transformed with their objects.

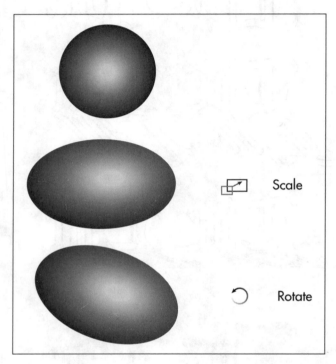

To create an effect similar to that of Figure 10-9, create a radial gradient inside a circle with no stroke. (Use a circle so that no portions of it are cropped outside of the shape when it is distorted.) Scale and shear the circle with the radial gradient, and the radial gradient becomes scaled and sheared as well.

Rotating into a path

Clever use of the Rotate tool can create a realistic, winding path by duplicating the same object at different rotational intervals, rotated from different origins.

Start by creating an object of some sort. The illustration in Figure 10-10 uses paw prints. Select the objects (I've found it best to group them together) and choose the Rotate tool. Click to set an origin a little distance from the side of the object. Click the other side of the object and drag. As you drag, you will see the outline of the shape of the object that you are dragging. When the object is a good distance away, press the Option key (to copy) and release the mouse button; then release the Option key. A copy of the object appears. Press ⌘-D (Repeat Transform) to create *another* object the same distance away.

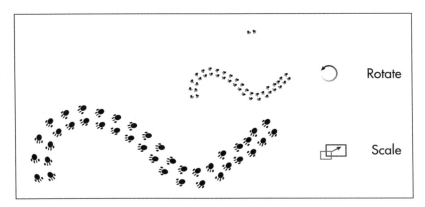

Figure 10-10:
Paw prints that have been rotated into a path.

After using the Repeat Transform command (⌘-D) a few times, click with the Rotate tool on the other side of the object to set another origin. Click and drag the outline of the object about the same distance; press the Option key and release the mouse button. Use the Repeat Transform command a few more times.

The farther you click from the objects to set the origin, the smaller the curve of the path of objects. Clicking right next to the objects causes them to turn sharply.

Making tiles using the Reflect tool

You can make symmetrical tiles by using the Reflect tool. You can use a set of four differently positioned yet identical objects to create artwork with a "floor tile" look, as shown in Figure 10-11.

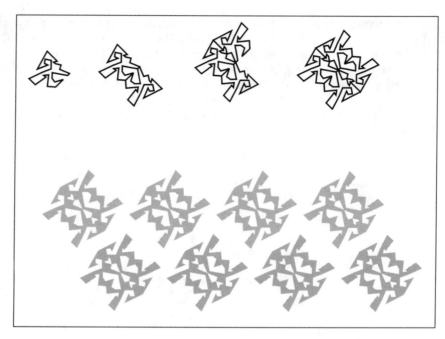

Figure 10-11:
Creating tiles with
the Reflect tool.

STEPS: Creating Symmetrical Tiles with the Reflect Tool

Step 1. Create the path (or paths) that you will make into the symmetrical tile. Group the artwork together.

Step 2. Take the Reflect tool and click off to the right of it to set the origin. Click and drag on the left edge of the object and drag to the right while pressing the Shift and Option keys. Using the Shift key will reflect the image at only 45° angles. When the object has been reflected to the right side, let go of the mouse button, still pressing the Option key. Release the Option key. You now have two versions of the object.

Step 3. Select the original and reflected object and reflect again, this time across the bottom of the objects. There will then be four objects, each mirrored a little differently, making up a tile, which can be used to create symmetrical patterns.

Using transformation tools on portions of paths

When using the transformation tools, you don't need to select an entire path. Instead, try experimenting with other effects by selecting single anchor points, line segments, and combinations of selected anchor points and segments. Another idea is to select portions of paths on different objects.

When you're working with portions of paths, one of the most useful transformation tool procedures is to select a smooth point with the Direct Selection tool and then choose a transformation tool, as shown in Figure 10-12.

Figure 10-12:
A smooth point selected and transformed with three different transformation tools.

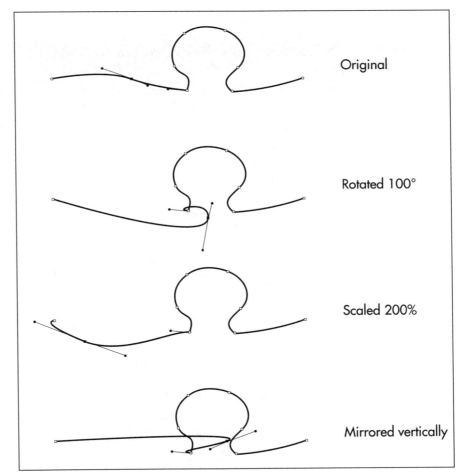

Original

Rotated 100°

Scaled 200%

Mirrored vertically

You can achieve precise control with the Rotate tool. Click the center of the anchor point and drag around the anchor point. Both direction points will move, but the distance from the direction points to the anchor point will remain the same. This task is very difficult to perform with just the Direct Selection tool, which you can also use to accomplish the same task.

You can accomplish the exact lengthening of direction lines by using the Scale tool. Click the anchor point to set the origin and then drag out from one of the direction points. Both direction points will grow from the anchor point in equal proportions.

When working on a smooth point, you can use the Reflect tool to switch lengths and angles between the two direction points.

The following are some more portion-of-path transformation ideas:

- Select all the points in an open path except for the end points and use all the different transformation tools on the selected areas.
- Select the bottommost or topmost anchor point in text converted to outlines and scale, rotate, and shear for interesting effects, as demonstrated in Figure 10-13.

Figure 10-13:
Text converted to outlines, with the bottom portion selected, reflected, and scaled.

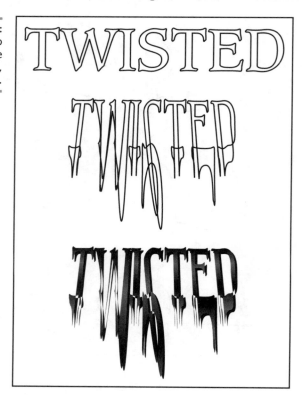

▓ Select two anchor points on a rectangle and scale and skew copies into a cube.

▓ Select just the inside anchor points on a star and scale to make the arms of the star wider and thinner. Use the Rotate tool to create Chinese throwing stars. Use the Shear tool to take the computery (precise) look away from the star.

Rotating into kaleidoscopes

By rotating and duplicating objects that have a stroke, you can make kaleidoscopic illustrations, such as the one in Figure 10-14. You may have trouble working with the last two or three objects, but this section shows you how to work through any difficulties.

Figure 10-14:
Objects that have been
rotated into kaleidoscopes.

First, select the object that you wish to rotate and duplicate. Choose the Rotate tool and Option-click at one end or corner of the object. Type in an angle that goes into 360 evenly in the Rotate dialog box, such as 18 (20x18=360), and press the Copy button (Option-Return). Choose Repeat Transform (⌘-D) until the object circles around the origin back to the beginning.

The trouble that you run into here is that if the objects have a fill and they overlap at all, the last object looks as if it's on the top, and the original object looks as if it's on the bottom, which destroys the perspective of the kaleidoscope. So either the original or the last object has to be fixed. It is generally easier to fix the original (bottommost) object.

Start by selecting the bottommost (original) object. Copy (⌘-C) it and paste it in front (⌘-F). Then use the Scissors tool to cut the path where it overlaps the second object; you will need to create two breaks in the path of the object, one on either side of the area that you wish to remove. Remove that portion of the path by deselecting (⌘-Shift-A) and selecting only that portion to be cut; then delete it. Many times this step alone will fix the path. If there is a fill and a stroke, however, your problems may not work out quite so easily. Copy the remaining piece of the copied object, choose Paste in Front (⌘-F) again, and change the fill to none. This procedure will correct any stroke deficiencies from the first copy.

Transforming patterns

The option in all transformation dialog boxes (and the Move dialog box) to apply transformations to patterns can produce some very interesting results, as shown in Figure 10-15.

Figure 10-15: A pattern that has been scaled up inside text and rotated.

One of the most interesting effects results from using patterns that have transparent fills. Select an object that has a pattern fill and double-click a transformation tool. Enter a value, check the Pattern tiles box, uncheck the Objects box, and then click Copy. A new object (which is unchanged) will overlap the original object, but the pattern in the new object will have changed. If desired, use the Repeat Transform command (⌘-D) to create additional copies with patterns that have been transformed even more.

Compound Paths and Masking

In This Chapter

- Understanding compound paths
- The difference between a fill of none and a hole
- How paths travel in directions, and reversing those directions
- Type and compound paths
- Faking a compound path
- Understanding masks
- Putting strokes and fills on masks
- Printing problems with masks
- Compound masks: an output nightmare

Compound Paths

Compound paths are one of the least understood areas of Illustrator, but after you understand a few simple guidelines and rules, manipulating and using them correctly is simple.

Compound paths are paths that are usually made up of more than one path. The one thing that often distinguishes compound paths from regular paths is that they appear to have holes in them (see Figure 11-1).

Creating compound paths

Compound paths of all sorts can be created by following the next steps. It is a good idea to make sure that none of the paths are currently compound paths or grouped paths before creating a new compound path.

Figure 11-1:
The frame of this
window looking
into space is a
compound path
with several
"holes" in it.

STEPS: Creating a Compound Path

Step 1. Create all the paths that you need for the compound path, including the outside path and the holes.

Step 2. Select all the paths and choose Object⇨Compound Paths⇨Make (⌘-8). The paths will now be treated as one path by Illustrator. When you click one of the paths with the Selection tool, the other paths in the compound path will be selected as well. Fill the object with any fill. (I used a custom radial gradient for the illustration in Figure 11-1.)

Step 3. Place the compound path over any other object. (I used a placed EPS image for this example). The inner paths act like holes that enable you to see the object underneath. Figure 11-2 shows these three steps.

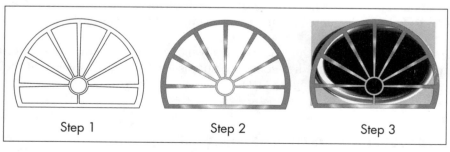

Step 1   Step 2   Step 3

Figure 11-2: The steps in creating a compound path.

You can select individual paths by clicking them once with the Group Selection tool. As always, you can select points and segments within each path by using the Direct Selection tool.

 Clicking only once with the Group Selection tool on paths that you wish to select is important. Clicking on those paths more than once with the Group Selection tool will select all the other paths in the compound path. To click (for moving or copying purposes) on the selected individual paths after they have been clicked by the Group Selection tool once, click on them with the Direct Selection tool.

 When you create a compound path, it takes on the Paint Style attributes of the bottommost path of all the paths that were selected and have become part of that compound path.

 You can create a compound path that is only one path, though there are very few reasons to do so. If the singular compound path is selected as part of a larger compound path (with either the Direct Selection tool or Group Selection tool), path directions may be altered. If you aren't sure whether an individual path is a compound path, select the path and choose Object⇨Compound Path. If the Release option is available, the path is a compound path; if it is not available, the path is not a compound path.

Compound paths do not work in a hierarchical process as groups do. If a path is part of a compound path, it is part of that compound path only. If a compound path becomes part of another compound path, the paths in the original compound path are compounded only with the new compound path.

 You cannot blend between multiple-path compound paths. Only the individual paths that you click with the Blend tool will be blended. You can blend each of the paths in a compound path separately; however, the blend step paths will not be compound paths.

 Blends are discussed in Chapter 12.

Releasing compound paths

When you want to release a compound path, select the path and choose Object⇨Compound Path⇨Release (⌘-9). The path changes into regular paths.

If any of the paths appeared as holes, they will, instead, be filled with the fill of the rest of the compound path. The results might be a little confusing because these holes then seem to blend right into the outer shape of the compound paths, as shown in Figure 11-3.

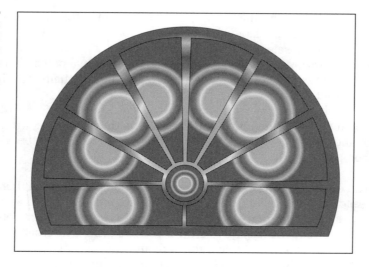

If the compound path that you are releasing contains other compound paths, they will be released as well because Illustrator doesn't recognize compound paths that are within other compound paths.

Understanding holes

Holes for donuts, Life Savers, and rings are quite simple to create. Just select two circles, one smaller than and totally within a larger circle, and choose Compound Path⇨Make (⌘-8). The inside circle is then a hole.

Holes in Illustrator really aren't holes at all. Instead, a compound path considers every path within it to lie along the borders of the compound path. Path edges within an object appear to you to be on the inside of an object, but they appear to Illustrator to be just another edge of the path.

With this concept in mind, you can create a compound path that has several holes, such as a slice of Swiss cheese or a snowflake. Just create the outermost paths and the paths that will be holes, select all the paths and then select Make Compound.

You aren't limited to one set of holes. You can create a compound path with a hole that has an object inside it with a hole. In that hole can be an object with a hole, and so on.

Overlapping holes

Holes, if they really are paths that are supposed to be empty areas of an object, should not overlap. If anything, you can combine multiple holes that are overlapping into one larger hole, possibly by using the Unite filter.

If holes within a compound path do overlap, the result is a solid area with the same fill color as the rest of the object. If multiple holes overlap, the results can be quite unusual, as shown in Figure 11-4. See the section "Reversing path directions" later in this chapter to learn more about multiple overlapping holes.

Figure 11-4:
Overlapping holes in compound paths, in Artwork mode (left) and Preview mode (right).

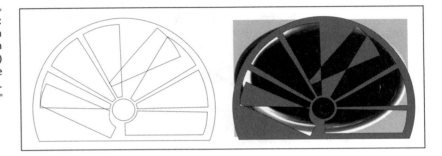

In most cases, you will get the desired results with holes only if the most outside path is under all the holes. As a rule, Illustrator uses the topmost objects to "poke" holes out of the bottommost objects. If you want holes to overlap, make sure that the holes are above the outside border.

Creating compound paths from separate sets of paths

Compound paths are very flexible. You can choose two sets of paths, each with an outline and a hole, and make them into one compound path. This technique is especially useful for making masks, but you also can use it to alleviate the repetition of creating several compound paths and selecting one of them at a time.

For example, if you have two shapes, a square and a circle, and want a round hole in each of them, you draw two smaller circles and put them into place. After you position the two shapes in the correct locations, you select them and the round paths inside each of them, and then you choose Object⇨Compound Path⇨Make (⌘-8). Each of the objects will have a hole, and they will act as if they are grouped.

To move separate objects that are part of the same compound path, select each object with the Group Selection tool, which selects an entire path at a time, and then move them. Remember that once selected, you should use the Direct Selection tool to move the selected portions of a compound path.

Type and compound paths

You have been using compound paths as long as you have been using a Mac with PostScript typefaces. All PostScript typefaces are made of characters that are compound paths. Letters that have holes, such as uppercase *B, D,* and *P* and lowercase *a, b,* and *d,* benefit from being compound paths. When you place them in front of other objects, you can see through the empty areas to objects behind them that are visible in those holes.

Each character in a PostScript typeface is a compound path. When you convert characters to editable outlines in Illustrator, each character is still a compound path. If you release the compound paths, the characters with empty areas appear to fill with the same color as the rest of the character, as shown in Figure 11-5, because the holes are no longer knocked out of the letters.

Figure 11-5:
Type as it normally appears after you convert it to outlines (top) and after you release compound paths (bottom).

 Many times, type is used as a mask, but all the letters used in the mask need to be one compound path. Simply select all the letters and choose Object⇨Compound Path⇨Make (⌘-8). This action creates a compound path in which all of the letters form the compound path. Usually, all the holes stay the same as they were as separate compound paths.

Any letters that overlap in a word that you make into a compound path can change path directions and thus affect the "emptiness" of some paths. If letters have to overlap, use the Unite filter on them first and then select all the letters and choose Object⇨Compound Path⇨Make (⌘-8).

Path Directions

Each path in Illustrator has a direction. For paths that you draw with the Pen or Free-hand tools, the direction of the path is the direction in which you draw the path. When Illustrator creates an oval or a rectangle, the direction of the path is counterclockwise.

 If you are curious about which way a path travels, click any spot of the path with the Scissors tool and then select Filter⇨Stylize⇨Add Arrowheads. In the Add Arrowheads dialog box, make sure that the End radio button is selected and click OK. An arrowhead appears, going in the direction of the path (Figure 11-6 shows several paths and arrowheads appearing for each path). If the path is filled, not stroked, you see only half the arrowhead in Preview mode. Choose the Undo command twice (once for the Arrowhead and once for the path splitting) to go back to where you started.

Paths have directions for one purpose (one purpose that you need to know about, anyway) and that is to determine what the solid areas of a compound path will be and what the empty areas will be. The individual paths in a compound path that create holes from solid paths go in opposite directions.

Figure 11-6:
The paths on the left are individual paths. The paths on the right make up a compound path. The arrows represent the direction of the paths. Notice that the only difference in direction is on the outermost path.

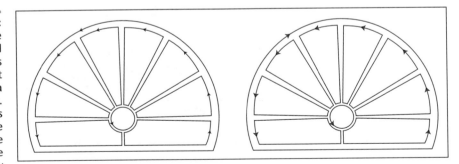

Create a large circle and put a smaller circle within it. Both circles are traveling in the same direction, counterclockwise. Select both of them and choose Object⇨Compound Path⇨Make (⌘-8). The outside circle changes its direction to clockwise so that the two circles can work together to form a doughnut-like shape.

If two smaller circles are inside the larger circle, they still punch holes in the larger circle because both of them are traveling in the same direction. But what happens when the two inside circles are overlapping? The area where they overlap is inside the empty areas, but both holes go in the same direction. The intersection of the two holes is solid because of the Even-Odd rule.

The Even-Odd rule, or what happened to my fills?

Understanding the Even-Odd rule is helpful when you are dealing with compound paths. The Even-Odd rule counts surrounded areas, starting with zero (outside the outermost edge) and working its way in. Any area with an odd number is filled, and any area with an even number (such as zero, the outside of the path) is empty, or a hole.

You can apply this rule to most compound paths — although taking the time to diagram the paths you've drawn and place little numbers in them to figure out what is going to be filled and what isn't is usually more time consuming than doing it wrong, undoing it, and doing it right. I've done the work for you in Figure 11-7.

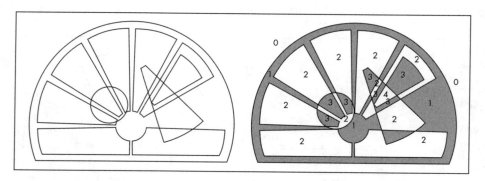

Figure 11-7: The Even-Odd Rule: Odd-numbered areas are filled; even-numbered areas are empty.

Reversing path directions

To change the direction of a path, select just that path (you may need to use the Group Selection tool) and choose Object⇨Attributes (⌘-Control-A). In the Object Attributes dialog box, you see a Reverse Path Direction check box.

When paths are changed into compound paths, their direction may change. The strange thing about this is that the Reverse Path Direction box is usually checked for objects that are traveling counterclockwise. The outermost path does not change direction from counterclockwise to clockwise until more than one overlapping path is made into a compound path. The paths that make up the holes don't change direction. They're still counterclockwise, but when you look at their Object Attributes, Reverse Path Direction is checked.

One thing that is consistent when dealing with path directions is that holes must travel in the opposite direction from the outside path. As a result, if the Reverse Path Direction check box is checked for the holes, it is not checked for the outside path. That scenario is the normal one when you create compound paths with holes. You can, if you so desire, check the Reverse Path Direction check box for the outside path and uncheck it for the inside paths. The resulting image will have the same holes as produced by the reverse. Figure 11-8 shows a compound path and its path directions before and after four of the paths were reversed.

 Never, never, never select Object⇨Attributes (⌘-Control-A) to change path direction when all paths of a compound path are selected. Doing so will display a gray box in the Reverse Path Direction check box in the Object Attributes dialog box. Clicking once on this gray check box will make it an empty box. Clicking twice on this box will change it to a filled (Xed) check box. Either way, all the paths in the compound path will be going in the same direction at this point, meaning that no holes will appear.

Figure 11-8:
Reversing the direction of four paths in the illustration on the left fills those holes.

Faking a Compound Path

At times, using a compound path just doesn't work. You may need to cheat a little. Except in the most extreme circumstances, you can fake compound paths, but you need to make quite an effort.

If the background is part of a gradient, select the hole and the object that is painted with the gradient, apply the gradient, and use the Gradient Vector tool to make the gradient spread across both objects in exactly the same way. This trick can fool even the experts.

 One way to fake a compound path is by selecting the background, making a copy of it, making the hole a mask of the background area, and grouping the mask to the copy of the background.

Masks

In Illustrator, you use masks to mask out parts of underlying objects that you don't want to see. The shape of the mask is defined by a path that you draw in Illustrator. Anything outside the mask is hidden from view in Preview mode and does not print.

You can make masks from any path, including compound paths and text that has been converted into outlines. You can use masks to view portions of multiple objects, individual objects, and placed EPS images.

 Masks caused a great deal of frustration in previous versions of Illustrator. The main problems were that you could not make grouped paths into masks and, causing confusion for everyone, masks were behind the objects that they were to mask. Masks are approached much differently in Illustrator 5.0, and they are much easier to understand. If you have used masks in previous versions of Illustrator, forget everything you know about masks and read this section. Even better, read the sidebar "Masking: changes from previous versions of Illustrator."

Creating masks

In order for you to create a mask, the masking object (the path that is in the shape of the mask) has to be in front of the objects that you want it to mask. You select the masking object and the objects that you want to mask. Then you choose

Figure 11-9:
The image on the left uses masks to hide portions of objects. The image on the right is the result of releasing those masks.

Object⇨Mask⇨Make. In Preview mode, any areas of the objects that were outside the mask vanish, but the parts of the objects that are inside the mask remain the same. Figure 11-9 shows an illustration with masks and without them.

 Masks are much easier to use and understand in Preview mode than in Artwork mode, which is another reason why masks seem to be easier to use in this version of Illustrator than in other versions.

If you want to mask an object that is not currently being masked, you need to select the new object and all the objects in the mask, including the masking object. You then choose Object⇨Mask⇨Make. The mask then applies to the new object as well as to the objects that were previously masked. The new object, like all others being masked, must be behind the masking object.

Like compound paths, masking does not work in hierarchical levels. Each time you add an object to a mask, the old mask that didn't have that object is released, and a new mask is made that contains all of the original mask objects as well as the new object. Releasing a mask affects every object in the mask, as described in the section "Releasing masks," which is later in the chapter.

 Usually, grouping all the objects in a mask is a good idea, but group them only after you have created the mask. Having the objects grouped facilitates moving the mask and its objects and selecting them when you want to add other objects to the mask.

Masking EPS images

There are two different ways to mask EPS images. The first way is by masking the EPS image in Photoshop by creating a *clipping path* and saving it with the EPS image in Photoshop. The second way is to use a mask in Illustrator.

The two methods have their strengths and weaknesses, with the best solution being a combination of both methods. The main advantage to creating a clipping path in Photoshop is that the path can be adusted while viewing the EPS image clearly at 1600% (viewing an EPS image at 1600% in Illustrator displays chunky, unrecognizable blocks of color). In this manner, the path can be precisely positioned over the correct pixels so that the right ones are selected to be masked. One disadvantage to using Photoshop's clipping path is that the Path tool and path editing controls in Photoshop are a limited version of Illustrator's Pen tool and path editing controls, making it more difficult to create and edit a path. The second disadvantage to using a clipping path is that compound paths in Photoshop adhere to one of two different fill rules, which control the way holes appear for differing path directions. Illustrator is much more flexible in this respect because you are able to change the path direction of each individual path with the Reverse Path Direction check box in the Object Attributes dialog box.

The best solution is to create the clipping path in Photoshop, and then, when the clipping path is selected, to select File⇨Export⇨Paths to Illustrator, which will save an Illustrator compatible file with the clipping path intact. Save the Photoshop image as an EPS and place it in Illustrator (File⇨Place Art). Then open the Illustrator file and copy the path to the document with the placed EPS image. The path will be sized to fit directly onto the EPS image.

Copying the selected path in Photoshop will allow you to paste it directly in Illustrator, even if you can run only one of those programs at a time. Just copy, quit Photoshop, run Illustrator, and paste it into the Illustrator document. This will work when going from Illustrator to Photoshop (paths only) as well.

Masking blends and other masks

You can mask objects that are masking other objects. Just make sure that you select all the objects in each mask and that, as with other objects, they are behind the path that you want to use for a masking object. You also can mask blends, as described in Chapter 12.

Masking: changes from previous versions of Illustrator

Along with the reorganization of the selection tools, masks have undergone a dramatic restructuring. The results are the same as in previous versions, but the method of setting up a mask is much different. The following information is a summary of the changes.

Objects that form the shape of the mask need to be in front of the objects that you want them to mask. In previous versions, masking objects had to be behind the objects to be masked.

When you create a mask, you need to select all the objects that you want to include in the mask, as well as the masking object. In previous versions, you needed to select only the path that made up the masking object.

Instead of using the Paint Style dialog box to create a mask, you choose Object⇨Mask⇨Make.

Only objects that you select with the masking object will be masked by the masking object. In previous versions, any objects in front of the mask would be masked, unless the mask was grouped with other objects.

To release a mask in Illustrator 5, you select the masking object and choose Object⇨Mask⇨Release. In previous versions, you selected the masking object and unchecked the Mask check box in the Paint Style dialog box.

In Illustrator 5, you cannot give masks a fill or stroke. In previous versions, because the masking object was the backmost object in the mask, you could fill it and stroke it, but you could see only half of the stroke on the inside of the masking object.

Stroking and filling masking objects

In Illustrator 5, creating a basic mask requires the following four steps:

STEPS: Creating a Mask and Stroking It

Step 1. Select the path that you want to use as a mask and bring it to the front.

Step 2. Select the mask and any objects that you want to mask and then select Object⇨Masks⇨Make. Group the masked objects with the mask for easier selecting in the future.

Step 3. Using the Group Selection tool, select the mask. Then change the stroke to 1-point black. Nothing will happen in Preview mode.

Step 4.   Select Filters⇨Stroke & Fill for Mask. A dialog box appears; click OK. The mask now has a 1-point black stroke. The result should resemble Step 4 in Figure 11-10.

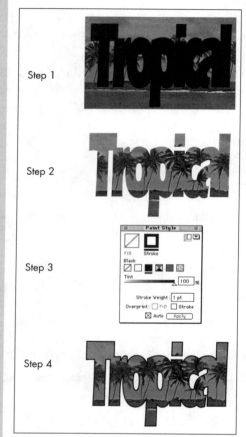

Step 1

Step 2

Step 3

Step 4

Figure 11-10: Steps for creating a stroked mask.

You cannot stroke or fill masking objects. Any Paint Style attributes that you applied to the masking object prior to transforming it into a mask are replaced by a fill and stroke of none. If you release the mask, the path that was the masking object continues to have a fill and stroke of none. You can, however, use two other methods to create a stroke or fill on a duplicate path of the masking object:

▓ The first method is to copy the masking object before you turn it into a masking object so that you can paste the copy onto the mask after you create it. To save a step, you can fill, and stroke the masking object before you copy it. After you create the mask, choose Edit⇨Paste in Front (⌘-F) to put a stroke on the mask (remove the fill or it will obscure all the objects that you are masking). Choose Edit⇨Paste in Back (⌘-B) and Arrange⇨Send to Back (⌘-hyphen) if you want the object to have a fill. If the object in the back has a stroke, the masking object will obscure half of it; the other objects in the mask may obscure other parts of it. If you want both a stroke and a fill, you need to paste two copies, one in front and one in back, to see both the fill and stroke accurately.

▨ The second method is to select the masking object and then from the Paint Style palette, choose the Paint Style attributes that you want for the masking object (it won't change in color, but you can change the attributes). Then choose Filter⇨Create⇨Fill & Stroke for Mask to create two more copies of the mask. Finally, paste the filled copy behind the mask's objects and the stroked copy in front of the masking object.

Releasing masks

To release a mask, first select the masking object (you may select other objects as well). Then select Object⇨Mask⇨Release, and the masking object will no longer be a mask.

If you aren't sure which object is the masking object or if you are having trouble selecting the masking object, then choose Edit⇨Select All (⌘-A) and choose Object⇨Mask⇨Release. Of course, this action releases any other masks that are in the document — unless they were separate masks that were being masked by other masks — got that?

To release all the masks in the document, even those masks that are being masked by other masks, Select All (⌘-A) and choose Release Mask repeatedly. Usually, three Release Masks gets everything, unless you went mask-happy in that particular document.

Masks and printing

As a rule, PostScript printers don't care too much for masks. They care even less for masks that mask other masks. And they really don't like masks that are compound paths.

Unfortunately, because of the way that Illustrator works, every part of every object in a mask is sent to the printer, even if only a tiny piece of an object will be used. In addition, controlling where objects are sliced by the masking object requires a great deal of computing power and memory. You can have a problem, for example, when you have more stuff to mask than the printer can handle.

The more objects in a mask, the more complex it is. The more anchor points, the more complex it is. The more direction points coming off those anchor points, the more complex the mask is. In other words, your printer would enjoy a mask if the masking object were a rectangle and no objects were being masked.

Masks are usually incredibly complex. This complexity causes many problems for printers (especially ones equipped with PostScript Level 1 and PostScript clones) and quite often results in PostScript printing errors. In addition, be careful not to go mask-crazy (using hundreds of masks), or your document may never see toner.

See Chapter 21 for more information on printing trouble and how to resolve these issues.

Masking with compound paths

Creating masks from compound paths is especially useful when you are working with text and want several separate letters to mask a placed EPS image or a series of pictures that you created in Illustrator.

The reason that you need to transform separate objects into compound paths is that a masking object can only be one path. The topmost object of the selected objects will become the masking object, and the others will be objects within the mask. Creating a compound path from several paths makes the Masking feature treat all the objects as one path and makes a masking object out of the entire compound path.

You can use compound paths for masking when you are working with objects that need to have "holes" as well as when you are working with text and other separate objects. Figure 11-11 was created by making one compound path from all of the parts of the window frame and using that compound path as a mask for the space scene.

Figure 11-11:
Creating a
compound path
out of all of the
parts of the
window frame
made the window
frame a mask for
the space scene.

Using compound paths and masks in an illustration

I used several compound paths and masks to achieve the effects in Figure 11-12. The compound paths are the word *Tropical* and the large strips of film across the lower half of the illustration. The masks are the word *Tropical,* the binocular shape, and the outside frame of the poster.

The first set of steps explains how to create the strip of film and place the island pic- tures into the film. You do not use masks in this process. I make this point so that you don't think that you always have to use masks, especially when another method is easier.

Figure 11-12:
This poster was created by using several different compound paths and masks.

STEPS: **Creating Complex Compound Paths**

Step 1. To create the film shape, draw a long horizontal rectangle with the Rectangle tool and place five rounded-corner rectangles inside the long rectangle.

Step 2. To create the sprocket holes in the film, place a right-side-up triangle next to an upside-down triangle and continue placing triangles until you have a row of triangles across the top of the film.

Step 3. After you group all the triangles together, Option-copy (drag the object with the Option key pressed, releasing the mouse button before the Option key) them to create a second row of triangles along the bottom of the film.

Step 4. Select all of the pieces of the film and choose Object⇨Compound Paths⇨Make (⌘-8). Fill the compound path with a dark purple color that is not quite black.

Step 5. This part looks as if you use a mask, but you don't need to do any masking here. Instead, place one EPS image, size it so that it just covers the hole, and Option-copy it across the remaining holes. Select each image in turn, choose File⇨Change Placed Art, and select a different image for each square. To complete the effect, simply bring the strip of film to the front.

Step 6. Before you place the film into the poster, group the images and the film and rotate them slightly. Grouping them prevents the hassle of selecting each one later if you need to move or transform them. Figure 11-13 shows the steps that you use to create the film.

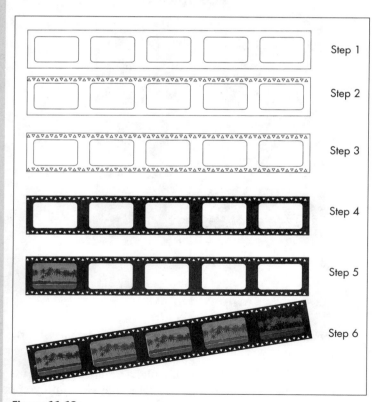

Figure 11-13:
Steps for creating a complex compound path to achieve a masking effect.

Instead of making the film a compound path, you could mask each of the photos and place each masked photo on top of the film. The method described in the preceding steps makes changing photos easier and takes less of a toll on the output device.

The next set of steps describes how to use the word *Tropical* to show the tropical island in Figure 11-12.

STEPS: Using Slightly Altered EPS Images with Masks

Step 1.   Place an EPS image in the document and create a masking path for the top of it. Before you make the objects into a mask, select the EPS image and choose Edit⇨Copy (⌘-C). You use this copy in Step 3.

Step 2.   Select both the masking path and the EPS image and choose Object⇨Mask⇨Make.

Step 3.   Select Edit⇨Paste In Back (⌘-B) to position the EPS image directly underneath the original image. Select FileÍChange Placed Art and substitute a slightly varied version of the original EPS image. The letters stand out decisively, as the third image in Figure 11-14 shows. The EPS image behind the word *Tropical* has been changed in Photoshop by using a Mosaic filter.

Figure 11-14: Using dissimilar EPS images as masked objects makes the word *Tropical* stand out in the image shown for Step 3.

Step 1   Step 2   Step 3

Use the outline of the masking path as a shadow by Option-copying it before you perform Steps 1 and 2. Change the fill in the copy to black and place the copy below and to the right of the original.

Blends and Gradations

- -

In This Chapter

- Comparing blends to gradations
- Creating blends of color
- Creating shape blends
- Understanding complex shape blends
- Using blends created in dimensions
- The magic of stroke blending
- Creating airbrush effects
- Understanding radial and linear gradations
- Creating gradations
- Using the Gradient Vector tool
- Using the Gradient palette
- Using gradients in software that doesn't like gradients

- -

Understanding Blends and Gradations

In Illustrator, a *blend* is a series of paths that Illustrator creates based on two other paths. The series of paths transforms from the first path into the second path, changing Paint Style attributes as it moves. *Gradations* are fills that change from one color to another in either linear or radial form.

Blends and gradations, at first glance, seem to do the same things but in different ways — so why have both? The Blend tool seems to be much harder to use than the Gradient Vector tool. On the surface, it seems that more can be done with gradients than with blends. Blends are limited to two colors; gradients can have tons of colors. Blends take a long time to redraw; gradients take up a fraction of the time.

After all, if gradients are so much easier to use and produce so much better results, is it really necessary to have a Blend tool? I've been asked this question quite often by students and clients, and they have a good point at first. Upon further study, however, it becomes apparent that blends are quite different than gradients, both in form and function.

Gradients are used only as fills for paths. Gradients can be either linear or radial, meaning that color can change from side to side, top to bottom, or from the center to the outside. Every gradient can have up to 34 distinct colors in it.

Blends, on the other hand, are series of transformed paths between two *end paths*. The paths between the end paths mutate from one end path into the other. All the attributes of the end paths change throughout the transformed paths, including shape, size, and all Paint Style attributes. The limiting feature of blends is that when you work with colors, you can blend only two colors at a time. Of course, you can blend between 34 different pairs of end paths, but that would be a little time-consuming, especially when you can use gradients to make the task much easier and quicker.

To summarize, gradients are an easier way to create blends that change only in color, not in shape or size. Figure 12-1 shows how you can use blends and gradients to create a similar result.

If you keep in mind that gradients work only with color, not with shapes, you should already have an idea of when to use which function. Linear and radial gradients usually look better than their blended counterparts because the quality is better and more colors can be added and manipulated. Changes to color are also another reason that gradients are better than blends. In addition, changes to angles and the placements of the gradients are much easier to make than if the same position changes needed to be accomplished with blends.

One drawback to using gradients is their "computery" look. Gradients are exact blends that are even from start to finish. Of course, with a little practice, additional colors or tints can be added, and the midpoint balance between two adjacent colors can be offset, giving the blend a more natural look. In general, though, realistic effects aren't all that easy to achieve with gradients.

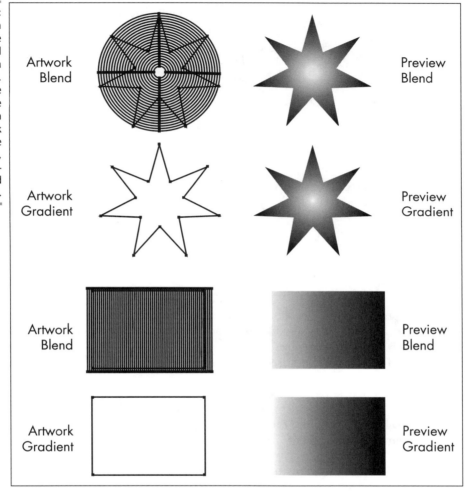

Artwork Blend — Preview Blend

Artwork Gradient — Preview Gradient

Artwork Blend — Preview Blend

Artwork Gradient — Preview Gradient

Blends, on the other hand, can be incredibly flexible when it comes to creating photo-realistic changes in color, if you plan ahead. Changes to blends aren't really changes at all; instead, they are deletions of the transformed objects and changes in the attributes of the end paths. If you know what you want, blending colors can take on an incredibly "real" look by changing the shapes of the blend's end paths just slightly.

But even more useful than creating realistic changes in color is blending's capability to transform shapes from one shape to another, as shown in the examples in Figure 12-2. With a bit of practice (and the information in this chapter), you can transform any illustration into another illustration. There is a limit to the complexity of the illustra-tions that can be transformed, but the limit is due more to the time it takes to create the blends than to limitations inherent in Illustrator.

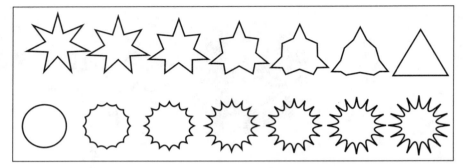

Figure 12-2:
Blending to
transform a
shape.

Because blends work on both stroke and fill attributes of objects, some really exciting effects can be created that aren't possible by using any other technique, electronic or traditional.

Blends

In past versions of Illustrator, blends were used predominantly for what gradients are used for now: to blend between different colors, normally just two different colors. But some artists took it upon themselves to stretch the capabilities of the Blend tool to create fantastic effects that amazed even the creators of the tool.

Originally, Adobe marketed the Blend tool (new to version 88) as a tool with the primary purpose of transforming shapes, not blending colors. Yeah, that's cool, designers said, but they instead used the tool for blending colors together to create what were known as vignettes, or gradients, to traditional artists.

For the most part, the blending function really hasn't changed since that version was released more than six years ago. Unfortunately, Adobe (or Aldus, which has a similar tool in FreeHand) never emphasized the incredible variations of effects that can be achieved with the Blend tool. In combination with some of the filters available in Illustrator 5.0, some pretty amazing effects can now be achieved.

The most noticeable change to the way the Blend tool works was in Version 3, when Illustrator began to automatically calculate blend steps and put the best number relative to color changes in the Steps field. This change was an indicator that Adobe realized that more people were using the Blend function for color blends than shape blends. In Version 5 of Illustrator, instead of making the Blend tool better, Adobe opted instead to create the Gradient feature, which does what most people were using the Blend tool for in past versions. Once again, the emphasis on the Blend tool is on shape transformation, rather than as away to create gradients.

Although any blend takes into account both color and shape, the following sections deal with color and shape separately because people using the Blend tool are often trying to obtain either a color effect or a shape effect, not both at the same time.

The Blend tool is the tool used to create blends, which are a group of paths (commonly referred to as *blend steps*) that change in shape and color as each path is created closer to the opposite *end path*.

STEPS: Creating a Basic Blend

Step 1. Using the Pen tool, create a small (1") vertical line segment. With the Selection tool, Option-copy the path a few inches to the side. Press Shift as you drag horizontally to constrain the movement of the path.

Step 2. On the left stroke, change the fill to none and the stroke to black with a 2-point weight. Change the right stroke to a fill of none and a stroke of 2-point white.

Step 3. Select both paths and choose the Blend tool. Click the top point of the left path and then the top point of the right path. This step tells Illustrator to blend between these two paths, and it uses the two end points as reference. The Blend dialog box appears after the second click.

Step 4. Click OK in the Blend dialog box. A mass of paths is created between the two end paths, all of them selected. Press ⌘-Shift-A to deselect all selected paths. The blend is made up of a total of 256 paths, including the two end paths. Each path is a slightly different tint of black.

You must use the Blend tool to click one point on each of two different paths, and those points must have been previously selected. Both paths must be open paths or closed paths. If the paths are open paths, only end points can be clicked.

 You should always click the corresponding points on both end paths. Figure 12-3 shows what can happen when opposite points are selected.

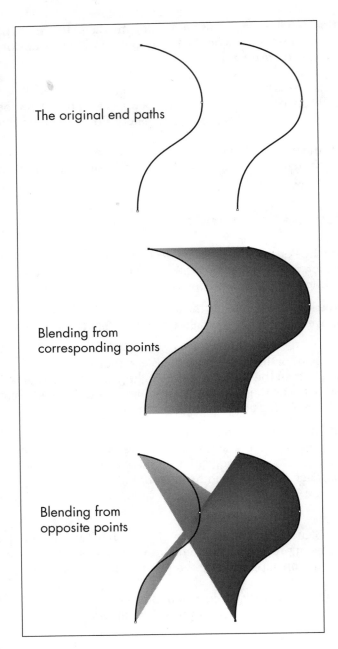

The original end paths

Blending from
corresponding points

Blending from
opposite points

Before you click any paths, the cursor looks like a crosshair. After the first click of the Blend tool, the cursor looks like a crosshair with three dots after it. After the second point has been clicked, the Blend dialog box appears.

There is no key command that accesses the Blend tool from any other tool.

Filter & Other Effects on this page were created using a wide variety of different filter effects. The steps to the right are explained fully in Chapter 17. Steps for creating the railroad track in the lower left are shown in Chapter 21. The embossed T was created using techniques found in Chapter 12. The patterns for the word "pasta" and the egg were created with steps from Chapter 13. The Star in the upper left corner was created using the Star and Divide filters, and the rounded corners were created with the Round Corners filter. The 2 and the Neptune flag were created in Adobe Dimensions (Chapter 24).

Step 1

Step 2

Step 3

Step 4

VW Corrado by Royce Copenheaver

Chapter 25 describes the steps taken to create
this illustration. Only gradients were used to create the
various nuances in the shading of the car and the
background. Blends were used to create the two clouds.

Timothy G. Freed Design created the artwork on this page. The billboard to the right, "A Natural Form of Expression" is dissected in Chapter 25.

The Loony Bird was created by using the Brush tool with a pressure sensitive drawing tablet. Techniques for using the Brush tool are shown in Chapter 6.

Juggling Charts

8
7
6
5
4
3
2
1
0

Bowling Balls
Clubs
Torches

Disoriented Convolution
Animated Suspension
The Flying Linguini

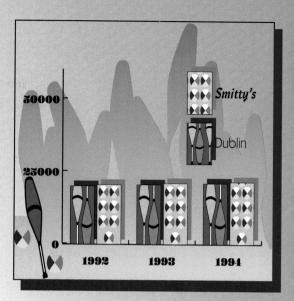

50000
25000
0

Smitty's
Dublin

1992   1993   1994

Summer Street Performing Income (weekly)

600
500
400
300
200
100
0

$ DISORIENTED CONVOLUTION
$ THE FLYING LINGUINI
$ ANIMATED SUSPENSION

MAY   JUNE   JULY   AUGUST   SEPTEMBER

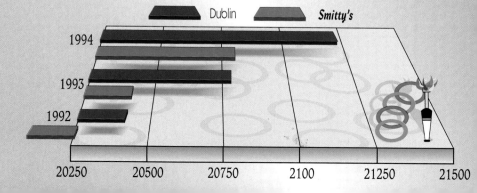

Dublin   Smitty's

1994

1993

1992

20250   20500   20750   2100   21250   21500

Graphs and Charts and techniques for creating them are in Chapter 13. The graphs on this page were all modified from original Illustrator graphs.

Ten Murders.
Ten Bodies.
One Clue.

The
PRINT

The greatest whodunit of our time.

MYSTERIOUS PICTURES Presents A MYSTERY RIDGE Production   A Film by WAYDE S. DELAFIELD

KEN WIRTH   DOLORES PENA   DIANE SCHMIDT   and Introducing SHNAY THE CAT

Written by ROBERT TEEPLE   based on MURDER, HE SPOKE   Directed by WAYDE S. DELAFIELD

BLOCKHEAD
FILMS

PG-13 | **PARENTS STRONGLY CAUTIONED**
SOME MATERIAL MAY BE INNAPPROPRIATE FOR CHILDREN UNDER 13

The Print was created using techniques found in Chapter 17.

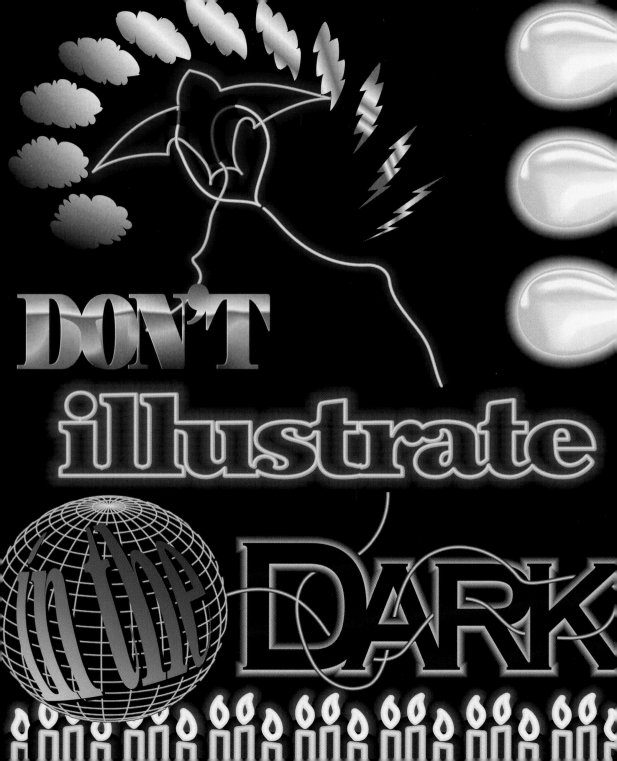

Tonight!

Live entertainment featuring

shattered dishes

ONLY AT

THINGS COOKED

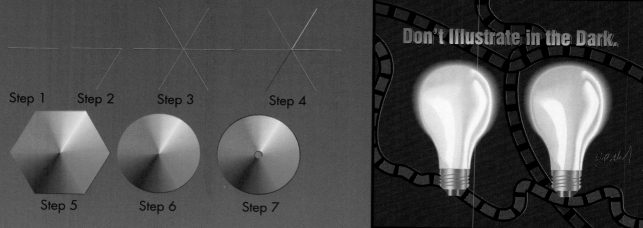

Don't Illustrate in the Dark.

Step 1 Step 2 Step 3 Step 4

Step 5 Step 6 Step 7

Filter Magic (top) was created by using several different Create filters. Each of the individual elements is part of a Step by Step tutorial in Chapter 16.

Steps for Creating a Color Wheel (lower left) are explained in Chapter 13.

Don't Illustrate in the Dark was created entirely with special blend effects. The original (lower right) contains overlapping strokes to achieve the "film" effect, while the enhanced version (opposite) uses blend techniques discussed in Chapter 13.

Backgrounds: These backgrounds were created with techniques discussed in Chapter 20.

Brush Horses (above) was drawn with a combination of drawing tools. Techniques for using the drawing tools are discussed in Chapter 6.

Snowman (below) was drawn from basic shapes. Tips on creating basic shapes are given in Chapter 5.

Ocean Heat (right) was created using several different gradients. Gradients are discussed in Chapter 13.

CHO
LIGHT
The Soft Drink
Gotta get some CHO. Where is that CHO store? It's got to be around here somewhere. I'm dying of thirst. The only thing that could take care of it is a big bottle of CHO. I love CHO. If I could be a soft drink, I would be a giant glass of crystal clear CHO. I wonder... if you gave steam engine trains CHO instead of water, would they go CHO CHO CHO? Just when you thought it was safe to drink the water...CHO! Obviously this lack of CHO is killing my brain cells. Wait, is that it up ahead? I think so! The giant CHO sign! Great! >sigh<.
CH2O
The Soft Drink for the Rest of Us

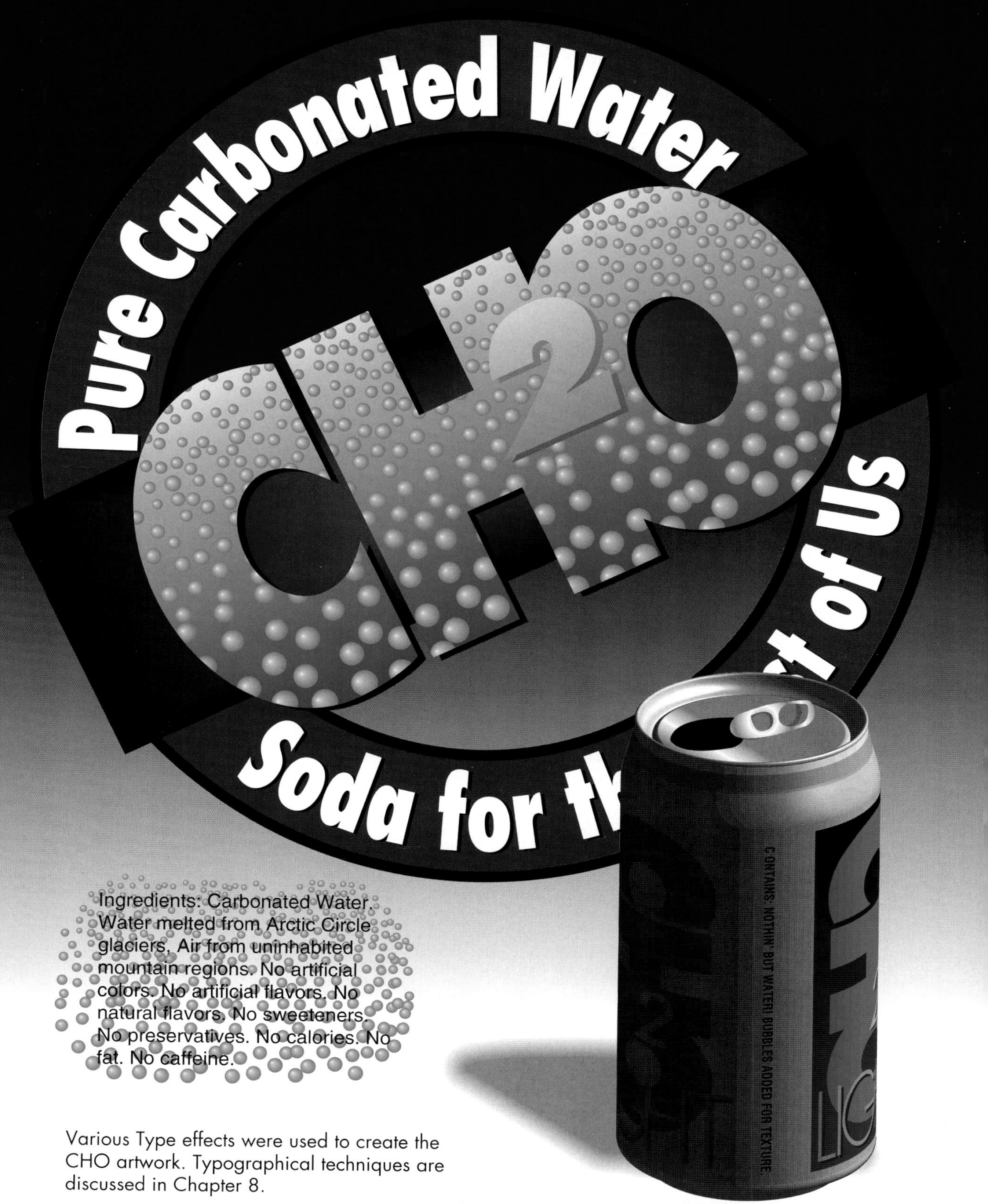

Pure Carbonated Water

CH₂O

Soda for the Rest of Us

Ingredients: Carbonated Water. Water melted from Arctic Circle glaciers, Air from uninhabited mountain regions. No artificial colors. No artificial flavors. No natural flavors. No sweeteners. No preservatives. No calories. No fat. No caffeine.

Various Type effects were used to create the CHO artwork. Typographical techniques are discussed in Chapter 8.

Traps: Follow the steps outlined in Chapter 21 to recreate the artwork trapping shown here. The trapping done on this page makes use of the Divide Fill filter, needed for trapping by 5.0 users only. Users of version 5.5 may use the Trap filter for quicker results.

Step 15

Step 4

Step 5

Step 6

Step 7

Step 16

Step 8

Step 9

Step 17

Step 10

Step 11

Step 18

Step 12

Step 13

Step 19

Step 20

Step 14

Step 21

Puzzle Pieces were created using concepts discussed in Chapter 10.

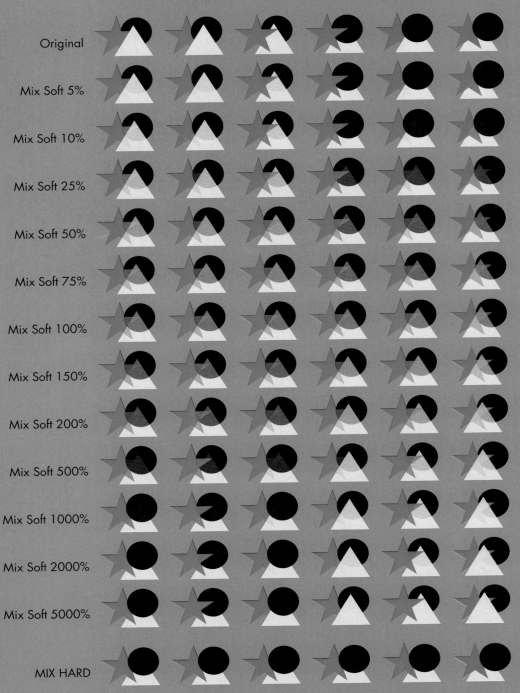

The Mix Chart shows how the Mix Soft filter works on three different overlapping objects when different objects are above and below other objects. Mix Soft, Mix Hard, and the other Pathfinder filters are discussed in Chapter 18.

Creating Linear Blends

Color blends are made by creating two end paths, usually identical in shape and size, giving each path different Paint Style attributes, and creating a series of steps between them with the Blend tool. The more end paths that are created, the more colors that you can create. Figure 12-4 shows the steps needed to create a basic linear blend.

Figure 12-4:
The steps needed to create a linear blend.

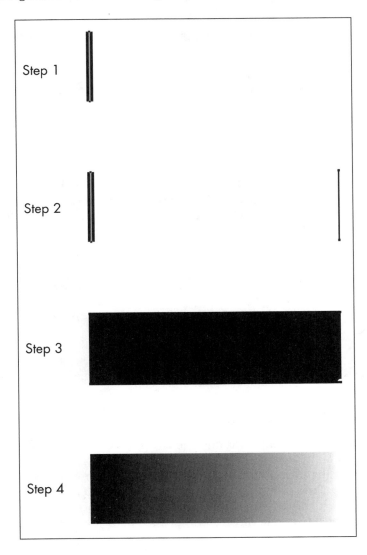

The examples in this chapter are easier to understand when you are working in Preview mode.

STEPS:	**Creating a Basic Linear Blend**
Step 1.	Draw a vertical path with the Pen tool. Give it a fill of none and a stroke of 2-points black in the Paint Style palette.
Step 2.	Option-copy the path to the right. Give the new path a stroke of 2-points white.
Step 3.	Select both paths. With the Blend tool, click the top point on the left path and then the top point on the right path. When the Blend dialog box appears, click OK.
Step 4.	Deselect all (⌘-Shift-A) to see the result.

 Whenever you create a blend, stop and select the blend steps (which are already grouped together) and the two end paths, and group them all together. This step makes selecting the blend easier in the future, especially if you use the Group Selection tool.

Multiple colors with linear blends

To create linear blends that have multiple colors, you must create intermediate end paths, one for each additional color within the blend.

STEPS:	**Creating Multiple Color Blends**
Step 1.	Create two end paths at the edges of where you want the entire blend to begin and end. Don't worry about colors at this time.
Step 2.	Select the two end paths and click the top point in each of them. In the Step field in the Blend dialog box, enter the number of additional colors you will be adding to the blend and click OK. For instance, if you want a blend to go blue, yellow, red, black, green, you would enter **3** in the Step field because there are three colors between the two end colors. For my example, I entered 3 to create three evenly spaced paths between the two end paths.

Step 3. Ungroup the newly created strokes, color each of the strokes of the paths differently, and give them a weight of 2 points. Select the first two paths and blend them together.

Step 4. Select the next pair and blend the next pair together. Continue blending until all the paths have been blended together. The result should look like the blend of colors at the bottom of Figure 12-5.

Figure 12-5:
The steps to create a multiple-color linear blend.

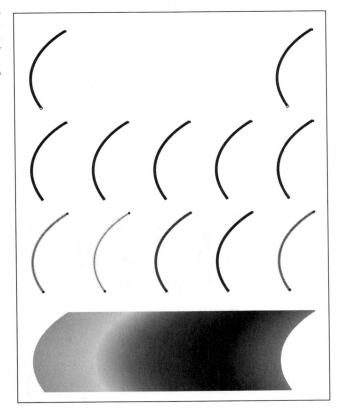

 Group all the end paths to all the blends after creating them. This step makes selecting the multiple color blend easy with the Group Selection tool.

Nonlinear blends

End paths created with two end points that make up blends don't have to be just horizontal or vertical. And when you create multiple color blends, the intermediate end paths don't have to be aligned in the same way as the end paths are aligned.

Careful setup of intermediate blends can create many interesting effects, such as circular and wavy appearances, all created with straight paths.

 End paths that cross usually produce undesirable effects, although, if carefully constructed, the blends can be quite intriguing. The result of blending crossed end paths presents the appearance of a three-dimensional blend, where one of the end paths blends "up" to the other.

To create nonlinear blends, set up the end paths and either rotate them or change their orientation by using the Direct Selection tool on one of the end points. Then blend from one end path to the intermediate end paths and then to the other end path. Figure 12-6 shows two examples of nonlinear blends.

Figure 12-6:
Blending end paths together to create a nonlinear blend.

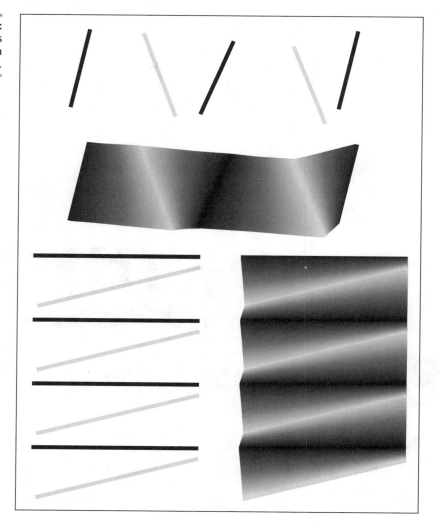

Masking blends

Blends by themselves are great, but when masked by other paths, they can really take on a life of their own. To illustrate this concept, follow these steps to create a color wheel (refer to Figure 12-7):

Figure 12-7:
Creating a
black-and-white
color wheel.

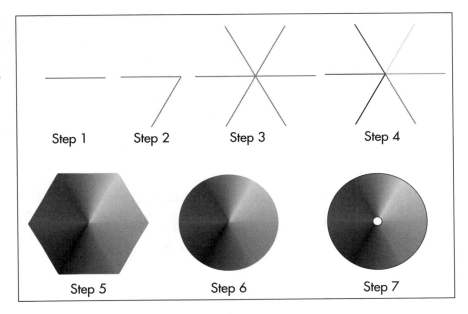

Step 1   Step 2   Step 3   Step 4

Step 5   Step 6   Step 7

STEPS: Creating a Color Wheel

Step 1. Using the Pen tool, draw a straight segment and give it a 2-point green (100% cyan, 100% yellow) stroke and a fill of none in the Paint Style palette.

Step 2. Choose the Rotate tool, press Option, and click one end point of the path to set the origin. Type in 60° for the angle in the Rotate dialog box and press the Copy button (Option-Return). This procedure creates a copy of the stroke at a 60° angle, with one end point directly on top of one of the existing ones.

Step 3. Select Arrange⇨Repeat Transform (⌘-D). Another stroke is created at a 60° angle from the second. Continue to Repeat Transform until there are six strokes. Each of these strokes is used as an end path.

Step 4.   Color each stroke as follows, moving clockwise: 1. green (100% cyan, 100% yellow); 2. yellow (100% yellow); 3. red (100% magenta, 100% yellow); 4. magenta (100% magenta); 5. blue (100% cyan, 100% magenta); 6. cyan (100% cyan).

Step 5.   Blend each pair of end paths together, a pair at a time. Click the outermost points to get the best results. When you are finished blending all the end paths together, the result is a beautifully colored hexagon. Because of the shape, the end paths really stand out as points on the hexagon. To complete the illusion of a perfect color wheel, the blend needs to be in the shape of a circle.

Step 6.   Using the Oval tool, draw a circle so that the edges are just inside the flat sides of the hexagon, with its center corresponding to the center of the hexagon. This process is easiest to do by Option-clicking with the Oval tool at the center of the hexagon and pressing the Shift key as the oval is being drawn. Select the circle, the blend steps, and the end paths, and select Object⇨Masks⇨Make.

Step 7.   For a more realistic color-wheel effect (one that resembles Apple's color wheel), create a black stroke on the mask and a small circle at the center that has a fill of white and a stroke of black.

 Blends can be masked with any object. For some really great effects, mask your blends with text (converted to outlines).

New and improved pseudolinear blends

There is very little difference in the end product of straight line linear blends and linear gradients. Both are very "computery" looking, but gradients are easier to create. The important thing about blends is that the end paths of linear blends *don't have to be straight lines*. This blend capability makes all the difference in the world and is why using linear blends takes on a "really cool" aspect.

By using a smoothly curving line, the blend takes on a fluidity and life of its own, gently caressing the objects it is behind, next to, or masked by. The curves (especially if the end paths are masked off) are not always visible to the eye, and this creates an effect that is both realistic and surreal, giving depth to your illustration in a way that flat linear blends can't.

Instead of smoothly curving lines, try broken, jagged paths, which can add fierce highlights to a blend. Once again, this type of blend is even more effective when the end paths are masked off. Figure 12-8 shows two examples of masked pseudolinear blends.

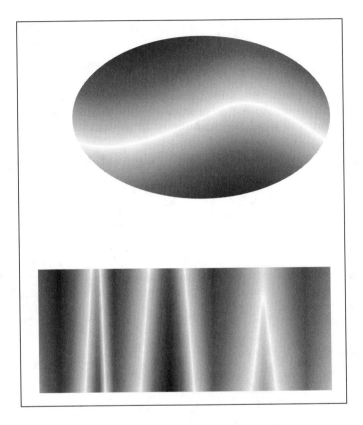

Figure 12-8: Masked pseudolinear blends.

When using end paths that have more than two anchor points, be sure to click the same end point on each path. Clicking an anchor point that is not an end point results in a dialog box telling you to . . . click an end point. If you click different end points, the result resembles an X shape, which is usually undesirable (see Figure 12-3).

Guidelines for creating color linear blends

Although the preceding procedure should have gone nice and smoothly, with no problems, you should follow these strict guidelines when creating blends to get good results each time you print:

* For linear blends, use straight paths with only two end points. If you use any more anchor points or if you use a line that isn't perfectly straight, you get extra information that isn't needed to create the blend, and printing will take much longer than usual.

When creating linear blends, use one line segment per end path and color the strokes of the paths, not the fills. Coloring the fills may appear to work, but it usually results in a moiré pattern when printed. Make sure that the fill is set to none, regardless of what the stroke is.

Don't change the number that appears in the Steps text field in the Blend dialog box. Making the number higher creates additional paths that can't be printed; making the number lower can result in banding when printed (see the sidebar).

Avoiding banding

The graphic artist's worst nightmare: Smooth blends and gradations turn into large chunks of tints, as shown in the accompanying figure, and suddenly get darker or lighter instead of staying nice and smooth. *Banding*, as this nightmare is called, is an area of a blend where the difference from one tint to the next changes abruptly and displays a defining line showing the difference between the two tints. Individual tints appear as solid areas called *bands*.

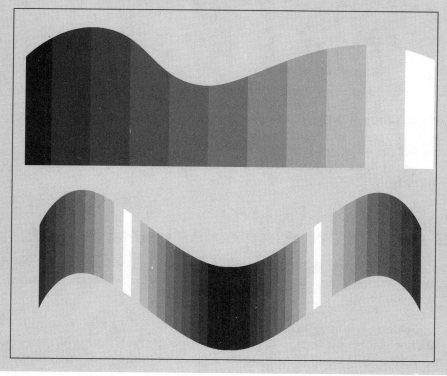

Avoiding banding is easier when you know what is causing it. Usually one of three things in Illustrator is the cause: too few blend steps, too much of a distance between end paths, or too little variation in the colors of the end paths. All these instances depend on the line screen setting and what the capability of your printer to print that line screen is.

These causes make pretty much sense. Take the linear blend example in a previous section. If there are only three intermediate steps between end paths, there will be only five colors in the blend, thus creating five bands. If the end paths are each on one side of a 17-inch span, each blend step created would take up the 5 points of width of the stroke, making each shade of gray 5-points wide, a noticeable size. If the color on the left were 10% black instead of 100% black, there would be only 26 color steps between the two end paths.

So to avoid banding, use the recommended number of steps over a short area with a great variation of color. See "Calculating the number of steps" in this chapter for more information on banding.

If you find it hard to fix the banding problem and the blend is made of process colors, try adding a small amount of an unused color (black, for instance) to cover up the banding breaks. A 5 percent to 30 percent change over distances may provide just enough dots to hide those bands. Keeping this in mind, there is more chance for banding if you use the same tints for different process colors. Alter the tint values for one of the colors at one of the end paths just a little, and this alteration will stagger the bands enough to remove them from sight.

End paths for linear blends

In the previous linear blend example, I used lines with stroke weights to create the blend. You can also use rectangles with fills and no strokes and achieve pretty much the same printed result. Figure 12-9 shows both lines and rectangles used for end paths.

There is no good reason to use a rectangle as an end path instead of a single line with two end points (at least, none that I can dig up). In fact, lines are better than rectangles for three reasons: First, lines use half as much information as rectangles because there are two anchor points on a line while there are four on a rectangle. Second, the width of a line (stroke weight) is much easier to change after the blend has been created (just select the lines and enter a new weight in the Paint Style palette) than the width of rectangles (you would have to use the Scale Each filter). Third, creating a linear blend with lines (strokes) creates a thick mess of paths, but creating a linear blend with rectangles creates a thicker mess, so much so that it is difficult to select specific rectangles.

Figure 12-9:
Lines (left) and
rectangles
(right) used for
end paths in
both artwork
and final
output.

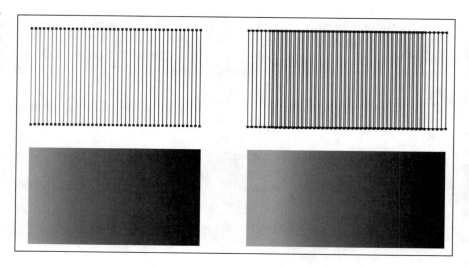

 An open path cannot be blended with a closed path or vice versa. Open paths can be blended to other open paths, as long as you click an end point on each with the Blend tool. Closed paths can be blended with another closed path.

Calculating the number of steps

Whenever you create a blend, Illustrator provides a default value in the Steps text field that assumes you are going to be printing your illustration to an imagesetter or other high-resolution device capable of printing all 256 levels of gray that PostScript allows.

The formula Illustrator uses is quite simple. It takes the largest change that any one color goes through from end path to end path and multiplies that percentage by 256. The formula looks like this:

$$(256 \times \text{largest color change \%}) = \text{number of steps to be created}$$

For instance, using our linear blend example, the difference in tint values is 100% (100%–0%=100%). Multiply 100% by 256, and you get 256. Because the total number of grays must be 256 or fewer, only 254 were created. When added to the two ends, there are 256 tints.

In the second example, where the first line was changed to a 10% stroke, the difference in tint values is 10% (10%–0%=10%). 10% x 256 is 26, the number of steps Illustrator calculates.

In a process color example, if the first end path is 20% cyan, 100% magenta, 40% yellow, and the second end path is 60% cyan, 50% magenta, and 0% yellow, the largest difference in any one color is cyan (100%–50%=50%). 50% x 256=126, the number of steps created.

But, of course, not everything you create is output on an imagesetter. Your laser printer, for example, cannot print out 256 grays, unless the line screen is set extremely low. To determine how many grays your laser printer can produce, you need to know both the dpi and the line screen. In some software packages, you can specify the line screen, but unless the printer is a high-end model, it is usually difficult to specify or change the dpi. Use the following formula to find out how many grays your printer can produce:

(dpi/line screen) x (dpi/line screen) = number of grays

For a 300 dpi printer with a typical (for 300 dpi) line screen of 53, the formula looks like this:

(300/53) x (300/53) = 5.66 x 5.66 = 32

A 400 dpi printer at a line screen of 71 has the following formula:

(400/65) x (400/65) = 6.15 x 6.14 = 38

A 600 dpi printer at 75 lines per inch uses this formula:

(600/75) x (600/75) = 8 x 8 = 64

Sometimes you may want to reduce the number of blend steps in a blend from the default because either your printer can't display that many grays or the distance from one end path to another is extremely small (see "Airbrushing and the Magic of Stroke Blends" later in this chapter).

When reducing the number of blends, start by dividing the default by two and then continue dividing by two until you have a number of steps that you are comfortable with. If you aren't sure how many steps you need, do a quick test of just that blend with different numbers of steps specified and print it out. If you are going to an imagesetter, don't divide by two more than twice, or banding (oh no!) can take place.

Creating radial blends

To create a radial blend, make a circle about two inches in diameter, filled with 100% black. Make a smaller circle inside the larger circle and fill it with white. Select both shapes, click the point at the top of the larger circle, and then click on the point at the top of the smaller circle. Click OK in the Blend dialog box and deselect.

Radial blends can be created with objects other than circles. In Figure 12-10, the radial blend was created with a star.

 As with most other blends, when blending from two identically shaped end paths, always click the anchor point in the same position on each object. Figure 12-10 shows the difference between clicking the anchor points in the same position and those that are not in the same position.

Figure 12-10: Clicking corresponding anchor points and noncorresponding anchor points for a radial blend.

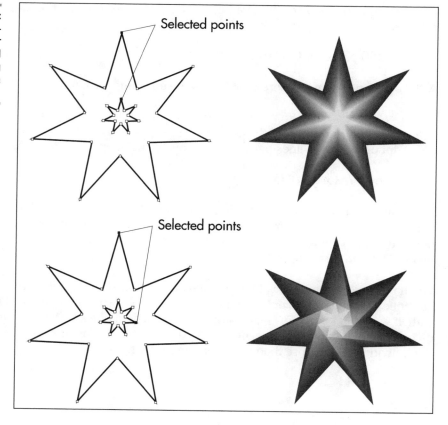

One of the nice things about creating radial blends manually (not using the gradient feature) is that by changing the location and the size of the inner object, the gradient can look vastly different. The larger the inner object, the smaller the blended area.

 The gradient feature allows you to change the highlight point on a radial gradient without changing the source, or angle, of the highlight.

Creating Shape Blends

The difference between color blends and shape blends is in their emphasis. Color blends emphasize a color change; shape blends emphasize blending between different shapes.

There are a number of things to keep in mind when creating the end paths that form a shape blend. Both paths must be either open or closed. If open, only end points can be clicked to blend between the two paths. If the shapes also change color, be sure to follow the guidelines in the preceding section related to color blends.

For best results, both paths should have the same number of anchor points selected before blending, and the selected points should be located in a relatively similar location. Illustrator pairs up points on end paths and the segments between them so that when it creates the blend steps, the lines are in about the same position.

Shape blend #1: computer vents

Look on the side of your monitor or on the side of a computer or hard drive case. You will undoubtedly see vents or simulated vents used for design purposes running back along these items. This type of blend (changing the angle of straight lines) is the most basic of shape blends and is rather easy to create, so I've added an extra tip at the end of this section to make these blends more realistic. Figure 12-11 shows the process for creating computer vents.

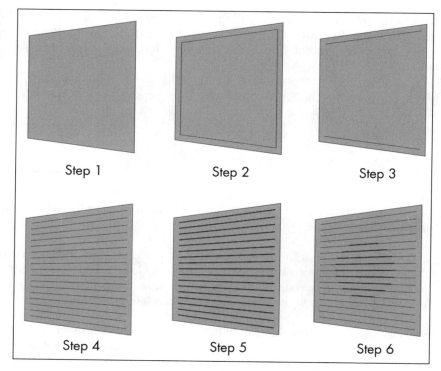

Figure 12-11: A computer-vent blend.

Step 1   Step 2   Step 3

Step 4   Step 5   Step 6

STEPS: Creating Computer Vents

Step 1.   Draw a rectangular shape that has been distorted to appear like the side of your monitor (use the Pen tool). Choose a fill of 25% black and a stroke of ½ point, 50% black in the Paint Style palette.

Step 2.   Select the shape and double-click the Scale tool. Enter 90% in the Uniform field of the Scale dialog box and click Copy (Option-Return).

Step 3.   With the Direct Selection tool, select and delete the two vertical segments of the shape. Select both of the horizontal segments and change the fill to none.

Step 4.   Blend the two paths together with 15 steps. One side of a monitor is now complete.

Step 5.   Select all the paths and copy them up ½ point by using the Copy button in the Move dialog box. Group the paths and change the stroke to 75% gray.

Draw a circle over the center of the group and select the group and the circle. Choose Object⇨Mask⇨Make, and you will have a "real" vent in the simulated one.

Shape blend #2: circle to star

The preceding blend slowly transformed one path to another, but the paths were basically the same. The real power of the Blend tool is evident when it is used to generate intermediate paths between two totally different, distinct paths, as in the following example (see Figure 12-12).

STEPS: Blending a Circle to a Star

Step 1. Create a 1-inch circle with the Oval tool. Create a 5-point star by selecting Filter⇨Create⇨Star and entering **5** in the Points text field. Enter **.19"** in the First Radius text field and **.5"** in the Second Radius text field.

Step 2. Fill both shapes with a color (I used light gray) and give each of them a 2-point stroke of another color. Change the view to Fit In Window (⌘-M) and place the two objects as far apart on-screen as possible.

Step 3. Choose the Direct Selection tool and select the entire circle. Press the Shift key and click four points on the star that closely match the four on the circle. If you accidentally click a point that you decide should not be selected, just click it again with the Direct Selection tool. As long as the Shift key is pressed, the tool deselects only that point while all the other points remain selected.

Step 4. After four points are selected on both the circle and the star, blend them together with the Blend tool. Click the corresponding points on each, such as the topmost point, and enter **7** in the Steps dialog box.

To see what happens if a different number of points are selected on each path, select both paths with the Selection tool. Click the topmost point of the circle with the Blend tool and then click the topmost point of the star. In the Blend dialog box, enter **7** in the Steps text field and then click OK. The star appears to work its way out of a growth on the circle. Figure 12-12 shows the difference between blending without corresponding anchor points selected and with corresponding anchor points selected.

Figure 12-12:
The difference between selecting the same number of anchor points on each path in a shape blend (top) and selecting a different number of anchor points on each path (bottom).

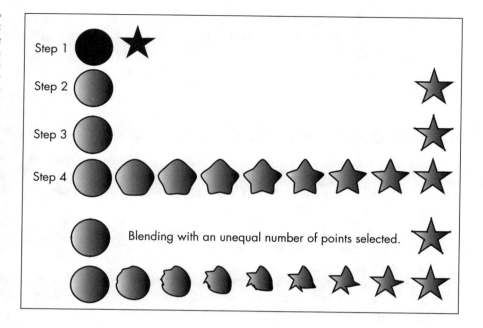

Blending with an unequal number of points selected.

 Another way to get a smooth transformation between two paths with different numbers of anchor points is to strategically add anchor points to the path with fewer points. By selecting both of the paths with the Selection tool, you can get results that are similar to selecting similarly positioned points. The results can actually be better when anchor points are added because they can be added in positions that correspond to the anchor points on the other path.

Complex shape blending

Whenever a shape is complex (it isn't a perfectly symmetrical shape, such as a circle or a star), a number of things may have to be done to create realistic and eye-pleasing effects. Figure 12-13 shows a complex shape blend.

One thing you can do to make the blend better is to add or remove anchor points from the end paths. Even if the same number of points are selected and those points are in similar areas on each path, the results can be anything but acceptable.

Figure 12-13:
Complex shape
blending.

The Add Anchor Point and Delete Anchor Point tools become quite useful here. By adding points in strategic locations, you can often fool Illustrator into creating an accurate blend; otherwise, the blend steps can resemble a total disaster.

 It is always better to add anchor points rather than to remove them. On most paths, removing any anchor points changes the shape of the path dramatically.

Another method of getting the paths to blend more accurately is to shorten them by splitting a long, complex path into one or two smaller sections that aren't nearly as complex. After the blends are finished — each path has to be blended separately and can't all be done at once — it takes just a few seconds to go through and Average/Join (⌘-Option-L or ⌘-Option-J) the paths back together.

And then there is the third method to blend paths, which is described in the next section.

Shape blend #3: cheating

There are times when blending together two different shapes produces results that end up being just plain grotesque no matter what you do with the anchor points. In these cases, a little fixing (which I will call cheating) is in order: The more blend steps you need, the more you benefit from this method.

To get more aesthetically pleasing results from shape blending, it is sometimes easier to create one or more intermediate (middle) end paths. Instead of blending from end to end, you blend from end to middle and then middle to end. Keep in mind that the middle should contain aspects of both end paths. Figure 12-14 shows how a blend would naturally appear (Steps 1 and 2) and how it appears after cheating (Steps 3 through 7).

Figure 12-14:
Blending a T to
an E without
cheating (Steps
1 and 2) and
with cheating
(Steps 3
through 7).

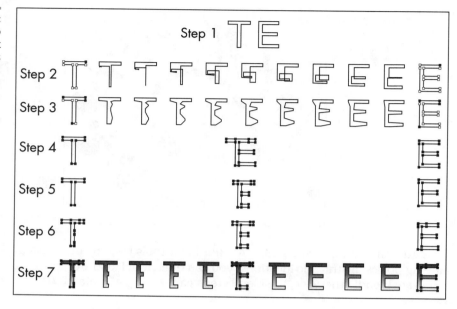

Figure 12-14: Blending a T to an E without cheating (Steps 1 and 2) and with cheating (Steps 3 through 7).

Remember, "cheating" is apparent only to you. The client or your boss will never know from seeing the final output that the results were "forced." Surprisingly, many illustrators actually feel guilty about creating another end path by using this method. If you can't live with yourself, by all means continue trying to select just the right points. However, I'll let you in on a secret: Adobe cheats, too. In one of the original ads for Illustrator 88 and in the accompanying videotape (watch it and check for the poor splicing!), you see an *S* transformed into a swan. Of course, in Adobe's case, it was misrepresenting the capabilities of the Blend tool by making it look like the tool automatically made eye-pleasing middle paths when, in reality, the "blended" paths were only loosely based on the real blends.

STEPS: Creating Complex Shape Blends by Cheating

Step 1. In this example, create a text area with a 100-point T and E in any font, though a sans serif font, such as Helvetica, is easier than a serif one, such as Times. Select the type with a Selection tool and select Type⊃Create Outlines. You are blending between these two letters. Change the fill to none and the stroke to 1-point black in the Paint Style palette.

Step 2. Select View⇨Fit In Window (⌘-M) and put each letter on either side of the document. Select both of them with the regular Selection tool and then blend them together with 10 steps by choosing the upper right point in each object. The results are quite ugly. A common shape-blending problem, called *blend arcing,* occurs when you choose none or very few anchor points on either the top or bottom of end paths. In this case, you selected an anchor point along the top and no anchor points along the bottom, so the blend arc formed along the bottom of the letters.

Step 3. Undo the blend. A better blending effect can be achieved by selecting the two upper right points, the upper left point, and the lower left point of the *T* and the *E* (see Figure 12-14), but then the blend takes on an ugly, lumpy look.

Step 4. Undo the blend again. The best thing to do in this case is to create an intermediate end path. Copy the *E* and *T* and place them over the top of each other between the two original letters.

Step 5. Select the overlapping letters and select Filter⇨Pathfinder⇨Unite. The two paths merge into one. Bring in the horizontal bars about halfway by using the Direct Selection tool.

Step 6. Select both the *T* and the merged letters. Make sure that there are corresponding points for each path by adding anchor points to the *T* with the Add Anchor Point tool. Both paths should have the same number of anchor points. Add corresponding anchor points to the *E,* as well.

Step 7. Blend the *T* to the merged path with the Blend tool by clicking the lower right point of each and creating four steps. Blend the *E* to the merged path by clicking the lower right of each and creating four steps. The transformation should be almost perfect. If necessary, individual points can be touched up with the Direct Selection tool.

 Some really interesting effects can be achieved by using the Rotate tool or the Rotate Each filter, which makes the paths appear to spin as they are transforming from one shape into another. Using these tools also serves to mask any unusual anomalies in the blend steps.

Creating realism with shape blends

To create a realistic effect with shape blends, the paths used to create the blends need to resemble objects you see in life. Take a look around you and try to find any object colored with a solid color. Doesn't the color appear to change from one part of the object to another? Shadows and reflections are everywhere. Colors change gradually from light to dark, but they do so not in straight lines but in smooth, rounded curves.

Blends can be used to simulate reflections and shadows. Reflections are usually created with shape blends; shadows are usually created with stroke blends.

In the first example, I show you how to simulate reflections with shape blends. This procedure is a little tricky for any artist because a reflection is determined by the environment. The artwork you create will be viewed in any number of environments, so the reflections have to compensate for most of them. Fortunately, unless you are creating a mirror angled straight back at the viewer (impossible, even if you know who the viewer is in advance), you can get the person seeing the artwork to perceive reflection without really being aware of it.

The chrome-like type in the word *DON'T* in Figure 12-15 was created by masking shape blends designed to look like a reflective surface.

STEPS: Creating Muted Reflective Surfaces in Type

Step 1. Type in the word or words you want to use for masking the reflective surface. The typeface and the word itself have an impact on how the finished artwork is perceived. I chose the word *DON'T* and the typeface Madrone. I also did a great deal of tracking and kerning so that all the letters touched, which makes the word look like one piece of material. In addition, I used baseline shift to move the apostrophe up several points.

Step 2. Select Type⇨Convert Outlines. Choose a fill of white for the text and a stroke of black. At this point, most of the serifs on the letters overlap.

Step 3. Select all the letters and select Filter⇨Pathfinder⇨Unite. This command gets rid of any unsightly seams between the letters. Create a rectangle and place it behind the letters.

Step 4. Set the Freehand tolerance option to 2 in the General Preferences dialog box (File⇨Preferences⇨General, ⌘-K). Using the Freehand tool, draw a horizontal line from left to right across the rectangle. With a low Freehand tolerance setting, this step should result in a path with many points.

Step 5. Option-copy several paths from the original down to the bottom of the rectangle. An easy way to copy the paths is to Option-drag down just a bit and then select Arrange⇨Repeat Transform (⌘-D) several times. In my

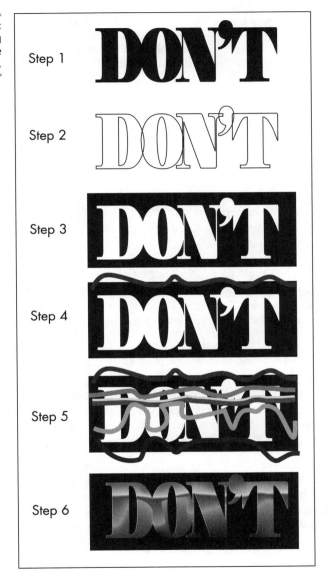

example, I created five more paths. With the Direct Selection tool, randomly move around individual anchor points and direction points on each path, but try to avoid overlapping paths. I left the third and fourth paths virtually identical and kept them close together so that there would be a swift change in color that brings out a "shine." Color the stroke of each path differently, going from dark to light to dark. In my example, I went from dark to light to dark to light and back to dark again.

Step 6.   Blend the stroked paths together and mask them with the type outlines. In my example, I did this step twice. The first time, I created the front piece; the second time, I used lighter colored strokes for a highlight, which I offset slightly up and to the left and placed behind the original type.

 I Option-copied the path in the preceding steps not only because it was easy, but also to ensure that the end paths in the blends would have the same points in the same locations. This technique is much more effective than adding or deleting points from one path or another.

 By using slight transformations, you can use the same reflection blend in other objects in the same illustration, with no one being the wiser. A method that I often use is to reflect the original, scale it to 200%, and then use only a portion of the blend in the next mask.

In the next example, I use shape blends to create the glowing surface of a light bulb. The key to achieving this effect successfully is to draw the light bulb first and then use a copy of the exact same path for the highlights. The relative locations of anchor points stay the same, and the number of anchor points never changes.

STEPS: Blending to Simulate Real Surfaces

Step 1.   Draw a light bulb. Take your time and get it exactly the way you want it because this path is the basis for everything else in this example. Fill the light bulb with 30% magenta, 80% yellow, and a stroke of none. The first four steps in Figure 12-16 show the light bulb in Artwork mode.

Step 2.   Option-scale the light bulb down just a little bit, setting the origin on the base of the bulb. Option-scale two more copies of the light bulb. Use the Direct Selection tool to change the shape of the paths until they resemble the paths in Step 2 of Figure 12-16. These paths are the basis for blends within the light bulb. Don't change the color of these paths.

Step 3.   Option-scale down three copies of the path on the left and shape them to resemble the paths in Figure 12-16. While your paths do not have to be exactly like the ones in the picture, be sure that each smaller path does not overlap the larger path. Color the paths as follows, from inside out: first (inside) path: 5% magenta, 10% yellow; next path: 10% magenta, 30% yellow; last path: 15% magenta, 40% yellow; the outermost path should still be 30% magenta, 80% yellow.

Step 4.   Option-scale one copy of each of the other two outermost paths and re-shape them. Color the new paths 5% magenta and 10% yellow.

Step 5. The paths should be in the correct top-to-bottom order, but if they are not, fix them. To see if they are in the correct order, go to Preview mode. If the smaller paths are not visible, then send the outer paths to the back.

Step 6. Blend the paths together by selecting similar anchor-point locations on each step.

Figure 12-16: Steps to creating real surfaces of a light bulb.

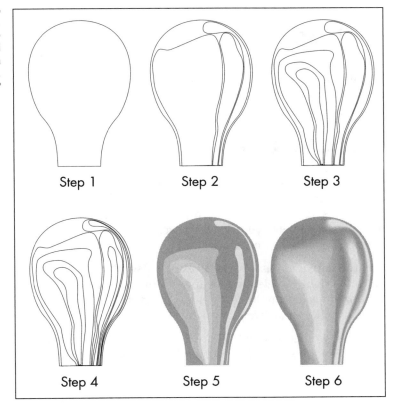

Step 1   Step 2   Step 3

Step 4   Step 5   Step 6

Airbrushing and the Magic of Stroke Blends

After wading through all the technical mumbo jumbo about blending information, you are ready to enjoy your newfound blending powers. Blending can create effects that are usually reserved for bitmap graphics software, such as Fractal Design Painter and Adobe Photoshop.

Most of the effects described in this section are created by blending identical overlapping paths together and varying their stroke weights and colors. This technique can provide some of the best effects that Illustrator has to offer.

Usually, the bottommost stroke has a heavier weight than the topmost stroke, and as the color changes from bottom stroke to top stroke, the colors appear to blend in from the outside.

Tubular blends

Creating tubular Blends with the Blend tool is quite often easier than creating any other type of stroke blend for one simple reason: the two paths, while identical, are not placed *directly* over each other, but instead are offset just slightly, giving the tube a three-dimensional appearance.

STEPS: Creating Tubular Blends

Step 1.   Draw a path with the Freehand tool. Smooth curves work better than corners, so make the Freehand tolerance high (7 to 10) in the General Preferences dialog box before drawing the curves. Change the fill to none and the stroke to 50% yellow, with a weight of ¼ point in the Paint Style palette. The path may cross itself.

Step 2.   Copy the path and Paste In Back (⌘-B). Offset the copy about ½ point up and to the right by selecting Arrange⇨Move (⌘-Shift-M) and entering the appropriate values in the text fields. Change the stroke on the copy to 50% yellow and 100% black and a weight of 4 points.

Step 3.   Blend the two paths together. Create a black rectangle and send it to the back. The result should look similar to the tube in Figure 12-17.

When you're creating stroke blends, the number of steps usually doesn't need to exceed 100. If the default is more than 100, divide it by two (as explained in a previous section, "Calculating the number of steps") until the number is less than 100.

In order to better see the end points on stroke blend end paths, draw a tiny marquee around one of the ends with the Zoom tool. If you still can't see the end points, switch to Artwork mode while creating the blend.

To create a stroke blend that has more "shine" to it, make the stroke lighter and thinner and do not offset it as far as in the preceding example.

To create a color stroke blend that has more depth, make two end paths and color the bottom darker and wider and the top lighter and thinner. Then blend the paths together with one step between the end paths. Add a bit of black (20% to 40%) to the bottom-most stroke and then blend from the bottom to the middle and from the middle to the top. The extra black usually creates a much more realistic appearance of depth than using just two colors, and it keeps black from being in the upper one half of the tube.

 Try not to use white as your topmost path when creating tubes because white not only looks bad, but can also cause problems when you print. The more subtle your color change, the more realistic your results. If necessary, you can always add highlights of much lighter colors after the stroke has been blended.

There are many shapes besides free flowing tubes that benefit from this type of stroke effect, including stars, spirals, and line drawings. Objects that appear in everyday life that can be created with tube-like stroke blends include wires, rods, paper clips, hangers, antennas, pins, and needles. The next section explains how to make one of the most confusing types of objects with blends — the spring tube.

Figure 12-17:
Creating a basic tubular blend.

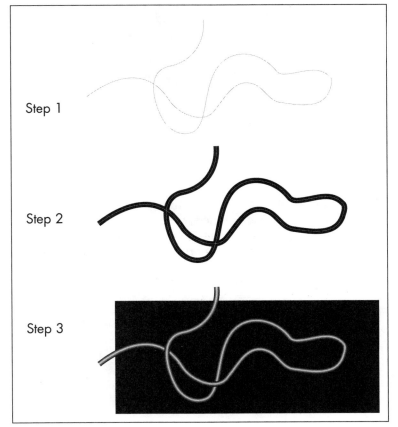

Spring tube blends

To create the curly section of a telephone cord (a spring tube), create a spiral with two winds (Filter⇨Create⇨Spiral) and get rid of the inner spiral. Select the outer spiral and go through the steps to create a tube. Make this particular tube look like a section of a telephone cord, like the illustration in Figure 12-18.

Figure 12-18:
A telephone cord created with tubular blends.

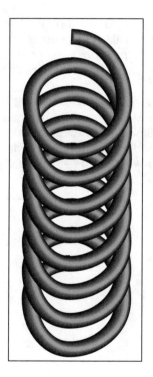

After the spring tube has been created, group the entire tube together and Option-copy it down until the one side of the spiral lines up with the other side of the spiral. Select Arrange⇨Repeat Transform (⌘-D) until the telephone cord is the desired length. To curve the phone cord, draw a marquee around one of the ends with the Direct Selection tool and move it, if necessary. Then use the Rotate tool to change the direction of the curve. Option-copy the next section and rotate that section into place.

For quicker but less effective changes in direction, select a small section of the telephone cord and just rotate that section.

Airbrushed shadows

To create a realistic shadow effect, the edges of an object must be a little fuzzy. The amount of fuzziness on the edges of the path is relative to the distance of the object from its shadow and the strength of the light source. These two areas also affect how dark the shadow is.

To make really cool shadows, you can use either the Pathfinder filter called Mix Soft, which can be used to darken areas, or the Color Adjust filter, which can be used to change the types of color in a selected area. The Drop Shadow filter creates hard-edged shadows, which are usually good only for creating text shadows quickly.

A second way to create cool shadows is to use stroke blends. Stroke blends can allow the shadows to smoothly fade into the background with a Gaussian blur-like effect. You can combine stroke blends with the Mix Soft filter for even better effects.

 For using the Mix Soft filter to create shadows, see Chapter 18.

STEPS: Creating Airbrushed Shadows

Step 1. Create a path (or copy from an original object) for which you want to create a shadow. At this point, you may want to hide the object from which the shadow is being made so that it doesn't get in your way, especially if this object is right above where the shadow will be. Fill the shadowed path with the color you want the shadow to be and then make the stroke the same color, with a ½-point stroke weight.

Step 2. Copy the shadow, select Edit⇨Paste In Back (⌘-B), and then change the stroke color to whatever the background color is (usually white, unless something else is under the shadow). Make the stroke weight twice the distance you want the shadow to fade out to. In my example, I made the stroke 12 points.

Step 3. The hard part (because they overlap each other) now is blending these two paths together. The easiest way to fix this problem is to offset the two paths by ½ point and then Zoom in to 1600% and blend them together. The shadow slowly fades in from the background color to the shadow color. Show the hidden objects (you may have to bring them to the front), and your shadow effect has been created (see Figure 12-19).

Figure 12-19:
Steps for creating airbrushed shadows with linear blends.

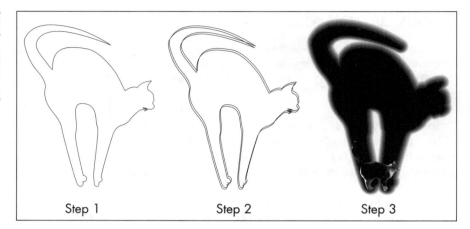

Step 1   Step 2   Step 3

Be careful not to overlap shadows. Because all the steps of a blend are grouped together, the steps should all be above or behind neighboring blends.

Creating glows

Glows are very similar to soft-edged shadows, but instead of a dark area fading into the background, a lighter area fades into the background. Using the light bulb from Figure 12-16, you now can create a glow for that light bulb by using stroke blending.

STEPS:	Creating Glows with Stroke Blends
Step 1.	Select the edge of the object on which you want to create the glow. In my example, I use the light bulb created in Figure 12-16. Copy the edge, Paste in Back (⌘-B), and press ⌘-Option-1. These steps lock everything that is not selected. Give the copied edge a stroke of 6% magenta and 62% yellow and a weight of 1 point.
Step 2.	Draw a black rectangle around the outside edge of the object and send it to the back. Copy the edge of the light bulb and Paste In Back (⌘-B) again. Change the stroke to 6% magenta, 60% yellow, and 100% black and make the stroke about 40-points wide. Move this path about ½ point to the right and up.
Step 3.	Blend the two edge paths together, which creates the glow of the light bulb (see Figure 12-20). The larger the weight of the second copied path from Step 2, the bigger the glow.

Figure 12-20:
Creating a glow around the
light bulb.

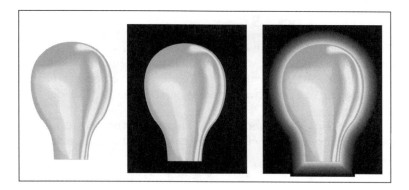

 When creating glows, make the initial glow area (around the edge of the object) *lighter* than the object edges if there are bright highlights in the object. Make the initial glow *darker* than the edges if the edges of the object are the brightest part of the object.

Softening edges

Edges of objects can be softened in a manner very similar to that of creating shadows. The reason that edges are softened is to remove the hard, computer-like edges from objects in your illustration. Softening edges can be done to an extreme measure so that the object appears out of focus or just a tiny little bit for an almost imperceptible change.

When determining how much of a distance should be softened, look at the whole illustration, not just that one piece. Usually, the softening area is no more than 1 or 2 points (unless the object is being blurred).

To soften edges on an object, select the object, copy, and hide the original object. Select Edit⇨Paste In Back (⌘-B) and then make the stroke on the object .1 point, the same color as the fill. Copy again, Paste In Back, make the stroke the color of the background, and make the weight 2 points (which makes the "softening" edge 1-point thick).

When softening objects, rather than moving the entire path in the background, try moving one anchor point out just far enough to be able to click it. Blend the two paths together and then show the original object (it may have to be brought to the front).

To blur an object, just make the bottom layer stroke extremely wide (12 to 20 points or more, depending on the size of the illustration) and blend as described in the preceding paragraphs.

Neon effects

To create neon effects with stroke blends, you need to create two distinct parts. Part one is the neon tubing, which by itself is nice, but it doesn't really have a neon effect. The second part is the tubing's reflection off the background, which usually appears as a glowing area. These two separate blends give the illusion of lit neon.

Neon effects work much better when the background is very dark, though some interesting effects can be achieved with light backgrounds.

STEPS:	Creating Neon Tubing
Step 1.	To make the tubing, create a path that will be the neon. I used two paths: a candle and a flame. Give the stroke of the paths a weight of 4 and color them 100% yellow. Make sure that the fill is set to none. Change the cap of the stroke to round and the join of the stroke to curved.
Step 2.	Create a rectangle that is larger than the area of the path. Send it to the back and color the fill black.
Step 3.	Select the neon path, copy it, and choose Arrange⇨Paste in Front (⌘-F). Offset the copy by .25 points and change the weight of the copy to .25 points. Hold down the Shift key and change the color of the stroke by dragging the sliders to the left to make the color lighter. Do not make the copy white, but make it noticeably lighter than the neon color.
Step 4.	Blend the two paths together and then group the two end paths with the blend. This is the neon tube part of the illustration. Hide this tube.
Step 5.	To create the reflected area of the background, select Arrange⇨Paste in Back (⌘-B). This step pastes a copy of the original path behind the bottom part of the existing neon tube. Give the path a stroke of 4 and change the color to be 100% yellow and 75% black.
Step 6.	Copy the stroke and Paste in Back (⌘-B) again, changing the color of the stroke to the same as the background and then making the weight of the stroke 24 points. Offset this copy by .25 points and blend the two together.
Step 7.	Select Arrange⇨Show All (⌘-4). Your result should look similar to the illustration in Figure 12-21.

Figure 12-21:
Neon candles.

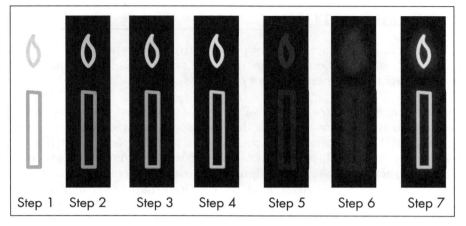

Step 1   Step 2   Step 3   Step 4   Step 5   Step 6   Step 7

Try crossing paths with neon or, for an even more realistic look, create "unlit" portions of neon by using darker shading with no reflective glow.

Backlighting

Backlighting effects can be accomplished by simply creating a glow for an object and then placing that same object on top of the glow. By making the topmost object filled with black or another dark color, a backlit effect is produced, as shown in Figure 12-22.

Figure 12-22:
Backlighting
the
word *dark*.

Gradations

Adobe has finally succumbed to the pressure from Illustrator users who have been asking why, since Version 88 of Illustrator, their drawing software didn't have a way to make gradient fills. "FreeHand users point at us and laugh," they said.

The gradient feature now has no rivals. It is by far the most powerful gradient-creating mechanism available for PostScript drawing programs. Gradients in Adobe Illustrator can have 34 different colors, from end to end in a linear gradient, and from center to outside in a radial gradient. Gradients can consist of custom colors, process colors, or just plain black and white. The midpoint of two adjacent colors can be adjusted smoothly and easily toward either color. The Gradient palette can be made available at all times because it is a floating palette, although it cannot be accessed or viewed with a key command, like all other palettes in Illustrator. And, for what they do, gradients are easier to use than blends.

Gradients can only be applied to the fills of paths, not to strokes or text objects. Gradients cannot be used in patterns, either.

Checking the Compatible Gradients check box (only available in 5.5) in the Document Setup box will prevent most gradient problems from occurring. When you're printing to PostScript Level 1 printers, checking this box will speed up gradient printing dramatically. Compatible Gradients bypasses a high-level imaging system within Illustrator that older printers and printers without genuine Adobe PostScript (commonly referred to as PostScript clones) cannot understand. Checking this box may cause documents to print slower on printers that would ordinarily be able to print those documents.

The Gradient Vector tool

Unlike blends, which can be created only with the Blend tool, gradients can survive quite nicely without the Gradient Vector tool. Gradients are created with the Gradient palette and applied from the Paint Style palette. The Gradient Vector tool controls the direction, length, and, in the case of radial gradients, the highlight of gradients.

To use the Gradient Vector tool, at least one path that is filled with a gradient must be selected. By dragging with the Gradient Vector tool on linear gradients, the angle and the length of the gradient can be changed as well as the start and end points. By dragging with the Gradient Vector tool on radial gradients, the start position and end position of the gradient is determined. By clicking with the Gradient Vector tool, the highlight is reset to a new location.

Using preset gradients

There are eight preset gradients in Illustrator; six of them are linear, and two are radial. The linear ones are Black & 50% Gray; Black & White; Green & Blue; Purple, Red, & Yellow; Red & Yellow; and Steel Bar. The radial gradients are White & Purple Radial and Yellow & Blue Radial.

To choose a preset gradient, select a path and make sure the Fill box is underlined in the Paint palette. On the right side of the Paint palette, click the seventh box along the top, which is the gradient fill box. The eight default gradient presets appear below the row of boxes. None of the options is selected until you click one of them.

Do you think it's strange that Illustrator doesn't have a preset radial fill that goes from white to black? You're not alone. This is one of the great mysteries of modern times, right up there with "Why is the # symbol on a phone called the *pound* key?"

These preset gradients appear in Illustrator because they exist in the Illustrator start-up file, which is discussed in Chapter 14.

Using the Gradient palette

The Gradient palette, if nothing else, is really *neat* looking, with all sorts of nifty little controls at your disposal for creating and modifying gradients, as shown in Figure 12-23.

Figure 12-23:
The Gradient palette.

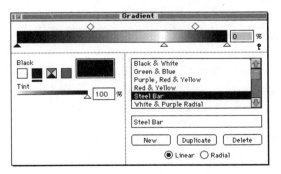

On the right side of the palette is a list of all the gradients that have been created, including the presets. Under the list is a group of buttons for creating new gradients, duplicating existing gradients, and deleting gradients.

On the left side of the Gradient palette is the area where you may choose colors and tints for individual gradient steps. The boxes across the top are white, black, process, and custom and correspond to the same boxes in the Paint Style palette.

The top of the Gradient palette is where you control what colors are in the gradient and where the colors are in relation to each other.

To add a new color to the bar, click below the bar where you want the new color to appear. Then change the lower left side of the palette to create the color you want for that *color stop* in the same way that colors are created in the Paint Style palette. You can enter up to 32 color stops between the two end colors. When a color stop is selected, entering a different percentage in the text field on the right changes the color stop's position.

The diamonds at the top of the color bar show where the midpoint between two color stops is. By moving the midpoint left or right, you alter the halfway color between two color stops. When a diamond is selected, entering a different percentage in the text field on the right changes the diamond's position.

The lever under the percentage text field changes the size of the palette from full size to just big enough to see the top section. Unfortunately, in this small position, you can't do much except alter existing gradients' color stops, moving them back and forth.

STEPS: Using Custom Gradients to Create a Cityscape

Step 1.   Draw a series of vertical rectangles, some overlapping, with their bases horizontally even. In my example (Figure 12-24), I angled the top of one of the rectangles.

Step 2.   Fill the rectangles with the Black & White gradient and be sure that the gradient angle in the Paint Style palette is 0°.

Step 3.   In the Gradient palette, duplicate the Black & White Gradient and name the copy "Buildings." Enter a new color stop at 31% across and make the color 70% black. Change the color of the leftmost color stop to 85% black. Apply the gradient "Buildings" to the rectangles.

Step 4.   Draw a rectangle and send it behind the buildings. Change the fill to the Black & White gradient and change the gradient angle to 90°.

For added dramatic impact in a cityscape, copy the buildings one by one and Paste In Front (⌘-F). Fill the front copies with a custom pattern of lights with a transparent background.

Figure 12-24:
A cityscape created from rectangles and gradients.

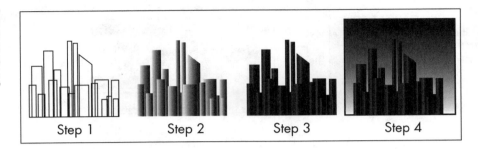

Step 1   Step 2   Step 3   Step 4

Shadows, highlights, ghosting, and embossing

Gradients can be used to simulate special effects by either duplicating and altering a gradient or by using the Gradient Vector tool on similar gradients.

Ghosting can be simulated by using the Gradient Vector tool to slightly alter the starting and ending locations of the gradient.

STEPS: Creating Ghosting Effects with Gradients

Step 1. Ghosting effects are easiest to see on text, so create a rectangle and then create large text on top of the rectangle.

Step 2. Convert the type into outlines and position the type outline just to the right and below the center of the rectangle.

Step 3. Select both type and rectangle and apply a gradient fill to them. I used the Red & Yellow gradient at 90°.

Step 4. Move the type to the center of the rectangle. The type appears to be "ghosted" there, as in Figure 12-25.

Embossed gradient images are created by offsetting two copies of the original graduated image. In one offset image, the gradient is lightened; in the other, the gradient is darkened.

Figure 12-25:
Ghosting with gradients.

Step 1

Step 2

Step 3

Step 4

STEPS: Embossing Text

Step 1. Create text and convert it to outlines.

Step 2. Select the outlined type and choose Filter⇨Pathfinder⇨Unite. Draw a rectangle around the type and send it to the back.

Step 3. Select both the type outline and the rectangle and fill them with a gradient. Use a process gradient for this example. Drag the Gradient Vector tool across the rectangle (keeping both objects selected) to set the gradient length and angle.

Step 4. In the Gradient palette, select the gradient used for both rectangle and type outlines, and make two duplicates of it. Make one duplicate lighter by selecting each color stop and moving it to the left. Create one gradient darker than the original by moving each color stop to the right.

Step 5. Using the Move dialog box, create a copy of the path offset a few points up and to the left. Create another copy offset a few points down and to the right.

Step 6. Fill the upper left path with the lighter duplicate and the lower right path with the darker duplicate.

Step 7. Select the middle type path and select Arrange⇨Bring to Front (⌘-Plus). The type appears embossed, as shown in Figure 12-26.

Figure 12-26:
Steps for making embossed type.

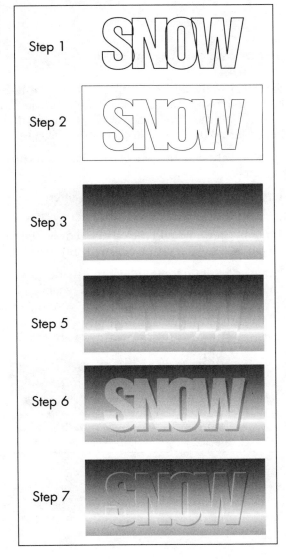

To make embossed images seem sunken rather than raised, make the lighter image below and to the right and the darker image above and to the left. To make the image seem further raised or recessed, increase the distance between the original path and the offset images.

Shadows can be simulated by creating darker gradients based on an existing gradient. The new, darker gradient is created in a path that is the same shape as the object causing the shadow.

STEPS: Creating Shadows with Gradients

Step 1. For this example, use the cityscape created in Figure 12-24. Create a rectangle at the bottom of the city and give it a blend from light to dark. Send the rectangle behind the city. In the Gradient palette, duplicate the gradient and add some black to the color stops in the duplicate.

Step 2. Select the city and choose the Reflect tool. Reflect a copy of the city across the base of the city.

Step 3. Unite the city buildings with the Unite filter (Filter⇨Pathfinder⇨Unite). Fill the united city with the darker gradient.

Step 4. Select both the background and the city, and draw the Gradient Vector tool across both paths. The shadow is automatically created.

Step 5. Using the Scale and Rotate tools, adjust the shadow to more accurately resemble the light source. The result should resemble Figure 12-27.

Figure 12-27:
Creating a
shadow on a
gradient.

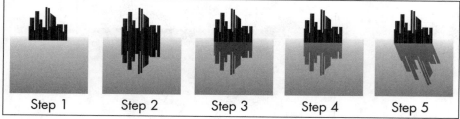

Step 1   Step 2   Step 3   Step 4   Step 5

Taking gradients where gradients fear to go

There are many pieces of software that accept Illustrator files but don't care for gradients very much. Photoshop, for instance, will replace gradients with black areas. Dimensions 1.0 just ignores them. And even Illustrator says "uh-uh" when you try to use a gradient in a pattern.

The solution to this problem is to save your Illustrator file with the gradient that has Illustrator 3 compatibility and then reopen it in Illustrator 5.0. All gradients in Illustrator 5.0 are changed into blends automatically.

After reopening the file, select the blends and choose Filter⇨Pathfinder⇨Merge Fill, which gets rid of the overlapping areas always present with blends in Illustrator.

In addition, gradients cannot be used in strokes of paths. To get around this limitation, select the path, make the stroke the correct weight, and select Filter⇨Object⇨Outline Stroked Path. The stroke is transformed into a closed path, which can then be filled with a gradient.

Before using the Outline Stroked Path filter, be sure that the weight of the stroke on the path to be outlined is the correct weight; otherwise, there is no way short of undoing the whole thing to convert outlined strokes back into a single path.

Patterns and Graphs

In This Chapter

- Using the default patterns
- Creating your own patterns
- Making patterns seamless
- Understanding how transparency works with patterns
- Modifying existing patterns
- Putting patterns and gradients into patterns
- Transforming patterns
- Creating graphs
- Entering information into graphs
- Working with different types of graphs
- Modifying existing graphs
- Using marker and column designs

Patterns

"The Perfect Pattern is one in which you cannot determine the borders of its tiles," so saith the Chinese *Book of Patterns*. If that is the case, you can use Adobe Illustrator to create perfect patterns.

The Pattern function in Illustrator is twofold. First, you can fill or stroke any path with a pattern, although strokes are not visible on-screen. Second, you can edit existing patterns or create new ones from Illustrator objects. The real strength of Illustrator's pattern features is that you can both create patterns and apply them on-screen in almost any way imaginable.

A pattern in Illustrator is a series of objects within a rectangle that is commonly referred to as a *pattern tile*. When you choose the Pattern option in the Paint Style palette, the selected pattern is repeated on each of the four sides of the rectangle as well as in the four corners, as shown in Figure 13-1.

Figure 13-1:
The area inside the solid rectangular outline in the center of the figure is the original pattern tile. The dotted line rectangles represent additional pattern tiles that are aligned with the original to create the pattern and fill up the object.

Illustrator places the pattern tiles together for you. After you apply a pattern to an object, you can use any of the transformation tools to transform it, and you can move within the object by using the Move command. You can move and transform patterns with or without the objects they are within.

 Tile patterns can have a background color, or they can be transparent. Transparent patterns can overlay other objects, including objects filled with patterns.

Using the default patterns

Eleven default, ready-made patterns are available all the time in Illustrator. You select Object⇨Pattern to see a list of the default patterns. If a pattern in the scrolling list is selected, the box to the right of the list is filled with that pattern.

To fill or stroke an object with a pattern, select the object and click on the sixth box (Pattern) in the Paint Style palette. A list of the available patterns appears, though none is selected yet. To select a pattern, click it, and it will fill or stroke the object that is selected in the document. Figure 13-2 shows the Paint Style palette when the Pattern option is checked, as well as samples of each of the patterns.

Figure 13-2:
The Paint Style palette with the Pattern square selected, and samples of each of the default patterns.

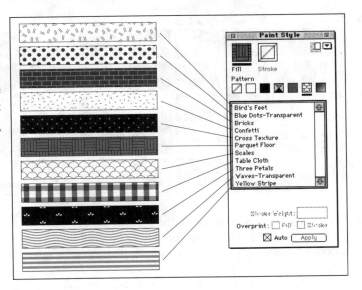

To some people, eleven patterns may seem like quite a few patterns. To others, eleven patterns may seem like hardly any. The amazing thing about the few supplied patterns is that you can use them to create a great number of different effects, and you can use the pattern tiles to create new patterns that have even more exciting effects. Figure 13-3 shows patterns that were created by using just five of the default patterns.

In Preview mode, patterns that are applied to fills show up, but patterns that are applied to strokes do not show up. Instead of the pattern, you see a gray stroke. When you print the illustration, however, patterns do appear in strokes. If you want to see a pattern in a stroke on-screen, apply the Outline Path filter (Filter➪Object➪Outline Path) to convert a stroke into outlines and fill the outlines with the pattern.

Figure 13-3:
These patterns are based on the Bird's Feet, Blue Dots, Bricks, Confetti, and Cross Texture patterns. I created all of these variations from the five base patterns in about 15 minutes.

After you select a pattern, you can see the pattern in the fill of selected objects if you are in Preview mode. Text with patterns appears only as gray text. To see patterns in text, you need to convert the text to outlines by selecting Type⇨Convert to Outlines.

If you see just a gray area in place of the pattern, you may not have the Preview and Print Patterns option selected in the Document Setup dialog box. This option is usually on by default.

In addition to the default patterns, you can choose from an incredibly wide variety of patterns that are in the Collector's Edition folder on the Illustrator CD-ROM. This folder contains borders and clip art as well as patterns. Open the pattern file to see large blocks that contain the patterns as well as the art that was used to create the patterns.

The default patterns are stored in the Adobe Illustrator Startup file. To learn how to modify the Startup file to have a specific set of patterns available every time you use Illustrator, see Chapter 14.

Creating custom patterns

In addition to using the patterns provided with Illustrator, you can create custom patterns by following these steps (as shown in Figure 13-4):

Figure 13-4:
The steps for creating and using a basic pattern.

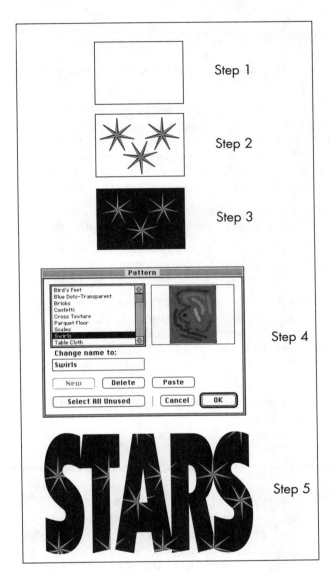

STEPS: Creating a Basic Pattern Tile

Step 1. Using the Rectangle tool, draw the rectangle that will be the boundary of the pattern tile.

You must use a rectangle that you have drawn with the Rectangle tool. You cannot transform the rectangle, except to scale it to any percentage, mirror it, or rotate it in an increment of 90°. You cannot use rectangles that you have created with the Pen tool, even if they are perfect. On the same note, if the constraining angle is not an increment of 90° when the rectangle is drawn, you have to rotate it to an increment of 90°.

Step 2. Create any shapes or objects that you want to make up the pattern. Make sure that the objects do not overlap the outside edge.

Step 3. Change the fill of the boundary rectangle to the color that you want to have for the background color of the pattern tile. If you put a stroke on the rectangle, each tile will have a stroke with the same color and weight on it.

Step 4. Select all of the objects — both the boundary rectangle and the objects in the rectangle. Choose Object⇨Pattern. Click the New button and type a name for the new pattern. The words *New Pattern 1* normally appear in the text box, but I recommend that you use a more descriptive name. The name of the new pattern then appears in the list of patterns in the Paint Style palette.

Step 5. Select an object to apply the pattern to and select that pattern from the Paint Style palette.

Why patterns aren't always seamless

In order for patterns to appear seamless, the edges of the rectangle cannot be apparent. Avoiding this problem sounds rather easy: You just avoid creating any objects that touch the edges of the rectangle. Well, that technique will do it, but when you use such a pattern, the pattern tiles become evident because of the lack of any objects along the borders.

So, then, you do want objects to cross the edges of the pattern rectangle. The catch is that those objects cannot appear to be broken. Doing an illustration the wrong way can help you understand this principle.

Start by drawing a background rectangle with a fill of none. Draw a 1-point black stroked wavy path from left to right, overlapping both edges. Draw a circle, filled with 50% gray, that overlaps the bottom of the rectangle. Select all the objects and choose Object⇨Pattern. Click the New button and then the OK button.

When you fill an object with the new pattern, the edges of the pattern will be very noticeable because the wavy path and the circle will both be cut at the edges of the pattern boundary. The figure shows the pattern tile and the original objects that formed the pattern.

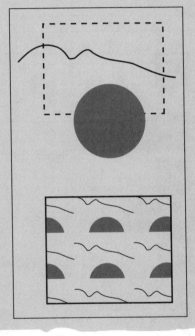

Making seamless patterns

In order to make patterns seamless, you need to remember that objects that lie across the edge of the pattern border will be cut into two sections, one of which will be invisible. You also need to make sure that lines that stretch from one edge of a pattern border to the other side connect to another line on the opposite edge of the boundary. The second problem is more difficult to deal with than the first one. To make a line match well from one side to the other, you usually have to move one or both of the ends up or down slightly.

The following steps describe how to fix objects that get sliced apart at the edges of the pattern tile boundary:

STEPS: Making Seamless Patterns, Part 1

Step 1. Create the boundary and the pattern tile objects. The objects may overlap any of the edges, including the corners. In the example that I created (see Figure 13-5), the stones overlap all four sides as well as one of the corners. I gave the edges of the pattern a stroke so that you can see the boundary clearly.

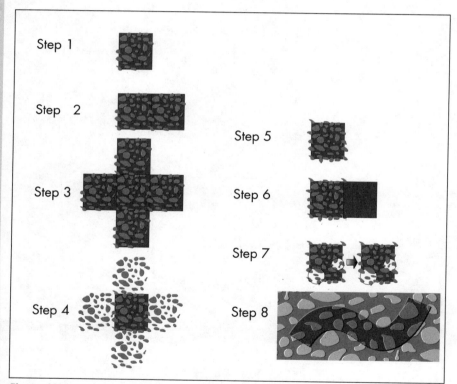

Figure 13-5: Steps for creating a seamless pattern.

Step 2. Select all of the objects, including the pattern boundary, and group them. Click the upper lefthand corner of the pattern and drag to the right until the arrow pointer is directly over the upper righthand corner (it will turn hollow at this point). Press Option and release the mouse button. A copy of the tile will be created to the right of the original.

Step 3. Repeat the process in Step 2 until all four sides have copies of the pattern up against them.

Step 4. Select all five sections and ungroup them. Select the boundary rectangles on the four copied sections and delete them.

Step 5. Delete all the paths (stones, in the example) that don't cross the border of the rectangle.

Step 6. Look at the corners of the rectangle. If an object overlaps any of the corners at all, it should overlap the other three corners. If it doesn't overlap the other three (as in the upper righthand corner in the example) Option-copy (drag the selected object, pressing the Option key, and release the mouse button *before* the Option key) that piece and the boundary to cover the empty corners. Move the boundary with a corner as before so that the piece lines up perfectly. Delete the rectangle after you finish.

Step 7. Look for any overlapping pieces of art in the artwork, including areas of objects that are "too close" for your liking. Move any pieces of art that are not overlapping a boundary.

Step 8. Make the boundary and objects into a pattern (Object ⇨Pattern); apply it to a shape and check the seams to make sure that it is correct. (If I am even the least bit doubtful that a pattern may be showing seams, I zoom in to 1600% to examine the questionable area.)

 If you deleted the original pattern artwork, select Object⇨Pattern. In the Pattern dialog box, select the pattern that was just created and click the Paste button to place a copy of the original artwork on the screen.

To fix lines that cross the edges of the pattern tile boundary, you need to adjust both the lines and the boundary rectangle itself.

STEPS: Making Patterns Seamless, Part 2

Step 1. Create the artwork that you will use in the pattern.

Step 2. Option-copy all of the artwork to the right. At a few points inside the original tile boundary, use the Scissors tool to cut along each path in order to prevent any change to the location and angle of the lines as they meet the opposite edge. You must cut the paths *inside* the original boundary, not outside. Join the paths together, moving only the end point of the path in the original tile boundary.

Step 3. Option-copy both the original and the copied artwork down. Use the Scissors tool to cut along the inside bottom edge of the tile boundary and join the pieces, moving only the end point of the paths inside the original tile boundary.

Step 4. Using the Scissors tool again, click about ½ " down the outside right and bottom edges of the tile boundary. Select all paths that do not go into the tile boundary and delete them.

Step 5. Select the tile boundary rectangle and move it ⅛ " down and to the right. Make sure that no new paths are overlapped on the top and left edges; if they are, do not move the rectangle so far.

Step 6. If you plan to use a blended line or a series of lines placed on top of each other, you may want to join the ends of the paths outside the rectangle to make blends merge together and keep layers of paths separate. I joined such ends in the example; if I hadn't, the pattern edges would not have lined up directly.

Step 7. Add any other elements of the pattern and change the background color if necessary. In the example, I added meatballs and a sauce-colored background. Select all the elements and make them into a pattern.

Step 8. Fill a path with the pattern. Three variations on the pattern appear at the top of Figure 13-6.

Symmetrical patterns

You can easily create symmetrical patterns in Illustrator. The key to creating them is to draw the bounding rectangle after you create the rest of the objects, drawing from the center point of one of the objects out.

When you are creating symmetrical patterns, the main difficulty is judging the space between the objects in the pattern. Objects always seem too close together or too far apart, especially in patterns that have different amounts of space between the objects horizontally and vertically.

Figure 13-6: Steps for creating seamless patterns with continuous paths.

Step 1

Step 2

Step 3

Step 4

Step 5

Step 6

Step 7

To have an equal amount of space from the center of one object to the center of the next object both vertically and horizontally, use a square as the pattern tile boundary.

Using the method described in the following steps (see Figure 13-7), you can visually adjust the amount of space between objects before you make the objects a pattern.

Figure 13-7: Creating perfectly symmetrical patterns.

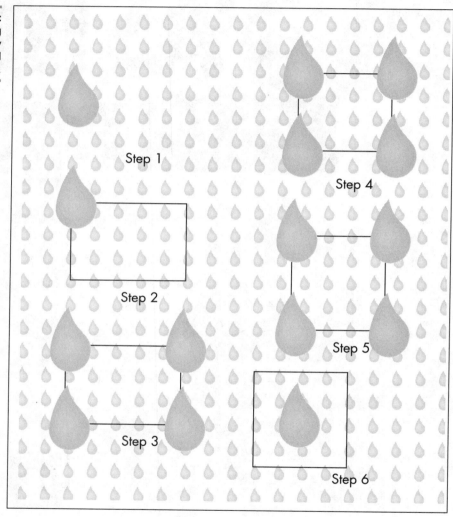

Technically, all the patterns in Illustrator are symmetrical patterns, but the patterns I am writing about here are meant to look symmetrical.

STEPS: **Making Symmetrical Patterns**

Step 1. Create the artwork to use in the pattern.

Step 2. Draw a rectangle from the center of the object so that the object is in the upper lefthand corner of the rectangle.

Step 3. Option-copy the object and the rectangle across and down. Delete the extra rectangles.

Step 4. Using the Direct Selection tool, drag to select the objects on the right and Shift-drag (move the object with the Shift key pressed, releasing the mouse button before the Shift key) them left or right to change the horizontal spacing.

Step 5. Drag the Direct Selection tool to select the objects on the bottom and Shift-drag up or down to adjust the vertical spacing.

Step 6. Move the rectangle so that it surrounds only the initial object and delete the other three objects.

Step 7. Make the objects into a pattern and apply them to a path. The pattern is the background for Figure 13-7.

Line patterns and grids

Using lines and grids for patterns is ideal because they are so easy to create. The key in both types of patterns is the size of the bounding rectangle.

To create a line pattern with horizontal 1-point lines that are aligned on every ½", do the following: Draw a rectangle that is exactly ½" tall, at any width, with a fill and stroke of none. Draw a horizontal line from outside the left edge of the rectangle to outside the right edge of the rectangle, with a fill of none and a stroke of 1 point.

Make a pattern out of the two objects. The new pattern will consist of 1-point horizontal strokes that are spaced ½" apart.

You can use this technique with vertical lines, as well. Just make the bounding rectangle the width of the distance from line to line.

Creating grids is even easier than creating evenly spaced lines. Create a rect-angle that is the size of the grid "holes" (for a ¼" grid, the rectangle would be ¼" x ¼") and apply a stroke to the object. Make the stroke the weight that you want the grid lines to be. Make that rectangle into a pattern. That's it. You now have a pattern grid that is as precise as possible.

If you want the space between gridlines to be an exact measurement, make the rectangle bigger by the stroke weight. A ¼" grid (18 points) with 1-point grid lines requires a rectangle that is 19 points by 19 points. Remember that four of these grids don't equal an inch; instead, they equal 4 points more than an inch.

Diagonal line and grid patterns

Creating diagonal line and grid patterns can be difficult if you try to make a rectangle, draw a path at an angle, and then use the rectangle with the path in it as a pattern. Joining diagonal lines at the edges of the pattern is nearly impossible.

A better method is to create line and grid patterns in horizontal or vertical alignment and then double-click on the Rotate tool. In the Rotate dialog box, enter the angle to change the lines and uncheck the Object check box. The pattern will rotate to the desired angle inside the path.

Using this technique is also a great way to avoid making several patterns when you need line patterns that are set at different angles. Just make one horizontal line pattern and rotate the patterns within the paths.

Transparency and patterns

To make the background of a pattern transparent, give the bounding rectangle a fill of none. Only the other objects in the pattern will be opaque.

To make the objects in a pattern transparent, copy the rectangle and then make the rectangle and the other objects into a compound path. Paste the copy of the rectangle in the back (select Edit⇨Paste In Back or press ⌘-B) and give the copy no fill or stroke. Select the compound path and the copy of the rectangle and make the objects into a pattern.

When you make the bounding rectangle part of a compound path, it is no longer a rectangle, and you cannot use it as the bounding rectangle. Always copy the rectangle before you make the objects and the rectangle into a com-pound path.

You can achieve some fascinating effects by using the transformation tools to make transformed copies of patterns on top of themselves.

Another way to achieve interesting effects is by making a copy of the object behind the original. Select the object, choose Edit⇨Copy (⌘-C), and then choose Edit⇨Paste In Back (⌘-B). Change the fill in the copy of the object to a solid or a gradient or change it to another pattern.

 Chapter 16 describes a technique for creating a "hollow honeycomb" effect.

Modifying existing patterns

To change an existing pattern, select Object⇨Pattern with no object selected. In the Pattern dialog box, select the pattern to change and press the Paste button. Then press the OK button. A copy of the original artwork will be placed in the document.

Select individual parts with any of the selection tools and change Paint Style attributes or change the shape of any of the objects with selection or transformation tools.

After modifying the artwork, select all the pattern-related objects and select Object⇨Pattern. Click the New button and name the pattern something close to but not exactly the same name as the original. Click OK to exit the Pattern dialog box.

Select one of the objects that contains the original pattern as a fill and choose Filter⇨Select⇨Same Paint Style. All the objects that have that pattern as a fill will be selected. Change the fill pattern from the old pattern to the new one that is in the Paint Style palette. If any objects have that pattern as a stroke, repeat the procedure for them.

Return to the Pattern dialog box and select the original pattern. Click the Delete button to remove that version of the pattern from the scrolling list.

Putting patterns and gradients into patterns

Under normal circumstances, you cannot put gradients into patterns or patterns into other patterns. But if Illustrator doesn't think of the objects as patterns or gradients, you can put patterns and gradients into patterns.

To put a pattern into another pattern, select Object⇨Pattern and select the pattern that you want to put into the new pattern. Click the Paste button and click OK to exit the Pattern dialog box. Group the pattern artwork and Option-copy several squares. Draw a rectangle around the squares and add any additional artwork for the new pattern. Select Object⇨Pattern and click the New button.

Including gradients in patterns is not quite so simple. First, create the object in the shape of the gradient and fill it with the gradient. Save the document as an Illustrator 3 document. (Saving an illustration in Illustrator 3 format converts any gradients into blends, which can be used in patterns.) Close the document and open it. The Illustrator 3 version of the file, with the gradient converted to a blend, is the one that will open. You can then use the blended object in any pattern.

 When you save gradients in Illustrator 3 format and bring them back into Illustrator 5 for placement in a pattern, check for masked areas. You cannot use masks in patterns, so you need to release the mask before you incorporate the blend into the pattern.

Transforming patterns

After you create patterns and place them within paths, they may be too big or at the wrong angle, or they may start in an awkward location. You can use the transformation tools and the Move command to resolve these problems.

To transform a pattern inside a path, select the path and double-click on the transformation tool that corresponds to the change that you want to make to the pattern. In the transformation tool's dialog box, uncheck the Object check box.

 The Pattern Tiles and Objects check boxes will be grayed out if the selected object does not contain a pattern.

Any changes that you make in the transformation tool's dialog box when only the Pattern check box is checked will affect only the pattern, not the outside shape. The default (which cannot be changed) is for both check boxes to always remain checked.

If you are using any of the transformation tools manually, the pattern inside the selected object will transform with the object only if the Transform pattern tiles option in the General Preferences dialog box is checked.

To move a pattern within a path, select Arrange⇨Move (press ⌘-Shift-M or Option-click on the Selection tool). The Move dialog box also contains Pattern and Objects check boxes. If you uncheck the Objects check box, only the pattern will be moved.

Graphs

The Graphs feature seems to be one of the most underused features in Illustrator. In Version 3, graphs have their own menu, and you can choose one of six graph styles right from the Toolbox. The current version still has the six graph styles, but you cannot access them as easily as you can in Version 3. Graphs have a submenu in the Objects menu, and all of the graph key commands have been eliminated.

One of the most exciting things about graphs in Illustrator is their fluidity. Not only can you create graphs easily, but after you create them, you can change them easily. In addition, if the data that you used to create a graph changes, you can enter the new data and have it show up in the graph instantaneously. Figure 13-8 shows the creation and modification of a graph.

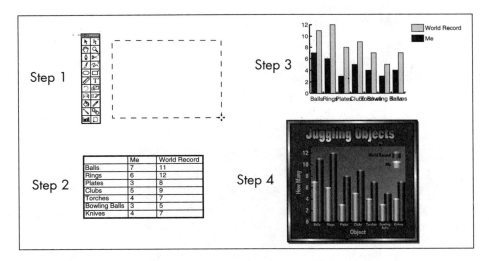

Figure 13-8: The basic steps for creating a graph in Illustrator: dragging to set the size of the graph, entering the graph data, and touching up the final graph.

The following steps describe the basics of creating a graph. The type of graph in this example is a grouped column graph, which is commonly used to compare quantities over time or between different categories.

STEPS: Creating a Graph

Step 1. Select the Graph tool and click and drag to form a rectangular area, similar to the way that you use the Rectangle tool. The size of the rectangle that you create will be the size of the graph.

Step 2. As soon as you release the mouse button, the Graph Data dialog box appears. Information that you enter in the Graph Data dialog box becomes formatted into graph form.

The top row in the Graph Data dialog box worksheet area should contain the labels for comparison within the same set. In the example, I compared how many things I can juggle to what the current world records are for juggling those particular objects. The items in the top row appear as *legends* outside the graph area.

In the leftmost column, you can enter labels that appear at the bottom of the grouped column graph as *categories*. I entered the types of objects that are to be compared in the graph.

In the remaining *cells,* enter the pertinent information.

Step 3. Click OK to have all the data that you entered used in the graph. The graph appears, and it should look something like the one in Figure 13-8.

Step 4. After I created the graph, I edited it by changing the paint style of the bars and legends, adding a background, changing the point sizes and font of the type in the graph, and adding the lightened circles at the top of each bar and legend to make the elements in the graph look more three-dimensional.

When to use graphs

Graphs are most useful when they show numerical information that would normally take several paragraphs to explain or that can't be expressed easily in words. Furthermore, you can express numerical information easily in graphs, and using graphs makes finding and understanding information easier than when the same information is in lines of text.

Numbers are fascinating concepts that most people have a good grasp of, but you can overlook their significance, especially when you are comparing different numbers. The numbers *2* and *9* are the same size when you type them; however, when you use them in a graph, they can represent a drastic difference.

Of course, although graphs are normally used to educate and inform, they are also suited very well for misinforming. Stretching or crushing a graph can cause a great difference in the way the information appears. Even worse is the ability to stretch or compress information in one part of the graph. The figure shows the same information in two radically different graphs.

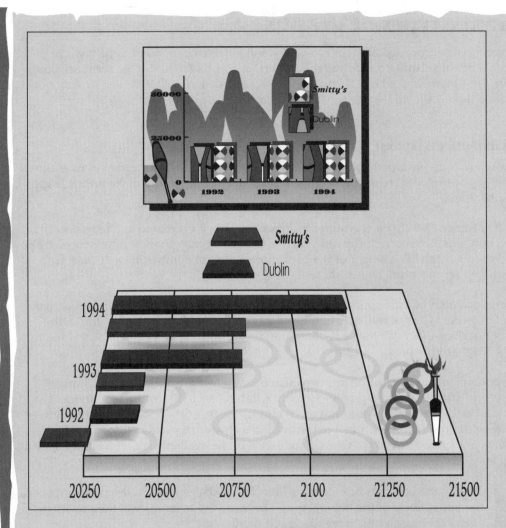

The information for the top graph, created by the Smitty's people, shows them to be even with their competitors. The text for the numbers, the column drop shadows, and the distracting images cause the data to make less impact on the reader than it does in the graph below. Dublin's graph indicates that Dublin is doing substantially better than Smitty's. The vast difference in the length of the bars is one way to show the difference, as is the numbering scheme, which starts at 20250, making the first Smitty's bar appear to be a negative number.

The six types of graphs

You can choose from six different types of graphs in Illustrator. Each type gives a specific kind of information to the reader. Certain graphs are better for comparisons, others for growth, and so on. The following sections describe the graphs, explain how to create them, and tell what you can use them for.

Grouped column graphs

You primarily use grouped column graphs to show how something changes over time. Often they are referred to as bar graphs because the columns that make up the graphs resemble bars.

Step 3 of Figure 13-8 shows a grouped column graph as it is created in Illustrator. This graph contains seven categories, and each of the seven categories is represented by two different totals. The height of the bars represents the number in each case, with higher bars representing higher values.

The real strength of a grouped column graph is that it provides for the direct comparison of different types of statistics in the same graph. For example, in this graph, the number of rings that I can juggle is compared to the bowling ball juggling world record by the height of the bars.

Both column and cluster width are two customizable options for grouped column graphs and stacked column graphs. Column width refers to the width of individual columns, with 100% being wide enough to butt up against other columns in the cluster. Cluster width refers to how much of the available cluster space is taken up by the columns in the cluster. At 80% (the default), 20% of the available space is empty, leaving room between clusters.

 Making the columns or clusters wider than 100% can have a dramatic impact on the appearance of the column graph because the columns will then overlap each other just a bit, giving the graph depth.

You can widen columns and clusters to 1,000% of their size and condense them to 1% of the width of the original column or cluster.

Stacked column graphs

Stacked column graphs are good graphs for presenting the total of a category and the contributing portions of each category. In Figure 13-9, I used objects once again as categories and split each object into the number of those objects being juggled. The total of the time it takes (in weeks) to learn to juggle that number of objects is the height of the object's bar. The time for each number of objects juggled represents a certain portion of the entire time, reflected in each of the smaller sections of the bars.

Figure 13-9:
Data for a stacked column graph, how the graph appears as it is first created in Illustrator, and the graph after it is altered.

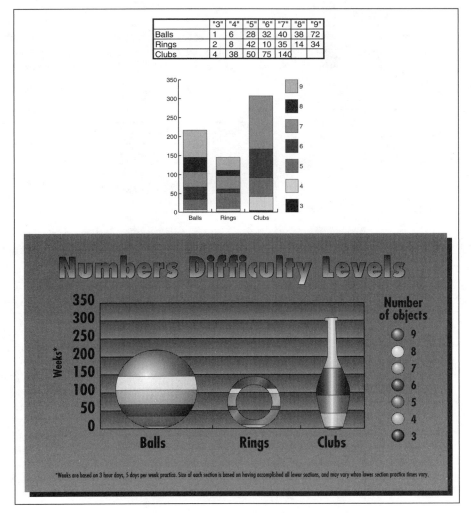

	"3"	"4"	"5"	"6"	"7"	"8"	"9"
Balls	1	6	28	32	40	38	72
Rings	2	8	42	10	35	14	34
Clubs	4	38	50	75	140		

 To get the labels on the legends to read numbers only, I had to put quotation marks (") around each of the numbers. If I had not used quotation marks, the numbers would have been considered data, not labels.

This graph shows the same amount of information as the grouped column graph, but the information is organized differently. The strength of the stacked column graph is in showing a total of all the legends, and the grouped column graph's strength is in showing how all individual legends in each category compare.

Line graphs

Line graphs (also known as line charts) show trends over time. They are especially useful for determining progress and identifying radical changes. For example, the line graph in Figure 13-10 shows the average income of three street performers on successive weeks throughout the summer.

Figure 13-10:
Line graph data (top), the graph as it first appears in Illustrator (middle), and the graph after it has been redesigned (bottom).

	Animated Suspension	The Flying Linguini	Disoriented Convolution
May	300	220	145
	240	190	120
	260	260	140
	320	300	200
June	380	360	150
	400	350	195
	395	320	230
	435	420	190
July	520	190	200
	600	290	195
	440	405	240
	380	340	150
August	300	210	200
	275	250	240
	360	280	230
	300	290	210
September	420	280	170
	220	140	110

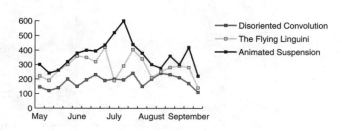

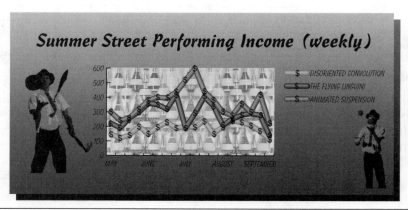

The Mark Data Points option in the Line graphs area of the Graph Style dialog box (Object➪Graphs➪Style) forces data points to appear as squares. If this box is not checked, the data points are visible only as direction changes in lines between the data points.

If the Connect Data Points option is checked, lines will be drawn between each pair of data points.

The Fill Lines option and the corresponding text box for line width create a line that is filled with the data point legend color and is outlined with black. The Fill Lines option changes the line from a single path with a stroke weight into a filled path with a black stroke.

The Edge to Edge lines option stretches the lines out to the left and right edges of the graph. Although the result is technically incorrect, you can achieve better visual impact by using this feature.

Pie graphs

Pie graphs are great for comparing percentages of the portions of a whole. In Figure 13-11, pie graphs show how much of a juggling performance was spent doing particular activities. The higher the percentage for a certain activity, the larger its wedge.

Figure 13-11:
A pie graph showing how much time each performer spent on certain activities.

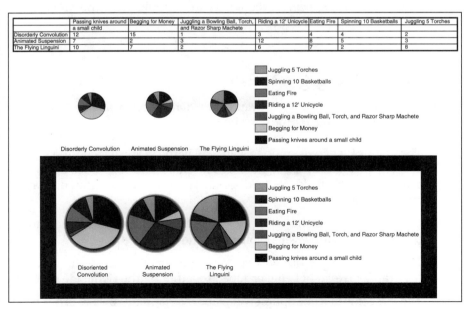

	Passing knives around a small child	Begging for Money	Juggling a Bowling Ball, Torch, and Razor Sharp Machete	Riding a 12' Unicycle	Eating Fire	Spinning 10 Basketballs	Juggling 5 Torches
Disorderly Convolution	12	15	1	3	4	4	2
Animated Suspension	7	2	3	12	8	5	3
The Flying Linguini	10	7	2	6	7	2	8

When you create pie graphs, you can remove the individual wedges from the central pie with the Group Selection tool to achieve an exploding pie effect.

The Legends in wedges option is the only option in the Graph Style dialog box that is specifically for pie graphs. If Legends in wedges is selected, the name of each wedge will be centered within that wedge. Illustrator doesn't do a very good job of placing the legend names, many times overlapping neighboring names. In addition, the letters in the legend names are black, which can make reading some of the names difficult or impossible.

Area graphs

Upon first glance, area graphs may appear to be just like line graphs that are filled. Like line graphs, area graphs show data points that are connected, but area graphs are stacked upon each other to show the total area of the legend subject in the graph.

Scatter graphs

Scatter graphs, which are primarily used for scientific charting purposes, are quite different from all the other types of graphs. Each data point is given a location by x-y coordinates instead of by category and label. The points are connected, as are the points in line graphs, but the line created by the data point locations can cross itself and does not go in any specific direction. Scatter graphs have the same customization options as line graphs.

Customizing graphs

When a graph is selected and the Graph Style dialog box is displayed, a number of options become available for most graphs:

- The Left or Right axis options will display the vertical values on either the left side (the default) or the right side. The Same axis both sides option will put the same axis on both sides. Clicking on the Left or Right button displays options for customizing axes.

- Checking the drop shadow option will place a black shadow behind the graph objects. The shadow will be offset up and to the right.

- The Legends on top option will make legends (if any) appear across the top of the graph, instead of being grouped together on the right side of the graph.

- The First row in front option will place overlapping rows in order from left to right, wherever columns, clusters, or other objects overlap.

Each type of graph has its own customization options. The preceding sections that describe each type of graph explain those options.

 It is usually quicker to press Apply and then (if necessary) move the Graph Data dialog box out of the way than it is to press OK and have to reopen the Graph Data dialog box.

 To make graphs stand out, use a combination of graph types. Simply use the Group Selection tool to select all the objects that are one legend type and then select Object⇨Graphs⇨Graph Style and enter the new graph type for that legend.

Using the Graph Data dialog box

You can change the numbers and the text in the Graph Data dialog box at any time by selecting the graph and choosing Object⇨Graphs⇨Data. Illustrator will re-create the graph to reflect the changes you make. If you have moved some of the graph objects around, they may revert to their original locations when Illustrator re-creates the graph.

 If a number does not have quotation marks around it, Illustrator assumes that you want the number to be entered as a value in the graph.

 Make sure that the graph is never ungrouped, at least not until you have finished making all graph data and graph style changes. If you ungroup the graph, you will not be able to use any of the graph options to change the ex-graph because it will be just a set of paths and text in Illustrator's view.

You can import graph data in a number of formats, including both spreadsheet data and tab-delimited word processing files. Tab-delimited files are text and numbers that are separated by tabs and returns. To import data from another file, click the Import button or click the Import button while you are in the Graph Data dialog box.

Illustrator is not really a graphing or spreadsheet program, so many of the controls for arranging data are not available, including inserting rows and columns and creating formulas.

The Cut, Copy, and Paste functions work within the Graph Data dialog box, so you can move and duplicate information on a very basic level.

One very useful feature in the Graph Data dialog box is the Transverse button. This function switches the x and y axes of the data, reversing everything that you have entered.

Using marker and column designs

The most exciting part about the graphing functions in Illustrator is the capability to give column graphs and line and area graphs special icons to indicate values on the graphs.

On line and area graphs, marker designs are created, which you can use in place of the standard markers. For each value in the graph, the marker design is placed, adding visual impact to the graph.

Column designs are created for grouped column graphs and stacked column graphs. The strength of using column designs is most evident in grouped column graphs, where images are placed side by side (see Figure 13-12).

Figure 13-12: Creating a column design and using it in four different grouped column graphs.

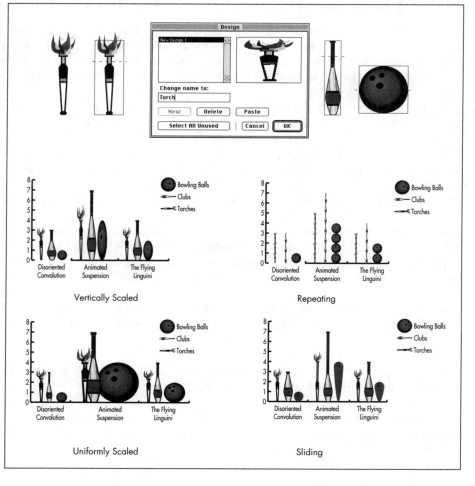

STEPS: Creating and Using a Column Design

Step 1. Create the graphic object in Illustrator.

Step 2. Draw a rectangle around the border of the object. Illustrator will use this border to determine the area of the object relative to the values entered for the graph.

Step 3. Draw a horizontal line across the rectangle at a good place for the image to stretch. Make the horizontal line into a guide (select Object⇨Guides⇨Make or press ⌘-5).

Step 3 is necessary only if you use the column design as a sliding design.

Select the rectangle, object, and guide, and select Object⇨Graphs⇨Design. Click the New button to make the selected object appear in the window. Name the design and click the OK button.

Step 5. Select just one legend type by clicking twice on the legend graphic with the Group Selection tool. Select Object⇨Graphs⇨Column Design and select the design from the list. Choose the column design type (see Figure 13-12 for examples of each type). Repeat this step for each legend.

You can combine column design types by selecting a different type for each legend.

Preferences and Layers

In This Chapter

- Personalizing Illustrator
- Modifying the Adobe Illustrator Start-up file
- Setting preferences that affect all documents
- Setting document-specific preferences
- Understanding layers
- Using the Layers palette
- Developing Layer creation strategies
- Working with layers

Preferences

No two illustrators work the same. To accommodate the vast differences in styles, techniques, and habits, Illustrator provides many settings that each user can change to personalize the software.

Illustrator provides four major ways to change preferences. The most dramatic and difficult changes are to a small file called Adobe Illustrator Start-up. The Start-up file changes how new documents appear and which custom colors, patterns, and gradients are available.

You also can control how Illustrator works by accessing the Preferences submenu (select File⇨Preferences). You make most of these changes in the General Preferences dialog box, which you access by choosing File⇨Preferences⇨General (⌘-K).

A third way to make changes is by changing preferences relative to each document. You usually make these changes in the Document Setup dialog box, but a few other options are available. See Chapter 9 for more information on document-specific preferences.

The fourth way that you can customize preferences happens pretty much automatically. When you quit Illustrator, it remembers many of the current settings until the next time you run it. These settings include palette placements and values in Toolbox settings.

Illustrator has a few settings that you cannot customize. These features can dig under your skin because most of them seem like things that you should be able to customize. See the "Things you can't customize" section later in this chapter for a list of these settings.

Modifying the Start-up File

When you first run Illustrator, the program looks to the Illustrator start-up file to check a number of preferences. Those preferences include window size and placement, as well as custom colors, gradients, patterns, and graph designs.

New documents (like the one created automatically when you first run the program) have all the attributes of the start-up file. Opened documents have all the gradients, custom colors, patterns, and graph designs of the start-up file.

STEPS: **Changing the Start-up File**

Step 1. Open the start-up file. The start-up file, called Adobe Illustrator Start-up, is located in the Plug-Ins folder in the Adobe Illustrator folder. The file is an Adobe Illustrator 5.0 document, so double-clicking the file opens Illustrator, as well.

Step 2. Figure 14-1 shows what the file looks like. Each square in the document contains a pattern, gradient, custom color, or color swatch square. Remove any square that contains patterns, gradients, or custom colors that you don't use.

If you remove a pattern, go to the Pattern dialog box (select Object⇔Pattern) and delete the pattern. Do the same for gradients and custom colors and save the file.

If you delete a pattern, custom color, or gradient from the start-up file, it is gone. Kaput. The only way to get it back is to replace the start-up file from the original disks or CD-ROM.

Step 3. To add something to the start-up file, create a rectangle and fill it with a new pattern, custom color, or gradient. In order for a pattern, custom color, or gradient to appear for use in new documents, it has to be part of an object.

To add a graph design, create the graph design and apply it to a graph. Place the graph in the start-up file.

Step 4. To change the window size, just save the start-up file with the window size that you want new documents to have.

Step 5. To change the color swatches on the Paint Style palette, add, replace, or delete color swatches while the start-up file is open and then save the start-up file.

Figure 14-1:
The default Adobe Illustrator
Startup file.

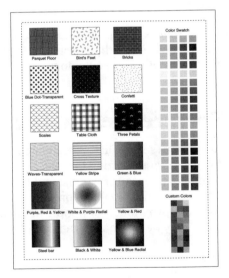

 If you delete the Adobe Illustrator Start-up file, most patterns, gradients, and custom colors will not be available until you create a new start-up file or place the original start-up file from the disks or CD-ROM in the Plug-Ins folder.

To check whether changes that you made in the start-up file will work, quit Illustrator and run the program again. You cannot tell whether the changes are in place until you quit and then reopen Illustrator.

 You can change not only the window size of new documents but also the viewing percentage. Most people like documents to fit in the window when it is created. For a 13-inch screen, use 50%; for a 16- or 17-inch screen, use 66%.

Changing Application Preferences

An *application preference* is a preference that affects the way the entire program works, regardless of which document you pull up. To alter application preferences, access the Preferences submenu (select File⇨Preferences).

 In most programs, Preferences is logically located on the Edit menu, not on the File menu. Preferences, unlike everything else on the File menu, deals with the entire program rather than with a specific document.

The General Preferences dialog box

The General Preferences dialog box (select File⇨Preferences⇨General or press ⌘-K) contains most of the "personalized" customizing options for Illustrator. The options in this box affect keyboard increments, measuring units, and the way that objects are drawn. These options are considered personalized options because they are specific to the way that each person uses the program. Few people have the same preference settings as others have (unless they never change the defaults).

For example, the preference settings on my system are quite different from the settings on the system used by Jennifer Garling, who has done a large number of the illustrations for this book. In fact, only 7 of the 18 options are the same. In discussing these options in detail, I explain what Jennifer's options are set at, what mine are set at, and why we have chosen those particular settings. Figure 14-2 shows both of our General Preferences dialog boxes.

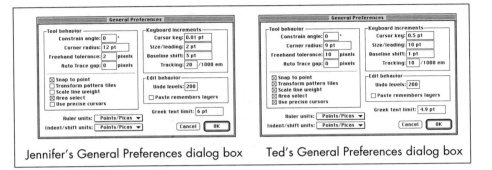

Figure 14-2:
Jennifer's and Ted's General Preferences dialog boxes.

Jennifer's General Preferences dialog box   Ted's General Preferences dialog box

One of the reasons that my settings are different from Jennifer's is the type of work we do. Most of my illustrations are type-heavy, or because of my lack of real drawing ability—they are based on shapes that are available in Illustrator. Jennifer, on the other hand, is a freelance artist who has been illustrating professionally for years, and she can draw and paint wonderfully. In addition, she specializes in technical art, so she needs to be extremely precise and accurate in her drawings. Keep these issues in mind as you read our reasons for certain preference settings.

The Constrain angle option

The Constrain angle option controls the angle on which all objects are aligned. Rectangles are always drawn "flat," aligning themselves to the bottom, top, and sides of the document window. When you press the Shift key, lines that you draw with the Pen tool and objects that you move will align to the constrain angle, or 45°, 90°, 135°, or 180°, plus or minus this angle.

The constrain angle also affects how the four transformation tools transform objects. The Scale tool can be very hard to use when the constrain angle is not 0°, and the Shear tool becomes even more difficult to use than normal at different constrain angles. Pressing Shift when you are using the Rotate tool constrains the rotational angle to 45° increments added to the constrain angle. (Chapter 3 discusses the Rotate tool and other transformational tools.)

In Illustrator, 0° is a horizontal line, and 90° is a vertical line. Figure 14-3 shows Illustrator angles.

Figure 14-3:
Illustrator
angles:
Negative
numbers are
shown because
remembering
an angle of –45°
is often easier
than remember-
ing an angle of
315°, and
Illustrator
accepts
negative angles
in text fields.

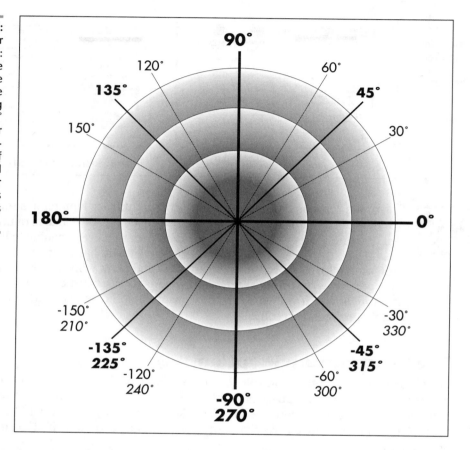

If you set the constrain angle at 20°, objects are constrained to movements of 20°, 65°, 110°, 155° , and 200°. Constrain angles of 90°, 180°, and –90° (270°) affect only type, patterns, gradients, and graphs; everything else works normally.

Preference practical jokes, part 1. Change the constrain angle on a friend's (or enemy's) machine to .5° for that "something just isn't right here" look. Change the constrain angle to 180° and everything will be fine . . . until the mark tries typing, when all text appears upside down! As with any practical joke, this may be much funnier to you than the unsuspecting victim, so don't try these on someone who can get you fired.

Both Jennifer and I have set our constrain angles to 0°, which is the default value. The only time I change the constrain angle is when I have to place a great deal of type at 90°.

Instead of rotating each piece 90° after typing it, I find that typing sideways is easier. Jennifer changes it mostly when certain drawings have 30° or 60° angles. You cannot access those angles by using Shift-Rotate when the constrain angle is 0°.

 When Option-copying objects, you can use the Shift key in conjunction with a constrain angle to duplicate objects at a specific angle. (*Option-copy* means press the Option key while dragging an object and then release the mouse button *before* releasing the Option key to produce a duplicate of the object at the new location.)

The Corner radius option

 The Corner radius option affects the size of the curved corners on a rounded rectangle. (For a complete explanation of the corner radius and rounded rectangles, see Chapter 5.)

The Corner radius value changes each time you enter a new value in the Rectangle dialog box. This dialog box appears when you click the Rectangle or Rounded Rectangle tools without dragging in a document. If, for example, you create one rounded rectangle with a rounded corner radius of 24 points, all rounded rectangles that you create from that point forward will have a radius of 24 points. The only ways to change the corner radius are to click a rectangle tool without dragging in a document and then enter a new value in the Rectangle dialog box or to enter a new value in the Corner radius text box in the General Preferences dialog box.

The real advantage to changing the corner radius in the General Preferences box is that the corner radius will affect manually created (dragged with the Rounded Rectangle tool) rounded rectangles immediately. Changing the corner radius in the Rectangle dialog box requires that you know the exact dimensions of the rectangle or that you draw a rectangle by entering information in the Rectangle dialog box (clicking with the Rectangle tool without dragging) and specifying the corner radius. That rectangle must then be deleted so that you can draw a rounded rectangle with the correct corner radius manually.

Jennifer has set the Corner radius option to 12 points, but she rarely pays attention to what the default setting is. She usually draws rounded rectangles to client specification, so the corner radius changes from day to day. When I draw rounded rectangles, I like the radius to be small relative to the rectangle I'm drawing. At 9 points, most corners still seem small, but not so small that they look as if I intended them to be a normal corner.

Because you can change the Corner radius setting easily, be sure to check it before you draw a series of rounded rectangles manually. No way exists to easily or automatically change the corner radius on existing rounded rectangles.

 If you use 0 pt as the Corner radius setting, the corners will not be rounded at all. If you click with the Rounded Rectangle tool and enter 0 pt as the corner radius, the Corner radius setting in the General Preferences dialog box will change to 0 pt.

The Freehand tolerance option

 The Freehand tolerance setting controls how accurate the paths that Illustrator creates are when you compare them to the area dragged with the Freehand tool and to any templates being traced with the Auto Trace tool. (Chapters 6 and 7 discuss Freehand tolerance settings and resulting paths. Chapter 3 explains the Freehand and Auto Trace tools and their uses.)

The lower the Freehand tolerance setting, the more exact the resulting path. A higher setting results in smoother, less accurate paths. You can enter a value from 0 to 10, in increments of $\frac{1}{100}$ of a point (two decimal places).

 The Freehand tolerance number is relative to the number of pixels on the screen that the resulting path may vary. A tolerance of 10 means that the resulting path may vary up to 10 pixels from the location of the actual dragged or traced area.

Jennifer uses a setting of 2, the default, because she finds that this setting keeps what she is drawing true to form but corrects for any shifts when she is drawing with her Wacom tablet. If she is using the mouse to draw, she changes the setting to 4, which corrects more errors. She uses a setting of 4 because the mouse is less precise and is prone to create more little bumps and skittles. When she does something that needs a great deal of detail, such as a map, she changes the Freehand tolerance to 0, regardless of which input device she is using.

I normally use a Freehand tolerance setting of 10 so that the paths I draw are smoothed out, with few or no extra bumps. Most of the paths that I draw with the Freehand tool are smooth, flowing paths. When I need more detail, I go as low as 2, but rarely less than that. When I use the Auto Trace tool to start tracing a logo, I usually set the tolerance to 3 or 4, depending on the complexity of the logo. Using a lower setting for auto tracing results in too many points that I need to remove later when I touch up the paths.

The Auto Trace gap option

When you use the Auto Trace tool to trace a template, the tool may encounter gaps, or white space, between solid areas. The Auto Trace gap option enables you to specify that if the Auto Trace tool runs into a white space gap of 1 or 2 pixels, it can jump over the gap and continue tracing on the other side of it.

A value of 0 prevents the Auto Trace tool from tracing over gaps. If you use a value of 1, the Auto Trace tool will trace over gaps that are up to 1 pixel wide. If you use a value of 2 (the highest allowed), it will trace over gaps that are 2 pixels wide.

 The Auto Trace gap setting not only goes over gaps, it also adheres less closely to the original template.

Jennifer's Auto Trace setting is 0, the default, and she rarely uses the Auto Trace tool. Because the Auto Trace tool produces results of questionable quality, she prefers to use Streamline 3.0 to have scans automatically traced. In fact, more often than not, she will trace placed EPS files manually. I also use a setting of 0 because when I bring any template into Illustrator, I examine it closely in Photoshop to make sure that it does not have any gaps. I can then be sure that the resulting paths will not be misshapen because of template tracing inaccuracies.

The Snap to point option

You turn on the Snap to point feature in Illustrator to automatically align a point that you are dragging with another point that already exists within the illustration. As soon as the cursor is within 2 screen pixels of an anchor point, the cursor will become hollow. If you release the mouse button when the cursor is hollow, the new point will precisely overlap the existing point.

 Be sure to click and drag on a *point* when you are dragging and using the Snap to point feature, or you may unintentionally align part of a line segment with the existing point.

Jennifer normally has Snap to point checked, but for drawings where objects need to be placed next to each other, rather than overlapping each other, this feature causes problems. For these drawings, she unchecks the option. To avoid confusion, she always turns Snap to point on as soon as she finishes one of these drawings. I usually keep the feature on to make sure that my points always align; the only trouble that I have is accidentally clicking and dragging segments rather than points.

Never assume that Snap to point is on, unless you know that you have not changed it. Watch for those hollow arrows, and if you don't see them, check the General Preferences box to see whether the feature is turned on.

The Transform pattern tiles option

Check the Transform pattern tiles option if you want patterns in paths to be moved, scaled, rotated, sheared, and reflected when you manually transform paths. When this option is checked, pulling up a transformation dialog box (either Move, Rotate, Scale, Reflect, or Shear) automatically checks the Pattern check box. When the option is not checked, the Pattern check box is not checked in the transformation dialog box.

Jennifer keeps this box unchecked because patterns that she places in objects should not change in size, location, or angle; nor should they be reflected or sheared. Usually, the patterns that she works with are a set size and angle, and any changes to one pattern have to be changed on all patterns. Keeping the box unchecked maintains consistency throughout, keeping all the patterns the same. If she has to transform a pattern, she selects a path that is filled with a pattern and chooses Filter⇨Select⇨Same Fill Color to select all the objects with that pattern as a fill. Then she double-clicks the Transformation tool or selects Arrange⇨Move (⌘-Shift-M). In the dialog box that appears, Jennifer checks the Pattern check box, unchecks the Object check box, and enters the transformation information.

I usually keep the Transform pattern tiles box checked, which sets all patterns to automatically transform and move with the objects that are being transformed and moved. This feature is especially useful when you want to create perspective in objects because the transformations of patterns can enhance the intended perspective.

The Scale line weight option

When the Scale line weight feature is on, it automatically increases and reduces line weights relative to an object when you uniformly scale that object manually. For example, if a path has a stroke weight of 1 point and you reduce the path uniformly by 50 percent, the stroke weight will be .5 point.

 Scaling objects nonuniformly (without the Shift key pressed) does not change the stroke weight on an object, regardless of whether the Scale line weight feature is on or off.

If an object is scaled uniformly throughout the Scale dialog box, the Scale line weight option in the Scale dialog box will default to checked if the Scale line weight check box is checked in the General Preferences dialog box.

 Unlike the Corner radius option, checking or unchecking the check box in the Scale dialog box for Scale line weight has no effect on the corresponding check box in the General Preferences dialog box.

By keeping this option unchecked, Jennifer specifies line weights and knows that no matter how much the object is reduced or enlarged, the line weight will stay the same. I usually have the Scale line weight option checked so that the line weight stays proportional to the size of the object.

The Area select option

When the Area select feature is on, you can select an object in Preview mode by clicking the object's fill. If the Area select feature is not on, you select an object the same way that you select it in Artwork and Preview selection mode: by clicking paths or anchor points of objects.

 The Area select feature has no effect on selecting objects in Preview selection mode, but after you select them, you can move them by clicking a filled area.

Both Jennifer and I always keep this option checked. I have yet to have a good reason to turn it off. The only reason that I can imagine for turning off this feature is if, for a particular illustration, I need to select specific paths from several overlapping, filled objects. To be honest, I think that selecting individual paths in Preview would still be difficult because you can't see most of them.

 The Area select feature does not enable you to select paths by clicking strokes, unless you click the center of the stroke where the path is (in which case you would be clicking the path anyway).

The Use precise cursors option

Precise cursors are cursors that appear as a variation of a crosshair instead of in the shape of a tool. Figure 14-4 shows cursors that are different when the precise cursors feature is on.

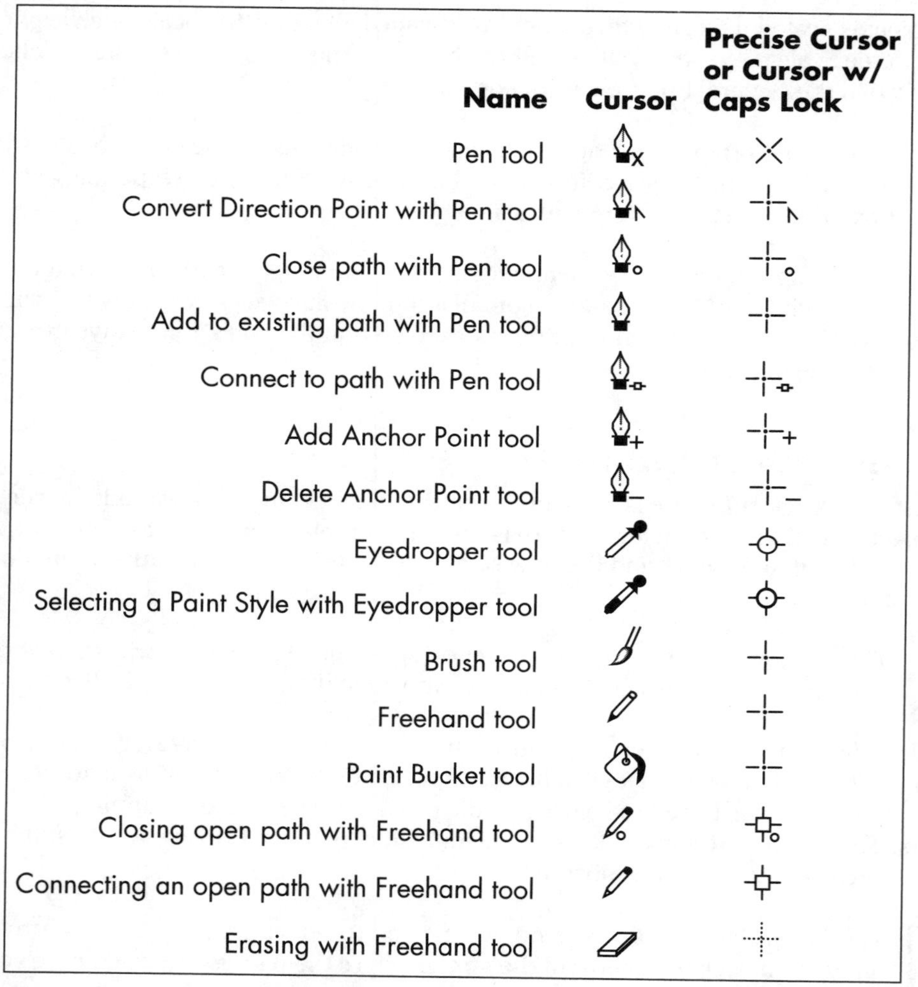

Name	Cursor	Precise Cursor or Cursor w/ Caps Lock
Pen tool		
Convert Direction Point with Pen tool		
Close path with Pen tool		
Add to existing path with Pen tool		
Connect to path with Pen tool		
Add Anchor Point tool		
Delete Anchor Point tool		
Eyedropper tool		
Selecting a Paint Style with Eyedropper tool		
Brush tool		
Freehand tool		
Paint Bucket tool		
Closing open path with Freehand tool		
Connecting an open path with Freehand tool		
Erasing with Freehand tool		

Figure 14-4: You use the Caps Lock key to switch between standard cursors and precise cursors.

The Caps Lock key toggles between standard cursors and precise cursors. When the Use precise cursors option is checked, the Caps Lock key makes the cursors standard. When the Use precise cursors option is not checked, Caps Lock activates the precise cursors.

Jennifer keeps this feature off and uses the Caps Lock key if she needs a certain cursor to be exact. An Illustrator veteran, Jennifer is quite used to, and even likes, the shaped cursors. I usually keep the option on and rarely engage the Caps Lock button to change the cursors back to normal. I find the precise cursor for the Brush tool to be the most useful because the standard Brush cursor is a giant blob. Jennifer likes the standard Brush cursor because it covers only one portion of the path that she is drawing, but the precise cursor for the Brush tool sticks lines in all four directions.

The Ruler units option

The pop-up menu for the Ruler units option changes the measurement system for the current document and all future new documents. This change affects most of the ways that dialog boxes, the Info palette, and the rulers display measurements.

Changing the Ruler units in the General Preferences dialog box changes the Ruler units in the Document Setup dialog box (select File⇨Document Setup or press ⌘-Shift-D).

Being aware of which measurement system you are working in is important. When you enter a measurement in a dialog box, any numbers that are not measurement system specific are applied to the current unit of measurement. For example, if you want to move something 1 inch and you open the Move dialog box (select Arrange⇨Move or press ⌘-Shift-M), you need to add either the inch symbol (") or the abbreviation *in* after you type a 1 in the dialog box if the measurement system is not inches. If the measurement system is points/picas, entering just a 1 moves the object one point, not one inch. If the measurement system is inches, though, entering just the number 1 is fine.

Usually the measurement system is indicated by a corresponding letter or letters: *in* for inch, *pt* for points, and *cm* for centimeters.

You can change the Ruler units setting in the General Preferences dialog box without entering the dialog box. Just press ⌘-Shift-P for points/picas, ⌘-Shift-N for centimeters, and ⌘-Shift-I for inches.

Both Jennifer and I use the points/picas system for several reasons. First, using points and picas is easier because you can specify smaller increments exactly (ever try to figure out what ½ inch is in decimals?). Second, type is measured in points, not inches. Third, points and picas are the standard in measuring systems for designers. The default is inches.

The Indent/shift units option

This option would be easier to understand if it referred to "type measuring units" instead of "Indent/shift units." This option controls how type is measured, how keyboard increments are defined, and how paragraph indents are measured.

The standard (and default) for this setting is points/picas. Both Jennifer and I see no reason to ever change this setting to inches or centimeters.

 As Chapter 8 explains fully, type is measured strangely, from ascender to descender.

The Cursor key option

The increment that you specify in this setting controls how far an object moves when you select it and press the keyboard arrows.

Jennifer normally has the Cursor key increment set to 0.01 pt. This setting makes her arrow keys work as "nudgers" by moving objects ever so slightly. I have the increment set to 0.5 pt. because that measurement is the smallest amount that I usually need to move things. I make my increment smaller when I am working in 800% or 1600% views.

The Size/leading option

You can use the keyboard to increase and decrease type size by pressing ⌘-Shift- > and ⌘-Shift- <, respectively. You can increase and decrease leading by typing Option- ↑ and Option- ↓, respectively. In the Size/leading text box, you specify the increment by which the size and leading change.

 You can increase or decrease the type size and leading only until you reach the upper and lower limits of each. The upper limit for type size and leading is 1296 points, and the lower limit for each is .1 point.

Jennifer has Size/leading set to 2 pt. the default, because her type size changes are relatively small. If she needs to dramatically change the size of the type, she uses the Scale tool. I keep my settings fairly high, at 10 pt., because I have found that I require large point changes, usually quite a bit more than 10 points. If I need to do fine-tuning, I either type in the exact size that I want or use the Scale tool.

The Baseline shift option

The Baseline shift feature moves selected type up and down on the baseline, independent of the leading. The increment specified in this box is how much the type will be moved when you press the keyboard commands. To move type up one increment, press Option-Shift-↑. To move type down one increment, press Option-Shift-↓.

Jennifer has the Baseline shift increment set at 3 pt. because that amount is how far she usually moves type to set superior and inferior numbers. I keep the Baseline shift increment at 1 pt. so that I can adjust Path type better; specifically, I want to be able to adjust the baseline shift of type on a circle.

The Tracking option

Tracking changes the amount of space between selected characters, and the setting in this text box represents the amount of space (measured in thousandths of an em space) that the keyboard command will add or remove. To increase tracking, you press ⌘- →; to decrease it, you press ⌘- ←.

To increase the tracking by five times the increment in the General Preferences dialog box, press ⌘-Option- →. To decrease the tracking by five times the increment, press ⌘-Option- ←.

The value in the Tracking text box also affects incremental changes in kerning. *Kerning* is the addition or removal of space between one pair of letters only. Kerning is done instead of tracking when a blinking insertion point is between two letters, as opposed to at least one selected character for tracking.

I have the Tracking increment set to 10 because that setting produces a result that corresponds to twice the tracking generated by the QuarkXPress key command. (In QuarkXPress, pressing Command-Option-Shift-[or Command-Option-Shift-] increases or decreases, respectively, tracking by ½₀₀ of an em space). Jennifer has set the Tracking increment to 20 because she doesn't require as much control for kerning.

The Undo levels option

The number that you specify in the Undo levels text box defines how many times you can undo. The maximum number is 200.

If you undo as far as you can, increasing the number of undo levels does not enable you to undo more.

The more undo levels you specify, the more memory the undos will take up, taking away from Illustrator's application memory.

Both Jennifer and I have Undo levels set to 200, the maximum number. If we run out of memory, a dialog box appears, asking whether we want to get rid of some of the oldest undos. Clicking the Always Discard option gets rid of them for us and frees up the necessary memory.

 Change this setting to 200 right now so that you don't forget. This feature is one of the most powerful features of Illustrator, and the default is a measly 10 undos.

The Paste remembers layers option

Checking the Paste remembers layers check box causes all objects to be pasted on the layer that they were copied from, regardless of which layer is currently active. Unchecking this box causes objects on the Clipboard to be pasted in the current layer.

This option is available in the Layers palette as well, and if it is on, a check mark appears next to Paste Remembers Layers in the pop-up menu. When you turn the Paste Remembers Layers menu item on or off, the preference setting changes in the General Preferences dialog box.

Both Jennifer and I always leave this option unchecked. Copying and pasting is one way to move objects from layer to layer, and when an object is not pasted into the layer where you expect to see it, the result can be very confusing.

The Greek text limit option

The number that you enter in this box defines the point at which Illustrator begins to greek text. Illustrator *greeks text* — turns the letters into gray bars — when the text is so small that reading it on the screen would be hard or impossible. This change reduces screen redraw time dramatically, especially when the document contains a great deal of text.

The size in this text box is relative to the viewing magnification of the document. At a limit of 6 points, 6-point type at 100%, 66%, 50%, 25%, or smaller will be greeked; but 6- point type at 150%, 200%, or larger will be readable. With the same limitations, 12-point type will be greeked at 50% and smaller, but it is readable at 66% and larger.

Preference practical jokes, part 2. Change the Greek text limit on a friend's (or enemy's) machine to 1296 points (the maximum) and then cover young children's ears in preparation for any verbal abuse given to the computer by the jokee. If you want to fess up to the joke, do so quickly so that the mark doesn't restart the system, thinking that there is a system problem.

Jennifer has the Greek text limit set to 6 pt. so that when she zooms out, the text redraws quickly. I have mine set to 4.9 pt. so that 10-point text (which I often use) is semireadable at 50%.

Other application preferences

The three other preference items in the File Preferences submenu deal with one issue apiece, as opposed to General Preferences, which is a catchall for most other preferences. By creating the submenu and these additional preference menu items, Adobe makes Illustrator's preference setup resemble Photoshop's preference setup. This similarity should make the transition between the two programs easier as both programs evolve.

With the release of Illustrator 5.5, Adobe has taken the two programs of Illustrator and Photoshop one step closer. The main change that makes the programs similar is how they open and save files. As files are opened, a "progress" bar appears. When files are saved, the saving process is very similar to Photoshop's saving process.

Other preferences are set automatically by Illustrator as it tries to keep the program the way you had it last.

The Color Matching dialog box

Select File⇨Preferences⇨Color Matching to bring up the Color Matching dialog box (shown in Figure 14-5). In this dialog box, you can specify how colors are to appear on the monitor. The way that colors appear on the monitor does not affect the output, but it may affect your perception of the colors on the screen. Changes that you make, based on what you see on the screen, may affect the output.

Figure 14-5:
The Color Matching
dialog box.

Color Matching
Cyan C	Magenta M	Yellow Y
Red MY	Green CY	Blue CM
White W	Black K	Black CMY

☒ CIE calibration

Ink: SWOP (Coated) ▼
Monitor: Apple 13" RGB ▼
Gamma: 1.8

Use Defaults   Cancel   OK

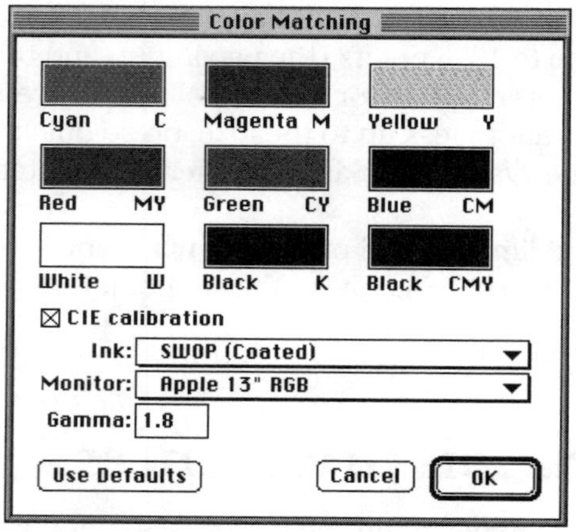

The nine boxes at the top of the dialog box show each color as it will appear in Illustrator. These colors should be fairly close to the colors in the *Adobe Illustrator Manual*. If they are not, you can adjust them by clicking the mismatched colors and changing them so that they resemble the printed colors more closely.

Preference practical jokes, part 3. Switch black to white and white to black in the Color Matching dialog box. Turn that buddy's "negative" attitude into a positive one. Lots of fun for all! Clicking the Use Defaults button will reset all the colors back to normal. Remember, this change will not affect output but could cause an unsuspecting mark to make all black objects white and all white objects black. Not to be used when the "buddy" has an important deadline or is going to send files to a service bureau.

When you check the CIE calibration check box, the color in the color boxes is determined by the specifications that you enter in the Ink and Monitor text boxes. You cannot change the color boxes manually when the CIE calibration check box is checked. The Gamma value is usually 1.8 for Macintosh monitors. Clicking the Use Defaults button automatically changes the options to the default values.

Because monitors and printed pieces are based on different display technologies, their colors are never exact matches. Certain monitors are better than others for color matching.

For more information on color matching and getting output to resemble what you see on-screen, see Chapter 21.

The Hyphenation Options dialog box

The Hyphenation Options dialog box (select File⇨Preferences⇨Hyphenation Options) contains options for customizing how Illustrator hyphenates words. At the top of the dialog box is a pop-up menu that lists various languages. Select the default language. At the bottom of the dialog box is an area where you can add hyphenation exceptions to the list of hyphenation exceptions. These exceptions are words that you don't want Illustrator to hyphenate under any circumstances.

The Plug-Ins Folder preference

The last preference item in the Preference submenu is a one-trick pony, the Plug-Ins Folder preference. This preference enables you to specify a folder in which Plug-Ins are located. The default is the folder called Plug-Ins in the Adobe Illustrator folder.

Placement and Toolbox value preferences

Most Illustrator users take many preferences for granted. But if Illustrator didn't remember most preferences, most Illustrator users would be quite annoyed.

Palettes (including the Toolbox) remain where they were when you last used Illustrator. Illustrator remembers their size, and even whether they were open. Values in the Toolbox remain whatever you set them to last. For example, the options in the Paint Bucket/Eyedropper dialog box remain the same between Illustrator sessions.

Things you can't customize

There are a few things that you cannot customize in Illustrator, and they can be annoying:

- Type information always defaults to 12-point Helvetica, Auto leading, 100% Horizontal Scale, 0 tracking, Flush left, Hyphenation off. There is no easy way around this set of defaults.

- Layers for new documents are limited to one, which is colored light blue and called "Layer 1." Layer Fixer, which sets up custom layers automatically, is described in the next section.

- When you create new objects, they are always 100% black fill and no stroke.

- The Selection tool is always the "active" tool.

If any of these things, or anything else, annoys you too much, call Adobe Tech Support (415-961-0911) and tell them about it. Usually (when you can get a human on the line), they are receptive to hearing your problem, and they may have an easy way for you to do something that you thought the program couldn't do.

Layers

The layering feature of Illustrator provides an easy and powerful way to separate artwork into individual sections. A layer is a separate section of the document that is on its own level, above, under, or in between other layers, but never on the same level as another layer. You can view these sections separately, locked, hidden, and rearranged around each other.

You create, control, and manipulate layers by using the Layers palette. Each layer can have its own color, and that color will show up when all paths and points of objects are selected.

 You can create as many layers as you want, up to the limitations of application memory. To make sure that the Adobe people were on the up and up about this, I set up a QuicKey to create 4,500 layers on my Quadra 800. The project took about 10 hours, but Illustrator created 4,500 usable layers. Why would you need 4,500 layers? I hope you wouldn't. But you shouldn't have any fears that you will not be able to create enough layers for an illustration.

 Of course, having 4,500 layers to work with slowed the operation of Illustrator to a crawl. I had to click the mouse button and hold on the menu bar for about 10 seconds before the menu appeared. Suffice to say, the more layers you create, the slower Illustrator will run.

Getting started with layers

After you realize that you need to use layers, what do you do? The only way to manipulate, create, and delete layers is by using the Layers palette.

When to use layers

Before you delve into the world of layers, here are some guidelines for deciding when to use layers in a document:

▓ If the drawing is complex, meaning that it has about a thousand paths, use layers to split the illustration into manageable sections. A thousand paths isn't that many; you can create a thousand paths with just four blends.

▓ If the drawing has patterns, blends, or other objects that take a long time to preview, you can place these hard-to-manage and time-consuming objects on a separate layer.

▓ If you frequently use Hide and Lock to send objects "out of the way," you will benefit from using layers.

▓ If you need to combine Artwork and Preview modes, perhaps to manually trace a scanned EPS image, layers give you the ability to set the EPS image to Preview mode but keep the paths that you are drawing in Artwork mode.

▓ If a drawing contains distinct sections, such as a background section, a type section, and a forward objects section, then it is a prime candidate for using layers.

STEPS: Creating and Customizing New Layers

Step 1. If the Layers palette is not showing, select Window⇨Show Layers (⌘-Control-L). When you open the Layers palette for the first time in a new document, you see only Layer 1 listed.

Step 2. To create a new layer, click the triangle in the upper right of the palette to display a pop-up menu. Drag over to the first item, New Layer, to see the New Layer dialog box.

Step 3. In the New Layer dialog box, the name of the new layer, Layer 2, is high-lighted. To change this name, type a new name, and it will replace the generic name.

Step 4. The options below the name affect how the layer works and is viewed. The first option is the color of the paths and points when objects on that layer are selected. Choose one of the preset colors from the pop-up menu or select the Other option to use a custom color.

The preset colors are faded colors that can easily blend into an illustration. For the most vibrant colors, use colors that you have picked from the color wheel at its outermost edges, where the brightness is as high as possible.

Step 5. Select any of the options that you want for this layer. Show makes the objects in the layer visible. Print enables you to print objects that are on this layer. Preview makes the objects on this layer preview. Lock prevents objects on this layer from being selected and prevents any objects from being put on this layer. Dim Placed EPS dims any EPS images on the layer, making them about 50 percent lighter than normal.

Step 6. Click OK after you have chosen all the options you want. The new layer appears above the existing layer in the Layers palette. If you want the objects on the new layer to appear below the objects on the existing layer, click the name of the new layer and drag it under Layer 1.

Step 7. To modify the existing layer, double-click it. You see the Layer Options dialog box, which looks just like the New Layer dialog box. Make the changes and choose the options that you want for this layer and then click OK.

The Layers palette

The Layers palette (shown in Figure 14-6) is the control center where all layer-related activities take place. Most activities take place on the main section of the Layers palette, which is always visible when the Layers palette is on-screen. Other activities take place in the pop-up menu that appears when you press the triangle in the upper right of the palette.

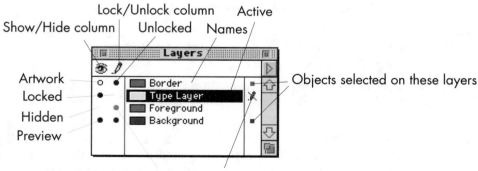

Figure 14-6: The Layers palette.

The main section of the Layers palette

Clicking the close box in the upper lefthand corner closes the Layers palette. Another way to close the Layers palette is to select Window⇨Hide Layers (⌘-Control-L).To bring the Layers palette back to the screen, select Window⇨Show Layers (⌘-Control-L).

 Clicking the resize box in the upper righthand corner of the Layers palette resizes the palette to as large as it needs to be to show all the layers and all the layer names in the document. The resize box never makes the Layers palette smaller than the one shown in Figure 14-6, and it does not make it taller than the height of the screen.

The eye in the upper left is above the Show/Hide Column. Clicking the eye toggles between showing only the Active layer (the one that is highlighted, which is Type Layer in Figure 14-6) and showing all the layers. Option-clicking the eye toggles between previewing all layers and previewing only the selected layer, changing the other layers to Artwork mode.

The bullets (circles) below the eye signify different things. Solid bullets represent a layer that is in Preview mode. Hollow bullets mean that the layer is in Artwork mode. No bullet means that the layer is hidden. Clicking a solid or hollow bullet toggles it from showing to hidden. Clicking in the Show/Hide Column when no bullet is present shows the layer. Option-clicking the bullet changes it from solid (Preview mode) to hollow (Artwork mode).

The pencil in the upper left is above the Lock/Unlock Column. Clicking the pencil toggles between unlocking all the layers and locking all the layers but the active one.

The bullets under the pencil signify whether each layer is locked or unlocked. A solid bullet means that the layer is not locked. No bullet means that the layer is locked from use. A light gray bullet means that the layer is hidden, but that when the layer is shown it will not be locked. You can move items to hidden layers as long as those layers are not locked, but you cannot change anything that is already on a hidden layer.

The column in the center of the palette lists all the layers in the document. When no documents are open, no layers are listed. If one layer is highlighted, it is the active layer. You create all new objects on the active layer. You can select more than one layer by dragging across several layers or Shift-clicking each layer to be selected. To deselect a layer, Shift-click it while it is selected. One layer must always be selected.

The layer at the top of the column is the layer that is on top of all the other layers. The layer at the bottom of the column is at the bottom of all the other layers. To move a layer, click it and drag it up or down. As you drag, a triangle pointer indicates where the layer will be placed when you release the mouse button.

You can undo all layer changes by selecting Edit⇨Undo (⌘-Z).

To the right of the layer names is a column that shows the object status of the layer. If a square appears in that column, at least one object on that layer is selected. If a pencil is in the column, that layer is active, and it is not locked. If a pencil with a slash through it is in that column, then that layer is active, and it is locked.

STEPS:	**Moving Objects from Layer to Layer**
Step 1.	Select the objects that you want to move from one layer to another. If the objects are on one layer, group them together so that you can reselect them easily.

 Do not group objects from different layers together, or all objects will be placed on the topmost layer.

Step 2. Open the Layers palette by selecting Window⇨Show Layers. A square should appear next to one of the layers. The square represents the selected objects.

 If you select objects on more than one layer, a square appears on each of the layers that has a selected object.

Step 3. Drag the square from its current layer to the target layer. The objects do not move left, right, up, or down, but now they may be in front of or behind other objects, depending on the layer that they are now upon.

The pop-up menu of the Layers palette

Clicking the triangle in the upper right of the Layers palette displays a pop-up menu that shows different options that are available relative to the selected layers.

The first option, New Layer, creates a new layer at the top of the list. When New Layer is selected, the New Layer dialog box appears, which is the same as the Layer Options dialog box, except for the title.

 If you press the Option key before you click the pop-up menu triangle, the first menu item will read New Layer Above First Layer or New Layer Above whatever the name of the active layer is.

The next option is Delete, which will delete the layer and any artwork on the layer. If the layer to be deleted contains artwork, a dialog box will warn you that you are about to delete it. If several layers are selected, the entry reads Delete Layers, and all selected layers will be deleted. You can undo layer deletions.

 The third menu item is Layer Options for Layer 1 (or Layer Options for whatever the name of the active layer is) — the menu item will read Layers Options if more than one layer is selected. Selecting Layer Options displays the Layer Options dialog box, in which you can choose a number of different options. If more than one layer is selected, the layer options will affect all selected layers. Double-clicking a layer name also brings up the Layer Options dialog box.

The next three options are different ways of changing the locking/viewing options. Hide Others/Show All does the same as clicking the eye. Artwork Others/Preview All is the same as Option-clicking the eye, and Lock Others/Unlock All is the same as clicking the pencil.

Checking the Paste Remembers Layers option causes all objects to be pasted on the layer they were copied from, regardless of which layer is currently active. Unchecking this menu item causes objects on the Clipboard to be pasted on the current layer.

Layer advice and strategies

Don't create layers unless you fall into one of the categories listed in the "When to use layers" sidebar. Layers take up RAM and computer power, and the more layers you have, the slower your system will be.

Do create layers when you believe that they will help you organize an illustration better. Even setting up one additional layer can dramatically ease selection and moving problems.

 One of the best uses for layers is for tracing EPS images. To learn exactly how to perform this procedure, see Chapter 7.

Use vivid, distinct colors for each layer. Using the same colors for all layers makes you miss out on half the power of layers. If you can't tell which layer an object is on, what good is it?

 A custom QuicKey called Layer Fixer that is on the *Macworld Adobe Illustrator Bible* CD-ROM automatically creates a series of layers, colors them differently, and names them. Instructions for installing and using the QuicKey are in the file on the CD-ROM.

Color Filters

	Black	Process	Custom	Fills	Strokes
Adjust Colors		◐		⊗	
Blend Front to Back	●	◐		⊗	
Blend Horizontally	●	◐		⊗	
Blend Vertically	●	◐		⊗	
Desaturate	●	◐	○	⊗	○
Desaturate More	●	◐	○	⊗	○
Invert Colors	●	◐		⊗	○
Saturate	●	◐	○	⊗	○
Saturate More	●	◐	○	⊗	○

The Filter menu in Illustrator is unlike any area of any other program. It can be remotely compared to the filters in Photoshop, but because Illustrator is vector based, the comparison falls short.

This section will take you on a journey of discovery into all the filters that Illustrator has to offer. More importantly, you will understand how and when to use these filters, and which filters are really useful and which ones are just for "fun."

Filter Basics

CHAPTER 15

In This Chapter

- An overview of filters
- Filters in Illustrator compared to filters in Photoshop
- Moving and using the Plug-Ins folder
- FPUs and the special Pathfinder/object filters
- Third-party filters
- Using filter combinations
- The mysterious Last Filter option

Filters in Illustrator

Adobe introduced Illustrator filters in Version 5.0. Most users of Illustrator expected Photoshop-type filters and were a little disappointed with the Illustrator filters. Actually, the only filters that are like Photoshop filters are the Distort filters and a few of the Stylize filters.

 Version 5.5 contains few "new" filters, mostly variations on the filters found in 5.0. The few exceptions are the new text filters and the "it's about time" Trap filter.

Instead of just changing the appearance of images, most of the filters in Illustrator perform tasks that took hours to do manually in previous versions of Illustrator. In a way, most of these filters work as intelligent macros, and they enable you to produce a variety of results.

Some filters, such as the Unite filter, seem to perform quite simple tasks. In reality, however, these filters are complex, mathematically based programs that accomplish certain tasks faster than the fastest illustrator could dream of performing without them.

After using the filters supplied with Illustrator 5.0, I can't imagine how I used Illustrator before they were part of the software package. I use the Select filters religiously, and the Pathfinder Divide Stroke filter enabled me to do trapping for color separations in Version 5.0 so fast that it was all a blur. Outline Stroked Path opens up a world of possibilities by enabling me to change strokes into filled paths. I use the Roughen filter to give Illustrator documents a bitmapped quality (I have my reasons). The Adjust Colors filter makes color adjustment incredibly simple.

 Version 5.5 has several filters that I would now be hard pressed to do without, as well. Instead of the Divide Stroke filter, the Trap filter (along with the Overprint filter) automates all areas of trapping, providing a much-needed function to one of the few areas of Illustrator that had been sorely lacking. The Document Info filter makes it easier than ever to take Illustrator files from system to system, or to have those files output at a service bureau. The combination of new text filters makes Illustrator's text functions rival that of page layout software.

Adobe, in its marketing wisdom, initially pushed the two filters with grunge-like names: Punk and Bloat. To be honest, I rarely use either of these filters, though I was quite intrigued the first time I saw them demonstrated. Cool names, little functionality. The same thing applies to the Twirl filter, which produces some really amazing effects. But once again, I don't use it very much (but I do use it more than the Punk and Bloat brothers). Yet I understand Adobe's marketing: I certainly wasn't that excited at first about the Select filters in comparison to the Distort filters.

66 Filters and No One Uses Them ___

Illustrator users don't use the filters enough. This fact has become shockingly apparent throughout the course of writing this book.

Jennifer Garling, the professional illustrator who did most of this book's illustrations, told me that she avoided using most filters until she was forced to use them when she began working on this book, several months after upgrading to Version 5.0. Like everyone else who uses Illustrator and has upgraded to Version 5.0, she was excited about the new filters. She also was apprehensive, and rightfully so, especially after fighting with Software FPU and suffering system crashes when she used the FPU filters on her

FPU-less Centris 610. FPUs (Floating Point Units) and FPU filters are discussed later in this chapter, in the section "The Great FPU Scare."

After testing the new Illustrator filters on some sample artwork, Garling promptly forgot about using them. But now that she has used them for real work, she uses them all the time. She has set up QuicKeys for the filters that she uses most, such as Add Arrowheads, Align Objects, Select Same Fill Color, and Scale Each.

Most users of Illustrator don't use filters because they're unfamiliar with the filters. A second obstacle is users' lack of understanding of when to use the filters in a real-life drawing situation. A third obstacle is that Illustrator has so many of the darn things. It wouldn't be too bad if there were 10 filters, or even 20. But Illustrator 5.0 shipped with 57 filters. That's right, most ordinary people don't have even that many fingers and toes to count 'em on.

 There are 66 filters (and one pseudofilter called Options for the Pathfinder submenu) now in Illustrator 5.5. Six of the new filters are text filters.

If the number of filters isn't enough to discourage you, consider that the Illustrator 5.0 manual contains just 11 pages of information about the filters and 4 pages that illustrate what the filters do. Because I think that filters are one of the most important parts of Illustrator 5.0, I have devoted five *chapters* to discussing filters in all their glory. These chapters provide examples, tutorials, and hints on using each of the 66 filters.

Comparing and Contrasting Illustrator and Photoshop Filters

The filters in Illustrator have to be different from the filters in Photoshop because Illustrator deals with vector-based images and Photoshop works with bitmapped graphics. Many electronic artists use Photoshop as a staple of their graphics work. For them, the word *filter* conjures up thoughts of blurring and sharpening, as well as some of the fantastic effects that they can achieve by using filters from third parties, such as Kai's Power Tools or Aldus's Gallery Effects.

The very term *filters* is based in photography terminology for special lenses that are attached to cameras to achieve special effects. Photoshop's filters are based on this concept, and they take it quite a bit further, creating controls for variety and exactness that a camera lens could never match.

Filters really isn't the best term for referring to the manipulations that Illustrator performs when you choose a filter. The following list compares some of the Illustrator filters with their Photoshop counterparts that perform similar functions:

- **Illustrator: Filter⇨Create⇨Mosaic**
  Photoshop: Filter⇨Stylize⇨Mosaic

  The mosaic filters take bitmap images and reduce the number of colored areas to large, single-colored squares.

  These two filters produce results that are the most alike of any of the Illustrator and Photoshop filters. The dialog boxes are a little different, but the results are the same. One big difference is that stylizing a mosaic in Photoshop is a fairly fast procedure, but creating a mosaic in Illustrator is a complex task that eats up tons of RAM and can take up to ten minutes to complete.

- **Illustrator: Filter⇨Distort⇨Twirl**
  Photoshop: Filter⇨Distort⇨Twirl

  Twirling spins an object or picture more in the center than around the edges.

  Both Twirl filters do about the same thing, but the result in Illustrator depends on the number of anchor points in the drawing. A greater number of anchor points creates a better effect, and a lesser number of points creates a choppy, poor effect. Photoshop's filter depends on the image resolution, but to a lesser extent.

- **Illustrator: Filter⇨Distort⇨Free Distort**
  Photoshop: Image⇨Effects⇨Distort

  Distorting gives you the ability to move the four corners of selected objects/ pictures to any new location, changing the perspective or just plain mangling the initial object/picture.

  A boon for Illustrator users, the Free Distort filter makes tedious perspective gridwork a thing of the past. Photoshop's Distort feature is not a filter per se but rather part of the Image control subsection.

- **Illustrator: Filter⇨Select⇨Inverse**
  Photoshop: Select⇨Inverse

  Selecting the inverse means that objects/portions of the picture that are not selected become selected, and objects/portions of the picture that are selected become deselected.

  In Photoshop, Inverse is not a filter but a capability built into the Select menu. In Illustrator, the Inverse filter selects objects that are not selected; in Photoshop, the Inverse feature selects pixels that are not selected.

███ **Illustrator: Filter⇨Select⇨Same Fill Color**
Photoshop: Select⇨Similar

Selecting objects that are the same color is useful for changing all objects that are a certain color, and both programs enable you to perform this function. The Similar feature in Photoshop is not a filter but a capability built into the Select menu. Photoshop's Similar feature is much more flexible than Illustrator's Same Fill Color filter because the Similar feature enables you to select different colors at the same time.

Some features that you would expect to do the same thing in each program are not the same:

███ **Illustrator: Filter⇨Colors⇨Invert Colors**
Photoshop: Image⇨Map⇨Invert

Illustrator's Invert Colors filter is annoying because you expect a negative image but don't get it. Instead, you get cyan, magenta, and yellow values that have been subtracted from 100, and a black value that is untouched. Photoshop's Invert command creates a true negative, and it is a feature, not a filter.

Illustrator: Filter⇨Colors⇨Saturate/Saturate More *and* Desaturate/Desaturate More
Photoshop: Image⇨Adjust⇨Hue/Saturation

The saturation filters in Illustrator increase the CMYK values for selected objects. In Photoshop, the color intensity is increased. Saturation in Illustrator is a misnomer.

The Plug-Ins Folder

All of the filters in Illustrator are in the Filter menu because a file with the same name as the filter is in the Plug-Ins folder. If the filter's file is not in the Plug-Ins folder, the filter will not appear in the Filter menu.

The Plug-Ins folder is put inside the first level of the Adobe Illustrator folder when Illustrator is installed. If you move the folder, you need to tell Illustrator where it is located:

STEPS: **Relocating the Plug-Ins Folder**

Step 1. In the Finder, with Illustrator *not* running, move or copy the Plug-Ins folder to the desired location.

Step 2. Double-click the Illustrator icon.

Step 3.   Select File⇨Preferences⇨Plug-Ins.

Step 4.   In the Plug-Ins dialog box, find the Plug-Ins folder and click the Select button at the bottom of the dialog box.

Step 5.   Quit Illustrator and double-click the Illustrator icon to restart Illustrator. The new Plug-Ins folder location is now used.

There are several Plug-Ins that are not located in the folder called Plug-Ins. These files are located in the Optional Plug-Ins folder, and include Artwork View Speedup (which isn't a filter at all but a way to marginally reduce the screen redraw speed in Artwork View by making all selected points black rather than the layer color), Custom to Process (added to the Color filters submenu), Overprint (added to the Other filters submenu), and Revert Text Path (added to the Text filters submenu). Many of these filters are discussed in detail later in this chapter. The FPU Plug-Ins folder also is located in this folder.

The Great FPU Scare

If you don't have an FPU, read this section. If you don't know whether you have an FPU, read this section. If you have an FPU, skip ahead to the "Third-Party Filters" section, later in the chapter, and congratulate yourself.

An FPU (Floating Point Unit) is a computer chip in your computer that is designed to handle logarithmic and trigonometric computations. The chip in most Macintosh computers is a 68881 or 68882. In most 68040 and all PowerPC machines, the FPU is built into the main processor. If your main processor chip is a 68LC040, there is not a math coprocessor in your main processor.

You may not have an FPU if you have any of the following computers: Macintosh LC, IIsi, Duo 210/230, Centris 610, Quadra 605/610, or any of the Performa computers. All Power Mac computers have an FPU built into their main processor.

If you installed Illustrator 5.0 on your system from the original (or duplicates of the original) disks/CD-ROM, run Illustrator and see whether the Filter menu has a Pathfinder menu item. If it doesn't, you don't have an FPU.

 Even if you copy Illustrator 5.0 to your system from another hard drive where it is installed, and the other system has an FPU and is able to use the FPU filters, they will not load on a system without an FPU.

Not having an FPU will prevent you from using all the Pathfinder filters and the Outline Stroked Path and Offset Path filters in Version 5.0.

Version 5.5 does not require an FPU for any filters. All the Pathfinder filters and Offset Path and Outline Path will run, albeit much slower, on machines without FPUs. To make the Outline Path and Offset Path filters run *much* quicker if you *do* have an FPU, you must manually copy the two filters in the FPU Plug-Ins folder to the Plug-Ins folder.

If you don't have an FPU and you have Illustrator 5.0, you may be able to get around the requirement to have an FPU by using Software FPU, a shareware utility that fools software into thinking that a real FPU is installed on a computer. This trick works relatively well; but in some instances, system crashes have occurred when FPU filters are used with Software FPU installed. (You can obtain Software FPU from America Online. Software for connecting to America Online is included on the *Macworld Illustrator 5.0/5.5 Bible* CD-ROM.)

Even though you don't need an FPU to use the 5.5 filters, an FPU *will* speed up Pathfinder/Offset Path/Outline Path filter operations by a tremendous amount. If you plan to use these filters or need to apply them to large or complex artwork, you will need an FPU to have the filters work in a reasonable amount of time.

Third-Party Filters

At press time, no other companies had produced Adobe Illustrator filters, but several were in the programming stages. If you are interested in creating a filter for yourself or for sale, contact Adobe Systems Technical Support. (The information on how to contact Adobe is in Appendix B.)

Filter Combinations and Relations

No filter is an island. Filters work best when you combine them with other filters. In fact, their functionality increases geometrically.

The following filters work well together:

▓ **Select Mask with Create Stroke & Fill for Mask:** These filters are natural buddies. Selecting a mask can be difficult, and if your eventual goal is to fill or stroke the mask, using these filters in tandem can move things right along.

▓ **Add Anchor Points with Distort and Stylize filters:** Most of the Distort filters, especially Twirl, give better results when an object has significantly more points than you originally gave it. Punk and Bloat also look better with more points.

▓ **Offset Path with Unite:** Unite zaps all the little skittles (tiny bumps and irregularities) that appear when you use the Offset Path filter.

▓ **Add Arrowheads with Outline Stroked Path and Unite:** Create the arrows, outline the original path, Select All, and select Filter⇨Pathfinder⇨Unite to create one object. You can set up a QuicKey for these filters.

Some filters are variations of other filters. The following filters are related:

▓ **Align Objects with Distribute Horizontally and Distribute Vertically:** Within Align Objects are controls for using both Distribute Horizontally and Distribute Vertically, even at the same time.

▓ **Bloat with Punk:** These two filters are opposites of each other. A negative Bloat is a Punk, and a negative Punk is a Bloat. Either way, they still have way cool names.

▓ **Scribble with Tweak:** I think the engineers at Adobe were trying to pull a fast one with these two filters. Both filters do the same thing, but Scribble is defined by a percentage, and Tweak is defined by an absolute measurement. Sneaky.

▓ **Saturate with Desaturate, Saturate More with Desaturate More:** Opposites, but three Saturate Mores followed by three Desaturate Mores will give you something darker than the original.

 See Chapter 16 for a discussion of how the saturation filters work.

Why You Can Choose the Last Filter but Never "Last Filter"

Whenever you start up Illustrator, the top menu item in the Filter menu reads "Last Filter," but it is grayed out. This causes some confusion initially. After you use a filter, its name appears where the menu once listed "Last Filter." Thereafter, the name of the last filter that you used appears at the top of the menu. The key command for reapplying the last filter is ⌘-Shift-E.

To return to the last filter's dialog box (if it has one), press Option and select Filter⇨*[Name of Last Filter]*.

Those Other Filters and Plug-Ins

A number of filters and Plug-Ins didn't fit into the following four chapters. This section discusses each of those filters.

Acrobat PDF File Format (5.5 only)

This Plug-In is automatically installed in the Plug-Ins folder. The Acrobat PDF File Format Plug-In allows Illustrator to open up PDF format files. If the PDF file consists of more than one page, then a screen will appear, asking which page to open in Illustrator. Text can be changed and modified as text, graphics can be manipulated, and the file can be saved as the PDF file or as an Illustrator document.

 Acrobat and PDF files are discussed in Chapter 9.

Artwork View Speedup

The Artwork View Speedup Plug-In is placed in the Optional Plug-Ins folder when Illustrator is installed. In order for it to be used, it needs to be moved to the Plug-Ins folder.

The Artwork View Speedup Plug-In speeds up screen redraw in Artwork View. This is achieved by using only black for all selected anchor points, direction lines, and direction points. By only using black, the screen redraw is quicker than if the selected objects were colored.

Document Info (5.5 only)

The Document Info filter is automatically placed inside the Plug-Ins folder. The filter can be selected in any document by selecting Filter⇨Other⇨Document Info.

After the filter is selected, a dialog box appears with a pop-up menu at the top. The pop-up menu consists of seven different ways to view information about the active document. At the bottom are two buttons: the Save button creates a TeachText format file with all eight categories of information about the document, while the Done button closes the dialog box.

The first option, Document, shows the document setup of the active document. All the relevant options from the Document Setup dialog box are shown, along with the name of the file.

The second menu option is Objects, which lists how many paths, masks, compound paths, custom colors, patterns, gradients, fonts, and placed EPS artwork are used in the document. This can be used as a rudimentary guide to how long a file may take to print.

 For instance, the puzzle pieces from the color insert (also available in Illustrator format on the CD-ROM) contain 4,394 paths, 6 masks, 141 compound paths, and 23 different gradients. These numbers give an indication that this file will take a bit of time to print. In fact, this file takes about 15 minutes to print to a low-end PostScript Level 2 printer at 300 DPI.

The remaining options show the names of any enclosed custom colors, patterns, gradients, and fonts. The final option, Placed Art, lists not only the name of the placed art but the disk path that tells Illustrator where to find it.

 The Save button saves the files, oddly enough, in TeachText format, a text format that cannot be read in Illustrator. To view the saved document info file you *must* double-click on the saved file or open it within a word processor.

Overprint Black (5.5 only)

The Overprint Plug-In is placed in the Optional Plug-Ins folder when Illustrator is installed. In order for it to be used, it needs to be moved to the Plug-Ins folder.

Selecting Filter⇨Other⇨Overprint Black displays the Overprint dialog box (shown in Figure 15-1), which will allow you to apply overprinting of black to selected paths. A number of options can be selected, including whether to add or remove overprinting from the selected objects. The next option is the amount of black percentage that is the minimum that will be used to overprint. Below this is a box with three radio buttons, where you can specify whether the overprinting will apply to strokes, fills, or both. Next to this box is an option to apply the new settings to the selected objects (my recommendation) or to all the objects in the document. The last options determine whether black will overprint when combined with CMY or when part of a custom color.

 The Overprint Black filter will only add overprinting to objects that are not currently overprinted when the Add button is selected, and it will remove overprinting from objects that currently have overprinting when the Remove button is selected. In no circumstances will overprinting be removed when the Add button is selected, even if the overprinting object does not fall within the parameters of the settings of the Overprint dialog box.

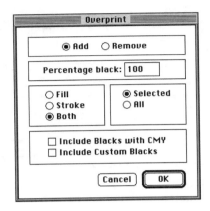

Figure 15-1:
The Overprint dialog box.

PICT File Format (5.5 only)

The PICT File Format Plug-In is automatically installed the Plug-Ins folder. This Plug-In allows you to open PICT files in Illustrator, converting them as they are opened. When a PICT file is selected in the Open dialog box and Open is selected, a dialog box appears, asking if the PICT file should be used as a template or imported into the document.

Pressure Support

The Pressure Support Plug-In is automatically installed in the Plug-Ins folder. This Plug-In allows you to use a pressure-sensitive tablet with the Brush tool to produce brush strokes of variable widths.

Make/Delete Riders

The Riders Plug-In is located in the Separator and Utilities folder, in another folder called Riders Folder. The Riders Plug-In must be moved to the Plug-Ins folder to become accessible from within Illustrator.

Riders are used to customize the output of an Illustrator file. To create a Rider, select Filter⇨Other⇨Make Riders. The Make Riders dialog box will appear, as shown in Figure 15-2.

There are six options in the Make Riders dialog box, along with a Cancel button and a Make button, which saves the Riders file. The first option, Screen Frequency, determines the halftone screen of the illustration. The second option, Flatness, determines

Figure 15-2:
The Make Riders
dialog box.

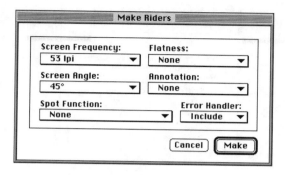

the number of pixels in the smallest segments of curved paths. The third option, Screen Angle, controls the halftone screen angle. The fourth option, Annotation, allows you to create a "note" for the illustration — you can even pick the font and font size of the note. The fifth option, Spot Function, determines the shape of the dots in halftone screens. The last option, Error Handler, determines how errors during printing are handled — whether they are printed, ignored, or displayed on-screen.

The Delete Riders filter (select Filter⇨Other⇨Delete Riders) deletes a Riders file that you specify.

The Color and Create Filters

■ ■

In This Chapter

※ How the color filters work

※ Using color to create highlights and shadows

※ Understanding the Create filters

※ Using the Fill & Stroke for Mask filter

※ Creating mosaics from PICT images

※ Adding trim marks

※ Creating stars, spirals, and polygons

※ Using advanced techniques for filters

■ ■

Manipulating Colors with the Color Filters

The color filters, which are located on the Colors submenu of the Filter menu, provide automated ways of changing colors for a variety of objects. Most of the filters work on paths that are filled with black or process color, and some of them work on the strokes of the paths as well. The table in Figure 16-1 lists all the filters and the attributes that they change.

Figure 16-1:
Illustrator's color
filters and the
attributes that
each filter
affects.

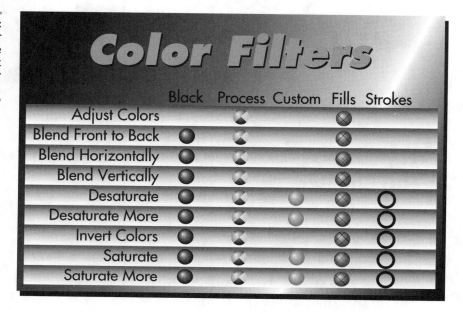

In the Color filter submenu of Illustrator 5.5, an additional filter, called Custom to Process, has been added. This filter automatically converts all custom colors to process colors, enabling most objects filled or stroked with custom colors to be affected by the color filters that do not change custom colors.

When you are working with color filters, keep in mind that using the color filters on custom colors produces process color results. Remember, too, that with the exception of the Adjust Colors filter, which works only with process colors, the color filters do not notify you when you have selected a color filter that does not work with the paths that you have selected.

Although most of the filters don't work correctly on custom colors, you can change custom colors to process colors very easily. Select an object that is filled with a custom color and choose Filter⇨Select⇨Same Fill Color. This action selects all of the objects with that tint of that custom color. Click the process color box in the Paint Style palette to have all of those objects filled with their respective process color counterparts.

Techniques for creating shadows and highlights

You can easily use color filters to create shadows and highlights for black and process colored paths.

You create most shadows by simply creating a copy of the object and placing it under, and slightly offset from, the original. You can darken the copy in a number of ways, but the easiest way is to use the Adjust Colors filter.

You create highlights in the same way as you create shadows, but instead of darkening the copy, you lighten it.

STEPS: Creating Shadows and Highlights with the Adjust Colors Filter

Step 1. Create an object that has several colors in it. I created a logo with quite a few different colors, as shown in Figure 16-2. Group the individual elements in the object.

Step 2. Copy the object and choose Edit⇨Paste In Back (⌘-B). Offset the copy down and to the right by a few points.

Step 3. Select Filter⇨Colors⇨Adjust Colors. To darken the shadowed copy evenly, add 20% to the cyan, magenta, and yellow text fields, and 40% to the black text field. Make sure that you click the Increase by radio button.

Step 4. To create the highlight, choose Edit⇨Paste In Back (⌘-B) again and decrease all four process colors by 40% if the background is dark or 20% if the background is light. My background is dark, so I reduced the color in the highlight by 40% of each color.

Figure 16-2 shows the four steps that you follow to create shadows and highlights (see Color Insert for color representation).

Creating extruded multiple path objects

You can normally make objects appear to be "extruded" by blending two objects together. If the objects contain multiple paths, however, you have to blend each of the paths separately. And if the objects contain compound paths, the blends that you create will not share the compound attributes of the original objects.

Figure 16-2: Steps for creating highlights and shadows on text (see also Color Insert).

Follow these steps to use the Blend Front To Back filter to make objects appear to be extruded.

STEPS:	**Creating "Extruded" Multiple Path Objects**
Step 1.	Release any compound paths in the object and group all the paths in the object together.
Step 2.	In the Move dialog box (select Arrange⇨Move, or press ⌘-Shift-M), enter **.25 pt** in the Horizontal text field and **.1 pt** in the Vertical text field. Click the Copy button (or press Option-Return).
Step 3.	Select Arrange⇨Repeat Transform (⌘-D) until the object has been duplicated far enough to appear 3-D. Copy the final duplicate object (it should still be selected).
Step 4.	Change the color of the final duplicate object to be the color of the frontmost part of the blend. In the example based on the steps in this chapter, I made the final duplicate object black ("Tonight" in Figure 16-9) and left the rest of the objects red. (The color insert shows the result.)
Step 5.	Select all the objects and choose Filter⇨Colors⇨Blend Front to Back.
Step 6.	Select Edit⇨Paste In Front (⌘-F) and give a different color to the object just pasted. In the example, I used yellow. Select Object⇨Compound Path⇨Make (⌘-8) and then Arrange⇨Hide (⌘-3).
Step 7.	Continue to select each grouped object, making each group a compound path and then hiding it, until all the paths are hidden. If you have QuickKeys or Tempo II, set up a macro to make this step a one-key procedure. I used F1. This process went really fast because all I had to do was click and press F1, click and press F1, and so on.
Step 8.	After you have hidden all the paths, choose Arrange⇨Show All (⌘-4) and then group all the paths together.

Do not make all the paths one compound path, or the color information for each path will be lost.

Creating negatives

You can produce negative images in Illustrator almost automatically by using the Invert Colors filters. For a process color, the Invert Colors filter subtracts the tints of cyan, magenta, and yellow from 100% and leaves black as is. On an object that is filled or stroked with black only, the filter subtracts the tint of black from 100%.

To get around the way that this filter works when creating negatives, select all the objects that you want to reverse. Next, choose Filter⇨Colors⇨Invert Colors and then select each path and check whether the paths have a process color fill that contains black. If you find any fills that contain black, manually change black to the correct value.

 After you check a path to see whether it is a process color that contains black, hide that path. Using this method can help you be sure that you have checked every path, and you do not have to worry about wasting time by rechecking paths.

Instant Creations with the Create Filters

The Create filters fall into two categories: special creations and shape creations. The special creations include using the Fill & Stroke for Mask filter, creating mosaics from PICT images, and adding trim marks to an object. Shape creations include stars, polygons, and spirals.

As with most filters, you can manually perform every function that the Create filters do, but using the filters is much easier.

Adding strokes and fills to masks

 When you turn a masking path into a mask, any Paint Style attributes that the masking path had before it was a mask are removed, and you cannot give it any Paint Style attributes. If you select a masking path, the Paint Style palette shows a fill and stroke of None. (Creating masks is discussed in Chapter 11.)

Follow these steps to add a stroke and fill to a mask.

STEPS:	Adding a Stroke and Fill to a Mask
Step 1.	Create a mask and masked object.
Step 2.	Select the masking path and choose the stroke and fill that you want to give to the masking path. As you choose and apply the fill and stroke, the mask will not show these changes.
Step 3.	Select Filter⇨Create⇨Stroke & Fill for Mask. The masking path will have the fill and stroke you requested.

The Create Stroke & Fill for Mask filter creates two copies of the original masking path. It places the first copy under all of the masked items and fills it with the fill that you chose in the Paint Style palette before you applied the filter. It places the second copy above the mask and gives it the stroke that you specified in the Paint Style palette.

 If either the fill or stroke for the masking object is set to None before you activate the filter, a dialog box appears, telling you that the Stroke & Fill for Mask filter applies the fill and stroke in the Paint dialog box to the mask. Whenever this message appears, I always look at my Paint Style palette to make sure that I did indeed select the mask before I made changes to the values in the Paint Style palette.

 Group the masking objects, the masking path, the filled masking path, and the stroked masking path to ensure that all the objects in the mask stay together.

Creating mosaics

Mosaics are images that are made up of a series of squares. Each of the squares contains one color. The more squares, the more detail in the mosaic. Bitmapped images are mosaics of a sort, with each pixel equal to 1 square.

Creating Mosaics in Illustrator changes a color or grayscale PICT image to a series of Illustrator squares. Each of the squares corresponds to a color in the original image.

 If you do not have software that creates PICT files, but you have created a file on-screen that you want to save as a PICT file, press ⌘-Shift-3. You will hear a noise that is similar to the sound that a shutter on a camera makes, and a PICT file will be created out of whatever is on-screen. The file is saved on the start-up drive as Picture 1. Additional screen shots are saved as Picture 2, Picture 3, and so on.

Follow these steps to create a fairly simple and basic mosaic in Illustrator.

STEPS: Creating a Mosaic

Step 1. Create or scan a PICT file. You do not need to use a high-resolution PICT file. The Illustrator mosaic will look just as good when you convert a 72 dots per inch (DPI) PICT file as when you convert a 300 DPI PICT file.

Step 2.   Choose Filters⇨Create⇨Mosaic. An open dialog box will appear. Select the file that you want to convert. In the Mosaic dialog box, enter the size that you want the mosaic to be and also the number of tiles across and down. Click the Use Ratio button to keep the same proportions as in the original image.

Step 3.   Click OK when you are satisfied with the information that you have entered in the Mosaic dialog box. Figure 16-3 shows the results that are produced by entering three different tile widths and heights into the Number of Tiles boxes.

   The number of tiles that Illustrator can produce is strictly limited and is directly related to the amount of RAM that is allocated to Illustrator. Exceeding the limit will cause Illustrator to create only a portion of the tiles.

You can create some very exciting effects with the Mosaic filter when you use it in conjunction with other filters. The best ones to use with it are Rotate Each, Scale Each, Move Each, Round Corners, all of the Distort filters, and most of the color filters. In the following example, I combined the Mosaic filter with the Round Corners and Move Each filters.

STEPS: Creating a Seurat-like Illustration

Step 1.   Create a mosaic with an average number of tiles (between 1,600 and 10,000 tiles, which would be from 40x40 to 100x100). In the example shown in Figure 16-4, I used a mosaic with 50x63 tiles, or 3,150 tiles total.

Step 2.   Select all the mosaic tiles and choose Filters⇨Stylize⇨Round Corners. In the Round Corners dialog box, enter a large number. I usually enter at least 10 pt. As long as the tiles are not larger than 20 points wide, the Round Corners filter will turn all the tiles into circles.

Step 3.   Copy all the tiles and choose Edit⇨Paste In Front (⌘-F). Select all the tiles (the image now has 6,300 tiles) and choose Filter⇨Objects⇨Move Each. In the Move Each dialog box, enter **5** in both text fields and check the Random check box. Click OK. If you want less white space between all the circles, choose Edit⇨Paste In Front (⌘-F) again and then choose Filter⇨Move Each (at the top of the Filter menu, ⌘-Shift-E). The results should look similar to Step 3 in Figure 16-4.

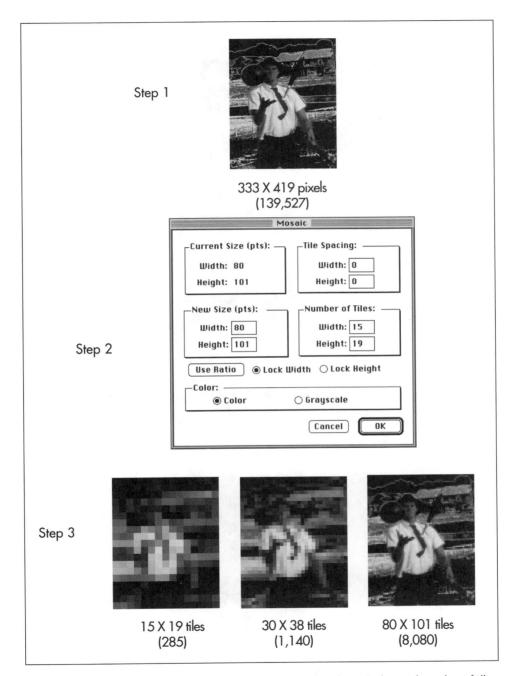

Figure 16-3: Steps for creating mosaics. (The number in parentheses is the total number of tiles required to create the mosaic.)

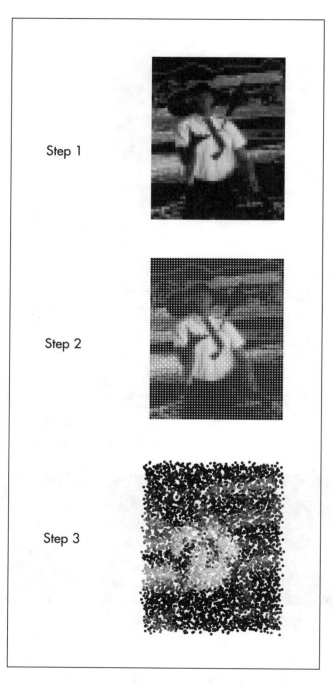

Step 1

Step 2

Step 3

The tiles created with the mosaic filter are placed on the page from top left to bottom right. The top left tile is underneath all the other tiles (in the back), and the bottom right tile is on top of all other tiles (in the front). The tiles are butted up against each other, so none of them overlap each other.

Because of the way that these tiles overlap each other, you can create a tiled or shingled roof quite easily, providing the original image is upside down. The steps below describe this process in detail.

STEPS: Creating a Tiled Roof

Step 1. Create a PICT file to be used as the roof. In the example shown in Figure 16-5, I created the name of a restaurant. Then I took a screen shot of it (⌘-Shift-3) that I opened in Photoshop so that I could delete the surrounding objects.

Step 2. In Photoshop or another bitmap image editing program, rotate the image 135° clockwise. Save it as a PICT file. In Illustrator, select Filter⇨Create⇨Mosaic. Open the file, make the number of tiles across about 50 or more, and click the Use Ratio button.

Step 3. Rotate the entire mosaic by 135°. Using the Selection tool, draw a marquee around any white squares above, below, to the left, and to the right of the roof area to select them. Delete all white squares. Because the squares are white, you may need to switch to Artwork mode to see them all.

It may seem strange that the mosaic gets rotated twice, but there is a method to this seemingly mad busywork. By placing the upper lefthand tiles on the bottom and the lower righthand tiles on the top, the image is rotated first in Photoshop so that the lower parts of the image are turned into squares first. By the way, if I hadn't helped put shingles on a roof recently (you have to work from the bottom up), I would never have been able to figure this out. So I guess that this is one of those "real life" examples, huh?

Step 4. Select the remaining tiles and group them. Choose Filter⇨Object⇨Add Anchor Points to add one anchor point to every side of every square in the mosaic. Choose Filter⇨Stylize⇨Punk to make all the points on each square come out a little.

Step 5. To round off the points and make the squares smoother, select Filter⇨Stylize⇨Round Corners, and enter **10 pt** in the text field. Choose Filter⇨Objects⇨Scale Each and enter **150** in both the width and height fields. Because the squares were scaled up, they now overlap.

Step 6.   Select Filter⊏>Objects⊏>Rotate Each, and enter **45°**. In the Paint Style palette, give each tile a black stroke of .25 point. Depending on the size of the tiles, the stroke weight may vary.

Step 7.   Use the Distort filter (select Filter⊏>Distort⊏>Free Distort) to change the shape of the roof to be more, well, rooflike.

Figure 16-5: Creating a tiled roof with the Mosaic filter.

The following steps describe how to make the tiles in a mosaic overlap with no white space between them. This technique can easily create a background image or a funky illustration, as shown in the steps and used in context in Figure 16-6.

Figure 16-6:
Creating a mosaic that has
uneven tile spacing.

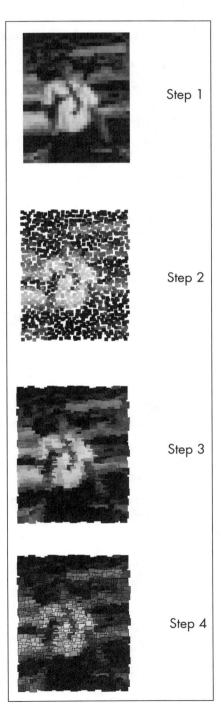

Step 1

Step 2

Step 3

Step 4

STEPS: **Creating Random Overlapping Tiles with No White Space**

Step 1. Create a mosaic from a PICT file.

Step 2. Select Filter⇨Object⇨Move Each, and enter the amount of movement for the tiles. Check the Random box. Measure one tile with the Measure tool. The tiles that I created for the example shown in Figure 16-6 are 3.3 points across, and the move distance that I used is 3.3 points. The most white space between any two tiles is 6.6 points.

Step 3. Select Filter⇨Object⇨Scale Each. Enter the percentage that the tile must be scaled up to eliminate the white space. In the example, I entered 200%.

Step 4. To see the edges of the tiles more easily, place a .25-pt. black stroke on them.

By using the Mosaic filter in combination with the blend colors filters, color sets can be created very easily. These color sets can be sampled for inclusion into the Paint Style palette or just used as a separate palette document (this is what I use them for), off to the side of your working document.

STEPS: **Creating Color Sets with the Mosaic Filter**

Step 1. Create a mosaic from any PICT file, making the total number of tiles equal to the number of different tiles that you want in the color set.

Step 2. Change the colors of the tiles that mark the beginning and end of each color set. In the example (Figure 16-7), I used primary colors and white as the beginning and end of each color set.

Step 3. Select one range of color and choose Filter⇨Color⇨Blend Front to Back to blend the colors from the upper lefthand tiles towards the lower righthand tiles. Repeat this step for each range of colors.

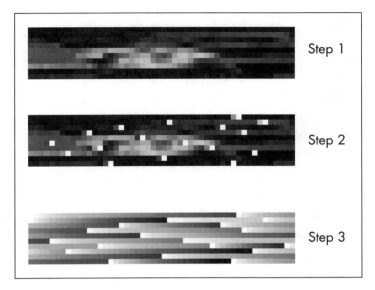

Figure 16-7:
Using the
Mosaic filter to
create color sets.

Step 1

Step 2

Step 3

Adding trim marks

Illustrator offers you the option of placing crop marks around any one rectangle by selecting the rectangle and choosing Object⇨Cropmarks⇨Make. This option works only on rectangles and only on one rectangle per document.

You can create more than one set of crop marks in a document manually, or you can use the Trim Marks filter.

To use the Trim Marks filter, select the objects that you want to place trim marks on and then choose Filter⇨Create⇨Trim Marks. Eight marks will appear for each object, two in each corner.

If the object is going to be color separated, you need to create additional trim marks on top of the original set of trim marks, making one set for each color in the illustration. If the illustration is a process color illustration with four process colors, you need to create three additional sets of trim marks.

The following steps describe how to create trim marks for process color illustrations and for illustrations that have spot colors.

STEPS: **Creating Trim Marks for Process Color Illustrations**

Step 1. Create the first set of trim marks by selecting the objects that the trim marks will surround and choosing Filter⇨Create⇨Trim Marks.

Step 2. Select the trim marks and change the stroke color to 100% of cyan, magenta, yellow, and black.

STEPS: **Creating Trim Marks for Illustrations with Spot Colors**

Step 1. Create trim marks and select them.

Step 2. Check the Overprint Stroke box in the Paint Style palette.

Step 3. Copy the trim marks and choose Edit⇨Paste In Front (⌘-F).

Step 4. Change the stroke color of the newly pasted trim marks to one of the spot colors.

Step 5. Repeat Steps 3 and 4 until you have a set of trim marks for each spot color.

 If the illustration does not contain any black, be sure to get rid of or change any black trim marks to a color that is in the illustration, or a black plate will be printed when the file is color separated.

Creating Polygons, Stars, and Spirals

The three Create filters that automatically generate polygons, stars, and spirals are enormous time-savers. Anyone who has had to create one of these objects without the filters can attest that the process is time consuming and monotonous.

 Chapter 5 discusses the basics of creating polygons and stars with the Create filters.

Using the Create filters to produce special effects

Illustrator enables you to use many special effects with the Create filters. For example, follow these steps to create a folded fan.

STEPS: **Creating a Folded Fan**

Step 1. Create a star with 20 points, a first radius of 20, and a second radius of 50.

Step 2. Select Object⇨Attributes and check the Show Center Point box. Use the Direct Selection tool to select every other inner point. With the Scale tool, click to set the origin on the center of the object. Press the Shift key and drag out towards the outer points of the star. Step 2 in Figure 16-8 shows what the illustration looks like at this stage.

Step 3. Select the remaining inner points and drag them towards the center of the star.

Step 4. Use the Pen tool to draw a line that precisely crosses the inner points of the outer edges, as shown in Figure 16-8. Use the Selection tool to select both the line and the star and then choose Filter⇨Objects⇨Align Objects. Click the Center radio buttons in each column to align both the pen drawn line and the star at their centers.

Step 5. Select just the line and double-click the Rotate tool. Enter **18°** in the Angle text field and click the Copy button (Option-Return). (You enter 18° in the Angle text field because 360°/20 (number of points on the star) = 18°.) To copy the line through each piece of the star, select Arrange⇨Repeat Transform (⌘-D) as many times as necessary.

Step 6. Select all the lines and the star and choose Filter⇨Pathfinder⇨Divide Fill to divide the fill of the star into separate sections.

Step 7. Select each piece of the star and color it differently. In the example, I used the same color for each piece and then made one half of each piece lighter than the other half.

Step 8. Double-click the Rotate tool and enter an angle that is a multiple of 36. In the example (see Figure 16-8), I then grouped the star, copied it, and chose Edit⇨Paste In Back (⌘-B). I offset the copy a few points down and to the right and filled the copied star with black to create a shadow.

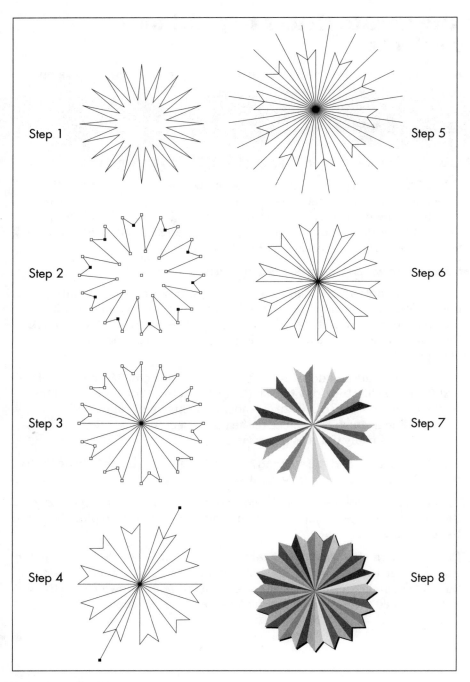

Figure 16-8: Creating a folded fan.

You can avoid Steps 2, 3, and 8 by creating a star with 40 points, instead of 20 points, and then rotating the line by 9° instead of by 18°.

Use the Direct Selection tool to select the inner points and drag the points off center to make the fan seem more 3-D.

You can use the Round Corners filter to turn a star into a seal.

STEPS: Creating a Seal

Step 1. Create a star with 20 – 30 points and make the first and second radius values different by about 10 points.

Step 2. Select the star and choose Filter⇨Stylize⇨Round Corners. Enter **10 pt** in the Round Corners dialog box to round off the points of the star and create a shape that looks like a seal. The result, when colored, looks something like the seal that you see in Figure 16-9 (see Color Insert for color representation).

You can give the seal a metallic look by filling it with a gradient that goes from a metallic color (silver or gold) to white and back to metallic a few times.

Figure 16-9:
A restaurant ad that includes many of the effects described in this chapter. The insert in the center of this book shows this ad in color.

If you want to create a star that has rounded tips but not rounded inner corners, follow these steps.

STEPS: Creating Stars That Have Rounded Tips

Step 1.   Create a star and copy it.

Step 2.   Select the star and choose Filter⇨Stylize⇨Round Corners. In the Round Corner dialog box, type **10.** The star will have rounded tips, but the inside corners will be rounded as well.

Step 3.   Select the star with the rounded corners and choose Edit⇨Paste In Back (⌘-B). The rounded-corner star will be directly under the pointed star.

Step 4.   Select both stars and choose Filter⇨Pathfinder⇨Crop Fill.

To create a star with pointed tips and rounded inside corners, choose Filter⇨Pathfinder⇨Unite instead of Crop Fill.

You can achieve interesting effects by combining spirals with shapes. Follow these steps to create a clay star.

STEPS: Creating a Clay Star

Step 1.   Create a five-point rounded tip star with $^{25}\!/_{100}$-point radii.

Step 2.   Create an eight-wind spiral with a 100-point radius. The spiral should appear directly on top of the star. Rotate the star 45° by double-clicking the Rotate tool and entering **45°** in the dialog box.

Step 3.   Select both the star and the spiral and choose Filter⇨Pathfinder⇨Divide Fill. Ungroup (⌘-U) all the pieces. (They become grouped when the Divide Fill command is used.) Delete all the excess pieces that are outside the star shape.

Step 4.   Select the innermost pieces individually and choose Filter⇨Pathfinder⇨ Unite for each of them. The Divide Fill command (especially in Version 5.0) may create some very odd anchor points that the Unite filter can fix.

Step 5.   Select all the pieces in the star and choose Filter⇨Stylize⇨Round Corners. In the Round Corners dialog box, enter **3 pt.**

Sometimes, some of the rounded paths may go a little wacky, sending part of the path outside the Artboard. When this happens, select Edit⇨Undo (⌘-Z) to undo the Round Corners filter and select the path that went wacky and then choose Filter⇨Pathfinder⇨Unite. Use the Unite filter on any paths that were out of control. The filter should keep problems from occurring when you round the paths.

Step 6. Color each of the pieces as you would clay. In the example (Figure 16-10), after I colored the pieces, I grouped them all and copied and pasted in back twice, using the Adjust Colors filter to lighten one copy and darken the other.

As the next example shows, you can use a spiral mask to create ripple effects, making it seem like the object is floating in liquid.

STEPS: **Creating Ripple Effects**

Step 1. Create a spiral with five winds and a radius of 50 points. Give the path a six-point stroke and choose Filter⇨Object⇨Outline Stroked Path.

Step 2. Place the path over the object to be masked and copy the object to the Clipboard by selecting Edit⇨Copy (⌘-C). The copy will be used later.

Step 3. Select both the object to be masked and the spiral path. Choose Object⇨Mask⇨Make.

Step 4. Scale the mask and masking object 115% from the center of the spiral. Choose Edit⇨Paste In Back (⌘-B). This will paste the original object (which you copied in Step 2) behind the spiral-masked object. Figure 16-11 shows these four steps and the results.

Creating patterns with polygons

You can use only three polygons to create patterns where all the tiles are the same size and shape and all of them butt up against each other evenly with no extra spaces. Those three polygons are triangles, rectangles, and hexagons. Any patterns that you create with polygons other than triangles, rectangles, and hexagons have either abnormal spacing between the polygons or bizarre shapes between some polygons.

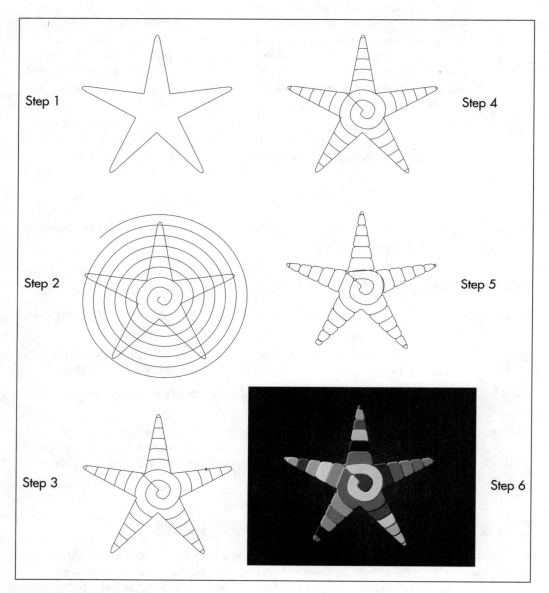

Figure 16-10: Steps for creating a clay star.

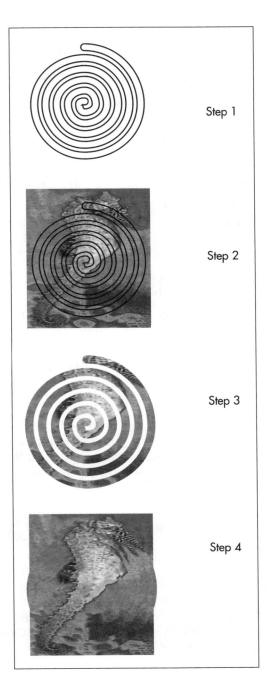

Step 1

Step 2

Step 3

Step 4

Don't waste time trying to prove me wrong; I've wasted enough time proving it for everyone reading this book. Instead, take advantage of the many ways to create interesting and different patterns by using just triangles, rectangles, and hexagons. By distorting, stretching, or filling these objects with other patterns, you can produce quite impressive results. For example, try the following instructions for creating 3-D block steps and an empty honeycomb.

STEPS: Creating 3-D Block Steps

Step 1. Create a six-sided polygon (a hexagon) with a 50-point radius.

Step 2. Using the Direct Selection tool, copy the two bottom segments and paste them. Move the copied sections under the two topmost segments, as shown in Figure 16-12. Copy a vertical segment and paste it, moving it to the center of the hexagon.

Step 3. Still using the Direct Selection tool, copy four segments at a time and paste them as shown in Figure 16-12. Delete the original hexagon.

Step 4. Use the ⌘-Option-J key command to average and join all the points together in each corner of the three sections. Fill each of the sections with a gradient for the best effect.

Step 5. Drag the pieces together and group them. Duplicate the entire cube as many times as necessary to form the pattern.

 In order to use gradients in a pattern, you need to replace the gradients with blends. To automatically convert any gradients to blends, save the file with gradients in Illustrator 3 and then close and reopen it. When you reopen the file, all the objects that contained gradients will contain blends instead.

STEPS: Creating an Empty Honeycomb Pattern

Step 1. Create a hexagon with a 50-point radius.

Step 2. Option-copy (hold down the Option key, drag an object, and release the mouse button *before* the Option key) the hexagon to the right, putting a small amount of space between the two hexagons. Select Arrange⇨Repeat Transform to create another evenly spaced hexagon. Figure 16-13 shows the distance I used in the example.

Step 3.   Manually moving objects at a precise angle is difficult unless the angle is a multiple of 45°. In this case, you can use two methods to copy and offset the hexagon equally from the other sides.

Choose Arrange⇨Move (⌘-Shift-M). In the Move dialog box, the distance that you moved the last object will still be in the Distance text field. If you select the center hexagon and change the Angle setting to 60°, you can copy another hexagon into the correct position and repeat this process until you have seven hexagons.

An easier method, though, is to select all three hexagons and then double-click the Rotate tool. Enter **60°** and click Copy (Option-Return). Select Arrange⇨Repeat Transform (⌘-D), which will move and duplicate the hexagon again. Delete the two extra center hexagons that were created, and the hexagons will be spaced apart perfectly.

Step 4.   Select all the hexagons, choose Object⇨Attributes (⌘-Control-A), and check the Show Center Point check box. Draw a rectangle from the center of one hexagon to the center of another (two diagonally opposite corners of the rectangle should each be positioned over the center of a hexagon). Copy the rectangle.

Step 5.   Select the hexagons and the rectangle and choose Filter⇨Pathfinder⇨Front Minus Back. Choose Edit⇨Paste In Back (⌘-B), change the fill of the rectangle to None, and change the stroke to None. Fill the hexagon path with the color that you want the honeycomb to be.

Step 6.   Select both the rectangle and the honeycomb shape and make it into a pattern by selecting Object⇨Pattern and clicking the New button in the Pattern dialog box.

Figure 16-12:
Creating a cube pattern from
a hexagon.

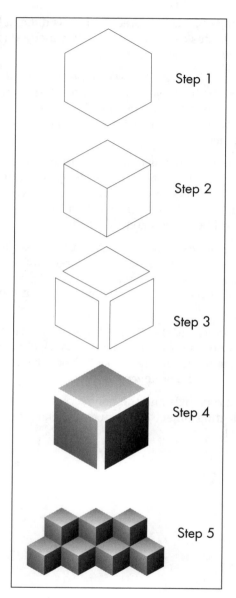

Step 1

Step 2

Step 3

Step 4

Step 5

Figure 16-13:
Creating an empty
honeycomb pattern.

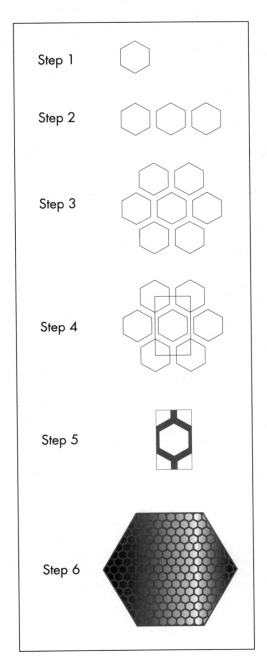

Step 1

Step 2

Step 3

Step 4

Step 5

Step 6

The Distort and Stylize Filters

In This Chapter

- Why the Distort and Stylize filters are so much alike
- Understanding the Distort filters
- Using the Free Distort filter
- Using the Twirl filter
- Using the three Random Mangle filters
- Understanding the Stylize filters
- Adding arrowheads to paths
- Bloating and punking
- Turning a path into "calligraphy"
- Creating drop shadows
- Rounding corners

See, I Told You So: There Are Real Filters in Illustrator

Most of the filters in Illustrator don't have any right to be called *filters,* but the filters in the Distort and Stylize submenus do. These filters twist and warp artwork in the best of filter traditions.

The only thing that puzzles me about these filters is why Adobe put them in the categories they're in. In particular, the Bloat and Punk filters seem to be better suited for the Distort submenu. I tend to think that the Stylize filters are in that category because Adobe didn't want to call the Stylize submenu the *Miscellaneous Junk submenu.* The Object submenu isn't much better, but you can read all about that in Chapter 18.

The filters in both submenus *do something* to selected paths. With the exception of the Add Arrowheads and Drop Shadow filters, all the Distort and Stylize filters reshape paths. They pull and push anchor points and direction points, and sometimes they even create new anchor points and direction points.

The Distort Filters

The Distort filters are the most "fun" filters that Illustrator has to offer as a group. Each one of the filters can turn an ordinary drawing into something really wacky. But the true power of the Distort filters becomes apparent when you use them sparingly with very small values entered in their text fields.

The Distort filters fall into two categories. The first category is the reshaping category, which includes the Free Distort filter and the Twirl filter. These filters change selected paths in a way that would be very difficult with conventional Illustrator tools and commands. When you work with these filters, you can know fairly accurately what the results will be.

In the second category are the Random Mangling filters. The Roughen, Scribble, and Tweak filters all mangle artwork in a random way. If you set their values too high, the filters will remove from the paths any resemblance to the way the paths looked before the filters distorted them. The Bloat and Punk filters, had Adobe chosen to make them Distort filters instead of Stylize filters, would be Nonrandom Mangling filters. Unlike with the reshaping filters, you cannot accurately determine what the results of using the Random Mangling filters will be, even though you have a great deal of control over them.

The Free Distort filter

Selecting Filter⇨Distort⇨Free Distort displays the Free Distort dialog box. Within this dialog box is a representative sample of the selected artwork surrounded by four corner handles. You adjust and move the four handles to change the shape of the object.

Reshaping artwork was very time consuming in previous versions of Illustrator. You used the Scale tool on individual points and segments, scaling a little more for each successive row of points. Before Illustrator 5.0 was released, the only widely used software that could distort freely was Broderbund's TypeStyler, but its exceedingly clunky and awkward interface and its requirement that artwork be in a font (with all colors removed) made the process cumbersome at best.

The following steps describe how to use the Free Distort filter:

STEPS: Using the Free Distort Filter

Step 1. Create the artwork that you want to distort. In the example in Figure 17-1, I used text converted to outlines.

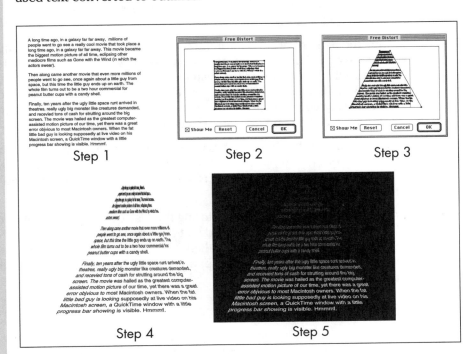

Figure 17-1: Steps for using the Free Distort filter.

Before you can distort text in the Free Distort dialog box, you have to convert it to outlines. Although you can distort Rectangle type, Path type, and Area type without converting it to outlines, only the paths that the type is in or on will be distorted.

The Free Distort filter does not work with placed EPS images or with type that has not been converted to outlines. Nor does the Free Distort filter affect patterns or gradients that are being used as fills.

Step 2.   Select Filter⇨Distort⇨Free Distort. The Free Distort dialog box appears, containing a line art (artwork only) view of the selected paths that you want to distort.

If the artwork is very complex, you may want to uncheck the Show Me check box. A rectangle will appear instead of the complex artwork. For this example, I found that adjusting the rectangle without seeing the artwork was much easier because the artwork contained several hundred compound paths that Illustrator had to redraw.

Step 3.   Move the handles around until the artwork is reshaped to your liking. If you don't have the Show Me button checked while you are moving the handles around, click it to preview the reshaped artwork when you think the handles are in a good position. Then if you realize that the artwork doesn't look the way you want it to look, you can make changes without having to choose the Undo command and select the filter again.

Step 4.   Click the OK button to have the reshaped artwork appear in the document. If the artwork is complex, you may want to group everything that was distorted. Or if you are really conscientious, you may have grouped everything already.

Step 5.   Add any finishing touches by coloring the distorted artwork. I placed a black background behind the distorted text and then filled the text with the Black & White gradient. I used the Gradient Vector tool to drag upwards, starting in the bottom-middle of the last paragraph and dragging up to the top line of type.

You can use the Free Distort filter to create artwork that twists. In the Free Distort dialog box, simply create an X pattern with the rectangle. To do so, switch the handles on one edge of the rectangle. Depending on the type of twist, the artwork will turn upside down or become reversed. By combining different twists, you can produce ribbonlike effects. For example, Figure 17-2 shows a banner that has two different twists.

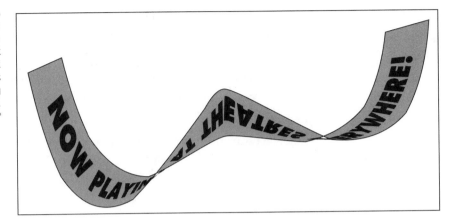

Figure 17-2:
A double twist in the Free Distort dialog box produced this flipping, twisting banner.

After you use the Free Distort filter, the handle positions are remembered in the dialog box. If you use the filter again during the same Illustrator session, those settings are immediately applied to the artwork. Press the Reset button to force the handles (and the artwork) back to their original positions.

You can pull the handles in the Free Distort dialog box right out of the dialog box and stretch them as far as the monitor is wide or tall. The catch in this maneuver is that when you release the mouse button on a handle that you have dragged outside the dialog box, you can no longer select that handle. The only way to recover the handle is to click the Reset button, which resets all the handles to their original positions, but does not change the previous distorted image much.

The Twirl filter

Like the Free Distort filter, the Twirl filter reshapes objects in ways that would be time consuming and tedious if you were using conventional Illustrator methods. The Twirl filter moves the innermost points a certain number of degrees around a circle. The farther away the points are from the center of the circle, the less they move; and the points at the outermost edges of the object hardly rotate at all.

The *Macworld Illustrator Bible* CD-ROM contains a Twirl filter chart that shows exactly what happens to various objects when you twirl them at various numbers of degrees and add different numbers of anchor points prior to twirling them.

To achieve twirl effects without the Twirl filter in older versions of Illustrator, I used the Rotate tool in the same way that I used the Scale tool to create effects that were similar to the ones that the Free Distort filter creates. No software could "twirl" PostScript outlines before Adobe introduced this filter, so no reasonable workaround existed. If you needed a twirl effect, the best thing to do was to convert your Illustrator drawing to a bitmap image and twirl the object in Photoshop, which has had a Twirl filter since Version 1.0.

The Twirl filter can twirl single paths or multiple paths. When it twirls multiple paths, the twirling takes place from the center of the entire group of objects, not from within each object. Follow these steps to use the Twirl filter:

STEPS: **Using the Twirl Filter**

Step 1. Create the artwork that you want to use with the Twirl filter. In the example in Figure 17-3, I created a star with several points and a tiny first (inner) radius. Then I selected the center points with the Direct Selection tool and dragged them down and to the left.

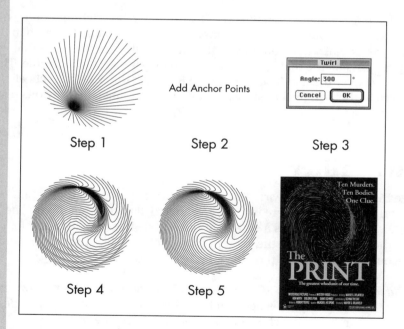

Figure 17-3: Steps for using the Twirl filter.

The constraints on the Twirl filter are similar to the constraints on the Free Distort filter. You cannot twirl EPS images, type that has not been converted to outlines, or patterns and gradients that are used as fills.

Step 2. Select the artwork that you want to twirl. Choose Filter⇨Object⇨Add Anchor Points to double the number of anchor points on the object. Add anchor points a few more times. The more anchor points you add, the better the end result of a twirl will be.

Adding too many anchor points may make the paths too complex to preview, and sometimes certain paths get too many points. If you see a dialog box that shows the progress for the Add Anchor Points filter on a 68040 or later machine, don't use the filter a second time.

Step 3. Select Filter⇨Distort⇨Twirl to see the Twirl dialog box. Enter the number of degrees that you want to twirl objects. In the example, I used 300°.

Entering a positive number in the Angle text field twirls the object clockwise; entering a negative number twirls the object counterclockwise. This setting works the opposite way from how the degree setting for the Rotate tool works.

Step 4. Examine the twirled artwork. If you didn't add enough anchor points, the edges may look like a bunch of broken twigs, which is usually an undesirable way for paths to appear. If the result is totally unacceptable, undo the Twirl filter (select Edit⇨Undo or press ⌘-Z) and select the Add Anchor Points filter until you think that you have added enough points; then twirl the object again.

Step 5. Select the artwork and choose Filter⇨Stylize⇨Round Corners. Enter a fairly large number to smooth out all the nasties that the Twirl filter created.

I wanted the twirled artwork in the example to resemble a fingerprint, so I used the Scale and Rotate tools and then the Scribble filter (see the section "The Scribble and Tweak filters" later in this chapter) to achieve the desired effect. After scribbling the artwork just .5 percent horizontally and vertically, I added the background and the accompanying text. A larger version of the resulting poster is in the color section of the book.

You can twirl paths up to 4,000° in both directions (4,000 and −4,000).

The Twirl filter by itself enables you to create many different effects. By moving different objects to different positions, the Twirl filter can produce entirely different results. For example, follow these steps to create an arc in an illustration:

STEPS:	Creating Arced Illustrations with the Twirl Filter
Step 1.	Create the type that you want to arc and convert it to outlines.
Step 2.	Make a copy of the type to the left of the original type and place an object between the two areas of type. Then place the same object at either end of the words. At this point, the illustration looks like Step 2 of Figure 17-4.
	In addition, you may want to add anchor points (select Filter⇨Object⇨Add Anchor Points) to the portions of the image you plan to keep. I added anchor points to the second rectangle from the right.
Step 3.	Select the objects and select Filter⇨Twirl. In the Twirl dialog box, enter **90°** and press OK.
Step 4.	Delete all the portions of the path except for the one shown.
Step 5.	Select the remaining portion and choose Filter⇨Distort⇨Free Distort. Move the handles so that the paths resemble the lower part of an arc.
Step 6.	Click OK.

The Random Mangle filters

The three Random Mangle filters — Roughen, Scribble, and Tweak — all do similar things to paths. Roughen adds anchor points and then moves them randomly by a percentage that you define. Scribble and Tweak randomly move existing anchor points and direction points by a percentage or by an absolute measurement that you define.

The *Macworld Illustrator Bible* CD-ROM contains a Distort Filter chart that shows what happens to various objects when you mangle them differently.

Because the mangle filters work randomly, you get different results when you apply the same settings of the same filter to two separate, identical objects. In fact, the results will probably never be duplicated. The mangle filters are a good reason for having the Undo command.

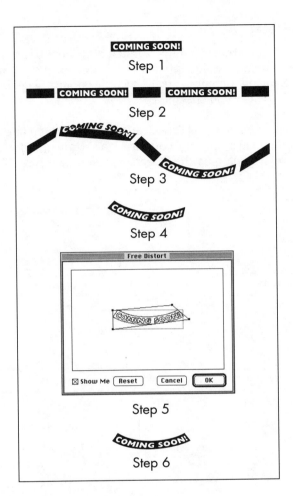

Figure 17-4:
Steps for creating arced illustrations with the Twirl filter.

 Using the keyboard, you can continuously reapply any filter that works randomly and get different results. Select the object and apply the filter by dragging the mouse to the menu item and entering the values. If you don't like the result, press ⌘-Z (Undo) and ⌘-Shift-E (reapply last filter).

One important limitation of the mangle filters is that they work on entire paths, even if only part of the path is selected. The only way to get around this limitation is to use the Scissors tool to cut the path into different sections.

The Roughen filter

The Roughen filter does two things at once. First, it adds anchor points until the selection has the number of points per inch that you defined. Second, it randomly moves all the points around, changing them into Straight Corner points (Jagged) or Smooth points (Rounded), whichever you specified.

Using the Roughen filter on a path is fairly straightforward, but using it on a portion of artwork is not. The following steps take you through setting up artwork so that only a portion of the artwork is affected by the Roughen filter (see Figure 17-5).

Figure 17-5:
Steps for
creating a
tear in a path.

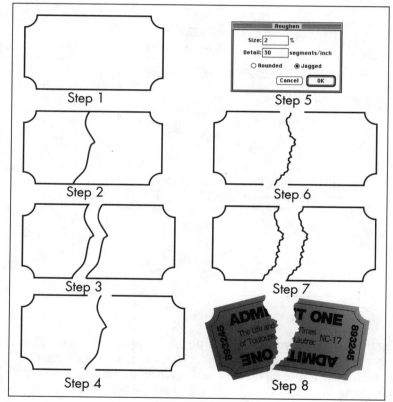

STEPS:	**Creating a Tear with the Roughen Filter**

Step 1. Create the artwork that you want to tear.

Step 2. Select the Pen tool and click from one edge of the artwork to another, crossing the path that you want to tear. If you don't want the tear to be straight, click additional points to change direction. If you want a curved tear, make the path curved. Connect the path by continuing around the outside of the artwork.

Step 3. Select the artwork and the path. Select Filter⇨Pathfinder⇨Divide. Ungroup and select Edit⇨Deselect All (⌘-Shift-A). Select the paths on one side of the tear and drag them away from the remaining paths.

Step 4. Using the Scissors tool, click on the ends of the tear on one side of the split path. Drag the cut section away from the rest of the path. On the other half of the tear, cut that tear away and delete it as well.

Step 5. Select Filter⇨Distort⇨Roughen to see the Roughen dialog box. In the Size text field, enter the percentage that you want the anchor points to be moved. In the example, I used 2% to move the points just slightly.

Next, determine how many points you want to add to the tear. I chose 30 points per inch. Then decide on the type of roughen: Rounded or Jagged. A Rounded roughen produces smooth points with direction points that stick out a very small amount from the anchor point, and a Jagged roughen has only Straight Corner anchor points.

Step 6. Click OK and check the newly roughened path to ensure that it is roughened correctly. If it isn't, or if you don't like the random movement of the anchor points, choose Edit⇨Undo (⌘-Z) and select the filter dialog box again (press Option and select Filter⇨Distort⇨Roughen). Continue undoing and roughening until the artwork is the way you want it or just adjust the anchor points with the Direct Selection tool.

Step 7. Option-copy the roughened path to the edge of the path that it was torn from. The best way to perform this task is to click on an end point with the Selection tool and drag to the end point of the existing path with the Option key pressed. Average and join the points (⌘-Option-J). Move the original roughened path to the other side of the path and average and join both points.

I usually zoom in, sometimes all the way to 1600%, to make sure that the two points are directly on top of each other and that only two points are selected.

Step 8. Add any other artwork to the torn paths. In the example, I rotated each of the sides a small amount.

The Roughen filter has a secret function that very few people know about: You can use it to add anchor points to paths. Simply enter **0%** in the first text field, and the points that are added will not be moved at all.

This method is especially useful as a substitute for the Add Anchor Points filter when some of the paths in a compound path don't need as many additional anchor points as others. The Roughen filter evens out the number of points for each of the paths in a compound path. I used the Roughen filter to add points to the artwork in Figure 17-4 before I twirled it. The type had a large number of anchor points, but the surrounding box did not. I used Roughen to give each path the same number of anchor points per inch.

If you want roughened edges to be *really* rounded, don't choose the Rounded option in the Roughen dialog box. Instead, choose the Jagged option and then select Filter⇨Stylize⇨Round Corners. The Round Corners option changes only Straight Corner points, so it will change all the points in the Jagged roughened object to smooth curves.

If you choose the Rounded option in the Roughen dialog box, the Round Corners filter will have no effect on the roughened object.

The Scribble and Tweak filters

Although they sound like characters from the Tiny Toons cartoon show, the Scribble and Tweak filters, as is true for most filters, create effects that would take an unrealistically long amount of time to do manually.

One important thing needs to be made clear right away: The Scribble and Tweak filters do the same thing (which makes my job easier). Their only difference is in the way that you enter the amount of random movement. Scribble understands percentages that are based on the size of the object's bounding box, but Tweak moves points based on absolute measurements.

Because of the measuring system that Tweak uses, I have found that using Tweak is much easier than using Scribble most of the time. Having to enter percentages in the Scribble dialog box can be very confusing, especially because you have to be concerned with both horizontal and vertical proportions.

Follow these steps to use the Scribble and Tweak filters:

STEPS: Using the Scribble and Tweak Filters

Step 1.   Create the artwork that you want to use with the filter.

The Tweak and Scribble filters do not work with type that has not been converted to outlines or with placed EPS images. Nor do they affect patterns or gradients that are being used as fills.

Step 2.   Select Filter⇨Distort⇨Scribble or Filter⇨Distort⇨Tweak.

I use the Scribble filter when I am not sure of the size of the selected artwork or when I can determine only that I want points moved a certain portion of the whole, but I cannot determine an absolute measurement.

In the Scribble or Tweak dialog box, enter the amount that you want points to be moved, both horizontally and vertically. Moving the points a large amount usually results in overlapping, crisscrossing paths that aren't very attractive.

Check the options that correspond to the points that you want to move randomly. Checking the Anchor Points check box will move anchor points randomly. Checking the "In" or "Out" Control Points check boxes will move those direction points.

The "In" Control Points are the direction points that affect the segment that precedes the anchor point relative to the path direction. The "Out" Control Points are the direction points that affect the segment that appears after each anchor point relative to the path direction. (Path direction is explained in Chapter 11.)

Step 3.   Click OK. If the artwork isn't what you expected, select Edit⇨Undo (⌘-Z) and then either reapply the filter (⌘-Shift-E) or press Option and enter new values in the dialog box (select Filter⇨Distort⇨Scribble or Filter⇨Distort⇨Tweak).

Step 4.   Add any further artwork to the completed object.

Figure 17-6 shows the four steps. At the bottom of the figure are eight different versions of the artwork. Each version has the same settings, but the points have been moved randomly eight different times.

Figure 17-6:
Steps for using the Scribble and Tweak filters. At the bottom are eight different examples that show the results of applying one of the filters to an object eight different times without changing any of the settings.

The percentages that you enter in the Scribble dialog box move points relative to the size of the bounding box.

The bounding box is an invisible box that surrounds each object. If the bounding box is 5 inches wide and 2 inches tall and you enter a percentage of 10% for width and height in the Scribble dialog box, the filter will move the points randomly up to .5 inch horizontally and .2 inch vertically in either direction.

The most important thing to remember when you are entering horizontal and vertical percentages in the Scribble dialog box is that the height and width of any object will usually be different. As a result, entering the same percentage in each box will usually cause different amounts of movement for each dimension.

The Stylize Filters

The six Stylize filters fall into two different categories. The first category contains the Add Arrowheads and Drop Shadows filters. Both of these filters create additional objects that are based on existing objects.

The Stylize filters in the second category work very similarly to the way that the Distort filters work. The Bloat and Punk filters move (and create, if necessary) anchor points and direction points on either side of each anchor point. The Calligraphy filter distorts the path, giving it a calligraphic appearance. The Round Corners filter removes corner points and replaces them with smooth points.

The Add Arrowheads filter

The Add Arrowheads filter is a boon to technical artists, sign makers, and anyone else in need of a quick arrow. The number one complaint about the Add Arrowheads filter is that Illustrator offers too many arrowheads to choose from. That may be a problem for some people, but I don't see it as one.

In the Add Arrowheads dialog box (select Filter⇨Stylize⇨Add Arrowheads), you can choose from 27 different arrowheads (see Figure 17-7).

Figure 17-7:
The arrowheads that are available in the Add Arrowheads dialog box.

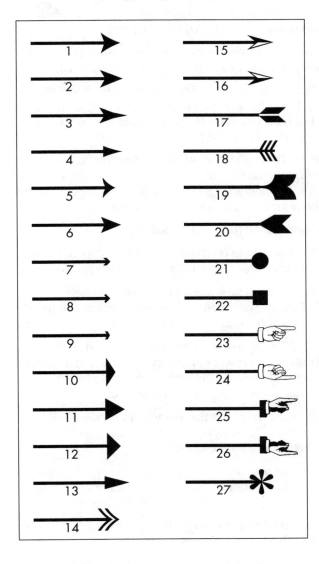

The size of the arrowheads is based on the width of the stroke, but you can alter each arrowhead's dimensions in the Scale text field in the Add Arrowheads dialog box. Follow these steps (illustrated in Figure 17-8) to create and customize an arrowhead:

STEPS: Creating a Customized Arrow

Step 1. Use the Pen or Freehand tool to create an open path. Set the width of the path to the width that you want it to be with an arrowhead attached to it.

You have to use an open path. Nothing happens when you select a closed path and apply the Add Arrowheads filter.

If you want just the arrowhead, and not the path, you still have to create a path first. You can delete the path after the arrowhead appears.

Step 2. Select Filter⇨Stylize⇨Add Arrowheads. The Add Arrowheads dialog box appears. Enter the size of the arrowhead (100% = normal size). Pick which end of the path you want the arrowhead to appear. If you want the arrowhead on both ends of the path, click the Start and End option.

If you drew the path yourself with either the Pen or Freehand tool, the path direction is the direction that you drew the path. Closed paths that were created with the Rectangle or Oval tools or the Create filters and were then cut usually go in a counterclockwise direction.

Pick an arrowhead from the 27 options.

Press down and hold on the directional arrows to flip through the arrowheads quickly. After arrowhead #27, you see arrowhead #1.

Step 3. Click OK. The path now has an arrowhead. Whenever arrowheads are created, they are grouped to the path. You have to use the Group Selection tool to select individual pieces of the arrow, or select Arrange⇨Ungroup (⌘-U).

Step 4. To add a different arrowhead to the other end of the path, select the path, press Option, and select Filter⇨Stylize⇨Add Arrowheads. Change the radio buttons to indicate that the new arrowhead should go at the other end of the path and select the type of arrowhead.

Step 5. Click OK. Make sure that the arrowhead is correct. If it isn't, select Edit⇨Undo (⌘-Z), press Option, and select Filter⇨Stylize⇨Add Arrowheads. Then add a different arrowhead.

Step 6. To make the arrowheads and path one path, select the path and select Filter⇨Object⇨Outline Path. Then select both the new outlined path and the arrowheads and select Filter⇨Pathfinder⇨Unite.

Now you can fill the new arrow object with anything, including gradients, and stroke the entire object at once.

Step 7. Add any other artwork that you want to the arrow.

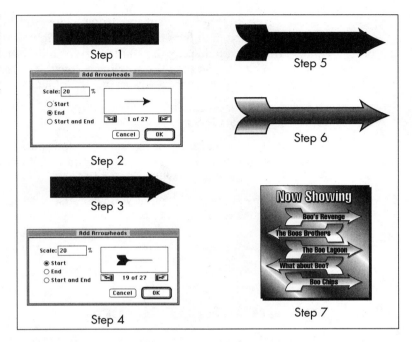

Figure 17-8:
Steps for creating and customizing an arrowhead by using the Add Arrowheads filter.

The Drop Shadows filter

The Drop Shadow filter makes creating drop shadows an easy task.

STEPS:	Creating a Drop Shadow

Step 1. Create and select the artwork that you want to give a drop shadow.

Step 2. Select Filter⇨Stylize⇨Drop Shadow. The Drop Shadow dialog box appears, as shown in Figure 17-9.

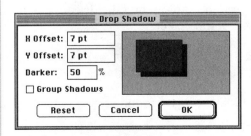

Figure 17-9: The Drop Shadow dialog box.

Step 3.   Enter the amount that you want the drop shadow to be offset. A positive value in the X text field puts the shadow to the right of the object; a negative value in the X text field puts the shadow to the left of the object. A positive value in the Y text field puts the shadow below the object; a negative value in the Y text field puts the shadow above the object.

The larger the offset amounts, the higher up the object will appear to float above the original object.

The value that you enter in the Darker field determines how much black will be added to the shadow to make it appear darker. If you check the Group Shadows box, the shadow will be grouped to the original object.

Step 4.   Click OK. If the shadow isn't what you want, use the Undo command (⌘-Z), press Option, select Filter⇨Stylize⇨Drop Shadow, and create a new drop shadow.

The Punk and Bloat filters

Although the Punk and Bloat filters undoubtedly have the coolest sounding names that Illustrator has to offer, these filters also are the least practical. But Illustrator is a fun program, right? And these filters make it lots of fun.

Punking makes objects appear to have pointy tips, and bloating creates lumps outside of objects. Punking and bloating are inverses; a negative punk is a bloat, and a negative bloat is a punk.

If you are constantly amazed at what the Punk and Bloat filters do, stop reading right here. The following information spoils everything.

The Punk and Bloat filters move anchor points in one direction and create two independent direction points on either side of each anchor point. The direction points are moved in the opposite direction of the anchor points, and the direction of movement is always toward or away from the center of the object.

The distance moved is the only thing that you control when you use the Punk and Bloat filters. Entering a percentage moves the points that percentage.

Nothing about the Punk and Bloat filters is random. Everything about them is controlled.

Follow these steps to use the Punk and Bloat filters (in Figure 17-10, I punked a circle).

STEPS: **Using the Punk and Bloat Filters**

Step 1. Create and select the artwork that you want to punk.

Step 2. Add Anchor points or use the Roughen filter at 0% to create additional anchor points if necessary. I selected Filter⇨Object⇨Add Anchor points twice, increasing the number of anchor points from 4 to 16.

Step 3. Select Filter⇨Stylize⇨Punk. You could, instead, select Bloat. In the dialog box, enter the amount that you want to punk or bloat the object.

Remember that a negative value in the Amount box in the Punk dialog box is a bloat, and a negative value in the Amount box in the Bloat dialog box is a punk.

Step 4. Check to see whether the result is what you intended.

Step 5. Add other artwork to the punked or bloated object.

Figure 17-10: Steps for punking and bloating. The sun was created by punking an object, and the cloud was created by bloating an object.

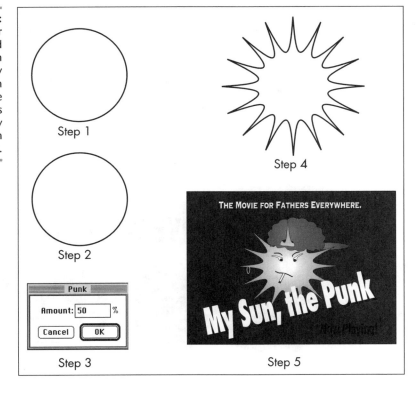

The Round Corners filter

You can use the Round Corners filter to create round corners easily. The Round Corners filter converts any corner points in a path into sets of smooth points, as described in the following example:

STEPS: Using the Round Corners Filter

Step 1. Select the artwork that will have its corners rounded. I used type converted to outlines in the example in Figure 17-11.

Step 2. Select Filter⇨Stylize⇨Round Corners. The Round Corners dialog box appears. Enter the amount that you want the corners to be rounded.

I wanted my corners rounded as much as possible, so I entered **100 pt** in the dialog box. Entering a large number usually ensures that all points will become as curved as possible.

Step 3. Click OK.

Step 4. Add other artwork to the final rounded artwork.

Figure 17-11: Using the Round Corners filter.

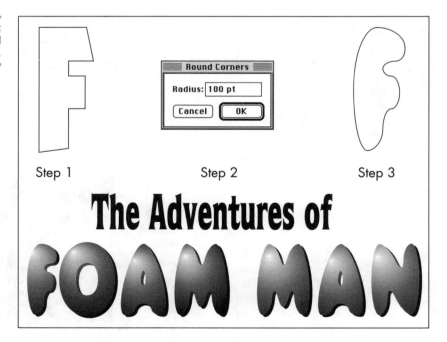

You can use the Round Corners filter to smooth out overly bumpy edges. Using the Round Corners filter with Roughen (and Jagged) can produce very smooth, flowing areas.

The Calligraphy filter

For those of us who are not blessed with the skill of calligraphy, Adobe has provided the Calligraphy filter. You can use it to turn any path into calligraphic art.

 Although you can turn any path into calligraphy, text converted to outlines looks just plain bad. If you've ever seen a calligrapher draw letters, you appreciate how wonderful calligraphic type looks. But because type outlines are just that — outlines — the result that you get from using this filter with text doesn't look like calligraphy at all. Instead, it looks like a giant mess. And no, script type isn't any better.

Why would you want to turn artwork into calligraphy? Well, the folks at Adobe were hard pressed to come up with an answer, but I've found one thing that it's good for: creating cookie cutters.

STEPS:	Creating Cookie Cutters with the Calligraphy Filter
Step 1.	Create the artwork that you want to use with the Calligraphy filter and select it. I used a pig shape for the example in Figure 17-12.
	Corners can look bad with the Calligraphy filter. If the artwork has too many corners, use the Round Corners filter to change the corners into curved areas.
Step 2.	Select Filter⇨Stylize⇨Calligraphy and enter the width and the angle of the calligraphic stroke.
Step 3.	Click OK.
Step 4.	To give the cookie cutter a metallic look, I applied a silver gradient to it and put it on a dark background.

Figure 17-12:
Creating a cookie cutter
with the Calligraphy filter.

Figure 17-12:
Creating a cookie cutter with the Calligraphy filter.

The Object and Pathfinder Filters

In This Chapter

- Understanding the Object and Pathfinder filters
- Why you may need an FPU
- Using and abusing the Add Anchor Points filter
- The alignment and distribution filters
- The individual transformation filters
- The path-based filters
- Changes in the Pathfinder filters from Version 5.0 to Version 5.5
- Using the five combine filters
- Using the four overlay filters
- Understanding the mix filters
- Applying the Trap filter
- Options for Pathfinder filters

The Object and Pathfinder Filters __

Although the Distort and Stylize filters are quite similar to some of the Photoshop filters, the Object and Pathfinder filters are Illustrator-specific power filters.

The Object filters do numerous things, including aligning multiple objects and transforming individual objects. The Pathfinder filters work with two or more paths to produce different results.

You need an FPU to run the Pathfinder filters, the Outline Stroked Path filter, and the Offset Path filter in Illustrator 5.0.

 You do *not* need an FPU (floating point unit) to use the Pathfinder filters, the Outline Path filter, and the Offset Path filter in Illustrator 5.5. If you *do* have an FPU, you should copy the Outline Path and Offset Path filters from the Optional Plug-Ins folder into the Plug-Ins folder for best performance.

FPUs are the math coprocessor chips found in most Macintosh computers. They allow certain mathematical computations to be done more quickly and precisely than with integer-based mathematical systems. Illustrator's Pathfinder filters are math-intensive, and having an FPU will make them operate faster than otherwise. With Illustrator 5.5, the issue is speed; having an FPU in your computer will increase the speed of the filter activity. With Illustrator 5.0, the issue is whether the Pathfinder filters, the Outline Stroked Path filter, and the Offset Path filter will work at all.

 With Illustrator 5.0, you may be able to "cheat" by using Software FPU, a shareware extension that fakes the computer into thinking it has an FPU.

Check with your Macintosh dealer to determine whether you have an FPU in your system. You may not have an FPU if you have any of the following computers: Macintosh LC, IIsi, Duo 210/230, Centris 610, Quadra 605/610, or any of the Performa computers. All Power Mac computers are considered to have an FPU built into their main processor.

Using the Object Filters

The nine different Object filters fall into four categories. The first category contains only the Add Anchor Points filter. The second category is the alignment and distribution category, which includes the Align Objects, Distribute Horizontally, and Distribute Vertically filters. The third category is the transformation category, in which objects are transformed individually by the Move Each, Scale Each, and Rotate Each filters. The last category contains the "pathfinder" object filters: the Offset Path and Outline Stroked Path filters.

If you look at the preceding categories, you quickly realize that the Object submenu is more of a miscellaneous grouping. The filters don't affect just individual objects because the alignment and distribution filters need more than one object to work. The other filters affect individual objects, regardless of how many objects are selected.

The Add Anchor Points filter

The Add Anchor Points filter (select Filter➪Object➪Add Anchor Points) doubles the number of points on an object. New anchor points are always added halfway between existing anchor points. Figure 18-1 shows an object that has had the Add Anchor Points filter applied once, twice, and three times.

Figure 18-1:
The Add Anchor Points filter doubles the number of anchor points, adding new anchor points directly between existing points.

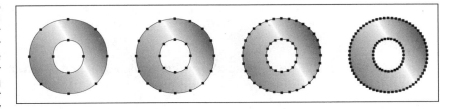

 Adding anchor points is useful before using the Twirl, Punk, Bloat, Scribble, and Tweak filters, and before using any other filter that bases results on the number and position of anchor points.

The alignment and distribution filters

The Align Objects filter provides ways to align and distribute objects horizontally and vertically. Choosing the Distribute option for Horizontal or Vertical in the Align Objects dialog box is exactly the same as choosing the Distribute Horizontally or Distribute Vertically filters, respectively.

Selecting Filter➪Objects➪Align Objects displays the Align Objects dialog box (shown in Figure 18-2). Radio buttons in this dialog box enable you to determine how selected objects will be aligned and distributed. The rightmost section of the Align Objects dialog box shows several objects aligned to the specifications in the other two sections.

Figure 18-2:
The Align Objects dialog box.

Align Objects

┌─ Horizontal ─┐
◉ None
○ Left
○ Center
○ Right
○ Distribute

┌─ Vertical ─┐
◉ None
○ Top
○ Center
○ Bottom
○ Distribute

[Cancel] [OK]

The None option in each column keeps objects the way they were when you first selected them. In the Horizontal area, choosing Left makes all objects align flush left. Choosing Center centers all objects from left to right. Choosing Right aligns objects flush right. Choosing the Distribute option evenly spaces objects between the leftmost object and the rightmost object.

In the Vertical area, choosing Top aligns all objects along the topmost edges of the objects. Choosing Center centers objects from top to bottom. Choosing Bottom makes all objects align flush bottom. The Distribute option moves objects between the topmost object and the bottommost object.

Figure 18-3 shows the 25 possible combinations of alignment and distribution.

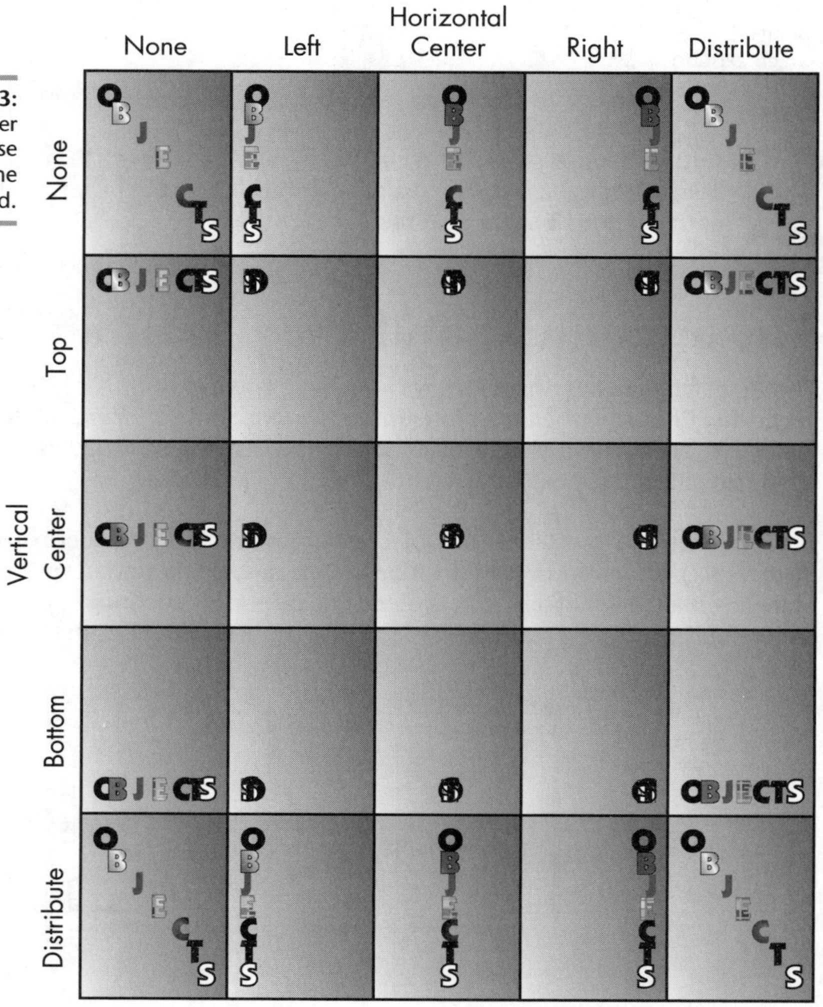

Figure 18-3: The Align Objects filter can produce all of these results, depending on the options selected.

QuicKeys software enables me to choose each of the 25 alignment and distribution combinations by pressing a combination of keystrokes. I use the arrow keys and the Home and End keys on my extended keyboard in combination with the ⌘ and Control keys.

The transform each filters

The Move Each, Scale Each, and Rotate Each filters work like their Illustrator counterparts, except for two big differences:

▓ Each object is transformed individually. The Move Each filter doesn't work differently from the way Arrange⇨Move (⌘-Shift-M) works, but the Scale Each and Rotate Each filters work quite differently from the Scale and Rotate tools.

▓ Each of the filters has a magical Random check box. When it is selected, you can move, scale, and rotate an object randomly up to the distance, percentage, or degree that you specify.

Figure 18-4 shows the steps to follow when using the transform each filters to create wacky letters.

Figure 18-4:
Steps for creating wacky type by using the transform each filters.

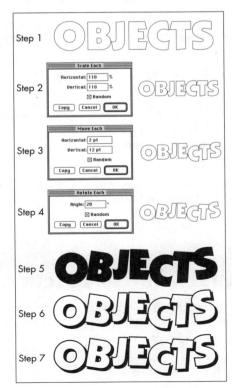

STEPS:	Creating Wacky Letters with the Transform Each Filters
Step 1.	Create the artwork that you want to make into wacky letters. Type doesn't have to be in outline format, but if it isn't, each letter needs to be a separate type area.
	Converting a line of type to outlines is easier than setting each character in separate type areas.
Step 2.	Select all the letters and choose Filter⇨Object⇨Scale Each. In the Scale Each dialog box, enter 110% in both the Horizontal and Vertical text fields and check the Random check box. Click OK.
	Do not group the letters together or make all the characters into one giant compound path. Doing so will transform the entire set of characters, not each individual character.
Step 3.	Select all the letters and choose Filter⇨Object⇨Move Each. In the Move Each dialog box, enter 2 points for the horizontal movement and 12 points for the vertical movement and check the Random check box. Click OK.
	Entering a small amount in the Horizontal text field prevents the letters from overlapping too much or having too much empty white space between them.
Step 4.	Select all the letters and choose Filter⇨Object⇨Rotate Each. In the Rotate Each dialog box, enter 20° in the Angle text field and check the Random check box. Click OK.
Step 5.	Group all the letters together. Change the stroke to 1 point black and the fill to black.
Step 6.	Option-copy (select and drag with the Option key pressed, releasing the mouse button before releasing the Option key — thus creating a duplicate of the originals) the letters up and to the left of the original letters. Change the fill to white.
Step 7.	If any of the letters overlap, ungroup all the letters, select the white and black parts of that letter, and bring the letter to the front or the back.

The "pathfinder" object filters

The Offset Path and Outline Path (called Outline Stroked Path in Version 5.0) filters create new paths around existing paths. The new paths are based on values that you enter in a dialog box or on the width of an existing stroke on a path.

Both filters require an FPU if you are using Version 5.0 of Illustrator.

In Version 5.5, if you don't have an FPU, the filters will work fine; however, if you *do* have an FPU, you will need to replace the Offset Path and Outline Path filters with filters of the same name located in the Optional Plug-Ins folder, in a folder called FPU Plug-Ins.

The main difference between these two filters and the filters in the Pathfinder filters submenu is that you need to select only one path to use these two filters, but you need to select at least two separate paths to use any of the Pathfinder filters.

The Offset Path filter

The Offset Path filter (select Filter➪Object➪Offset Path) draws a new path around the outside or inside of an existing path. The distance from the existing path is the distance that you specify in the Offset Path dialog box, which is shown in Figure 18-5.

Figure 18-5:
The Offset Path dialog box.

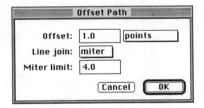

A positive number in the Offset Path dialog box creates the new path "outside" the existing path, and a negative number creates the new path "inside" the existing path. When the path is closed, figuring out where the new path will be created is easy. For open paths, the "outside" is the left side of the path, as it runs from start to end, and the "inside" is the right side of the path, as it runs from start to end.

For an in-depth explanation of path directions, see Chapter 11.

The Line join pop-up menu enables you to select from different types of joins at the corners of the new path. The choices are miter, round, and bevel, and the result is the same effect that you get if you choose those options as the stroke style for a stroke.

The Miter limit affects the miter size only when the miter option is selected from the Line join pop-up menu, but the option is available when round and bevel joins are selected. Just ignore the Miter limit when you are using round or bevel joins. (You cannot use a value that is less than 1.)

Often, when you are offsetting a path, the new, resulting path will overlap itself, creating undesirable *skittles* (small, undesirable bumps in a path). If the skittles are within a closed path area, select the new path and choose Filter⇨Pathfinder⇨Unite. If the skittles are outside the closed path area, choose Filter⇨Pathfinder⇨Divide and then select and delete each of the skittles.

The Outline Stroked Path filter

The Outline Stroked Path filter creates a path around an existing path's stroke. The width of the new path is directly related to the width of the stroke.

 I use the Outline Stroked Path filter for two reasons. The first reason is the most obvious: to fill a stroke with a gradient or to be able to view a pattern that is inside a stroke. The second reason is that when you transform an outlined stroke, the effect is often different from the effect that results from transforming a stroked path. Scaling an outlined stroke changes the width of the stroke in the direction of the scale, sometimes resulting in a nonuniform stroke. The same is true when using the Free Distort filter, which also changes the width of the stroke in the direction of the scale, sometimes resulting in a nonuniform stroke.

 The End and Join attributes of the stroke's style determine how the ends and joins of the resulting stroke look.

The Outline Stroked Path filter creates problems for tight corners. It causes overlaps that are similar to those generated by the Offset Path filter and the Brush tool when you use them on sharp corners.

Use the Unite filter to remove the skittles that result from overlapping paths. Not only will the Unite filter make the drawing look better as artwork and prevent overlapping strokes, but it also will reduce the number of points in the file, making the illustration smaller so that it can print faster.

 Using a Dash pattern on the stroke prevents the Outline Stroked Path filter from working at all. Make sure that the Dash pattern is set to None before you use this filter.

The Pathfinder Filters

The most powerful and "nifty" filters in Illustrator 5.0 are the Pathfinder filters. They do things that would take hours to do by using Illustrator's traditional tools and methods.

The Pathfinder filters change the way that two or more paths interact. The cute little symbols next to each of the filters are supposed to clue you in to what the filters do, but the pictures are small and most don't accurately depict how the filters work.

 The names of the Pathfinder filters can be a little confusing. The names were undoubtedly chosen to signify filters what the filters do, but most filters can't be defined easily in just one word (or in a few words in Version 5.0).

The Pathfinder filters fall into four categories (dotted lines in the submenu separate the categories). The first five filters are the combine filters, which for the most part combine two or more paths. The next five filters are the overlay filters, which generate results from two or more paths that overlap. The next two filters, the mix category, mix the colors of overlapping paths. The last filter (besides Option, which really isn't a filter) is the Trap filter, which generates trapping automatically, according to your specifications.

Changes from Version 5.0 to Version 5.5

 Adobe gave the Pathfinder filters a complete overhaul in Version 5.5, but the only real differences are the addition of the Trap filter and the Options "filter." (Most of the filters had name changes or organizational changes.) Figure 18-6 shows the Illustrator 5.0 Pathfinder filters and their 5.5 counterparts. The two crop filters have been eliminated because the divide filters support masks. The name changes are not referenced by more Illustrator 5.5 icons in this chapter, but functionality differences between the 5.0 and 5.5 filters are discussed.

 Although Version 5.5 does not require that you have an FPU to use the Pathfinder filters, an FPU dramatically improves the speed of the filters.

The Pathfinder Options dialog box

The new Options menu item (select Filter⇨Pathfinder⇨Options) displays a dialog box, shown in Figure 18-7, that enables you to customize the way that the Pathfinder filters work.

The value in the "Calculate results to a precision of x points" text field tells Illustrator how precisely the Pathfinder filters should operate. The more precisely they operate, the better and more accurate the results are, but the longer the processing time is. This speed differential is most apparent when you apply the Pathfinder filters, especially Trap, to very complex objects. The default value is .028 point, which seems to be accurate enough for most work. If you have Version 5.5 and no FPU in your system, increasing this value will dramatically speed up the processing of the Pathfinder filters.

Figure 18-6:
Changes in the Pathfinder filters from Illustrator 5.0 to Illustrator 5.5.

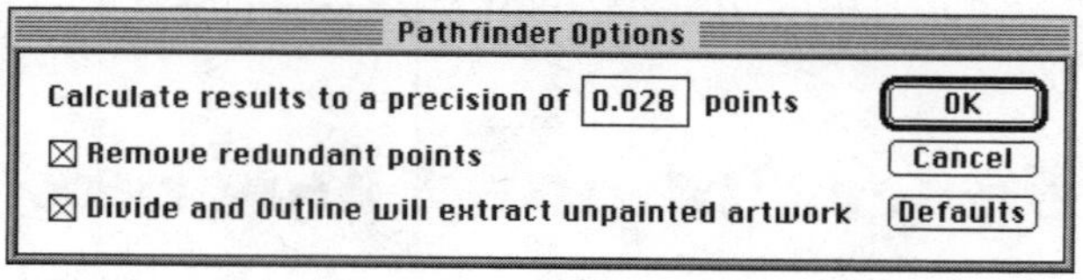

Figure 18-7:
The Pathfinder Options dialog box.

The Remove redundant points option gets rid of overlapping points that are side by side on the same path. I can't think of why you would want overlapping points, so using the default setting of checked is a good idea.

The last option, if checked, automatically deletes "unpainted artwork." Checking this option keeps you from having to remove all those paths that Divide always seems to produce that are filled and stroked with None.

Usually, the defaults in the Pathfinder Options dialog box are the best options for most situations. If you change the options, be aware that the Pathfinder Options dialog box will reset to the defaults when you quit Illustrator.

The combine filters

Five filters are in the combine filters category. I use the Unite filter more than the other four put together. The Unite filter combines two or more paths into one path, as described in the following steps:

STEPS: Using the Unite Filter

Step 1.   Create and select the artwork that you want to apply the Unite filter to. In the example in Figure 18-8, the artwork is type converted into outlines.

Figure 18-8: Using the Unite filter.

 The Pathfinder filters work only with paths. You have to convert type into outlined paths, and you cannot use EPS images.

Step 2.   Select Filter⇨Pathfinder⇨Unite. Any overlapping artwork is united into one path.

 The color of the united path is always the color of the path that was the topmost selected path before you used the Unite filter.

When you use the Unite filter, paths that don't overlap but are outside of other paths become part of a group. Illustrator draws paths between end points of open paths before it unites those paths with other paths. Compound paths remain compound paths.

The next two filters, Intersect and Exclude, are opposites. Using one filter results in the opposite of what you get from using the other filter.

 After you select two or more paths and choose Filter⇨Pathfinder⇨Intersect, only the overlapping portions of the paths remain. If you select three paths, the only area that remains will be the area where all three selected paths overlap each other.

 If you use the Exclude filter, only the areas that don't overlap will remain. The Exclude filter follows the Even-Odd Rule (sometimes called the Winding Number rule), which is discussed in Chapter 11.

 The color of the Intersected or Excluded path is always the color of the path that was the topmost selected path before you used the filter.

The last two combine filters are the Back Minus and Front Minus filters (select Filter⇨Pathfinder⇨Back Minus or Filter⇨Pathfinder⇨Front Minus). Each filter works on the principle that one path, either the frontmost or backmost of the paths selected, will have all the other overlapping paths subtracted from it.

 When you apply the Back Minus filter, the color of the remaining path is the color of the backmost path before you applied the filter. When you apply the Front Minus filter, the color of the remaining path is the color of the frontmost path before you applied the filter.

Figure 18-9 shows the same paths with each of the combine filters applied to them.

The overlay filters

The four overlay filters divide and merge overlaying paths. Each of the filters works a little differently, but all are based on the premise that the paths overlap.

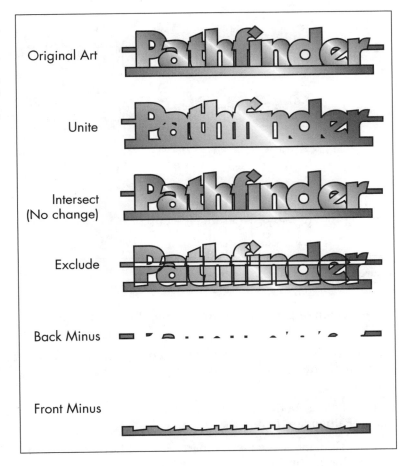

Figure 18-9:
Selected
paths, with
each of the
combine filters
applied to the
paths.

Original Art

Unite

Intersect
(No change)

Exclude

Back Minus

Front Minus

The Divide filter

The Divide filter (select Filter⇨Pathfinder⇨Divide) divides overlaying paths into
individual closed paths, as described in the following steps (Figure 18-10 shows these
steps):

STEPS: Using the Divide Filter

Step 1. Create the artwork that you want to divide into sections.

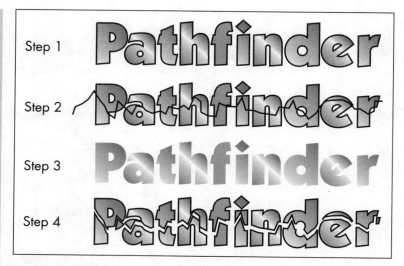

Figure 18-10: Using the Divide filter.

Step 2. Create a path or paths where you want to divide the object.

If the division lines consist of more than one path, you do not need to make those paths into a compound path, though it doesn't hurt.

Step 3. Select all paths, both artwork and dividing paths, and choose Filter⇨Pathfinder⇨Divide.

Step 4. If you wish to move the pieces apart, you first have to ungroup them (the Divide filter groups them automatically).

The Outline filter

The Outline filter creates smaller path pieces than the Divide filter does; but instead of making each section a closed path, each path maintains its individuality (becomes separate from adjoining paths). The result of outlining is several small stroke pieces. Instead of maintaining the fill color of each piece, each piece is filled with None and stroked with the fill color.

The Divide and Outline filters completely ignore the stroke color.

The Reduce and Merge filters

Both the Reduce and Merge filters delete extra paths that are hidden by objects, but Merge also combines colors that are the same. The following steps describe how to use the Merge filter (see Figure 18-11):

STEPS: Using the Merge Filter

Step 1. Create the artwork that you want to use the Merge filter for.

Figure 18-11: Using the Merge filter.

Step 2. Select the artwork to be merged and choose Filter⇨Pathfinder⇨Merge. All paths that were overlapped are removed, leaving only the paths that had nothing in front of them. All adjacent areas that contained identical colors are united.

 When you use either the Reduce or Merge filter, Illustrator deletes the stroke color from the resulting paths.

The Mix Filters

The two mix filters simulate transparency or shadows between two or more paths. The Soft filter enables you to specify the amount of color from each path that shows up in the intersecting paths. The Hard filter combines the colors at their full amount. The following steps describe how to use the Soft filter (see Figure 18-12):

STEPS: Using the Soft Filter

Step 1. Create and select the overlapping paths that you want to use the Mix Soft filter for.

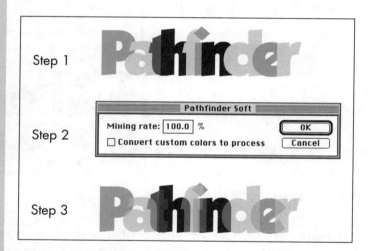

Figure 18-12: Using the Soft filter.

Step 2. Select Filter⇨Pathfinder⇨Soft. The Pathfinder Soft dialog box (called Mix Soft in Version 5.0) appears. Enter the amount that you want the colors to mix.

How the colors mix depends not only on the Mixing rate percentage, but also on the drawing order of the objects. Check the Mix Soft chart in the color insert to see how different overlaying objects react to the Soft filter.

Step 3. Click OK.

The Mix Soft filter can be a little difficult to understand at first. The Mix Soft filter determines how much of the background color will bleed through the foreground color. If each of the colors is at 100% and you use a setting of 50% for the filter, the background color will be 33.3%, and the foreground color will be 66.6% (50% of 66.6% = 33.3%, and 33.3% + 66.6% = 100%).

At 100%, those same colors would each be at 50% of their original values. The color section of the *Macworld Illustrator 5.0/5.5 Bible* contains a Mix Soft/Hard chart that shows how different colors blend together at 12 different percentages, ranging from 5% to 5,000%, with six different front and back positions for the three objects in each percentage.

 The Mix Soft and Mix Hard filters create the same path sections as the Divide filter creates.

 Checking the box for Convert custom colors to process in the Mix Hard and Mix Soft dialog boxes will do just that, even to sections of paths that don't overlap other paths.

The Trap Filter

The Trap filter takes the drudgery away from trapping. The only limitation for the Trap filter is that it doesn't work on extremely complex illustrations.

 For more information on trapping, see Chapter 21.

Follow these steps to use the Trap filter (see Figure 18-13):

STEPS: Using the Trap Filter

Step 1. Create and select the artwork that you want to trap.

 If the artwork is overly complex, you may want to select only a small portion of the artwork before you continue.

Step 2. Select Filter⇨Pathfinder⇨Trap. In the Trap dialog box, enter the width of the trap in the Thickness text field. The default is 0.25 point.

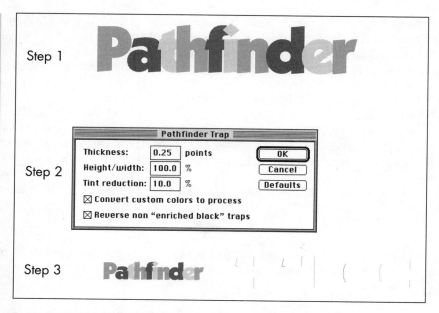

Figure 18-13: Using the Trap filter.

Enter the amount that you want the height of the trap to be different from the width. Entering 400% (the maximum) widens the horizontal thickness of the stroke to four times the amount set in the Thickness text field and leaves the vertical thickness the same. Changing this value allows for different paper-stretching errors.

The Tint reduction setting determines how much the lighter of the two colors is tinted on that area.

Checking the Convert custom colors to process check box converts custom colors to process equivalents only in the resulting trap path that is generated from the Trap filter.

Checking the Reverse non "enriched black" traps check box converts any traps along the object that are filled with 100% black but no other colors to be less black and more of the lighter abutting color.

Step 3.   Click OK. Figure 18-13 shows the trap as a separate piece to the right of the original object.

All traps generated by the Trap filter result in filled paths, not strokes, and are automatically set to overprint in the Paint Style palette.

The Select and Text Filters

19
CHAPTER

In This Chapter

- Understanding the Select filters
- Using the four Paint Style selection filters
- Using the Select Inverse filter
- Using the Select Masks filter
- Using the Select Stray Points filter
- Understanding the Text filters
- Using the Text Export filter
- Using the Text Find filter
- Using the Change Case filter
- Using the Check Spelling filter
- Using the Find Font filter
- Using the Revert Text Path filter
- Using the Rows & Columns filter
- Using the Smart Punctuation filter

The Select Filters

The Select filters are a welcome addition to Illustrator. More than any other type of filter, the Select filters make mundane, repetitive tasks easy to accomplish by doing all the nasty work for you.

To choose the Select filters, you select Filter⇨Select⇨ and the appropriate selection filter.

The four Paint Style selection filters make changing certain Paint Style attributes for selected objects a snap. They compare the selected path or paths to other paths in the document and select all the paths that have similar Paint Style attributes.

The Select Inverse filter is perfect for selecting all paths that aren't selected. You can use this filter to instantly select paths that are hidden, guides, and other objects that are hard to select.

The Select Masks filter makes the process of manipulating masks much easier by showing you where masks are in the document.

The Select Stray Points filter selects all isolated anchor points. Individual anchor points don't print or preview, and you can see them in Preview mode only when they are selected. After you cut portions of line segments, stray points often appear; and often these individual points interfere with connecting other segments. You can't use this filter enough.

The Paint Style Selection Filters

Four selection filters use the Paint Style attributes of currently selected objects to select additional objects. Using these filters makes object selection quick and intuitive. The main limitation of these filters is that they are limited to four categories of comparison, each of which must be used independently of the others. This limitation causes problems in selecting objects that share more than one attribute, such as objects that have the same stroke color and the same stroke weight.

The Same Fill Color filter

The Same Fill Color filter (Filter⇨Select⇨Same Fill Color) selects objects that have the same fill color as the selected object. This filter selects objects regardless of their stroke color, stroke weight, or stroke pattern.

 The Select Same Fill Color filter considers different tints of custom colors to be the same color. This filter works in two ways. First, if you select one object with any tint value of a custom color, the Select Same Color filter will select all other objects with the same custom color, regardless of the tint. Second, you can select more than one object, no matter what tint each object contains, provided that the selected objects have the same custom color.

To be selected with the Same Fill Color filter, process color fills have to have the same tint as the original. Even single colors, such as yellow, have to be the same percentage. The Same Fill Color filter considers 100% yellow and 50% yellow to be two separate colors.

 Don't select more than one fill color if you select more than one object. If you have different fill colors selected, even if they are just different tints of the same process color, the filter will not select any objects at all.

If you use custom colors often, the Select Same Fill Color filter is extremely useful. It enables you to instantly select all objects that are filled with the custom color, regardless of the tint of the selected object or the tints of the objects to be selected.

 The Same Fill Color filter also selects objects that are filled with the same gradient, regardless of the angle or the starting or ending point of the gradient. This filter does not, however, select objects that have the same pattern fill.

The Same Paint Style filter

The Same Paint Style filter (Filter⇨Select⇨Same Paint Style) selects objects that have almost exactly the same paint style as the paint style of the selected object. The following information has to be the same:

- The fill color (as defined in the preceding section, " The Same Fill Color filter")
- The stroke color
- The stroke weight

Some things in the paint style palette that don't matter (that is, they don't prevent the Same paint style filter from selecting an object) are any of the stroke style attributes and the overprinting options.

 Don't select more than one paint style if you select more than one object. If you have different paint styles (as defined previously) selected, no objects will be selected by the filter. The best thing to do with the Same Paint Style filter, as with the Same Fill Color filter, is to select only one object.

The Same Stroke Color filter

The Same Stroke Color filter (Filter⇨Select⇨Same Stroke Color) selects objects that have the same stroke color, regardless of the stroke weight or style and regardless of the type of fill.

The color limitations that are defined in "The Same Fill Color filter" section earlier in the chapter apply to the Same Stroke Color filter.

Although you can choose a pattern for a stroke that makes the stroke look gray, the Same Stroke Color filter does not select other objects that have the same stroke pattern.

The Same Stroke Weight filter

Illustrator's Same Stroke Weight filter (Filter➪Select➪Same Stroke Weight) selects objects that have the same stroke weight, regardless of the stroke color, style, or fill color.

Even if the stroke is a pattern, other paths that have the same stroke weight as the patterned stroke will be selected when you use the Same Stroke Weight filter.

Don't select more than one stroke weight if you select more than one object. If you select different stroke weights, no paths will be selected. The best thing to do with the Same Stroke Weight filter, as with the Same Fill Color and Same Paint Style filters, is to select only one object.

Combining the Paint Style selection filters

Unfortunately, you cannot do multiple-type selections with any of the Paint Style filters. You cannot, for example, select at one time all of the objects that have the same stroke color and fill color, but have different stroke weights.

The Lock Unselected command (press Option and select Arrange➪Lock or press ⌘-Option-1) is the key to specifying multiple selection criteria. The following instructions describe how to perform multiple-type selections in a few steps:

STEPS:	Selecting Objects That Have the Same Stroke and Fill Colors
Step 1.	Select a representative object that has the stroke and fill color that you want.
Step 2.	Choose Filter➪Same Fill Color. All objects that have the same fill color as the original object will be selected, regardless of their stroke color.
Step 3.	This step is the key step. Press Option and select Arrange➪Lock (⌘-Option-1) to lock any objects that are not selected. The only objects that you can modify or select now are the ones that have the same fill color.

Step 4. Deselect All (⌘-Shift-A) and select the original object, which has both the fill color and the stroke color that you want to select.

Step 5. Choose Filter⇨Select⇨Same Stroke Color. Only objects that have the same stroke and fill colors will be selected.

The Select Inverse Filter

The Select Inverse filter (Filter⇨Select⇨Select Inverse) quickly selects all objects that are not currently selected. For example, if one object is selected and the document contains fifteen other objects, the fifteen objects will become selected, and the one object that was selected originally will become deselected.

 The Select Inverse filter does not cause locked or hidden objects to be selected and does not select guides unless guides are not locked. Objects on layers that are locked or hidden will not be selected either.

The Select Inverse filter is useful because selecting a few objects is usually quicker than selecting most objects. After you select the few objects, the Select Inverse filter does all the nasty work of selecting everything else.

 When no objects are selected, the Select Inverse filter selects all the objects, just as the Edit⇨Select All (⌘-A) command would. When all objects are selected, the Select Inverse filter deselects all the objects, just as the Edit⇨Deselect All (⌘-Shift-A) command would.

The Select Masks filter

The Select Masks filter (Filter⇨Select⇨Select Masks) selects all the objects that are currently being used as masks. The only masks in the document that are not selected are the masks that are locked or hidden and the masks that are on layers that are locked or hidden.

 The Select Masks filter does not select fills and strokes that were created with the Fill and Stroke Mask filter (Filter⇨Create⇨Fill & Stroke for Mask). These separate paths are the same size as the masks, but they are not masks.

See Chapter 11 for detailed information on creating and using masks and Chapter 16 for information regarding the Fill & Stroke for Mask filter.

Use the Select Masks filter before you select the Fill & Stroke for Mask filter. Knowing whether the path that you have selected is really a mask can be difficult, but by using the Select Masks filter you can be sure that the selected objects are indeed masks.

The Select Stray Points filter

The Select Stray Points filter (Filter⇨Select⇨Select Stray Points) selects individual anchor points in the document.

Individual anchor points are nasty beasts, because although they don't show up in preview or printing, they contain fills and strokes that often cause separation software to print additional blank color separations that aren't needed.

You create stray points in various ways:

- You click once with the Pen tool, creating a single anchor point.

- You delete a line segment on a path that has two points by selecting the line segment with the Direct Selection tool and pressing Delete. This action leaves behind the two anchor points.

- You use the Scissors tool to cut a path, and while deleting one side or another of the path, you do not select the points. These points become stray points.

- When you ungroup an oval or rectangle in Version 3.2 or an older version of Illustrator, the center point remains.

Bringing an Illustrator 3.2 or older document that has still-grouped rectangles or ovals into Version 5.0 automatically deletes the center point and turns on the Show Center Point option in the Object Attributes dialog box (choose Object⇨Attributes or press ⌘-Control-A).

Be careful not to think that center points of object are stray points. They aren't, and you cannot select them without selecting the object they belong to. Center points of objects are visible when the Show Center Point option is checked in the Object Attributes dialog box (choose Object⇨Attributes or press ⌘-Control-A). Selecting the center point of an object selects the entire object, and deleting the center point deletes the entire object.

The Text Filters

The two Text filters that shipped with Illustrator Version 5.0, Export and Find, are considered filters only because their files are in the Plug-Ins folder in the Adobe Illustrator folder. Export and Find provide Illustrator with additional text features to give the software more word processing power.

Version 5.5 added six more Text filters, making this submenu worthy of the Filters menu. The six filters added to Illustrator 5.5 are discussed after the Text Find filter is explained below.

Chapter 8 discusses working with Type.

The Text Export filter

To export text, select Filter➪Text➪Export. A Save dialog box will appear, asking in what format and where you want to save the text.

To use the Text Export filter, you need to have the Claris XTND folder in your System Folder.

You can save text in most of the common formats, and you can import it back into Illustrator with the Import Text command (choose File➪Import Text when a text area is active with a Type tool). Word processing software, page layout software, or any other software that can read text files can open and use text that you saved in Illustrator.

The Text Find filter

The Text Find filter (Filter➪Text➪Find) uses the Text Find dialog box that is shown in Figure 19-1 to search for and, if necessary, replace certain letters, words, or character combinations.

Figure 19-1:
The Text Find
dialog box.

```
┌──────────────────────── Text Find ────────────────────────┐
│ Find what:                    Replace with:                 │
│ ┌─────────────────────────┐  ┌─────────────────────────┐   │
│ └─────────────────────────┘  └─────────────────────────┘   │
│                                                             │
│ ⊠ Whole Word ⊠ Case Sensitive ⊠ Search Backward ⊠ Wrap Around │
│ [ Find Next ] [ Replace, then Find ] [ Replace ] [ Replace All ] │
└─────────────────────────────────────────────────────────────┘
```

STEPS: Finding and Replacing Text

Step 1.   Select Filter⇨Text⇨Find. The Text Find dialog box appears.

Step 2.   Type the word, phrase, or characters that you want to find in the Find what text field.

You do not need to select areas of type with the Selection or Type tools. All that is necessary is that the document that you want to search be the active document.

Step 3.   Check the appropriate options from the four that follow:

Whole Word: The Whole Word option tells Illustrator that the characters you type in the Find what box are an entire word, not part of a word.

Case Sensitive: If Case Sensitive is checked, Illustrator will select the characters only if they have the same uppercase and lowercase attributes as the characters you type in the Find what text field.

Search Backward: Search Backward tells Illustrator to look before the current word for the next instance of the characters, instead of using the default, which is to look after the current word.

Wrap Around: Wrap Around keeps Illustrator going through all the text blocks and makes Illustrator continue looking and finding next throughout each text block. When it reaches the last text block, it starts where it originally began and continues finding the word or characters that you specified in the Find what box.

Step 4.   Click the Find Next button to find the first occurrence of the word or characters.

Step 5.   In the Replace with box, type the word or characters that you want to use to replace the text that Illustrator found.

Step 6.   Click the Replace button to replace the selected text. Click the Replace button and then the Find button to replace the selected text and automatically highlight the next matching word or characters. Click the Replace All button to replace all occurrences of the word or characters throughout the document.

Illustrator cannot find words or characters that you have converted to outlines.

The Change Case filter

 New to Version 5.5 of Illustrator is the Change Case filter, which converts selected text to a variety of case options.

Select type with a Type tool and then select Filter⇨Text⇨Change Case. The Change Case dialog box will appear, as shown in Figure 19-2.

Figure 19-2:
The Change Case dialog box.

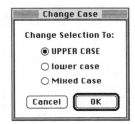

 Type *must* be selected with the Type tool (i.e., characters must be highlighted) to use the Change Case filter. If type is selected with a Selection tool, then the filter will not work, and a dialog box stating this will be displayed.

All three options affect only letters, not numbers, symbols, or punctuation. The options are as follows:

UPPER CASE makes all selected letters into uppercase, regardless if any letters were uppercase or lowercase.

lower case makes all selected letters into lowercase, regardless if any letters were uppercase or lowercase. It also doesn't matter if those letters were originally uppercase because they were typed with the Caps Lock key engaged, or if the uppercase letters were uppercase because of a style format.

Mixed Case makes all selected words into lowercase, with the first letter of each word becoming uppercase, regardless if any letters were originally uppercase or lowercase. It also doesn't matter if those letters were originally uppercase because they were typed with the Caps Lock key engaged, or if the uppercase letters were uppercase because of a style format. The Mixed Case option separates words by making *any* character that is between letters end one word and begin another. At the time of this writing, even apostrophes in contractions caused words like "don't" and "can't" to display as "Don'T" and "Can'T".

The Check Spelling filter

 New to Version 5.5 of Illustrator is the Check Spelling filter, which checks all text in a document to see if it is spelled (and capitalized) correctly.

Select Filter➪Text➪Check Spelling. The Check Spelling dialog box will appear, as shown in Figure 19-3.

Figure 19-3:
The Check Spelling dialog box and the Learned Words dialog box.

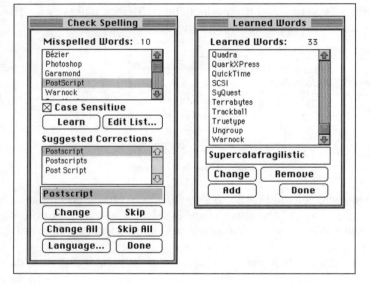

If all words are spelled correctly, a congratulatory message will appear telling you that your spelling is "excellent."

 If you are having a bad day and want some instant encouragement, there is no better way to get it than by creating a new document with no text and selecting the Check Spelling filter. The "Your spelling is excellent" message will appear, making you feel just dandy.

If you have any misspelled words or words that are not in the spelling dictionaries, those words will be listed at the top of the Check Spelling dialog box in the Misspelled Words window. Selecting a word in this list will display similar words below in the window titled Suggested Corrections.

If the Case Sensitive option is checked, the capitalization of words must match the words in the spell checker's dictionary, or they will appear as misspelled words. For instance, in Figure 19-3, the word "PostScript" is selected in the Misspelled Words window. This appeared in the window only because the Case Sensitive check box was checked. Below, in the Suggested Corrections window, one of the suggestions is "Post-script" which is spelled the same but is capitalized differently.

Under the Case Sensitive check box are two buttons. The button on the left, Learn, is used when you would like to add the selected "misspelled" word to your custom dictionary. Clicking the Edit List button displays the Learned Words dialog box (on the right side of Figure 19-3), showing you which words are currently in the user dictionary. The Learned Words dialog box allows you to add, remove, or change entries in the User dictionary.

STEPS: Adding Words to the User Dictionary

Step 1: To add a new entry to the user dictionary, select the Edit List button in the Check Spelling dialog box, which will display the Learned Words dialog box.

Step 2: Type in the word that you would like to add to the user dictionary. Click the Add button, and the word will be added to the list of words in the User dictionary.

Capitalization is very important when adding words, so be sure to place initial caps on proper nouns and to use correct capitalization on all words that require it.

If the word you are trying to add exists in the User dictionary or the Main dictionary, a dialog box will be displayed telling you that it is already a dictionary entry.

Step 3. Repeat Step 2 until all the words have been added.

Step 4. If at any time you make a mistake, you may change the spelling of an entered word by selecting it in the window above, typing in the correct spelling, and then clicking the Change button. If you wish to delete an entry that exists in the Learned Words window, select that word and click the Remove button.

Step 5. When you are finished, click the Done button.

The user dictionary words are saved in a file called "AI User Dictionary," which is stored in the Plug-Ins folder. The file is a TeachText-compatible format, but the character that separates the words is indistinguishable (it appears as an open rectangle, the symbol for a symbol that is not available in that typeface), so there is no way to add words to the dictionary by using TeachText or another word processor.

 Be careful not to delete or remove the AI User Dictionary file when reinstalling the software or moving the files in the Plug-Ins folder. Doing so will cause Illustrator to create a new User Dictionary file with no words in it. There is no way to combine two different user dictionary files.

While you're checking your spelling in the Check Spelling dialog box, clicking the Change button will change the misspelled word with the highlighted word in the Suggested Corrections list below. Clicking the Change All button will replace all misspelled occurrences of that word throughout the entire document with the correctly spelled word.

Clicking the Skip button will ignore that occurrence of the misspelled word. Clicking Skip All will skip all occurrences of that word in the document.

Clicking the Language button will use another dictionary for the language you are using. Illustrator 5.5 supplies dictionaries for the United States and the United Kingdom, both located in the Plug-In filters files.

 Oddly enough, dictionaries for other languages are *not* available through Adobe, even though there are Hyphenation dictionaries available for several different languages, including Danish, Dutch, Finnish, French, German, Hungarian, Italian, Norwegian, Spanish, and Swedish.

Clicking the Done button will close the Check Spelling dialog box.

The Find Font filter

 New to Version 5.5 of Illustrator is the Find Font filter, which looks for certain fonts in a document and replaces them with fonts you specify.

Select type with either a Selection tool or with a Type tool. Then select Filter⇨Text⇨Find Font to use this filter. The Find Font dialog box will appear, as shown in Figure 19-4.

Figure 19-4:
The Find Font dialog box.

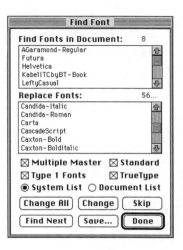

To change all occurrences of a certain font to another font, select the font to be changed in the top window, titled Find Fonts in Document. Then select a font in the Replace Fonts window and click the Change All button. To change one particular instance, click the Change button. To find the next occurrence of that font, select Find Next. The Skip button skips over the currently selected text and finds the next occurrence of that font.

Pressing the Save button will allow you to save your font list as a text file.

 After the fonts are found, you have to select type with the Type tool, no matter how it was selected before the Find Font filter was used.

The Revert Text Paths filter

 New to Version 5.5 of Illustrator is the Revert Text Paths filter, which converts selected text paths into standard Illustrator paths. This is useful for working with paths that have had text on them but don't work like normal paths anymore.

 Creating Text Paths (Path type and Area type) is discussed in Chapter 8.

Before you use this filter, the text path to be converted must contain *no* text. If it does contain text, click on the text path with a Type tool, select Edit⇨Select All (⌘-A), and press Delete. Select the type path with a Selection tool. Then select Filter⇨Text⇨Revert Text Path. The Revert Text Path dialog box will appear.

You have one choice in the Revert Text Path dialog box: whether or not to delete the original text path. If you check the check box, the original text path will be converted into an Illustrator path. If you do *not* check the check box, the original text path will remain, and a new Illustrator path of the exact same size will be placed directly on top of the original path.

 This filter works for Path type, Area type, and Rectangle type.

The Rows & Columns filter

 New to Version 5.5 of Illustrator is the Rows & Columns filter, which divides rectangular paths (text or standard Illustrator rectangles) into even sections. This is as close to a "grid" feature as Illustrator gets.

To use the Rows & Columns filter, select a path and select Filter⇨Text⇨Rows & Columns. The Rows & Columns dialog box will appear, as shown in Figure 19-5.

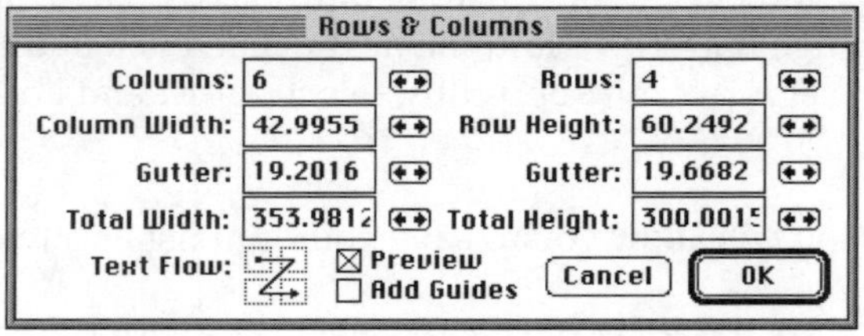

Figure 19-5:
The Rows & Columns
dialog box.

Rows & Columns			
Columns: 6	⟨⟩	Rows: 4	⟨⟩
Column Width: 42.9955	⟨⟩	Row Height: 60.2492	⟨⟩
Gutter: 19.2016	⟨⟩	Gutter: 19.6682	⟨⟩
Total Width: 353.981	⟨⟩	Total Height: 300.001	⟨⟩

Text Flow: ⊠ Preview ☐ Add Guides   [Cancel] [OK]

Any path, open or closed, can be selected and divided into rows and columns, with one catch: the object will become a rectangular shape, the size of the original path's *bounding box* (the smallest box that could completely contain the path). There is no way to divide a nonrectangular path automatically. See the steps below for a way to do this without Illustrator knowing about it.

The left side of the Rows & Columns dialog box determines the width of the columns. The right side determines the height of the rows. At the bottom of the dialog box is a Preview check box; checking this will display changes as you make them in the Rows & Columns dialog box.

 All measurements in the Rows & Columns dialog box are displayed in the current measurement system.

The first text field, Columns, determines how many columns the selected path will be cut into. Below that, Column Width text field determines the width of the columns. The column width must be less than the Total Width (fourth field) divided by the number of columns. The third text field is Gutter, which is the space between columns. The Total Width is how wide the entire rectangle is.

As the Column Width is increased, the Gutter will decrease. When Column Width is decreased, the Gutter will increase. Likewise, as the Gutter is increased, the Column Width will decrease. When Gutter is decreased, the Column Width will increase.

On the right side, the first text field is the number of Rows that the original path will be divided into. The second text field, Row Height, is the height of each of the rows. The Row Height must be less than the Total Height (fourth field on right) divided by the number of rows. The third text field on the right is Gutter, which is the space between rows. The Total Height is how high the entire rectangle is.

As the Row Height is increased, the Gutter will decrease. When Row Height is decreased, the Gutter will increase. Likewise, as the Gutter is increased, the Row Height will decrease. When Gutter is decreased, the Row Height will increase.

Remember that using the Rows & Columns filter actually divides the selected rectangle into several pieces.

The Text Flow option determines the direction of text as it flows from one section to the next. You may choose between text that starts along the top row and flows from left to right, and then goes to the next lowest row, flowing from left to right, and so on. The other option is to have text start in the left column, flowing from top to bottom, and then to the next column to the right, flowing from top to bottom. The Text flow is changed by clicking on the graphic once that is next to the words "Text Flow."

The Add Guides check box will create guides that extend off each edge of the page. These guides align with the edges of each of the boxes created from the Rows & Columns filter.

The following steps show how to create rows and columns in a nonrectangular object.

STEPS:	**Creating Rows and Columns in a Nonrectangular Object**
Step 1:	Create the object that you wish to divide into rows and columns. In my example (see Figure 19-6) I used type converted into outlines and made the entire word one compound path. Copy it to the Clipboard (select Edit⇨Copy, or press ⌘-C).

Step 2: Select Filter⇨Text⇨Rows & Columns and divide the object into the number of rows and columns desired. Click OK. The object will become rectangular.

Step 3: Paste in Front. The original object will appear in front of the rectangle that is divided into rows and columns.

Step 4: Select all objects and select Filter⇨Pathfinder⇨Crop. The result will be a nonrectangular shape that has been divided into rows and columns.

Figure 19-6:
Step for creating nonrectangular columns and rows.

Step 1

Step 2

Step 3

Step 4

STEPS: Creating Angled Rows and Columns

Step 1: Create an oversized object that the rows and columns will be made of.

Step 2: Select Filter⇨Text⇨Rows & Columns and divide the object into the rows and columns, but this time specify the size of the rows and columns, not how many you want. Click OK.

Step 3: Rotate the columns and rows you have just created.

Step 4: Create the object that you would like the angled rows and columns to be inside, and place it in front of the rows and columns. I used a plain rectangle, shown in Figure 19-7.

Step 5: Select all objects and select Filter➪Pathfinder➪Crop. The result will be an object with angled rows and columns within it.

Figure 19-7:
Steps for creating angled rows and columns. The sections have been outlined for easier viewing.

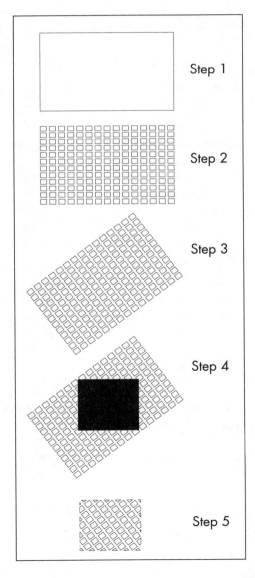

Step 1

Step 2

Step 3

Step 4

Step 5

The Smart Punctuation filter

New to Version 5.5 of Illustrator is the Smart Punctuation filter, which looks for certain fonts in a document and replaces them with fonts you specify.

Select type with either a Selection tool or with a Type tool. Then select Filter⇨ Text⇨Smart Punctuation. The Smart Punctuation dialog box will appear (see Figure 19-8).

Figure 19-8:
The Smart Punctuation
dialog box.

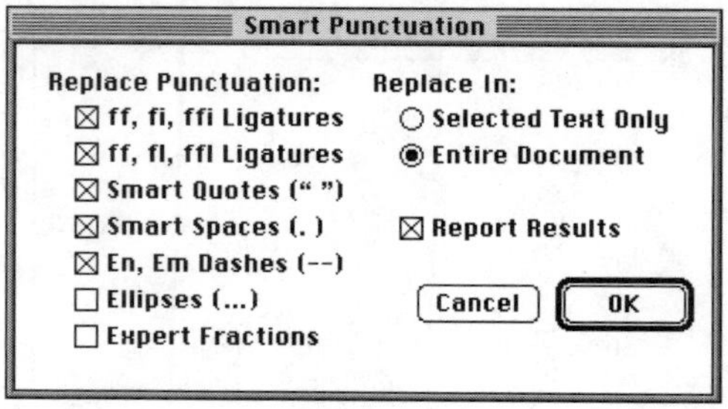

```
╔══════════════ Smart Punctuation ═══════════════╗
║                                                  ║
║  Replace Punctuation:      Replace In:           ║
║  ⊠ ff, fi, ffi Ligatures   ○ Selected Text Only  ║
║  ⊠ ff, fl, ffl Ligatures   ⦿ Entire Document     ║
║  ⊠ Smart Quotes (" ")                            ║
║  ⊠ Smart Spaces (. )       ⊠ Report Results      ║
║  ⊠ En, Em Dashes (--)                            ║
║  ☐ Ellipses (...)          ┌────────┐ ┌──────┐   ║
║  ☐ Expert Fractions        │ Cancel │ │  OK  │   ║
║                            └────────┘ └──────┘   ║
╚══════════════════════════════════════════════════╝
```

The Smart Punctuation filter works "after the fact," making changes to text already in the Illustrator document. There are no settings, for instance, to convert quotes to curved quotes as you are typing them. The types of punctuation to be changed are determined by a set of check boxes in the Smart Punctuation dialog box. A checked box means that Illustrator will look for these certain instances and, if it finds them, correct them with the proper punctuation.

The first two options are used for replacing ff, fi (or fl), and ffi (or ffl) with *ligatures*. Ligatures are characters that represent several characters with one character that is designed to let those characters appear nicer when placed next to each other. Most fonts have fi and fl ligatures, which look like fi and fl, respectively.

Smart Quotes will replace straight quotes (" ", ' ') with curly quotes, known as typesetter's quotes or printer's quotes (" ",' ').

Smart Spaces will replace multiple spaces after a period with one space. In typesetting, there should only be one space following a period.

En, Em Dashes will replace hyphens (-) with En dashes (–) and double hyphens (- -) with Em dashes (—).

Ellipses will replace three periods (...) with an ellipsis (…).

Expert Fractions will replace fractions with expert fractions if you have the expert fractions available in the font family you are using. Adobe sells "Expert Collection" fonts that contain these fractions. If you do *not* have expert fractions, your fractions will remain unchanged.

Checking the Report Results box will display a dialog box when the filter is finished, telling you how many of the punctuation changes were made, divided into several categories.

Areas Related to Illustrator

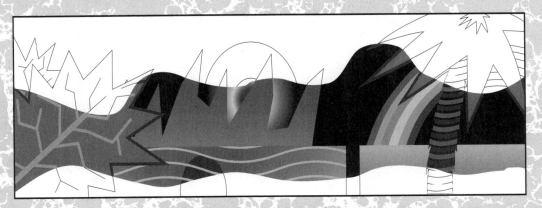

There are many concepts in Illustrator that don't fall under one of Illustrator's menus or tools. There are also several software packages that add features to Illustrator's already immense capabilities.

This section discusses a wide variety of areas and techniques that will help round out your knowledge of Illustrator. At the end of the section, several case studies are dissected so that you can see advanced Illustrator techniques at work.

Strokes and Backgrounds

In This Chapter

- Understanding what you can do with strokes
- The Outline Stroke filter
- Stroke effects for letters
- Blends and strokes
- Rough and feathered edges
- Creating designs on a stroke
- Path type and strokes
- Creating backgrounds
- Blends and gradient backgrounds

Using Strokes

The ability to stroke a path in Illustrator is greatly underrated. Strokes can do more than just outline shapes and vary thicknesses and patterns.

In the first part of this chapter, I explain some of the greatest mysteries and unlock some of the deepest secrets that surround strokes. If that sounds at all boring, take a look at the figures in the first half of this chapter. I created most of them by using strokes, not filled paths. Amazing, ain't it?

Stroke essentials

Strokes, which I introduced in Chapter 5, act and work differently than fills do. Keep the following basics and rules (no pun intended) in mind when using strokes:

- The most important thing to remember when you are using strokes is that stroke weight width is evenly distributed on both sides of a path. In other words, on a stroke with a 6-point weight, there will be 3 points of the stroke on both sides of the stroke's path.

- Patterns can be put into strokes, but patterns cannot be viewed in Preview mode when they are on strokes.

- Gradients may *not* be used to color strokes.

- Using the Outline Stroke filter (Filter⇨Object⇨Outline Stroke) creates path outlines around the width of the stroke. When a stroke has been converted into an outline, it is really an outlined path object and can be filled with patterns and gradients (both of which will appear when previewing and printing).

- Stroke weight *never* varies on the same path.

- A stroke with a color of none has no stroke weight.

- Strokes are, for the most part, ignored when combining/splitting/modifying paths with the Pathfinder filters. Strokes may result but are never taken into account when the Pathfinder filter looks to see the locations of the paths.

The secret magic of strokes

You create most effects with strokes by overlaying several strokes on top of one another. By copying and selecting Edit⇨Paste In Front (⌘-F), you place an exact duplicate of the original path on top of itself.

Changing the weight and color of the top stroke gives the appearance of a path that is a designer, or custom, stroke. You can add strokes on top of or under the original stroke to make the pattern more complex or to add more colors or shapes.

Follow these steps to create a specialty stroke that looks like parallel strokes (see Figure 20-1).

STEPS: Creating "Parallel Strokes"

Step 1. Use the Freehand tool to draw a short line. I usually set the Freehand tolerance (select File⇨General Preferences or press ⌘-K) to 10 for a very smooth path. Change the fill to none and stroke the path with 18-point black.

Step 2. Copy the stroke and paste the copy in front (⌘-F). Change the copied (pasted in front) stroke to 6-point white. Select both paths, copy them (⌘-C), and lock them (⌘-1). The 6-point stroke looks as if it has been subtracted from the 18-point stroke. The result appears to be two separate 6-point black strokes.

Step 3. Select Edit⇨Paste In Back (⌘-B). Deselect All (⌘-Shift-A) and click the top path. Change the weight of the stroke to 30 points. Lock the path and select the remaining path. Change the stroke on this path to 42. The 30 points is 12 points more than the 18 points of the black stroke, or 6 points on each side. The 42 points is 12 more than the white 30 points.

Figure 20-1:
Creating
parallel strokes.

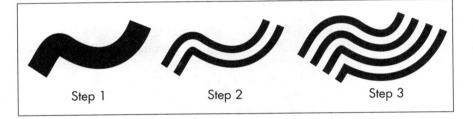

Step 1   Step 2   Step 3

When you are creating "parallel strokes," determine how thick the visible strokes should be, multiply that number times the black *and* white visible strokes that you want for the base stroke, and work up from there. For example, if you want 10-point strokes, and there are four white strokes and five black strokes, the first stroke would be 90 points thick and black. The next stroke would be 70 points white, and then 50 points black, 30 points white, and 10 points black.

This example is just the tip of the iceberg in creating custom strokes. Not only can you have paths that overlap, but you also can give the stroke on each path different dash patterns, joins, and caps. You can even add fills to certain paths to make the stroke different on both sides of the path. And if all that isn't enough, you can use the Outline Stroke filter to outline strokes.

Knowing the secrets doesn't let you in on the really good stuff, though. Read on to learn more.

Using the stroke charts

Figures 20-2, 20-3, 20-5, and 20-6 are charts that show how some of the basic stroke-dash patterns look with various options checked, at different weights, and in different combinations.

All of the paths in the charts were taken from an original shape that included a straight segment, a corner, and a curve. The charts should help you determine when to use certain types of stroke patterns because, as you can see, some patterns work better than others with curves and corners.

The first chart (Figure 20-2) consists of 32 3-point stroked paths that have a variety of dash patterns and end and join attributes. The second chart (Figure 20-3) shows 18 10-point stroke paths with similar attributes. These two charts show stroke effects with only one path. In the charts, text in the middle of each path describes the path. To see what the names of the caps and joins correspond to, see the Stroke section of the Paint Style palette, which is shown in Figure 20-4.

The third chart (Figure 20-5) and fourth chart (Figure 20-6) contain paths that have been copied on top of the original by using the Paste In Front command. The paths are listed in the order that they were created. The first path is described at the top of the list. The first path is copied, pasted in front (⌘-F), and given the Paint Style attributes of the second item in the list. The changes progress from the top left of each chart to the bottom left and then from the top right to the bottom right.

 In some cases, paths are blended from one to another. To be able to select an end point on each stroke (usually they will overlap), offset one of the paths by .1 point. When blending, use a number that is less than 100 for the number of blend steps, dividing the suggested number by 2 until it is small enough.

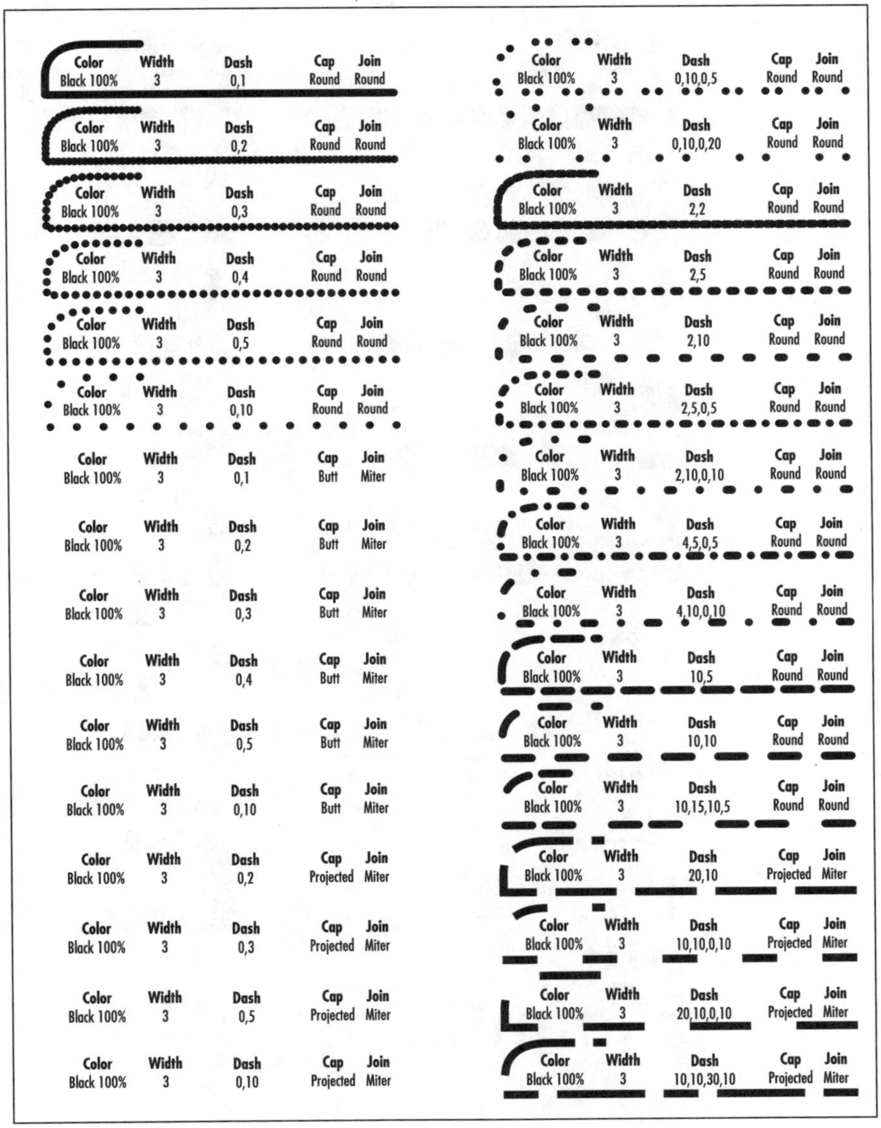

Figure 20-2:
Stroke Chart 1.

Figure 20-3:
Stroke Chart 2.

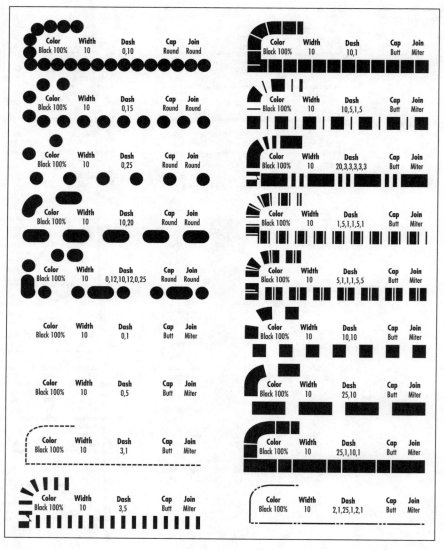

Figure 20-3:
Stroke Chart 2.

Figure 20-4:
The Stroke
section of the
Paint Style
palette.

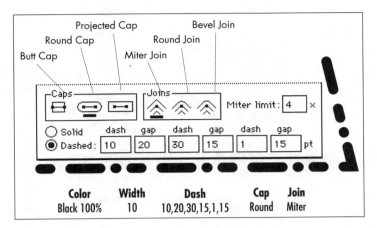

 When you're creating the various stroke patterns, many times the original path will be selected, copied, and then pasted in front or back (⌘-F or ⌘-B) several times. There is usually no need to recopy the original path after it has been copied. It can continue to be pasted again and again on top of or under the original path.

In the middle of the righthand column in Stroke Chart 4 is a stroke that looks like a strip of film. Follow these steps to create it:

STEPS: Creating the Film Stroke from Stroke Chart 4

Step 1. The film stroke from Stroke Chart 4 is a basic stroke that produces a stunning effect. Draw a wavy path with the Freehand tool.

Step 2. Change the stroke of the path to black, 18 points, and the fill to None.

Step 3. Copy (⌘-C) the path and select Edit⇨Paste In Front (⌘-F). Change the stroke to white, 16 points, and use a dash pattern of dash 1, gap 2.

Step 4. Select Edit⇨Paste In Front (⌘-F) again and change the stroke to black, 14 points, solid.

Step 5. Select Edit⇨Paste In Front (⌘-F) one last time and change the stroke to 75% black, 12 points, with a dash pattern of dash 20, gap 10.

Figure 20-7 shows these steps. You can use this procedure to create any of the strokes in Stroke Chart 4 (see Figure 20-6) by substituting the values that are listed in the chart for the stroke that you want.

Figure 20-5:
Stroke
Chart 3.

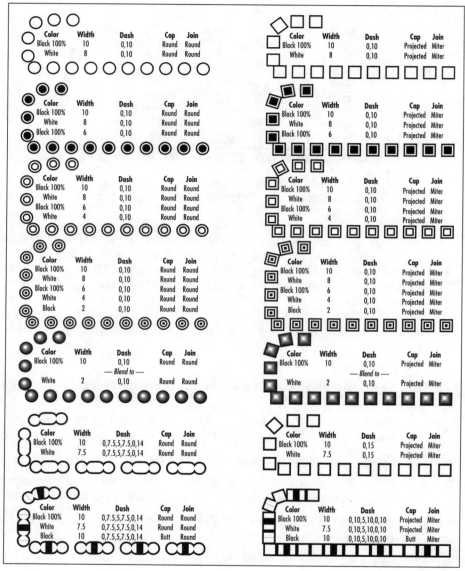

Figure 20-6:
Stroke
Chart 4.

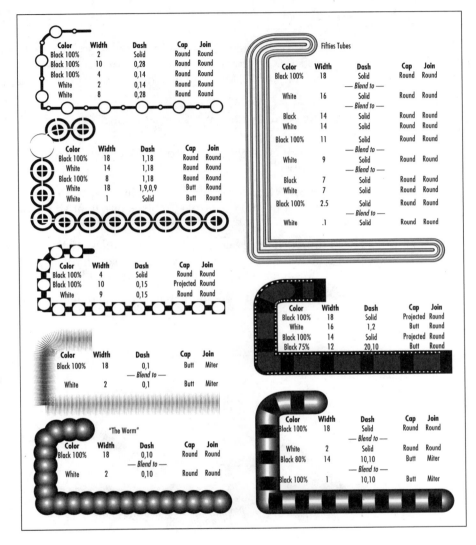

Color	Width	Dash	Cap	Join
Black 100%	2	Solid	Round	Round
Black 100%	10	0,28	Round	Round
Black 100%	4	0,14	Round	Round
White	2	0,14	Round	Round
White	8	0,28	Round	Round

Color	Width	Dash	Cap	Join
Black 100%	18	1,18	Round	Round
White	14	1,18	Round	Round
Black 100%	8	1,18	Round	Round
White	18	1,9,0,9	Butt	Round
White	1	Solid	Butt	Round

Color	Width	Dash	Cap	Join
Black 100%	4	Solid	Round	Round
Black 100%	10	0,15	Projected	Round
White	9	0,15	Round	Round

Color	Width	Dash	Cap	Join
Black 100%	18	0,1	Butt	Miter
		— *Blend to* —		
White	2	0,1	Butt	Miter

"The Worm"

Color	Width	Dash	Cap	Join
Black 100%	18	0,10	Round	Round
		— *Blend to* —		
White	2	0,10	Round	Round

Fifties Tubes

Color	Width	Dash	Cap	Join
Black 100%	18	Solid	Round	Round
		— *Blend to* —		
White	16	Solid	Round	Round
		— *Blend to* —		
Black	14	Solid	Round	Round
White	14	Solid	Round	Round
Black 100%	11	Solid	Round	Round
		— *Blend to* —		
White	9	Solid	Round	Round
		— *Blend to* —		
Black	7	Solid	Round	Round
White	7	Solid	Round	Round
Black 100%	2.5	Solid	Round	Round
		— *Blend to* —		
White	.1	Solid	Round	Round

Color	Width	Dash	Cap	Join
Black 100%	18	Solid	Projected	Round
White	16	1,2	Butt	Round
Black 100%	14	Solid	Projected	Round
Black 75%	12	20,10	Butt	Round

Color	Width	Dash	Cap	Join
Black 100%	18	Solid	Round	Round
		— *Blend to* —		
White	2	Solid	Round	Round
Black 80%	14	10,10	Butt	Miter
		— *Blend to* —		
Black 100%	1	10,10	Butt	Miter

Stroking type

 You can use strokes to enhance type in a number of ways. The first example (shown in Figure 20-8) is based on stroke blends. For more information on stroke blends, see Chapter 12; for more information on type, see Chapter 8.

STEPS: **Creating Ghosted Type with Strokes**

Step 1. Type a few words in a heavily weighted font, like Helvetica Black, Futura Extra Bold, or Kabel Ultra.

Step 2. Select the type with the Selection tool and select Type⇨Create Outlines and change the fill to None and the stroke to black or a light shade of gray. Change the weight of the stroke to .1 point.

Step 3. Copy (⌘-C) the words and Select Edit⇨Paste In Back (⌘-B). Move the copy a few points up and to the right. Change the stroke on the copy to 4-point white and blend each set of paths together with the Blend tool.

Step 4. Select Edit⇨Paste In Front (⌘-F) and change the fill to white and the stroke to None.

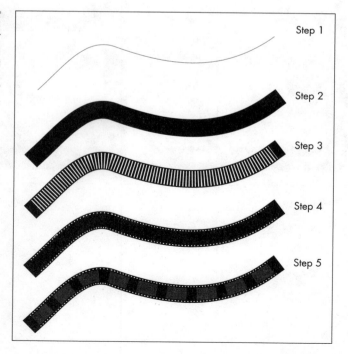

Figure 20-7:
The steps for
creating the film
stroke from Stroke
Chart 4.

Step 1

Step 2

Step 3

Step 4

Step 5

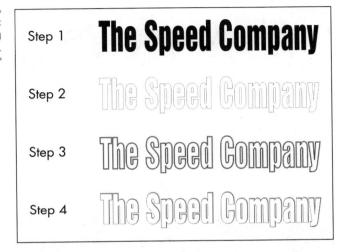

Figure 20-8:
Steps for creating
ghosted type.

Another popular effect (OK, it was popular in the '70s, but the style made a comeback) for type is to create several strokes for each stroke of a letter, as shown in Figure 20-9.

STEPS: **Creating Type That Has Multiple Strokes**

Step 1. Create a word or words in a lightweight typeface.

Step 2. Use the Pen tool to re-create the letters in the typeface. I colored the letters in the original word light red and then locked those letters in place so that I could trace the letters easier.

Step 3. Group all the paths that you have drawn and give them a heavy stroke. I used 18 points in the example. Change the join and cap style in the Paint Style palette to rounded.

Step 4. Copy (⌘-C) and paste in front (⌘-F) in gradually decreasing stroke weights. Change between white and a darker color as the weight decreases.

Figure 20-9:
Making type
that has
multiple
strokes.

Step 1

Step 2

Step 3

Step 4

Creating rough edges

You can create some of the most interesting stroke effects by using the Roughen filter in combination with a heavily weighted stroke. Even with a Roughen filter setting of 1% or 2%, a heavily weighted stroke can have many sharp, long points, as the following example shows:

STEPS:	Using Strokes to Create Multiple Jagged Edges
Step 1.	Create an object to which you want to add jagged or explosive edges. I used text that was converted to outlines in the example (see Figure 20-10). Copy the object off to the side before continuing.
Step 2.	Use the Offset Path filter to create a path that is offset by 20 points or more. Select all the paths and choose Filter⇨Pathfinder⇨Unite.

Step 3.   Copy the path again, roughen the path Filter⇨Distort⇨Roughen (2%, 40 per inch), and apply a 20-point stroke to it. Paste the roughened path in front and roughen it again; then apply a 20-point stroke in a different color. Continue to paste in front, roughen, and thicken the stroke until you have created a satisfactory number of paths.

Step 4.   Paste in front one last time and roughen as before, but give the stroke a lesser weight and fill the path with the same color as the stroke. Place the original art (which you copied off to the side in Step 1) on top of the roughened paths.

Figure 20-10:
Creating roughened
paths with strokes.

Using fills to create half-stroked paths

One technique that I don't think is used enough is hiding one side of the stroke as the path layers are built up. To hide half of the stroke at any level, paste in front as you normally do and then press ⌘-Option-1. This command locks everything that isn't selected; in other words, only the path that you just pasted (and which is currently selected) will not be locked.

Using the Pen tool, connect the ends of the just-pasted path and fill it with the background color and a stroke of None. This action obliterates one side of the stroke because the file of the path covers the "inside" part of the stroked path. Any strokes that you place on top of this object will be visible on both sides of the path.

Workin' on the railroad

Several effects that you can create with paths have a traveling theme, mainly because a path starts somewhere and finishes somewhere else. Railroad tracks, roads, highways, trails, and rivers all have a tendency to conform very nicely to stroke effects with paths.

 If you are using Illustrator 5.0 and do not have an FPU on your system, you will not be able to use the Outline Stroke filter described below. As an alternative, ignore those steps and instead stroke the path with a comparable color (that is, light blue-gray for metallic).

One of the trickiest traveling paths to create is railroad tracks. To get the real railroad track look, some advanced "cheating" is necessary, as shown in the following steps:

STEPS: Creating Railroad Tracks

Step 1. Draw a path to represent the railroad. Create a background shape and fill the background with a color. In the example (see Figure 20-11), I used dark green.

Step 2. Copy the path. Give the path a stroke weight of 30 points. Select Edit⇨Paste In Front (⌘-F) and give this path a stroke weight of 20 points.

Step 3. Select both paths. Choose Filter⇨Object⇨Outline Stroke to change the paths into outlined paths because strokes cannot contain gradients. Fill the paths with a metallic gradient.

Step 4. Select both paths and choose Filter⇨Pathfinder⇨Exclude. This command subtracts the inner section of the track from the two outer sections.

Step 5. Check the ends of the path and delete any excess paths that are not part of the tracks. In the example, I also joined the ends on each individual track.

Step 6. Paste in back (⌘-B) and give the new path a stroke weight of 40 points. Choose Filter⇨Object⇨Outline Stroke and fill this path with a gradient consisting of several woodlike browns. This path is the wood that underlies the tracks.

Step 7. The last thing to do is split the pieces of wood into individual railroad ties. Select the wood path and choose Edit⇨Paste In Front (⌘-F). This command will paste a path right on top of the wooden area. Give this stroke the same color as the background and give it a dash pattern of dash 20, gap 10. The gaps will be the "see through" areas, showing the wood-filled path below them.

To easily change the color of the new path in Step 7, select the new path, choose the Eyedropper tool, and double-click the background.

The Outline Stroke filter is often used on this type of stroke design because strokes can't have gradient fills. The reason that the railroad ties were not given a dash pattern before the Outline Stroke filter was applied is that the Outline Stroke filter doesn't work with dash patterns.

Figure 20-11:
Steps for
creating
railroad tracks.

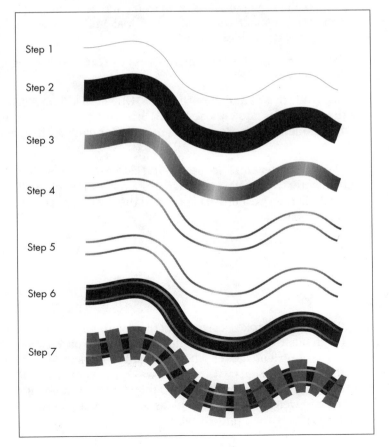

The wild river

A wild river is another path that you can create easily by using strokes. One problem in getting rivers to look good is that creating the rough, in-out texture of a river's bank is difficult. Also, because different parts of rivers are different weights, connecting the parts smoothly is difficult. The following example describes how to create a river:

STEPS: Creating a River

Step 1. Draw the paths for the river. In the example (see Figure 20-12), I created a *Y* at one end of the river and an island. For these features, I used the Pen tool to draw additional paths next to the river.

Step 2. Give the river a stroke weight and color. In the example, I gave the main part of the river a stroke of 18 points and the two additional parts 14-point strokes. Copy all of the paths, paste in front, and color the copy a little darker than the original river stroke color. Make the strokes on the copy a few points less wide than on the original.

Step 3. Blend (Filter➪Colors➪Blend Front To Back) the two strokes together, using three blend steps.

Step 4. Select all of the strokes and choose Filter➪Object➪Outline Stroke. Select one of the new paths and choose Filter➪Select➪Same Fill Color. Choose Filter➪Pathfinder➪Unite. Repeat this process for each of the five different colors.

Step 5. Select all of the paths and choose Filter➪Distort➪Roughen. In the Roughen dialog box, enter **.3** and **40** segments per inch and then click OK. The edges of the river will now be a little ragged, and they will appear to have ripples, or waves, in them.

The highway

Figures 20-13 and 20-14 show a stroke design that I discovered a few years back while I was playing around with Illustrator. It has the makings of a cute parlor magic trick that you can use to impress your friends. Back when you had to work in Artwork mode, before Illustrator 5.0, creating designs with strokes was much more difficult. Artists couldn't see what they were drawing on-screen, so they had to envision it in their minds. Editing dashes and weights is almost a pleasure now that you can use the Auto feature of the Paint Style palette and undo multiple changes.

Figure 20-12:
Steps for making
a river.

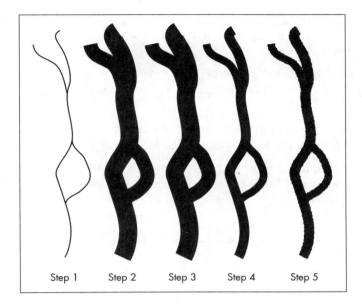

Step 1   Step 2   Step 3   Step 4   Step 5

After creating the Railroad Tracks stroke design, which I thought was pretty clever, I yearned for a similar effect — turning one path into an object. I especially liked the effect of doing several paths and several stroke attributes in Artwork mode and then switching to Preview mode when I was finished.

Figures 20-13 and 20-14 show the following steps that you take to create a four-lane highway by drawing just one path.

STEPS: Creating a Highway

Step 1. Use the Freehand tool to draw a slightly wavy path from the left side of the Artboard to the right side and then group the path.

Step 2. Change the Paint Style of the stroke to a fill of None and create a 400-point stroke that is colored as follows: cyan 100, magenta 25, and yellow 100. This path is the grass next to the highway.

Step 3. Copy the path and paste in front. Change the paint style of the stroke to cyan 25, yellow 25, and black 85, with a weight of 240 points. This path is the shoulder of the highway.

Step 4. Paste in front and change the paint style to cyan 5 and black 10, with a weight of 165 points. This path is the white line at the edge of the highway.

Step 5. Paste in front and change the paint style to cyan 15, yellow 10, and black 50, with a weight of 160 points. This path is the highway's road surface.

Step 6. To create the dashed white lines for passing, paste in front and change the paint style to cyan 5 and black 10, with a weight of 85 points, a dash of 20, and a gap of 20.

Step 7. Paste in front and change the paint style to cyan 15, yellow 10, and black 50, with a weight of 80 points. This path is the inner part of the highway's road surface.

Step 8. To create the double yellow line, paste in front and change the paint style to cyan 15, magenta 20, and yellow 100, with a weight of 8 points.

Step 9. Paste in front and change the paint style to cyan 15, yellow 10, and black 50, with a weight of 3 points. This path is the piece of highway that divides the double yellow line.

Figure 20-13:
The first five steps in creating a highway.

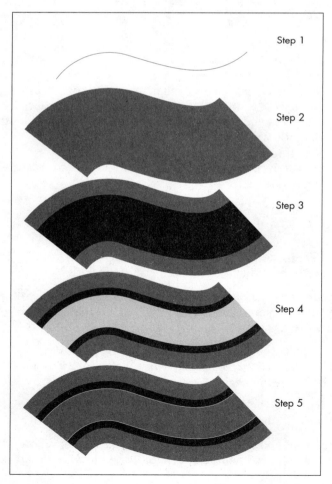

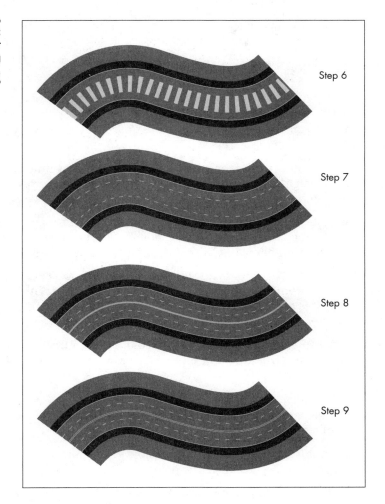

Figure 20-14:
The last four
steps in creating
a highway.

Step 6

Step 7

Step 8

Step 9

With the Outline Stroke filter included with Illustrator 5.0, I have taken the highway concept a step or two further by adding a passing zone to the highway.

 If your computer does not have an FPU and you are using Illustrator 5.0, you will not be able to use the Offset Path filter and will not be able to create a passing zone for your highway.

Follow these steps to create the passing zone, as shown in Figure 20-15:

STEPS:	Adding a Passing Zone to the Highway
Step 1.	Delete the top two paths of the original highway. Select all of the paths and choose Arrange⇨Hide (⌘-3) to hide the base of the road temporarily. You don't need to change anything about these parts of the highway to create the passing zone effect.
Step 2.	Paste in front and change the paint style to cyan 15, magenta 20, and yellow 100, with a weight of 8 points. This path is the same double yellow line as the one in Step 8 of the preceding instructions, but it is not yet split.
Step 3.	Copy and paste in front. Keep the paint style at cyan 15, magenta 20, and yellow 100 but change the weight to 3 points. This line is the same width as the road from number 9, but the color is the double yellow-line color.
Step 4.	Select All (⌘-A). This command selects the last two paths that you placed on the illustration. Choose Filter⇨Object⇨Outline Stroke. This command create outlines around the edges of the stroke so that it results in two filled objects instead of two overlapping stroked paths.
Step 5.	Select Filter⇨Pathfinder⇨Exclude. This command subtracts the top object (the 3-point path) from the bottom one, resulting in two filled objects that are grouped together. Ungroup the two objects by selecting Edit⇨Ungroup (⌘-U).
Step 6.	Deselect one of the two paths by Shift-clicking it once and deleting the selected object.
Step 7.	Paste in front to put the line with the double yellow-line stroke in front of the remaining filled object. Change the paint style to dash 20, gap 20.
Step 8.	Paste in front and change the paint style to cyan 15, yellow 10, and black 50, with a weight of 3 points. These settings create a gray line that divides the dashed section from the solid section of line. The dashed section is actually on both sides of the 3-point gray divider line, but you cannot see the part that overlays the solid line because it is the same color and size as the solid line.
Step 9.	Select Arrange⇨Show All. The highway has a dashed/solid yellow line.

You can see the highway, and many of the other effects described in this chapter, in Figure 20-16.

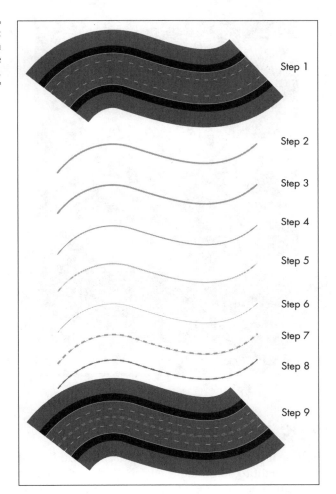

Step 1
Step 2
Step 3
Step 4
Step 5
Step 6
Step 7
Step 8
Step 9

Figure 20-15:
Steps for creating a passing zone for the highway.

Figure 20-16:
This poster incorporates
many of the effects
described in this
chapter. The Color
Insert in the center of
this book shows the
poster in color.

Putting type into strokes

You can put type into strokes by creating Path type and giving the path a heavy enough stroke weight to surround the type, as described in the following steps. Using symbols and special typefaces, you can create almost any pattern at all when you put type inside strokes. (For more information on creating Path type, see Chapter 8.)

STEPS: Making Type into a Stroke Pattern

Step 1.   Draw a path that you want the type to appear upon.

Step 2.   Click the path with the Path Type tool. Type the letters, numbers, or symbols that will make up the pattern.

Step 3.   Select the characters, copy, and paste. Paste until the path is full of characters.

Step 4.   Using the Direct Selection tool, change the fill on the characters and the stroke of the path.

If you are blessed with font creation software, such as Altsys Fontographer, you can achieve even better results. Simply incorporate any artwork that you create in Illustrator into a font and then use that artwork as Path type by using that font when you type.

Creating Backgrounds for Illustrations

This section contains examples of backgrounds (see Figure 20-17) and suggestions for creating backgrounds for illustrations. You can create backgrounds in a number of ways. For example, you can use gradients, EPS images, blends, and patterns. When you are deciding what type of background to use, remember that you need to consider how well a background will interact with the front artwork.

Figure 20-17:
A variety of backgrounds for illustrations. The Color Insert in the center of this book shows these examples in color.

Using gradients for backgrounds

Gradients can be very effective backgrounds all by themselves, providing that they don't detract from the front artwork.

In the following example, I combined linear and radial gradients for an impressive effect.

STEPS: **Using Gradients to Create a Sunset**

Step 1. Draw a rectangle to serve as the background area. Create a bottom edge (I used mountains) that will sit in front of the background. For sunsets and other sky-related backgrounds, try to avoid a flat, horizontal base. Color the mountains or bottom edge with a solid fill color and then select the background for the rectangle.

You create the gradient after you create the object that it will fill so that you can instantly see how the gradient will appear in that object in the illustration.

Step 2. Double-click the Gradient Vector tool to display the Gradient palette. Click the New button and call the gradient Sunset. In the Paint Style palette, replace the fill of the rectangle with the sunset gradient and change the angle of the gradient to 90°.

Step 3. In the Gradient palette, make the following color stops: at 0%, white; at 5%, yellow 100%; at 15%, yellow 100%; at 25%, yellow 100% and magenta 50%; at 35%, magenta 50%; at 50%, cyan 15% and magenta 10%; at 80%, cyan 25%; and at 100%, cyan 50%.

The first two 100% yellow color stops create a solid area of yellow within the gradient.

Step 4. Draw a circle in the solid yellow area of the gradient. In the gradient palette, create a new radial gradient called Sunset Sun and create the following color stops: at 0%, white; at 5%, yellow 30%; at 80%, yellow 60%; at 100%, yellow 100%. Because the sun blends into the color of the solid band in the sunset gradient, it appears to blend very nicely. In the example, I partially hid the sun behind some of the clouds.

Using the same technique, I created the sun for a blue sky. In the sun gradient, the last color stop is the same color as the sky.

By themselves, gradients can be effective backgrounds. When you combine gradients with patterns, blends, or other objects, they can form a complex, sometimes realistic, backdrop.

Using blends and blend effects for backgrounds

You can use a number of different methods to create backgrounds by using blends:

▩ One method is to blend two shapes together, one larger and one smaller. You can achieve different effects by choosing different shapes.

▩ By blending from a large circle to a small circle, you can create a very smooth blend that produces better results than using a radial gradient.

▩ One of the best ways to get a smooth, unobtrusive background when you are using gradients is to blend smoothly curved lines together and mask them in the shape of the background rectangle.

▩ You can achieve interesting highlights between two blend shapes by blending to different points on objects.

Printing Separations and Traps

■ ■

CHAPTER 21

In This Chapter

▓ Understanding the difference between composites and separations

▓ Determining when to use process versus spot color separations

▓ Printing out of Adobe Separator

▓ Understanding line screens

▓ Printing separations from other programs

▓ Understanding trapping

▓ Using the Overprint features for trapping

▓ Using filters for trapping

▓ Trapping after you create an image in Illustrator

■ ■

Printing

You can print Illustrator documents in two ways. The first method is to print a composite, which is a combination of all the colors and tints on one printout. To print a composite, you select File⇨Print (⌘-P). The other way to print a document is by printing color separations. This method divides the output into several different printouts, one for each color. Printing color separations is needed when the illustration will be printed on a printing press.

Printing composites

A composite printout looks very much like the image that appears on the screen when you preview the document (select View⇨Preview or press ⌘-Y). If you have a color printer, the image appears in color; otherwise, the colors are replaced by gray tints (see the "Gray Colors" sidebar).

Composites print to the maximum dots per inch of the printer. You align the objects on the page in the Page Setup dialog box (File⇨Page Setup). (See Chapter 9 for more information on setting up a document to print composite images.)

Objects that are hidden or that exist on layers that are currently hidden will not print, and neither will objects that exist on layers that have the printing option unchecked in the Layers Option dialog box.

Gray colors

When you are printing a full color illustration to a black-and-white printer, Illustrator substitutes gray values for colors. In this way, the program creates the illusion that each color has a separate, distinct gray value.

Of course, each color can't have only certain gray values, so the colors have to overlap at some point. Illustrator converts each of the process colors into specific gray values when it prints to a black-and-white printer.

Magenta is the darkest process color, ranging from 0% to 73% gray. Therefore, at 100% magenta, it prints at 73% gray. Cyan is second darkest, ranging from 0% to 57% gray. Yellow is extremely light, ranging from 0% to only 11% gray. The figure shows a comparison of the four process colors at various settings and their printed results. The four bars show different values for each process color, as indicated above the bars. Within each bar is the percent of black that prints when you are printing that color at that percentage to a black-and-white printer.

Different printers may produce different tints of gray. Lower-resolution printers, such as 300 dpi (dots per inch) laser printers, do not create an accurate gray tint because they use dots that are too large to create accurate tint patterns.

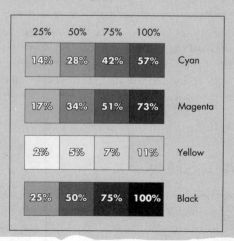

Printing color separations

Illustrator cannot print separations, so you have to use additional software if you want to print separations. To get around this problem, Adobe designed a program called Separator, which creates color separations from Illustrator documents. Separator is packaged with Illustrator. Another way to create color separations is to place an Illustrator file in a page layout program, such as QuarkXPress or PageMaker, and color separate the file along with the rest of the page layout document.

Color separations are necessary for printing a color version of an illustration on most printing presses. Each separation creates a plate that is affixed to a round drum on a printing press. Ink that is the same color as that separation is applied to the plate, which is pressed against a sheet of paper. Because the ink adheres only to the "printing" areas of the plate, an image is produced on paper. Some printing presses have many different drums and can print a four-color job in one run. Other printing presses have only one or two drums, so the paper has to pass through the press four or two times, respectively, to print a four-color job.

Learning printing from the experts

If you have never visited a printing company, make a point to visit one and take a tour. Most printing companies have staff members who are more than willing to explain their equipment and various printing processes. In a 30-minute tour with a knowledgeable guide, you can learn enough to save yourself hours of work, money, and misunderstandings.

When you are talking to a representative at the printing company, find out what type of media they want your work on. Printing companies commonly have imagesetters that can output the job for you, and some companies even perform this service at no charge if you have the job printed there.

Imagesetters are similar to laser printers, except that they produce images with a very high dpi, from 1273 to 3600, and sometimes higher. Imagesetters can print directly to RC (resin-coated) paper or to film negatives (or positives). The paper or film runs through the imagesetter and then must run through a developing process for the images and text to appear.

Most printing company salespeople are fluent to a minor degree in desktop publishing speak, though few will know the difference between a TIFF and an EPS. They can tell you when to give them negs (film negatives) and paper and which service bureau to use if they don't have an imagesetter in-house. Many of them can tell you which software their clients prefer and which software packages create problems, and they can give you tips that can help you get your project through smoothly.

(continued)

(continued)

A service bureau is a company or part of a company that has on its premises an imagesetter, and whose function is to provide the general community of desktop publishers with imagesetter output for a cost between $7 and $40 per page. Service bureaus often have color output capabilities, offer disk-conversion services, and other services that are sometimes needed by desktop publishers.

Better yet, do what I did: work at a printing company for a short period of time. The first job I had out of college at Y/Z Printing taught me more than I learned in four years of school and entrenched in me some of the most important basic skills for graphics design that I still use and need every day. Ever wonder why your printer gets so grumpy when you tell him that your negs won't be available to him until two days after you told him? Working inside a printing company can give you an understanding of job scheduling, an art of prophecy and voodoo that gives ulcers to printing company managers and supervisors.

The more you know about printing and your printer, the better your print job will turn out, and the fewer hassles you will have to deal with.

The two types of color separation are process color separation and spot color separation. Each type has its own advantages and drawbacks, and you can use either type or a combination of both types for any print job. You should always determine which type of separation you want *before* you begin to create a job electronically.

Spot color separation

Jobs that are printed with spot colors are often referred to as "two-color" or "three-color" jobs when two or three colors are used. Although you can use any number of colors, most spot color jobs contain only a few colors.

Spot color printing is most useful when you are using two or three distinct colors in a job. For example, if I needed only black and green to create a certain illustration, I would use only black and a green custom color for all of the objects in the illustration.

One use for spot color separations is in screen printing, which is a printing process where a flexible, taut screen is coated with ink and the ink is then applied to items that are not made of paper, such as T-shirts, towels, and mugs.

The three reasons for using spot color separation, rather than process color separation, are

▓ It's cheaper. Spot color printing requires a smaller press with fewer drums. For process color separation, you usually need to use a press with four drums or run the job through a smaller press a number of times.

▓ Spot colors are cleaner, brighter, and smoother than the same colors that you create as process colors. To get a green process color, for example, you need to mix both cyan and yellow on paper. Using one spot color will result in a perfectly solid area of color.

▓ You cannot duplicate certain spot colors, especially fluorescent and metallic colors, with process colors.

Illustrator creates spot colors whenever you specify a custom color. If you use six different custom colors and black, you could print out seven different spot color separations.

Spot colors have limitations and disadvantages. The primary limitation of using only spot colors is that the number of colors is restricted to the number of color separations that you want to produce. Remember that the cost of a print job is directly related to the number of different colored inks in the job.

The cutoff point for using spot colors is usually three colors. When you use four spot colors, you limit yourself to four distinct colors and use as many colors as a process color job that can have an almost infinite number of colors. Spot color jobs of six colors are not unusual, however. Sometimes people use more than three spot colors to keep colors distinct and clear. Each of the six colors will be bright, vibrant, and distinct from its neighbors, whereas different process colors seem to fade into one another due to their similarity.

 Spot colors are often incorrectly referred to as Pantone colors. Pantone is a brand name for a color matching system. You can select Pantone colors as custom colors and use them in Illustrator, and you can print them as either spot colors or as process colors.

Process color separation

Process color separation, also known as four-color separation, creates almost any color by combining cyan, magenta, yellow, and black inks. By using various combinations of different tints of each of these colors, you can reproduce most colors that the human eye can see.

You use process color separation when

- The illustration includes color photographs.
- The illustration contains more than three different colors.

By now, you have probably used the process color square to create illustrations within Illustrator. This square, which has the four process colors in it, enables you to pick from any percentage of any of the colors to create all the different colors you need.

How many colors?

Everyone always says that you can create as many colors as you could ever want when you are using process colors. Maybe.

In Illustrator, you can specify colors up to $\frac{1}{100}$ percent accuracy. As a result, 10,000 different shades are available for each of the 4 process colors. So, theoretically, $10,000^4$, or 10,000,000,000,000,000, different colors should be available, which is 10 quadrillion, or ten million billion. Any way you look at it, you have a heck of a lot of color possibilities.

Unfortunately, PostScript Level 2 can produce only 256 different shades for each color. This limitation drops the number of available colors to 256^4, or 4,294,967,296, which is about 4.3 billion colors — only 1 billionth of the colors that Illustrator can create.

That limitation is fortunate for us humans, however, because the estimate is that we can detect a maximum of 100 different levels of gray, probably less. As a result, we can view only 100^4, or 100,000,000, different colors.

We can run into a problem when we preview illustrations, however. An RGB monitor (used on computers) can display up to 16.7 million colors, theoretically, if each red, green, and blue pixel can be varied by 256 different intensities. Most recent Macintoshes can create only 32,768 colors with their on-board video, and some are limited to 256 colors. You need to add special video cards or additional VRAM (Video RAM) to Macintosh computers to display the 16.7 million colors that monitors can produce.

Another problem is that about 30 percent of the colors that you can view on an RGB monitor can't be reproduced by using cyan, magenta, yellow, and black inks on white paper. You can't create these unprintable colors in Illustrator, but you can create them in most other drawing and graphics software packages. The only use these colors have is to view them on screen.

The secret to process color separation is that the four colors that make up all the different colors are themselves not visible. Each color is printed as a pattern of tiny dots, angled differently from the other three colors. The angles of each color are very important. If the angles are off even slightly, a noticeable pattern that is commonly known as a *moiré* will emerge.

The colors are printed in a specific order—usually cyan, magenta, yellow, and black. Although the debate continues about the best order in which to print the four colors, black is always printed last.

To see the dots for each color, use a magnifying device to look closely at something that is preprinted and in full color. Even easier, look at the Sunday comics, which have bigger dots than most other printed pieces. The different colored dots in the Sunday comics are quite visible, and their only colors are magenta, cyan, yellow, and black.

The size of the dots that produce each of these separations also is important. The smaller the dots, the smoother the colors appear. Large dots (such as in the Sunday comics) can actually take away from the illusion of a certain color because the viewer sees the different colored dots.

See the section, "Setting the halftone screen," later in this chapter, for more information on how dot size relates to the quality of the illustration, as well as what the common sizes are.

The figure shows how process colors are combined to create new colors. In the figure, the first four rows show very large dots. The top three rows are cyan, magenta, and yellow. The fourth row is all four process colors combined, and the bottom row shows how the illustration looks when you print it.

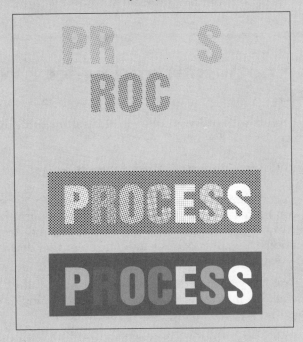

(continued)

(continued)

Process color printing is best for photographs because photographs originate from a *continuous tone* that is made on photographic paper from film, instead of being made of dots on a printing press.

In Illustrator, you can convert custom colors to process colors before printing or during printing. To convert custom colors to process colors *before* printing, select any objects that have a specific custom color and tint and click the process color icon. The color will be converted to its process color counterpart, and all selected objects will be filled with the new process color combination.

After you click the process color icon, if the selected objects become filled with white and the triangles for each process color are at 0%, you have selected objects that contain different colors or tints. Undo the change immediately.

To make sure that you select only objects that have the same color, select one of the objects and choose Filter⇨Select⇨Same Paint Style. Objects that have different strokes or objects with different tints of the same color will not be selected.

You can convert custom colors to process colors in the Adobe Separator Separation dialog box (see the "Working with Different Color Separations" section, later in this chapter) and in many page layout programs.

Combining both spot and process color separations

You can couple spot colors with process colors in Illustrator simply by creating both process and custom colors in a document.

Usually, you add spot colors to process colors for the following reasons:

- You are using a company logo that has a specific color. By printing that color as a spot color, you make it stand out from the other coloring. In addition, color is more accurate when it comes from a specific ink rather than from a process color combination. Often, the logo is a Pantone color that doesn't reproduce true to form when you use process color separation.

- You need a color that you can't create by using process colors. Such colors are most often metallic or fluorescent, but they can be any number of Pantone colors or other colors that you can't match with process colors.

- You need a varnish for certain areas of an illustration. A varnish is a glazed type of ink that results in a shiny area wherever you use the varnish. You commonly use varnishes on titles and logos and over photographs.

▓ You need a light color over a large area. The dots that make up process colors are most noticeable in light colors, but by using a spot color to cover the area with a solid sheet of ink that has no dots, you can make the area smoother and enhance it visually.

In some circumstances, you need to use a spot color as a spot color and also use it as a process color. Normally, you can't do both, but the following steps describe one way to get around this problem:

STEPS:	Using a Custom Color as Both a Spot Color and a Process Color
Step 1.	Select Object⇨Custom Color. In the Custom Color dialog box, choose the custom color and change the name of the color by adding the word *spot* after it.
Step 2.	Memorize or write down the process color combination of the custom color.
Step 3.	Click the New button and change the process color values to match the existing values. Name the color the same as the original, but instead of the word *spot,* add the word *process*.
Step 4.	Change all objects that have that custom color and should print as process colors into the custom color with the word *process* after it.
Step 5.	When printing out of Separator or other software that provides a means for printing color separations, select the "spot" custom color to print as a spot color and the "process" custom color to print as a process color.

Adobe Separator

One of the biggest disappointments I've experienced recently is seeing Adobe Separator in the Adobe Illustrator 5 folder on my hard drive for the first time.

Actually, nothing is wrong with Separator. The problem is that you need Separator at all. Adobe includes Separator because Illustrator can't print color separations. Separator has but one function, and that function is to print color separations from Illustrator files. On the plus side, it performs this feat extremely well.

Follow these steps to run Separator for the first time (see Figure 21-1):

STEPS: **Running Separator for the First Time**

Step 1. The first time that you run Separator, it sets up parameters for the future. To set them up, Separator asks for a number of different files, or so it seems. Before running the software, select the correct printer in the Chooser by choosing Apple Menu⇨Chooser, clicking the printer icon on the left side of the dialog box, and then selecting the name of the printer.

When you select a printer in the Chooser, it remains chosen until you select a new printer in the Chooser.

Step 2. Double-click the Adobe Separator icon.

Step 3. A dialog box appears, asking you to open an Illustrator file. Select an Illustrator file.

You cannot open Illustrator files in Separator if you have not saved them as EPS (None-Omit EPSF Header preview in Version 5.0). You can open files with the None-Include EPSF Header preview, but you can't view them for placement.

Step 4. Another dialog box appears, asking you to locate a PPD (PostScript Printer Description) file for the printer. The PPD file gives Separator information about the printer, such as the dots per inch, paper size, and so on. Locate the PPD for your printer. After you choose the PPD, Separator does not ask for a PPD each time you open it; it asks only for an Illustrator file.

If you can't find a PPD for your particular printer, choose LaserWriter IINT if you have a laser printer and Linotronic 200 if you have an imagesetter. The settings in these files are more "generic" and seem to work somewhat with most printers and imagesetters. You can change the PPD at any time in the main Separator window.

Using Separator

The two major sections of Separator are the main Separator window and the Separation window. The main window controls what elements are on printed pages, how the elements will appear, and how the illustration is set up on the page. The Separation window controls which separations print and whether custom colors are printed as spot colors or divided into process colors.

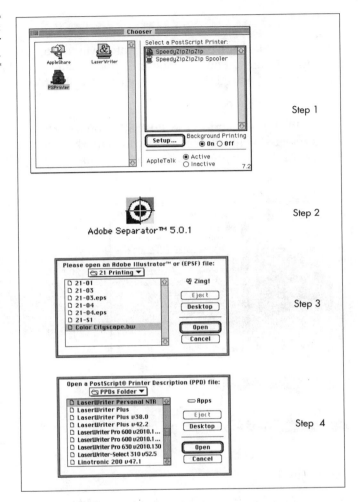

Figure 21-1:
Running Separator
for the first time.

Before using Separator, prepare the illustration in Illustrator by saving it with a color preview. This type of preview enables you to see the illustration in color in Separator. If you save the illustration without a preview, a box with the words *No Preview Available* appears in place of the illustration. If you save the illustration with a black-and-white preview instead of a color preview, the result is usually a big black blob because black-and-white Illustrator previews have no gray values.

The main Separator window

After you select a file to be separated, the main Separator window appears. The left side shows how the illustration is aligned on the page and which elements will print with the illustration. The right side contains all the options for how the illustration is to print on the page.

The picture on the left side initially shows the illustration on a portrait-oriented page, even if landscape was selected in Illustrator. The various marks shown on the page in Figure 21-2 are the defaults. You can move or rearrange them simply by clicking and dragging them.

Figure 21-2:
You can rearrange the default marks by clicking and dragging on them.

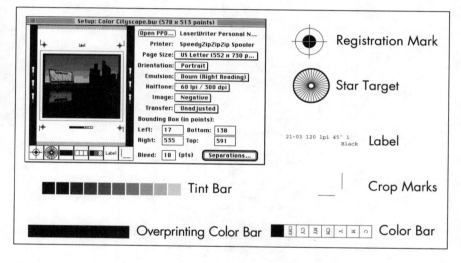

Margin marks

Below the picture are several different marks that you can add to the page above by dragging. You can use any number of the marks on the page. After you place the marks on the page, all of them except the colored parts of the color bars will appear on each of the separations. The colored parts of the color bar will appear only on the separations for their particular colors.

Usually, you place these marks outside the dotted area (called the *bounding box*) so that they don't interfere with the illustration. Sometimes you put them in the middle of the page if they won't overlap the illustration and will be cut out by die-cutting or some other procedure.

If you have moved margin marks around, added some, and taken away others, you can restore the original marks to the page, delete any that you have added, and move the original marks back to their initial locations by selecting Settings⇨Use Default Marks (⌘-M). For temporary fixes, select Edit⇨Undo (⌘-Z) to undo the last move, deletion, or addition.

You use the first two marks to position separations over each other when they are printed. By making sure that both registration marks and star targets align perfectly, press operators can be sure that the separations are directly on top of one another. Both marks are usually placed on both sides, the top and bottom, or all four sides. Sometimes paper and negatives can stretch or shrink, and aligning all the marks that are on each separation ensures that each separation is the same size. Ordinarily, you use four registration marks: one on each side of the illustration and two star targets in opposite corners. On large jobs, you can use additional marks and targets to make them easier to find.

The first symbol is a registration mark, which you use to align different separations. The phrase "in register" refers to making sure that all registration marks align exactly. Usually, you don't need more than four registration marks for an illustration, but each separation page has eight registration marks by default.

The default placement of the registration marks is a little closer to the edge of the illustration than many strippers like to deal with. You may want to move them out from the edges a bit or ask what placement the printer prefers.

To move all the margin marks away from the bounding box by an equal distance, enter the distance in points in the Bleed text field at the bottom right of the main panel. All default-placed marks will be a minimum of that many points from the bounding box.

The second symbol is a star target, which is a variation of a registration mark. Star targets have more lines than registration marks so that you can more easily see how different separations are lining up. Because the different lines in each star target are in close proximity, star targets are ideal for illustrations that have many separations, as even a slight misfit will result in an obvious star target misalignment. Usually, you place one star target in the upper righthand corner and another in the lower righthand corner.

Amateurs may like to use bunches of registration marks and star targets, but professionals don't. Got that? If you use many of them, especially on a large job, you will be perceived as an amateur, and no one wants to look like an amateur.

The third symbol is the overprinting color bar. Each color appears in this bar on its own separation, with black overprinting each color. The colors are in the same order as shown in the following list for the color bar, but black overprints each square. By default, one overprinting color bar appears on the right center of the page, just outside the bounding box.

The fourth symbol is the color bar, which shows each process color and then combinations of each color, in the following order:

1. Cyan

2. Magenta

3. Yellow

4. Cyan/magenta

5. Magenta/yellow

6. Cyan/yellow

7. Cyan/magenta/yellow

8. Black

The color bar is useful for showing press operators and strippers who are creating proofs that the colors are accurate. Initially, one color bar appears in the left center of the page, outside the bounding box.

The fifth symbol is the tint bar, which prints tints of each plate in 10 percent increments from 10 percent to 100 percent. You can use the tint bar to quickly check whether the output device is producing the proper tints. If each box in the bar is not very distinct from the boxes on either side of it, the output device is not producing the proper range of tints, and you need to adjust it. One tint bar normally appears at the bottom center of the page.

 You only need to print the color bars and tint bar once on a page; having several of them will just annoy the strippers and press operators. Occasionally, on very large pieces (more than 28 inches wide or long), you can use two color bars or two tint bars to ensure that the ink is consistent over a large area.

The second-to-last symbol is the label symbol. When you place a label on an illustration, each separation includes information about the job. Each color separation will contain the name of the file being printed, the line screen in lines per inch, the screen angle, and the page number. In addition, the name of the color of that specific separation will be printed below the other information. One label is usually sufficient for each illustration, and a label is placed at the top center of the illustration by default.

Always include at least one label when you are printing separations. Different colors are indistinguishable from each other without the printed label.

The label is a great help in determining which side of the Illustration is "right reading," even without any other text on the page.

The last symbol is the crop mark symbol. Unlike all the other marks, you cannot place as many crop marks as you would like. You can remove them, however. Crop marks will only go to the corners of the bounding box; you cannot place them at any other location within the illustration. When the illustration first appears in Separator, you see four sets of crop marks, one set at each corner.

The bounding box, bleed, and page direction

The page with the illustration on it is above the margin marks. The illustration is surrounded by a bounding box, and only the parts of the illustration that are within this bounding box will print. Anything outside of the bounding box will be cropped off. When you first open the illustration in Separator, the bounding box is the size of the illustration. The bounding box is as wide and as tall as necessary to include all the printable objects in the illustration.

You can resize the bounding box by clicking and dragging on either the edges or the corners of the box. When you move the edges of the bounding box, you also change the location of all crop marks and margin marks that were placed by default. The color bars, the tint bars, and the label will remain centered between the crop marks, and the registration marks and star targets will move relative to their original position. Note, however, that margin marks that you dragged to the page in Separator do not move when you move the edges of the bounding box.

When you resize the bounding box manually, the numbers in the Bounding Box text fields change because the four text fields correspond to the location of each of the edges of the bounding box. You also can resize the bounding box by typing new values in the Bounding Box text fields. The bounding box will instantly reflect changes that you make in these text fields.

You can move the illustration within the bounding box by placing the cursor within the bounding box and clicking and dragging. As you move the illustration out of the bounding box, the illustration will be cropped off at its edges.

The Bleed text field in the lower right of the Separator window does two different things. First, it defines how much of the illustration can be outside of the bounding box and still print. Second, it forces default margin marks away from the edges of the bounding box. The default for bleed is 18 points, regardless of the size of the bounding box.

To change the bleed, enter a distance in points in the Bleed text field. As you type the numbers, the bleed will change dynamically.

Bleed is useful when you want an illustration to go right up to the edge of the page. You need to account for bleed when you create an illustration in Illustrator so that the illustration is the correct size with X amount of bleed.

Selecting Settings⇨Use Default Bounding Box (⌘-B) changes the bounding box back to the size that it was when you first opened the illustration in Separator and changes the bleed back to 18 points.

The white arrows on the black background show the direction of the paper (or film) as the image is being printed. When you select different printing orientation (portrait or landscape) in the main panel, these arrows may change in direction. The direction of the arrows is often more important for imagesetters than for laser printers.

Changing printer information

To change the PPD, click the Open PPD button in the upper right of the main panel. The Open a PostScript Printer Description (PPD) file window appears, as shown in Step 4 of Figure 21-1.

Select the PPD file that is compatible with your printer and click the Open button. The PPD folder is placed in the Separator and Utilities folder by the Adobe Illustrator Installer automatically, and you return to the main panel.

PPDs were created with specific printers in mind. Unpredictable and undesirable results can occur when you use a PPD for a different printer than it is intended for. If you don't have a PPD for your printer and must use a substitute, always test the substitute PPD before relying on it to perform correctly.

If you have two or more printers in your workplace, chances are that you will be changing the PPD file in Separator from time to time. To make this task easier, open the PPD folder on the hard drive, select all the PPD files that you don't use, and drag them to the trash. Having a shorter list to choose from makes finding the right PPD much easier and frees up space on the hard drive. If you get a new printer at a later date and need a different PPD, you can get it from the Illustrator floppy disk or CD-ROM.

If your printer's PPD is not included with Illustrator, contact the dealer from whom you purchased the printer and ask for it. If you bought the printer by mail order or from a retail store, the dealer will probably not have a PPD for you and may not even know what a PPD is, for that matter. In this case, contact the printer manufacturer directly. Another place to find PPDs from manufacturers is on on-line services such as America Online. Adobe does *not* have PPDs for printers other than the ones supplied with the software.

When you choose a different PPD file, the information in the main panel changes to reflect the new selection. Certain default settings in the pop-up menus will be activated at this time. You can change the settings at any time, but most of them will revert to the defaults if you choose a new PPD. To revert to the default settings without picking a new printer, select Settings⇨Use Default Settings (⌘-T).

Right below the Open PPD button is the word *Printer*, followed by the name of the printer that you have selected in the Chooser. Look at the Printer line *every time* that you open Separator. Until I learned to check this line, my laser printer used to spit out negatives, which is not a pretty sight and is something that eats through toner like nobody's business. Checking which printer is selected in the Chooser is a pain, and Adobe has taken the trouble to create an additional line in the main panel so that all you have to do is look at that line to make sure that the right printer is selected.

Changing page size

The Page Size pop-up menu lists the available page sizes for the printer whose PPD is selected, *not* the printer selected in the Chooser. For laser printers, few page and envelope sizes are supported. For imagesetters, many sizes are supported, and an Other option enables you to specify the size of the page that you want to print on.

When you choose Other in the Page Size pop-up menu, you see the Other dialog box. The default measurements in the box are the smallest size area that the current illustration can fit within. Enter the width and height of the desired page in their respective boxes. You can use the Offset option to move the illustration a certain distance from the right edge of the page, and you can save media by using the Transverse option to turn the image sideways on the paper or film that it is printing on.

Imagesetters print on rolls of paper or film. Depending on the width of the roll, you may want to print the image sideways. For example, on a Linotronic 200 or 230 imagesetter, paper and film rolls are commonly 12 inches wide. For letter-size pages, you should check the Transverse option to print the letter-size page with the short end along the length of the roll. For a tabloid page (11 x 17 inches), do not check the Transverse option because you want the long edge (17 inches) of the page to be printed along the length of the roll. If you check Transverse for a tabloid-size document, 5 of the 17 inches will be cropped off because the roll is not wide enough. As always when trying something new with printing, run a test or two before sending a large job.

 The page size that you select in the Page Size pop-up menu determines the size of the page on the left side of the main panel. The measurements next to the name of the page size are not the page measurements; instead, they are the measurements of the Imageable area for that page size. The Imageable area dimensions are always less than the dimensions of the page so that the margin marks can fit on the page with the illustration.

Changing the orientation

The Orientation setting controls how the illustration is placed on the page. You have two choices from the pop-up menu: Portrait and Landscape.

Selecting Portrait causes the illustration to print with the sides of the illustration along the longest sides of the page. Selecting Landscape causes the illustration to print with the top and bottom of the illustration along the longest sides of the page.

Usually, the orientation reflects the general shape of the illustration. If the illustration is taller than it is wide, you usually choose Portrait orientation. If the illustration is wider than it is tall, you usually choose Landscape orientation.

 Separator does not care whether the illustration fits on the page in one or both of these orientations. If you can't see all four edges of the bounding box, chances are the illustration will be cropped.

 Orientation is quite different from Transverse in the Other Page Size dialog box. Orientation changes the orientation of the illustration on the page, but Transverse changes the way that the page is put onto the paper. A seemingly small difference, but a distinct and important one to understand.

Figure 21-3 shows an illustration that is placed onto a page in both Portrait and Landscape orientations, with and without the Transverse option selected.

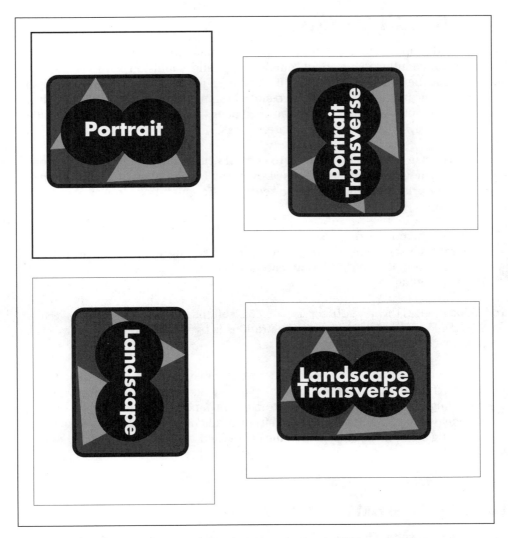

Figure 21-3: An illustration is placed onto a page in Portrait orientation (upper left), Landscape orientation (lower left), Portrait with Transverse checked (upper right), and Landscape with Transverse checked (lower right).

Understanding emulsion

Hang out around strippers (at a printer's . . . get your mind out of the gutter), and you will hear them constantly talking about "emulsion up" and "emulsion down." What they are referring to is the black "stuff" on film. If you have a piece of film from a printer lying around, look at it near a light. One of its two sides is shinier than the other. That side is the side without emulsion. When you are burning plates for presses, the emulsion side (dull side) should always be toward the plate.

In Separator, you use the Emulsion option to control which side the emulsion goes on. If you are printing negatives on film, choose Down (right reading) from the Emulsion pop-up menu. For printing on paper, just to see what the separations look like, choose Up (right reading).

 Although "wrong reading" isn't an option in Separator, you can reverse an illustration by choosing the opposite emulsion setting. In other words, Down (right reading) is also Up (wrong reading), and Up (right reading) is also Down (wrong reading).

Reversing text creates the kind of secret code illustrations that you can send to your friends. The only way to understand the illustrations is by viewing them in a mirror. This technique works best with text, of course.

Thinking of the emulsion as the toner in a laser printer may help you understand this concept better. If the toner is on the top of the paper, you can read it fine, as always (Up, right reading). If the toner is on the bottom of the paper, and you can read the illustration only when you place the paper in front of a light, the emulsion is Down, right reading. Thinking along these lines helped me back when I was a scrub, and it should help you as well.

Setting the halftone screen

The halftone screen setting is one of the great mysteries of life to the graphic designer who has not been informed about it. A too-low halftone screen setting will render an illustration terribly, making text and pictures unclear and fuzzy, sometimes even showing the dots that create the tints in the illustration. But if the halftone screen setting is too high, blends and gradations will show "banding," and some areas or the entire illustration may look posterized. The halftone setting can be too high for a particular press, resulting in smeary, terrible looking results.

 Blends, gradations, and how to avoid banding are discussed in Chapter 12.

Understanding halftone line screens

The most common mistake that graphic designers make is confusing dots per inch with lines per inch. Lines per inch (lpi) is another way of saying line screen or halftone line screen.

The number of dots per inch of the output device controls what the potential lines-per-inch settings are. The higher the dpi, the higher the lpi can be, but the higher the lpi, the lower the number of grays (see the formula later in this sidebar).

In bitmap graphics software, such as Photoshop, the dpi of the image is also important. In Illustrator, objects that you create are based on locations of points rather than on dots per inch. Trust me, dealing with an image's dots per inch is no picnic, and the fact that Illustrator can bypass this specification entirely is a great boon.

Line screens are made up of a combination of halftone cells. Each halftone cell has a certain number of dots within it that can be turned on and off. Usually the dots are turned on and off in a round pattern to create a halftone dot.

As an example, consider a common dpi/lpi ratio, that of a 300 dot-per-inch laser printer with a 60-line screen. Each halftone dot is made up of a 5 x 5 halftone cell (300 / 60 = 5). The number of pixels within each cell is 25. The following figure shows 5 x 5 halftone cells at different percentages.

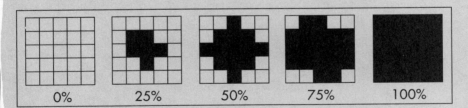

| 0% | 25% | 50% | 75% | 100% |

At a 25% tint, 25 percent of the dots are black. In a halftone cell of 25 dots, 6.25 dots would be black. Because you cannot print a quarter of a dot with this method, 6 dots are black.

Because the halftone cell has 25 pixels, only 26 different "levels" of gray are available when you are using a 300 dpi laser printer with a 60 lpi screen (1 level for each of the 25 pixels, plus 1 level for no pixels on at all, yields a total of 26). To get more grays, you need to lower the line screen.

Lower line screens seem rougher than higher line screens. The cutoff point for line screens is about 105; anything higher is considered a "fine" line screen, and anything lower is a "coarse" line screen.

A 300 dpi laser printer prints 9,000 dots for every square inch (300 x 300 = 9,000). The second figure shows 1 square inch blown up 500 percent so you can see the different dot patterns in a small gradient.

In deciding on a halftone screen, you need to consider many things, the most important of which are the type of paper or other media that the image will eventually be printed on and the press that it will be printed on.

Common settings for different types of print jobs are as follows: newsprint and photocopiers, 85 lpi; standard magazines, 133 lpi; better quality magazines, 150 lpi; and high-quality book images, 150 or 175 lpi.

In Separator, you can specify the line screen only by selecting one of the choices in the Halftone pop-up menu. This restriction can be very limiting, but you can get around it by doing a serious amount of tinkering:

STEPS: **Adding New Halftone Screens to PPD Files**

Step 1.   Make a copy of the PPD file that you want to add halftone screens to and add a suffix, such as *NEW,* to its name (for example, Laserwriter.NEW). Open the copy with TeachText or another word processor.

Step 2.   Scroll down to a section that looks very similar to what you see in Figure 21-4. The halftone screen numbers may be different from the ones shown in the figure, depending on the PPD chosen. Select the entire section and copy it. Press the left arrow once and paste.

Step 3.   In the copy, change the numbers highlighted in Figure 21-4 to whatever line screen you choose. Paste the copy and repeat this step for every new halftone screen that you want to include in the PPD file.

Step 4.   Save the changes.

Step 5.   Open the new PPD in Separator. If all went well, new pop-up menu items will reflect your recent changes.

Figure 21-4:
The areas of a PPD that need to be changed to add halftone screen settings in Separator.

```
*%  For  60  lpi  /  300  dpi  =================================

*ColorSepScreenAngle ProcessBlack.60 pi.300dpi.60 lpi / 300 dpi: "45"
*ColorSepScreenAngle CustomColor.60 pi.300dpi.60 lpi / 300 dpi: "45"
*ColorSepScreenAngle ProcessCyan.60 pi.300dpi.60 lpi / 300 dpi: "15"
*ColorSepScreenAngle ProcessMagenta.60 pi.300dpi.60 lpi / 300 dpi: "75"
*ColorSepScreenAngle ProcessYellow.60 pi.300dpi.60 lpi / 300 dpi: "0"

*ColorSepScreenFreq ProcessBlack.60 pi.300dpi.60 lpi / 300 dpi: "60"
*ColorSepScreenFreq CustomColor.60 pi.300dpi.60 lpi / 300 dpi: "60"
*ColorSepScreenFreq ProcessCyan.60 pi.300dpi.60 lpi / 300 dpi: "60"
*ColorSepScreenFreq ProcessMagenta.60 pi.300dpi.60 lpi / 300 dpi: "60"
*ColorSepScreenFreq ProcessYellow.60 pi.300dpi.60 lpi / 300 dpi: "60"
```

The final thing to think about when you are choosing a halftone screen is the type of media that the illustration will be output on from an imagesetter. If the output will be on paper, the halftone screen needs to be lower than if the output will be on film.

The printing process and saving $$ with your computer

The following brief rundown of the process that a printer goes through when taking a job from start to finish can help you understand some of the choices that you need to make when you are printing out of Separator. Of course, the following is a generalization, and all printers do things a little differently.

First, the printer gathers all of the materials for the print job. These materials may include artwork, logos, photos, and copy. The materials may go to different places, depending on what equipment the printer has. A typical commercial printer has limited prepress equipment in-house.

Color artwork and color photos are sent to a color separation house that specializes in creating film separations from full-color originals. The cost for each piece of artwork can range from $20 to $100, depending on the quality desired and the quantity.

Black-and-white artwork is shot with a camera (usually in-house) and resized to fit. Text is sent to a typesetting firm and set.

Black-and-white artwork and text are pasted up onto pasteboards, proofed, and then shot with a camera. A stripper takes the resulting film to a light table, where any seams in the film are opaqued out.

Film from the separation houses is stripped into the film from the artwork and type. This particular process is the most time consuming and adds substantially to the prepress portion of the labor bill.

At this point, proofs are created. Printers may use many different proofing methods, but the least expensive and most basic is the blueline, so called for the blue color of the text and artwork that appears on the sheets.

After the blueline is approved (or *if,* to be more exact), each piece of film is used to create a printing press plate for each color.

The plates are applied to presses, and the number of copies specified by the customer is run, plus several more copies to account for errors in printing and cutting.

After the ink on the printed paper dries, the copies are cut along crop marks, bound, and folded along fold marks. Depending on the type of product, the printed pieces may be bound, folded, and cut in any order.

The final piece is boxed and shipped to the client.

If you do everything you can with your system, you can save substantial amounts of money in all of the prepress areas. If possible, do as many of the following as possible to save money and avoid problems:

▓ Do as much as you can electronically. This rule is one you should live by.

▓ Have someone else proof your work *before* you output it to film. Objectivity for your own work decreases geometrically in relationship to the time you spend working on it. Your subconscious doesn't want to find mistakes.

▓ Get a separation house to scan photos and traditionally created artwork and then provide you with the files on disk. Sure, you can buy a flatbed desktop scanner inexpensively, but color pictures from them can look like mush next to scans from a drum scanner at a separation house.

▓ Assemble all your artwork, type, and photos in QuarkXPress. Don't bother with PageMaker or other lesser page layout software. *Everyone* in high-end printing and publishing has QuarkXPress, but only about half of them have PageMaker. Even employees of the companies that have PageMaker will have more experience with QuarkXPress, so you shouldn't have many problems.

PageMaker versus QuarkXPress is an ages-old battle that neither side will ever win. More people use PageMaker regularly, but more professionals use Quark regularly. You figure it out.

▓ Have all film negatives output by a reputable service bureau. If your job contains a large amount of color artwork or photos, or if you need the artwork and color photos to be of the best possible quality, take everything back to the color separation house, where your job will be outputted at a better quality than most imagesetters can produce.

Changing from positive to negative to positive

You use the Image pop-up menu to switch between printing positive and negative images. Usually, you use a negative image for printing film negatives and a positive image for printing on paper. The default for this setting, regardless of the printer chosen or PPD selected, is Negative.

Modifying the Transfer function

You adjust the Transfer function by selecting the Adjust Tints menu item from the Transfer pop-up menu. The Unadjusted tint densities dialog box appears, as shown in Figure 21-5.

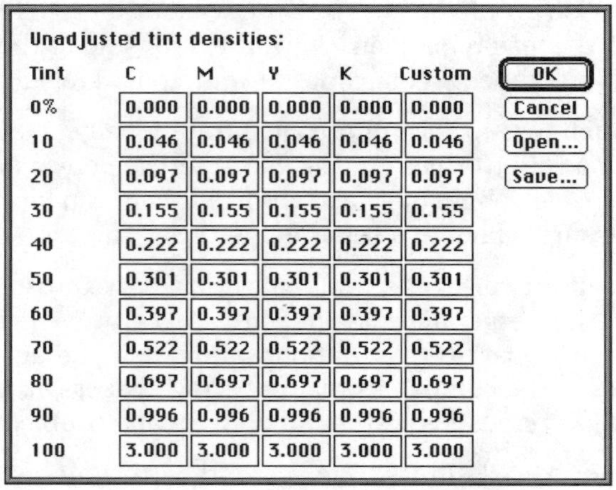

Figure 21-5:
The Unadjusted tint densities dialog box appears when you select Adjust Tints from the Transfer pop-up menu.

Tint	C	M	Y	K	Custom	
	Unadjusted tint densities:					
0%	0.000	0.000	0.000	0.000	0.000	OK
10	0.046	0.046	0.046	0.046	0.046	Cancel
20	0.097	0.097	0.097	0.097	0.097	Open...
30	0.155	0.155	0.155	0.155	0.155	Save...
40	0.222	0.222	0.222	0.222	0.222	
50	0.301	0.301	0.301	0.301	0.301	
60	0.397	0.397	0.397	0.397	0.397	
70	0.522	0.522	0.522	0.522	0.522	
80	0.697	0.697	0.697	0.697	0.697	
90	0.996	0.996	0.996	0.996	0.996	
100	3.000	3.000	3.000	3.000	3.000	

The Transfer function skews the tints from one output device to the next. If you look at paper output from two different imagesetters, even the same make and model of imagesetters, the output will look different from one to the next.

 Only a well-trained eye can spot differences in individual film tint separations unless they are extreme. The difference *will* be quite clear, however, when the final, color image is printed.

By adjusting the Transfer function, you can customize the tints of gray that are created out of Separator to your imagesetter. A 90% tint should look like 90%, not 92%, or 88%. By modifying the Transfer function, you can correct the tint.

To decide which values to change in the Unadjusted tint densities dialog box, you need to use a film densitometer to measure the film density. You also need to be able to output to a film-producing device.

 Certain densitometers measure only paper density. These reflective densitometers give really wacky readings if you try to measure film density with them. A film densitometer is also called a *transmission densitometer*.

STEPS: Adjusting the Transfer Function

Step 1. In Separator, open the Densitometer Control Chart file, which is located in the Separator and Utilities folder in the Adobe Illustrator folder. The Densitometer Control Chart is shown in Figure 21-6.

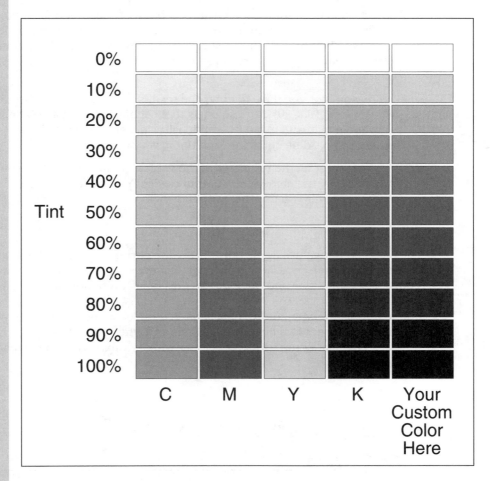

Figure 21-6: The Densitometer Control Chart.

Step 2. Open the PPD file for the output device you are using and choose the following settings: Page Size, Letter; Orientation, Portrait; Emulsion, Down (Right Reading); Image, Negative; and Transfer, Unadjusted. Select the halftone screen that you will be using.

Do *not* print the Densitometer Control Chart with the Transfer set to anything but Unadjusted, or the results will be incorrect.

Step 3. Select File⇨Print All Separations (⌘-P). Process the film.

Step 4. Select the Adjust Tints option from the Transfer pop-up menu. The Unadjusted tint densities dialog box will appear.

Step 5. With the film densitometer, measure each tint of each color and enter the results into the corresponding text field in the Unadjusted tint densities dialog box. You press Tab to select the next text field in each column. At the bottom of each column, press Tab to highlight the first text field in the next column.

The reason that you have to enter the results from each color, instead of just a general 10%, 20%, and so on, is that each color is set at a different angle and may result in a different density. In fact, having all the values across the board be equal for each tint is very rare.

Step 6. After you enter all the values, save the values by clicking the Save button and the file by the name of the output device. You can then recall it in the future whenever you use that output device.

The changed tint values apply only during the current session of Separator. The next time you open Separator, you have to choose Adjust Tints from the Transfer pop-up menu and open the saved Transfer function data.

Run new densitometer control charts often — at least once every two weeks. Chemicals in processors change over time, and when you replace old chemicals with fresh ones or combine old developer with new fixer, the density can vary dramatically.

Working with Different Color Separations

Clicking the Separations button in the main panel of Separator displays the Separation window, where you can select different colors and set them to print, set custom colors to process separate, and change the label for the file (see Figure 21-7).

Figure 21-7:
The Separation
window.

Color	Print	Convert To Process	Frequency	Angle
ProcessCyan	Yes	n/a	60	15
ProcessMagenta	Yes	n/a	60	75
ProcessYellow	Yes	n/a	60	0
ProcessBlack	Yes	n/a	60	45
Dark Blue	n/a	Yes	60	45
Gold	Yes	No	60	15
Grass Green	n/a	Yes	60	75

Separation: Color Cityscape.bw

Label: Color Cityscape.bw

To change the label, simply type a new name. The name of the original file will not be affected, but when the file is separated, the label will be what you have typed in this box. This method is the best way to give files with nasty names (such as "Crustball's Artwork") more respectable labels (such as "Cool Dude's Artwork").

The list of color separations contains only the colors that are used in that particular illustration. At the top of the list of separation colors are the four process colors, if they or custom colors that contain those process colors are used in the illustration. Below the process colors is a list of all the custom colors in the document.

If the illustration has any guides in it, their colors are reflected in the Separation window. If you choose Print All Separations from the File menu (⌘-P), separations with the guide colors will print, but they will be blank. From looking at the preview of the illustration in Separator, you can't easily determine that these blank separations will print. The best thing to do is release all guides and delete them.

By default, all process colors are set to print, and all custom colors are set to convert to process colors. Clicking the Print or Convert To Process column toggles between Yes and No.

N/A means that the selection isn't applicable. For example, when a custom color is set to process separate, it can't print as a custom color, and the print column for that color will read n/a. Process colors can't be converted to process, so the Convert To Process column reads n/a for the four process colors.

Clicking either the Frequency or Angle column displays a dialog box that asks you to enter the frequency (halftone screen) and angle for that color. Don't change the angle or frequency for process colors because Separator has automatically created the best values for the process colors. Instead, make sure that any custom colors that may be printing have different angles from each other so that no patterns develop from them.

Closing the Separation window does not cancel changes you have made. As soon as you type new values or check different options, they are applied. The Separation window does not have to be closed when you print.

Getting information about an illustration

In the Finder, selecting File⇨Get Info (⌘-I) displays the Get Info dialog box (see Figure 21-8), which contains important printing information about your document.

Figure 21-8:
The Get Info
dialog box.

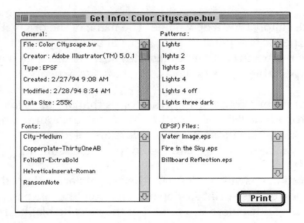

The General window lists the name of the file, the program that created it, the type of file, the date the file was created, and the date it was last modified. This window also lists Data and Resource fork size information (both irrelevant to how the job prints), the default bounding box size, the type of preview that the file was saved with, the internal version of PostScript and EPSF format, and the number of pages. (You scroll to see all the information.)

 The version of PostScript in the Get Info window is not the same as the versions of PostScript that are in laser printers and the RIPs (*raster image processor*) of imagesetters.

The Fonts window lists all the fonts used in the document, but it does not list fonts that you have converted to outlines. After you convert fonts to outlines, they lose all of their "typeface" origins and are only paths.

The Patterns window lists all the patterns that you used in the process of creating the illustration. When I created the illustration for this example, I experimented with many different patterns to put lights on some of the buildings, but I didn't get the desired results, so I deleted them. Separator lists all of the patterns that I tried.

The (EPSF) Files window shows all the EPS files that are included in the illustration. This list is the single most useful feature of the Get Info dialog box because it is the only place where you can get a list of all the EPS files that are in a document.

Open an Illustrator file in Separator when you need to send the Illustrator file to be output and you aren't sure which EPS files are in a document. You need to include the EPS files that are placed in the Illustrator file, and the Get Info window will list all of those EPS files.

The Print button in the Get Info window prints a list of all of the information in the Get Info windows. The list appears in one column, in 12-point Helvetica.

Normally, the printer in the Chooser is set to an imagesetter for printing out of Separator. If you click the Print button in the Get Info window, you will print this info to the imagesetter or to whichever printer is selected in the Chooser.

Use this Print function to print an information sheet to give to the service bureau when you send them an illustration to print. This information is incredibly valuable to the service bureau, and it takes care of the most common problems that they will encounter, including not knowing which fonts are included in the illustration.

Printing separations

Separator's File menu offers three different options for printing. The first option is to print a composite, which will produce similar results to printing directly from Illustrator. The main advantage to printing a composite from Separator instead of from Illustrator is that in Separator you can specify the line screen, whereas in Illustrator the illustration is printed at the "optimal" line screen for the printer.

Another printing option is to select File⇨Print All Separations (⌘-P), which prints all the separations listed in the Separation window. This command often prints cyan, magenta, yellow, and black separations, even if an illustration does not include all four colors.

The last printing alternative is Print Selected Separations, which prints according to the options that you have specified in the Separation window. This option is grayed out when no separations are selected in the Separation window.

Saving separations

Instead of printing separations, you can save them for later printing. You cannot import the separation files that Illustrator creates for saving into any other Macintosh software (including Illustrator and Separator) for viewing.

To save a separation, select File⇨Save Selected Separations or File⇨Save All Separations (⌘-S). A standard Save As dialog box appears, where you name the file and specify where you want to store it.

You can use a PostScript printing utility such as PSPrint, LaserWriter Utility, or Font Downloader to print the saved separation file.

Separator secrets

Separator has some helpful features that you may not find out about just by using the software:

* Separator saves additional information with each Illustrator file so that the next time you open the file in Separator any changes that you made to it will be in place. For example, Separator saves the margin marks and bounding box sizing with the illustration.

* The magic Option key works its spells in Separator. Pressing Option when you select Save All Separations, Save Selected Separations, Print All Separations, or Print Selected Separations makes two additional dialog boxes appear.

    The first dialog box asks whether you want black to overprint all the other colors. If you click Yes (or press Return), any black in the illustration will overprint every other color instead of being knocked out as usual.

    Click the Cancel button to return to the last window you were working with in Separator. Click either the Yes or No button to see the next dialog box.

    The next dialog box asks whether all custom colors printed as spot colors should appear on the same plate. If you check Yes, only one separation will be created for all the custom colors.

Printing Separations from Other Applications

Many other software programs, particularly page layout software programs, incorporate color separation capabilities. These programs usually enable you to import Illustrator files.

When you produce color separations from other software, make sure that any custom colors that are in the Illustrator illustration are present and accessible in the document that the illustration is placed within. Usually, you can set the custom colors to process separate or to spot separate.

 You cannot change the colors of an imported Illustrator EPS document in a page layout program, so be sure that the colors are correct for the illustration while it is in Illustrator.

Traps

Trapping is one of the most important but least understood issues in all of printing. In the past, desktop publishing has been noted for its inefficiency in trapping, but QuarkXPress 3.1 and a few other after-the-fact trapping software packages, such as Aldus TrapWise and Island Trapper, have gradually bettered the trapping capabilities of electronic publishing.

 Illustrator 5.0 is not a trap-friendly program. That said, I also need to say that Version 5.5 makes trapping correctly easier than ever before. Still, to be honest, setting up traps correctly is still a hassle.

Understanding what traps do

Traps solve alignment problems when color separations are produced. The most common problem that occurs from misalignment is the appearance of white space between different colors.

The thought of trapping scares many graphic designers — not just because they don't know how to do it, but also because they aren't sure what trapping is and what purpose it serves. Understanding the concept of trapping is the hard part; trapping objects is easy (though somewhat tedious in Illustrator).

Figure 21-9 shows a spot color illustration with four colors. The top row shows each of the individual colors. The first illustration in the second row shows how the illustration prints if all the separations are aligned perfectly. The second illustration in the second row shows what happens when the colors become misaligned. The third illustration in the second row shows how the illustration looks when trapped, with black indicating where two colors overprint each other.

This example shows extreme misalignment and excessive trapping; I designed it just as a black-and-white illustration for this book. Ordinarily, the overprinting colors may appear a tiny bit darker, but they do not show as black. I used black so that you can see what parts of the illustration overlap when trapping is used. The trapping in this case is more than sufficient to cover any of the white gaps in the second illustration.

You create trapping by spreading or choking certain colors that touch each other in an illustration. To spread a color, you enlarge an object's color so that it takes up more space around the edges of the background area. To choke a color, you expand the color of the background until it overlaps the edges of an object.

The major difference between a spread and a choke has to do with which object is considered the background and which object is the foreground. The foreground object is the object that traps. If you spread the foreground object, you expand the color of the foreground object until it overlaps the background by a certain amount. If you choke the foreground object, you expand the color of the background around the foreground object until it overlaps the foreground object by a certain amount.

To determine whether to use a choke or a spread on an object, compare the lightness and darkness of the foreground and background objects. The general rule of thumb is that lighter colors expand into darker colors.

Figure 21-10 shows the original misaligned illustration and two ways of fixing it with trapping. The middle star has been spread by 1 point, and the third star has been choked by 1 point.

Figure 21-9:
A spot color illustration
that shows individual
colors (top) and aligned,
misaligned, and trapped
composites.

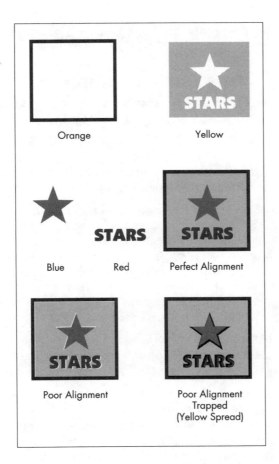

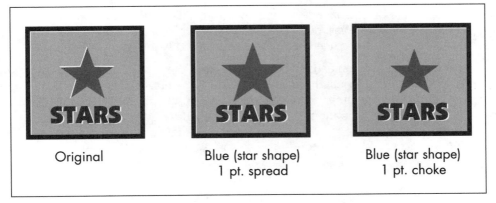

Figure 21-10: The original illustration (left), fixing the star by spreading it 1 point (middle), and fixing the star by choking it 1 point (right).

Why you need trapping

Trapping is a solution for covering gaps that occur when color separations do not properly align. Maybe this sidebar should have been called, "Why Color Separations Do Not Properly Align," but now the book has been printed and it can't be changed.

The three reasons why color separations don't align properly are that the negatives are not the same size, the plates on the press are not aligned perfectly when printing, or the gods have decided that a piece is too perfect and needs gaps between butting colors.

Negatives can be different sizes for a number of reasons. When the film was output to an imagesetter, the film may have been too near the beginning or the end of a roll, or separations in the same job may have been printed from different rolls. The pull on the rollers, while fairly precise on all but top-of-the-line imagesetters — where it should be perfect — can pull more film through when there is less resistance (at the end of a roll of film), or less film when there is more resistance (at the beginning of a roll of film). The temperature of the film may be different if a new roll is put on in the middle of a job, causing the film to shrink (if it is cold) or expand (if it is warm).

The temperature of the processor may have risen or fallen a degree or two while the film was being processed. Once again, cooler temperatures in the chemical bays and in the air dryer as the film exits the process have an impact on the size of the film.

Film negatives usually don't change drastically in size, but they can vary up to a few points on an 11-inch page. That distance is huge when a page has several butting colors throughout it. The change in a roll of film is almost always along the length of the roll, not along the width. The quality of the film is another factor that determines how much the film will stretch or shrink.

Most strippers are quite aware of how temperature affects the size of negatives. A common stripper trick is to walk outside with a freshly processed negative during the colder months to shrink a negative that may have enlarged slightly during processing.

Check with your service bureau staff to see how long they warm up the processor before sending jobs through it. If the answer is less than an hour, the chemicals will not be at a consistent temperature, and negatives that are sent through too early will certainly change in size throughout the length of the job. Another question to ask is how often they change their chemicals and check the density from their imagesetter. Once a week is acceptable for a good-quality service bureau, but the best ones will change chemicals and check density once a day.

The plates on a press can be misaligned by either an inexperienced press operator or a faulty press. An experienced press operator knows the press and what to do to get color plates to align properly. A faulty press is one where plates move during printing or are not positioned correctly. An experienced press operator can determine how to compensate for a faulty press.

No press is perfect, but some of the high-end presses are pretty darn close. Even on those presses, the likelihood that a job with colors that butt up against one another can print perfectly is not very great.

If a job doesn't have some sort of trapping in it, it probably will not print perfectly, no matter how good the negatives, press, and press operator are.

Trapping Illustrator 5.0 files

In both Illustrator 5.0 and 5.5, you accomplish trapping by selecting a path's stroke or fill and setting it to overprint another path's stroke or fill. The amount that the two paths' fills or strokes overlap and overprint is the amount of trap that is used.

How much trap?

The amount of trap that you need in an illustration depends on many things, but the deciding factor is what your commercial printer tells you is the right amount.

The most important thing to consider is the quality of the press that the printer will use. Of course, only the printer knows which press your job will run on, so talking to the printer about trapping is imperative.

Other factors to consider include the colors of ink and types of stock used in the job. Certain inks soak into different stocks differently.

Traps range from $2/1000$ inch to $6/1000$ inch. Most traditional printers refer to traps in thousandths of inches, but Illustrator likes values in points for this sort of thing. The figure shows a chart with traps in increments of $1/1000$ inch, from $1/1000$ inch to $10/1000$ inch, and gives their point measurements. The trapped area is represented by black to be more visible in this example.

(continued)

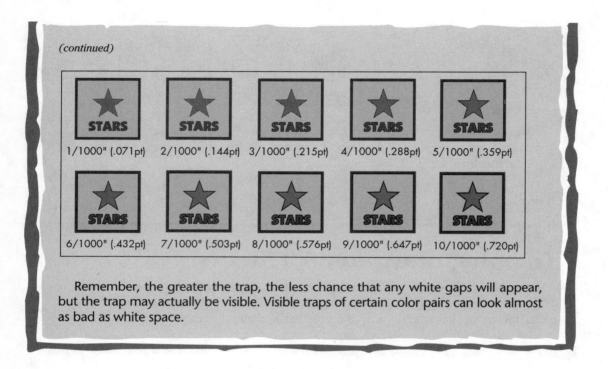

(continued)

STARS — 1/1000" (.071pt) STARS — 2/1000" (.144pt) STARS — 3/1000" (.215pt) STARS — 4/1000" (.288pt) STARS — 5/1000" (.359pt)

STARS — 6/1000" (.432pt) STARS — 7/1000" (.503pt) STARS — 8/1000" (.576pt) STARS — 9/1000" (.647pt) STARS — 10/1000" (.720pt)

Remember, the greater the trap, the less chance that any white gaps will appear, but the trap may actually be visible. Visible traps of certain color pairs can look almost as bad as white space.

The most basic way to create a trap on an object is by giving it a stroke that is either the fill color of the object (to create a spread) or the fill color of the background (to create a choke).

 Be sure to make the width of any stroke that you use for trapping twice as wide as the intended trap because only half of the stroke (one side of the path) actually overprints a different color. In some circumstances, fixing a stroke that is not wide enough initially can be difficult.

The following sets of steps describe how to create basic choke and spread traps in Illustrator 5.0:

STEPS: Creating a Basic Choke Trap in Illustrator 5.0

Step 1. For a choke trap, the foreground object in the illustration should be darker than the background. In the illustration on the left in Figure 21-11, the star is the object that will be choked by the background.

Step 2. Click the background to find the color of the background. Write the color down or commit it to memory (remembering the color is always much easier when the color is a custom color and more difficult when the color is a process color).

Step 3. Click the foreground object and change the stroke to the color of the background with a width that is double that of the desired trap. I used a $\frac{5}{1000}$-inch trap for the example on the left in Figure 21-11.

Step 4. Check the Overprint Stroke box in the Paint Style palette. The object will now be choked by $\frac{5}{1000}$ inch.

Figure 21-11: The star on left was trapped by choking it with the background color because the star is darker than the background. The star on the right was trapped by spreading it into the background because the star is lighter than the background. The overprinting area was darkened in this illustration so that it could be seen better in black and white.

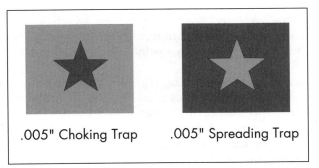

.005" Choking Trap   .005" Spreading Trap

STEPS: Creating a Basic Spread Trap in Illustrator 5.0

Step 1. For a spread trap, the foreground object in the illustration should be lighter than the background. In the illustration on the right in Figure 21-11, I spread the star into the background by $\frac{5}{1000}$ inch.

Step 2. Click the foreground object and change the stroke to the fill color of the foreground object with a width that is double that of the desired trap. I used a $\frac{5}{1000}$-inch trap for the example on the right in Figure 21-11.

Step 3. Check the Overprint Stroke box in the Paint Style palette. The object will now be spread into the background by $\frac{5}{1000}$ inch.

Complex trapping techniques in Illustrator 5.0

The preceding examples of creating basic spread and choke traps are very simplified examples of trapping methods in Illustrator 5.0. In reality, objects never seem to be a solid color, and if they are, they are never on a solid background. In addition, most illustrations contain multiple overlapping objects that have their own special trapping needs.

Complex trapping involves several different techniques, which are described in the following list. I consider trapping to be complex when I can't just go around adding strokes to objects and causing them to overprint, which is most of the trapping that I do.

- **Create a separate layer for trapping objects.** By keeping trapping on its own layer, you make a myriad of options available that are not available if the trapping is intermixed with rest of the artwork. Make the new layer above the other layers. Lock all the layers but the trapping layer so that the original artwork is not modified. You can turn trapping on and off by hiding the entire layer or turning off the Print option in the Layers Options dialog box.

- **Use the round joins and ends options in the stroke portion of the Paint Style palette for all trapping strokes.** Round ends and joins are much less conspicuous than the harsh corners and 90° angles of other joins and ends, and they blend smoothly into other objects.

When doing the trapping yourself just isn't worth it

Before you spend the long amounts of time that complex trapping entails and modify your illustration beyond recognition (at least in Artwork mode), you may want to reconsider whether you should do the trapping yourself.

If you estimate that trapping your job will require several hours of work, the chances of doing it correctly dwindle significantly. If the illustration includes many crisscrossing blends and gradations or multiple placed EPS images, you may not have the patience to get through the entire process with your sanity intact.

If you have Illustrator 5.5, the amount of time it will take to trap will be *much* less than the time it takes to trap using 5.0.

If you determine that you cannot do the trapping yourself, you can have it done after the fact with Aldus TrapWise or Island Trapper, or you can have a service bureau with special output devices create trapping automatically. These services will undoubtedly cost more than doing the trapping yourself, but it will get done right, which is the important thing.

> ▨ **Trap gradations by stroking them with paths that are filled with overprinting gradients.** You cannot fill strokes with gradients, but you can fill paths with gradients. You can make any stroke into a path by selecting it and choosing Filter➪Object➪Outline Stroked Path. After you have transformed the stroke into a path, fill it with the gradient and check the Overprint Fill box for that path.

 Whenever I start a heavy-duty trapping project, I always work on a copy of the original illustration. Wrecking the original artwork is just too easy when you add trapping.

 Figure 21-12 shows the steps for the following exercise on trapping a complex object in Illustrator 5.0. To see the steps in color, turn to the color section of the book.

 If your system does not have an FPU, then the Pathfinder filters are not available. In this case, I recommend upgrading to Illustrator 5.5, which contains a trapping filter, letting you avoid all this mess.

Figure 21-12:
Steps for trapping a complex object in Illustrator 5.0.

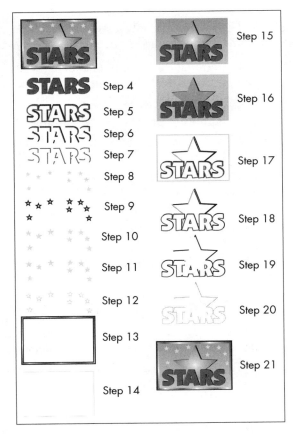

STEPS:	**Trapping a Complex Object in Illustrator 5.0**

Step 1. The first thing to do when you want to trap something complex is to copy the original drawing and work on the copy. I usually copy the file in the Finder by selecting it and choosing File⇨Duplicate (⌘-D).

You can follow along with these steps by opening the Complex Trapping file from the Tutorial Folder on the *Macworld 5.0/5.5 Illustrator Bible* CD-ROM.

Step 2. Create a new layer just for trapping purposes. I called my new layer Trapping Layer because I couldn't think of anything wittier.

Step 3. Look at the illustration and try to figure out which areas are going to create the most trouble for trapping. I look for gradations and multiple overlaps. Most of the objects in the example are filled with gradations, so you know that most areas are going to cause some trouble. The background is a gradient of cyan to a lighter cyan; the little stars are linear gradients; the big star is a radial magenta gradient; and the inside frame is a linear black gradient.

Multiple overlaps exist between only a few colors in this illustration, namely where the word *STARS* and its shadow overlap the big star and the background.

One area where no trapping will have to take place is between the word *STARS* and the magenta gradient of the big star because both of these elements contain only magenta.

The colors in the example are process colors because the color insert of this book was printed with process colors. To make the colors behave as spot colors, I did not mix two process colors together in any object.

Normally, trapping process colors is much easier than trapping spot colors because slight tints of neighboring colors can be added to the "other" color, eliminating the possibility of white gaps.

Step 4. Start with the "easiest" traps first. The easiest trap to create is the one between the word *STARS* and the shadow for the same word. A magenta spread into the black will be necessary for the two objects to trap together successfully.

Copy *STARS* in both magenta and black. Select the Trapping Layer to make it the active layer and choose Edit⇨Paste In Front (⌘-F). This command pastes a copy of the word *STARS* on the Trapping Layer, directly above the original. Lock Layer 1 so that nothing on it can be accidentally changed.

Sometimes I hide the original artwork layers so that all I have to deal with is the Trapping Layer.

Step 5. Select both the magenta and black letters in the Trapping Layer and select Filter⇨Pathfinder⇨Merge Stroke. Merge Stroke will produce paths that are stroked with a 1-point stroke around all the edges of the letters. The paths that are created are divided wherever different fills are encountered.

The paths are grouped together, so select Arrange⇨Ungroup (⌘-U) to ungroup them so that you can select them individually.

Step 6. Delete all the magenta paths that are not up against a black path. Select all the remaining paths and change the weight of the paths to .01 inch, which is twice .005 inch, the amount you want to trap. Select the Overprint Stroke check box. Change the ends and joins of the strokes to round.

When the Merge Fill filter is applied, ends and bends of strokes are automatically changed to round.

Step 7. Delete all the black strokes. An easy way to delete them is to select one of them, select Filter⇨Select⇨Same Stroke Color, and then press Delete. Select all the paths, group them, and lock them.

Step 8. The next easiest thing to trap is the yellow stars into the cyan background. Select the stars.

Step 9. Give the stars a .01-inch stroke. The color of the stroke doesn't matter at this point.

Step 10. Select Filter⇨Object⇨Outline Stroked Path and fill the resulting paths with the gradient that is in the stars (called, appropriately, Stars). Ungroup all the stars.

When multiple objects are selected and the Outline Stroked Path filter is activated, all the original and new paths will be grouped together.

Step 11. Select each star individually by dragging a marquee around it with the Selection tool. This action selects both the original path and the new path created from the Outline Stroked Path filter. Use the Gradient Vector tool to drag across each star in the direction the gradient should go. Repeat this step for each of the stars.

Step 12. Select the paths created from the Outline Stroked Path filter of each of the stars, group them, and select Edit⇨Cut (⌘-X). Select the Trapping Layer and paste in front. These actions put the star outlines directly above where they were originally. Select the Overprint Fill check box and lock the star outlines.

Step 13. The next area to be trapped is the silver frame (Steel Frame gradient) into the cyan background. The frame is a little lighter than the cyan, so spread the color of the frame into the cyan background.

Select the frame and copy and paste in front on the Trapping Layer. Give the path a .01-inch stroke.

Technically, this process should be considered a choke of the cyan because the cyan is surrounded by the frame. The frame acts as the background. The terminology doesn't matter because the method and results are the same.

Step 14. Select Filter⇨Object⇨Outline Stroked Path. Fill the inside path with the Steel Frame gradient. Delete the original path and the outside path from the trapping layer and lock the remaining path.

Step 15. Select the cyan background, the big star, and the word *STAR* and copy them. Make the Trapping Layer active and paste in front.

Step 16. Change the cyan gradient to a fill of 50% cyan and the magenta gradient to a fill of 50% magenta.

The Merge Stroke filter, which is used in Step 17, does not work properly when objects have gradient fills, so you need to fill objects with solid colors before using the Merge Stroke filter.

Step 17. Select all the objects and choose Filter⇨Pathfinder⇨Merge Stroke. Change the weight of the strokes to .01 inch and set the strokes to overprint.

Step 18. Delete the cyan frame around the outside of the illustration and delete all the paths that were used for the first trap between the word *STARS* and its shadow.

Step 19. Select all the strokes that would touch the big star and choose Filter⇨Object⇨Outline Stroked Path. Make the new stroked paths into a compound path (select Object⇨Compound Path⇨Make or press ⌘-8). Fill the new compound path with the magenta gradient that you used for the big star.

Step 20. Select all the remaining paths by pressing Shift and dragging a marquee around the illustration. Choose Filter⇨Object⇨Outline Stroked Path. Make a compound path out of the new paths and fill the compound path with the cyan gradient used for the background.

Because the strokes were set to overprint, Illustrator automatically changes them to overprint fill after you outline them.

Step 21. Show all and print the illustration.

Trapping in Illustrator 5.5

If you have Illustrator Version 5.5, most of your trapping problems can be solved, but you will still need to know the basics. Because it is hard to understand just what the Trap filter in Illustrator 5.5 is doing, you may want to review the above steps.

The Trap filter is discussed in Chapter 18.

Adobe
Streamline™

In This Chapter

- Understanding Streamline
- Streamline versus Illustrator's Auto Trace tool
- The tools in Streamline
- The commands in Streamline
- Converting bitmapped art into Illustrator paths

The Streamline Software

Imagine Illustrator's Auto Trace tool on steroids. That's the Streamline package: a super-powerful bitmap tracing tool. The options for converting images are staggering, and the results can be dramatically better than the results that you can achieve with the Auto Trace tool. A demo version of Adobe Streamline is included on the *Macworld Illustrator Bible* CD-ROM.

The Auto Trace tool in Illustrator traces one solid part of a PICT template. Sure, you can adjust the Freehand tolerance to make the created path stay closer to the image or be drawn a little less constrained, but the options end there. The biggest advantage to using the Auto Trace tool instead of Streamline is that the Auto Trace tool is free, while Streamline costs about $100. (The Auto Trace tool and tracing within Illustrator are discussed in Chapter 7.)

On the other hand, Streamline can perform all of the following tasks:

- Trace bitmapped artwork that has been saved in the PICT, TIFF, TIFF Compressed, MacPaint, PCX, and Photoshop 2.0 and 2.5 formats.

- Convert artwork into EPS and PICT formats, creating editable paths that you can manipulate in Illustrator.

- Edit bitmapped artwork before converting it into paths.

- Adjust paths that were created by converting bitmaps.

- Support Adobe PostScript on the Clipboard for instant copy/paste capability between Illustrator, Photoshop, and Dimensions.

- Provide complex control over how images are traced.

- Convert line art and grayscale and color artwork to editable Illustrator paths.

The Streamline Toolbox and Menu Items

The following pages contain an overview of the functions of the Streamline toolbox and the menu items. Later in the chapter, I discuss some of the items in greater detail. Although Streamline is a fairly small program, I can't possibly cover all the facets of the software in one chapter, so I focus on information that's important and relevant to Illustrator.

The next few sections contain general information. Use them as a reference when you can't figure out what a tool or menu item does.

Streamline tools

The toolbox in Streamline (see Figure 22-1) is a Photoshop/Illustrator hybrid. It has to be a hybrid because you use it to edit both bitmapped and path-based portions of images.

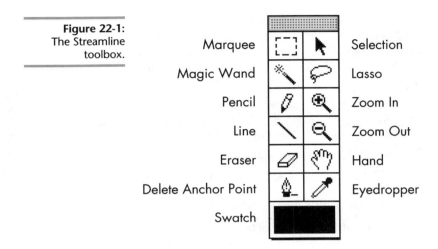

Figure 22-1:
The Streamline toolbox.

Marquee · Selection

Magic Wand · Lasso

Pencil · Zoom In

Line · Zoom Out

Eraser · Hand

Delete Anchor Point · Eyedropper

Swatch

The toolbox contains the following tools. If you cannot use a tool on the type of image that you are currently editing, the tool is grayed out.

- **The Marquee tool:** You use the Marquee tool to select an area in a bitmapped image. You can move, delete, copy, or cut the selected area. You also can convert the selected area into paths. You use the tool by clicking and dragging — just as you do with Illustrator's Rectangle tool. The Shift and Option keys have no effect on the Marquee tool. You can use the Marquee tool only when you are editing bitmapped images.

- **The Magic Wand tool:** You use the Magic Wand tool to select areas in a bitmapped image that are similar in color. The color at the point where you click with the Magic Wand tool determines which areas are selected. Double-clicking on the Magic Wand tool displays the Magic Wand dialog box, where the "spread" of the wand is determined by a setting of Tight (little spread; only colors very closely related to the original are selected) or Loose (colors even loosely related to the original are selected). You can use the Magic Wand tool only when you are editing bitmapped images.

- **The Pencil tool:** You use the Pencil tool to draw on bitmapped images. It is most useful for touching up small areas that were problematic when you scanned an image. Double-clicking on the Pencil tool displays the Pencil dialog box, where you can specify the width of the Pencil. You choose the color that the Pencil draws from the Paint Style palette (select Options⇨Paint Style or press ⌘-I). You can use the Pencil tool only when you are editing bitmapped images.

- **The Line tool:** The Line tool creates lines in the same way that the Pencil tool creates individual points. Double-clicking on the Line tool enables you to specify the width of the line. The color that the Line tool draws is determined by the color in the Paint Style palette. You can use the Line tool only when you are editing bitmapped images.

- **The Eraser tool:** The Eraser tool erases bitmapped images by painting them with white. Double-clicking on the Eraser tool displays a dialog box in which you can specify the width of the Eraser. You can use the Eraser tool only when you are editing bitmapped images.

- **The Delete Anchor Point tool:** The Delete Anchor Point tool deletes individual anchor points that are created in the conversion process. You can use the Delete Anchor Point tool only for editing converted images.

- **The Swatch:** The Swatch at the bottom of the toolbox isn't a tool. Instead, it's a color indicator. Clicking on the Swatch displays the Paint Style palette.

- **The Selection tool:** You use the Selection tool to select points and paths that have been converted. You can use the Selection tool only when you are editing converted images.

- **The Lasso tool:** You use the Lasso tool to select either a group of pixels or a set of paths and points. You drag the tool around the objects or pixels that you want to select.

- **The Zoom In tool:** The Zoom In tool magnifies both bitmapped and converted images.

Unlike in Illustrator, Dimensions, and Photoshop, you can use the Zoom In tool in Streamline to enlarge an image to *any* percentage.

- **The Zoom Out tool:** You use the Zoom Out tool to zoom out from an image.

- **The Hand tool:** You use the Hand tool to scroll around the document window.

- **The Eyedropper tool:** You use the Eyedropper tool to sample color from pixels or paths in both bitmapped and path-based images. Pressing the Control key accesses the Eyedropper. To use the tool, drag a marquee around the desired area.

You can access the Selection, Zoom In, Zoom Out, and Hand tools by using the same shortcuts that you use in Illustrator. Press ⌘ for the Selection tool, ⌘-spacebar for the Zoom In tool, ⌘-spacebar-Option for the Zoom Out tool, and the spacebar for the Hand tool.

Streamline menus

The menus in Streamline act like the toolbox; at any time you may find more than half of the options unselectable (grayed out) because of the mode you are in.

Figure 22-2 shows the Streamline menus and keyboard commands.

Figure 22-2:
The Stream-
line menus.

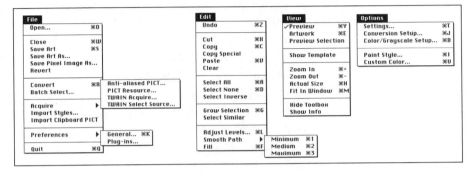

- **The File➪Open command** (⌘-O) opens a bitmapped image for conversion. Images that Streamline can open are MacPaint, PICT, PCX, Photoshop 2.0 and 2.5, TIFF, and TIFF Compressed.

Streamline can open only bitmapped images. It cannot open Illustrator documents or images that have been converted into paths by Streamline. It also cannot open bitmapped images that are in the EPS format.

- **The File➪Close command** (⌘-W) closes the active document. If you made changes to the image, Streamline asks whether you want to save changes. It saves changes to both bitmapped and converted images.

- **The File➪Save Art command** (⌘-S) saves converted artwork as Illustrator paths.

- **The File➪Save Art As command** saves converted artwork as Illustrator paths with a different name than it was originally saved as.

- **The File➪Save Pixel Image As command** saves a bitmapped image as a different file. This command is useful when you are scanning right out of Streamline.

- **The File➪Revert command** causes a converted image to revert to its bitmapped image.

- **The File➪Convert command** (⌘-R) converts artwork from bitmapped images into Illustrator paths.

▓ **The File➪Batch Select command** enables you to select several files in different locations and have all of them converted, one after the other, into Illustrator paths. This command is useful when you have several similar images to convert, all with the same settings, and you want to go to lunch. Set them up and go!

▓ **The File➪Acquire command** displays the Acquire submenu, which enables you to acquire an anti-aliased PICT, a PICT resource, or a TWAIN mechanism. You use the TWAIN Acquire command to activate scanners through Streamline. The TWAIN Select Source command enables you to determine which TWAIN source will be activated when you activate the TWAIN Acquire command.

▓ **The File➪Import Styles command** imports styles from an Illustrator document, specifically custom colors for use in Streamline.

▓ **The File➪Import Clipboard PICT command** enables you to use a PICT image on the Clipboard as the bitmapped source art. This command is necessary because Streamline does not have a New document command.

▓ **The File➪Preferences command** displays a submenu of either General Preferences (⌘-K) or Plug-Ins.

▓ **The File➪Quit command** (⌘-Q) quits Streamline. If you have made changes (to either bitmapped or Illustrator path artwork) since the last save, Streamline asks whether you want to save changes before quitting.

▓ **The Edit➪Undo command** (⌘-Z) undoes your last action. Streamline does not support multiple undos.

▓ **The Edit➪Cut command** (⌘-X) cuts selected objects and sends them to the Clipboard.

▓ **The Edit➪Copy command** (⌘-C) copies selected objects to the Clipboard.

▓ **The Edit➪Copy Special command** copies objects in the Adobe Illustrator Clipboard format.

▓ **The Edit➪Paste command** (⌘-V) pastes objects that are on the Clipboard into the Streamline document.

▓ **The Edit➪Clear command** deletes selected objects.

▓ **The Edit➪Select All command** (⌘-A) selects all pixels in bitmap mode and all paths in path mode.

▓ **The Edit➪Select None command** (⌘-D) deselects anything that is currently selected.

▓ **The Edit➪Select Inverse command** selects whatever is currently *not* selected.

▓ **The Edit➪Grow Selection command** (⌘-G) selects additional pixels in bitmap mode relative to the Magic Wand settings in the toolbox.

- **The Edit⇨Select Similar command** selects pixels that have the same color as the pixels that are currently selected.

- **The Edit⇨Adjust Levels command** (⌘-L) displays the Levels dialog box.

- **The Edit⇨Smooth Path command** displays the Smooth Path submenu, in which you can select Minimum (⌘-1), Medium (⌘-2), or Maximum (⌘-3) to smooth out the selected paths.

- **The Edit⇨Fill command** (⌘-F) allows you to fill a selected bitmap area with a certain color.

- **The View⇨Preview command** (⌘-Y) shows converted Illustrator paths in Preview mode.

- **The View⇨Artwork command** (⌘-E) shows converted Illustrator paths in Artwork mode.

- **The View⇨Preview Selection command** shows selected converted Illustrator paths in Preview mode.

- **The View⇨Show Template command** shows the original bitmapped image under the converted Illustrator paths.

- **The View⇨Zoom In command** (⌘-plus) zooms in one level.

- **The View⇨Zoom Out command** (⌘-hyphen) zooms out one level.

- **The View⇨Actual Size command** (⌘-H) shows the image at 100% magnification.

- **The View⇨Fit In Window command** (⌘-M) displays the image at a size that can fit entirely within the document window.

- **The View⇨Hide Toolbox command** hides the toolbox. When the toolbox is hidden, this menu item reads Show Toolbox.

- **The View⇨Show Info command** shows the Info palette. If the Info palette is showing, this menu item reads Hide Info.

- **The Options⇨Settings command** (⌘-T) displays the Settings dialog box.

- **The Options⇨Conversion Setup command** (⌘-J) displays the Conversion Setup dialog box.

- **The Options⇨Color/Grayscale Setup command** (⌘-B) displays the Color/ Grayscale Setup dialog box.

- **The Options⇨Paint Style command** (⌘-I) displays the Paint Style palette.

- **The Options⇨Custom Color command** (⌘-U) displays the Custom Color dialog box.

Using Streamline

The three basic steps in using Streamline are opening and editing a pixel bitmapped image, converting the pixel image into a vectored path drawing, and editing and saving the resulting Illustrator paths. Follow these steps to convert a bitmapped image into paths:

STEPS: **Converting Bitmapped Art to Paths**

Step 1. Open the bitmap image file (select File⇨Open or press ⌘-O) or use the TWAIN Acquire command to scan in the artwork.

Step 2. Use any of the bitmap editing tools to clean up stray pixels. If the area that you want to convert is only part of an image, use the Marquee tool to select that portion.

Step 3. Select Options⇨Settings (⌘-T) and choose the type of bitmapped image that you are converting. The list that you choose from contains the best generalized settings for each type of bitmapped image.

If none of the settings seems to fit your bitmapped image, select Options⇨Conversion Setup (⌘-J) and adjust the settings within the Conversion Setup dialog box.

Step 4. Select File⇨Convert (⌘-R) to have Streamline begin to do its magic.

Streamline can outline any size bitmapped artwork; it is limited only by the amount of RAM you allocate to the software. Streamline will, however, stop converting artwork before it finishes if it does not have sufficient memory. If the bitmapped artwork is overly complex (lots of colors or a big file), increase the RAM that is allocated to Streamline.

To increase the RAM allocated to Streamline, quit Streamline, select the Streamline icon from the Desktop, select File⇨Get Info (⌘-I), and change the bottom box (called "Preferred Size" in System 7.1 and 7.5) to the amount of memory that you want to allocate to Streamline. If you aren't sure how much memory you can spare, select Apple⇨About This Macintosh from the Apple menu to display the amount of RAM installed and the amount that the system and other software are using.

Step 5. Edit the new paths with the path editing tools.

Step 6. If you have Illustrator running at the same time as Streamline, you can copy converted paths in Streamline, go to Illustrator, and Paste (⌘-V) in Illustrator. The copied paths will be pasted in the Illustrator document.

If you want to save the converted file that you have just created, select File⇨Save Art (⌘-S).

Case Studies and Discovering Cool Stuff on Your Own

In This Chapter

- Looking at how art pieces are designed and assembled
- Creating a billboard — from concept to final painting
- Creating photo-realistic artwork
- Incorporating a logo into business cards and getting text shadows to overprint
- Discovering new techniques and practices

Case Study #1: "A Natural Form of Expression"

In the fall of 1993, a stunning, colorful billboard appeared across central Pennsylvania. The board featured five bright animals (well, four and an insect, if you want to get technical) on a tropical background. The images themselves were fairly basic and straightforward, with only the words "A Natural Form of Expression" across the top and an "Outdoor Advertising" banner in smaller letters below the larger text. The billboard, which is shown in Figure 23-1, also appears in the color section of this book, along with a few other samples of Tim Freed's work.

Figure 23-1:
"A Natural
Form of
Expression."

Timothy G. Freed Design created this billboard for Penn Advertising during the summer of 1993. The following pages document the steps that took the project from Tim Freed's mind to the computer screen and then eventually onto a roadside billboard.

The concept

The original idea consisted of giving a "natural" look to a billboard to promote outdoor advertising. The thought of several animals in their natural habitat became the theme of the illustration.

As Freed pondered and drew rough sketches, he kept in mind that he wanted a number of separate elements that would create a "natural" atmosphere when combined. The elements had to work together, yet retain enough individuality to make each one worth observing.

Freed drew and sketched individual animals and pondered different layouts and backgrounds. Eventually, he decided on a selection of animals and a basic layout.

The animals

Freed created each of the animals in a separate Illustrator document to save time and memory. He based most of the animals on a series of ovals or circles to give them a uniform, related kind of look; he also used concentric blends for each.

It was tempting to use different perspectives for each of the animals, but Freed decided that both the fish and the parrot would look better straight on, and he gave the other animals either a three-quarter or a one-quarter view.

The fish

The wide-eyed, panic-stricken fish consists almost entirely of ovals. Figure 23-2 shows the fish's separate shapes with white fills, layered in the order in which they appear in the illustration.

Figure 23-2:
The fish's basic outlines, before blends or blend end paths were added.

For most of the blends that give the fish texture, Freed created a smaller version of the outside shape, used a slight color variation, and blended the two shapes together. On the topmost fin, he created two ovals because the shape was very odd and would have produced strange and noticeable highlights if he had blended it.

After he finished creating the fish, he grouped all the pieces together so that he could move the fish as one unit.

The bug

Two ovals, each blended slightly to lighter, smaller ovals make up the bug (Figure 23-3). The bug gets its continuity not just from the two ovals, but also from the spots on its back.

Figure 23-3:
The bug.

Freed created the spots as an Illustrator pattern so that he could experiment with both the size and location of the dots after he applied them. He used an existing Adobe Collectors' Edition Patterns and Textures pattern that is rather large and contains nine equally sized dots placed in various locations. The pattern that Freed chose was designed so that it would look random without having to be rotated.

Freed used two dots from the pattern to create the bug's eyes. He changed the dots by converting a direction point right at the already existing opposite points and moving the far point in to form a crescent.

Using the Pen tool, Freed created the antennae separately to give the bug more of a perspective. Two circles, blended together, form the nubs on the ends of the antennae.

The salamander and its rock

The salamander, shown in three separate stages in Figure 23-4, is the most complex composition of all the animals. The image at the top of Figure 23-4 shows the composition's basic shapes.

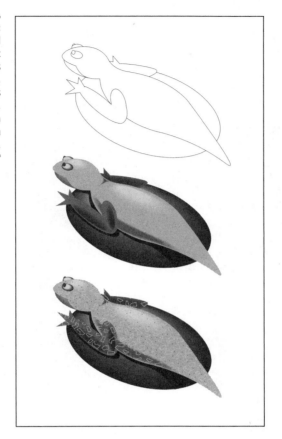

Most of the shapes in the salamander are irregular, so Freed once again used various ovals to create blends that give the salamander depth. The rock was easy to blend because it was already an oval.

After creating the blends, Freed found a pattern to use for the salamander's body, arms, and head. The pattern (from Adobe's Collectors' Edition Patterns and Textures) consists of various yellow stroked shapes and darker dots. This pattern, which contains more than a hundred shapes, is incredibly complex.

To make the pattern appear to actually wrap around the salamander, Freed created separate shapes for each arm of the salamander, as well as for its body. He then applied the pattern to each of the shapes individually. If you look closely at the left arm of the salamander, you can see that the pattern looks as if it wraps around.

To create the shadow on the rock, Freed pasted the salamander shape over the rock, filling it with a dark gray, and then changed the shape so that it conformed to the rock.

The snake

The snake stands out because it is actually two pieces and because it seems to be the most three-dimensional of all the animals, coming under the letters and in front of the rainbow and tree. Its shape, with the neck getting thicker near the head, reinforces this "comin' at ya" perspective.

The snake is one main piece, with additional paths for the chin, eyes, nose, and tongue. Instead of using the main path and creating a blend throughout the entire piece, Freed used smaller paths within the main body path and blended those paths together to provide depth. The middle image in Figure 23-5 shows the paths that were used for blends that provide depth. The outer path on each of these blends is the same color as the snake, and the inner path of the blend has a lighter or darker fill, depending on the position of the blend.

Freed drew the "bumps" for the eyes and the tongue and then created two different linear blends so that both paths showed depth along with the rest of the illustration. The eye shape is a mask that covers an oval-shaped blend.

Figure 23-5:
The snake's basic outline (top), with blend end paths added (middle), and the blended final version (bottom).

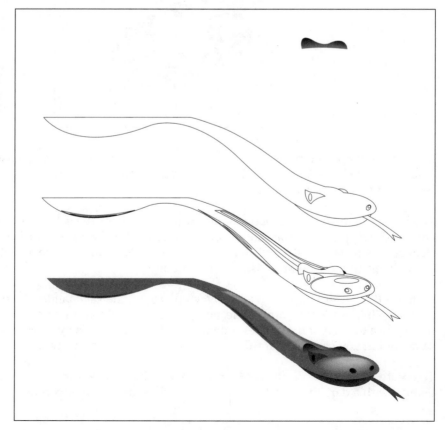

The parrot

The parrot, shown in cutaway in Figure 23-6, has three blends that create depth. In the parrot's head, a linear blend changes the color from top to bottom. In the beak, an oval blend at the point where it curves provides the "curved" perspective, and a triangular shaped blend is at its tip.

Figure 23-6:
The parrot in
cutaway view.

Freed did not use a blend to create the eyes of the parrot for two reasons. He felt that if he used a blend for the eyes, they would look just like the fish's eyes, which had their own bulgy look and were quite indicative of a fish. He also felt that using just a few concentric circles with distinct divisions made the eyes look sharper and more intelligent than a blend would make them look. The fish looks panicked, but the parrot is staring right at you, wondering if you are really paying attention to the ad.

 Figure 23-6 was created by masking half of a black-and-white line art version of the parrot with a rectangle. The original parrot was masked with another rectangle, and the two pieces fit together quite nicely.

The background

The background for "A Natural Form of Expression" works with each of the individual animals. Most of the background elements have sharp corners that offset some of the smoother curves of the animals. The various background elements, although specific to each animal, overlap each other and blend the background together. The background is shown in Figure 23-7, in dual cutaway mode.

Figure 23-7:
The background in dual cutaway mode.

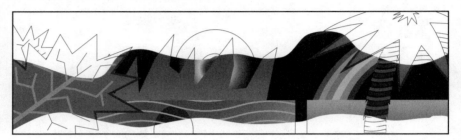

Because Freed created all the animals separately, he could bring them into the final illustration one at a time. He grouped each animal so that he could select and move them easily.

The circle-based bug contrasts with the sharp edges of the leaf, which Freed created with the Pen tool. A shadow on the leaf gives the bug more depth, and a second, smaller leaf behind the original leaf adds depth to the first leaf.

The standard Wave pattern provides water for the fish. To make the fish fit into the curve easily, Freed placed a dark shadow under the fish and moved and enlarged the wave pattern. Behind the fish, jutting, mountain-like rocks give the water the appearance of being close to the front of the drawing.

The salamander already had a rock as a partial background, and Freed added a sun.

To offset the gray of the snake, Freed created a rainbow and placed it just behind and to the right of the snake. The snake ends up using the black background of the entire ad as its own personal background, giving the snake a three-dimensional feeling.

The parrot was already brightly colored, but Freed had a problem with having both the rainbow and the parrot so bright. He didn't want the rainbow to detract from the parrot, but he couldn't very well move the rainbow in front of the sun so that it wouldn't be behind the parrot. After experimenting a bit, he added a palm tree behind the parrot and shaped it so that it blocked off the rainbow on every side of the parrot. The spiky green leaf on the right side balances the leaves on the left side very nicely.

After all the elements were in place, Freed cropped the edges to 12 inches wide by 3.5 inches high.

The type

As always, choosing a typeface was difficult. Freed chose a squarish font that has a serif and made it white with a dark shadow. The shadow gives the type depth where it is in front of the snake and the tree.

The "Outdoor Advertising" banner is bright to make sure that people notice it. Freed figured that because "A Natural Form of Expression" doesn't name a product or a service, people viewing the billboard would look to any other words for what the billboard was referring to. The nice thing about keeping the words small is that the banner doesn't overshadow the artwork, and therefore, the artwork has more impact.

The production

To get the layout approved, Freed printed the ad on paper at full size (12 inches x 3.5 inches) on a color laser printer. This printout would serve as a color guide to the painters who actually did the painting on a billboard.

Artists usually sketch billboard designs on the board at full size. As a guide, they use outlines of the artwork that are traditionally drawn by artists and projected on the billboard by an overhead projector. Penn Advertising streamlines the procedure by using Illustrator to print the outlines of the artwork onto a transparency for projection. This method keeps the artwork as close as possible to the computer-generated design.

To create the outlines of the artwork for the transparency, Freed followed these steps:

STEPS:	Changing Full-Color Art into Outlines
Step 1.	Change the Paint Style of the original artwork to a fill of white and a stroke of .25 point 100% black.
Step 2.	Release all the masks in the artwork by choosing Edit⇨Select All (⌘-A) and choosing Object⇨Mask⇨Release. Check to see whether all the masks were released by selecting Object⇨Mask. If Release is still an option, not all the masks have been released. Release until the Release option is no longer available.

Step 3.   Delete all blend-generated paths by using the Group Selection tool. Click any blend-generated path twice to select all the paths generated by the blend. Repeat this process for each blend.

You may want to keep the end paths for blends, as Freed did in this example, to help show the painters where the colors begin to change and where they end.

Step 4.   Make any necessary adjustments. For example, the rainbow's strokes are heavily weighted. After checking the original to determine the weight of the strokes, change the outline of those paths to that weight and then select Filter⇨Object⇨Outline Stroked Paths. The completed outlines for the illustration appear in Figure 23-8.

Figure 23-8:
Outlines for "A
Natural Form of
Expression."

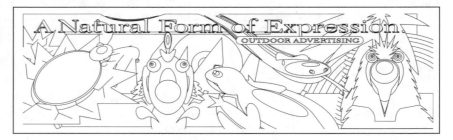

If an illustration includes a photograph or imagery created in Photoshop, you need to posterize it and outline it in Streamline to produce the outlining you need for a transparency.

See Chapter 22 for more information on Streamline.

Case Study #2: "VW Corrado"

Royce Copenheaver created the "VW Corrado" illustration for this book (see Figure 23-9 and the color section) as an example of how he uses Illustrator techniques to create a photo-realistic image.

Unlike the illustration for the billboard, this illustration is almost completely made up of gradients, which makes the file smaller and easier to work with than if Copenheaver had used blends. He used a few blends, but only in areas where gradients couldn't work, such as in the irregular shadow under the car.

Figure 23-9:
"VW Corrado"
— a photo-
realistic image
created in
Illustrator.

Preparing to illustrate

Although taking a picture of the car and scanning the photograph was tempting, Copenheaver decided not to use that method. He thought that using a photograph would force him to make the car look too mechanical and precise, and he still had lighting and background problems to deal with. Besides, he thought that scanning a photograph would make the whole process too easy.

Copenheaver decided instead to create a detailed line art drawing of the car and scan the drawing. He scanned the image at 576 dpi with a Scanjet IIcx scanner. In Photoshop, Copenheaver changed the image size of the file to 72 dpi, keeping the File Size check box checked. These changes increased the dimensions of the artwork to eight times the original size.

By scanning at a high resolution and saving at a lower resolution without changing the file size, you produce an image that you can reduce in Illustrator to much smaller than its blown-up size. You can then use this image for zooming in to high levels of magnification without sacrificing clarity. (See the sidebar on figuring out which EPS image size to use.)

Figuring out EPS image size for tracing

To produce the best possible image to trace in Illustrator, you have to save the file at the correct size and number of dots per inch. As a result, you need to know the original image's size and at what resolution (dpi) it was scanned.

To figure out what dpi to scan at, you first need to decide how much detail you want to be able to see in Illustrator. By detail, I am referring to the level at which you want to zoom in and still be able to see the scan clearly. The following table shows the zoom level as a percentage and the required dpi for scanning to achieve detail at that zoom level. The table also shows how much you need to reduce the EPS image with the Scale tool to return it to the original size.

Zoom	Scan dpi	Scale EPS	Size (3" x 5" CMYK Color)
100%	72 dpi	100%	.30MB
150%	108 dpi	66.67%	.68MB
200%	144 dpi	50%	1.19MB
300%	216 dpi	33.33%	2.67MB
400%	288 dpi	25%	4.75MB
600%	432 dpi	16.67%	10.70MB
800%	576 dpi	12.5%	19.00MB
1200%	864 dpi	8.33%	42.70MB
1600%	1152 dpi	6.25%	75.90MB

If you will use the image at less than 100%, scanning at 72 dpi is still a good idea.

After you have scanned the image at the proper resolution, open it in Photoshop and select Image⇨Image Size. In the Image Size dialog box, make sure that the File Size and Proportions check boxes are checked. Use a setting of 72 in the dpi text field and press OK. Save the file as an EPS image with an 8-bit preview.

Even if the artwork is black and white, do not save it with a 1-bit preview because this setting will make the artwork appear terrible in Illustrator. Always use an 8-bit preview.

In Illustrator, place the EPS image and double-click the Scale tool. Enter the reduction amount from the third column of the list in the Uniform text field. You can now trace the image up to and including the zoom specified.

Keep in mind that the size of an EPS file may make an Illustrator file unmanageable. A 75MB EPS image requires an enormous amount of time for redrawing and also uses a healthy chunk of the hard drive.

Copenheaver created a new Illustrator document and placed the art in it. In the Layers palette (select Window⇨Show Layers or press ⌘-Control-L), he changed the current layer to Dim EPS images and renamed the layer Scan. (Refer to Chapter 14 for an in-depth discussion of layers.)

He then locked the layer so that the image wouldn't move. Because Copenheaver put the EPS image on its own layer, he was able to easily hide or show the EPS image, and he did not have to worry about accidentally sending artwork that he created behind the EPS image.

Copenheaver created a new layer to draw the car on. He made the points and paths bright green, which was a color he didn't plan to use in the illustration.

Creating the body

Copenheaver used the Pen tool to draw the body panels, tracing over most of the illustration that he had scanned. Figure 23-10 shows the individual body pieces.

Figure 23-10:
The Corrado's
body panels.

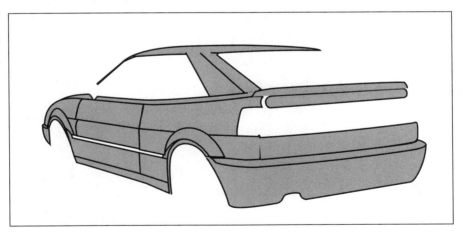

Instead of creating the gradients for the car panels at this point, Copenheaver focused on getting the shapes just right. He wasn't concerned about setting up the light source until more of the car was done.

The most difficult part about creating the panels was deciding how large to make each piece. Nobody likes to have to split up larger paths into smaller ones that have to fit very tightly. Copenheaver considered creating paths for each panel on the car; but he knew that shading could be a big problem with such large pieces if he were to use mostly gradients, and he didn't want to have to split the pieces later.

Although Copenheaver didn't want to be too concerned with the lighting initially, he decided to put a highlight down the driver's side and create two separate paths above and below the highlight area. He also decided to ignore any areas that have body molding until he had finished creating the panels.

Creating the panel gradients

After Copenheaver had the panels in place, he opened the Gradient palette and created two new gradients based on yellow, which was to be the color of the car. The primary gradients were white-to-yellow gradients that were both linear and radial.

He created the linear gradient with the white color stop at the 35% mark and the center of the gradient offset to 54%. The radial gradient consisted of a white color stop and a yellow color stop, with the midpoint set to 28%.

Using only two gradients seems limiting, but Copenheaver used the two gradients in many different ways, stretching the gradients across different paths with the Gradient Vector tool. Because Copenheaver had the highlight shapes in mind when he created the panels, applying gradients realistically was much easier than if the gradients had been an afterthought.

Molding and pieces

The next step was to create all the body molding and extraneous surface pieces such as the door handle, mirror, and antenna. Copenheaver used the Pen tool to create shapes for most of these pieces.

After he drew the outside mirror, he gave the reflective surface of the glass a slight blue tinted gradient to make it appear as realistic as possible.

He created the molding pieces mostly by drawing a path along the center of where the molding was to go and then changing the weight of the stroke to make the molding the right thickness. This method was much easier than trying to draw an outer shape for moldings of varying thicknesses. Copenheaver used the Outline Stroked Path filter for molding that needed a slight gradient.

Interior design

The inside of the car was very important to the way the car would look in its entirety. Copenheaver felt very strongly about this area, and consequently, he spent a good deal of time drawing and perfecting it. In his words, "I didn't want to take the easy way out by just having a gradient where the windows would be. Instead, I wanted the viewer to have trouble believing this was only a drawing and not a photograph."

The interior detail enhances this illustration. Not that the interior has so much detail, but the shapes and shading are done so well that the detail is implied. Sometimes achieving that effect is more difficult than creating the detail for real, and it is usually more effective.

One of the little things that Copenheaver took the time to add and craft carefully is the seat belt on the passenger's side. The belt looks as if it is actually being twisted as it descends toward the seat. If you look closely, you also can see the seat belt clasp on the driver's side.

One of the other little things is the rearview mirror, which adds to the complexity and believability of the interior. The shading of the mirror gives it a reflective appearance.

Copenheaver drew most of the pieces of the interior with different tints of dark gray. By making most of the interior shapes just a little different, he was able to create even more implied detail.

Glass and taillights

The glass panels were easy to draw because they ended up behind openings that already existed. Copenheaver created each pane as a separate path and then filled it with a gray-based gradient.

The most troubling problem about creating the glass pieces was that Copenheaver could not create driver's side and rear windows because they would have concealed the interior and the other windows. To compensate for the missing windows, Copenheaver darkened much of the interior and darkened the front and passenger windows. He had to angle each of the glass gradients differently to create the correct effect and to compensate for the missing glass sections.

He drew the taillights and the third brake light next. The third brake light was easy to draw because it is outside the rear door and is rather small and simple. The other tail-lights are much more complex. They contain different colors (orange, white, and red) that have to be part of the base unit, and they are ridged. Copenheaver had to create separate horizontal paths with different colored strokes for each section of the taillights.

Next, Copenheaver added the black license plate strip. It is a solid color because the plastic rubbery material on the actual car does not reflect light at all.

Creating the trunk lock

The trunk lock, although a small part of the car, is one of those little make-it or break-it pieces that has to look good. Because the lock is inset and outset at the same time, figuring out how to create it took a little thought. Copenheaver achieved the right effect by using the same gradient in opposite directions. To duplicate his work, follow these steps:

STEPS: Creating an Inset/Outset Key Lock

Step 1.   Draw three circles that have the same center. Use the Option key to draw each circle from the center out to the edges. Draw a little line in the center to represent the keyhole. In the example in Figure 23-11, the circles are skewed slightly to fit the angle of the part of the car that the lock is on.

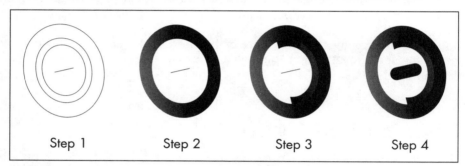

Step 1   Step 2   Step 3   Step 4

Figure 23-11: Steps for creating an inset/outset key lock.

Step 2.   Color the outermost circle with a black-and-white gradient. If it doesn't already appear horizontal, drag across the circle with the Gradient Vector tool.

Step 3.   Select the middle circle and fill it with the black-and-white gradient as well, but this time use the Gradient Vector tool to drag across the circle in the opposite direction.

When you drag the same gradient in opposite directions within an object in an illustration, you naturally produce the effect of depth. You can enhance this effect by giving other objects in the illustration reflections, highlights, or shadows.

Step 4.   Change the keyhole line Paint Style to a fill of None and a black stroke of 10 points.

The wheels

The rims and tires were time consuming to create because, once again, Copenheaver wanted to make the pieces look as real as possible. He created them in a separate document, copying just the edges of the car that were near the wheel so that he would have a reference for the perspective. Figure 23-12 shows one wheel in cutaway view.

Figure 23-12:
Cutaway view of a wheel from the Corrado. The bottom part shows the wheel in Artwork mode, without showing the blend on the inside of the tire.

Copenheaver first created the rims by using the Oval tool and then shearing the shape to the correct angle. Then he added the tires. After trying many different approaches, he finally settled on using a blend for the sides of the tires and a gradient for the edges of the tires. The edges contain a linear gradient that is really a darkened version of the Steel Bar gradient.

To add the tread, Copenheaver stroked paths with different weights and shades of gray and black. After completing the major parts of the wheel, he added details such as the lug nuts, stem, hubcap emblem, and highlights.

Copenheaver copied the wheel and placed it into the rest of the document with the car. Then he scaled it up just a little so that it fit perfectly in the rear wheel opening. For the front wheel, Copenheaver copied the rear wheel and rotated the inside rim just a bit so that the two wheels wouldn't be identical. Then he scaled down the entire wheel and placed it in position. He filled the wheel well on the rear of the driver's side with a gradient to add depth even to the underside of the car.

Adding all the little things

At this point, Copenheaver started adding all the little things that make the car look real. He added lines for the door, hatch, spoiler, and bumper gap to show the gaps between these parts. Where the factory had welded body panels, Copenheaver used two paths, one stroked lighter and one stroked darker, placed next to each other. Later, he added the exhaust pipe, rear wiper, and emblems.

Getting the lighting just right

What took the most time was getting the lighting to look just right. Look at any car on the street, and you will see a dull, flat reflection on its sides and body. In order to be able to place the car on any background, Copenheaver wanted to emulate this reflection as well as possible without making the reflection indicative of a certain setting.

After Copenheaver realigned and angled the gradients just right, he added small crescent-shaped highlights by transforming the yellow radial blend to fit the crescents. More than anything else, these highlights give the body panels their "reflective" appearance.

He added other little finishing touches, including making the mirror show up in the reflection of the window on the driver's side and showing the reflection of the antenna on the back window.

Creating the background

Copenheaver had created several backgrounds to use with the car, but all of them presented a common problem: he would have to alter the windows of the car when he added the background.

He finally settled on using an open-air background with colors that complemented the car. The front window gradient didn't show a very distinct mountain, so he created a new piece in the shape of the part of the mountain that should have been visible through the front window.

Case Study #3: The Bézier Logo, Business Cards, Letterhead, and Envelopes

This case study describes how to create a logo in Illustrator and prepare it for use in printing business cards, letterhead, and envelopes.

The concept and the logo

The concept for the logo is simple. It needs to contain the word *Bézier,* which is part of the name of the company, and somehow represent Bézier curves. The final logo design is a curve that runs from left to right, with the letters in the word *bézier* interspersed in lowercase through the curve. The logo is shown in Figure 23-13.

Figure 23-13:
The Bézier logo.

The logo colors are black and Pantone 340, which is a dark green. The color is in a top-to-bottom gradient that goes from solid green to 50 percent of the Pantone color.

Designing the cards, letterhead, and envelopes

Two versions of business cards were used for the company: a vertical design and a horizontal design. The green part of the logo bleeds off the bottom and the lower right and left of the cards. The letterhead and the envelopes have the logo at a right angle, bleeding off the left edges and the left side of the top and bottom. Figure 23-14 shows these designs.

To make the concept more in tune with computer graphics, the cards and letterhead have a reverse side that shows the text in what Illustrator sees as Artwork format. The reverse side is an actual reverse that shows the text and objects backwards. Creating it is fairly simple:

STEPS: **Creating Reversed Outlines**

Step 1. Select the original artwork. Copy and paste it; work only with the copy.

Step 2. Select all the paths in the copy and double-click the Reflect tool. Click the Horizontal or Vertical axis radio button and press OK. In the example (Figure 23-15), I reflected across the vertical axis.

Step 3. Convert any text to outlines.

Step 4. Select all the paths in the copy. Change the stroke weight to .25 point and black and the fill to None. In some cases, you may want to fill all the paths with white to knock out excessive lines that would not show up in the original artwork.

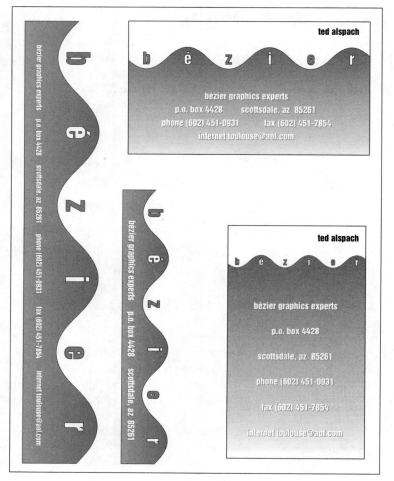

Figure 23-14: Designs for business cards, letterhead, and envelopes.

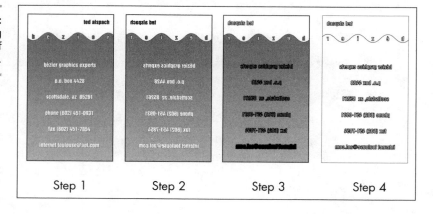

Figure 23-15: Steps for creating reversed outlines of artwork.

Step 1 Step 2 Step 3 Step 4

Printing the job

The most difficult aspect of creating the artwork for these pieces is making it work on a printing press. The main obstacle is the hairline rules, which are on everything from the letters and curve in the logo to the shadow on all the text in the green gradated area.

Because the cards, letterhead, and envelope contain a gradation, the different colors have to be dead-on center. Very little, if any, variation can exist. This requirement creates a problem regarding trapping for the hairline stroke and the artwork. The hairline is black and can overprint, but the way the artwork was created as a shadow for most of the text, as shown in Figure 23-16, causes a big problem.

Figure 23-16:
Black objects set to overprint on the horizontal version of the Bézier Graphics Experts business card.

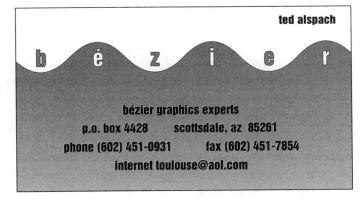

Instead of simply setting all the black objects to overprint, you need to create the shadows of the text as separate objects and then set them to overprint. Because the black objects will overprint entirely, no extra trapping (that is, widening of strokes) is necessary. Follow these steps:

STEPS: Creating Overprinting Areas for Shadows

Step 1.   Position the shadow correctly under the object.

Step 2.   Copy the object, lock it (choose Arrange⇨Lock or press ⌘-1), and paste in front (⌘-F).

Step 3.   Select both the object and the shadow and choose Filter⇨Pathfinder⇨Front Minus. All the shadowed areas will be cropped to the size of just the shadow. Figure 23-17 shows the pieces of shadow that result when you follow these steps for the horizontal business card text.

Step 4.   Check the Overprint fill check box in the Paint Style palette.

Figure 23-17:
The pieces of shadow that result from subtracting the front from the back in outline form.

bézier graphics experts
p.o. box 4423   scottsdale, az 85261
phone (602) 451-0931   fax (602) 451-7854
internet toulouse@aol.com

Discovering Cool Stuff on Your Own

This book contains many really neat tips and techniques. I discovered most of them by doing some really hard "playing" with Illustrator.

If you are excited and enthusiastic about Illustrator, you will undoubtedly discover things that I didn't include in this book because of a lack of space or a lack of time — or most likely, because I didn't know anything about them.

I have stuffed within these pages all of the best things about Illustrator that other graphic artists who contributed to this book and I could come up with, but I know that in the short time between writing the chapters and having the book appear on bookshelves, I will discover many more things that I could have included.

Illustrator is one of the, if not *the,* most versatile software packages around. There are limits to what you can do with it, but those limits are being pushed further and further each time an upgrade appears and every time computer systems become more powerful, faster, and cheaper. New technologies will continue to enhance Illustrator's capabilities, but the core of the product will always be the same.

How I figured out cool stuff

My observation in the area of finding "new" things that Illustrator can do is that any time I say to myself, "Golly! This sure does take a long time to do!" there is probably a shorter way to do it that I haven't figured out yet.

Very rarely do I exclaim "Golly!" but when I do, I take note. Others hearing this outburst take note as well, and yes, they have recommended counseling.

Like everyone else, I can't just sit and play with Illustrator all day in order to come up with techniques and tips that no one else has yet discovered. But when I do use Illustrator, I make the best use of my time, and I try to use key commands for everything. If I have to pull down a menu because I don't know a key command, it is a sad day in my life.

As I am using Illustrator, I try different ways of doing ordinary things. For example, I often select almost everything in an illustration and lock it. The first method that I used for this procedure was to select everything by choosing All, which selected all the objects in the Illustration. I then deselected particular objects by Shift-clicking them and selected Arrange⇨Lock (⌘-1). This method wasn't too productive because I usually had the other items selected (the ones that I didn't want locked), and I had to deselect all of them before I could lock the others.

The second method that I tried was a little better, but I knew that somehow there had to be a better way. Because all the things that I didn't want locked were selected, I selected View⇨Fit In Window (⌘-M), pressed the Shift key, and dragged a marquee around everything. This action selected all the unselected objects and deselected all the selected objects. I then locked the selected objects.

The third method was the best up to that time. Because everything that I wanted to select and lock wasn't selected, I chose Filter⇨Select Inverse, which selected everything that wasn't selected and deselected the selected objects. That way I didn't have to select the other objects with the mouse, which always slows me down. Then I locked the selected objects.

Have you noticed that these paragraphs are getting shorter? The method I now use is almost too easy. The objects that I want locked are the only things not selected, so I press Option and choose Arrange⇨Lock (⌘-Option-1), which locks everything that isn't selected.

Back when I was Shift-clicking, if I had known that ⌘-Option-1 locked everything that wasn't selected, I could have avoided a great deal of wasted time and frustration. But because I tried to do this operation so many different ways, I *know* that command, and I use it more than ever.

Knowing versus memorizing

If you memorize all the key commands in this book and then take the time to memorize all the tips and techniques listed in these pages, you will still not be able to use Illustrator as well as the pros.

To get the most out of Illustrator, you need to use the software until the commands and techniques become intuitive. Memorizing the menus may help you find menu items faster, but knowing what each menu item does in depth will score that information into your subconscious and enable you to use Illustrator better than otherwise possible.

Very few people in the graphic arts industry know Illustrator inside and out; yet the ones who do are producing the best-quality illustrations. What does it take to know Illustrator? If you can see in your mind how to create an entire illustration, step by step, you know the software. On the other hand, if you make a mistake in real life and type a mental ⌘-Z, it's time for therapy.

What you can do to learn more

Read this book inside and out and think to yourself, "Gee, I can do that better *and* faster," and sit down and figure it out. Strangely enough, the first time you discover that you can do something faster than before, doing it will take twice as long as it used to take.

Look at the last set of steps in Chapter 21 and figure out how you can reduce the number of steps from 21 to 10. Before I came up with the printed version of the steps for creating a rounded rectangle with reversed corners, I must have thought of five other ways to create it. The method that appears in this book is the fastest, most accurate way to do it. Now if only I could come up with a better, tighter *name* for the darned things.

If you have to Option-copy (to duplicate a selected object, drag with the Option key and then release the mouse button before the Option key) a hundred things, decide whether it would be better to select Arrange⇨Repeat Transform (⌘-D) 99 times or by doing it ten times you can select all the objects, Option-copy *them,* and select Repeat Transform only eight more times. Which method is faster for your job? Why?

Is it better to create an object and change the Paint Style information after it is selected or to deselect all (⌘-Shift-A), change the Paint Style, and then create an object? Or maybe an object on the page already exists, so you can create the object and use the Eyedropper/Paint Bucket tools to copy the color from one to the other. Or, if an object with that color exists, you can select the object, which will change the Paint Style to that color, and then create the new object.

If you think about all these things as you are drawing, your illustration time will decrease, the quality of your drawings will increase, and you will have more time for using Illustrator to design a solar-powered hang glider, or whatever you do when you aren't using Illustrator for real work.

Getting answers and information from Adobe

When you can't find an answer to a problem or want to know whether a way exists to do some tedious task faster, call the Adobe Tech support line.

 The main problem with most software company support these days is the "not our fault" answer. (Whatever problem or question you have, it isn't the software company's fault.) You don't find this attitude at Adobe. Most of the support staff are polite, and they will help even the most befuddled user along, as well as give additional tips and techniques. The main problem with Adobe tech support is the difficulty in reaching a human being. When you call, you get routed through a series of questions ("If you are having trouble designing a hang glider with Adobe Illustrator, press 465.") that hardly ever seem to pertain to your particular problem. After a grueling mechanical question-and-answer session, you put on hold while some tech people argue about who has to answer the call, (and other tech people place bets on how long it will be before you hang up). Actually, I am kidding about the tech support staff's behavior while you are on hold, and I am sure they jump from one call to the next without pausing to catch a breath. Adobe now has a special support line that you pay a premium for, where the tech people are the first to answer, and most of them pick up within the first movement of the classical music you are forced to listen to.

If you don't need an answer right away, you can fax Adobe. You should get a response within one business day, by either phone or return fax. Faxing is great because you can send along your illustration so the tech people can actually look at it.

In addition, Adobe has a free BBS running at 14.4 that anyone can call. Adobe tech people regularly answer posted questions, and you can send your Illustrator file along with your questions.

Appendices

One of the best ways to begin using this book is a quick skim through the following appendices. This is especially true if you have just upgraded your Illustrator software to either 5.0 or 5.5.

This section contains six appendices with all sorts of juicy tidbits, including a thorough discussion of the keyboard commands used in the software.

Your System and Illustrator

System Requirements

To run Adobe Illustrator 5.0 and 5.5 for the Macintosh, there are certain requirements you need to fulfill with your computer system. Of these, the CPU and RAM are the most important. Previous versions of Illustrator worked with almost any Macintosh — from the Mac Plus on up — with very little RAM requirements. This capability has changed with Version 5.0, however.

The computer

The following is a list of the Macintosh computers you *can't* use to run the latest version of Illustrator. Don't attempt to load Adobe Illustrator 5.0/5.5 on any of the following systems:

- Macintosh 128 (original Mac)
- Macintosh 512K or 512KE
- Macintosh Plus
- Macintosh SE
- Macintosh Portable
- Macintosh Classic
- Macintosh PowerBook 100

There are more than 20 Macintosh models Illustrator *can* run on, including all members of the following classes (or families):

- Macintosh II
- Macintosh LC
- Macintosh Performa

- Macintosh PowerBook, including Duos (except PowerBook 100)
- Macintosh Centris
- Macintosh Quadra
- Macintosh SE/30, Classic II, Color Classic
- Power Macs—PowerPC-based Macintosh systems

The rule here is that your system must have a 68020 or greater processor or a PowerPC processor. The systems that don't make the cut are 68000-based.

RAM

Illustrator 5.0/5.5 needs a minimum of 3.1MB to run. What this means is that your system should have *at the very least* 5MB of RAM total. The system software usually takes up between 1 – 2MB of RAM.

A good way to check how much RAM you have available for Illustrator is to restart your system. After the desktop appears, go under the Apple in the upper lefthand corner and pull down either About This Macintosh (System 7) or About the Finder (System 6). The number in the Largest Unused Block box needs to be 3,100K or larger. If not, then you need to buy some RAM.

Other attachments

You also need a hard drive with about 5MB of free space on it, a monitor (black and white will work), a keyboard, and a mouse.

System Recommendations

If you have the minimum system that Adobe recommends, Illustrator will work — kind of. If you have armloads of patience and plenty to do between certain operations, this minimum setup may work for you.

CPU and FPU

Although a 68020 is fast compared to a 68000, it crawls compared to a 68040, and it stops compared to a PowerPC. To do color work, investigate your options regarding a 68040 or better. Systems with 68040s include Centris, Quadra, LCIV, and some of the latest PowerBooks and Performas.

There is a catch, however. If you are using Illustrator 5.0, make sure that your computer has a math coprocessor (also called a floating point unit, or FPU). Most computers do, but some don't. Here is a list of systems with a 68020 or greater processor that do *not* have a math coprocessor:

- Macintosh IIsi (FPU comes on the NuBUS adapter card), IIvi
- Macintosh LC, LCII, LCIII (optional)
- Macintosh Classic II, Color Classic (optional)
- PowerBook 140, 145, 145B, 160
- PowerBook Duos (available on Duo Dock)
- Performa 200, 400, 600 (optional), 405, 430, 450 (optional)
- Centris 610
- Quadra 605
- Quadra 610 (base 8/160 model; all others have it)

Why does your system need an FPU? The Pathfinder filters and two object filters (Outline Stroked Path and Offset Path) do not load in Illustrator 5.0 if there is no FPU present.

A way to get around this limitation if your computer does *not* have an FPU is to get Software FPU (included on this book's CD-ROM), a shareware utility that fools Illustrator into thinking that there *is* an FPU installed. Unfortunately, this utility loads *all* the filters, and not all the filters work with Software FPU (the two object filters and Mix Soft have the most trouble).

 Probably the best thing you can do to become compatible is to upgrade to Version 5.5 of Illustrator, which does not require an FPU for any of the filters mentioned above.

Too much RAM is never enough

Through the Get Info box (in the Finder, select the Illustrator icon and then choose File⇨Get Info or press ⌘-I), you can allocate as much RAM to Illustrator as you like; of course, if you don't have much RAM available, Illustrator uses as much RAM as it can.

A good setting for Preferred Memory size of RAM (on the Get Info box) is 10,000K. This is twice as much RAM as Adobe recommends, but this amount allows you to work with medium-sized documents at a pretty fast clip.

No matter how much RAM you add to your system and allocate to Illustrator, there will surely be times when you get various types of "Out of Memory" errors. One of the most common of these errors is the `Not enough memory for Undo/Redo` error, which occurs when the computer doesn't have enough memory to keep some of the oldest undos in your system. Because different operations take up different amounts of memory and more complex drawings take up more memory than simpler ones, the amount of RAM you need at any one time can vary.

Other areas that need lots of RAM are patterns (especially transparent ones), blends, mullet-color gradients, masks, compound paths, and the use of some filters (Free Distort and Create Mosaic are notorious for RAM usage).

Adobe Illustrator on Floppy Disks __

Illustrator comes in two forms: on floppy disks and on CD-ROM. Both give you everything you need to run the software correctly, but the CD-ROM gives you much more (extra fonts, tutorials, a slide show) for only $100 – $150 more.

Installing Illustrator from disks

The normal way to install Illustrator is to insert Disk 1 in your computer and double-click the Adobe Illustrator Installer icon. After the Installer dialog box comes up, click Install for a normal installation. The Installer checks to see what type of computer you have and installs the appropriate software. A good rule of thumb: Whenever you install a brand new version of software, keep the version you've been using on your hard drive for a while because — believe it or not — there could be problems with the new version!

It isn't always necessary, but starting up with extensions off (hold down the Shift key when powering up) prevents your start-up inits (extensions and control panel devices) from loading, including virus protection software that may interfere with the installation process. Two popular virus checkers, SAM and Virex, allow you to control when and if floppies are scanned when inserted; if you have these programs, change this option so the floppies are *not* scanned when inserted.

The following is a list of the contents of each of the disks. Note that under normal circumstances, you don't need to insert any of the floppies except when installing. If a file or a folder's content becomes *corrupted* (part of the file is damaged; the code has changed; or the part of the disk where the file was stored becomes bad), it can be quicker to copy just the files you need instead of going through the installation process.

Most of the files and folders are compressed with the Stuffit 1.5.1 technology. Most software that can decompress Stuffit files can decompress these files and folders.

Disk 1

- Adobe Illustrator Installer
- Install Script
- Read Me Version 5.0/5.5
- Samples *f* (Any time you see an *f*, it is usually computer lingo for *folder.*)
- TeachText (For some reason, Adobe is still shipping TeachText Version 1.2, which Apple claims is incompatible with System 7.)
- Tutorial *f*

Disk 2

- Adobe Illustrator.1 (The first part of two Stuffit parts; the two need to be joined before decompressing.)

Disk 3

- Adobe Illustrator.2
- Plug-Ins *f*
- PPDs *f*

Disk 4

▓ Adobe Type ƒ.1 (first part of three)

Disk 5

▓ Adobe Type ƒ.2 (second part of three)

Disk 6

▓ Adobe Type Manager

▓ Adobe Type ƒ.3 (third part of three)

▓ ATM 680x0

▓ Plug-Ins FPU ƒ (Plug-Ins that work only when an FPU is installed)

▓ Utilities ƒ

Disk 7

▓ Gradients ƒ (Gradients and Patterns folder)

▓ XTND

▓ XTND System

Custom installation

When doing a custom installation, you can pick and choose which parts of the Illustrator software you want installed on your system. For instance, you may not want the tutorial files and samples installed, so a custom installation allows you to install everything *but* the tutorial and sample files. Of course, you can do what most people do — simply drag the folders you don't want to the trash after you have looked at them. This is the cooler way to pare down your folders. But be careful not to trash the wrong files!

Actually, as time goes on, there are more and more reasons to do a custom installation. Adobe and other software manufacturers are constantly updating their software, making changes and improvements, fixing things, and making sure that all the new software from other manufacturers works with their software. Using custom installation prevents you from putting an older version of ATM on your system than is currently available.

Probably the most important reason to do a custom installation is for users who have no FPU. The standard installation will *not* install the Plug-Ins that work only with an FPU installed. Makes sense, right? Well, not if you have SoftFPU or another software-based FPU installed. In this case, you need to do a custom installation to ensure that those Plug-Ins are installed.

The following list discusses each option in the Custom box (seen when doing a custom installation) and what it does:

Adobe Illustrator installs Illustrator 5.0 applications into a folder at the root level of your hard drive.

Plug-Ins folder installs a folder called Plug-Ins inside the Illustrator folder. The Plug-Ins requiring an FPU are *not* installed when this option is selected.

FPU-Based Plug-Ins installs additional Plug-Ins into the Plug-Ins folder that only work when an FPU is present. Even if you don't have an FPU or software that emulates an FPU, you can install these Plug-Ins. They are *not* available in the Filter menu until you have either a real FPU or a software emulation of one installed.

Tutorial folder installs a folder called Tutorial with illustrations from the Tutorial book.

Color Systems folder installs a folder in the Illustrator folder that contains Pantone, Trumatch, Focoltone, and Toyo88/91 color finder files. These files contain a set of the colors used in each system. A folder called Pantone Color Look-Up Tables is also installed.

Samples folder installs a folder called Sample Files, which contains three folders: Sample Artwork, Grids and Layout, and Graphs and Graph Designs.

Gradients & Patterns folder installs a folder with sample gradients and patterns.

Separator & Utilities installs a folder that contains all sorts of really neat stuff, including Adobe Separator 5.01, which you need to print color separations of Illustrator files. The "Densitometer Control chart" file, a Read Me file concerning PPDs (PostScript Printer Description files), and the PPDs folder are also included. A filter called Artwork View Speedup, which not many people know about, is tucked away in here. This filter changes Artwork view handles and anchor points to black. The Riders Folder and Riders Maker, in the folder called Third-Party Utility, are also located here.

Claris XTND System creates a folder in your System folder containing all the necessary files for importing text.

XTND Translators loads all the different translators into the System folder.

Adobe Type folder installs Adobe PostScript Typefaces into the Illustrator folder in a folder called, appropriately, Adobe Type.

Adobe Type Manager (68020 or greater) installs Version 3.6.1 of ATM into your System folder's Control Panels folder and the ATM 68020/030/040 file into the root level of the System folder.

Illustrator on CD-ROM

CD-ROMs are very hip (hey, we included one with this book for that very reason). In fact, more and more software publishers are supplying their applications on CD-ROM in addition to floppies.

Installing Illustrator from CD-ROM is easier than installing from floppies because you don't have to switch floppy disks. Using the installer on the CD-ROM is just like using the installer from floppies.

There are a number of additional files on the CD-ROM that are not available on floppy disks. One such file, Adobe Illustrator Deluxe, is a multimedia production with digitized movies, a self-contained installer, demos of other Adobe products, and a slide show of artwork done in Illustrator. Other files/folders include the following:

Acrobat Installer is a folder that consists of an installer for Adobe Acrobat. Just the software for reading PDF files is installed, but an added bonus takes place when you use the installer: duplicate fonts are removed from your System folder, including the base TrueType fonts that Macintosh System Software automatically installs.

Adobe Illustrator 5.5 is a folder that contains much of the same information that is installed onto your hard disk, but there's a catch. Every time you run Illustrator from the CD, you must enter your serial number. It doesn't remember that you just typed it in two hours ago, before that fatal system crash that tore up your multimedia production of *Evita.*

PSPrinter 8 contains the installer for a replacement to Apple's LaserWriter extension, PS Printer 8.

Adobe Type Library is a folder that holds all the typefaces that come with the Deluxe CD-ROM edition.

AI Manuals and Tech Notes is a folder that has technical notes in a variety of formats: Acrobat, Macwrite II, Microsoft Word 5.0, and TeachText. Another folder contains the four Illustrator manuals, *in their entirety*, in PDF format for use within Acrobat.

Adobe Products contains demo versions of Premiere, Dimensions, and Photoshop. Each program is disabled with no save function.

Adobe Collector's Edition is a folder with patterns and borders ready for use in Illustrator.

QuickTime contains the installation software for QuickTime (you need QuickTime for the Adobe Illustrator Deluxe software on the CD-ROM).

Puzzle is a larger-than-life rendition of the Illustrator 5 picture in puzzle form.

Third Party Clip Art is a folder containing various Illustrator-format clip art.

Resources

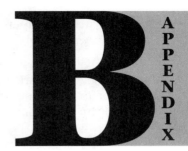

This appendix contains resources for related products, services, and other information you may find useful. All phone numbers, addresses, and version numbers are subject to change without notice, of course.

People and Service Company Resources

The following individuals and companies contributed artwork to the *Macworld Illustrator 5.0/5.5 Bible* for use in the book, CD-ROM, or both. All are experts in their particular fields:

Sandee Cohen, 33 Fifth Ave., New York, NY 10003. Phone: 212-677-7763. Fax: 212-979-0740 (call first). AOL address: SandeeC. Sandee works as a Macintosh desktop trainer and consultant. She also teaches at New York's New School for Social Research and has written training materials for many Macintosh training facilities. Sandee contributed the filter charts in Illustrator form that are available on the *Macworld Illustrator 5.0/5.5 Bible* CD-ROM.

Royce Copenheaver of Academy ArtWorks, Inc., located at 52 Grumbacher Road, York, PA 17402. Phone: 717-767-4086. Fax: 717-767-5044. Royce contributed the VW Corrado, created exclusively for the *Macworld Illustrator 5.0/5.5 Bible* and used for Case Study #2 in Chapter 23. The VW Corrado artwork is available for study on this book's CD-ROM.

Tim Freed of Timothy G. Freed Design, located at 443 Park Street, York, PA 17404. Phone: 717-854-3976. Tim created the billboard entitled "A Natural Form of Expression," used in Case Study #1 in Chapter 23. Tim also creates a wide variety of artwork. The "Natural Form of Expression" artwork is available for study on this book's CD-ROM.

Jennifer Garling of Bézier Graphics Experts, located at P.O. Box 4428, Scottsdale, AZ 85261. Phone: 602-451-0931. Fax: 602-451-7584. AOL address: Lucyfer. Internet: Lucyfer@aol.com. Jennifer is a graphic designer/artist and graphic software trainer.

She drew most of the art, including all the nasty-to-draw technical art (showing paths, anchor points, and so on) in this book. All of the artwork she created for the color insert is available for inspection on this book's CD-ROM.

Teeple Graphics, 100 Brown Street, Middletown, PA 17057. Phone: 717-944-2034. Fax: 717-944-2088. Teeple Graphics is a Macintosh VAR specializing in desktop publishing and high-end graphic training and systems integration.

Software Company Resources

3G Graphics, Inc., 114 Second Ave. South, Suite 104, Edmonds, WA 98020. Phone: 206-774-3518. Fax: 206-771-8975. Publisher of *Images with Impact!* (clip art). Includes many different varieties of clip art on both CD-ROM and floppy disk. Sample artwork is included on the *Macworld Illustrator 5.0/5.5 Bible* CD-ROM.

Adobe Systems, Inc., 1585 Charleston Road, P.O. Box 7900, Mountain View, CA 94039-7900. Customer Service: 800-833-6687. Technical Support (available to registered users with a valid serial number only): 415-961-0911. BBS (First Class software): 408-562-6839. Publisher of Illustrator 5.5, Photoshop 2.5, Streamline 3.0, and Dimensions 2.0. A demo version of Streamline is included on this book's CD-ROM.

Altsys Corp., 269 W. Renner Pkwy., Richardson, TX 75080. Phone: 214-680-2060. Fax: 214-680-0537. Publisher of Fontographer 4.0, typeface creation and editing software.

America Online, 8619 Westwood Center Drive, Vienna, VA 22182. Phone: 800-827-6364. America Online is an on-line service featuring several resources, electronic mail, access to the Internet, and thousands of different conferencing areas. Software to access AOL is included on this book's CD-ROM.

Artbeats, Box 1287, Myrtle Creek, OR 97457. Phone: 503-863-4429. Fax: 503-863-4547. Publisher of Artbeats clip art, samples of which are included on this book's CD-ROM.

Bruce Jones Design Inc., 31 St. James Ave., Boston, MA 02116. Phone: 800-843-3873. Fax: 617-350-8764. Publisher of Maps! Maps! Maps!, clip art map for Macintosh and PC on floppy disk and CD-ROM. Vol. 1 World Maps, Vol. 2 USA State by State, Vol. 3 World Hot Spots. Sample artwork is included on this book's CD-ROM.

Cartesia Software, 5 South Main Street, P.O. Box 757, Lambertville, NJ 08530. Phone: 609-397-1611. Fax: 602-397-5724. Publisher of Map Art volumes 1 through 4 and World Data Bank Maps. Sample artwork is included on this book's CD-ROM.

Educorp, 7434 Trade St., San Diego, CA 92121-2410. Phone: 619-536-9999. Fax: 619-536-2345. Suppliers of clip art samples for this book's CD-ROM.

Dynamic Graphics, Inc., 6000 N. Forest Drive, Peoria, IL 61614-3592. Phone: 309-688-8800. Fax: 309-688-3075. Publisher of Electronic Clipper, Designer's Club, Electronic Volk, and ArtAbout clip art collections and subscriptions. Sample artwork is included on this book's CD-ROM.

Image Club Graphics, Inc., 729 Twenty-Fourth Ave. Southeast, Calgary, Alberta, Canada T2G 1P5. Phone: 800-661-9410. Fax: 403-261-7013. Image Club products include DigitArt clip art, the Image Club Typeface Library, the PhotoGear CD-ROM Series, and other related products. Sample artwork is included on this book's CD-ROM.

Innovation Advertising & Design, 41 Mansfield Ave., Essex Junction, VT 05452. Phone: 800-255-0562. Fax: 802-878-1768. Publishers of AdArt EPS clip art, available on CD-ROM and floppy disk. Sample artwork is included on this book's CD-ROM.

Letraset USA, 40 Eisenhower Drive, Paramus, NJ 07653. Phone: 201-845-6100. Fax: 201-845-6100. Publisher of FontStudio 2.0, software for custom font, symbol, logo, and typeface design.

Pixar, 1001 West Cutting Blvd., Richmond, CA 94804. Phone: 510-236-4000. Publisher of Pixar Typestry, software for creating 3-D images from type and Illustrator paths. A demo version of Typestry is included on this book's CD-ROM.

How Illustrator Versions 5.0 and 5.5 Differ

Illustrator 5.0

Illustrator 5.0 was released in August 1993, following the introduction of the Newton at Macworld Boston.

Packaged inside a purple box, Illustrator now comes (like its sister product Photoshop) in a regular or Deluxe CD-ROM version. Weighing in at a hefty seven disks, Illustrator 5.0 is the biggest Illustrator ever. CD-ROM purchasers receive a tutorial that covers some of the new features and a small sampling of techniques.

Version 5.0 requires at least a Mac II series, a hard drive, and 4MB of RAM. An illustration drawn in Illustrator 5.0 is shown in Figure C-1.

Figure C-1:
An illustration created
with Illustrator 5.0.

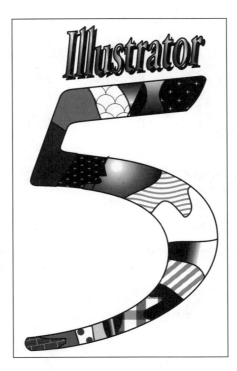

New stuff

Illustrator 5.0 boasts gradients, layer support, PostScript on the Clipboard, the capability to work in Preview/Preview Selection mode, custom views, Plug-In filters, and multiple undo/redo levels.

The interface was totally revamped, making use of palettes for Gradients, Paint Style, Tools, Info, Layers, Character, and Paragraph.

Cursors are also interactive: they "know" where you are and what will happen when you click. Cursors change as you drag in Illustrator 5.0.

Tools

The redesigned Toolbox (see Figure C-2) has 26 tools; Adobe eliminated a lot of dead-weight tools. Tools that lead to pop-up tools are now clearly indicated with a little triangle.

Figure C-2:
The standard Illustrator 5.0 Toolbox (left) and the Illustrator 5.0 Toolbox with pop-up tools.

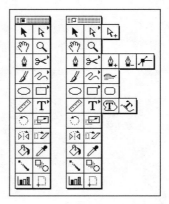

Tools deleted from the Illustrator 3 version are

- Object Selection
- Zoom In/Out
- Centered versions of Oval, Rectangle, and Rounded Corner Rectangle (they can be accessed by double-clicking the standard versions of these tools)
- The four transformation dialog tools
- Five of the graph tools (actually, you now must pick them from the Graph Style dialog box)

New tools are

- Group Selection (formerly Direct-Up Selection)
- Brush (for drawing free-form closed paths with or without a pressure-sensitive tablet
- Eyedropper (for sampling)
- Paint Bucket (for carrying colors from shape to shape)
- Gradient Vector (for controlling gradients' angle and distance)

Most of the tools were redesigned slightly; the Freehand and Blend tools look the most different.

Menus

Tons of new menu items and submenus were added. The Paint menu is now the Object menu, and the Graph menu was made a submenu of the Object menu. And there are two Type menus: one for just fonts, the other for other type options. Other changes include

- **File menu:** Revert to Saved was added in Version 5.0.1, Import Styles was added, Change Art replaces Place Art when Placed Art is selected in the document, and Preferences is a submenu with four options.
- **Edit menu:** Redo and Select None were added. Move, Bring to Front, and Send to Back were moved to the Arrange menu. Show Clipboard was relocated from the Window menu of Version 3. A Publishing submenu (for Publish and Subscribe) was added.
- **Arrange menu:** Transform Again was renamed Repeat Transform. Move, Bring to Front, and Send to Back were transplanted from the Edit menu. Make/Release Guides, Set/Release Cropmarks, Join, and Average were moved to the Object menu.
- **View menu:** Artwork and Template, Template Only, and Hide/Show Unpainted Objects were zapped. Show/Hide Template, Show/Hide Page Tiling, Show/Hide Edges, Show/Hide Guides, Zoom In, Zoom Out, New View, and Edit Views were added.
- **Object menu:** This menu used to be Paint. Contains Paint Style, Custom Color, Pattern, Gradient, Attributes (object attributes), Join, and Average. There are five new submenus: Guides, Masks, Compound Paths, Cropmarks, and Graphs.
- **Font menu:** A new menu. Lists all the fonts installed on your system.

█ **Type menu:** Font is its own menu. Character has replaced Type Style. Paragraph and Fit Headline were added.

█ **Window menu:** Show Layers, Show Paint Style, Show Gradient, Show Character, and Show Paragraph were added. Show Clipboard was moved to the Edit menu. Reset Toolbox has vanished.

Shortcuts

⌘-W used to mean Artwork Only mode, but with Illustrator 5.0, Adobe changed the key command to Close (as in most other Mac applications). ⌘-E is now the shortcut for Artwork mode.

The main differences from previous versions are

Key Command	Action	Old Key Command
⌘-8	Make Compound	⌘-Option-G
⌘-9	Release Compound	⌘-Option-U
⌘-Option-J or ⌘-Option-L	Averages and joins in one step	
⌘-Shift-T	Shows/hides the Paragraph palette	
⌘-Control-L	Shows/hides the Layers palette	
⌘-Control-T	Shows/hides the Toolbox	
⌘-Control-I	Shows/hides the Info palette	
⌘-Control-A	Displays the Object Attributes dialog box	
⌘-Return or ⌘-Enter	Closes the currently active palette (this only works for palettes with text fields)	
⌘-Shift-M	Displays the Move dialog box	

Illustrator 5.5

Illustrator 5.5 was a surprise upgrade to most, timed by Adobe to closely coincide with Apple's PowerPC release. It was the first major application from Adobe to have native code for the PowerPC Macs, known as the Power Mac 6100, 7100, and 8100.

The new features focus on making Illustrator *the* high-end illustration program. With no cute little bells and whistles, all the new features for this upgrade are top-notch stuff.

The way Illustrator works didn't really change that much, and, in fact, the common, everyday user will see little difference between 5.0 and 5.5. The most obvious difference, however, is a small but noticeable one: the Save dialog box is different.

The requirements for 5.5 are the same as 5.0.

New Features in 5.5

Unlike the preceding sections, which provide just a summary of new features for reference purposes, this section explains most of the new features of 5.5 individually. Throughout the rest of the *Macworld Illustrator 5.0/5.5 Bible,* there are notes and comments where the changes take place from Version 5.0 to 5.5.

Text changes

The most striking differences in 5.5 are in the powerful text-editing features added to the software through six new text filters and the Tab palette. These changes are undoubtedly in response to reviews and comparisons of FreeHand 4 to Illustrator 5.5, where FreeHand's new text-editing features were indeed superior to Illustrator. Adobe has changed this by providing options that rival most word processors.

The new text filters are as follows:

Change Case: A basic, yet helpful filter, Change Case lets you choose between UPPER, lower, and Mixed Case.

Check Spelling: Just like it sounds.

Find Font: A filter that finds and replaces fonts within the document.

Revert Text Path: Changes text paths back to nontext paths after all the characters on the path have been deleted.

Rows and Columns: Divides text or another rectangle into rows and columns.

Smart Punctuation: Changes punctuation to the correct typographical format, such as converting inch marks to curly quotes or hyphens to en or em dashes.

A pseudo-grid filter, Rows & Columns, is included with Version 5.5 of Illustrator. Used correctly, it can simulate setting up grids in a document.

The other really big change is the Tab Ruler. The Tab Ruler floats above a text rectangle and allows the four basic tabs to be set (left, right, center, decimal). It was modeled after the tabs in Microsoft Word, and it works like those tabs, too.

Pathfinder filter changes

What is the biggest change in the Pathfinder filters? Now you don't need an FPU to use them. (You still need one to use the FPU Object filters, though.)

The Pathfinder submenu has been completely reorganized; Adobe has eliminated the annoying subheadings and some of the unnecessary filters. There are now four categories of Pathfinder filters: Combine, Overlay, Mix, and Trap. They have no headings; they are split with a dotted line.

- The Combine filters are Unite, Intersect, Exclude, Minus Back, and Minus Front.
- The Overlay filters are Divide, Trim, Outline, Merge, Reduce, and Crop.
- The Mix filters are the same as before with just slightly different names: Mix Hard is now Hard, and Mix Soft is now Soft.
- The new category is Trap, which contains just the Trap filter. It actually does trapping the way that trapping should be done, with user controls.
- An Options menu item is added to the bottom to control all aspects of how the Pathfinder filters work.

Other filter changes

In the Colors submenu, the Custom to Process filter has been added, which changes objects with custom colors into their process color equivalents.

The filter category Other, used in Version 5.0 only with the Riders filter, has had two filters added to it: Document Info and Overprint Black. Document Info returns information about the document for viewing in the dialog box or for printout. Overprint Black lets you specify how the color black is to automatically overprint other colors in your document.

Other changes

When you save a file, you now have the option of saving it as a straight, no-EPS Illustrator file in any Illustrator version or as an EPS file with different preview options, similar to those found in Photoshop.

In addition, the capability to save files as Adobe Acrobat PDF files was added, as well as all of the Acrobat software.

Saving choices are for Illustrator 5.0 format, not for 5.5. Files saved in Illustrator 5.5 can be opened by Illustrator 5.0.

Illustrator 5.5 Tools

The tools and their functions are the same as in Version 5.0.

Illustrator 5.5 Menus

The main difference in menus is the Filter menu, where several filters have been added and the Pathfinder submenu has been rearranged.

A new entry for the Window menu is Show/Hide Tab Ruler.

Illustrator 5.5 Shortcuts

The differences from Version 5.0 are as follows:

⌘-Shift-T displays/hides the Tab Ruler.

⌘-Shift-P displays/hides the Paragraph Ruler.

⌘-Shift-W shows and hides templates, if available.

⌘-Shift-P, ⌘-Shift-I, and ⌘-Shift-N no longer change the measurement system to picas, inches, and centimeters. Instead, ⌘-Control-U toggles between all three of the measurement systems.

Upcoming Versions

Certainly, Adobe will produce new versions of Illustrator, but we probably won't see another major revision (Version 6, 6.5, 7.2 or maybe Illustrator II or Illustrator Pro) for the Power Mac until 1997.

Of course, many other things will change in the meantime. Everyone who is anyone will have Photoshop 3.0; Acrobat will be revved to Version 2; Premier 5.0 will have shipped; QuarkXPress 4.0 will be the standard; Apple will have a System 8; and 68040s should be a thing of the past.

I can't wait.

Taking Files from a Mac to a PC and Back

A Brief History of Computing's "Tower of Babel"

As the computer world evolves, the dividing line between IBM-compatible computers (PCs) and Macintosh computers is getting fuzzier and fuzzier. Until the line disappears, though, the task of taking files from a Mac to a PC and back is always a challenge.

Software manufacturers, including Adobe, are well aware of this problem and have taken great steps over the last few years to ensure compatibility between their products on both platforms. PageMaker has been the most stable cross-platform product for years, but recently QuarkXPress (Version 3.3) has become completely compatible.

Illustrator has been compatible since its inception, but there has been trouble along the way. Initially, the trouble resulted from translation programs that, in their eagerness to please, translated everything to WordPerfect format.

Even Version 1.1 of Illustrator had the capability of saving files as PC Illustrator. The files could then be opened up on a PC machine running the same version of Illustrator. Things really started to mesh with Version 3 of Illustrator, but there were still preview and font problems. Windows 3.1 solved most of these problems, but then Adobe released Illustrator 4 for Windows. PC users had to save their files as Illustrator 3 so that Mac users could read them.

At the present time, Illustrator for the Mac is at Version 5.5, and Illustrator for Windows is at Version 4.0. Mac users need to save their files as Illustrator 4.0 (or earlier) for their PC counterparts to be able to read the file.

Transferring Illustrator Files across Platforms

STEPS: Taking an Illustrator File from a Mac to a PC

Step 1. Save the Illustrator file as a PC Illustrator file in the version of Illustrator being used on the PC (usually Version 4).

Step 2. Save the file on an IBM-compatible floppy disk. This task is usually achieved by installing software on the Macintosh that allows it to read IBM-formatted disks, inserting an IBM disk, and dragging the icon of the file to the disk.

Two popular products for mounting IBM disks on a Macintosh are DOSMounter and Access PC.

Step 3. Remove the IBM disk from the Macintosh and open the file on a PC.

STEPS: Opening an IBM Illustrator File on a Mac

Step 1. Insert the IBM floppy disk with the IBM Illustrator file on it into the Macintosh. To do this task, you must have software on the Macintosh that allows it to read IBM-formatted disks.

Step 2. Copy the file from the IBM floppy disk to your Macintosh's hard disk and remove the IBM floppy disk.

Step 3. In Illustrator, select File⇨Open (⌘-O) and select the IBM PC Illustrator file.

If these steps sound simple, don't worry, they are. People may run into problems with mounting IBM-formatted disks. Even these disk problems don't amount to much, however, because IBM floppy disk-mounting software has steadily improved over the past few years.

About the Enclosed CD-ROM

The CD-ROM enclosed with this book is packed full of all sorts of surprises. The most important and useful of these surprises is the tutorial software, which demonstrates many of the techniques and tips in the book. The CD also includes most of the illustrations used in the book, clip art from selected companies that use Illustrator to create their clip art, and Illustrator charts of filters.

 The demonstrations were done by the author, so if you are wondering who is behind that squeaky voice. . . .

Because you happen to be the diligent type — reading about the CD-ROM before you use it (or after you use it or while you're using it) — I'll let you in on a little secret: when you click at a certain spot on the help screen, you will bring up a personalized message from me, so you can actually *see* who is behind that squeaky voice on the demos. There are some other secret messages besides this. Of course, if I told you where to click and what keys to press to see those, it wouldn't be any fun. I'm sure you can figure it out. I've already spoiled most of the fun by telling you that a message exists, although I tried to conceal it in a big, ugly paragraph like this one, which will surely be overlooked by those who only skim through the book. Just remember the initials of this book....

Running the Tutorials

To run the tutorial program, you *must* have QuickTime 1.6.1 or later installed on your computer, and you should have as much RAM available as you can spare.

The tutorial is designed for 13" and larger monitors. It may take a few minutes for the start-up screen to appear on slower machines, and it will take at least 30 seconds on faster ones. Be patient. If the playback seems jumpy, turn off any extensions besides QuickTime and any needed CD extensions and make sure that no other programs are running. Move the cursor from the tutorial window to the brick background to prevent cursor flicker. Change the number of colors on your monitor to thousands or more to achieve the best results.

Double-click the CD-ROM tutorial file, located in the tutorial folder, to run the tutorial program, which contains over 1.5 hours of tutorials. There are 40 different tutorials, ranging from simple activities to complex projects. You can quit at any time by pressing ⌘-period. Press the buttons to go to an area of your interest and press even more buttons to watch the tutorials. It just doesn't get any more intuitive than this.

 The tutorials were recorded with CameraMan software and assembled within Macromedia Director.

 If you are having trouble running the tutorial program, remove any unnecessary extensions and control panels from your System folder and try again. Most popular extensions and control panels do not interfere with the operation of the software, but "Sammy's Wacky Finder Extension" may.

 If it makes you feel more confident, I have more than two complete rows of icons that appear when I start up my Macintosh — and the demo works flawlessly.

Examining the Artwork

The artwork used in the color section of this book is included on the CD-ROM in Illustrator format.

 You may *not* use the artwork or any portion of the artwork for anything except to study how it was created. It is supplied for educational purposes only.

Take a look at some of the more complex illustrations to see how "we professionals" created the artwork. I have always found this dissection of artwork extremely fascinating.

 Look for areas where the artists "cheated" by overlapping with white boxes, by using fills for strokes and strokes for fills, and where objects are made up of several pieces when you expect only one. See what stuff we masked (an awful lot). We do these things all the time, and you can learn from our cheating techniques.

The Filter Charts

The filter charts are provided for you to get a look at how filters affect paths in a document. Printed illustrations show only the results, not necessarily the makeup of the paths after filters have been applied. Like the illustrations of the figures in the book, these charts aren't to be used for any purpose other than opening them and looking at them on-screen.

The Fonts

Also included on the CD-ROM are two PostScript Type 1 fonts: Lefty Casual 2.1 and Ransom Note 2.1.

To use the fonts, select the screen font (little suitcase) and the printer font (little printer) for each typeface and drag it to your System folder. Your Macintosh asks you whether it is OK that these items get shuffled into the Font folder. Just nod like you understand and click the OK button.

Both Lefty Casual and Ransom Note were used in some of the Illustrations that appear throughout the book.

Lefty Casual 2.1

Lefty Casual 2.1 font is an update to the popular left-handed handwriting font, which has been available as shareware for the last two years. Lefty Casual now sports three weights: Casual (the original), Bold (a little heavier), and Marker (what Casual would look like if written with a Sharpie marker). New characters have been added since the initial release of the font.

Lefty Casual was originally intended to fool people into thinking they were seeing real handwriting, while providing a consistency that allows the typeface to be quite legible. The original Lefty Casual is currently being used as the title typestyle for Pixar's Typestry 2.0 software and has also appeared in the August 1992 issue of *Popular Science*, in the cover article about Apple's Newton.

The additional weights were provided at the request of the registered users of Lefty Casual 1.1.

Ransom Note 2.1

Ransom Note 2.1 font is a significantly updated version of the classic Ransom Note typeface that has been available as shareware for the past two years.

Ransom Note consists of letters and words that appear to have been cut from a magazine and pasted down quickly. In response to the registered users of Ransom Note 1.02, the following new features have been added:

※ More reversed and outlined letters

※ Letters whose edges appear torn or ripped

※ Commonly used words in one style accessible with one keystroke

※ Better kerning pairs

The words tend to follow a ransom note theme. All words can be accessed by typing an Option-letter or Shift-Option-letter combination. (The maker of Ransom Note assumes no responsibility for its contents being used in a real-life hostage or kidnapping situation.)

The Clip Art

Several companies have asked that samples of their clip art be included on the CD-ROM, and being the nice author that I am, I have graciously included the samples on the CD-ROM.

 Information about each clip art company is found in Appendix B. This clip art is included for sample purposes only and is intended to give you an idea of the variety and quality each company has to offer.

The Demo Software

Adobe has included a demo version of Adobe Streamline 3.0 on the CD-ROM. Everything is fully operational, but you can't save or copy out of it. After you see its great conversion of bitmapped artwork to paths, you'll probably run right out to the local Software Shack and pick up your own copy, anyway.

 Chapter 22 contains a basic primer and tutorial on using Streamline.

In addition, there is a demo of Pixar's Typestry software. Typestry allows users to take Illustrator outlines and type into Typestry and to give them 3-D like qualities, including 3-D animation.

Keyboard Commands and Shortcuts

Menu Commands

The File Menu

Command	Shortcut
New document	⌘-N
New document with template	⌘-Option-N
Open document	⌘-O or ⌘-Option-O
Close document	⌘-W
Save document	⌘-S (Save As does not have a key command)
Document Setup	⌘-Shift-D
Print document	⌘-P
General Preferences	⌘-K
Quit	⌘-Q

The Edit Menu

Command	Shortcut
Undo last activity	⌘-Z
Redo last undo	⌘-Shift-Z
Nice do	"Like your hair"
Cut	⌘-X
Copy	⌘-C
Paste	⌘-V
Select All	⌘-A
Select None	⌘-Shift-A
Paste In Front	⌘-F
Paste In Back	⌘-B

The Arrange Menu

Command	Shortcut
Repeat Transform	⌘-D
Move	⌘-Shift-M or Option-click the Selection tool
Bring To Front	⌘-=
Send To Back	⌘-hyphen
Group	⌘-G
Ungroup	⌘-U
Lock selected	⌘-1 (to lock deselected, ⌘-Option-1)
Unlock All	⌘-2
Hide	⌘-3 (to hide deselected, ⌘-Option-3)
Show All	⌘-4

The View Menu

Command	Shortcut
Preview	⌘-Y
Artwork	⌘-E
Preview Selection	⌘-Option-Y
Show/Hide Rulers	⌘-R
Show/Hide Edges	⌘-Shift-H
Zoom In	⌘-]
Zoom Out	⌘-[
Actual Size	⌘-H or double-click the Zoom tool
Fit In Window	⌘-M or double-click the Hand tool
New View	⌘-Control-V

The Object Menu

Command	Shortcut
Paint Style	⌘-I
Attributes	⌘-Control-A
Join	⌘-J
Average	⌘-L
Join and Average	⌘-Option-J or ⌘-Option-L
Make Guides	⌘-5
Release Guides	⌘-6 or double-click while pressing Shift-Control
Lock/Unlock Guides	⌘-7
Make Compound Path	⌘-8
Release Compound Path	⌘-9

The Type Menu

Command	Shortcut
Other size	⌘-Shift-S
Other font	⌘-T, ⌘-Shift-F, or ⌘-Option-Shift-M
Left alignment	⌘-Shift-L
Center alignment	⌘-Shift-C
Right alignment	⌘-Shift-R
Justify alignment	⌘-Shift-J
Justify last line alignment	⌘-Shift-B
Tracking/Kerning	⌘-Shift-K
Spacing	⌘-Shift-O
Character	⌘-T
Paragraph (Version 5.0)	⌘-Shift-T or ⌘-Shift-O
Paragraph (5.5 only)	⌘-Shift-P or ⌘-Shift-O
Link Blocks	⌘-Shift-G
Unlink Blocks	⌘-Shift-U

The Filter Menu

Command	Shortcut
Last Filter	⌘-Shift-E
Last Filter dialog box	Press Option while choosing Filter⇨Last Filter

The Window Menu

Command	Shortcut
Show/Hide Toolbox	⌘-Control-T
Show/Hide Layers	⌘-Control-L
Show/Hide Info	⌘-Control-I
Show/Hide Paint Style	⌘-I
Show/Hide Character	⌘-T
Show/Hide Paragraph (Version 5.0)	⌘-Shift-T
Show/Hide Paragraph (5.5 only)	⌘-Shift-P
Show/Hide Tab Ruler (5.5 only)	⌘-Shift-T

Tool Time

▨ To Show/Hide Toolbox, press ⌘-Control-T (if the Toolbox is hidden by another palette, press ⌘-Control-T twice to display it).

▨ Press ⌘ to access the most recently used selection tool; press ⌘-Tab to toggle between selection tools.

▨ To bring up the Hand tool, press spacebar or with the Type tool selected, press ⌘-spacebar and then release ⌘.

Accessing tools

You can access many tools by pressing a modifier when another tool is already selected:

Tool	Selected Tool-Modifier
Add Anchor Point	Scissors or Delete Anchor Point-Option
Centered Oval	Oval-Option (or double-click the Oval tool)
Centered Rectangle	Rectangle-Option (or double-click the Rectangle tool)
Centered Rounded Rectangle	Rounded Rectangle-Option (or double-click the Rounded Rectangle tool)
Convert Direction Point	Any selection tool-Control or Pen-Option-Control or All tools but Scissors, Add Anchor Point, and Delete Anchor Point-⌘-Option-Control
Delete Anchor Point	Add Anchor Point-Option
Eyedropper tool	Paint Bucket-Option
Group Selection	Direct Selection-Option
Oval	Centered Oval-Option (or double-click the Centered Oval tool)
Paint Bucket tool	Eyedropper-Option
Pen	Freehand or Auto Trace-Control
Rectangle	Centered Rectangle-Option (or double-click the Centered Rectangle tool)
Rounded Rectangle	Centered Rounded Rectangle-Option (or double-click the Centered Rounded Rectangle tool)
Type	Area Type or Path Type-Control
Zoom In	⌘-spacebar*
Zoom Out	⌘-Option-spacebar

Note: SCSI Probe, a popular Control Panel used for mounting SCSI devices (such as SyQuest cartridges), has a default setting of ⌘-spacebar to mount unmounted volumes (hard drives, CDs, and so on). Even if everything is mounted, SCSI Probe always attempts to mount, wasting about 1.5 seconds to look for more drives. To change the key command, access the Options box of SCSI Probe (I suggest changing the default to ⌘-Control-spacebar).

Using tools

Learning keyboard shortcuts helps you use the tools more efficiently. *Note:* Knowing when to release keys is crucial.

Action	Shortcut
Create smooth anchor point	Click-drag Pen tool
Create straight corner anchor point	Click Pen tool
Convert anchor point to smooth anchor point	Click-drag Convert Direction Point tool on anchor point
Convert anchor point to straight corner anchor point	Click anchor point with Convert Direction Point tool
Convert smooth anchor point to combination anchor point	Click smooth anchor point with Pen tool
Convert smooth anchor point to curved anchor point	Option-drag Pen tool on smooth anchor point
Convert straight corner anchor point to combination anchor point	Click-drag Pen tool on straight corner anchor point
Deselect object	Shift-click (or Shift-drag across) object with a selection tool
Deselect all objects	⌘-Shift-A or click in an empty area with a selection tool
Select inverse	Shift-drag across entire document

(continued)

Action	Shortcut
Select objects	Shift-click (or Shift-drag across) objects with a selection tool
Drag 45°-direction lines	Pen-Shift-drag (release mouse button before Shift)
Draw 45°-angle lines	Pen-Shift-click
Draw circle from center	Oval-Option-Shift keys (release mouse button before Option-Shift)
Draw circle	Shift-Oval (release mouse button before Shift)
Draw oval at specified size	Oval-click in document (displays Oval dialog box)
Draw oval at specified size from center	Option-Oval-click in document
Draw rectangle or rounded corner rectangle at specified size	Rectangle or Rounded Corner Rectangle-click in document (displays Rectangle dialog box)
Draw rectangle or rounded corner rectangle at specified size from center	Option-Rectangle or Rounded Corner Rectangle-click in document
Draw rounded corner square	Shift-Rounded Corner Rectangle tool (release mouse button before Shift)
Draw rounded corner square from center	Option-Shift-Rounded Corner Rectangle (release mouse button before Option-Shift)
Draw square	Shift-Rectangle (release mouse button before Shift)
Draw square from center	Option-Shift-Rectangle (release mouse button before Option-Shift)
Duplicate entire path	After using the Group Selection or Selection tool to move a path, press Option while releasing the mouse button
Duplicate portion of path	After using the Direct Selection tool to move point(s) and/or segment(s), press Option while releasing the mouse button

Action	Shortcut
Erase Freehand tool path	⌘-retrace path
Fill selected objects with another object's Paint Style	Double-click source object with Eyedropper
Constrain object movement to 45°	Shift-move object with a selection tool (release mouse button before Shift)
Measure at 45° angle	Shift-drag (anytime a path is passed over, the Measure tool snaps to the path or its fill)
Measure to edge of path	In Artwork mode, Shift-Measure and go near any path (if you aren't near any paths, the Measure tool is constrained to a 45° angle)
Reflect at 45° angles only	Press Shift before releasing the mouse while setting the axis of reflection
Rotate at 45° angles only	Press Shift before releasing the mouse while setting the angle
Scale horizontally or vertically or proportionally	Set the origin and then Shift-drag as desired (left/right or up/down or diagonally)
Set the gradient from anchor point to anchor point	Shift-drag from anchor point to anchor point
Set the radial gradient highlight	With an object with a radial gradient selected, click in the location of the highlight with the Gradient Vector tool
Shear horizontally or vertically	Set the origin and then Shift-drag as desired (left/right or up/down)
Zoom marquee drawn from center	Control-draw marquee

Viewing Shortcuts

Action	Shortcut
Zoom in one level	⌘-]
Zoom out one level	⌘-[
Zoom in to a specific area	Drag Zoom tool around area
Fit in window	⌘-M (or double-click the Hand tool)
Actual size	⌘-H (or double-click the Zoom tool)
6.25 percent	Option-double-click the Hand tool
Artwork mode	⌘-E
Preview mode	⌘-Y
Preview Selection mode	⌘-Option-Y
Toggle between Preview and Artwork	Option-click the layer's leftmost column in the Layers palette
Define new view	⌘-Control-V
Go to first custom view	⌘-Control-1
Go to next custom view	⌘-Control-view number
Show/Hide Edges	⌘-Shift-H
Show/Hide Rulers	⌘-R
Change Ruler Units to picas (Version 5.0)	⌘-Shift-P
Change Ruler Units to inches (Version 5.0)	⌘-Shift-I
Change Ruler Units to centimeters (Version 5.0)	⌘-Shift-N
Cycle through Ruler Units from picas to inches to centimeters (5.5 only)	⌘-Control-U

Generic Dialog Box Commands

Command	Shortcut
Cancel	⌘-. (period)
OK (or dark-bordered button)	Return (or Enter)
Highlight next text field	Tab
Highlight preceding text field	Shift-Tab
Highlight any text field	Double-click the text field

Save As/Open/Import/Place/Export Dialog Boxes Commands

Command	Shortcut
Go to Desktop	⌘-D
Next disk	⌘-left arrow
Open selected file/folder	⌘-down arrow
Preceding disk	⌘-right arrow
Preceding folder	⌘-up arrow
Select certain file/folder	With the file window active, type the name of the file/folder (the more letters you type, the more accurate the search); to go to the bottom of the list, press Z
Select next file/folder	Down arrow
Select preceding file/folder	Up arrow
Toggle between file window and name window	Tab (when active, the file window has a dark border)
Create new folder (Save As/Import/Export dialog boxes)	⌘-N

Other Dialog Boxes Commands

Command	Shortcut
Display the Rotate/Scale/Reflect/Shear dialog boxes	Corresponding tool-Option-click the origin location
Copy (Move/Rotate/Scale/Reflect/Shear dialog boxes)	Option-Return or Option-Enter (or Option-click the OK button)
Don't Save (Do You Wish to Save Changes? dialog box)	D
None (New template dialog box)	⌘-N (if you have Super Boomerang or Norton Utilities Directory Assistance, you will get a New folder)

Type Command Shortcuts

Type Tool Shortcuts

Action	Shortcut
Access the Area Type tool	Drag Type tool over closed path or Option-drag Type tool over open path
Access the Path Type tool	Drag Type tool over open path or Option-drag Type tool over closed path
Access the Type tool	Area Type or Path Type-Control
Copy type on a path	Drag any selection tool on the I-bar, press Option, and release the mouse button (this shortcut actually creates two paths as well as two text stories)
Deselect all type	With any tool and anything selected, ⌘-Shift-A

Action	Shortcut
Flip type on a path	Double-click the I-bar with any selection tool or just drag it to the opposite side
Move insertion point to next character	Right arrow
Move insertion point to next line	Down arrow
Move insertion point to next paragraph	⌘-down arrow
Move insertion point to next word	⌘-right arrow
Move insertion point to preceding character	Left arrow
Move insertion point to preceding line	Up arrow
Move insertion point to preceding paragraph	⌘-up arrow
Move insertion point to preceding word	⌘-left arrow
Place type in area	With the Type tool, pass the cursor over a closed path or pass the cursor over an open path and press Option
Place type on path	With the Type tool, pass the cursor over an open path or pass the cursor over a closed path and press Option
Select (by highlighting) all type in story	With any type tool selected and either a visible blinking insertion point visible or highlighted text, ⌘-A or ⌘-. (period)
Select (by not highlighting) all type in story	With the Selection tool selected, click either the baseline of the type or the path that the type is in; with the Group Selection or Direct Selection tool selected, click the baseline of the type

(continued)

Action	Shortcut
Select all type in document	With any tool but the type tools selected, ⌘-A (*Caution:* Type-related changes will affect only the type, but object changes will affect everything)
Select next character	Shift-right arrow
Select next line	Shift-down arrow
Select next paragraph	⌘-Shift-down arrow
Select next word	⌘-Shift-right arrow
Select paragraph	Triple-click in the paragraph with any type tool
Select preceding character	Shift-left arrow
Select preceding line	Shift-up arrow
Select preceding paragraph	⌘-Shift-up arrow
Select preceding word	⌘-Shift-left arrow
Select word	Double-click the word with any type tool

Command	Shortcut
Increase baseline shift*	Option-Shift-up arrow
Increase leading*	Option-down arrow
Increase tracking/ kerning*	⌘-right arrow or ⌘-Shift-]
Increase tracking/ kerning five times*	⌘-Option-right arrow
Increase type point size*	⌘-Shift->
Link text blocks	⌘-Shift-G
Unlink text blocks	⌘-Shift-U
Insert discretionary hyphenation	⌘-Shift-hyphen

* You specify the increment in the General Preferences dialog box (⌘-K).

Note: Character formatting affects only selected characters, while paragraph functions affect entire paragraphs regardless of how many characters are selected with a type tool.

Type Formatting Shortcuts

Command	Shortcut
Alignment: center	⌘-Shift-C
Alignment: justify	⌘-Shift-J
Alignment: justify last line	⌘-Shift-B
Alignment: left	⌘-Shift-L
Alignment: right	⌘-Shift-R
Change font	⌘-T, ⌘-Shift-F, or ⌘-Option-Shift-M
Decrease baseline shift*	Option-Shift-down arrow
Decrease leading*	Option-up arrow
Decrease tracking/ kerning*	⌘-left arrow or ⌘-Shift-[
Decrease tracking/ kerning five times*	⌘-Option-left arrow
Decrease type point size*	⌘-Shift-<

Palette Commands and Shortcuts

Generic Commands and Shortcuts

Command	Shortcut
Show/Hide Info palette	⌘-Control-I
Show/Hide Tab Ruler palette (5.5 only)	⌘-Shift-T
Hide active palette	⌘-Return (this command only works when a text field is highlighted or a blinking insertion point is in a text field on the active palette)
Highlight next text field	Tab
Highlight preceding text field	Shift-Tab

Paint Style Palette

Command	Shortcut
Show/Hide Paint Style palette	⌘-I
Switch to full view & back	Click the upper right corner box on the title bar
Change to specific view	Use the pull-down menu in the upper right corner of the title bar
Change to show/hide Paint Style palette parts	Click the part to be hidden/viewed in the little diagram in the upper right corner of the Paint Style palette
Delete custom swatch	⌘-click swatch
Delete custom swatch (no warning dialog box)	⌘-Option-click swatch
Delete multiple swatches	⌘-drag across swatches
Delete multiple swatches (no warning dialog box)	⌘-Option-drag across swatches
Reset swatch to original	⌘-Shift-click swatch
Move process sliders proportionally	Shift-drag any slider
Move slider in 1% increments	Option-click either side of the slider
Move slider in 5% increments	Shift-Option-click either side of the slider
Bring up Custom Color palette	Double-click the custom color name

Gradient Palette

Command	Shortcut
Show Gradient palette	Double-click the Gradient Vector tool or double-click the gradient name in the Paint Style palette
Move Process sliders proportionally	Shift-drag any slider
Move slider in 1% increments	Option-click either side of the slider
Move slider in 5% increments	Shift-Option-click either side of the slider
Select more contiguous gradients	Shift-click
Select more individual gradients	⌘-click
Duplicate gradient color triangle	Option-drag triangle
Duplicate gradient color triangle at 1% less	Option-click either side of the color triangle
Duplicate gradient color triangle at 5% less	Shift-Option-click either side of the color triangle
Change selected triangle color to existing Artwork color	Control-Eyedropper-click the color
Move midpoint 2% less	Option-click left of midpoint
Move midpoint 2% more	Option-click right of midpoint
Move midpoint 5% less	⌘-Option-click left of midpoint
Move midpoint 5% more	⌘-Option-click right of midpoint
Add color triangle	Click below gradient bar
Delete color triangle	Pull triangle below gradient bar

Layers Palette

Command	Shortcut
Show/Hide Layers palette	⌘-Control-L
View/Hide layer	Click View column (eye)
Lock/Unlock layer	Click Lock column (pencil)
Move layer up/down	Drag layer to new location
Select more than one layer	Shift-click
Deselect layer	Shift-click
Toggle between Artwork and Preview for layer	Option-click View column
Hide all but selected layer	Click eye at top of View column
Preview only selected layers	Option-click eye at top of View column
Lock all but selected layer	Click pencil at top of Lock column
Create new layer above selected layer	Option-click pop-up menu and choose Create new layer above
Show layer options	Double-click the layer

Character Palette

Command	Shortcut
Show/Hide Character palette	⌘-T, ⌘-Shift-F, or ⌘-Option-Shift-M
Highlight Font field	⌘-T, ⌘-Shift-F, or ⌘-Option-Shift-M
Highlight Size field	⌘-Shift-S
Highlight Leading field	⌘-Shift-S and Tab
Highlight Tracking/Kerning field	⌘-Shift-K

Paragraph Palette

Command	Shortcut
Show/Hide Paragraph palette (Version 5.0)	⌘-Shift-T
Show/Hide Paragraph palette (5.5 only)	⌘-Shift-P
Highlight Left Indent	⌘-Shift-T
Highlight Spacing field	⌘-Shift-O

Miscellaneous

- 52 different keys on standard keyboard x 16 different combinations of 4 basic modifier keys (Command (⌘), Shift, Option, Control) = 832 key combinations

- 832 possible key combinations – 128 standard ASCII characters – 100 special characters = 604 available key combinations

- 46 menu items do not have key commands

- None of the Illustrator filters has a key command (although you can press ⌘-Shift-E to reapply the last filter)

- The Control key was rarely used in previous versions of Illustrator because most Macintosh Plus models did not have Control keys. But Illustrator 5 will not run on a Mac Plus.

- Several keyboard commands are undocumented.

- To see special status line categories, Option-click the status line (at the lower left corner of Illustrator's window).

- The right-, left-, up-, and down-arrow keys move selected objects in the increment set in the General Preferences dialog box.

Index

A

About Adobe Illustrator
command, 196
About Plug-Ins command, 196
About the Finder command, 736
About this Macintosh command,
196, 736
dialog box, 45
Academy ArtWorks, Inc., 745
Acrobat Installer, 742
Acrobat PDF File Format Plug-In,
535
actions
redoing, 76–77, 136
undoing, 76–77, 136, 513–514
active document, closing, 130
Actual Size command, 146
⌘-H keyboard shortcut, 98,
146, 355
Add Anchor Points filter, 101–103,
181–182, 386, 447, 449,
573, 591
Distort filter, 534
Stylize filter, 534
Add Arrowheads filter, 189–190,
580–582
dialog box, 189, 411, 581–582
Outline Stroked Path filter, 534
Unite filter, 534
Adjust Colors filter, 171–172, 528,
540
dialog box, 171
shadows and highlights, 541
Adobe Collector's Edition, 743
Adobe Illustrator Startup file,
474, 499
adding graph design, pattern,
custom color, or gradient,
501
deleting, 501
modifying, 500–502
preferences, 500–502
removing pattern, gradient,
custom color, or color
swatches, 500–501
resizing window, 501
verifying changes, 502
Adobe Systems, Inc., 746
getting answers and information from, 731
points and picas, 351
products, 743
Adobe Type folder, 742
Adobe Type Library, 742

Adobe Type Manager (ATM),
38–40, 168, 742
AI Manuals and Tech Notes, 743
AI User Dictionary file, 618
airbrushing, 453–461
shadow blends, 457–458
Align Objects filter, 182, 591–593
dialog box, 182, 591–592
Distribute Horizontally filter,
534
Distribute Vertically filter, 534
alignment and distribution filters,
591
Alignment⇨Center command,
162
Alignment⇨Justified command,
163
Alignment⇨Justify Last Line
command, 164
Alignment⇨Left command, 162
Alignment⇨Right command, 163
All Tools Default (⌘-Shift)
keyboard shortcut, 87
Altsys Corp., 746
America Online, 746
contacting author, 9
software for connecting, 4
anchor points, 53, 63–66, 385–388
adding, 101, 181–182, 386,
576–578
as transitional points, 264
Bézier curves, 68
combination corner points,
100, 257
combining two into one, 390–393
converting, 393–395
corner points, 64–66
curved corner points, 100, 257
Direct Selection tool, 94
direction lines, 68–70
direction points, 68–70, 258
doubling number on object, 591
Freehand tool, 105, 249, 254
moving around, 576–578
ovals, 212
paths, 56, 255
Pen tool, 256
removing, 102, 387–388
Scissors tool, 388
selecting, 62, 608, 612
smooth points, 63, 100, 257,
262, 386, 388
stars, 221
straight corner points, 100,
201, 257, 386, 388

stray, 189, 612
Twirl filter, 573
two independent direction
points, 249
types, 102, 256
Apple LaserWriter driver,
printing, 380–381
Apple menu, 196
Apple menu⇨Chooser command,
376, 664
application preferences
Color Matching dialog box,
515–516
Hyphenation Options dialog
box, 517
modifying, 502–518
applications: See programs
arcs, 212
Area Graph tool, 122–123
area graphs, 494
Area type, 293, 296–303
coloring type anchored to
path, 301
designing with, 301–303
outlining areas, 297–298
path, 296
unusual things done with,
299–300
selecting good shapes for, 297
text linking, 326
Area Type tool, 109–111, 296, 304
Arrange menu, 89, 91, 139–141, 751
commands, 763
keyboard shortcuts, 763
Arrange⇨Bring To Front
command, 234, 273, 467
Arrange⇨Group command, 274
Arrange⇨Hide command, 141,
146, 291, 543, 648
Arrange⇨Lock command, 141,
290, 610, 727
Arrange⇨Move command, 109,
285, 291, 454, 486, 508, 511,
543, 563, 593
Arrange⇨Paste In Back command, 460
Arrange⇨Paste In Front
command, 460
Arrange⇨Repeat Transform
command, 269, 396, 435,
450, 456, 543, 555, 562–563
Arrange⇨Send To Back com-
mand, 217, 273, 419
Arrange⇨Show command, 291
Arrange⇨Show All command,
460, 543, 648

Arrange⇨Ungroup command, 275, 582, 697
Arrange⇨Unlock command, 290
arrow keys, 311
Arrowheads dialog box, 234
arrows, 189–190, 581–582
  as one object, 534
  customized, 582
Artbeats, 746
Artboard, 82
  changing dimensions, 82
  clearing objects, 136
  fitting in window, 147
  options, 346–347
  orientation, 347
  sizes, 347
artwork
  guide alignment, 288
  previewing, 142
  viewing, 142–148
Artwork command, 142
  ⌘-E keyboard shortcut, 142–143
Artwork mode, 77, 142–143, 359
  combining with Preview mode, 362
  displaying placed images, 348
  EPS images, 359
  fills, 223
  Measure tool, 109
  paths, 59, 77, 143, 145, 223, 359
  rectangles, 201
  unselected objects, 360
  vs. Preview mode, 358–362
artwork view, increasing speed of operation, 535
Artwork View Speedup Plug-In, 143, 532, 535
attributes and strokes, 237–238
Attributes command, 151
  ⌘-Control-A keyboard shortcut, 151, 334, 413
  dialog box, 151
Auto tab stops, 328
Auto Trace tool, 106, 281, 699
  Freehand tolerance, 254
  tracing, 506–507
Average command, 151–152, 389
  ⌘-L keyboard shortcut, 151–152, 389, 392
  dialog box, 389–390, 392
averaging points, 389–390

B

Back Minus filter, 186, 600
Back Minus Front filter, 186

background printing, 376
backgrounds, 271–273, 651–653
  blends, 653
  gradients, 652–653
bar graphs: *See* grouped column graphs
Baseline Shift Down
  Option-↓ keyboard shortcut, 304, 306–307, 309
  Option-Shift-↓ keyboard shortcut, 513
Baseline shift feature, 304, 513
  Character palette, 316
Baseline Shift Up
  Option-↑ keyboard shortcut, 304, 307, 309
  Option-Shift-↑ keyboard shortcut, 513
Bézier curves, 53, 67–68, 100–101
Bézier Graphics Experts, 745
Bézier logo, 725
  designing, 725
  printing, 727
Bézier, Pierre, 67
Bill's Dingbats, 338
binary, 43
bitmap fonts, 35–36
bitmap paint application, moving objects, 201
bitmapped images
  areas similar in color, 701
  color to large square blocks, 530
  converted images to revert to, 703
  converting to Illustrator paths, 703
  converting to paths, 706
  deleting anchor points, 702
  drawing on, 701
  erasing, 702
  filling area with color, 705
  group of pixels or set of paths and points, 702
  magnifying, 702
  opening, 703
  sampling color, 702
  saving as different file, 703
  selecting area, 701–702
  viewing original under Illustrator paths, 705
  zooming out, 702
bits, 43
black-and-white printer, gray values for color, 656
bleed, 669–670
blend arcing, 449

Blend dialog box, 429, 432, 442
Blend Front To Back filter, 172, 542–543
Blend Horizontally filter, 172
Blend tool, 86, 120, 122, 426, 428–430, 445
Blend Vertically filter, 172
blends, 122, 425–430
  airbrushed shadows, 457–458
  backgrounds, 653
  backlighting, 461
  basics, 429
  color, 431
  glows, 458–459
  linear, 431–443
  masking, 435–436
  nonlinear, 433–434
  pseudolinear, 436–437
  radial, 442–443
  shape, 443–453
  shape transformation, 429
  softening object edges, 459
  spring tube, 456
  steps, 429, 440–441
  stroke, 453–461
  tubular, 454–455
Bloat filter, 190, 528, 580, 584–585
  adding anchor points, 591
  dialog box, 190, 585
  Punk filter, 534
bounding box, 580, 620, 666, 669–670
boxes and drop shadow, 204
Bring To Front command, 140, 326
  ⌘-= keyboard shortcut, 140, 234, 467, 273
Bruce Jones Design Inc., 746
Brush dialog box 245, 247
brush strokes
  bends and ends, 246
  caps, 246
  joins, 246
  looking bad, 244
  vs. strokes, 243
Brush tool, 103
  brush strokes, 243, 246
  calligraphy, 245
  changing cursor into crosshair, 244
  consistency of width, 245
  drawing, 241–247
  Horse and Tall Grass drawing, 241–256
  options, 104
  paths, 239
  pressure-sensitive tablet, 241, 244, 247, 537

trackballs, 244
undoing mistakes, 241
variable widths, 247
bytes, 43

C

calligraphy, 245, 587
  brush angle, 245
  pen width, 191
Calligraphy filter, 191, 245, 580, 587
  cookie cutters, 587
  dialog box, 191
CameraMan, 760
Cancel (⌘-period) keyboard
        shortcut, 142–143, 204,
        313, 360, 372, 381–382, 760
cap style, 224
Caps Lock key, changing cursor
        to crosshair, 244, 249, 251
Carta, 338
Cartesia Software, 747
case studies
    A Natural Form of Expression,
        707–716
    Bézier Logo, Business Cards,
        Envelopes, and Letter,
        724–727
    VW Corrado, 716–724
Caution icons, 8
CD-ROM drives, 28–29
CD-ROMs and memory, 44
center points, 108, 201, 612
Centered Alignment (⌘-Shift-C)
        keyboard shortcut, 162,
        306, 322
Centered Oval Tool, 214
Centered Rectangle tool, 205
Centered Rounded Rectangle
        tool, 207
Change Case filter, 340, 615, 753
  dialog box, 615
Change Placed Art command, 132
character attributes, 312–319
    Character palette, 312–313
    incremental changes, 312
Character command, 164
    ⌘-T keyboard shortcut, 164
Character palette, 80, 160, 312–313
    baseline shift, 304, 316
    closing, 313
    features, 313–316
    Font family field, 313
    Font field, 160, 164, 314
    Horizontal Scale field, 316
    Leading text field, 315
    listing typefaces, 314

showing/hiding, 195, 312
    Size field, 314
    Style field, 313
    Tracking/Kerning field, 316–319
characters
    outlining, 319
    spacing between, 513
Check Spelling filter, 340, 616–618,
        753
    dialog box, 616–618
Chinese throwing stars, 403
Chooser
    Background Printing option, 376
    printing, 376–377
    selecting printer, 664
CIE calibration, 360
circles, 211–214, 305
    constrain angle, 212
    diameter, 210
    measuring distances between
        objects, 286
    radius, 210
    tracing, 212
Claris XTND folder, 132, 613
Claris XTND System, 741
Clear command, 73, 136
Clear key, 136
clicking, 16
clip art examples, 4
Clipboard, 74–75
    pasting from, 73
    placing objects on, 73
    showing/hiding, 139
    viewing contents, 74–75
close box, 83
Close command, 130
    ⌘-W keyboard shortcut, 130
Close palette (⌘-Return) keyboard
        shortcut, 313, 321
closed paths, 58, 60, 102–104, 110
    filling with type, 111
    fills, 60
CMYK (cyan, magenta, yellow,
        and black), 119–120, 531
Cohen, Sandee, 745
color
    adding equal amounts to
        objects, 173–174
    adding together based on
        percentage, 188
    automatically converting
        custom to process, 540
    background bleed through
        foreground, 605
    blends, 172, 431
    CMYK values, 531
    combining the same, 603

fills, 230–234
filters, 171–174
gray values for, 656
information lines, 237
inverting, 173
limitations, 660–662
linear blends, 437–438
manipulating, 539–544
Preview mode, 360
removing from objects, 173
spreading or choking, 688
stroke blends, 455
strokes, 224, 230–234
type, 300–301
unprintable, 660
Color Adjust filter, 457
color filters, 539–544
    extruded multiple path
        objects, 541–543
    negatives, 543–544
    shadows and highlights, 541
Color Macintosh preview, 665
Color Matching command, 135
    dialog box, 135, 515–516
color monitors, 26
color separations
    alignment, 667, 687–688
    combining spot and process
        color, 662–663
    labeling, 668
    printing, 134, 375, 655, 657–658,
        663, 685, 687
    process color, 659–660
    saving, 686
    spot color, 658–659
    trim marks, 553–554
    why they don't align, 690
    working with different, 682–686
color sets, 552
Color Swatch panel, 227, 236–237
color swatches, 236–237
Color Systems folder, 741
color wheel, 435–436
Colors submenu, 171–174, 539
columns
    angled and curved, 301
    by text linking, 326
combination corner points, 66,
        100, 257, 267, 395
Combine filters, 599–600, 754
Command key, 21, 251–252, 311
commands: See individual
        commands
    keyboard shortcuts, 763–771
composites, printing, 655–656
compound paths, 59, 155, 268,
        329, 334, 405–411

⌘-8 keyboard shortcut, 155, 334, 406, 409–410, 412, 422, 543, 698
bounding rectangle, 484
complex, 421–423
creation, 155, 405–407
directions, 411–413
Even-Odd rule, 412
faking, 414
from separate sets of paths, 409–410
Group Selection tool, 407
holes, 408–409
masks, 420
moving separate objects, 410
Paint Style attributes, 407
PostScript characters, 410
releasing, 155, 407–416
reversing direction, 413
type and, 410–411
Compound Paths⇨Make command, 155
Compound Paths⇨Release command, 155
computers, 24, 735–736
CPU (central processing unit), 24
constrain angle, 503–505
changing, 504
circles, 212
shapes, 222
continuous tone, 662
control handles: *See* direction points
Control key, 22
Control Panels
Adobe Type Manager (ATM), 38–40
SCSI Probe, 765
Super ATM, 41
Convert Direction Point tool, 101–103, 393
cool stuff
discovering on your own, 728–731
getting answers and information from Adobe, 731
how author figured it out, 728–729
knowing vs. memorizing, 729–730
what you can do to learn more, 730
Copenheaver, Royce, 716, 745
Copy Button (Option-Return) keyboard shortcut, 113, 403, 543, 555, 563

Copy command, 73–74, 136
⌘-C keyboard shortcut, 136, 327, 404, 423, 485, 559, 621, 631, 635, 638–639
corner points, 64–66
combination, 66
curved, 65
rounding, 586–587
straight, 64
to smooth points, 192
corner radius
changing values, 505–506
limitations, 208
rounded rectangles and squares, 207
corners, overlapping, 244
CPU (Central Processing Unit), 24, 737
Create filters, 544–563
adding strokes and fills to masks, 544–545
adding trim marks, 553–554
folded fan, 555
mosaics, 545–550
special effects, 555–559
Create Mosaic filter, 738
Create Outlines command, 160, 168–169
Create Polygon dialog box, 176, 218
Create Publisher command, 138
Create Spiral dialog box, 176
Create Star dialog box, 176, 220
Create Stroke & Fill for Mask filter, 533
Create submenu, 174–177, 218
Crop Fill filter, 187
Crop filter, 187
crop marks, 155–157, 553–554, 669
Crop Stroke filter, 188
Cropmarks⇨Make command, 156
Cropmarks⇨Release command, 157
Cross Reference icon, 8
cursors, 17
changing into crosshair, 244
precise, 509–511
curve handles: *See* direction points
curved corner points, 65, 100, 395
curved-corner anchor point, 257, 265–267
Freehand tool, 249, 254
path creation, 266–267
vs. smooth point, 265
curves and Pen tool, 259–262
Custom Color command, 149

dialog box, 149, 663
custom colors
as spot and process colors, 663
converting to process color, 172, 540, 662
displaying, 149
spot color, 659
tint, 232
custom dictionary, adding words, 617
custom gradients, 464
custom installation, 740–742
Adobe Illustrator, 741
Adobe Type folder, 742
Adobe Type Manager, 742
Claris XTND System, 741
Color Systems folder, 741
FPU-Based Plug-Ins, 741
Gradients & Patterns folder, 741
Plug-Ins folder, 741
Samples folder, 741
Separator & Utilities, 741
Tutorial folder, 741
XTND Translators, 742
custom patterns, 474–476
Custom to Process filter, 172, 532, 540, 754
custom views, 142, 147–148, 364
editing or renaming, 148
naming, 364
Cut command, 73–74, 136
⌘-X keyboard shortcut, 136, 697

D

DAT (digital audio tape) format, 29, 44
Decrease Baseline Shift (Option-Shift-↓) keyboard shortcut, 316
Decrease Leading (Option-↓) keyboard shortcut, 316, 512
Decrease Point Size (⌘-Shift-¨) keyboard shortcut, 314
Decrease Tracking
⌘-¨ keyboard shortcut, 513
⌘-Shift-[keyboard shortcut, 318
Decrease Tracking Five Times (⌘-Option-¨) keyboard shortcut, 513
Decrease Tracking/Kerning (Option-→) keyboard shortcut, 317
Decrease Type (⌘-Shift-<) keyboard shortcut, 161, 512

Default Bounding Box (⌘-B) keyboard shortcut, 670
Default Marks (⌘-M) keyboard shortcut, 667
Default Settings (⌘-T) keyboard shortcut, 671
default tools, 86
Delete Anchor Point filter, 447
Delete Anchor Point tool, 101–103, 386, 388
Delete key, 73, 137, 269, 311, 385
Delete Riders filter, 537–538
Delete Swatch (⌘-Option) keyboard shortcut, 237
Densitometer Control Chart file, 681
Desaturate filter, 173
  Saturate filter, 534
Desaturate More filter, 173
  Saturate More filter, 534
Deselect All (⌘-Shift-A) keyboard shortcut, 92, 429, 432, 577, 611, 631
Deselect Paths (⌘-Shift-A) keyboard shortcut, 388, 404
Design dialog box, 158
desk accessories, 335–336
Desktop Mouse II, 25
device independent, 37
diagonal line and grid patterns, 484
dialog boxes, 19–20, 127
  accepting options, 203
  canceling, 204
  check boxes and radio buttons, 19
  editable text fields, 20
  exiting, 20
  for particular filters, 170
  generic commands, 767
  highlighted text, 20
  moving between fields, 20, 203
  number or character out of range, 20
  returning to last filter, 534
Dimensions, 2, 136, 364
  gradients, 469
Direct Selection tool, 89, 93–94, 151–152, 165, 183, 190, 211, 299, 301, 307, 309, 326, 331, 333, 389–390, 410, 434, 444–445, 449, 452, 483, 555, 557, 562, 572, 612
  Command (⌘) key, 93
  curved corner points into combination corner points, 395

direction points, 393–394
  examining semistraight segments, 251
  moving paths, 268
  selecting portion of path, 269
  Shift key, 94
  smooth points, 393–394
Direct Selection/Selection tool (⌘-Tab) keyboard shortcut, 276
direction lines, 68–70
  Direct Selection tool, 94
  lengthening, 402
direction points, 53, 68–70
  Bézier curves, 68
  converting, 393–395
  Direct Selection tool, 94
  linked to independent, 393
  moving, 102, 393
discretionary hyphen, 323
  ⌘-Shift-hyphen keyboard shortcut, 323
distances, measuring, 285–287
Distort filters, 177–181, 550, 568–580
  Add Anchor Points filter, 534
  Free Distort, 568–571
  Random Mangling filters, 568
  reshaping category, 568
  Twirl filter, 571–574
distorting, 530
Distribute Horizontally filter, 182, 591
  Align Objects filter, 534
Distribute Vertically filter, 182, 591
  Align Objects filter, 534
Divide Fill filter, 187
  clay star, 558–559
Divide filter, 187, 601–602
Divide Stroke filter, 187
Document Info filter, 528, 535–536, 754
Document Setup command, 133
  ⌘-Shift-D keyboard shortcut, 133, 346, 352, 359, 363, 377, 511
  dialog box, 133, 346–350, 352, 359, 376–377, 474, 535
Document Setup file, 130
document window, 81–83, 345
  artboard, 82
  close box, 83
  current viewing zoom percentage, 83
  elevator box, 83
  manual resize box, 83

pasteboard, 81
scroll bars, 83
status bar, 83
title bar, 83, 345
documents
  actual size, 146–147
  Artwork mode, 359
  changing setup, 346–352
  closing, 130–131
  custom views, 364
  defaults, 130, 345
  deselecting items, 92
  Document Setup dialog box information, 535
  fonts used, 684
  grids, 348
  how long it may take to print, 536
  importing attributes from other documents, 132
  importing styles, 375
  magnification, 97–99, 353
  maximum printable size, 346
  navigating, 97, 353–358
  new active, 129
  new window for current, 362
  opening, 34, 130
  previewing, 359–360, 655
  printable area, 124, 145
  printing, 134
  redoing undo, 136
  resizing themselves, 98
  saving, 130, 366–367, 486
  scrolling, 357–358
  selecting all paths, 137
  selecting everything, 91
  selecting unselected, 189
  setting up new, 343–345
  spell-checking, 616–618
  undoing actions, 136
  viewing, 347–348, 535–536
  way type appears, 300–301
  zooming, 353–356
  zooming out, 146
Don't Save button (⌘-D) keyboard shortcut, 372
dot leader tabs, 329
double-clicking, 16, 21
dpi (dots per inch), 51, 675
dragging, 16
Draw from Center mode, 108
Draw from Corner mode, 108
Draw Square from Center (Option-Shift) keyboard shortcut, 208
drawing, 199–217

accidentally scrolling windows, 244
Brush tool, 241–247
circles, 211–214
Freehand tool, 247–255
getting objects out of the way, 519
juggler, 215–217
layers, 519
ovals, 211–214
Pen tool, 255–267
perfect squares, 206
rectangles, 201–205
rounded rectangles, 206–210
rounded squares, 206–210
sections, 519
splitting into manageable sections, 519
ungrouping all objects, 275
zooming in, 146
Drop Shadow filter, 191, 457, 580, 583–584
dialog box, 191, 583
drop shadows, 191, 204, 583–584
drum scanners, 29
Duplicate (⌘-D) keyboard shortcut, 696
Dynamic Graphics, Inc., 747

E

edges, showing/hiding, 363
Edit menu, 21, 73–77, 135–139, 751
commands, 763
keyboard shortcuts, 763
Edit Views command, 148
dialog box, 148
editable type outlines, 168–169, 329–335, 341
arcing words and phrases, 332–333
avoiding font conflicts, 334–335
distorting letters, 330–331
gradients, 333–334
logos, 331–332
masking, 333–334
patterns, 333–334
type (and path) effects, 335
Edit⇨Copy command, 423, 485, 621, 559
Edit⇨Cut command, 697
Edit⇨Deselect All command, 92, 577, 611
Edit⇨Paste In Back command, 156, 419, 423, 457, 459, 484–485, 541, 543, 546, 554–555, 558–559, 563, 631, 638
Edit⇨Paste In Front command, 156, 273, 325, 419, 630, 635, 638, 642-643, 696
Edit⇨Select All command, 91, 154, 275, 290, 310, 326, 419, 611, 619, 715
Edit⇨Undo command, 241, 313, 522, 559, 573, 577, 579, 582, 667
Edit⇨Ungroup command, 648
Educorp, 747
elevator box, 83
em space, 318
emulsion, 674
enclosed CD-ROM, 4, 759–762
Adobe Streamline demo version, 4
clip art, 4, 762
Collector's Edition folder, 474
demo software, 762
examining artwork, 760
filter charts, 760
fonts, 761–762
Lefty Casual font, 4
Ransom Note font, 4
software for connecting to America Online, 4
tutorials, 759–760
end paths and linear blends, 439–440
end points
combining into single anchor point, 390
determining location, 393
joining, 151, 390–393
overlapping, 391–392
Scissors tool, 389
EPS (Encapsulated PostScript) files, 364
Artwork and Preview mode, 374
bringing into document, 131
linking to Illustrator, 374
listing for illustration, 685
placing, 374–375
replacing with another EPS file, 132
tracing, 374
transforming, 374
EPS images
Artwork mode, 359
as full-color template, 283
changing on-screen resolution, 283
clipping path, 416
dimming, 282–284, 520
masks, 416
Preview mode, 519
sizing for tracing, 718
tracing, 214, 523
equilateral shapes, 218
erasing in real time, 252
Eric's Ultimate Solitaire, 16
Even-Odd Rule, 412, 600
Exclude filter, 186, 600
Export filter, 193, 340
dialog box, 193
extended keyboards, 24
extensions
Laserwriter 8, 377
PS Printer, 377
turning off, 40, 739
external speakers and microphones, 31
Eyedropper tool, 119–120

F

F/A-18 Hornet, 41
file compatibility options
Illustrator 1.1 option, 372
Illustrator 3 option, 371
Illustrator 4 option, 371
Illustrator 5 format, 371
Illustrator 88 option, 372
File menu, 21, 42, 129–135, 751
commands, 763
keyboard shortcuts, 763
file preview options, 368–370
File⇨Change Placed Art command, 422–423
File⇨Close command, 372
File⇨Document Setup command, 82, 346, 352, 359, 363, 377, 511
File⇨Duplicate command, 696
File⇨General Preferences command, 212, 214, 217, 631
File⇨Get Info command, 377, 684, 738
File⇨Import Styles command, 132, 375
File⇨Import Text command, 613
File⇨New command, 343, 373
File⇨Open command, 372, 373
File⇨Page Setup command, 378, 656
File⇨Place Art command, 282, 374, 416
File⇨Preferences command, 499, 502

File⇨Preferences⇨Color
Matching command, 360,
515
File⇨Preferences⇨General
command, 76, 105, 109,
113–116, 136, 204, 208, 211,
222, 248, 253–352, 450, 499,
502
File⇨Preferences⇨Hyphenation
Options command, 517
File⇨Preferences⇨Plug-Ins
command, 532
File⇨Print All Separations
command, 682, 685
File⇨Print command, 380, 655
File⇨Quit command, 373
File⇨Save All Separations
command, 686
File⇨Save As command, 367
File⇨Save command, 365
File⇨Save Selected Separations
command, 686
files, 343–382
Adobe Illustrator Startup, 474,
499
AI User Dictionary, 618
copying, 34
customizing output, 537–538
deleting, 34
Densitometer Control Chart, 681
Document Setup, 130
Horses/Snowman, 214
locating, 34
managing, 364
manipulation, 34
moving, 34
naming, 130–131, 366
new in Version 5.5, 527
None-Omit EPSF Header
option, 368
opening, 364, 372–373
organizing, 33
preview options, 368–370
Riders, 537–538
saving, 130, 364–372
taking from Macintosh to PC
and back, 757–758
types, 367–368
when to save, 366
Fill & Stroke for Mask filter, 174,
544, 611
fills
Artwork mode, 223
black option, 231
color, 230–234

combining with strokes, 226
custom color, 232
foreground/background
relationship to strokes, 273
gradients, 233
half-stroked paths, 641–642
patterns, 233
Process box, 232
transparent, 231
White option, 231
film stroke, 635
Filter menu, 91, 169–193, 531, 539
checking for Pathfinder
command, 532
commands, 764
keyboard shortcuts, 764
Filter⇨[Name of Last Filter]
command, 534
Filter⇨Add Arrowheads
command, 234
Filter⇨Colors command, 171
Filter⇨Colors⇨Adjust Colors
command, 541
Filter⇨Colors⇨Blend Front To
Back command, 543, 552,
644
Filter⇨Colors⇨Desaturate/
Desaturate More com-
mand, 531
Filter⇨Colors⇨Invert Colors
command, 531, 544
Filter⇨Colors⇨Saturate/Saturate
More command, 531
Filter⇨Create command, 174, 218
Filter⇨Create⇨Fill & Stroke for
Mask command, 419, 544,
611
Filter⇨Create⇨Mosaic com-
mand, 530, 546, 549
Filter⇨Create⇨Polygon com-
mand, 218
Filter⇨Create⇨Spiral command,
456
Filter⇨Create⇨Star command,
220, 222, 445
Filter⇨Create⇨Trim Marks
command, 155, 157, 553–554
Filter⇨Distort⇨Free Distort
command, 333, 530, 550,
568, 570, 574
Filter⇨Distort⇨Roughen
command, 577, 641, 644
Filter⇨Distort⇨Scribble
command, 579
Filter⇨Distort⇨Tweak command,
579

Filter⇨Distort⇨Twirl command,
530, 573–574
Filter⇨Object⇨Add Anchor
Points command, 549,
573–574, 585, 591
Filter⇨Object⇨Align Objects
command, 555, 591
Filter⇨Object⇨Move Each
command, 546, 552, 594
Filter⇨Object⇨Offset Path
command, 287, 298, 595
Filter⇨Object⇨Outline Path
command, 473, 582
Filter⇨Object⇨Outline Stroke
command, 642, 644, 648
Filter⇨Object⇨Outline Stroked
Path command, 469, 559,
630, 695, 697–698, 716
Filter⇨Object⇨Rotate command,
222
Filter⇨Object⇨Rotate Each
command, 550, 594
Filter⇨Object⇨Scale Each
command, 549, 552, 594
Filter⇨Other⇨Delete Riders
command, 538
Filter⇨Other⇨Document Info
command, 535
Filter⇨Other⇨Make Riders
command, 537
Filter⇨Other⇨Overprint Black
command, 536
Filter⇨Pathfinder⇨Back Minus
command, 600
Filter⇨Pathfinder⇨Crop
command, 622–623
Filter⇨Pathfinder⇨Crop Fill
command, 558
Filter⇨Pathfinder⇨Divide
command, 577, 596, 601–602
Filter⇨Pathfinder⇨Divide Fill
command, 555, 558
Filter⇨Pathfinder⇨Exclude
command, 642, 648
Filter⇨Pathfinder⇨Front Minus
Back command, 563, 600,
727
Filter⇨Pathfinder⇨Intersect
command, 600
Filter⇨Pathfinder⇨Merge
command, 603
Filter⇨Pathfinder⇨Merge Fill
command, 469
Filter⇨Pathfinder⇨Merge Stroke
command, 697–698

Filter⇨Pathfinder⇨Options
   command, 597
Filter⇨Pathfinder⇨Soft command, 604
Filter⇨Pathfinder⇨Trap
   command, 605
Filter⇨Pathfinder⇨Unite
   command, 244, 287, 449–
   450, 466, 468, 558–559, 582,
   596, 599, 640, 644
Filter⇨Same Fill Color command,
   610
Filter⇨Select command, 607
Filter⇨Select⇨Inverse command,
   530
Filter⇨Select⇨Same Fill Color
   command, 508, 531, 540,
   608, 644
Filter⇨Select⇨Same Paint Style
   command, 274, 485, 609, 662
Filter⇨Select⇨Same Stroke Color
   command, 609, 611, 697
Filter⇨Select⇨Select Inverse
   command, 611
Filter⇨Select⇨Select Masks
   command, 611
Filter⇨Select⇨Select Stray Points
   command, 62, 612
Filter⇨Star command, 222
Filter⇨Stroke & Fill for Mask
   command, 418
Filter⇨Stylize⇨Add Arrowheads
   command, 234, 411, 581–582
Filter⇨Stylize⇨Calligraphy
   command, 587
Filter⇨Stylize⇨Drop Shadow
   command, 583–584
Filter⇨Stylize⇨Punk command,
   549, 585
Filter⇨Stylize⇨Round Corners
   command, 208, 546, 549,
   557–558, 573, 578, 586
Filter⇨Text⇨Change Case
   command, 615
Filter⇨Text⇨Check Spelling
   command, 616
Filter⇨Text⇨Export command,
   613
Filter⇨Text⇨Find command,
   613–614
Filter⇨Text⇨Find Font command, 618
Filter⇨Text⇨Revert Text Path
   command, 619
Filter⇨Text⇨Rows & Columns
   command, 620, 622

Filter⇨Text⇨Smart Punctuation
   command, 624
filters, 169–193, 527–538, 567–587
   Add Anchor Points, 181–182,
      447, 449, 573, 591
   Add Arrowheads, 189–190,
      580–582
   Adjust Colors, 171–172, 528,
      540–541
   Align Objects, 182, 591–593
   Back Minus, 186, 600
   Back Minus Front, 186
   Blend Front to Back, 172,
      542–543
   Blend Horizontally, 172
   Blend Vertically, 172
   Bloat, 190, 528, 580, 584–585
   Calligraphy, 191, 245, 580, 587
   Change Case, 340, 615, 753
   Check Spelling, 340, 616–618,
      753
   color, 171–174, 539–544
   Color Adjust, 457
   combinations and relations,
      533–534
   cool shapes with, 217–222
   Create, 544–554
   Create Mosaic, 738
   Crop, 187
   Crop Fill, 187
   Crop Stroke, 188
   Custom to Process, 172, 540
   Delete Anchor Point, 447
   Delete Riders, 537–538
   Desaturate, 173
   Desaturate More, 173
   dialog box for particular, 170
   Distort, 177–181, 550, 568–580
   Distribute Horizontally, 182, 591
   Distribute Vertically, 182, 591
   Divide, 187, 601–602
   Divide Fill, 187
   Divide Stroke, 187
   Document Info, 528, 535–536
   Drop Shadows, 191, 457, 580,
      583–584
   Exclude, 186, 600
   Export, 193, 340
   Fill & Stroke for Mask, 174, 544,
      611
   Find, 193, 340
   Find Font, 340, 618–619, 753
   FPU, 528
   Free Distort, 177, 530, 568–571,
      738
   Front Minus, 186, 600

Front Minus Back, 186
Hard, 188, 604
Illustrator Version 5.5 and FPU,
   533
Illustrator vs. Photoshop,
   529–531
Intersect, 186, 600
Inverse, 530
Invert Colors, 173, 531, 543–544
Make Riders, 537–538
Merge, 187, 603
Merge Fill, 187
Merge Stroke, 187
missing in Illustrator version
   5.0, 170–171
Mix, 604–605
Mix Hard, 188
Mix Soft, 188, 457, 605
Mosaic, 175–176, 530, 545–550
Move Each, 182–183, 546,
   593–594
Object, 181–184, 589–596
obstacles to using them,
   528–529
Offset Path, 171, 183, 287, 298,
   533, 594–596, 737
Options, 188
Outline, 187, 602–603
Outline Path, 183, 473, 594
Outline Stroked Path, 171, 183,
   528, 533, 559, 594, 596, 737
Overprint, 528
Paint Style selection, 608–611
Pathfinder, 184–188, 533,
   589–590, 596
Pathfinder Divide Stroke, 528
Photoshop, 169
Plug-Ins folder, 531–532
Polygon, 176, 218
Punk, 191–192, 528, 580, 584–585
Random Mangle, 574–580
reapplying last used, 170, 534
Reduce, 603
returning to last filter dialog
   box, 534
Revert Text Path, 340, 619–620,
   753
Rotate Each, 184, 449, 593–594
Roughen, 177–179, 528, 568,
   574, 576–578
Round Corners, 192, 208, 546,
   557, 580, 586–587
Rows & Columns, 340, 620–623,
   753
Same Fill Color, 188, 531, 608–609
Same Paint Style, 188, 609

Same Stroke Color, 188, 609–610
Same Stroke Weight, 189, 610
Saturate, 173
Saturate More, 174
Scale Each, 184, 593–594
Scribble, 179, 568, 573–574, 578–580
Select, 188–189, 528, 607–608
Select Inverse, 189, 608, 611
Select Masks, 189, 608, 611–612
Select Stray Points, 189, 608, 612
Smart Punctuation, 340, 624–625, 753
Soft, 188, 604
special shapes, 174–177
Spiral, 176
Star, 176, 218, 220–222, 555
Stylize, 189–192, 568, 580–587
Text, 193, 340, 613–625
Text Export, 613
Text Find, 613–615
third-party, 533
Trap, 185, 188, 528, 605–606
Trim, 187
Trim Marks, 176–177, 553–554
Tweak, 180, 568, 574, 578–580
Twirl, 180–181, 528, 530, 568, 571–574
Unite, 186, 244, 287, 528, 599
Find Again feature, 34
Find filter, 193, 340
Find Font filter, 340, 618–619, 753
dialog box, 618–619
Finder, 33–34, 41
Fit Headline command, 166–167
Fit In Window command, 147
⌘-M keyboard shortcut, 98, 147, 445, 449
flatbed scanners, 29
floppy disk drives, 27
floppy disks, 43–44
Flush Left (⌘-Shift-L) keyboard shortcut, 321
Flush Right (⌘-Shift-R) keyboard shortcut, 322
Font
⌘-Option-Shift-M keyboard shortcut, 160
⌘-Shift-F keyboard shortcut, 160
Font Downloader, 686
Font Field (⌘-Option-Shift-M) keyboard shortcut, 318
Font menu, 159, 751
FontMonger, 340
Fontographer, 340, 651
fonts, 35–41: *See also* type

Adobe Type Manager (ATM), 39–40
avoiding conflicts, 334–335
below 8 points on-screen, 39
Bill's Dingbats, 338
bitmap, 35–36
Carta, 338
customizing, 339–340
enclosed CD-ROM, 761–762
greeking, 39
Illustrator and, 39–41
Lefty Casual, 4, 339, 761
listing, 160, 314
Madrone, 450
Mathematical Pi, 338
Multiple Master, 40, 166–167, 340
outputting files, 340
PostScript, 36–38, 168, 334
Ransom Note, 4, 339, 761–762
saving list as file, 619
searching and replacing, 618–619, 624–625
selecting, 314
sets of characters, 336
specifying, 313
Super ATM, 41
Symbol typeface, 336
TrueType, 38–39, 168, 334
types, 35
viewing characters available and keyboard shortcuts, 336
Zapf Dingbats, 336
FontStudio, 340
foreground, 271–273
four-color separation, 659
FPU (Floating Point Unit), 170, 528, 532–533, 590, 737
Offset Path filter, 590, 594
Outline Path filter, 590
Outline Stroked Path filter, 590, 594
Pathfinder filters, 590
FPU Plug-Ins folder, 532
FPU-Based Plug-Ins, 741
Fractal Design Painter, 31, 79, 453
Free Distort filter, 177, 568–571, 738
arcing letters, 333
changing width of stroke, 596
dialog box, 177, 568, 570
handle positions, 571
Freed, Tim, 708, 745
freeform path, 242, 247
FreeHand, 77
Freehand tool, 104, 281, 327, 450, 454, 582, 631, 645
adding to existing open path,

254–255
anchor points, 105, 249, 254
cursor changing to pencil with black eraser, 254
curved-corner anchor point, 249, 254
drawing, 247–255
drawing paths, 239
erasing, 105, 252
Freehand Tolerance setting, 105, 506
Horse and Tall Grass drawing, 248–256
huge eraser cursor, 251
jagged and smooth paths, 252–254
limitations, 247
open paths and closed paths, 250–251
Paint Style attributes, 248
pencil shape to crosshair cursor, 249
semistraight segments, 251–252
smooth anchor points, 249, 254
straight-corner anchor points, 249
Front Minus Back filter, 186
Front Minus filter, 186, 600

G

Garling, Jennifer, 528, 745
General command, 134
General Preferences dialog box, 134, 136, 145, 248, 312, 316, 328, 450, 499, 502–515
⌘-K keyboard shortcut, 109, 113–116, 134, 136, 145, 214, 217, 248, 253, 281, 312, 316, 352, 450, 499, 502, 631
Area select option, 509–515
Auto Trace gap option, 507
Baseline shift option, 304, 306, 513
Constrain angle option, 222, 503–505
Corner radius option, 208, 505–506
Cursor key option, 512–515
Freehand tolerance option, 253–254, 281, 454, 506
Greek text limit option, 514–515
incremental character attribute changes, 312
Indent/shift units option, 512

measurement systems, 352
Paste remembers layers
option, 514
Ruler units option, 511
Scale line weight option, 508–509
Size/leading option, 512
Snap to point option, 285, 392,
507–508
Tracking option, 513
Transform pattern tiles option,
508
Undo levels option, 76, 513–514
Use precise cursors option,
509–511
Geo-port, 31
Geshke, Chuck, 68
Get Info dialog box, 684-685, 738
⌘-I keyboard shortcut, 377,
684, 738
(EPSF) Files window, 685
gigabyte (GB), 43
glows, 458–459
Gradient command, 150
Gradient palette, 150, 462–464, 652
accessing, 233
adding new color, 464
showing/hiding, 195
Gradient Vector tool, 86, 120–121,
426, 462, 465–468, 570, 652
gradients, 121–122, 150, 425–428,
426, 462–468
backgrounds, 652–653
custom, 464
Dimensions 1.0, 469
editable type outlines, 333–334
embossing text, 466–467
fills, 233
ghosting effects, 465
Illustrator 3 compatibility, 469
modifying, 463–464
Photoshop, 469
preset, 463
putting into patterns, 485–486
shadows, 468
strokes, 469
sunset, 652
transforming, 398
Gradients & Patterns folder, 741
Graph Column Design dialog box,
158
Graph Data dialog box, 158, 488,
495
Graph Marker Design dialog box,
158
Graph Size dialog box, 122

Graph Style dialog box, 123, 157,
493–494
Graph tool, 86, 122–123, 157, 487
graph tools, 122
Area Graph tool, 122–123
Graph tool, 122–123
Line Graph tool, 122–123
Pie Graph tool, 122–123
Scatter Graph tool, 122–123
Stacked-column Graph tool,
122–123
Graph⇨Column command, 158
Graph⇨Data command, 158
Graph⇨Design command, 158
Graph⇨Marker command, 158
Graph⇨Style command, 157
graphs, 122–123, 157–158, 487–497
area, 494
categories, 488
cells, 488
changes over time, 490
column design, 158, 496–497
combining types, 495
comparing percentages of
portions of whole, 493–494
customizing, 494–495
data, 158
graph design, 158
grouped column, 490
importing data, 495
line, 492–493
marker design, 158, 496–497
numbers and text, 495
pie, 493–494
scatter, 494
scientific charting purposes, 494
stacked column, 490–491
switching x and y axes, 495
total and contributing portions
of categories, 490–491
total area of legend subject, 494
trends over time, 492–493
types, 157, 490–494
ungrouping, 495
when to use, 488
greeking, 39, 514–515
grids, 348
Group command, 140
⌘-G keyboard shortcut, 140
Group Selection tool, 89–91, 93–96,
151–152, 190, 276, 299, 390,
410, 417, 494–495
accessing, 96
⌘-Option keyboard shortcut, 276
compound paths, 276, 407
quickly selecting, 276

paths, 276
Shift key, 95
grouped column graphs, 490
groups, 140, 274
selecting, 93, 95–96, 276
ungrouping, 141
guides, 152–154, 288–290
changing into path, 289–290
creation, 153, 288–290
locking/unlocking, 154, 289
Magic Rotating, 289
moving, 289
pulling from ruler, 289
releasing, 153, 289–290
selecting all, 290
Separator, 683
showing/hiding, 146, 363
transforming paths into, 289
Guides (⌘-5) keyboard shortcut,
289–290, 497
Guides⇨Lock command, 154
⌘-7 keyboard shortcut, 154
Guides⇨Make command, 153
⌘-5 keyboard shortcut, 153
Guides⇨Release command, 153
⌘-6 keyboard shortcut, 153

H

halftone line screens, 352, 675–678
Halftone pop-up menu, 676
Hand tool, 86, 96
Fit In Window view, 355
scrolling documents, 357–358
spacebar keyboard shortcut,
88, 97
hanging indents, 322
hanging punctuation, 322–323
hard disks, 27
memory, 43–44
physical sizes, 27
sizes, 44
speed measurements, 44
Hard filter, 188, 604
hardware, 23–31
CD-ROM drives, 28–29
external speakers and
microphones, 31
floppy disk drives, 27
Geo-port, 31
hard disks, 27
Illustrator version 5.0
requirements, 749
imagesetters, 30
joysticks, 26
keyboards, 24–25

laser printers, 30
modems, 31
monitors, 26–27
mouse, 25–26
optical drives, 28
scanners, 29
Syquest drives, 27–28
tape drives, 29
trackballs, 25–26
video in and out, 31
Hide Borders command, 138
Hide Character command, 195
Hide Clipboard command, 139
Hide command, 141, 519
⌘-3 keyboard shortcut, 141,
291, 543, 648
Hide Edges command, 145–146
Hide Gradient command, 195
Hide Guides command, 146
⌘-3 keyboard shortcut, 363
Hide Info command, 194
⌘-Control-I keyboard shortcut,
108
Hide Layers command, 194
⌘-Control-L keyboard
shortcut, 521
Hide Page Tiling command, 145
Hide Paint Style command, 195
Hide Paragraph command, 195
Hide Rulers command, 145
Hide Template command, 145
Hide Toolbox command, 194
highlights, 541
Horse and Tall Grass drawing
Brush tool, 241–256
duplicating weeds, 269
Freehand tool, 248–256
grouping objects, 274
Pen tool, 256, 267
Horses/Snowman file, 214
hyphenation, 323
customizing, 517
discretionary hyphen, 323
exceptions, 135
preferences, 135
Hyphenation dictionaries, 618
Hyphenation Options command,
135
dialog box, 135, 517

I

icons, 8–9
Caution, 8
Cross Reference, 8
Illustrator 5.5, 9
Note, 8
Power Tip, 8
illustrations
backgrounds, 651–653
Color Macintosh preview, 665
information about, 684–685
juggler, 215–217
masks and compound paths,
421–423
previewing color, 660
roughening up, 177–196
showing/hiding parts, 362–363
Illustrator, 41, 741
automatic or computer-
assisted manipulations, 92
credits, 196
custom installation, 740–742
default measurements, 204
defining, 2
fonts and, 39–41
history, 48
Installer icon, 738
installing, 738–742
learning curve, 47–50
quitting, 135
resources, 745–747
Stuffit files, 739
techniques for learning more,
48–50
upcoming versions, 755
vs. Photoshop filters, 529–531
what you cannot customize,
517–518
Illustrator on CD-ROM, 742–743
Illustrator 3, saving documents as,
486
Illustrator 5.0, 749–752
basic choke trap, 692–693
basic spread trap, 693
checking for FPU (Floating
Point Unit), 532
complex trapping techniques,
694–698
FPU (Floating Point Unit), 590
getting around not having FPU,
533
hardware requirements, 749
keyboard shortcuts, 752
menus, 751–752
missing filters, 170–171
new features, 750
preview options, 368–370
tab problems, 326–327
tools, 750–751
trapping files, 691–693
Illustrator 5.5, 2, 742, 752–756
Acrobat PDF File Format Plug-
In, 535
Color filter submenu, 540
Document Info filter, 528,
535–536
FPU (Floating Point Unit), 590
FPU and filters, 533
icon, 9
keyboard shortcuts, 755
menus, 755
new features, 753–755
new filters, 527–528
Offset Path filter, 533
Outline Path filter, 533
Overprint Black Plug-In, 536
Overprint filter, 528
Pathfinder filters, 533, 754
PICT File Format Plug-In, 537
PowerPCs and, 3
preview options, 368–370
Save As dialog box, 126, 131
saving files, 754
Tab Ruler palette, 327–330
text changes, 753–754
text filters, 340
tools, 755
trapping, 698
Trap filter, 528
Image Club Graphics, Inc., 747
Image pop-up menu, 679
images, tracing, 106–107
imagesetters, 30, 657, 671
calculating blend steps, 440
page size, 671
PostScript, 30
ImageWriter Page Setup dialog
box, 380
Import Styles command, 132
dialog box, 375
Import Text command, 132
importing text formats, 132
Increase Baseline Shift (Option-
Shift-↑) keyboard
shortcut, 316
Increase Leading
Option-↑ keyboard shortcut,
316, 512
Increase Point Size (⌘-Shift-→)
keyboard shortcut, 314
Increase Tracking
⌘-→ keyboard shortcut, 513
⌘-Shift-] keyboard shortcut,
318
Increase Tracking Five Times
⌘-Option-← keyboard shortcut,
317

⌘-Option→ keyboard shortcut, 513
Increase Tracking/Kerning (Option←) keyboard shortcut, 317
Increase Type (⌘-Shift→) keyboard shortcut, 161, 512
Info palette
  opening, 296
  showing distances, 285
  showing/hiding, 108, 194
Innovation Advertising & Design, 747
Installer dialog box, 738
Internet, contacting the author, 9
interruptable redraw, 78
Intersect filter, 186, 600
Inverse filter, 530
Invert Colors filter, 173, 531, 543–544
Island Trapper, 694

J

jaggies, 52
Join and Average
  ⌘-Option-J keyboard shortcut, 151, 389, 392, 447, 562, 577
  ⌘-Option-L keyboard shortcut, 447
Join command, 151
  ⌘-J keyboard shortcut, 151, 390, 393
  dialog box, 390
join style, 224
joining, 389, 390–393
  brush strokes, 246
joysticks, 26
juggler drawing, 215–217
Justify command, 297
  ⌘-Shift-J keyboard shortcut, 163, 297, 322
Justify Last Line (⌘-Shift-B) keyboard shortcut, 164, 322

K

kaleidoscopes, rotating objects into, 403–404
Kern (⌘-Shift-K) keyboard shortcut, 312
kerning, 316–319, 513
  Path type, 307
  preset values, 318
  values, 318
keyboard shortcuts: *See also individual keyboard*

shortcuts
  commands, 763–771
  Illustrator Version 5.0, 752
  Illustrator Version 5.5, 755
keyboards, 24–25
  defining increments, 512
  extended, 24
  selecting items from menus, 21–22
  standard, 24
  touch, 25
KeyCaps, 335
KeyFinder, 336
kilobyte (K), 43

L

Language pop-up menu, 319
laser printers, 30, 51
  calculating blend steps, 441
  dpi (dots per inch), 51, 676
  page size, 671
  PostScript, 30
  things to consider when purchasing, 30
LaserWriter, 52
LaserWriter 8 extension, 133, 377
LaserWriter IINT PPD, 664
LaserWriter Page Setup dialog box, 378–379
  Faster Bitmap Printing option, 379
LaserWriter Utility, 686
Last Filter command, 170
  ⌘-Shift-E keyboard shortcut, 170
Layer Fixer QuicKey, 523
Layer Options dialog box, 282, 520, 523
layers, 518–523
  active, 521
  advice and strategies, 523
  Artwork mode, 519, 521
  changing order, 520
  color of paths and points, 519
  custom colors, 519
  customization and creation, 519–520
  deleting, 523
  deselecting, 521
  dimming EPS images, 520
  displaying, 362
  distinct colors, 523
  hidden, 521
  listing, 521
  locking/unlocking, 520–521, 523
  making objects visible, 520

modifying existing, 520
  moving, 521
  moving objects between, 522
  naming, 519
  new top, 522
  number limitations, 518
  pasting objects, 523
  placing hard to manage objects on separate, 519
  preset colors, 519
  Preview mode, 519–521
  printing objects on, 520
  splitting drawing into manageable sections, 519
  top and bottom, 521
  tracing EPS images, 523
  undoing changes, 522
  when to use, 519
Layers Option dialog box, 656
Layers palette, 80, 518–523
  ⌘-Control-L keyboard shortcut, 282, 519, 719
  active layer, 521
  Artwork mode, 521
  Artwork Others/Preview All option, 523
  combining viewing modes, 362
  Delete option, 523
  deselecting layers, 521
  Dim EPS images option, 214
  Hide Others/Show All option, 523
  layer is hidden, 521
  Layer Options option, 523
  listing layers, 521
  Lock Others/Unlock All option, 523
  locking/unlocking all layers, 521
  main section, 521–522
  moving layer, 521
  New Layer option, 282, 522
  opening, 282, 522
  Paste Remembers Layers option, 514, 523
  pop-up menu, 522–523
  Preview mode, 521
  resizing, 521
  showing/hiding, 194, 521
  top and bottom layers, 521
  viewing, 519
leading, 161–162, 316
  entering values, 315
  increasing/decreasing, 512
  increments, 316
  upper and lower size limits, 512
Leading command, 161–162

Learned Words dialog box, 617
Left Alignment (⌘-Shift-L)
    keyboard shortcut, 162
Lefty Casual, 4, 339, 761
Letraset USA, 747
ligatures, 624
line and grid patterns, 483–484
Line Graph tool, 122–123
line graphs, 492–493
line screens, 675–676
line segments, 94
line weights, 508–509
linear blends, 431–443
    basic, 432
    color, 437–438
    end paths, 439–440
    multiple colors, 432–433
linear gradient, 121–122
lines, 702
    measuring distance in one
        direction, 286
lines per inch (lpi), 352, 675
Link Blocks command, 165–166
    ⌘-Shift-G keyboard shortcut,
        165–166, 326
linked direction points, 63
Linotronic 200 PPD, 664
Lock command, 141, 519
    ⌘-1 keyboard shortcut, 141,
        290, 631, 727
Lock Unselected command, 610
    ⌘-Option-1 keyboard shortcut,
        141, 610, 641
Lock/Unlock Guides (⌘-7)
    keyboard shortcut, 289
logos, 331–332

M

Macintosh, 13–45
    advantages, 14–15
    basic concepts, 15–22
    computer itself, 24
    consistency, 15–16
    CPU (central processing unit), 24
    cursors, 17
    dialog boxes, 19–20
    Edit menu, 21
    File menu, 21
    Finder, 33–34
    floppy disk drives, 27
    fonts, 35–41
    FPU (Floating Point Unit), 590
    hard disks, 27
    hardware, 23–31
    hooking up scanners, 29

joysticks, 26
keyboards, 24–25
megahertz (MHz), 24
menus, 21
models, 532, 735
monitors, 26–27
mouse, 16, 25–26
PowerPCs, 24
processors, 24
program similarities, 15
selecting before doing, 21
several ways to complete
    action, 16
speed, 24
system software, 32–33
terminology, 22–23
tools, 20
trackballs, 25–26
windows, 17–19
MacPaint images, tracing, 106–107
Macromedia Director, 41, 760
Madrone font, 450
Magic Rotating guide, 289
Main panel, 227, 230–234
    Custom Color box, 232
    Gradient box, 233
    overprinting options, 234
    Pattern box, 233
    Process box, 232
    slider bar, 231
Make Riders filter, 537–538
    dialog box, 537–538
Make Wrap command, 166
manual resize box, 83
marquee, 93–94
masks, 154, 414–423, 533
    blends, 435–436
    changes from previous
        versions of Illustrator, 417
    compound paths, 420
    creation, 154, 414–415
    editable type outlines, 333–334
    EPS images, 416
    fills and strokes, 174, 417–419,
        544–545
    manipulating, 608
    masking blends and other
        masks, 416
    printing and, 419–420
    releasing, 154, 419
    ripple effects with spiral, 559
    selecting, 189, 611–612
    slightly altered EPS images, 423
    turning path into mask, 544–545
Masks⇨Make command, 154
Masks⇨Release command, 154

Mathematical Pi, 338
mean method, 390
Measure tool, 86, 108–109, 285
measurement systems, 351–352
    ⌘-Control-U keyboard
        shortcut, 328
    default, 204
    modifying, 363, 511
    points/inches/centimeters
        conversions, 204
measuring distances, 285–287
megabyte (MB), 43
megahertz (MHz), 24
memory, 42–45
    allocation, 196
    application number limitations,
        42
    bits, 43
    bytes, 43
    CD-ROMs, 44
    DAT tape drives, 44
    floppy disks, 43–44
    gigabyte (GB), 43
    hard disks, 43–44
    kilobyte (K), 43
    megabyte (MB), 43
    programs and, 44–45
    random access memory
        (RAM), 42, 44
    storage, 42
    Syquest drives, 44
    System 6 requirements, 33
    System 7 requirements, 33
    temporary, 44
    terminology, 43
    terrabytes, 43
menus, 21, 125–196
    avoiding when possible, 128
    effective use, 127–128
    ellipsis (. . .), 21, 127
    Illustrator 5.0, 751–752
    Illustrator 5.5, 755
    keyboard shortcuts, 21, 127
    keyboard item selection, 21–22
    memorizing commands on, 128
    noun/verb terms, 128
    pop-up menus, 21, 127
    rules, 127
    selecting item, 127
    viewing items, 21
Merge Fill filter, 187, 697
Merge filter, 187, 603
Merge Stroke filter, 187, 697
Microsoft Windows, 17
Microsoft Word, 41
mirror images, 396

miter limit, 224
Mix filters, 604–605, 754
Mix Hard filter, 188
   dialog box, 605
Mix Soft filter, 188, 457, 605
   dialog box, 188, 604–605
modems, 31
moiré, 660
monitors, 26–27
   attaching, 26
   CIE calibration, 360
   color, 26
   multiple, 26
   setting number of colors,
      515–516
   video cards, 26
Mosaic filter, 175–176, 530,
      545–550
   color sets, 552
   dialog box, 175, 546
   Seurat-like illustration, 546
   tiled roof, 549–550
mosaics, 545–550
   number of tiles, 546
   random overlapping tiles with
      no white space, 552
   rotating, 549
mouse, 16, 25–26
   clicking, 16
   Desktop Mouse II, 25
   double-clicking, 16
   dragging, 16
   drawing with, 244
Move command, 140
   ⌘-Shift-M keyboard shortcut,
      109, 140, 183, 285, 291, 454,
      486, 508, 511, 543, 563
   dialog box, 109, 140, 285,
      291–292, 444, 466, 486, 511,
      543, 563
Move Each filter, 182–183, 546,
      593–594
   dialog box, 546, 594
Multiple Master fonts, 40, 166–167,
      340

N

A Natural Form of Expression,
      707–716
   animals, 708
   background, 714–715
   bug, 709–710
   concept, 708
   fish, 709
   parrot, 713

production, 715–716
salamander and its rock,
      710–711
snake, 712
type, 715
negatives
   color filters, 543–544
   reasons they are different
      sizes, 690–691
New command, 129
   ⌘-N keyboard shortcut, 129, 343
New Layer dialog box, 282, 519, 522
New Template (⌘-Option-N)
      keyboard shortcut, 373
New View 1 command, 148
   ⌘-Control-1 keyboard
      shortcut, 148
New View command, 147
   ⌘-Control-V keyboard
      shortcut, 147, 364
   dialog box, 147, 364
New Window command, 194
nonlinear blends, 433–434
Not enough memory for Undo/
      Redo error message, 738
Note icon, 8

O

Object filters, 181–184, 589–596
   Add Anchor Points filter, 591
   alignment and distribution
      filters, 591–593
   pathfinders, 594–596
   transform each filters, 593–594
Object menu, 89, 91, 148–158, 751
   commands, 764
   keyboard shortcuts, 764
Object⇨Attributes command,
      108, 155, 334, 413, 555, 563,
      612
   ⌘-Control-A keyboard
      shortcut, 108, 563, 612
   dialog box, 413, 612
Object⇨Average command, 389,
      392
Object⇨Compound Path
      command, 407
Object⇨Compound Path⇨Make
      command, 334, 406,
      409–410, 412, 422, 543, 698
Object⇨Compound Path⇨Release
      command, 407
Object⇨Cropmarks⇨Make
      command, 553
Object⇨Custom Color command,
      663

Object⇨Graphs⇨Column Design
      command, 497
Object⇨Graphs⇨Data command,
      495
Object⇨Graphs⇨Design
      command, 497
Object⇨Graphs⇨Graph Style
      command, 495
Object⇨Graphs⇨Style command,
      493
Object⇨Guides command, 289
Object⇨Guides⇨Lock command,
      289
Object⇨Guides⇨Make command,
      146, 286, 289–290, 497
Object⇨Guides⇨Release
      command, 289–290
Object⇨Join command, 390, 393
Object⇨Mask command, 715
Object⇨Mask⇨Make command,
      334, 415, 417, 423, 436, 445,
      559
Object⇨Mask⇨Release com-
      mand, 417, 419, 715
Object⇨Paint Style command,
      204, 226
Object⇨Pattern command, 472,
      476–477, 479, 485–486, 500,
      563
Object⇨Release command, 154
Object⇨Show Rulers command,
      289
objects, 290–292
   adding points, 534
   aligning, 181–184, 503–505, 534,
      591
   anchor points, 576–578, 591
   angled rows & columns, 622–623
   attributes, 151, 226
   back of current layer, 140
   background, 271–273
   blending, 172
   bounding box, 580
   center points, 612
   clearing from Artboard, 136
   constraining to equal propor-
      tions, 115
   copying, 73–74, 113, 136
   cropping, 187
   cutting, 73–74, 136
   deselecting selected, 137
   distributing centers, 182
   distribution on pages, 139–141
   drop shadow, 191, 583–584
   duplicating at specific angle, 505
   extruded multiple path, 541–543

filling or stroking, 223, 473
flipping, 115
foreground, 271–273
front of current layer, 140
grouping, 274
hiding, 141, 291
how far it moves with arrow
    keys, 512
how much they will spin,
    180–181
locking, 141, 290–292
lumps outside, 584–585
magnifying, 97–99
measuring distances, 286–287
mirror image, 116, 396
moving, 140, 271, 291–292, 522,
    530, 571–574
nonuniformly scaling, 508
Option-copying, 505
overprinting, 536
Paint Style attributes, 149, 608
pasting, 73–74, 136, 138, 514
pointy tips, 584–585
preventing selection on layer,
    520
previewing selected, 143
redoing last transformation,
    140
releasing masked, 154
reshaping, 568–571
rotating, 113–114, 184, 398–399
rows & columns in non-
    rectangular object, 621–622
same Paint Style attributes,
    188, 609
same stroke and fill colors,
    188, 609–611
same stroke weight, 189, 610
scaling, 115, 508–509
selecting/deselecting, 89–96,
    274, 360, 509, 531, 608–611
shadow creation, 396–397
shearing, 117–118
showing hidden, 141
sliced apart at edges of pattern
    tile boundary, 478–479
softening edges, 459
spinning more in center than at
    edges, 530
strokes, 224
tracing, 106–107, 212
transforming, 112, 395–404, 593
twisting, 570
ungrouping, 275–276
uniting, 186
unlocking, 141, 290

unselectable, 141
viewing attributes, 227
zooming, 146
Objects submenu, 171
Offset Path filter, 171, 183, 298,
    533, 594–596, 640, 737
    dialog box, 183, 595
    FPU (Floating Point Unit), 590,
        594
    Illustrator 5.5, 533
    inset type areas, 298
    measuring distances, 287
    Unite filter, 534
Open command, 130
    ⌘-O keyboard shortcut, 130,
        372–373
    dialog box, 16, 372
Open a PostScript Printer
    Description (PPD) file
    window, 670
open paths, 58, 102, 111, 582
    filling with type, 111
    fills, 60
    strokes, 60
optical drives, 28
Option key, 22, 204–205, 207, 214,
    306, 396, 399
Optional Plug-Ins Folder, 532
Options filter, 188
    dialog box, 382
origin point, 202
    rounded rectangles and
        squares, 206
Outline filter, 187, 602–603
outline fonts: See PostScript fonts
Outline mode, 329
Outline Path filter, 183, 473, 594:
    See also Outline Stroked
    Path filter
    FPU (Floating Point Unit), 590
    Illustrator 5.5, 533
Outline Stroked Path filter, 171,
    183, 528, 533, 559, 594, 596,
    630, 642–643, 697, 737
    Add Arrowheads filter, 534
    Dash pattern, 596
    FPU (Floating Point Unit), 590,
        594
    overlapping paths, 596
outlined stroke, 596
outlining type, 319
Oval dialog box, 214
Oval tool, 108, 211, 214, 305, 436,
    445
ovals, 211–214
Overlay filters, 600–603, 754

Overprint Black filter, 536, 754
Overprint filter, 528, 532
    dialog box, 536
overprinting, 142
    Main panel options, 234
    objects, 536

P

page description language, 53
page direction, 669–670
page guides, 363
page outlines, 348
Page Setup command, 133
Page Setup dialog box, 133, 656
    ImageWriter, 380
    LaserWriter, 378–379
    printing, 376
    PS Printers, 380
Page Size pop-up menu, 671–672
Page tool, 86, 124, 145, 348
PageMaker, 51, 657
pages, tiling, 124
Paint Bucket tool, 119, 120
Paint Bucket/Eyedropper dialog
    box, 119
Paint file format templates, 278
Paint palette, 463
Paint Style command, 149
    ⌘-I keyboard shortcut, 149, 226
Paint Style palette, 226–238, 432,
    435, 550
    applying paint style, 120
    Apply button and Auto check
        box, 230
    Color Swatch panel, 227, 236–237
    default view, 229
    Fill square, 204
    fills, 545
    gradients, 462
    instantly applying changes, 230
    Main panel, 227, 230–234
    moving sliders around, 235–236
    Overprint Stroke box, 156, 554
    Paint Style attribute, 216, 248
    pattern list, 476
    Pattern option, 472–473
    storing paint style information,
        120
    Stroke square, 204, 632
    Stroke Style panel, 227
    viewing/hiding, 149, 195, 226–229
Paint Style selection filters, 608–611
    combining, 610–611
palettes
    commands, 769–771

keyboard shortcuts, 769–771
placement preferences, 517
toolbox, 81
vs. windows, 79–81
Pantone colors, 659
Paragraph command, 164
⌘-Shift-P keyboard shortcut, 164
⌘-Shift-T keyboard shortcut, 164
Paragraph palette, 320–321
⌘-Shift-O keyboard shortcut, 320
Auto hyphenate box, 164, 323
closing, 313
Hang punctuation option, 164
hanging indents, 322
Leading before ¶ text field, 164, 323
Left Indentation field, 164
⌘-Shift-P keyboard shortcut, 320
⌘-Shift-T keyboard shortcut, 320, 327
paragraph indentation, 322
showing/hiding, 195
paragraphs
alignment, 162–169, 321–322
attributes, 320–324
Centered, 322
Flush Left, 321
Flush Right, 322
hanging punctuation, 322–323
hyphenation, 323
indentation, 322–323
Justified, 322
Justify Last Line, 322
leading, 161
measuring indents, 512
selecting, 110
spacing, 322
word and letter spacing, 324
parallel strokes, 631
Paste command, 73–74, 136
⌘-V keyboard shortcut, 136, 327
Paste In Back command, 138
⌘-B keyboard shortcut, 138, 419, 423, 454, 457–460, 484–485, 541, 555, 558–559, 563, 642
Paste In Front command, 138
⌘-F keyboard shortcut, 138, 273, 325, 404, 419, 460, 464, 543, 546, 554, 631–632, 639, 642, 696, 727
pasteboard, 81
path creation tools, 100–108
Auto Trace tool, 106
Brush tool, 103

Freehand tool, 104
Pen tool, 100
shape creation tools, 108
path editing tools, 100–103
Add Anchor Point tool, 101–103
Caps Lock key, 101
Convert Direction Point tool, 101–103
Delete Anchor Point tool, 101–103
Scissors tool, 101–103
Path Type tool, 109–111, 293, 303–309, 650
Pathfinder Divide Stroke filter, 528
Pathfinder filters, 184–188, 533, 589–590, 596–603, 630, 737
Changes from Version 5.0 to Version 5.5, 597
combine filters, 599–600
customizing, 597–599
FPU (Floating Point Unit), 590
Illustrator 5.5, 533, 754
overlay filters, 600–603
Pathfinder Options dialog box, 597–599
specifying exactness, 188
Pathfinder Options dialog box, 597–599
Pathfinder Soft dialog box, 604
Pathfinder submenu, 171
paths, 56–62, 100–101, 104–105, 239–276
adding to existing open path, 254–255
adding values of overlapping fills, 188
anchor points, 56, 101-102, 181–182, 255, 385–388
Area type, 296
around an existing path's stroke, 596
arrowheads, 189–190
Artwork mode, 59, 77, 359
as group, 268
averaging every point, 390
back of current layer, 140
backmost, 186
blends, 122
bloating, 190
bounding box, 620
changing Paint attributes, 301
changing way two or more interact, 597–603
closing, 58, 102–104, 223, 254, 259, 265

coloring type anchored to, 301
combining two or more into one, 599
common attributes, 188–189
compound, 59, 268, 329, 334
converting text paths into standard paths, 619–620
copying, 136
corners, 256
crossing, 250, 259
curve changes from clockwise to counterclockwise, 256
curve changing intensity, 256
curved corner points, 266–267
deleting, 186, 603
detail without all straight lines, 248
directions, 411–413, 582
distorting, 177
dividing overlaying into individual closed, 601–602
drawing, 239–240
duplicating portions, 271
editing, 101–103, 385–404
filling or stroking with patterns, 472
fills, 60, 187, 641–642
first-level selecting, 89
freeform, 242, 247
Freehand tool erasing, 252
front of current layer, 140
frontmost, 186
frontmost or backmost selected, 600
grouping, 140
in Artwork mode, 519
intersection, 186
jagged and smooth, 252–254
joining, 391
maintains its individuality, 602
merging, 187
modifying patterns during transformation, 508
moving, 182, 269, 486
new, 187, 594–596
offsetting from original, 183
open, 58, 102, 223, 250–251, 582
overlapping, 244
pasting from other programs, 136
Pen tool, 259
point locations, 256
Preview mode, 59, 77, 359
rectangles, 201
removing overlapped sections, 187

reversing direction, 413
rotating into, 398–399
running type along, 111
saving portions, 600
scaling, 184
selecting, 89–96, 137, 268–271
selecting unselected, 608
showing/hiding, 145–146
simulate transparency or
    shadows between two,
    604–605
skittles, 596
specify amount of color in
    intersecting, 604
splitting, 101, 348–350, 388–389
stroke color, 187–188
strokes, 60
tall spikes, 191
transformation
transforming, 286, 289, 401–403,
    486
type into editable paths, 329
Pattern command, 150
    dialog box, 150, 479, 485, 500,
        563
pattern tile, 472, 476, 479–480
patterns, 150, 471–486
    aren't only seamless, 476
    custom, 474–476
    default, 472–474
    diagonal line and grid, 484
    displaying, 347
    editable type outlines, 333–334
    editing, 472
    empty honeycomb, 562–563
    fills, 233
    lines and grids, 483–484
    listing, 472, 684
    modifying, 485
    moving in paths, 486
    naming, 476
    pattern tile, 472
    polygon creation, 559–563
    Preview mode, 377, 473
    putting patterns and gradients
        into, 485–486
    seamless, 477–480
    strokes, 233
    symmetrical, 480–483
    transforming, 113, 404, 472,
        486, 508
    transparent, 404, 472, 484–485
    viewing, 473–474
PDF format files, 535
Pen tool, 100, 240, 281, 429, 432,
        435, 444, 555, 577, 582, 612,
        639, 642, 644

anchor points, 256, 263–264
angled straight segment, 259
basic curve, 260
basic S curve, 261
closing paths, 259, 265
combination-corner anchor
    points, 257, 267
commandments, 262–264
curved-corner anchor points,
    257, 265–267
curves, 259–262
direction lines, 263
direction point, 263
drawing, 255–267
misdrawn curve, 264
paths, 239, 259–260
segments as long as possible,
    263
signifying line finished, 259
smooth anchor points, 257
straight lines, 256, 258–259
straight-corner anchor points,
    257
photographs, 662
Photoshop, 41, 79, 136, 453
    clipping path, 416
    color intensity increase, 531
    Filter⇨Distort⇨Twirl command,
        530
    Filter⇨Stylize⇨Mosaic
        command, 530
    filters, 169
    gradients, 469
    Image⇨Adjust⇨Hue/Saturation
        command, 531
    Image⇨Adjust⇨Levels
        command, 279
    Image⇨Effects⇨Distort
        command, 530
    Image⇨Image Size command,
        284
    Image⇨Map⇨Invert command,
        531
    Levels dialog box, 279
    Mode⇨Bitmap command, 279
    ⌘-L (Levels) keyboard
        shortcut, 279
    Path tool, 240
    Select⇨Inverse command, 530
    Select⇨Similar command, 531
    setting up Illustrator templates,
        279–280
    Similar feature, 531
    true negatives, 531
    vs. Illustrator filters, 529–531
picas, 204, 351

PICT File Format Plug-In, 537
PICT files
    as bitmapped image, 704
    mosaics, 545
    opening, 364, 537
    saving files as, 545
    templates, 278, 373
    tiling images, 175–176
    tracing, 106–107
pictures, 530
Pie Graph tool, 122–123
pie graphs, 493–494
    exploding pie effect, 494
Pixar, 747
Place Art command, 131
placed art name and disk path,
    536
Plug-Ins, 170, 535–538
    Acrobat PDF File Format, 535
    Artwork View Speedup, 143, 535
    listing, 196
    Overprint Black, 536
    PICT File Format, 537
    Pressure Support, 537
    specifying folder location, 517
Plug-Ins command, 135
    dialog box, 135, 532
Plug-Ins folder, 130, 170, 531–532,
    741
    Adobe Illustrator Startup file, 500
    location, 135
    preferences, 517
    relocating, 531–532
    Startup document, 345
Point type, 293–294
points, 62, 204, 351
    aligning with existing points,
        507–508
    averaging location, 151–152
    determining center by mean
        method, 390
    lining up, 389–390
    measuring distance between
        two, 108–109
    moving, 179–180, 183
    selecting, 94
points/inches/centimeters
    conversions, 204
Polygon filter, 176, 218–219
polygons, 176, 218–219
    3-D block steps, 562
    adding to Snow Scene, 218–219
    empty honeycomb pattern,
        562–563
    maximum number of sides, 218
    pattern creation, 559–563

pop-up menu, 21
pop-up tools, 86–87
PopChar, 336
PostScript, 30, 364
  benefits, 54–56
  laser printers, 30
  printing, 51–56
  transforming objects, 395–404
  what it does, 52–53
PostScript fonts, 36–39, 334–335
  mixing with TrueType fonts, 341
PostScript page description
  language, 37
Power Tip icon, 8
PowerPCs, 24
  FPU (Floating Point Unit), 590
  Illustrator 5.5 and, 3
PPD (PostScript Printer Description) file, 664, 670–671
  adding new halftone screens, 677
precise cursors, 509–511
preferences, 134–135, 499–500
  Adobe Illustrator Startup file,
    499–502
  document-specific changes, 500
  general, 134
  hyphenation, 135
  Illustrator remembering last
    settings, 500
  modifying application, 502–518
  palette placement, 517
  Plug-Ins Folder, 517
  Preferences submenu, 499
  setting, 133
  Toolbox placement, 517
Preferences command, 134–135
Preferences General (⌘-Shift-D)
  keyboard shortcut, 208
Preferences submenu, 129, 499, 502
preset gradients, 463
Pressure Support Plug-In, 537
pressure-sensitive tablet, 241,
  244, 247, 537
Preview command, 142
  ⌘-Y keyboard shortcut, 142, 655
Preview mode, 77–78, 142, 359–360
  color, 360
  combining with Artwork mode,
    362
  drawback, 78
  editing artwork, 142
  fills, 223
  interruptable redraw, 78
  Measure tool, 109
  paths, 59, 77, 145, 359
  patterns, 473–474

rectangles, 201
selected objects, 360, 509
strokes, 224
  vs. Artwork mode, 358–362
Preview Selection command, 143
  ⌘-Option-Y keyboard shortcut,
    143, 360
Preview Selection mode, 143, 358,
  360–361
preceding field (Shift-Tab)
  keyboard shortcut, 20,
  203, 321
preceding slider (Shift-Tab)
  keyboard shortcut, 236
Print All Separations (⌘-P)
  keyboard shortcut, 682–683,
  685
print area, 82
Print command, 134
  ⌘-P keyboard shortcut, 134,
    380, 655
  Print dialog box, 376, 380–381
printer fonts, 37, 39
printers
  changing information in
    Separator, 670–671
  PPD (PostScript Printer
    Description) file, 664
  screen default, 352
  selecting, 376–377, 664
printing, 134, 375–382, 655–663
  Apple LaserWriter driver,
    380–381
  background, 376
  Chooser, 376, 376–377
  color separations, 134, 375,
    655, 657–658, 663, 685, 687
  composites, 655–656
  direction of paper, 670
  Document Setup dialog box,
    376–377
  imagesetters, 657
  learning from experts, 657
  masks, 419–420
  Page Setup dialog box, 376
  positive and negative images,
    679
  PostScript, 51–56
  Print dialog box, 376
  process, 678–679
  process color, 662
  PS Printer driver, 381–382
  saving money with your
    computer, 678–679
  spot color, 658
  varnishes, 662

printing companies, 657
PrintMonitor, 376
process color, 660–661
  color separations, 659–660
  converting custom color to,
    172, 540, 662
  dots, 660
  fills and strokes, 232
  increasing/decreasing fills, 171
  limitations, 660– 662
  moving sliders, 236
  new colors, 661
  printing, 662
  reasons for adding spot colors,
    662
  separation secrets, 660
processors, 24
programs, 41–42
  Adobe Type Manager (ATM), 168
  automatic adaptation to
    environment, 16
  CameraMan, 760
  consistency on Macintosh, 15
  Dimensions, 2, 136, 364
  disk space needed, 45
  double-clicking icon, 16
  Edit menu, 15
  Eric's Ultimate Solitaire, 16
  F/A-18 Hornet, 41
  File menu, 15
  Finder, 33–34, 41
  Font Downloader, 686
  FontMonger, 340
  Fontographer, 340, 651
  FontStudio, 340
  Fractal Design Painter, 31, 79, 453
  FreeHand, 77
  how they operate, 41–42
  Island Trapper, 694
  LaserWriter Utility, 686
  launching, 41, 44
  Macromedia Director, 41, 760
  memory and, 44–45
  Microsoft Word, 41
  number limitations, 42
  opening desktop publishing
    and graphics, 345
  PageMaker, 51, 657
  Photoshop, 41, 79, 136, 453
  PrintMonitor, 376
  PSPrint, 686
  QuarkXPress, 41, 79, 142, 657,
    679
  QuicKeys, 593
  QuickTime 1.6.1, 759
  quitting, 42

random access memory (RAM)
needed, 45
SAM, 739
Separator, 2, 134, 142, 375,
663–664
Software FPU, 171, 533, 590, 737
Streamline, 2, 107, 136, 364,
699–706, 762
Stuffit, 739
TrapWise, 694
Typestry, 335, 762
TypeStyler, 340
Virex, 739
PS Printer 8.01, 133, 377, 381–382
PS Printers Page Setup dialog
box, 380
pseudolinear blends, 436–437
PSPrint, 686
PSPrinter 8, 742
Publish and Subscribe feature,
138–139
Publisher Options command, 138
Publishing command, 138–139
Punk filter, 191–192, 528, 534, 580,
584–585, 591
dialog box, 585
Puzzle, 743

Q

QuarkXPress, 41, 79, 142, 657, 679
⌘-Option-Shift-[(Decrease
Tracking) keyboard
shortcut, 513
⌘-Option-Shift-] (Increase
Tracking) keyboard
shortcut, 513
QuicKeys, 593
Layer Fixer, 523
QuickTime, 743, 759
Quit command, 42, 129, 135
⌘-Q keyboard shortcut, 42, 135

R

radial blends, 442–443
radial gradients, 121–122, 398
RAM (Random Access Memory),
42, 44, 736, 738
Random Mangle filters, 568,
574–580
Roughen filter, 576–578
Scribble filters, 578–580
Tweak filter, 578–580
Ransom Note, 4, 339, 761–762

Reapply Last Filter (⌘-Shift-E)
keyboard shortcut, 534,
575, 579
Rectangle dialog box, 203–208,
210, 295, 505
Rectangle Size dialog box, 296
Rectangle tool, 108, 201, 204, 476,
505
origin point, 202
Rectangle type, 295
rectangles from center, 205
tracing EPS image shapes, 214
Rectangle type, 110, 293, 295–296
text linking, 326
rectangles, 201–204
Artwork mode, 201
black, 204
corner radius, 210
drawing from center, 201, 205
measuring different horizontal
and vertical distances, 286
path, 201
Preview mode, 201
reverse rounded, 210–211
rounded corners, 203, 206–210
specific size, 203
straight corner anchor points,
201
straight line segments, 201
rectangular paths dividing into
equal sections, 620–623
Redo command, 76–77, 136
⌘-Shift-Z keyboard shortcut, 136
Reduce filter, 603
Reflect dialog box, 116
Reflect tool, 111, 116, 396–397, 468
switching lengths and angled
between direction points,
402
symmetrical tiles, 399–400
Release Compound Path (⌘-9)
keyboard shortcut, 155, 407
Release Guides (⌘-6) keyboard
shortcut, 289, 290
Release Wrap command, 166
removable cartridge drives: See
Syquest drives
Repeat Transform command,
140, 404
⌘-D keyboard shortcut, 140,
396, 399, 403–404, 435, 450,
543, 555, 563
Reset Color Swatch (⌘-Shift)
keyboard shortcut, 237
resources

people and service company,
745–746
software company, 746–747
Return key, 20
reverse rounded rectangle, 210–211
Revert Text Path filter, 340, 532,
619–620, 753
dialog box, 619
Revert To Saved command, 131
Riders files, 537–538
Right Alignment (⌘-Shift-R)
keyboard shortcut, 163
Rotate dialog box, 403, 435, 484
Rotate Each filter, 184, 449,
593–594
dialog box, 184, 594
Rotate tool, 111, 113, 184, 435,
449, 456, 484, 555, 558, 563,
593
Chinese throwing stars, 403
constrain angle, 503
dialog box, 113
dragging anchor point, 402
reverse rounded rectangle,
210–211
rotating, 214, 403
winding path, 398–399
Roughen dialog box, 177–178,
577–578, 644
Roughen filter, 177–179, 528, 568,
574, 576–578, 640–641
adding anchor points to paths,
578
artwork tears, 577–587
Round Corners dialog box, 192,
208, 546, 557–558, 586
Round Corners filter, 192, 208,
546, 557–558, 580, 586–587
rounded rectangle, 505–506
Rounded Rectangle tool, 108, 206,
505
rounded rectangles, 206–210
corner radius, 207, 208
origin point, 206
roundness of corners, 208
rounded square, 206–210
corner radius, 207
drawing from center, 208
origin point, 206
Rows & Columns dialog box,
620–621
Rows & Columns filter, 340,
620–623, 753
Ruler Centimeters (⌘-Shift-N)
keyboard shortcut, 145,
286, 352, 363, 511

Ruler Inches (⌘-Shift-I) keyboard shortcut, 145, 286, 352, 363, 511
Ruler Picas (⌘-Shift-P) keyboard shortcut, 145, 286, 352, 363, 511
rulers
    dotted lines corresponding to the cursor's position, 286
    measurement system, 145, 286, 328, 351–352, 363, 511
    measuring distances, 285–286
    on/off, 285
    origin, 285, 363
    pulling guides from, 289
    showing/hiding, 145, 363

S

SAM, 739
Same Fill Color filter, 188, 531, 608–609
Same Paint Style filter, 188, 609
Same Stroke Color filter, 188, 609–610
Same Stroke Weight filter, 189, 610
Samples folder, 741
Saturate filter, 173, 534
Saturate More filter, 174, 534
Save All Separations (⌘-S) keyboard shortcut, 686
Save As command, 130
    dialog box, 16, 130–131, 365, 372
    Illustrator version 5.5, 126, 131
Save command, 130
    ⌘-S keyboard shortcut, 130, 365, 366
Scale dialog box, 115, 444, 509
Scale Each filter, 184, 593–594
    dialog box, 184, 594
Scale tool, 111, 115, 333, 396, 444, 593, 718
    constrain angles, 503
    lengthening direction lines, 402
    resizing type, 161
    setting object origin, 555
scanners, 29
Scatter Graph tool, 122–123
scatter graphs, 494
Scissors tool, 101–103, 411, 479, 577, 612
    anchor points, 388
    cutting overlapping path, 404
    end points, 389
    splitting paths, 388–389
screen
    color representation, 135

redraw speed, 532
Screen Capture (⌘-Shift-3) keyboard shortcut, 545, 549
screen fonts, 36: *See also* bitmap fonts
    linking with printer fonts, 39
scribble, 179
Scribble dialog box, 179, 578, 579, 580
Scribble filter, 179, 568, 573–574, 578–580
    adding anchor points, 591
    Tweak filter, 534
scroll bars, 19, 83, 357
SCSI Probe, 765
seamless patterns, 477–480
Select All command, 137, 301
    ⌘-A keyboard shortcut, 91, 137, 275, 290, 301, 326, 327, 419, 611, 619, 648, 715
    ⌘-period keyboard shortcut, 137, 143
Select filters, 188–189, 528, 607–608
Select Inverse filter, 189, 608, 611
Select Masks filter, 189, 533, 608, 611–612
Select None command, 137
    ⌘-Shift-A keyboard shortcut, 137
Select Stray Points filter, 189, 608, 612
selecting before doing, 21
Selection tool, 89–91, 93, 110, 151–152, 165–166, 301, 306, 390, 392, 406, 429, 448–449, 549, 555
    Command (⌘) key, 93
    dragging objects, 248, 256
    drop shadow, 204
    groups, 140
    Option-clicking, 285
    paths, 268–269
    selecting, 93, 268, 274, 388
selection tools, 89–96
    Direct Selection tool, 89, 94
    Group Selection tool, 89, 94–96
    Selection tool, 89, 93
    Shift key, 92
Selection/Direct Selection tools (⌘-Tab) keyboard shortcut, 89, 93
selections, clearing, 73
semistraight segments, 251–252
Send To Back command, 140, 326
    ⌘-hyphen keyboard shortcut, 140, 217, 273, 396, 419
Separator, 2, 134, 142, 375, 663–664

bleed, 669–670
bounding box, 669–670
changing page size, 671–672
changing printer information, 670–671
color bar, 668
converting custom color to process color, 662
crop marks, 669
customizing tints of gray, 680
emulsion, 674
guides, 683
imageable area, 346
Illustrator files as EPS files, 664
label symbol, 668
Landscape orientation, 672
list of color separations, 683
main Separator window, 664, 666
margin marks, 666–669
modifying Transfer function, 680–682
overprinting color bar, 668
page direction, 669–670
page orientation, 672
Portrait orientation, 672
printing color separations, 685
printing composite, 685
printing positive and negative images, 679
registration mark, 667
relabeling file, 683
running for first time, 664
saving color separations, 686
secrets, 686–687
Separation window, 664, 682–686
setting halftone screen, 674–678
star target, 667
tint bar, 668
Separator & Utilities, 741
service bureaus, 658
Settings⇨Use Default Bounding Box command, 670
Settings⇨Use Default Marks command, 667
Settings⇨Use Default Settings command, 671
shadows, 396–397, 541
shape blends, 443–453
    circle to star, 445–446
    complex, 446–448
    computer vents, 443–445
    muted reflective surfaces in type, 450–451
    realism, 450–453
    simulating real surfaces, 452–453
shape creation tools

Oval tool, 108
Rectangle tool, 108
Rounded Rectangle tool, 108
shapes, 53, 108
  angling, 222
  basic, 199–217
  combining strokes and fills, 226
  constraining, 108, 222
  cool shapes with filters, 217–222
  drawing from center, 108
  equilateral, 218
  filling, 223
  origin point, 202
  rectangles, 201–204
  strokes, 224
  tracing EPS image with basic
    shapes, 214
Shear dialog box, 118
Shear tool, 111, 117–118, 396, 403,
  503
Shift key, 22, 40, 87, 92, 206, 208,
  214, 396
Show All command, 141
  ⌘-4 keyboard shortcut, 141,
    460, 543
Show Borders command, 138
Show Character command, 195
Show Clipboard command, 74–75,
  139
Show Edges command, 146
Show Gradient command, 195
Show Guides command, 146
Show Info command, 194
  ⌘-Control-I keyboard shortcut,
    296
Show Layers command, 194
  ⌘-Control-L keyboard
    shortcut, 521
Show Object (⌘-4) keyboard
    shortcut, 291
Show Page Tiling command, 145
Show Paint Style command, 195
Show Paragraph command, 195
Show Rulers command, 145
Show Tab Ruler (⌘-Shift-T)
    keyboard shortcut, 195
Show Template command, 145
Show Toolbox command, 194
Show/Hide Character (⌘-T)
    keyboard shortcut, 195
Show/Hide Edges (⌘-Shift-H)
    keyboard shortcut, 145–146,
    363
Show/Hide Info (⌘-Control-I)
    keyboard shortcut, 194

Show/Hide Layers (⌘-Control-L)
    keyboard shortcut, 194
Show/Hide Paint Style (⌘-I)
    keyboard shortcut, 195
Show/Hide Paragraph
  ⌘-Shift-P keyboard shortcut, 195
  ⌘-Shift-T keyboard shortcut, 195
Show/Hide Rulers (⌘-R)
    keyboard shortcut, 145,
    285, 289, 363
Show/Hide Toolbox (⌘-Control-T)
    keyboard shortcut, 88, 194
SIMMS (single in-line memory
    modules), 44
Size command, 160–161
  ⌘-Shift-S keyboard shortcut,
    160–161
  submenu, 160
skittles, 596
Smart Punctuation filter, 340,
  624–625, 753
  dialog box, 624–625
smooth anchor points, 257
  Freehand tool, 249
smooth points, 63, 100, 262
  combination corner points, 394
  converting, 393–394
  curved corner points, 394
  Freehand tool, 254
  linked direction points, 63
  straight corner points, 393
  switching lengths and angles
    between direction points,
    402
  two direction lines of different
    lengths, 262
  vs. curved corner points, 265
Snap to Point feature, 392, 507–508
Snow Scene
  adding polygon, 218–219
  coloring background and sign,
    234
  coloring hat and barn, 232
  coloring snow and snowman,
    231
  coloring stars, 233
  coloring walls, 233
  drawing sky, 222
  finishing touches, 234
Soft filter, 188, 604
Software FPU, 171, 533, 590, 737
special characters, 335–338
  Symbol typefaces, 336–338
special shapes, 174–177
spell-checking text, 616–618

Spiral filter, 176
spirals, 176
spot color
  color separation, 658–659
  custom color, 659
  limitations, 659
  printing, 658
  reasons for adding to process
    colors, 662
spring tube blends, 456
Square from Center (Option-Shift)
    keyboard shortcut, 206
squares, 206
  measuring horizontal and
    vertical distances, 286
stacked column graphs, 490–491
Stacked-column Graph tool,
  122–123
standard keyboard, 24
Star filter, 176, 218, 220–222, 555
  ⌘-Shift-E keyboard shortcut, 222
stars, 176, 220–222
  anchor points, 221
  point limitations, 221
Startup file: *See* Adobe Illustrator
    Startup file
status bar, 83
storage memory, 42
stories, 110, 160
straight corner anchor points,
  201, 257
straight corner points, 64, 100,
  249, 386, 394
straight line segment, 201
  when it is selected, 270
Streamline, 2, 107, 136, 364,
  699–706, 762
  100% magnification, 705
  acquiring anti-aliased PICT,
    PICT resource, or TWAIN
    mechanism, 704
  additional pixels relative to
    Magic Wand, 704
  closing active document, 703
  Color/Grayscale Setup dialog
    box, 705
  commands, 700–705
  Conversion Setup dialog box, 705
  converted Illustrator paths, 705
  converting bitmapped art to
    paths, 706
  converting multiple files, 704
  copying objects, 704
  Custom Color dialog box, 705
  cutting objects, 704
  Delete Anchor Point tool, 702

deleting objects, 704
demo version, 4
deselecting objects, 704
displaying Paint Style palette, 702
Edit⇨Adjust Levels command (⌘-L), 705
Edit⇨Clear command, 704
Edit⇨Copy command (⌘-C), 704
Edit⇨Copy Special command, 704
Edit⇨Cut command (⌘-X), 704
Edit⇨Fill command (⌘-F), 705
Edit⇨Grow Selection command (⌘-G), 704
editing same color pixels, 705
Edit⇨Paste command (⌘-V), 704
Edit⇨Select All command (⌘-A), 704
Edit⇨Select Inverse command, 704
Edit⇨Select None command (⌘-D), 704
Edit⇨Select Similar command, 705
Edit⇨Smooth Path command, 705
Edit⇨Undo command (⌘-Z), 704
Eraser tool, 702
Eyedropper tool, 702
File⇨Acquire command, 704
File⇨Batch Select command, 704
File⇨Close command (⌘-W), 703
File⇨Convert command (⌘-R), 703
File⇨Import Clipboard PICT command, 704
File⇨Import Styles command, 704
File⇨Open command (⌘-O), 703
File⇨Preferences command, 704
File⇨Quit command (⌘-Q), 704
File⇨Revert command, 703
File⇨Save Art As command, 703
File⇨Save Art command (⌘-S), 703
File⇨Save Pixel Image As command, 703
General Preferences or Plug-Ins, 704
Hand tool, 702
hiding toolbox, 705
image document window size, 705
importing styles from Illustrator, 704

Info palette, 705
Lasso tool, 702
Levels dialog box, 705
Line tool, 702
Magic Wand tool, 701
Marquee tool, 701
menus, 703–705
Options⇨Color/Grayscale Setup command (⌘-B), 705
Options⇨Conversion Setup command (⌘-J), 705
Options⇨Custom Color command (⌘-U), 705
Options⇨Paint Style command (⌘-I), 705
Options⇨Settings command (⌘-T), 705
Paint Style palette, 705
pasting objects, 704
Pencil tool, 701
quitting, 704
saving converted artwork, 703
scrolling document window, 702
selecting all pixels or paths, 704
selecting unselected, 704
Selection tool, 702
Settings dialog box, 705
smoothing paths, 705
Swatch, 702
toolbox, 700–702
tracing images, 281
undoing last action, 704
View⇨Actual Size command (⌘-H), 705
View⇨Artwork command (⌘-E), 705
View⇨Fit In Window command (⌘-M), 705
View⇨Hide Toolbox command, 705
View⇨Preview command (⌘-Y), 705
View⇨Preview Selection command, 705
View⇨Show Info command, 705
View⇨Show Template command, 705
View⇨Zoom In command (⌘-+), 705
View⇨Zoom Out command (⌘-hyphen), 705
Zoom In tool, 702
Zoom Out tool, 702
zooming one level, 705
stroke blends, 453–461
color, 455

glows, 458–459
neon effects, 460–461
Stroke Style panel, 227, 237–238
strokes, 629–651
adding passing zone to highway, 648
attributes, 237–238
Black option, 231
cap style, 224
charts, 632–635
color, 224, 230–234
combining with fills, 226
custom color, 232
end caps, 238
essentials, 630
film, 635
foreground/background relationship to fills, 273
ghosted type, 638
gradients, 469, 596
highway design, 644–648
join style, 224
joins, 238
magic, 630–632
miter limit, 224, 238
multiple for type, 639
multiple jagged edges, 640–641
no stroke, 231
on path surrounding Area type, 297–298
outlining, 183
parallel, 631
paths, 60
patterns, 233, 596
Preview mode, 224
Process box, 232
putting type into, 650–651
railroad tracks, 642–643
rough edges, 640–641
shapes, 224
solid or dashed, 238
style, 224
type, 638–639
vs. brush strokes, 243
weight, 224
White option, 231
wild river, 644
Stuffit, 739
styles, importing, 132, 375
Stylize filters, 189–192, 568, 580–587
Add Anchor Points filter, 534
Add Arrowheads, 581–582
Bloat filter, 584–585
Calligraphy filter, 587
Drop Shadows filter, 583–584

Punk filter, 584–585
Round Corners filter, 586–587
Subscribe To command, 138
Super ATM, 41
Superdrives, 27
Symbol typefaces, 336–338
symmetrical patterns, 480–483
Syquest drives, 27–28
  memory, 44
  sizes, 28
System 6, 32–33
System 7, 32–33
System 7.1, 32–35
System 7.5, 32, 736–738
  CPU (Central Processing Unit), 737
  FPU (Floating Point Unit), 737
  RAM (random access memory), 738
system requirements
  additional hardware, 736
  computer, 735–736
  RAM (random access memory), 736
system software, 32–33

T

Tab key, 20, 203
Tab Ruler palette, 327–329
  ⌘-Shift-T keyboard shortcut, 327
  showing, 195
tabs
  Auto tab stops, 328
  deselecting all, 329
  Illustrator 5.0 problems, 326–327
  setting, 328
  style changes, 329
tape drives and DAT (digital audio tape) format, 29
Teeple Graphics, 746
templates, 106, 277–284
  clarity, 278
  EPS image as full-color template, 283
  opening, 373
  Paint file format, 278
  PICT file format, 278
  quality, 277
  setting up Illustrator in Photoshop, 279–280
  showing/hiding, 145, 362
  tracing, 281, 506–507
  when are they not templates, 282–284

terrabytes, 43
text
  changing case, 615
  copying, 74
  cutting, 74
  default values, 294
  exporting, 613
  finding and replacing, 613–615
  format to save, 193
  hyphenation, 323
  importation formats, 132
  linking, 165–166, 325–326
  pasting, 74
  searching, 193
  selecting, 21
  spell-checking, 616–618
  styles, 313
  unlinking blocks, 166
  viewing patterns, 474
  wrapping around objects, 166
Text Export filter, 613
Text filters, 193, 340, 613–625, 753–754
Text Find filter, 613–615
  dialog box, 193, 613–614
text string, foreground and background, 273
3G Graphics, Inc., 746
third-party clip art, 743
third-party filters, 533
tiles, symmetrical, 399–400
Timothy G. Freed Design, 745
title bar, 83, 345
Toolbox, 20, 85–89, 764–766
  ⌘-Control-T keyboard shortcut, 201
  accessing tools, 765
  Blend tool, 86
  close box, 88
  Gradient Vector tool, 86
  Graph tool, 86
  Hand tool, 86
  keyboard shortcuts, 764
  Measure tool, 86
  Page tool, 86
  placement preferences, 517
  selecting tools, 86
  showing/hiding, 88, 194, 201
  Type tool, 86
  Zoom tool, 86
tools, 20, 85–124
  accessing, 765
  Add Anchor Point, 101–103
  Area Type, 110–111
  Auto Trace, 106
  Blend, 120, 122

Brush, 103
Convert Direction Point, 101–103
default, 86
Delete Anchor Point, 101–103
Direct Selection, 89, 94
Eyedropper, 119–120
Freehand, 104
Gradient Vector, 120–121
Graph, 122
Group Selection, 89, 94–96
Hand, 96
Illustrator 5.0, 750–751
Illustrator 5.5, 755
keyboard shortcuts, 765
Measure, 108–109
Oval, 108
Page, 124
Paint Bucket, 119–120
Path Type, 110–111
paths, 100–108
Pen, 100
pop-up, 86
Rectangle, 108
Reflect, 116
Rotate, 113
Rounded Rectangle, 108
Scale, 115
Scissors, 101–103
selecting, 86
Selection, 89–96
shape creation, 108
Shear, 117–118
transformation, 111–118
Type, 109–111
viewing, 96–99
Zoom, 97–99
Zoom In, 353–355
Zoom Out, 353–355
Track (Kern) (⌘-Shift-K) keyboard shortcut, 317
trackballs, 25–26
  Brush tool, 244
tracking, 316–319, 513
  values, 318
Transfer function, modifying, 680–684
transform each filters, 593–594
transformation tools, 111–118
  Constrain Angle setting, 113
  on portions of paths, 401–403
  Reflect tool, 111, 116, 396–397
  repeating usage, 396
  Rotate tool, 111, 113
  Scale tool, 111, 115, 396
  shadow creation, 396
  Shear tool, 111, 117–118, 396

transforming objects, 395–404
    creating shadows, 396–397
    gradients, 398
    making tiles, 399–400
    patterns, 404
    portions of paths, 401–403
    rotating into kaleidoscopes,
        403–404
    rotating into path, 398–399
transparent patterns, 472
Trap dialog box, 605–606
Trap filter, 185, 188, 528, 605–606,
    698, 754
trapping, 188, 605–606, 687–698
    amount necessary, 691
    basic choke trap, 692–693
    basic spread trap, 693
    complex techniques in
        Illustrator 5.0, 694–698
    Illustrator 5.0 files, 691–693
    Illustrator 5.5, 698
    round joins and ends options,
        694
    separate layer for trapping
        objects, 694
    trap gradations by stroking
        them, 695
    what it does, 687–688
    when it is not worth doing
        yourself, 694
    why it is necessary, 690–691
TrapWise, 694
Trim filter, 187
Trim Marks, 176–177, 553–554
    color separations, 553–554
Trim Marks filter, 155, 176–177,
    553–554
TrueType fonts, 38–40, 168, 334
    mixing with PostScript fonts, 341
tubular blends, 454–455
Tutorial folder, 741
tutorials, 759–760
Tweak dialog box, 180, 579
Tweak filter, 180, 568, 574, 578–580
    adding anchor points, 591
    Scribble filter, 534
Twirl filter, 180–181, 528, 530,
    568, 571–574
    anchor points, 573, 591
    arced illustrations, 574
    constraints, 573
    dialog box, 180–181, 573–574
twirling, 530
type, 109–111, 159–169, 293–341
    alignment, 162–169, 304
    arcing, 332–333

Baseline shift feature, 513
becoming path, 303–309
below path, 304
centered, 162
character attributes, 312–319
color, 300–301
compound paths and, 410–411
constricted to rectangular
    area, 295–296
controlling flow, 324–329
defining beginning for
    greeking, 514–515
editable outlines, 168–169,
    329–335
editing, 311
entire area selection, 309
expanding/condensing, 316
fitting in space, 166
flush left, 162
flush right, 163
heavy weights, 301
increasing/decreasing size or
    leading, 512
justified, 163–164
kerning, 301, 316–319
keyboard shortcuts, 768–769
leading values, 315
measuring, 314, 512
multiple strokes, 639
on top and bottom of circle,
    304–306
outlining, 319
paragraph, 160
placing in any area, 296–303
putting into strokes, 650–651
replacing as you type, 311
running along paths, 111
scaling, 160
selecting, 110, 309–311, 326
shadows, 396–397
Shift key selection, 311
single point defining location,
    294
sizes, 160–161, 314
special characters, 335–338
specifying fonts, 313
stories, 160
strokes, 638–639
styles, 313
text linking, 325–326
tracking, 316–319
upper and lower size limits, 512
wrapping, 325
x-height, 301
Type 1 PostScript fonts, 168
type areas, 293

all text selection, 310
Area type, 293, 296–303
individual character selection,
    310
paragraph selection, 310
Path type, 293, 303–309
Point type, 293–294
Rectangle type, 293, 295–296
selecting, 309–310
Type Insertion bar, 304
Type menu, 159–169, 752
    commands, 764
    keyboard shortcuts, 764
Type tool, 86, 110, 294–295, 306
    rectangle type, 110
type tools
    Area Type, 109, 111
    intelligent switching, 110
    Path Type, 109, 111
    Type, 110
typefaces, listing, 314
Type⇨Alignment command, 320
Type⇨Alignment⇨Centered
    command, 306, 322
Type⇨Alignment⇨Flush Left
    command, 321
Type⇨Alignment⇨Flush Right
    command, 321
Type⇨Alignment⇨Justify
    command, 322
Type⇨Alignment⇨Justify Last
    Line command, 322
Type⇨Character command, 160,
    312
Type⇨Convert Outlines
    command, 450, 474
Type⇨Create Outlines command,
    273, 329, 341, 448, 638
Type⇨Kern command, 312
Type⇨Leading⇨Other command,
    312
Type⇨Link Blocks command, 326
Type⇨Make Wrap command,
    325, 327
Type⇨Paragraph command, 320
Type⇨Size⇨Other command, 312
Type⇨Spacing command, 320
Type⇨Track (Kern) command, 317
Typestry, 335, 762
TypeStyler, 340
typestyles, missing, 341

U

Unadjusted tint densities dialog
    box, 680

Undo command, 76–77, 136
⌘-Z keyboard shortcut, 136,
241, 313, 329, 522, 559, 573,
575, 577, 579, 582, 584, 667
undoing actions, 513–514
Ungroup command, 141
⌘-U keyboard shortcut, 141,
558, 582, 648, 697
ungrouping, 275–276
Unite filter, 186, 468, 528, 599
Add Arrowheads filter, 534
clay star, 558–559
cleaning up overlapping brush
strokes, 244
eliminating overlapping areas
that appear as loops, 287
Offset Path filter, 534
path color, 599
reducing skittles, 596
Unlink Blocks command, 166
⌘-Shift-U keyboard shortcut, 166
Unlock command, 141
⌘-2 keyboard shortcut, 141, 290
Untitled Art 1 command, 195
User dictionary, 617

V

varnishes, 662
video in and out, 31
View menu, 141–148, 355–356, 751
commands, 763
keyboard shortcuts, 763
View⇨Actual Size command, 81,
98, 355
View⇨Artwork command, 59, 359
View⇨Fit In Window command,
81, 98, 355, 449
View⇨Hide Edges command, 363
viewing tools, 96–99
Hand tool, 96
Zoom tool, 97–99
View⇨New View command, 364
View⇨Preview command, 59,
359, 655
View⇨Preview Selection
command, 360
View⇨Show Guides command, 363
View⇨Show Page Tiling
command, 363
View⇨Show/Hide Rulers
command, 285, 363
View⇨Show Template command,
362
View⇨Zoom In command, 355

View⇨Zoom Out command, 355
views, custom, 142, 147
Virex, 739
VW Corrado, 716–724
adding little things, 723
background, 724
body creation, 719–720
getting lighting just right, 724
glass and tail lights, 721
interior design, 720–721
molding and pieces, 720
panel gradients, 720
preparing to illustrate, 717–719
trunk lock, 722
wheels, 723

W

Wacom pressure-sensitive tablet,
247
Warnock, John, 68
Window menu, 80, 194–195, 752
commands, 764
keyboard shortcuts, 764
Window⇨Hide Info command, 108
Window⇨Hide Layers command,
521
Window⇨Hide Paint Style
command, 226
Window⇨New Window command,
362
Window⇨Show Character
command, 312
Window⇨Show Info command, 296
Window⇨Show Layers command,
214, 282, 519, 521–522, 719
Window⇨Show Paint Style
command, 226
Window⇨Show Paragraph
command, 320
Window⇨Show Tab Ruler
command, 327–328
windows, 17–19
accidentally scrolling while
drawing, 244
active, 17
closing, 19
functions, 16
moving, 17
multiple, 362
new, 194, 362
resizing, 19
scroll bars, 19
toggling between sizes, 19
vs. palettes, 79–81

wireframe mode, 142
words, double-clicking, 21
WYSIWYG (What You See Is What
You Get), 51

X

XTND Translators, 742

Z

Zapf Dingbats, 336
Zoom In command, 146
⌘-] keyboard shortcut, 146
⌘-spacebar keyboard
shortcut, 353
Zoom In Level (⌘-]) keyboard
shortcut, 355
Zoom In tool, 146, 353–355
⌘-spacebar keyboard
shortcut, 88
marquee, 355
where you click, 354
Zoom Out command, 146
⌘-[keyboard shortcut, 146
⌘-Option-spacebar keyboard
shortcut, 355
Zoom Out Level (⌘-[) keyboard
shortcut, 355
Zoom Out tool, 146, 353–355
Zoom tool, 86, 97–99, 353–355
100% view, 355
instantly zooming out, 355
marquees, 98
Option key, 98

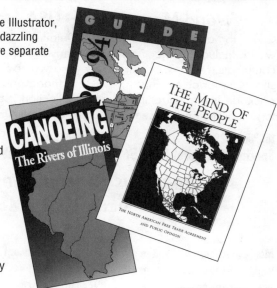

Dynamic Graphics, Inc.

Dynamic Graphics, Inc., the "How-To Company," is the leading name in quality, affordable subscription art and idea services in both traditional and electronic formats. Established in 1964, the company offers a wide range of subscription art services for graphic communicators, including Electronic Clipper®, Electronic Print Media Service®, Designer's Club®, and Electronic Volk® for electronic designers and Clipper®, Print Media Service®, and Volk® for traditional designers.

For product and ordering information:
In the United States and Canada, call toll-free 800/255-8800 and specify Priority Code #50510500. Outside the United States, contact your local Dynamic Graphics sales representative.

Dynamic Graphics, Inc.
6000 N. Forest Park Drive, Peoria, IL 61614-3592
800/255-8800 FAX 309/688-5873

MacWorld Illustrator Bible
Special Pricing
You've seen the demo..now you're ready for the real thing!

Pixar Typestry

Pixar Typestry is exciting software which invokes RenderMan magic to turn fonts and Adobe Illustrator files into extraordinary three-dimensional images. Pixar Typestry is ideal software for those who are creating logos, brochures, newsletters, ads, and slide or multimedia presentations.

System Requirements:
Macintosh - Any MacII running 6.07 or higher, Multifinder, FPU recommended, 32-bit QuickDraw, 8MB of RAM, a color display and 5 MB of disk space.

Pixar One Twenty Eight

Pixar One Twenty Eight is Pixar's private collection of high-quality, photographic textures. The 128 unique 512x512x24 bit images in TIFF format can be easily accessed through plug-ins for Photoshop and PhotoStyler. The CD can be read by any application that can read TIFF files on Windows, Macintosh and UNIX.

System Requirements:
Macintosh - Any Apple Macintoch computer with color monitor and card. 4MB of RAM, hard drive, System 6.07 or later and 32 bit QuickDraw 1.2.

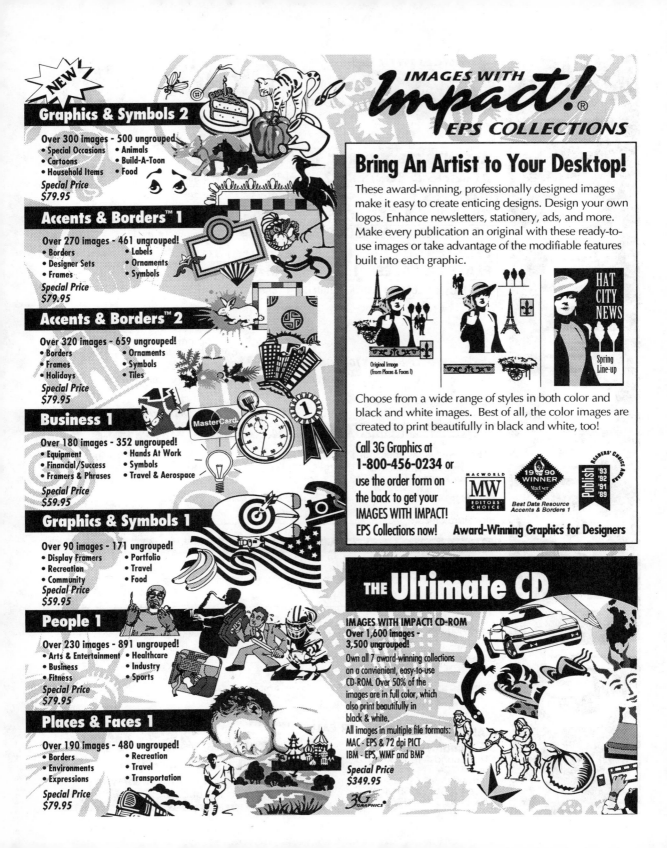

Order Form

Order Center: (800) 762-2974 (8 a.m.-5 p.m., PST, weekdays) or (415) 312-0650

For Fastest Service: Photocopy This Order Form and FAX it to: (415) 358-1260

Quantity	ISBN	Title	Price	Total

Shipping & Handling Charges

Subtotal	U.S.	Canada & International	International Air Mail
Up to $20.00	Add $3.00	Add $4.00	Add $10.00
$20.01-40.00	$4.00	$5.00	$20.00
$40.01-60.00	$5.00	$6.00	$25.00
$60.01-80.00	$6.00	$8.00	$35.00
Over $80.00	$7.00	$10.00	$50.00

In U.S. and Canada, shipping is UPS ground or equivalent.
For Rush shipping call (800) 762-2974.

Subtotal _____

CA residents add
applicable sales tax _____

IN and MA residents add
5% sales tax _____

IL residents add
6.25% sales tax _____

RI residents add
7% sales tax _____

Shipping _____

Total _____

Ship to:

Name _____

Company _____

Address _____

City/State/Zip _____

Daytime Phone _____

Payment: ❏ Check to IDG Books (US Funds Only)   ❏ Visa   ❏ Mastercard   ❏ American Express

Card# _____ Exp._____ Signature_____

Please send this order form to: IDG Books, 155 Bovet Road, Suite 310, San Mateo, CA 94402.

Allow up to 3 weeks for delivery. Thank you!

IDG BOOKS
WORLDWIDE
LICENSE AGREEMENT

**Important — read carefully before opening the software packet(s). This is a
legal agreement between you (either an individual or an entity) and IDG
Books Worldwide, Inc. (IDG). By opening the accompanying sealed packet(s)
containing the software disc, you acknowledge that you have read and
accept the following IDG License Agreement. If you do not agree and do not
want to be bound by the terms of this Agreement, promptly return the book
and the unopened software packet(s) to the place you obtained them for a
full refund.**

1. License. This License Agreement (Agreement) permits you to use one copy of the
enclosed Software program(s) on a single computer. The Software is in "use" on a
computer when it is loaded into temporary memory (i.e., RAM) or installed into permanent memory (e.g., hard disc, CD-ROM, or other storage device) of that computer.

2. Copyright. The entire contents of this disc and the compilation of the Software are
copyrighted and protected by both United States copyright laws and international
treaty provisions. You may only (a) make one copy of the Software for backup or
archival purposes, or (b) transfer the Software to a single hard disc, provided that you
keep the original for backup or archival purposes. The individual programs on the disc
are copyrighted by the authors of each program respectively. Each program has its own
use permissions and limitations. To use each program, you must follow the individual
requirements and restrictions detailed for each in Appendix E of this Book. Do not use a
program if you do not want to follow its Licensing Agreement. None of the material on
this disc or listed in this Book may ever be distributed, in original or modified form, for
commercial purposes.

3. Other Restrictions. You may not rent or lease the Software. You may transfer the
Software and user documentation on a permanent basis provided you retain no copies
and the recipient agrees to the terms of this Agreement. You may not reverse engineer,
decompile, or disassemble the Software except to the extent that the foregoing restriction is expressly prohibited by applicable law. If the Software is an update or has been
updated, any transfer must include the most recent update and all prior versions.

IDG BOOKS WORLDWIDE REGISTRATION CARD

RETURN THIS REGISTRATION CARD FOR FREE CATALOG

Title of this book: Macworld Illustrator 5.0/5.5 Bible

My overall rating of this book: ❑ Very good [1] ❑ Good [2] ❑ Satisfactory [3] ❑ Fair [4] ❑ Poor [5]

How I first heard about this book:

❑ Found in bookstore; name: [6]

❑ Advertisement: [8]

❑ Word of mouth; heard about book from friend, co-worker, etc.: [10]

❑ Book review: [7]

❑ Catalog: [9]

❑ Other: [11]

What I liked most about this book:

What I would change, add, delete, etc., in future editions of this book:

Other comments:

Number of computer books I purchase in a year: ❑ 1 [12] ❑ 2-5 [13] ❑ 6-10 [14] ❑ More than 10 [15]

I would characterize my computer skills as: ❑ Beginner [16] ❑ Intermediate [17] ❑ Advanced [18] ❑ Professional [19]

I use ❑ DOS [20] ❑ Windows [21] ❑ OS/2 [22] ❑ Unix [23] ❑ Macintosh [24] ❑ Other: [25]_____
(please specify)

I would be interested in new books on the following subjects:
(please check all that apply, and use the spaces provided to identify specific software)

❑ Word processing: [26]

❑ Data bases: [28]

❑ File Utilities: [30]

❑ Networking: [32]

❑ Other: [34]

❑ Spreadsheets: [27]

❑ Desktop publishing: [29]

❑ Money management: [31]

❑ Programming languages: [33]

I use a PC at (please check all that apply): ❑ home [35] ❑ work [36] ❑ school [37] ❑ other: [38] _____

The disks I prefer to use are ❑ 5.25 [39] ❑ 3.5 [40] ❑ other: [41]_____

I have a CD ROM: ❑ yes [42] ❑ no [43]

I plan to buy or upgrade computer hardware this year: ❑ yes [44] ❑ no [45]

I plan to buy or upgrade computer software this year: ❑ yes [46] ❑ no [47]

Name: _____ Business title: [48] _____ Type of Business: [49] _____

Address (❑ home [50] ❑ work [51]/Company name: _____)

Street/Suite# _____

City [52]/State [53]/Zipcode [54]: _____ Country [55] _____

❑ **I liked this book!** You may quote me by name in future
IDG Books Worldwide promotional materials.

My daytime phone number is _____

IDG BOOKS
THE WORLD OF
COMPUTER
KNOWLEDGE

 **YES!**
Please keep me informed about IDG's World of Computer Knowledge.
Send me the latest IDG Books catalog.

COMPUTER
BOOK SERIES
FROM IDG

NO POSTAGE
NECESSARY
IF MAILED
IN THE
UNITED STATES